Joseph A. DeVito

Hunter College of the City University of New York

THE INTERPERSONAL COMMUNICATION BOOK

Fourth Edition

HARPER & ROW, PUBLISHERS, New York
Cambridge, Philadelphia, San Francisco, Washington,
London, Mexico City, São Paulo, Singapore, Sydney

1817

Photograph Credits

The following are the pages on which the photographs appear: Page 9, © Reno, 1984, Jeroboam; p. 23, © Siteman, 1981, Jeroboam; p. 34, © Schaefer, The Picture Cube; p. 47, © Eckert, Jr., EKM-Nepenthe; p. 62, Gatewood, The Image Works; p. 76, Johnson, Jeroboam; p. 96, © Wood, 1982, The Picture Cube; p. 106, Siteman, The Picture Cube; p. 123, Blankfort, Jeroboam; p. 140, © Arms, Jeroboam; p. 151, Buck, The Picture Cube; p. 161, Herwig, Stock, Boston; p. 178, Houghton, Stock, Boston; p. 189, Albertson, The Picture Cube; p. 202, © Ansin, The Picture Cube; p. 217, © Maher, 1980, EKM-Nepenthe; p. 227, © Ballard, EKM-Nepenthe; p. 245, © Druskis, Jeroboam; p. 259, Antman, The Image Works; p. 274, © Gelles, 1981, Stock, Boston; p. 289, Sedwick, The Picture Cube; p. 305, © Siteman, 1983, EKM-Nepenthe; p. 324, Gatewood, The Image Works; p. 332, © Cox, Stock, Boston; p. 346, Thompson, 1980, The Picture Cube; p. 362, Wollinsky, Stock, Boston.

Sponsoring Editor: Louise H. Waller
Project Editor: Eleanor Castellano
Text Design: Suzanne Dyer Company
Cover Design: CATED
Cover Art: Jack Youngerman, *Roundabout,*
  1970, acrylic on canvas, 96" diameter.
  Albright-Knox Art Gallery, Buffalo, New York.
  Gift of Seymour H. Knox, 1971.
Text Art: Vantage Art, Inc.
Photo Research: Mira Schachne
Production: Delia Tedoff
Compositor: Ruttle, Shaw & Wetherill, Inc.
Printer and Binder: R. R. Donnelley & Sons
  Company

The Interpersonal Communication Book, Fourth Edition

Library of Congress Cataloging-in-Publication Data

DeVito, Jospeh A., 1938-
  The interpersonal communication book.

  Includes index.
  1. Interpersonal communication. I. Title.
BF637.C45D49 1986   158'.2   85-17675
ISBN 0-06-041669-6

86 87 88 89 9 8 7 6 5 4 3 2

CONTENTS IN BRIEF

CONTENTS IN DETAIL

v

xi

A HANDBOOK OF EXPERIENTIAL VEHICLES AND REVIEW QUIZZES IN INTERPERSONAL COMMUNICATION 371

PREFACE

The fourth edition of *The Interpersonal Communication Book,* while remaining in the tradition of earlier editions, incorporates significant improvements. The philosophical basis of the text rests on the concept of choice and provides readers with viable options and alternatives for a wide variety of interpersonal situations and thus expands the choices for acting in any given communication context.

Choice is central to interpersonal communication, because the speaker, listener, and communication analyst are constantly confronted with choice points at each and every stage of the communication process. After finishing this text the reader should be better equipped to analyze communication situations and to make more reasoned, reasonable, and more effective communication decisions. Throughout the text I discuss the theory, research, and evidence bearing on the various interpersonal communication choices. Theory and research clearly demonstrate the efficiency of certain choices over others, and these insights are presented as clearly and directly as possible. Where no such evidence is available, reasoned arguments, sometimes concerning effectiveness and sometimes concerning values and ethics, are presented.

Purpose, Format, and Content

The text provides readers with the opportunity and specific means for learning, internalizing, and actually experiencing relevant concepts. That function is served throughout the text in discussion of various concepts and principles, and by the Experiential Vehicles at the end of the book.

Also in the vehicles are useful dialogues written especially to clarify central issues in interpersonal communication. These dialogues serve to make general and abstract theory specific and concrete.

Five review quizzes, summary exercises in which some of the central terms or principles of each of the parts are presented, follow the experiential vehicles in the "Handbook" at the end of the text. The quizzes do not test student knowledge but provide a means for recalling major concepts, theories, and research findings and for stimulating and organizing more thorough review sessions.

The text consists of 26 short units, which makes them easier and more enjoyable to read. Since most studying is done in short periods, these units allow for the most efficient use of readers' available time. Yet each unit is sufficiently developed to give readers a sense of having mastered a significant whole.

Each unit opens with *behavioral objectives,* which identify major behaviors which readers should be able to demonstrate after finishing the unit. They also highlight the most pertinent principles and skills in the unit.

The units are followed by a *Summary: Contents in Brief* that presents the major concepts covered in the unit in the form of a chart. These serve as convenient summaries of essential concepts in the unit and to identify the most essential theories and principles.

The units are arranged in five parts—preliminaries, the self, verbal messages, nonverbal messages, and relationships. Each part is followed by *Skills in Brief* in which major, relevant interpersonal skills are clearly identified. Approximately 125 skills are included and provide a convenient summary of those skills most important to the mastery of interpersonal communication.

Each part begins with *universals* that explain the essential concepts and points of view for topics covered in the part.

The book aims to provide readers with greater insight into their own interpersonal relationships and the skills needed to make more reasoned choices, as well as to establish and maintain more productive and more satisfying relationships.

Major Additions and Revisions

Just a few of the major changes for the improvement and clarification of this new edition are listed here:

1. The concept of interpersonal effectiveness (Unit 6) has been expanded to include effectiveness principles derived from a pragmatic as well as from a humanistic model of interpersonal communication.
2. A new unit on power in interpersonal relationships (Unit 20) has been included.
3. Another new unit on the principles of language and verbal interaction (Unit 12) develops seven principles for effective language use.
4. Relational deterioration has been expanded to Unit 25 on understanding deterioration and Unit 26 on managing relational deterioration.
5. The units on friendship and love (Units 22 and 23) have been expanded to incorporate more information on both verbal and nonverbal communication.
6. Listening (Unit 4) has been completely rewritten, and a discussion of active listening has been added.
7. The unit on universals of verbal messages has been revised to include directive and nondirective language and direct and indirect speech.

Other material has been expanded or revised, notably the discussions of apprehension, self-awareness, self-disclosure, eye communication, development of relationships, initiating relationships, conflict, and gender differences.

Six new Experiential Vehicles have been added to the Handbook at the end of the text; and the *glossary* has been updated and expanded to include over 400 terms.

Instructor's Manual

The *Instructor's Manual,* available from the publisher, covers additional experiential vehicles, suggestions for using the vehicles, suggestions for teaching the course, additional references, and a testbank organized by units. The testbank is also available on computer disks (Microtest) and may be secured from the publisher.

Acknowledgments

It is a pleasure to record my indebtedness to those who helped me in conceptualizing, writing, and producing this book. As with my other books, my major debt is to Boo who contributed to my development as a teacher, as a writer, and, most important, as a thinking-feeling individual. From the beginning, Maggie provided me with the support and encouragement so essential in this type of endeavor, and the students in my interpersonal communication classes helped me to clarify my ideas and provided numerous insights of their own. I especially appreciate the comments from the students of Professors Bernard Brommel of Northeastern Illinois University; Hal Dalrymple of Kent State, Ashtabula Campus; Ken Leibowitz of Philadelphia College of Pharmacy and Science; and Kathy Wenell of Wartburg College. This type of feedback was most helpful and most reinforcing; it made the task of writing this edition a positive learning experience for me.

I am most grateful to those persons who reviewed the first two editions and the manuscript for this edition and who made many valuable suggestions that I tried to incorporate here; many of these people went far beyond the normal responsibilities of reviewers. Needless to say, they are neither responsible for any deficiencies that may remain nor are they necessarily in agreement with what appears here. For their time, their energy, and their willingness to share their expertise and insights, I am most thankful to: Ronald Bassett, University of Texas; Charles Berger, Northwestern University; Bernard Brommel, Northeastern Illinois University; Matt Campbell, Johnson County Community College; Sumitra Chakrapani; James Chesebro, Queens College; Ronald Coleman, Edinboro State College; Harold R. Dalrymple, Kent State University; Sue DeWine, Ohio University; Robert C. Dick, Indiana University at Indianapolis; Paul Feingold, University of New Mexico; Mary Anne Fitzpatrick, University of Wisconsin; Rex Gaskill, Normandale Community College; James E. Hasenauer, California State University; Michael Hecht, Arizona State University; Randy Y. Hirokawa, Penn State University; Thomas E. Jewell, The University of New Mexico; Lynne Kelly, University of Hartford; Catherine Konsky, Illinois State University; Larry Miller, Western Kentucky University; Charles Rossiter, Hood College; Alan L. Sillars, Ohio State University; Dennis Smith, San Francisco State University; Jim Towns, Stephen F. Austin State University; Paul Westbrook, Telex Computer Products; and W. Gill Woodall, University of New Mexico.

JOSEPH A. DeVito

Interpersonal Communication Preliminaries

In this first part we introduce the study of interpersonal communication and identify the elements and the principles that apply to this unique and most important form of communication. The processes of message reception—perception and listening—are also considered with a view toward increasing the efficiency and effectiveness of our own message reception. The moral or ethical dimension of interpersonal communication is considered, because we are concerned with the morality of communication as well as with effectiveness. Last, we focus on what makes interpersonal communication effective and how we might increase our own effectiveness as senders, receivers, and analyst-critics of interpersonal messages.

As a kind of preview, here are some of the questions we focus on in this first part:

What is interpersonal communication? ■ Can we not communicate? ■ What is double-binding? ■ How is it created? ■ How can it be avoided? ■ On what basis do we form impressions of other people? ■ What makes for accuracy in our judgments of people? ■ Why do we expect a person we like to like us in return and also to like our friends and dislike our enemies? ■ Why do we believe some people and disbelieve others? ■ How can listening be improved? ■ What is feedback, and how can we learn to use it more effectively in interpersonal communication? ■ When is interpersonal communication unethical? ■ Is it unethical to lie? ■ To use fear and emotional appeals? ■ To prevent others from engaging in certain interpersonal interactions? ■ What makes interpersonal communication effective? ■ How can you improve your own effective-

UNIT OUTLINE

Universals of Interpersonal Communication

Axioms of Interpersonal Communication

Perception in Interpersonal Communication

Listening and Feedback in Interpersonal Communication

Ethics in Interpersonal Communication

Effectiveness in Interpersonal Communication

Skills in Brief

1

ness in one-to-one communication encounters? ■ What skills can you master that will enable you to perceive messages more accurately, to increase your listening abilities, and to communicate more effectively in a wide variety of interpersonal contexts?

Universals of Interpersonal Communication

OBJECTIVES

Upon completion of this unit, you should be able to:

1. define *interpersonal communication* using a componential, a developmental, and a relational definition
2. cite examples of interpersonal communication from your own observations and experiences
3. explain the nature of *universals* in interpersonal communication
4. define each of the following terms and explain their role in interpersonal communication: *source-receiver, encoding-decoding, competence* and *performance, message, channel, noise (physical, psychological,* and *semantic), feedback, context, field of experience, effect,* and *ethics*
5. explain at least two implications for interpersonal communication of the competence-performance distinction
6. diagram the model of communication presented in this unit and label all its parts
7. explain Lasswell's or Gerbner's model of communication
8. construct an original model of communication that incorporates at least the following components: context, source-receiver, message, encoding-decoding, noise, feedback, field of experience, and effect
9. identify and explain at least five purposes of interpersonal communication

You enter your interpersonal communication class and spot a person you would like to date. You get the person's phone number from a mutual friend and call that evening. A previous engagement prevents this person from saying yes, and you decide to call next week. At the same time, you wonder if this "previous engagement" was merely another way of saying no.

You are sitting on a bus reading a book when a person who smells of cigar smoke sits next to you. The odor is so strong that you change your seat.

You are on a basketball team and are discussing strategy for the next quarter with the other members. The captain wants to do certain things, while other members want to do something else. The members argue and fight.

TABLE 1.1: Lasswell's Model of Communication

Who
Says what
In what channel
To whom
With what effect

You are having dinner with your family and the conversation covers a variety of topics—what each person did during the day, the accident that happened down the street, the plans for tomorrow, and so on.

These and thousands of similar examples are interpersonal communication situations. We all know what interpersonal communication is, and, for most purposes, this intuitive understanding is adequate. For our in-depth study of interpersonal communication, however, we need definitions that are more specific and more revealing. To achieve this greater understanding we explore the nature of interpersonal communication from the perspectives afforded by a componential, a developmental, and a relational definition.

A COMPONENTIAL DEFINITION OF INTERPERSONAL COMMUNICATION

In constructing a componential definition—one that identifies the components or elements of the interpersonal communication process—there are many time-honored sources on which to draw. One of the most popular was presented by political scientist Harold Lasswell, who viewed communication as concerned with five basic questions, presented in Table 1.1. In a similar vein, George Gerbner identified ten components (Table 1.2).

Both "models" are relatively linear; they imply that communication begins at one end and moves through discrete steps to the other end. By studying Lasswell's or Gerbner's model of communication, you can easily visualize a message being traced through space from left to right. Such linear views of communication are much too limiting, however, because they fail to emphasize the circular nature of communication and fail to take into consideration the fact that each participant in the communication act both sends and receives messages. These aspects of communication need to be reflected in any visual or verbal description of communication. For our purposes, then, the model presented in Figure 1.1 should prove more helpful. It is a bit more complex, but it is a more accurate reflection of what interpersonal communication is—namely, the process of sending and receiving messages between two persons, or among a small group of persons, with some effect and some immediate feedback.

Each of the concepts discussed here may be thought of as a universal of interpersonal communication in that each is integral to any and all interpersonal communication encounters. Universals are the concepts or features that are present in all interpersonal communication acts.

TABLE 1.2: Gerbner's Model of Communication

Someone
Perceives an event
And reacts
In a situation
Through some means
To make available materials
In some form
And context
Conveying content
Of some consequence

Source–Receiver

Interpersonal communication involves at least two persons. Each of these persons formulates and sends messages (source functions) and also perceives and comprehends messages (receiver functions). The hyphenated term *source-receiver* is used to

FIGURE 1.1: A Model of Some Universals of Interpersonal Communication.

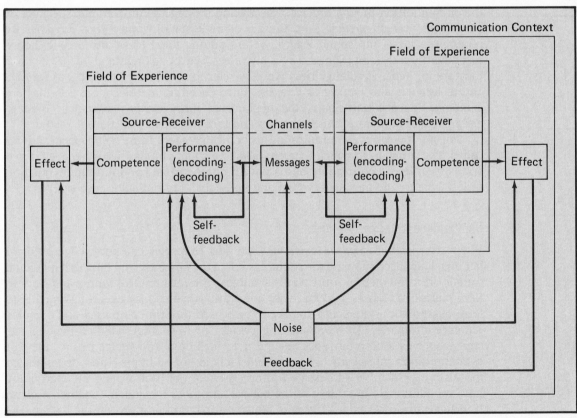

emphasize that these source and receiver functions are performed by each individual engaging in interpersonal communication.

A number of additional and related issues require explanation. First, interpersonal communication cannot occur with oneself. Communication with oneself is termed *intra*personal communication. It is essential to understand intrapersonal communication if we are fully to understand interpersonal communication. Yet it is best to keep these two forms of communication separate. Second, interpersonal communication deals with human beings. Communication by or with animals, machines, plants, pictures, and the like are not interpersonal communication experiences. Third, interpersonal communication occurs between two people or among a small group of people. It excludes mass communication and public speaking situations, in which there is a large audience and the messages go essentially in one direction—from speaker to audience but not from audience to speaker.

Who people are, what they know, what they believe, what they value, what they want, what they have been told, how intelligent they are, what their attitudes are, and so on, all influence what they say and how they say it, what messages they receive, and how they receive them. Each person is unique; each person's communications are unique.

Encoding–Decoding

In communication theory, the act of producing messages—for example, speaking or writing—is termed *encoding,* and the act of understanding messages, *decoding.* By putting our ideas into sound waves, we are putting these ideas into a code, hence *en*coding. By translating sound waves into ideas, we are taking them out of the code they are in, hence *de*coding. Thus we may refer to speakers and writers as *encoders* and to listeners and readers as *decoders.* Since encoding and decoding activities are combined in each participant, the hyphenated form *encoding-decoding* is used to designate and emphasize this important and inevitable dual function.

For interpersonal communication to occur, messages must be encoded and decoded. The situation in which a parent talks to a child who has his or her eyes closed and is wearing stereo headphones is not an interpersonal communication situation simply because the messages, verbal and nonverbal, are not being received.

Competence and Performance

When we speak of *language competence,* we refer to a speaker's knowledge of his or her own language: knowing the sound system of the language and how the individual sounds are combined to form words, knowing the meanings of words and how to form plurals and tenses, and knowing how various words may be strung together to form questions or statements that are in turn used to form compound and complex sentence structures. *Communication competence,* on the other hand, uses language competence as a base but goes beyond it to include a knowledge of the rules for communication interaction. These would include, for example, rules pertaining to the ways in which we address each other, the role that status plays in determining how we address the president of the college, and how we address another student. It includes the knowledge of how to adjust our communications on the basis of the context in which we are interacting, the person with whom we are interacting, and a host of other variables to be discussed throughout this text. Communication competence also includes a knowledge of the nonverbal rules of interaction—when to speak and when to remain silent, when silence is uncomfortable and when it is welcomed, and the appropriateness of touching, vocal volume, and physical closeness.

Performance refers to the actual sending and receiving of both verbal and nonverbal signals. Whereas competence is concerned with a *knowledge* of the elements and rules that go into language and communication, performance is concerned with the *application of the knowledge* of these elements and rules in the actual sending and receiving of the message.

Many writers on communication effectiveness use the term *communication competence* to refer to both the knowledge of the rules of communication effectiveness (what we have called competence) *and* the skill or ability to apply these rules in actual communication interactions (what we have called performance). In this view "competence" and "competent" are equated: one who possesses communication competence is a competent communicator; conversely, a competent communicator is, by definition, one who possesses competence. Although the distinction between competence and performance is not always crucial, several important corollaries or implications (that would be obscured if we did not make this distinction) are worth noting.

IMPLICATIONS FOR INTERPERSONAL COMMUNICATION

First, competence is essential if performance is to be consistently effective. That is, to communicate effectively, we must have the relevant knowledge or competence. Second, competence is not translated automatically or directly into performance. On a language level this can be illustrated by noting that although we know the rules of language, we nevertheless make errors: We make false starts, use double negatives, speak ungrammatically, and the like. Performance is actually a combination of our competence and other factors—attention level, level of fatigue, anxiety, interest, and so on. Similarly, in communication we may know what should be done—we may know the rules for meeting another person and asking for a date, for example, and sometimes we can almost see ourselves doing it in our heads—yet our performance often falls short of this idealized competence. This is because in communication, as in language, a great number of factors influence performance. For example, shyness or nervousness may prevent us from asking for a date or a raise.

Third, we continue to acquire communication competence throughout our lives. Although we learn the basic rules early, say by the time we are 10 or 12, we are forever refining these basic rules, and, as a result, refining our performance, as we learn more and more about communication. Fourth, and perhaps most important, if we are to improve our performance—that is, if we are to communicate more effectively—we must do so in at least two steps. The first is to acquire the appropriate competence, the knowledge of how communication should operate. This will be covered in the following units and can be acquired by learning the relevant theories and research in communication. This competence is identified specifically in the behavioral objectives that preface each of the units in the text. The second step is to put this knowledge into practice, to experience applying the rules to different situations. Opportunities for applying competence to performance are provided by the Handbook of Experiential Vehicles at the end of this book as well as by our everyday experiences. Specific performance skills are discussed throughout the book and are highlighted in the Skills Summary sections that follow each of the five major parts of the text. Because we are social creatures who cannot exist without communication, we are forever engaging in communication performance. The key is to put these experiences to good use by practicing effective communication patterns.

Messages

For interpersonal communication to exist, messages—signals that serve as stimuli for a receiver—must be sent and received. These messages may be auditory, visual, tactile, olfactory, gustatory, or any combination of these. Interpersonal communication does not have to be oral; we can communicate by gestures, touch, smell, or taste as well as by sound.

For example, the clothes we wear communicate something to other people and, in fact, probably communicate to us as well. The way we walk communicates, as does the way we shake hands, cock our heads, comb our hair, sit, smile, or frown. In fact, everything about us communicates. These signals constitute our interpersonal communication message.

Interpersonal communication does not have to occur face to face. It can occur over the telephone, through prison-cell walls, or through videophone hookups. Note, too, that messages need not be sent intentionally. Through slips of the tongue, a lingering body odor, or a nervous twitch we also communicate.

Channel

The communication channel is the medium through which the messages pass; the channel functions as a bridge connecting source and receiver. Communication rarely takes place over only one channel; two, three, or four channels are normally used simultaneously. Thus, for example, in face to face interactions, we speak and listen (vocal-auditory channel), but we also gesture and receive these signals visually (gestural-visual channel), and we emit odors and smell those of others (chemical-olfactory channel). Often we touch one another, and this too communicates (cutaneous-tactile channel).

Another way to categorize channels is in terms of the means of communication; thus we would identify as channels face to face, telephone, electronic and "regular" mail, movies, television, radio, smoke signals, telex, telegraph, and ESP, to name but a few.

Noise

Noise enters into all communication systems, no matter how well designed or technically proficient. Noise is anything that distorts or interferes with message reception. It is present in a communication system to the extent that the message received differs from the message sent. Three main types of noise may be identified: physical, psychological, and semantic.

PHYSICAL NOISE

Physical noise interferes with the physical transmission of the signal or message. The screeching of passing cars, the hum of an air conditioner or computer, the lisp of a speaker, and sunglasses may all be regarded as physical noise in that they interfere with the transmission of signals from one person to another. Physical noise is also present in written communication and would include blurred type, print that shows through from the back of the page, creases in the paper, and anything that prevents a reader from getting the message sent by the writer.

PSYCHOLOGICAL NOISE

Psychological noise refers to any form of psychological interference and includes biases and prejudices in senders and receivers that lead to distortions in receiving and processing information, and closed-mindedness—perhaps the classic example of psychological noise preventing information from being received or being received fairly.

SEMANTIC NOISE

In semantic noise the interference is due to the receiver's failing to grasp the meanings intended by the sender. Semantic noise in its extreme occurs between people speaking different languages. In more common form, semantic noise is created by the speaker's use of jargon, technical, or complex terms not understood by the

Noise is present in all communication acts. The physical noise (sounds from others, motors running, cameras clicking) is easy to detect and relatively easy to control. The psychological noise or semantic noise, however, is difficult to detect and even more difficult to control.

listener or in the assignment by the listener of meanings different from those intended by the speaker (as would frequently be the case with ambiguous or highly emotional terms and statements).

Perhaps the most important point to keep in mind concerning noise is that it is inevitable; all communication transactions contain noise of some kind. And while we cannot eliminate noise completely, we can reduce noise and its effects. Making our language more precise, acquiring the skills for sending and receiving nonverbal messages, improving our perceptual, listening, and feedback skills—covered throughout this text—are just a few of the ways in which we can effectively combat the effects of noise.

Feedback

Another type of message is feedback. When we send a message, say, in speaking to another person, we also hear ourselves. We get feedback from our own messages— we hear what we say, we feel the way we move, we see what we write, and so on. On the basis of this information, we may correct ourselves, rephrase something, or perhaps smile at a clever turn of phrase. This is self-feedback. Also significant is the feedback we get from others. In speaking with another individual, not only are we constantly sending messages, but we are also constantly receiving messages. Both parties are sending and receiving messages at the same time. The messages that are sent in response to other messages are termed *feedback*. This feedback, like other messages, can be in many forms—auditory, tactile, or visual, for example. A frown or a smile, a yea or a nay, a pat on the back or a punch in the mouth are all feedback.

Effectiveness in interpersonal communication seems largely due to the ability of the communicator to respond appropriately to feedback. Teaching effectiveness may be seen in the same way. Effective teachers seem to be those who can read the responses of their students accurately and adjust their messages accordingly. Ineffective teachers seem oblivious to how students are responding and just carry on as usual.

Context

Communication always takes place within a context. At times this context is not obvious or intrusive; it seems to be so natural that it is ignored, like background music. At other times the context stands out, and the ways in which it restricts or stimulates our communications are obvious. Compare, for example, the differences in communicating in a funeral home, in a football stadium, in a quiet restaurant, and at a rock concert.

The context of communication has at least three dimensions: physical, social-psychological, and temporal. The room or hallway or park in which communication takes place—the tangible or concrete environment—is the *physical dimension*. This physical dimension exerts some influence on the content as well as the form of our messages. The *social-psychological dimension* includes, for example, status relationships among the participants, roles and games that people play, norms and cultural mores of the society in which they are communicating, friendliness or unfriendliness of the situation, formality or informality, and seriousness or humorousness. The *temporal dimension*—in addition to the obvious time of day and time in history—refers to where a particular message fits into the sequence of communication events. For example, a joke about sickness told immediately after the illness of a friend has been disclosed will be perceived differently and will have quite different effects from the same joke told as one of a series of similar jokes.

These three dimensions of context interact with one another; each influences and is influenced by the others. If, for example, the temperature in a room becomes extremely hot (a physical change), it would probably lead to changes in the social-psychological dimension as well. General discomfort seems to make people more talkative, as many have witnessed when a subway train or bus gets stuck. A change in the context, then, may be brought about from outside influences, for example, a train failure; from a change in one of the basic dimensions, for example, time change or temperature change; or from interaction among the dimensions, for example, talkativeness increasing as a result of a train breakdown.

Field of Experience

The squares that overlap in Figure 1.1 refer to what is called the *field of experience*. The assumption is that effective communication takes place to the extent that the participants share the same experiences. Communication is ineffective to the extent that the participants do not share the same experiences. Parents have difficulty communicating with their children, in this view, because the children cannot share the parental experience and because the parents have forgotten what it is like to be children. When management forgets what it is like to be labor and labor does not share any of management's experiences, communication becomes difficult. Differences among people make communication more and more difficult; the larger the differences, the more difficult communication becomes. Although many differences cannot be eliminated, communication is still not impossible. Though we cannot always share the experiences of others, we can learn to empathize with people different from ourselves—to feel what they are feeling—and thus extend the overlap in our respective fields of experience.

Effect

Communication always has some effect. For every communication act, there is some consequence, and the effect may be on one person or on both. When communication affects the environment or context, it is done through people. The effects of communication, then, occur first on people and are always personal. Even when we cannot observe an effect (which is perhaps most of the time), we assume that for every interpersonal communication act there is an effect, somewhat like ''for every action there is a reaction.'' As students of communication, part of our task is to determine what these effects are.

Ethics

To the degree that interpersonal communication has an effect, it also has an ethical dimension. Because communication has consequences, there is a rightness or wrongness aspect to any communication act. Unlike principles of effective communication, however, principles of ethical communication are difficult if not impossible to formulate. We can often observe the effect of communication and on the basis of these observations formulate principles of effective communication. But we cannot observe the rightness or wrongness of a communication act. The ethical dimension of communication is further complicated by the fact that it is so interwoven with one's personal philosophy of life that it is difficult to propose universal guidelines. Given these difficulties, we nevertheless include ethical considerations as being integral to any communication act. The choices that we make concerning communication must be guided by considerations of ethics as well as effectiveness, satisfaction, or whatever other effects may seem desirable.

A DEVELOPMENTAL DEFINITION OF INTERPERSONAL COMMUNICATION

In addition to distinguishing interpersonal communication from, say, mass or intrapersonal communication on the basis of its components, as we do in a componential definition, we might also distinguish it from *im*personal communication. Not only is interpersonal communication a special form of communication in terms of its components, but it is also special in that it is personal rather than impersonal. To distinguish interpersonal or personal from impersonal communication, we need what has been called a *developmental approach*. I here follow Gerald Miller's analysis in "The Current Status of Theory and Research in Interpersonal Communication."

In the developmental approach, communications are viewed as existing on a continuum ranging from impersonal at one end to increasingly interpersonal or intimate at the other end. Interpersonal communication is characterized by, and distinguished from, impersonal communication on the basis of at least three factors.

Predictions Are Based on Psychological Data

First, interpersonal interactions are characterized by the participants' basing their predictions about each other on psychological data—that is, the ways in which this person differs from the members of his or her group. In impersonal encounters we respond to each other according to the class or group to which we belong. For example, initially we respond to a particular college professor in the way we respond to college professors in general. Similarly, the college professor responds to a particular student in the way professors respond to students generally. As the relationship becomes more and more personal, however, both the professor and the student begin to respond to each other not as members of their groups but as individuals; each begins to respond to the other on the basis of the individual's uniqueness. Another way of putting this would be to say that in impersonal encounters, the social or cultural role of the person tells us how to interact, while in personal or interpersonal encounters, the psychological role of the person tells us how to interact.

Interactions Are Based on Explanatory Knowledge

Second, interpersonal interactions are based on an explanatory knowledge of each other. When we know a particular person, we can better predict how that person will react in a variety of situations. In interpersonal situations, we can not only predict how a person will act but can also advance explanations for that person's behaviors. The college professor may, in an impersonal relationship, know that Pat will be five minutes late to class each Friday. That is, the professor is able to predict Pat's behavior. In an interpersonal situation, however, the professor can not only predict Pat's behavior but can also offer generally valid explanations for the behavior—in this case, give reasons why Pat is late.

Interactions Are Based on Personally Established Rules

Third, in impersonal situations, the rules of behavioral interaction are set down by social norms. Students and professors behave toward one another—at least in impersonal situations—according to the social norms that have been established by the culture or subculture in which they are operating. However, as the relationship between a student and a professor becomes interpersonal, the rules established by the social norms are no longer the important ones and no longer totally regulate their interaction; the individuals establish rules of their own. To the extent that the individuals establish their own rules for interacting, the situation is interpersonal.

These three characteristics vary in degree. We respond to each other on the basis of psychological data *to some degree;* we base our predictions of another's behavior *to some degree* on the basis of our explanatory knowledge; and we interact on the basis of mutually established rules rather than on socially established norms *to some degree.* As already noted, a developmental approach to communication implies a continuum ranging from highly impersonal to highly intimate. "Interpersonal communication" occupies a broad area of this continuum, although each person might draw its boundaries a bit differently. Therefore, although this developmental view does not enable us to make universally agreed-on decisions concerning what is or what is not interpersonal, the three characteristics noted should give us some added insight into interpersonal communication and how it might be distinguished from formal or impersonal communication.

One frequent misconception about interpersonal communication (and particularly about its developmental definition) is that an interpersonal relationship is one characterized by liking or loving. This is not the case. We may have an interpersonal relationship and engage in interpersonal communication with people we dislike intensely as well as with people we love. Our interactions may be interpersonal in conflict as well as in love, in competition as well as in cooperation, in relationships that are getting stronger as well as in relationships that are deteriorating.

A RELATIONAL (DYADIC) DEFINITION OF INTERPERSONAL COMMUNICATION

In a relational definition interpersonal communication is defined as communication that takes place between two persons who have a clearly established relationship between them; the people are in some way "connected." Interpersonal communication would thus include that which takes place between a waiter and a customer, a son and his father, two sisters, a teacher and a student, two lovers, two friends, and so on.

Note that under this definition, it is almost impossible to have dyadic (two-person) communication that is not interpersonal, and not surprisingly, this approach is often referred to as the dyadic definition of interpersonal communication. Almost invariably, there is some relationship between two persons who are interacting. Even the stranger who asks directions from a resident has an identifiable relationship with that person as soon as the first message is sent.

These three definitions of interpersonal communication are not as separate and distinct as they may at first appear. All are useful in explaining what interpersonal communication is, each giving a somewhat different perspective to this important form of human behavior. The developmental definition serves to emphasize the types of interactions that are most significant to people—the kinds of relationships that make a substantial difference in our lives. This definition clearly defines the more intimate types of interpersonal interaction. The componential definition serves to emphasize the numerous elements and processes that have to be taken into consideration before an adequate understanding of interpersonal communication can be achieved. This definition enables us to recognize the nature of each part of the interpersonal communication process. The relational definition presents an extremely broad view of interpersonal communication while emphasizing that the interaction is—in some ways, at least—structured. There are, for example, socially established (rather than personally established) rules for appropriate and inappropriate behavior, mutual role expectations (based largely on sociological data), and a focused attention by each on the other.

SOME PURPOSES OF INTERPERSONAL COMMUNICATION

Interpersonal communication may serve a variety of purposes. Here six of the most important are identified briefly. These purposes need not be conscious at the time of the interpersonal encounter, nor do they need to be the intended purposes of the encounter; purposes may be conscious or subconscious, intentional or unintentional.

To Discover Oneself

One of the major purposes of interpersonal communication is personal discovery. When we engage in an interpersonal encounter with another person, we learn a great deal about ourselves as well as about the other person. In fact, our self-perceptions are in large part a result of what we have learned about ourselves from others during interpersonal encounters.

Interpersonal communication provides an opportunity for us to talk about our favorite subject—ourselves. Nothing seems as interesting, as exciting, or as worthy of discussion as our own feelings, thoughts, and behaviors. By talking about ourselves with another individual we are provided with an excellent source of feedback on our feelings, thoughts, and behaviors. From this type of encounter we learn, for example, that our feelings about ourselves, others, and the world are not so different from someone else's feelings. The same is true about our behaviors, our fears, our hopes, and our desires. This positive reinforcement helps to make us feel "normal." Through these communications we also learn how we appear to others, what our strengths and weaknesses are, and who likes us and who dislikes us and why.

To Discover the External World

Just as interpersonal communication enables us to understand better ourselves and the person with whom we are communicating, it also enables us to understand better the external world—the world of objects, events, and other people. Much of the information we now have comes from interpersonal interactions. Although a great deal of information comes to us from the mass media, it is often discussed and ultimately "learned" or internalized through interpersonal interactions. In fact, our beliefs, attitudes, and values have probably been influenced more by interpersonal encounters than by the media or even by formal education.

To Establish and Maintain Meaningful Relationships

One of the greatest desires (some would say needs) people have is establishing and maintaining close relationships with other people. We want to feel loved and liked, and in turn we want to love and like others. Much of the time we spend in interpersonal communication is devoted to establishing and maintaining social relationships with others. Such relationships help to lessen loneliness and depression, enable us to share and maximize our pleasures, and generally make us feel more positive about ourselves.

To Change Attitudes and Behaviors

Many times we attempt to change the attitudes and behaviors of others in our interpersonal encounters. We may wish them to vote a particular way, try a new diet, buy a particular item, listen to a record, see a movie, read a book, enter a particular field, take a specific course, think in a particular way, believe that something is true or false, value some idea, marry us—the list is endless. We spend a good deal of our time engaged in interpersonal persuasion.

It is interesting to note that studies on the effectiveness of the mass media versus interpersonal situations in changing attitudes and behaviors point to the conclusion that we are more often persuaded through interpersonal than through mass media communication.

To Play and Entertain

Play includes all activities from which deriving pleasure is the primary goal. Talking with friends about our activities over the weekend, discussing sports or dates, telling stories and jokes, and, in general, just talking to pass the time serve this function. Far from being insignificant or frivolous, this purpose is an extremely important one. It gives our activities a necessary balance and gives our minds a needed break from all the seriousness around us. We all have a child within us, and we all must allow that child time to play.

To Help

Psychiatrists, clinical psychologists, and therapists of various kinds serve a helping function professionally. Their task is to offer guidance through interpersonal interaction. But we all serve this function in our everyday interactions: We console a friend who has broken up a love affair, we counsel a fellow student about courses to take, we offer advice to a colleague about work, we give comfort to a crying child. Whether professional or nonprofessional, success in providing this helping function depends on one's knowledge and skill in interpersonal communication.

We may also look at these purposes of interpersonal communication from two other perspectives. First, these purposes may be seen as motivating factors or as reasons why we engage in interpersonal communication. Thus we can say we engage in interpersonal communication to obtain pleasure, to help, to change someone's attitudes or behaviors. Second, these purposes may be viewed as outcomes or as general effects of interpersonal encounters. Thus we can say that as a result of interpersonal communication we derive self-knowledge, establish a more meaningful relationship, and acquire an increased knowledge of the external world.

It should be clear, of course, that interpersonal communication is usually motivated by a combination of factors and has not one but a combination of outcomes or effects. Any given interpersonal interaction, then, serves a unique combination of purposes, is motivated by a unique combination of factors, and produces a unique combination of outcomes or effects.

Summary: Contents in Brief

Interpersonal Communication Definitions	Interpersonal Communication Purposes
Componential: the process of sending and receiving messages between two persons, or among a small group of persons, through one or more channels, distorted by noise, with some effect and some immediate feedback	Self-discovery
	Discovery of the external world
	Establishing and maintaining meaningful relationships
Relational: communication between two or a few connected individuals	Changing attitudes and behaviors
	Playing and entertaining
Developmental: communication between two persons in which interactions are based on (1) psychological data, (2) explanatory knowledge, and (3) personally established rules	Helping

---

Sources

The nature of interpersonal communication is surveyed in a number of excellent sources. See, for example, Murray S. Davis, *Intimate Relations* (New York: Free Press, 1973); Kurt Danziger, *Interpersonal Communication* (Elmsford, N.Y.: Pergamon Press, 1976); and Mark L. Knapp, *Interpersonal Communication and Human Relationships,* 2d ed. (Boston: Allyn & Bacon, 1984). An interesting eclectic view of interpersonal communication is presented by George L. Shapiro, Jerie M. Pratt, and Maryan Schall, "The Eclectic Perspective on Interpersonal Communication: An Explanation and a Description," *Communication Education* 30 (April 1981): 133–145. Communication concepts are considered in most of the available texts on communication. One starting place would be my reader, *Communication: Concepts and Processes*, 3d ed. (Englewood Cliffs, N.J.: Prentice-Hall, 1981). An excellent introduction to communication terminology is provided by Wilbur Schramm and William E. Porter, *Men, Women, Messages, and Media: Understanding Human Communication*, 2d ed. (New York: Harper & Row, 1982). Also see my *The Communication Handbook: A Dictionary* (New York: Harper & Row, 1986).

On communicative competence, see John M. Wiemann, "Explication and Test of a Model of Communicative Competence," *Human Communication Research* 3 (Spring 1977): 195–213. For an excellent discussion of communication competence and performance, see James C. McCroskey, "Communication Competence and Performance: A Research and Pedagogical Perspective," *Communication Education* 31 (January 1982): 1–7. For a more comprehensive presentation of competence, see Brian H. Spitzberg and William R. Cupach, *Interpersonal Communication Competence* (Beverly Hills, Calif.: Sage, 1984).

Two excellent articles that influenced this discussion are Gerald R. Miller, "The Current Status of Theory and Research in Interpersonal Communication," *Human Communication Research* 4 (Winter 1978): 164–178, and Art Bochner, "On Taking Ourselves Seriously: An Analysis of Some Persistent Problems and Promising Directions in Interpersonal Research," *Human Communication Research* 4 (Winter 1978): 179–191.

The purposes or functions of communication are thoroughly surveyed in Carroll C. Arnold and John Waite Bowers, eds., *Handbook of Rhetorical and Communication Theory* (Boston: Allyn & Bacon, 1984). See especially the article by Arthur P. Bochner (pp. 544–621).

Axioms of Interpersonal Communication

OBJECTIVES

Upon completion of this unit, you should be able to:

1. explain the transactional nature of interpersonal communication
2. explain why one cannot *not* communicate
3. identify the alternatives available when one person does not wish to communicate but another person does
4. explain the concept of irreversibility as applied to interpersonal communication
5. distinguish between the content and the relationship dimensions of interpersonal communication
6. explain the principle that interpersonal communication involves a process of adjustment
7. explain the concept of punctuation in interpersonal communication
8. distinguish between symmetrical and complementary interactions

Interpersonal communication is a very special process. It is nothing like running a race, drinking a soda, or working out a math problem. Nor is it like writing an essay, delivering a public speech, or designing an advertising campaign. In this unit, the very special nature of interpersonal communication is explained in two ways. First, the nature of interpersonal communication as a transactional process is examined. We identify some of the assumptions concerning interpersonal communication and some of the implications entailed in making these assumptions. Second, we examine six transactional axioms or postulates of interpersonal communication. Taken together, these two approaches should clarify what interpersonal communication is and especially how it operates in the real world of person-to-person communication.

INTERPERSONAL COMMUNICATION AS A TRANSACTIONAL PROCESS

When we say that interpersonal communication is transactional, we mean that (1) interpersonal communication is a process, (2) whose components are interdependent and (3) whose participants act and react as whole beings.

Interpersonal Communication Is a Process

Interpersonal communication is a process; it is an act, an event, an activity. It is not something static and at rest; it is an ongoing process. Everything involved in interpersonal communication is in a state of change: we are constantly changing, the people we are communicating with are changing, and our environment is changing. Sometimes these changes go unnoticed, sometimes they intrude in obvious ways, but always the changes are occurring.

The interpersonal communication process is best described as a circular and continuous one. When we consider communication as the transmitting of messages from speaker to listener, we imply that the process begins with the speaker and ends with the listener. This is a linear view. In reality, interpersonal communication is a circular process with each person serving both functions—each is simultaneously a speaker and a listener, an actor and a reactor.

The interpersonal communication process is continuous. It has no clear-cut beginning and no clear-cut end; it is perpetual. Although we may, for convenience, appear to stop the process and talk about when a particular communication act began, in reality the process has not stopped, and a beginning may never be clearly distinguished.

Consider a "simple" interpersonal act: You meet and talk with another person. Because it is convenient, we may say that this interaction began when you started to speak or when you first saw each other. But that is too simplistic because what each of you says and how each of you responds during the interaction are greatly dependent on factors that began at some unidentifiable earlier time, for example, your self-confidence, your previous experience, your fears, your communicative competencies, your expectations, your needs, and hundreds of other factors.

Components Are Interdependent

The elements in interpersonal communication are integrally related to one another; they are interdependent (never independent). Each element—each part of interpersonal communication—exists in relation to the other parts and to the whole. For example, there can be no source without a receiver; there can be no message without a source; there can be no feedback without a receiver. Each aspect of the interpersonal communication process is intimately connected with all other aspects, and because of this interdependency, a change in any one element leads to changes in the others. For example, you are talking with a group of fellow students about a course or a recent examination and the teacher enters the group. This change in participants will lead to other changes—perhaps in the content of what is said, perhaps in the manner in which it is expressed. But regardless of what change is introduced, other changes will occur as a result.

Because of this interdependency and change, no action or reaction is exactly repeatable. No person ever does the same thing in exactly the same way. The major reason for this is that no human being is the same from one moment to the next. Changes have occurred. More formally, we might say that interpersonal communication possesses the feature of *unrepeatability* so that all interpersonal interactions are novel experiences.

Participants Act and React as Wholes

In a transactional process, each person acts and reacts as a whole. We are designed to act as whole persons. One cannot react, for example, solely on an intellectual level or solely on an emotional level; we are not so compartmentalized. Rather, we respond intellectually and emotionally, with body and mind. Our reactions in interpersonal communication, then, are not based solely on what is said or on body gestures, but on our entire beings—our previous experiences, our present emotions, our knowledge, our physical health, and a multitude of other factors.

SIX TRANSACTIONAL POSTULATES

In Unit 1 we presented several definitions of interpersonal communication in order to highlight its unique and special nature. Here, six postulates or general principles that further characterize interpersonal communication are explained. These postulates are largely the work of transactional psychologists Paul Watzlawick, Janet Helmick Beavin, and Don D. Jackson, presented in their landmark *Pragmatics of Human Communication*. Together with the previously presented definitions, these postulates should complete our characterization of interpersonal communication.

Communication Is Inevitable

Often we think of communication as being intentional, purposeful, and consciously motivated. In many instances it is. But in other instances we are communicating even though we might not think we are or might not even want to communicate. Take, for example, the student sitting in the back of the room with an "expressionless" face, perhaps staring at the front of the room, perhaps staring out the window. Although the student might say that she or he is not communicating with the teacher or with the other students, that student is obviously communicating a great deal—perhaps disinterest, perhaps boredom, perhaps a concern for something else, perhaps a desire for the class to be over as soon as possible. In any event, the student is communicating whether she or he wishes to or not; we cannot *not* communicate. Further, when we are in an interactional situation with this person, we must respond in some way. Even if we do not respond actively or overtly, that lack of response is itself a response and communicates. Like the student's silence, our silence in response also communicates.

Further, as Paul Watzlawick observes in *The Language of Change*, "One cannot *not* influence." Persuasion, like communication, is also inevitable. The issue to be considered, in any and every interactional situation, is not whether we will persuade or influence another but rather how we will exert our influence. This corollary raises interesting questions concerning both interpersonal effectiveness (to which we turn in Unit 6) and interpersonal ethics (to which we turn in Unit 5).

Another way in which we communicate without wanting to and without conscious awareness is in mirroring. When interacting with another person, we frequently mirror (mimic or imitate) that person's nonverbal behaviors. Research *suggests* that mirroring generally signals agreement, attraction, interest, and a desire to continue the interaction. In fact, a great deal of our nonverbal behavior occurs without any conscious control and communicates a wide variety of messages: shyness, aggression, confidence, sexual attraction, fear, surprise, dominance, and numerous others considered in our discussion of nonverbal communication (Units 14–17).

Communication Is Irreversible

The processes of some systems can be reversed. For example, we can turn water into ice and then reverse the process by turning the ice back into water. And we can repeat this process of reversing back and forth between ice and water for as long as we wish. Other systems, however, are irreversible; the process can go in only one direction; it cannot go back again. Interpersonal communication is an irreversible process. We can never undo what has already been done. What has been communicated remains communicated; we cannot uncommunicate. Although we may try to qualify, negate, or somehow reduce the effects of our message, the message itself, once it has been sent and received, cannot be reversed.

This principle has a number of important implications. For example, in interpersonal interactions, we need to be especially careful that we do not say things we may be sorry for later. Especially in conflict situations, where tempers run high, we have to be especially vigilant that we not say things we may wish to withdraw later. Similarly, commitment messages—"I love you" messages and their variants—must be similarly monitored lest we commit ourselves to a position with which we may be uncomfortable later.

Communications Have Content and Relationship Dimensions

Communications, to a certain extent at least, refer to the real world, to something external to both speaker and listener. At the same time, however, communications also refer to the relationship between the parties. For example, a teacher may say to a student, "See me after class." This simple message has a content aspect that refers to the behavioral responses expected—namely, that the student see the teacher after class—and a relationship aspect that tells us how the communication is to be dealt with. Even the use of the simple command shows that there is a status difference between the two parties that allows the teacher to command the student. This can perhaps be seen most clearly if we visualize this command being made by the student to the teacher. It appears awkward and out of place because it violates the normal relationship between teacher and student.

In any communication, the content dimension may be the same but the relationship aspect different, or the relationship aspect may be the same and the content dimension different. For example, the teacher could say to the student, "You had better see me after class" or "May I please see you after class?" In each case the content is essentially the same; that is, the message being communicated about the behavioral responses expected is the same in both cases. But the relationship dimension is very different. The first signifies a very definite superior-inferior relationship, even a put-down of the student, whereas the second signals a more equal relationship and shows respect for the student. Similarly, at times the content may be different but the relationship essentially the same. For example, a son might say to his parents, "May I go away this weekend?" or "May I use the car tonight?" The content is clearly very different in each case, but the relationship dimension is essentially the same. It is clearly a superior-inferior relationship in which permission to do certain things must be secured.

RELATIONAL CONFLICTS

Many problems between people are caused by the failure to recognize the distinction between the content and the relationship levels of communication. For example, consider the engaged couple arguing over the fact that the woman made plans to study during the weekend with her friends without first asking her fiancé if that would be all right. Probably both would have agreed that to study over the weekend was the right choice to make; thus the argument is not primarily concerned with the content level. The argument centers on the relationship level; the man expected to be consulted about plans for the weekend; the woman, in not doing this, rejected this definition of their relationship. Similar situations exist among married couples when one person will buy something or make dinner plans or invite a guest to dinner without asking the other person first. Even though the other person would have agreed with the decision made, the couple argue because of the message communicated on the relationship level.

Let me give you a personal example. My mother came to stay for a week at a summer place I had. On the first day she swept the kitchen floor six times, though I had repeatedly told her that it did not need sweeping, that I would be tracking in dirt and mud from the outside, and that all that effort was just wasted. But she persisted in sweeping, saying that the floor was dirty and should be swept. On the content level, we were talking about the value of sweeping the kitchen floor. But on the relationship level we were talking about something quite different. We were each saying, "This is my house." When I realized this (though only after considerable argument), I stopped complaining about the relative usefulness of sweeping a floor that did not need sweeping. Not surprisingly, she stopped sweeping.

Arguments over the content dimension are relatively easy to resolve. Generally, we may look something up in a book or ask someone what actually took place or perhaps see the movie again. It is relatively easy to verify facts that are disputed. Arguments on the relationship level, however, are much more difficult to resolve, in part because we seldom recognize that the argument is in fact a relationship one. One of the clearest examples of the confusion between the content and the relationship aspects was reported in a letter to Ann Landers. A woman and her husband were playing bridge with her sister and her husband. The writer notes that her husband had a habit of overbidding his hand and on this particular evening made a "reckless bid of six spades." The writer reports that all she said was, "Either you are crazy or I'm blind." The husband then said, "Why don't you just keep your mouth shut and play the hand." "The dumb remark of yours," he later continued, "cost us the game. I don't want to play cards with you ever again." On one level this argument concerns content—the bridge game, proper bidding, winning strategies, and the like. On another level, however, the argument concerns the relationship between the husband and wife. We might venture to postulate that the relationship level involved such issues as the husband's feeling that his wife should be supportive regardless of what he does, the appropriateness of the wife's public criticism of her husband and of the husband's criticism of his wife, who was really the offended party, and probably many more. As long as the husband and wife assume that their conflict is totally content oriented, they are probably never going to resolve it. A resolution can only come about, it seems, if the relational aspect is understood and confronted.

Communication Involves a Process of Adjustment

Communication may take place only to the extent that the parties communicating share the same system of signals. This is obvious when dealing with speakers of two different languages; one will not be able to communicate with the other to the extent that their language systems differ.

This principle takes on particular relevance when we realize that no two persons share identical signal systems. Parents and children, for example, not only have different vocabularies to a very great extent but, even more important, have different meanings for the terms they have in common. Different cultures and subcultures, even when they share a common language, often have greatly differing nonverbal

The generation gap—a phrase used widely in the 1960s to describe the difficulty in communicating between people who differ widely in age—has always and will always be with us. Differences in experiences, in expectations, in attitudes, in goals, and in language, for example, all contribute to make communication between the generations difficult (but surely not impossible).

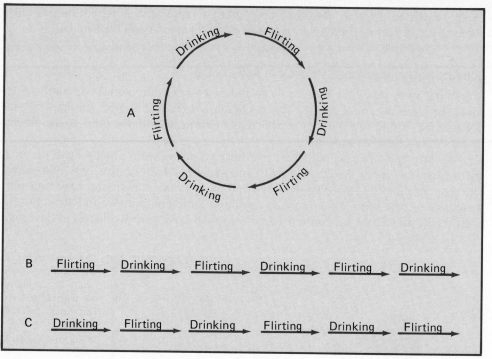

FIGURE 2.1: Punctuation and the Sequence of Events.

communication systems. To the extent that these systems differ, communication will not take place.

Part of the art of communication is learning the other person's signals, how they are used, and what they mean. Persons who are in close relationships with others—either as intimate friends or as romantic partners—realize that learning the other person's signals takes a great deal of time and, often, a great deal of patience. If we want to understand what another person means (by a smile, by saying "I love you," by arguing about trivial matters, by self-deprecating comments), rather than simply what the other person says or does, we have to learn the other person's system of signals.

Relationships Are Defined by Punctuation

Communication events are continuous transactions. They are broken up into short sequences only for purposes of convenience. What is stimulus and what is response is not very easy to determine when we, as analysts of communication, enter after the communication transaction is under way.

Consider, for example, the following incident. A couple is at a party. The husband is flirting with the other women and the wife is drinking; both are scowling at each other and are obviously in a deep nonverbal argument with each other. In explaining the situation, the husband might recall the events by observing that the wife drank and so he flirted with the sober women. The more she drank, the more he flirted.

The only reason for his behavior was his anger over her drinking. Notice that he sees his behavior as the response to her behavior; her behavior came first and was the cause of his behavior.

In recalling the "same" incident, the wife might say that she drank when he started flirting. The more he flirted, the more she drank. She had no intention of drinking until he started flirting. To her, his behavior was the stimulus and hers was the response; he caused her behavior. Thus he sees the behavior as going from drinking to flirting, and she sees it as going from flirting to drinking. This example is depicted visually in Figure 2.1.

In Figure 2.1(a) we see what we assume to be the actual sequence of events. We see this as a continuous series of events with no absolute beginning and no absolute end. Each action (drinking and flirting) stimulates another action, but no initial cause can be identified. In Figure 2.1(b) we see the same sequence of events, punctuated by the wife. She sees the sequence as beginning with the husband's flirting. She sees her drinking behavior as a response to her husband's stimulus (flirting). In Figure 2.1(c) the same sequence of events is portrayed from the husband's point of view. He sees the sequence beginning with the wife's drinking. He sees his flirting as a response to his wife's stimulus (drinking).

This tendency to divide various communication transactions into sequences of stimuli and responses is referred to by Watzlawick, Beavin, and Jackson as the *punctuation* of the sequences of events. They do not argue that punctuation is wrong; obviously, it is a very useful technique in providing some organization for thinking about and talking about communication transactions. At the same time, because we each see things differently, we each punctuate events differently. To the extent that these differences are significant, the possibility for a communication breakdown exists.

Interactions May Be Viewed as Either Symmetrical or Complementary

Some 40 years ago anthropologist Gregory Bateson formulated the concepts of symmetrical and complementary relationships while studying the interactions between the Sepik and Fly River people of New Guinea. Bateson and others soon realized that the concepts were applicable to all forms of interpersonal relationships.

In a symmetrical relationship, the two individuals mirror each other's behavior, with the behavior of one reflected in the behavior of the other. If one member nags, the other member responds in kind. If one member expresses jealousy, the other member expresses jealousy. If one member is passive, the other member is passive. The relationship is one of equality, with the emphasis on minimizing the differences between the two individuals.

In a complementary relationship, the two individuals engage in different behaviors, with the behavior of one serving as the stimulus for the complementary behavior of the other. In complementary relationships, the differences between the parties are maximized. It is necessary in a complementary relationship for both parties to occupy different positions, one the superior and one the inferior, one passive and one active, one strong and one weak. At times such relationships are established by the culture, as, for example, the complementary relationship existing between teacher and student or between employer and employee.

Problems may arise in both symmetrical and complementary relationships. In the symmetrical relationship, it is easy to appreciate that two individuals who mirror each other's jealousy will find very little security. The jealous behavior is likely to escalate to the point where one or both parties will quit from exhaustion. As Watzlawick, Beavin, and Jackson put it, "In marital conflict, for instance, it is easy to observe how the spouses go through an escalation pattern of frustration until they eventually stop from sheer physical or emotional exhaustion and maintain an uneasy truce until they have recovered enough for the next round."

A problem created in complementary relationships, familiar to many college students, is that of *rigid complementarity*. Whereas the complementary relationship between mother and child was at one time vital and essential to the life of the child, that same relationship when the child is older becomes a handicap to further development, when essential change is not allowed to occur.

The problem of *progressive differentiation* may result from either type of relationship—a condition Bateson called *schismogenesis*. Consider this development first in the complementary relationship. Let us say that we have two brothers and that the older brother overprotects the younger. This overprotection fosters increased dependency from the younger brother. As the younger brother becomes more and more dependent, the older brother becomes more and more protective. The result is often a breakdown in the relationship, with each coming to resent the behavior of the other and perhaps coming to dislike or even hate the other.

Progressive differentiation may also occur in a symmetrical relationship. Consider the situation of a husband and wife, both of whom are very aggressive. The aggressiveness of the husband fosters aggressiveness in the wife; the aggressiveness of the wife fosters aggressiveness in the husband. As this escalates, the aggressiveness can no longer be contained, and the relationship blows up.

These axioms seem essential to any introductory or advanced analysis of interpersonal communication. They provide us with insight into the nature and function of human communication as well as into the intricacies of human interpersonal relationships and interactions.

Summary: Contents in Brief

Transactional Postulates	Implications
Inevitability: We cannot *not* communicate; all behavior communicates.	Seek out nonobvious messages and meanings.
Irreversibility: We cannot uncommunicate.	Beware of messages you may later wish to take back, for example, conflict and commitment messages.
Content and relationship dimensions: All communications refer to both content and to the relationships existing between the participants.	Seek out and respond to relational (as well as content) messages.

Summary: Contents in Brief (continued)

Transactional Postulates	Implications
Adjustment: Communication depends on participants' sharing the same system of signals and meanings.	Expand common areas and learn each other's system of signals and meanings to increase interpersonal effectiveness.
Punctuation: Each person divides up the communication sequences into stimuli and responses from his or her own perspective.	View relationship punctuation as arbitrary and adopt the other's point of view to increase empathy and understanding.
Symmetrical and complementary transactions: Interpersonal communications may stimulate similar or complementary behavior, and relationships may be described as basically symmetrical or complementary.	Beware of rigid complementarity, mirroring destructive behaviors, and progressive differentiation (schismogenesis).

Sources

For the axioms I relied on Paul Watzlawick, Janet Helmick Beavin, and Don D. Jackson, *Pragmatics of Human Communication: A Study of Interactional Patterns, Pathologies, and Paradoxes* (New York: Norton, 1967). Another useful work in this area is Jurgen Ruesch and Gregory Bateson, *Communication: The Social Matrix of Psychiatry* (New York: Norton, 1951). Many of the ideas set forth in *Pragmatics* may be found in the work of Bateson. For a useful collection of Bateson's writings, see *Steps to an Ecology of Mind* (New York: Ballantine Books, 1972). An interesting interview with Paul Watzlawick that elaborates on some of the topics presented here may be found in *Journal of Communication* 28 (Autumn 1978): 35–45. Popular accounts of these principles may be found in Paul Watzlawick, *How Real Is Real? Confusion, Disinformation, Communication* (New York: Random House [Vintage Books], 1976) and *The Language of Change: Elements of Therapeutic Communication* (New York: Basic Books, 1978). A useful review article is Carol Wilder, "The Palo Alto Group: Difficulties and Directions of the Interactional View for Human Communication Research," *Human Communication Research* 5 (Winter 1979): 171–186. For the discussion of the nature of the transactional view of interpersonal communication, I used the insights of Dean C. Barnlund, "A Transactional Model of Communication," *Language Behavior: A Book of Readings in Communication*, comp. J. Akin, A. Goldberg, G. Myers, and J. Stewart (The Hague: Mouton, 1970), and William W. Wilmot, *Dyadic Communication*, 2d ed. (Reading, Mass.: Addison-Wesley, 1979). An excellent discussion of these and related principles as applied to improving interpersonal relationships may be found in William J. Lederer, *Creating a Good Relationship* (New York: Norton, 1984).

Perception in Interpersonal Communication

OBJECTIVES

Upon completion of this unit, you should be able to:

1. define *interpersonal perception*
2. explain the three major stages in the perception process
3. explain the process of attribution and identify the operation of the three criteria used in making causal judgments
4. explain how self-attribution differs from other-attribution
5. define *self-serving bias* and explain its operation in causal attribution
6. explain what is meant by an *implicit personality theory* and describe its influence on interpersonal perception
7. define and explain the relevance in interpersonal perception of the following: *self-fulfilling prophecy, perceptual accentuation, primacy, recency, consistency,* and *stereotype*
8. explain at least three variables related to the accuracy of interpersonal perception

Perception is the process by which we become aware of objects and events in the external world through our various senses: sight, smell, taste, touch, and hearing. Perception is an active rather than a passive process. Our perceptions are only in part a function of the outside world; in large measure they are a function of our own past experiences, our desires, our needs and wants, our loves and hatreds. Hans Toch and Malcolm MacLean express the essence of this transactional view of perception most clearly. "Each percept [that which is perceived], from the simplest to the most complex, is the product of a creative act. . . . We can never encounter a stimulus before some meaning has been assigned to it by some perceiver. . . . Therefore, each perception is the beneficiary of all previous perceptions; in turn, each new perception leaves its mark on the common pool. A percept is thus a link between the past which gives it its meaning and the future which it helps to interpret."

In this unit our concern is with explaining the nature of perception, particularly its role in interpersonal communication. First, we consider the stages in the perception process and what happens between the occurrence of an event and a person's interpretation and evaluation of that event. Second, we explore attribution—the process by which we attempt to understand behavior, especially the reasons or motivations for behavior. Third, we consider six major perceptual processes—the processes we use to perceive people and make inferences about them. Fourth, we focus on the issue of accuracy in interpersonal perception: How accurate are our perceptions of others? What characteristics make some people more accurate perceivers than others?

THE PERCEPTION PROCESS

The process of perception may be viewed as occurring in three stages or steps. These stages are not discrete; they are continuous and blend into one another.

1. Sensory Stimulation Occurs

At this first stage, the sense organs are stimulated—we hear the Rolling Stones's new record, we see someone we have not seen for years, we smell perfume on the person next to us, we taste a juicy steak, we feel a sweaty palm as we shake hands.

Even when we have the sensory ability to perceive stimuli, we do not always do so. For example, when you are daydreaming in class, you do not hear what the teacher is saying until your own name is called. Then you wake up. You know your name was called, but you do not know why. This is a clear and perhaps too frequent example of our perceiving what is meaningful to us and not perceiving what is not meaningful (or at least what we temporarily judge to be meaningless).

An obvious implication of this is that what we do perceive is only a very small portion of what could be perceived. Much as we have limits on how far we can see, we also have limits on the quantity of stimulation that we can take in at any given time. One of the goals of education, or so it would seem, is to train us to perceive and make sense of what exists, whether it be art, politics, music, communication, social problems, or any other conceivable source of sensory stimulation.

2. Sensory Stimulation Is Organized

At the second stage, the sensory stimulations are organized in some way and according to some principles. Experts do not agree on exactly how our sensory stimulations are organized and what principles such organization follows. Two principles, proximity and resemblance, however, seem useful in interpersonal perception and illustrate how sensory stimuli might be organized. The principle of *proximity* states that persons who are physically close to one another (persons who are often seen together or who live close to each other) will be perceived as a group, as having some commonality. The principle of *resemblance* states that people who are similar in appearance (members of the same race or persons who dress in similar ways) will also be grouped together and distinguished from people of a different race or who dress very differently.

3. Sensory Stimulation Is Interpreted–Evaluated

The third step in the perceptual process is interpretation-evaluation (hyphenated to emphasize that the two cannot be separated). This third step is inevitably subjective.

Our interpretations-evaluations are not based solely on the external stimulus but are greatly influenced by our past experiences, needs, wants, value systems, beliefs about the way things are or should be, physical and emotional state at the time, expectations, and so on. Obviously, there is much room here for disagreement. Although we may all be exposed to the same external stimulus, the way it is interpreted-evaluated will differ from person to person and from one time to another for the same person.

ATTRIBUTION

Perhaps the most interesting and most insightful theoretical approach to interpersonal perception is that of *attribution theory,* developed largely by E. E. Jones and K. E. Davis and expanded and clarified greatly by H. H. Kelley. Attribution is a process through which we attempt to understand the behaviors of others (as well as our own), particularly the reasons or motivations for these behaviors. Most of our inferences about a person's motivations—a person's reasons for behaving in various ways—come from our observations of the person's behaviors.

If our eventual aim is to discover the causes of another's behavior, our first step is to determine if the individual is responsible for the behavior or if some outside factor is responsible. That is, we first have to determine if the cause of the behavior is *internal* (for example, if the behavior is due to the person's personality or to some such enduring trait) or *external* (for example, if the behavior is due to some situational factor). Internal and external are the two kinds of causality with which attribution theory is concerned.

Consider an example. We look at a teacher's grade book and observe that ten F's were assigned in cultural anthropology. In an attempt to discover what this behavior (assignment of the ten F's) reveals about the teacher, we first have to discover if the teacher was in fact responsible for the behavior or if it could be attributed to outside or external factors. If we discover that the examinations on which the grades were based were made up by a faculty committee and that the committee set the standards for passing or failing, we could not attribute any particular motives to this individual teacher since the behavior was not internally caused. It was externally caused—in this case by the department committee in conjunction with each student's performance on the examination.

On the other hand, let us assume that the following occurred: This teacher made up the examination without any assistance from other faculty members, and no department or university standards were used; the teacher made up a personal set of standards for passing and failing. Now we would be more apt (though perhaps not fully convinced) to attribute the ten F's to internal causes. We would be strengthened in our beliefs that there was something internalized within this teacher, some personality characteristic, for example, that led to this behavior if we discovered that (1) no other teacher in anthropology gave out nearly as many failures, (2) this particular teacher frequently gives out lots of F's in cultural anthropology, and (3) this teacher frequently gives many F's in other courses as well. These three bits of added information would lead us to conclude that there was something in this teacher that motivated the behavior.

Three Principles of Attribution

These three new items of information each represent one of the three principles we use in making causal judgments in interpersonal perception: (1) consensus, (2) consistency, and (3) distinctiveness. We use each of these principles every day in making judgments about people, though we talk about them with a different jargon.

CONSENSUS

When we focus on the principle of *consensus*, we ask essentially, "Do other people react or behave in the same way as the person on whom we are focusing?"—that is, is the person acting in accordance with the consensus? If the answer is no, we are more likely to attribute the behavior to some internal cause. In the teacher example, we were strengthened in our belief that there was something internal causing the F's when we learned that other teachers did not do this—there was low consensus. When only one person acts contrary to the norm, we are more likely to attribute that person's behavior to some internal motivation. If all teachers gave a great number of F's (that is, if there was high consensus), we would be more likely to look for causality outside the individual teacher and conclude, for example, that the anthropology department uses a particular curve in determining grades, that the students were not very bright, or any other reason external to the specific teacher.

CONSISTENCY

When we focus on the principle of *consistency*, we ask if this person repeatedly behaves in the same way in similar situations. If the answer is yes, there is high consistency, and we are likely to attribute the behavior to the person, to some internal motivation. The fact that this teacher frequently gives lots of F's in cultural anthropology leads us to attribute the cause to the teacher rather than to outside sources. If, on the other hand, there was low consistency—that is, if this teacher rarely gives F's—we would be more likely to look for reasons external to the teacher. We might consider, for example, the possibility that this specific class was not terribly bright or that the department required the teacher to start giving out failures, and so on. That is, we would look for causes external to the teacher.

DISTINCTIVENESS

When we focus on the principle of *distinctiveness*, we ask if this person reacts in similar ways in different situations. If the answer is yes, there is low distinctiveness, and we are likely to conclude that there is an internal cause. Low distinctiveness indicates that the situation is not distinctive and that this person reacts in similar ways in different situations. The fact that the teacher reacted the same way (gave lots of F's) in similar situations led us to conclude that this particular class was not distinctive and that the reason or motivation for the behavior could not be found in this unique situation. We further concluded that this behavior must be due to the teacher's inner motivation. Consider the alternative: If this teacher gave all high grades and no failures in all other courses (that is, if the cultural anthropology class situation was highly distinctive), we would conclude that the motivation for the failures was to be found in sources outside the teacher and for reasons unique to this class.

Low consensus, high consistency, and low distinctiveness lead us to attribute a person's behavior to internal causes. High consensus, low consistency, and high distinctiveness lead us to attribute a person's behavior to external causes. A summary with a specific example is presented in Table 3.1.

Revealing and Unrevealing Behaviors

Of course, not all behaviors are equally revealing of internal motivations. Some behaviors tell us a great deal about an individual, while other behaviors fail to separate this person from thousands of others. First, behaviors that are produced by one motivation are more revealing than are behaviors produced by various and numerous motivations. Consider attempting to account for the reason why a friend took a position with Hulk Industries. The job is boring, the work required is physically demanding and unpleasant, but it pays well. Further, our friend has turned down easier and more exciting jobs that did not pay well. From this we would likely conclude that this individual was motivated by money. The behavior of taking the position with Hulk Industries could be accounted for (assuming we had all the facts) only on the basis of the money factor. This behavior is therefore more revealing of motivation than would taking a position with Wonder, Inc., where the job was interesting, the work easy and pleasant, and the money good. Here we would not be able to make a strong inference concerning which motive operated to produce the given behavior.

Second, behaviors that are uncommon or are drastically different from those produced by others are more revealing than are behaviors common to everyone. Consider the mother who buys her children new clothes, sees that they go to bed on time, and supervises their homework. These are the functions of many mothers and hence would not be particularly revealing; they would not enable us to separate this mother from thousands of other mothers. However, take the mother who beats her child for hanging her new dress on a wire hanger—as depicted in the book and film *Mommie Dearest*. This bit of behavior is uncommon enough for us to find it revealing; this behavior tells us something about this particular individual and enables us to distinguish her from thousands of other mothers.

TABLE 3.1: A Summary of Consensus, Consistency, Distinctiveness in Causal Attribution

Situation: A student is observed complaining about a grade received in a philosophy course. On what basis will we conclude whether this behavior is internally or externally caused?

Internal If:	External If:
1. No one else complained. (Low consensus)	1. Many others have complained. (High consensus)
2. Student has complained in the past. (High consistency)	2. Student has never complained in the past. (Low consistency)
3. Student has complained to other teachers in other courses. (Low distinctiveness)	3. Student has never complained to other teachers. (High distinctiveness)

Self-attribution

In *self-attribution*—the attempt to account for our own behaviors—we follow the same general patterns, with two main differences. First, there is a general tendency to see the behaviors of others as internally caused but our own behaviors as externally caused. In part this seems due to the fact that in accounting for our own behaviors, we have a great deal more information than we do when accounting for the behaviors of others. For example, we know that we have acted differently in other situations and therefore can more easily attribute this specific behavior to this specific situation. Also, since we cannot focus directly on our own behaviors and see them as objectively as we see the behaviors of others, we focus most of our attention on the environment or situation. Both of these tendencies, then, lead us to attribute the majority of the causes of our own behaviors to situational or external factors.

The second major difference in self-attribution involves what has been called the *self-serving bias*. Generally, this bias leads us to take credit for the positive and to deny responsibility for the negative. Thus, when attempting to account for our negative behaviors, we would be more apt to attribute them to situational or environmental factors, and when accounting for our positive behaviors, we are likely to attribute them to internal factors.

Generally, then, in self-attribution, we attribute our behaviors to situational factors—especially when they are negative. When our behaviors are positive, the self-serving bias tends to have greater force and leads us to attribute the cause to some internal factor, to our positive personality characteristics.

PERCEPTUAL PROCESSES

A number of significant processes govern interpersonal perception. These processes greatly influence what we observe and what we fail to observe, what we infer and what we fail to infer about another person. These processes help to explain the reasons why we make some predictions and why we decline to make other predictions about people. These processes help us to impose some order on the enormous amount of data that impinge on our senses. They enable us to simplify and categorize the vast amount of information around us. In some cases, as is noted in the following discussions, they lead to oversimplification and to a distortion of information. Six perceptual processes are identified and described here: implicit personality theory, the self-fulfilling prophecy, perceptual accentuation, primacy-recency, consistency, and stereotyping.

Implicit Personality Theory

We each have a theory of personality, a system of rules that tells us which characteristics of an individual go with which other characteristics. Consider, for example, the following brief statements. Note the characteristic in parentheses that best seems to complete the sentence:

> *John is energetic, eager, and (intelligent, stupid).*
> *Mary is bold, defiant, and (extraverted, introverted).*
> *Joe is bright, lively, and (thin, fat).*

Jane is attractive, intelligent, and (likable, unlikable).
Susan is cheerful, positive, and (attractive, unattractive).
Jim is handsome, tall, and (flabby, muscular).

Certain of the words "seem right" and others "seem wrong". What makes some seem right is our *implicit personality* theory, the system of rules that tells us which characteristics go with other characteristics. The theory tells us that a person who is energetic and eager is also intelligent, not stupid, although there is no logical reason why a stupid person could not be energetic and eager.

The widely documented "halo effect" is a function of our implicit personality theory. If we know an individual to possess a number of positive qualities, we make the inference that she or he also possesses other positive qualities. There is also a "reverse halo effect" that operates in a similar way. If we know a person to possess

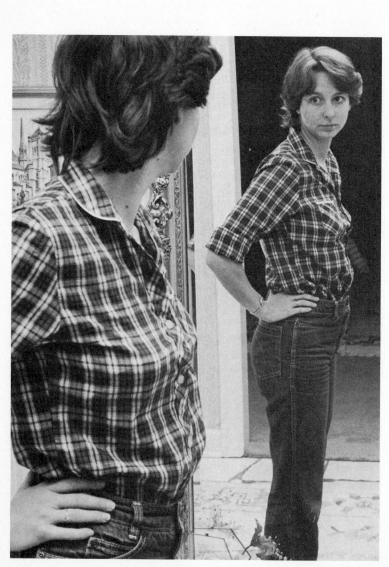

The processes that influence interpersonal perception—implicit personality theory, self-fulfilling prophecy, perceptual accentuation, primacy-recency, consistency, and stereotyping—also influence self-perception (the way we see ourselves). And this self-perception will greatly influence how we communicate with others and how we respond to the communications of others. In turn, our interpersonal interactions—the successes, the failures, the reinforcement, the stroking—will influence the view we have of ourselves. It is a transactional process in which our self-image influences how we communicate, and our communications influence our self-image.

a number of negative qualities, we are more likely to infer that the person also possesses other negative qualities. Implicit personality theories, with their halo and reverse halo effects, often lead to self-fulfilling prophecies, our second perceptual process.

The Self-fulfilling Prophecy

A *self-fulfilling prophecy* is a phenomenon that occurs when we make a prediction or formulate a belief that comes true because we made the prediction and acted on it as if it were true. Identifying the four basic steps in the self-fulfilling prophecy should clarify this important concept and its implications for interpersonal perception.

1. We make a prediction or formulate a belief about a person or a situation. (For example, we make a prediction that Pat is awkward in interpersonal encounters.)
2. We act toward that person or situation as if that prediction or belief were in fact true. (For example, we act toward Pat as if Pat were in fact awkward.)
3. Because we act as if the belief were true, it becomes true. (For example, because of the ways in which we act toward Pat, Pat becomes tense and manifests awkwardness.)
4. We observe *our* effect on the person or the resulting situation, and what we see strengthens our beliefs. (For example, we observe Pat's awkwardness, and this reinforces our belief that Pat is in fact awkward.)

If we expect people to act in a certain way or if we make a prediction about the characteristics of a situation, our predictions will frequently come true because of the phenomenon of the self-fulfilling prophecy. Consider, for example, people who enter a group situation convinced that the other members will dislike them. Almost invariably they are proved right; the other members do dislike them. What they may be doing is acting in such a way as to encourage people to respond negatively. Such people fulfill their own prophecies.

THE PYGMALION EFFECT

A widely known example of the self-fulfilling prophecy is the Pygmalion effect. In one study of this effect, teachers were told that certain pupils were expected to do exceptionally well, that they were late bloomers. The names of these students were actually selected at random by the experimenters; the results, however, were not random. The students whose names were given to the teachers actually did perform at a higher level than the other students. In fact, these students even improved in IQ score more than did the other students.

SCRIPTS

Eric Berne, in *Games People Play,* and Thomas Harris, in *I'm O.K., You're O.K.,* both point out the same type of effect in a somewhat different context. These transactional psychologists argue that we live by the scripts (discussed in detail in Unit 7) given to us by our parents and that we act as we are told to act. Much like the children who were expected to do well, we all, according to transactional psychology, live by the scripts given to us as children. In a sense, these internalized scripts provide us with directives that influence the prophecies we make about ourselves. If our script tells us that we are socially inept, we make prophecies that predict social failure. If our script tells us that we are mechanically inclined, we make prophecies that predict success in mechanical matters.

THE LAW OF EXPECTATIONS

The self-fulfilling prophecy is much like social psychologist George Kelly's so-called law of expectations, which states that our behaviors will be determined, in large part, by our expectations or how we think an event will turn out. If we have negative expectations ("We're going to have a fight when I get home late tonight" or "This dinner party is going to be a disaster"), our behavior will assist in making these negative expectations come true. If we have positive expectations ("This blind date is going to be the best yet" or "This semester I'm going to make some really good friends"), our behavior will assist in making these positive expectations come true.

The practical advice to be derived from this important process is not that we should avoid making prophecies or developing expectations; these are inevitable and helpful to normal functioning. Rather, it is to become aware of how our prophecies and expectations influence our behavior and to use this awareness to achieve the interpersonal outcomes we want. If we want to make more friends, this law suggests, negative expectations will hinder us and positive expectations will help us.

Perceptual Accentuation

"Any port in a storm" is a phrase that appears in various guises throughout our communications: To many people an ugly date is better than no date at all. Spinach may taste horrible, but when you are starving, it can taste like filet mignon. And so it goes.

In a classic study on need influencing perception, poor and rich children were shown pictures of coins and later asked to estimate their size. The poor children estimated the size as much greater than did the rich children. Similarly, hungry people perceive food objects and food terms at lower recognition thresholds (needing fewer physical cues) than people who are not hungry.

In terms of interpersonal perception, this process, called *perceptual accentuation*, leads us to see what we expect to see and what we want to see. We see people we like as being better-looking than people we do not like; we see people we like as being smarter than people we do not like. The obvious counterargument to this is that we actually prefer good-looking and smart people, not that people whom we like are seen as being handsome and smart. But perhaps that is not the entire story.

In a study reported by Zick Rubin, male undergraduates participated in what they thought were two separate and unrelated studies that were actually two parts of a single experiment. In the first part, each subject read a passage; half the subjects were given an arousing sexual seduction scene to read, and half were given a passage about sea gulls and herring gulls. In the second part of the experiment, subjects were asked to rate a female student on the basis of her photograph and a self-description. As might be expected, the subjects who read the arousing scene rated the woman as significantly more attractive than did the other group. Further, the subjects who expected to go on a blind date with this woman rated her as more sexually receptive than did the subjects who were told that they had been assigned to date someone else. How can we account for such findings?

Although this experiment was a particularly dramatic demonstration of perceptual accentuation, this same general process occurs every day. We magnify or accentuate that which will satisfy our needs and wants. The thirsty person sees a mirage of water; the sexually deprived person sees a mirage of sexual satisfaction.

Primacy–Recency

Assume for a moment that you are enrolled in a course in which half the classes are extremely dull and half the classes are extremely exciting. At the end of the semester, you evaluate the course and the instructor. Would the evaluation be more favorable if the dull classes constituted the first half of the semester and the exciting classes constituted the second half of the semester or if the order were reversed? If what comes first exerts the most influence, we have what is called a *primacy effect*. If what comes last (or is the most recent) exerts the most influence, we have a *recency effect*.

In an early study on the effects of primacy-recency in interpersonal perception, Solomon Asch read a list of adjectives describing a person to a group of subjects and found that the effects of order were significant. A person described as ''intelligent, industrious, impulsive, critical, stubborn, and envious'' was evaluated more positively than a person described as ''envious, stubborn, critical, impulsive, industrious, and intelligent.'' The implication here is that we use early information to provide us with a general idea as to what a person is like, and we use later information to make this general idea or impression more specific. Numerous other studies have provided evidence for the effect of first impressions. For example, in one study, subjects observed a student (actually a confederate of the experimenter) taking a test. The task of the subject was to estimate the number of questions the student got right and to predict how well he would do on a second trial. The confederate followed two different orders. In one order, the descending order, the correct answers were all in the beginning. In the ascending order, the correct answers were toward the end. In each case, of course, there were the same number of correct and incorrect answers. Subjects judged the descending order to contain more correct responses. They also estimated that students in the descending order would do better on a second trial and judged them to be more intelligent.

The obvious practical implication of primacy-recency is this: The first impression you make is likely to be the most important. It is through this first impression that others will filter additional information to formulate eventually a picture of who you are. At the same time, recognize that your first impressions of others may not be accurate descriptions of the entire person. Hence, try to keep an open mind; do not allow your first impressions to blind you to further incoming data or lead you to misinterpret additional (and perhaps contradictory) information.

Consistency

There is a strong tendency to maintain balance or consistency among our perceptions. We strive to maintain balance among our attitudes; we expect certain things to go together and other things not to go together. On a purely intuitive basis, for example, respond to the following sentences by noting the expected response.

1. I expect a person I like to (like, dislike) me.
2. I expect a person I dislike to (like, dislike) me.
3. I expect my friend to (like, dislike) my friend.
4. I expect my friend to (like, dislike) my enemy.
5. I expect my enemy to (like, dislike) my friend.
6. I expect my enemy to (like, dislike) my enemy.

According to most consistency theories, our expectations would be as follows: We would expect a person we liked to like us (1) and a person we disliked to dislike us (2). We would expect a friend to like a friend (3) and to dislike an enemy (4). We would expect our enemy to dislike our friend (5) and to like our other enemy (6). All of these should be intuitively satisfying.

Further, we would expect someone we liked to possess characteristics we liked or admired. And we would expect our enemies not to possess characteristics we liked or admired. Conversely, we would expect persons we liked to lack unpleasant characteristics and persons we dislike to possess unpleasant characteristics.

In terms of interpersonal perception, this tendency for balance and consistency may influence the way in which we see other people. It is easy to see our friends as being possessed of fine qualities and our enemies as being possessed of unpleasant qualities. Donating money to the poor, for example, can be perceived as an act of charity (if from a friend) or as an act of pomposity (if from an enemy). We would probably laugh harder at a joke told by a well-liked comedian than at that very same joke told by a disliked comedian.

Stereotyping

One of the most frequently used shortcuts in interpersonal perception is stereotyping. Originally *stereotype* was a printing term that referred to the plate that printed the same image over and over again. A sociological or psychological stereotype is a fixed impression of a group of people. We all have stereotypes, of national groups, religious groups, or racial groups, perhaps of criminals, prostitutes, teachers, or plumbers.

If we have these fixed impressions, we often, upon meeting a member of a particular group, see that person primarily as a member of that group and apply to that person all the characteristics we have in our minds for members of that group. If we meet someone who is a prostitute, for example, we have a host of characteristics for prostitutes that we are ready to apply to this one person. To complicate matters further, we will often see in this person's behavior the manifestation of various characteristics that we would not see if we did not know that this person was a prostitute. Stereotypes distort our ability to perceive other people accurately. They prevent us from seeing an individual as an individual rather than as a member of a group.

ACCURACY IN INTERPERSONAL PERCEPTION

Children can tell what a person is really like, even though adults might have difficulty.

Women are just naturally better judges of people than men.

Pat is so popular with everyone; Pat must be an excellent judge of people.

After going on an encounter weekend, we should be able to judge people more accurately.

These statements reflect our concern with accuracy in interpersonal perception. Some of these statements seem logical on the basis of our experience. Some seem logical because of some rule of analogy—we went on an encounter weekend, improved our accuracy, and therefore conclude that encounter weekends improve perception accuracy for people in general. Some seem logical because some authority told us so.

Actually, much experimental research, clearly synthesized by Mark Cook, has been directed at testing these and similar statements to determine the characteristics of persons who are particularly accurate in interpersonal perception. Some of the prominent factors or variables are age, sex, intelligence, popularity, personality characteristics, and training.

AGE

Contrary to the popular notion that children can tell what a person is really thinking or is really like, accuracy of interpersonal perception increases rather than decreases with age. For example, it has been found that judgments of emotion from facial and vocal cues as well as sociometric judgments increase in accuracy with age.

SEX

The popular notion that women are more accurate interpersonal perceivers than men has some—but not overwhelming—support. Differences on the basis of sex have been found in some studies. In the studies that have found differences, women have performed at a higher level than men. It is interesting to note that the emotions of women are perceived more accurately than the emotions of men. This may be due to the fact that in our culture women have been ''allowed'' to express emotion more freely than have men. Consequently, the expression of emotion in women may be more complete and less inhibited than in men. Or perhaps women have learned emotional expression better than have men.

INTELLIGENCE

Although intellectual brilliance does not ensure interpersonal perceptual accuracy, generally the more intelligent the person, the better he or she is at accurately judging other people. This is due in part to the fact that people of superior intelligence generally have more categories—more names and labels—for describing people. They are therefore less apt to group people into broad and general (and inaccurate) classes as much as people with fewer categories. Having a great number of categories for describing people's personalities and behaviors probably assists us in focusing our attention on small differences that others, without these finely differentiated categories, might not see. Surely it enables those with these extra categories to appear to be more accurate and more sophisticated in their interpersonal perceptions.

POPULARITY

It is generally assumed that people who are popular and socially favored have achieved their standing because they are accurate judges of people. A number of studies have sought to investigate this, but no definite conclusions seem warranted. At times, of course, accurate perception may prove a hindrance to popularity if this skill enables the individual to see all the faults in others. On the other hand, if it gives an individual better insight into other people, it probably functions to improve social relationships.

PERSONALITY

A great deal of research has focused on the personality characteristics of accurate perceivers. Are accurate perceivers more sociable or less sociable, more empirically oriented or less empirically oriented, more independent or more dependent? Here there is much confusion. Generally, the personality characteristics of accurate judges include sociability, tough-mindedness, empiricism, nonconformity, independence, strong will, and dominance. When the sex of the judge is controlled, however, a somewhat different picture emerges. "The picture of the good male judge that emerges," says Cook, "is rather unexpected. The good male judge of males is described as a rather insensitive aggressive person while the good male judge of females is described as very ineffectual. The good female judges are described slightly more favorably."

TRAINING

Training, it is assumed, increases one's ability at almost anything. We seem to have an undying faith in the ability of individuals to be educated to the point where they can do just about anything. With interpersonal perception, however, training has not been found to be effective, at least not generally. Interpersonal perception has been improved when judges were given immediate knowledge of results, but T-groups and clinical training, for example, have not resulted in improved interpersonal perception. Such training does provide people with a host of new labels and terms, and this makes it appear that their accuracy has improved. Actually, however, it has not. Or so say the experimental studies.

Perceiving another person's characteristics or traits is a particularly complex task, and it should come as no surprise that we have difficulty with it. We are especially poor at perceiving people who are very different from ourselves and best at perceiving people who are very similar to ourselves.

Summary: Contents in Brief

Definitions	Processes
Perception: the process by which we become aware of objects and events in the external world through our various senses in three stages: (1) occurrence of sensory stimulation, (2)	*Implicit personality theory:* expectations that certain characteristics go with certain other characteristics *Self-fulfilling prophecy:* predictions influence behaviors

Summary: Contents in Brief (continued)

Definitions	Processes
organization of sensory stimulation, and (3) interpretation-evaluation of sensory stimulation	*Perceptual accentuation:* we perceive what we expect to perceive *Primacy-recency:* first impressions (primacy) influence later perceptions *Consistency:* perception is influenced by our expectation of consistency or balance *Stereotyping:* fixed impressions of groups influence perceptions of individuals
Attribution: the process through which we attempt to understand the behaviors of others (and our own in *self-attribution*), particularly the reasons or motivations for these behaviors	*Consensus:* the degree to which others behave similarly *Consistency:* the degree to which the same behavior occurs in other, similar situations *Distinctiveness:* the degree to which the same behavior occurs in different situations
	Internal motivation is identified in cases of low consensus, high consistency, and low distinctiveness. *External motivation* is identified in cases of high consensus, low consistency, and high distinctiveness.

Sources

A thorough summary of perception is contained in Mark Cook, *Interpersonal Perception* (Baltimore: Penguin, 1971). Standard reference works in this area include Michael Argyle, *Social Interaction* (London: Methuen, 1969), and Renato Tagiuri and Luigi Petrullo, eds., *Person Perception and Interpersonal Behavior* (Stanford, Calif.: Stanford University Press, 1958). A brief but insightful account of interpersonal perception is provided by Albert Hastorf, David Schneider, and Judith Polefka, *Person Perception* (Reading, Mass.: Addison-Wesley, 1970). I found Zick Rubin, *Liking and Loving: An Invitation to Social Psychology* (New York: Holt, Rinehart and Winston, 1973), a most useful source. Much of the discussion of the perceptual processes is based on the insights provided by Rubin. The cited study by Solomon Asch is "Forming Impressions of Personality," *Journal of Abnormal and Social Psychology* 41 (1946): 258–290. The cited study on forming impressions of exam-taking students was conducted and reported by Edward E. Jones, Leslie Rock, Kelley G. Sharver, and Lawrence M. Ward, "Pattern of Performance and Ability Attribution: An Unexpected Primacy Effect," *Journal of Personality and Social Psychology* 10 (1968): 317–340. Both of these studies are discussed by Rubin. On scripts see Eric Berne, *Games People Play* (New York: Grove Press, 1964), Thomas A. Harris, *I'm O.K., You're O.K.* (New York: Harper & Row, 1969), and any of the more recent works cited in Unit 7. On the role of perception in interpersonal communication, see Don. E. Hamachek, *Encounters with Others: Interpersonal Relationships and You* (New York: Holt, Rinehart and Winston, 1982), Hans Toch and Malcolm S. MacLean, "Perception and Communication: A Transactional View," *Audio-Visual Communication Review* 10 (1967): 55–77, and Gary Cronkhite, "Perception and Meaning," in Carroll C. Arnold and John Waite Bowers, eds., *Handbook of Rhetorical and Communication Theory* (Boston: Allyn & Bacon, 1984), pp. 51–229. In-depth coverage of selected issues in interpersonal perception is provided in *Issues in Person Perception,* ed. Mark Cook (New York: Methuen, 1984).

On attribution theory, see E. E. Jones and K. E. Davis, "From Acts to Dispositions: The Attribution Process in Person Perception," in *Advances in Experimental Social Psychology,* vol. 2, ed. L. Berkowitz (New York: Academic Press, 1965), pp. 219–266. Harold H. Kelley offers "The Process of Causal Attribution," *American Psychologist* 28 (1973): 107–128 and *Personal Relationships: Their Structures and Processes* (Hillsdale, N.J.: Erlbaum, 1979). For recent reviews of attribution theory, see Harold H. Kelley and John L. Michela, "Attribution Theory and Research," in *Annual Review of Psychology,* ed. M. R. Rosenzweig and L. W. Porter (Palo Alto, Calif.: Annual Reviews, 1980), pp. 457–501, and Susan T. Fiske and Shelley E. Taylor, *Social Cognition* (Reading, Mass.: Addison-Wesley, 1984).

The self-fulfilling prophecy was originally formulated by Robert K. Merton in *Social Theory and Social Structure* (New York: Free Press, 1957). For the original Pygmalion studies, see R. Rosenthal and L. Jacobson, *Pygmalion in the Classroom* (New York: Holt, Rinehart and Winston, 1968). Although a number of studies failed to replicate these original findings, most recent studies seem again to support the Pygmalion effect. See, for example, W. B. Seaver, "Effects of Naturally Induced Teacher Expectancies," *Journal of Personality and Social Psychology* 28 (1973): 333–342. An excellent collection of articles on the self-fulfilling prophecy may be found in Paul M. Insel and Lenore F. Jacobson, eds., *What Do You Expect? An Inquiry into Self-Fulfilling Prophecies* (Menlo Park, Calif.: Cummings, 1975).

Listening and Feedback in Interpersonal Communication

OBJECTIVES

Upon completion of this unit, you should be able to:

1. explain the importance of listening
2. define *listening*
3. identify and define the three types of listening
4. define and distinguish between *active* and *passive listening*
5. define and distinguish between *empathic* and *objective listening*
6. define and distinguish between *nonjudgmental* and *judgmental listening*
7. define and distinguish between *surface* and *deep listening*
8. define *active listening*
9. identify at least three functions of active listening
10. describe three techniques for practicing active listening
11. define *feedback*
12. identify and explain at least four suggestions for giving feedback effectively
13. identify and explain at least four suggestions for receiving feedback effectively

There can be little doubt that we listen a great deal. Upon awakening we listen to the radio. On the way to school we listen to friends, to people around us, and perhaps to screeching cars, singing birds, or falling rain. In school our listening day starts in earnest, and we sit in class after class listening to the teacher, to comments by other students, and even to ourselves. We listen to friends at lunch and return to class to listen to more teachers. We arrive home and again listen to our family and friends. Perhaps we then listen to records, radio, or television. All in all, we listen for a good part of our waking day.

THE IMPORTANCE OF LISTENING

If we measured importance in terms of the time we spend at an activity, listening would be our most important communication activity, for we spend most of our communication time engaged in listening. A glance at Figure 4.1, which diagrams the results of two studies, illustrates this point. Note that in both studies (one conducted in 1929 using adults as subjects and one conducted in 1980 using college students as subjects), listening occupied more time than any other communication activity. The results of other studies, using, for example, people in business, further support the importance of listening.

That we listen a great deal of the time, then, can hardly be denied. Whether we listen effectively or efficiently, however, is another matter. In actual practice, most of us are relatively poor listeners, and our listening behavior could be made more effective. Given the amount of time we engage in listening, the improvement of that skill would seem well worth the required effort. And it does take effort. Listening is not easy; it takes time and energy to listen effectively.

THE NATURE OF LISTENING

Because listening is often only vaguely and sometimes inaccurately understood, we need to examine briefly the nature of listening—specifically, the definition of listening and the major types or purposes of listening.

What Is Listening?

Listening is an active process of receiving aural stimuli. Contrary to popular conception, listening is an *active* rather than a passive process. Listening does not just happen; we must make it happen. Listening takes energy and a commitment to engage in often difficult labor.

Listening involves *receiving* stimuli and is thus distinguished from hearing as a physiological process. The word *receiving* is used here to imply that stimuli are taken

FIGURE 4.1: The Time Spent in Listening.

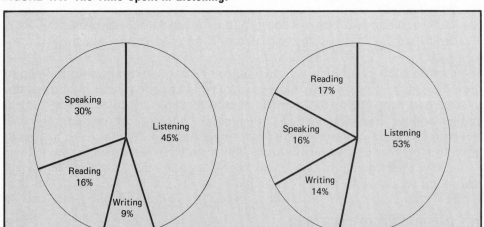

in by the organism and are in some way processed or used. For at least some amount of time, the signals received are retained.

Listening involves *aural* stimuli—that is, signals (sound waves) received by the ear. Listening, therefore, is not limited to verbal signals but encompasses all signals sent by means of fluctuations in air—noises as well as words, music as well as prose.

Jesse S. Nirenberg, in *Getting Through to People*, distinguishes three levels of listening; these may further clarify what we mean by listening. First, there is the level of *nonhearing*. Here the individual does not listen at all; rather, he or she looks at the speaker and may even utter remarks that seem to imply attention such as "OK," "yes," and "mm," but there is really no listening. Nothing is getting through. The second level is the level of *hearing*. Here the person hears what is being said and even remembers it but does not allow any of the ideas to penetrate beyond the level of memory. Third is the level of *thinking*, where the listener not only hears what the speaker is saying but also thinks about it. The listener here evaluates and analyzes what is being said. It is this third level, the level of *listening-thinking*, that we are defining as listening.

Why We Listen

Just as we speak for a variety of purposes, we also listen for different purposes. Three general types of listening may be distinguished: listening for enjoyment, for information, and for help.

LISTENING FOR ENJOYMENT

Listening for enjoyment occupies a good deal of our listening time. We listen to music, to a sports broadcast, and to a television comedy or drama basically for enjoyment. We suspend our critical faculties, rid ourselves of competing stimuli, relax, and enjoy the stimulation.

LISTENING FOR INFORMATION

As students your primary listening responsibilities center on listening for information; in class you listen to the instructor and to other students. When you turn on the car radio to listen for the ball scores, your objective again is to listen for information. In small group and interpersonal situations, much of your time is spent listening for information—what happened to Chris and Pat last weekend, what friends are planning to do over the holiday, what happened in the sociology class you missed. At times our goal is simply the acquisition of new information, to learn some isolated bits of data we did not already know. At other times we listen for information so that we can acquire some new skill or engage in some behavior more effectively—how to operate a computer, how to throw a curve, how to prepare a particular dinner. In still other cases we listen for information so that we can eventually render some kind of evaluation or judgment or criticism.

Listening for enjoyment and listening for information are interrelated: Seldom do we not learn something from our entertainment, and, likewise, seldom are we not entertained during our informative listening. The mass media have been particularly sensitive to the importance of mixing entertainment with their "informative programs" and have recently made great changes, for example, in their news broadcasts. Programs such as "60 Minutes" and "20/20" illustrate the close connection of entertainment and information.

LISTENING TO HELP

The helping function of listening is a crucial one, one to which we turn repeatedly. When we listen to people complain, talk about personal problems, or attempt to make a decision, we often listen with a view to helping them. Perhaps the help will come simply from providing them with a receptive and supportive audience. Just being there, ready to listen and willing to help, is often a great comfort. At other times, the help we give may be more direct, as when we make suggestions or offer advice.

Listening and the Law of Least Effort

Generally, the law of least effort states that, given a choice, we will take the road of least effort, the path of least resistance. Applied to listening, this law refers to the practice of listening to messages that require little effort and avoiding messages that require us to expend much energy and effort. Probably the easiest messages for us to receive come from television, and perhaps this is one reason why we watch so much television. This is not to say that it is the only reason, but clearly it seems to be one reason why people spend more time watching television than they do reading.

Messages that are complicated and thus take a great deal of energy to decipher are less popular than messages that require little effort. Other things being equal, we listen to the messages that require the least effort to interpret and the least expenditure of energy and avoid messages that will require a greater effort and energy expenditure. As speakers, we must recognize this tendency and assist our listeners by making our messages as interesting, as clear, and as easily comprehensible as possible. As listeners, we need to guard against the least-effort tendency lest we fail to listen to complex but valuable and important messages.

EFFECTIVE LISTENING

Because we listen for different reasons and purposes, the principles we follow in listening effectively should vary from one situation to another. Here we identify four dimensions of listening and illustrate the appropriateness of different listening modes for different communication situations.

Active and Passive Listening

The art of effective listening in interpersonal situations is to be an active participant. Perhaps the best preparation for active listening is to act like an active listener, physically and mentally. This may seem trivial and redundant. In practice, however, it may be the most abused rule of effective listening. Students often, for example, come into class, put their feet up on a nearby desk, nod their head to the side, and expect to listen effectively. It just does not happen that way. Recall, for example, how your body almost automatically reacts to important news. Almost immediately you assume an upright posture, cock your head to the speaker, and remain relatively still and quiet. We do this almost reflexively because this is how we listen most effectively. This is not to say that we should be tense and uncomfortable, only that our bodies should reflect our active minds. Even more important than this physical alertness is mental alertness, an active listening attitude. As listeners, we need to enter the communication interaction—whether interpersonal, small group, or public speaking—as coequal partners with the speakers, as persons emotionally and intellectually ready to engage in the mutual sharing of meaning.

Passive listening, however, is not without merit, and some recognition of its values is warranted. Passive listening—listening without talking and without directing the speaker in any nonverbal way—is a powerful means for communicating acceptance. Passive listening allows the speaker to develop his or her thoughts and ideas in the presence of another person who accepts but does not evaluate, who supports but does not intrude. Almost invariably, our comments direct the communications and the thought processes of others, so passive listening serves the often useful purpose of allowing the other person free reign. Listening passively, we provide a supporting and receptive environment; once that has been established, we may wish to participate in a more active way, verbally and nonverbally.

Another form of passive listening is to just sit back, relax, and let the auditory stimulation massage you without your exerting any significant energy or effort and

Effective listening is characterized by the subtle adjustments among the four major dimensions of listening: passive and active listening, empathic and objective listening, supportive and judgmental listening, and surface and deep listening.

especially without your directing the stimuli in any way. Listening to music for pure enjoyment (rather than as a music critic) is perhaps the best example. But listening to the wind howl, the birds sing, the chatter of a crowd of people are better appreciated when listened to passively.

Empathic and Objective Listening

If we are to understand what a person means and what a person is feeling, we need to listen with empathy. To empathize with others is to feel with them, to see the world as they see it, to feel what they feel. Only when we achieve this can we understand another's meaning fully.

There is no fast method for achieving empathy. But it is something we should work toward. It is important, for example, that a student see the teacher's point of view through the eyes of the teacher. And it is equally important for the teacher to see the student's point of view from the student's perspective.

We often witness behavior that seems foolish or ridiculous. We see, for example, a child cry because he or she lost a coin. From our point of view, the amount lost is insignificant, and it therefore seems foolish to cry over it. What we need to do, however, is to see the situation from the point of view of the child—to realize that the amount of money is not insignificant to the child or that perhaps the consequences of losing the money are extremely serious. Popular students might intellectually understand the reasons why an unpopular student might feel depressed, but that will not enable them to understand emotionally the feelings of depression. To accomplish that, they must put themselves in the position of the unpopular student, to role-play a bit and begin to feel that student's feelings and think that student's thoughts. Then the popular students will be in a somewhat better position truly to understand, to empathize.

Although for most communication situations, empathic listening is the preferred mode of responding, there are times when we need to go beyond standing in the other person's shoes and measure the meanings and feelings against some objective reality. It is important to listen to a friend tell us how the entire world hates him or her and to understand how our friend feels and perhaps why he or she feels this way. But then we need to look a bit more objectively at our friend and at the world and perhaps see the paranoia or the self-hatred. Sometimes we have to put our empathic responses aside and listen with objectivity and detachment.

Nonjudgmental and Judgmental Listening

Effective listening is characterized by both nonjudgmental and judgmental responses—listening with an open mind with a view toward understanding and also listening critically with a view toward making some kind of evaluation or judgment. Clearly, we should listen for understanding while suspending judgment first; only after we have fully understood the relevant messages should we evaluate or judge. Listening with an open mind is extremely difficult. It is not easy for us, for example, to listen to arguments against some cherished belief or to criticisms of something we think is just great. We need to listen fairly, despite the red flag of an out-of-place expression or a hostile remark. Listening often stops when such a remark is made.

Admittedly, to continue listening with an open mind is difficult, yet it is particularly important in such situations that we do continue to listen.

If meaningful communication is to take place, however, we need to supplement open-minded listening with critical listening. Listening with an open mind will help us to understand the messages better; listening with a critical mind will help us to analyze that understanding and to evaluate the messages judiciously. As intelligent and educated citizens, it is our responsibility to evaluate critically what we hear. This is especially true in the college environment. It is very easy simply to listen to a teacher and take down what is said; it is extremely important that what is said be evaluated and critically analyzed. Teachers have biases too; at times consciously and at times unconsciously, these biases creep into scholarly discussions. They need to be identified and brought to the surface by the critical listener. Contrary to what most students will argue, the vast majority of teachers appreciate the responses of critical listeners. They demonstrate that someone is listening and stimulate further examination of ideas.

Two relevant listening problems that should be identified are prejudging messages and filtering out difficult or undesirable messages.

PREJUDGING MESSAGES

We have to be especially careful of what is referred to as prejudgment. There is often a strong tendency to prejudge the communications of others as uninteresting or irrelevant or invalid before we even hear them. By prejudging a communication, we are in effect lifting the burden of listening from our shoulders. So we just tune out the speaker and let our minds recapture last Saturday night. It's an easy trap to fall into. Most communications are, at least potentially, interesting and relevant. If we prejudge them and tune them out, we will never be proved wrong. At the same time, however, we close ourselves off from potentially useful information. Most significant, perhaps, we do not give the other person a fair hearing.

FILTERING OUT MESSAGES

Another listening problem that we have to be careful to avoid is that of filtering out difficult or undesirable messages. Depending on our own intellectual equipment, many of the messages that we confront will need careful consideration and in-depth scrutiny. Listening will be difficult, but the alternative—missing out on what is said—seems a lot less acceptable than stretching and straining our minds a bit.

Perhaps more serious than filtering out difficult messages is filtering out unpleasant ones. None of us wants to be told that something we believe in is untrue, that people we care for are disliked, or that ideals we hold are self-destructive. Yet these are the very messages we need to listen to most attentively. These messages will lead us to examine and reexamine our unconscious assumptions. If we filter out this kind of information, we will be left with a host of unstated and unexamined assumptions that will influence us without our influencing them.

Surface and Deep Listening

In Shakespeare's *Julius Caesar*, Marc Antony, in giving the funeral oration for Caesar, says: "I come to bury Caesar, not to praise him. / The evil that men do lives after them, / The good is oft interred with their bones." And later: "For Brutus is an honourable man; / So are they all, all honourable men." But Antony, as we know, did not come to bury Caesar and certainly not to convince the crowd that Brutus was, in fact, an honorable man. Instead he came to incite the crowd to avenge the death of Caesar, his friend.

In most messages there is an obvious meaning that a literal reading of the words and sentences enables us to derive. But there is often another level of meaning; sometimes, as in *Julius Caesar,* it is the opposite of the expressed literal meaning; sometimes, it seems totally unrelated. In reality, few messages have only one level of meaning; such messages seem the exception. Most messages function on two or three levels at the same time. Consider some of the frequently heard messages: A friend asks you how you like his new haircut. Another friend asks you how you like her painting. On one level, the meaning is clear: Do you like the haircut? Do you like the painting? But it seems reasonable to assume that on another level, perhaps a more important level, your friends are asking you to say something positive about them—about his appearance, about her artistic ability. They seem to be asking for positive stroking, asking you to say something pleasant and positive. The parent who seems at first to be complaining about working hard at the office or in the home may in reality be asking for some expression of appreciation. The child who talks about the unfairness of the children in the playground may be asking for affection and love, for some expression of caring, for some indication that you understand. The college student who expresses the desire to quit school and get a full-time job may be asking for encouragement or perhaps preparing for the impact of soon-to-be-received, not-so-great grades.

In interpersonal listening, we have to be particularly sensitive to different levels of meaning because if we respond only to the surface-level communication (the literal meaning), we miss the opportunity to make meaningful contact with the other person's feelings and real needs. If we say to the parent, "You're always complaining. I bet you really love working so hard," we are failing to meet the needs of this call for understanding and appreciation.

EXAMINING THE LEVELS OF MEANING

In attempting to decipher the different levels of meaning, a few principles might prove useful. Meaning is communicated both verbally and nonverbally, by what is said as well as by what is done with the face, eyes, hands, and so forth. Sweating hands, shaking knees, a limp handshake, a wink of the eye, the avoidance of direct eye contact, in conjunction with verbal messages, alter the verbal messages in significant ways and clue us in to the likelihood that there is more to the message than its literal meaning. Further, we must recognize that the meaning of a communication lies also in what is omitted. The parents of teenagers who talk about the drug problem of everyone else's teenagers but never once mention their own children (and may never even think of their own children in this connection) are communicating important information that deserves looking into.

Earlier we noted that all messages have a content and a relationship dimension. Listening for different levels of meaning will be aided if we focus on both relational and content aspects. The student who constantly criticizes or challenges the teacher is on one level communicating disagreement over content; the student is debating the issues. On another level—the relationship level—however, the student may well be voicing objections to the instructor's authority or perhaps to the instructor's authoritarianism. If the instructor is to deal effectively with the student, both types of messages must be listened to and responded to.

In listening for the different levels of meaning, recognize that a person inevitably talks about oneself, from one's own point of view, colored by one's needs, wants, and desires, on the basis of one's own previous experiences, and so on. Whatever a person says is, in part, a function of who that person is, and listening for the different levels of meaning is to attend to those personal, self-reference messages.

All this is not to say that we should disregard the literal meaning of interpersonal messages or that we should constantly focus attention on what else the speaker might be attempting to communicate. If we do this, we will quickly find that our listening problems are over; no one will be talking with us anymore. We need to walk a reasonable line between the literal and the underlying meanings in the messages we receive. We need to become sensitive to the underlying meanings in many messages but not preoccupied with them to the point that we see and hear nothing else. We need to be ready to respond to the underlying messages without becoming obsessed with uncovering everyone's hidden meanings. Perhaps the best guideline to use is to respond to the various levels of meaning in the messages of others as you would like others to respond to yours—sensitively but not obsessively, readily but not overambitiously.

ACTIVE LISTENING

Earlier we noted the distinction between active and passive listening and observed that generally we should be active participants in the communication encounter. There is, however, another kind of active listening that should be considered. This type of active listening is one of the most important communication skills we can learn, so we need to consider it in some depth.

Consider the following brief comment and some possible responses that might be made to it:

> **Speaker:** That creep gave me a C on the paper. I really worked on that project and he gives me a lousy C.
> **Listener 1:** That's not so bad; most people got around the same grade. I got a C too.
> **Listener 2:** So what? This is your last semester. Who cares about grades anyway?
> **Listener 3:** You should be pleased with a C. Peggy and Michael both failed, and John and Judy got D's.
> **Listener 4:** You got a C on that paper you were working on for the last three weeks? You sound really angry and hurt.

All four listeners are probably eager to make the speaker feel better. But they go about it in very different ways and, we can be sure, with very different outcomes. The first three listeners give fairly typical responses. Listeners 1 and 2 both try to minimize the significance of a C grade. This is an extremely common response to someone who expresses some kind of displeasure or disappointment. It is also, I think, a most inappropriate response, a response that may be well intended but one that does little to foster meaningful communication and understanding. Listener 3 tries to make the C grade take on a more positive meaning. Note, however, that in the process all three listeners are also saying a great deal more. All are also saying that the speaker should not be feeling as he or she does; that the feelings are not legitimate ones and should be replaced with other feelings. These responses deny the validity of the speaker's feelings. They put the speaker into the position of having to defend his or her own feelings.

Listener 4, however, is different; listener 4 uses what is called *active listening*, a process of sending back to the speaker what you as a listener think the speaker meant, both in terms of content and in terms of feelings. Active listening takes into consideration both verbal and nonverbal signals.

Active listening is not a process of repeating the speaker's exact words; it is rather one of putting into some meaningful whole the listener's understanding of the speaker's total message—the verbal and the nonverbal, the content and the feelings.

Purposes of Active Listening

Active listening serves a number of important purposes. First, it enables the listener to check on the accuracy of understanding what the speaker said and, more important, what the speaker meant. By reflecting to the speaker what the listener perceived to be the speaker's meanings, the speaker is given an opportunity to confirm or amend the listener's perceptions and to clarify whatever may need clarification. In this way, future messages will have a better chance of being relevant and purposeful.

Second, through the process of active listening, the listener expresses acceptance of the speaker's feelings. Note that in the sample responses given, the first three listeners challenged the speaker's feelings; they refused to give these feelings legitimacy. The active listener, who reflected to the speaker what he or she thought was said, gave the speaker acceptance. The speaker's feelings were not challenged; rather, they were echoed in a sympathetic and empathic manner. Note, too, that in the first three responses, the feelings of the speaker are denied without ever actually being identified. Listener 4, however, not only accepts the speaker's feelings but identifies them explicitly, again allowing for the opportunity for correction.

Third, and perhaps most important, active listening stimulates the speaker to explore his or her feelings and thoughts further. With the response of listener 4, the speaker has an opportunity to elaborate on these feelings without having to defend them. Active listening sets the stage for meaningful dialogue, a dialogue of mutual understanding. In stimulating this further exploration, active listening also encourages the speaker to solve his or her own problems.

Techniques of Active Listening

Three "simple" techniques may prove useful in learning the process of active listening. At first, the application of these principles may seem awkward and unnatural. With practice, however, they will flow and blend into a meaningful and effective dialogue.

PARAPHRASE THE SPEAKER'S MEANING

State in your own words what you think the speaker meant. This paraphrase helps to ensure understanding, since the speaker is able to correct or modify your restatement. It also serves to show the speaker that you are interested and that you are attending to what is being said. Everyone wants to feel attended to, especially when angry or depressed. The active-listening paraphrase confirms this to the speaker. The paraphrase also provides the speaker with the opportunity to elaborate or extend what was originally said. Thus when the listener echoes the thought about the C grade, this provides the speaker with the opportunity to elaborate on why that grade was important. Paraphrases should be objective; be especially careful that you do not lead the speaker in the direction you think he or she should go.

EXPRESS AN UNDERSTANDING OF THE SPEAKER'S FEELINGS

In addition to paraphrasing the content, echo the feelings you felt were expressed or implied. Just as the paraphrase enables you to check on the accuracy of your perception of content, the expression of feelings enables you to check on the accuracy of your perception of the speaker's feelings. This expression of feelings also provides the speaker with the opportunity to see these feelings more objectively. This is particularly helpful when an individual is feeling angry, hurt, or depressed. We need that objectivity; we need to see our feelings from a somewhat less impassioned perspective if we are to deal with them effectively.

When we echo the speaker's feelings, we also provide a stimulus for elaboration and extension of these feelings. Most of us hold back our feelings until we are certain that they will be accepted; once we feel they are accepted, we feel free to go into more detail, to elaborate. Active listening provides the speaker with this important opportunity. In echoing these feelings, be careful that you do not maximize or minimize the speaker's emotions and feelings. Just try to echo these feelings as accurately as you can.

ASK QUESTIONS

Ask questions to ensure your own understanding of the speaker's thoughts and feelings and to secure additional relevant information. The questions should be designed to provide just enough stimulation and support for the speaker to express the thoughts and feelings he or she wants to express rather than to pry into areas that are not germane to the issue or to challenge the speaker in any way.

INTERPERSONAL FEEDBACK

Throughout the listening process, we give the speaker feedback—the messages we send back to the speaker concerning our reactions to what is said. In sending feedback, we inform the speaker of the progress or lack of it being made; we tell the speaker what effect he or she is having on us. On the basis of this feedback information, the speaker may or may not adjust, modify, strengthen, deemphasize, or change the content or the form of the messages.

A few suggestions may be offered for making feedback more effective, both in giving and in receiving.

Giving Feedback Effectively

The process of giving effective feedback seems characterized by at least five qualities: immediateness, honesty, appropriateness, clarity, and informativeness.

IMMEDIATENESS

The most effective feedback is that which is most immediate. Ideally, feedback is sent immediately after the message is received. Feedback, like reinforcement, loses its effectiveness with time; the longer we wait to praise or punish, for example, the less effect it will have.

HONESTY

Feedback should be an honest reaction to communication. This does not imply license for overt hostility or cruelty, but it does mean that feedback should not merely be a series of messages that the speaker wants to hear and that will build up his or her ego. Feedback concerning one's understanding of the message as well as one's agreement with the message should be honest. We should not be ashamed or afraid to admit that we did not understand a message, nor should we hesitate to assert disagreement.

APPROPRIATENESS

Feedback should be appropriate to the communication situation. For the most part, we have learned what is appropriate and what is not appropriate from observing others as we grew up, so there is no need to spell out what is and what is not appropriate here. Recognize, however, that appropriateness is a learned concept; consequently, what is appropriate in our culture is not necessarily appropriate in another culture. For example, for students to stamp their feet when a teacher walks in might signal approval or respect in one culture but hostility in another.

Feedback to the message should be kept distinct from feedback to the speaker. Make clear when disagreeing with speakers, for example, that you are disagreeing with what they are saying and not necessarily rejecting them as people. You may dislike what a person says but like the person who is saying it.

CLARITY

Feedback should be clear on at least two counts. It should be clear enough so that the speaker can perceive that it is feedback to the message and not just a reflection of something you ate that did not agree with you. Feedback should also be clear in meaning; if it is to signal understanding, it should be clear to the speaker that that is what you are signaling. If you are disagreeing, that too should be clear.

INFORMATIVENESS

The feedback you send to speakers should convey some information; it should tell them something they did not already know. To always respond in the same way conveys no information. To communicate information, responses must be, in part at least, unpredictable. If speakers are able to completely predict how you will respond to something they say, then your response conveys no information and does not serve any useful feedback function.

Receiving Feedback Effectively

It probably takes a great deal more effort and ingenuity to respond appropriately to feedback than to give feedback to others. The process of receiving feedback effectively is characterized by sensitivity, supportiveness, open-mindedness, helpfulness, and specificity.

SENSITIVITY

Develop a sensitivity to feedback—a sensitivity that will enable you to perceive feedback in situations where it might normally go unnoticed. We are given feedback at all times, both verbally and nonverbally. Most often the feedback comes in the form of nonverbal messages—puzzled face, a wide smile, a limp handshake. These are examples of feedback to which we have to learn to become sensitive. And, of course, verbal feedback also comes in many forms. At times the verbal feedback is obvious; it is said directly and without any attempt at subtlety: "Your humor is gross." "You walk like an elephant," "When you look at me that way, I want to kiss you." But most often verbal feedback comes to us in more subtle ways—a quick, almost throwaway remark about your method of approaching someone; a slow, belabored effort to say something good about your newly decorated apartment. Feedback may also be given by silence, as when someone would normally be expected to say something but says nothing. When you ask someone for a date and at three different times are given three different excuses and the person does not suggest an alternative time, perhaps the person is saying no in an imperfect and indirect way.

SUPPORTIVENESS

Support the person giving feedback in order to avoid, or at least suspend, defensive responses. Your own responsiveness to the feedback in large measure determines the comprehensiveness and depth of the feedback you receive. Defensiveness is usually taken as a sign to stop giving feedback. If the feedback is stopped, we stand to lose a great deal of insight that we might otherwise have gained. Often, for example, in hearing negative feedback there is a tendency to respond in kind: "If you think I come on strong, you should have seen yourself last night." This, of course, does nothing to help the cause of responsible and helpful feedback. If we make the assumption that the person giving the feedback has our own betterment in mind, and this seems a reasonable enough assumption, and if we keep this clearly in mind, our defensiveness should be lessened.

OPEN-MINDEDNESS

Listen to feedback with an open mind. If the feedback is negative, and especially if it centers on some issue of high ego involvement, it becomes particularly difficult to accept, and we tend to block it out very quickly, even before we hear the entire message. We obviously need to listen to the entire feedback message and to suspend judgment until we have learned and understood it all. This is not to say that we must uncritically accept everything anyone else says about us; certainly we should not. We need to evaluate critically what is said, accept what seems reasonable and useful, and reject what seems unreasonable and not useful. But we should make these decisions only after we have listened carefully and fully understood what the individual is saying.

HELPFULNESS

It seems strange to advise someone to help out the person giving the feedback, especially if that feedback is negative. Yet that is exactly what we must do. Giving feedback is a difficult task, and the person giving the feedback needs to be helped along. Feedback is often given initially in general and highly abstract terms. In this form, the feedback is not very useful. Most of these general and abstract comments can be made more specific and more useful, and hence some energy may be profitably devoted to enabling the person giving the feedback to become more specific. For example, it might help if, in hearing the feedback, we say, "Do you mean when I said . . . ?" or "Are you referring to the time I . . . ?" This type of behavior also demonstrates supportiveness, and the feedback giver will probably be more willing to supply additional and more specific feedback. Be helpful to the feedback giver in an encouraging way. Create conditions conducive to the giving of clear and honest feedback.

SPECIFICITY

When listening to feedback, translate it into very specific, preferably behavioral, terms. Think of the feedback in terms of what it means to your own specific behavior. Ask what you can learn on the basis of this feedback: How can you adjust your interpersonal verbal and nonverbal messages on the basis of this feedback?

Summary: Contents in Brief

Definitions	Functions and Purposes	Techniques and Guidelines
Listening: an active process of receiving aural stimuli	Enjoyment Information Help	Active-passive Empathic-objective Nonjudgmental-judgmental Surface-deep
Active listening: a process of sending back to the speaker what you think the speaker meant in content and in feeling	To enable listener to check on accuracy of understanding To express acceptance of the speaker's feelings To stimulate speaker to explore further feelings and thoughts	Paraphrase Express understanding Ask questions
Feedback: messages sent back to the speaker concerning the listener's reaction to what is said or the effect that the message has on the listener	To inform the speaker of the listener's reactions To provide guidance for speaker to modify or change the content or form of the messages	*In giving feedback:* Immediateness Honesty Appropriateness Clarity Informativeness *In receiving feedback:* Sensitivity Supportiveness Open-mindedness Helpfulness Specificity

Sources

A number of excellent works on listening are currently available, for example, Lyman K. Steil, Larry L. Barker, and Kittie W. Watson, *Effective Listening: Key to Your Success* (Reading, Mass.: Addison-Wesley, 1983); Robert L. Montgomery, *Listening Made Easy: How to Improve Listening on the Job, at Home, and in the Community* (New York: American Management Association, 1981); and Andrew D. Wolvin and Carolyn Gwynn Coakley, *Listening* (Dubuque, Ia.: Brown, 1982). A philosopher discusses listening in Mortimer J. Adler, *How to Speak, How to Listen* (New York: Macmillan, 1983).

On empathic listening, see Carl R. Rogers, "Communication: Its Blocking and Its Facilitation," in *Communication: Concepts and Processes*, rev. ed., ed. Joseph A. DeVito (Englewood Cliffs, N.J.: Prentice-Hall, 1976). On active listening, see Carl R. Rogers and Roger E. Farson, "Active Listening," in *Communication: Concepts and Processes*, 3d ed., ed. Joseph A. DeVito (Englewood Cliffs, N.J.: Prentice-Hall, 1981) and Thomas Gordon, *P.E.T.: Parent Effectiveness Training* (New York: New American Library, 1975).

The sources for the studies cited in Figure 4.1 are (a) Paul Rankin, "Listening Ability," *Proceedings of the Ohio State Education Conference's Ninth Annual Session* (1929) and (b) Larry Barker, R. Edwards, C. Gains, K. Gladney, and F. Holley, "An Investigation of Proportional Time Spent in Various Communication Activities by College Students," *Journal of Applied Communication Research* 8 (1980): 101–109.

A review of the factors that influence listening and listening tests is provided by Kittie W. Watson and Larry L. Barker, "Listening Behavior: Definition and Measurement," *Communication Yearbook 8*, ed. Robert N. Bostrom (Beverly Hills, Calif.: Sage, 1984), pp. 178–197.

UNIT 5

Ethics in Interpersonal Communication

OBJECTIVES

Upon completion of this unit, you should be able to:

1. explain Karl Wallace's ethical basis of communication
2. explain Paul Keller and Charles Brown's interpersonal ethic for communication
3. explain the concept of choice as it relates to ethics in interpersonal communication
4. formulate your own tentative theory of ethics in interpersonal communication

All interpersonal communication interactions have an ethical dimension. All interpersonal interactions must therefore be considered not only in terms of effectiveness-ineffectiveness or satisfaction-dissatisfaction, for example, but also in terms of right-wrong, justified-unjustified, moral-immoral. Ethical considerations are an essential and integral component of all interpersonal interactions.

This unit outlines three systems of ethics—three positions on the ethics of interpersonal interaction—and raises a number of questions concerning this right-wrong dimension of communication by focusing on three communication situations that raise ethical issues. This discussion is intended to stimulate you to develop and crystalize your own position concerning the ethics of interpersonal communication rather than to persuade you to accept any of the positions explained here.

POSITION 1: AN ETHICAL BASIS FOR COMMUNICATION

Karl Wallace, in "An Ethical Basis of Communication," offers four principles or guidelines for ethical communication. These guidelines, contends Wallace, are not external to communication; rather, "communication carries its ethics within itself. Communication of any kind is inseparable from the values which permeate a free and democratic community."

Wallace's ethic is based on the essential values of a free and democratic society. According to Wallace, these values include the dignity and worth of the individual, equality of opportunity, freedom, and the opportunity of an individual to grow and develop to the limits of his or her capacity. On the basis of these four democratic values, Wallace suggests four "moralities," four principles that should govern communication behavior.

1 "A communicator in a free society must recognize that during the moments of his utterance he is the sole source of argument and information." This calls for communicators' having a thorough knowledge of their topic, an ability to answer any relevant questions, and an awareness of the significant facts and opinions.

2 "The communicator who respects the democratic way of life must select and present fact and opinion fairly." The communicator must, in Wallace's words, "preserve a kind of equality of opportunity among ideas." This principle calls upon the communicator to provide the listener with an opportunity to make fair judgments.

3 "The communicator who believes in the ultimate values of democracy will invariably reveal the sources of his information and opinion." The communicator must assist the audience in evaluating any prejudices and biases that might be inherent in the sources by revealing them to listeners.

4 "A communicator in a democratic society will acknowledge and will respect diversity of argument and opinion." The ethical communicator should be able to admit the weight of the opposing argument and evidence if he or she intends to defend ethically an opposing position. This principle calls for a "tolerance of dissent."

There are a number of difficulties in putting this system into operation. What constitute a "thorough knowledge of the topic" and "an ability to answer relevant questions" are not easy to determine. Similarly, what constitute a fair presentation of facts and opinions, a full presentation of (all) sources of information, and a respect for diversity of argument and opinion are equally difficult to determine. Yet the four principles provide some guidance in this difficult area.

POSITION 2: AN INTERPERSONAL ETHIC FOR COMMUNICATION

For the most part, traditional approaches to ethics have focused on the message. They have concerned themselves with, for example, falsification of evidence, lying, distortion of facts and figures, and extreme emotional appeals. To Paul Keller and Charles Brown, these message aspects, although important, are not the only factors to consider in developing an ethic for communication.

Keller and Brown propose an interpersonal ethic for communication—an ethical perspective that focuses on the speaker and the listener and their attitudinal and behavioral responses to each other. In this system, communication is ethical (or, perhaps more correctly, communicators are ethical) when there is acceptance of the responses of others. Assume, for example, that a listener does not agree with something for which you have argued. Although you have presented what to you is incontrovertible evidence and argument, the listener remains adamant in his or her contradictory belief. Your communications, according to this position, are ethical to the extent that they are accepting of this listener's freedom to agree or not to agree.

This point of view is based on the democratic value that "conditions be created and maintained in which the potential of the individual is best realized." The assumption, based on this value, which leads to the formulation of the ethical perspective of Keller and Brown, is that people will best be able to realize their potential when they are psychologically free; when they are not afraid to disagree; when their beliefs, opinions, and values are accepted rather than rejected.

The crucial questions to consider in this system, then, are, "How does the speaker respond to the listener's responses?" and "How does the listener respond to the speaker's responses?" Speakers communicate ethically if they react to enhance the self-determination of others. Speakers communicate unethically if they react to inhibit the self-determination of others.

Keller and Brown's system is particularly interesting because it lends an ethical dimension to matters not normally considered questions of ethics. For example, the instructor who tolerates no disagreement and belittles students who disagree is, according to this system, unethical. Group members who sulk and withdraw whenever they do not get their way are likewise unethical. The instructor and the group members are guilty of unethical behavior because they are acting in a manner that inhibits rather than enhances the self-determination of others.

This system raises the problem of operationalizing the processes by which an individual's self-determination is enhanced. To what extent does disagreement (verbal or nonverbal) restrict an individual's freedom? How does one behave so that an individual feels free, unafraid to disagree, and accepted? How do we disagree with someone and still conform to the principles set forth in this system of interpersonal ethics?

POSITION 3: AN ETHICAL BASIS FOR CHOICE

Although the first two positions have much to recommend them, I find this third approach more satisfying, more complete, and applicable to a greater number of situations. In this system, the major determinant of whether communications are ethical or unethical is to be found in the notion of choice. It is assumed that individuals have a right to make their own choices. Interpersonal communications are ethical to the extent that they facilitate the individual's freedom of choice by presenting the other person with accurate bases for choice. Communications are unethical to the extent that they interfere with the individual's freedom of choice by preventing the person from securing information relevant to the choices he or she will make. Unethical communications, therefore, would be those that force the individual (1) to make choices he or she would not normally make or (2) to decline to make choices he or she would normally make (or both).

DIALOGUE VERSUS MONOLOGUE

An interpersonal ethic based on choice, an ethic based on the belief that each person has a right to make his or her own choices, assumes a view of interpersonal communication as dialogue rather than monologue. The distinction between these two forms of communication should further clarify this ethical position. *Monologue* refers to a form of communication in which one person speaks and the other listens; there is no interaction among participants. The focus is clearly and solely on the one person doing the speaking. The term *monologic communication*, or "communication as monologue," is a kind of extension of this basic definition and refers to communication in which there is no genuine interaction, in which one speaks without any real concern for the other person's feelings or attitudes, in which one is concerned only with his or her own goals and is interested in the other person only insofar as the other person is of benefit to oneself.

In dialogue there is two-way interaction; each person is both speaker and listener, both sender and receiver. In *dialogic communication,* or "communication as dialogue," there is deep concern for the other person and for the relationship formed between the two individuals. The objective of dialogic communication is mutual understanding and empathy. There is respect for the other person not because of what this person can do for you but simply because this person is a human being and therefore deserves to be treated with honesty, caring, and sincerity.

In monologic interaction, one communicates to the other that which will advance one's own goals, that which will prove most persuasive, that which will benefit oneself. In dialogic interaction, the individual respects the other person enough to allow that person the right to make his or her own choices without coercion, without the threat of punishment, without fear or social pressure. A dialogic communicator respects other people enough to believe that they can make decisions that are right for them and will implicitly or explicitly let them know that whatever choices they make, they will still be respected as people. In Carl Rogers's terms, the dialogic communicator gives unconditional positive regard to others. This is true regardless of whether one agrees or disagrees with their choices. When we feel that the choices other people make are illogical or unproductive, we may attempt to persuade them to do otherwise, but we do not withdraw (or threaten to withdraw) our positive regard for them as human beings who, because they are human beings and for no other reason, have the right to make their own choices (and mistakes).

A FEW QUALIFICATIONS

The ethical communicator, then, provides others with the kind of information that is helpful in making their own choices. In this ethic based on choice, however, there are a few qualifications that may restrict one's freedom of choice. It is assumed that these individuals are of the age and mental condition to allow free choice to be reasonably executed and that they are in situations in which their free choice does not prevent the free choice of others. A child of 5 or 6 is not ready to make certain choices, so someone else must make them instead. Similarly, some mentally incompetent individuals need others to make certain decisions for them. The circumstances under which one is living also can restrict free choice; for example, persons in the military will at times have to give up free choice and eat hamburger rather than steak, wear uniforms rather than jeans, and march rather than stay in bed. By entering the armed forces, one voluntarily waives, at least partially, the right to make one's own choices. The free choices we make must not prevent others from making their free choices. We cannot permit a thief to have freedom of choice to steal, because in the granting of that freedom we are preventing the victims from exercising their free choice.

These, then, are some of the qualifications that must be considered in any theory of choice as an ethical guide. Admittedly, it is not always easy to determine when people possess the mental ability to make their own decisions or when the choice of one person actually prevents the choices of another from being exercised. These are the vagaries we must contend with in any theory concerned with the morality of human behavior.

With these qualifications recognized, some of the applications of this position to specific situations may be pointed out. It is easier to proceed in this type of situation from the negative, and so I will explain the situations in which interpersonal communications are unethical.

Lying

Lying or otherwise hiding the truth is unethical because it prevents another person from learning about possible alternative choices. Consider the situation in which a patient is given six months to live. Is it ethical for the doctor or for family members to tell the patient that he or she is doing fine and that the tests were all negative? Applying our notion of choice, we would have to conclude that this is unethical. In not telling the patient the truth, we are making choices for him or her; we are in effect preventing the individual from living these last six months or so as he or she might want to, given the knowledge of imminent death. Similarly, parents who keep the truth about their child's adoption secret (after the child has become "of age") are eliminating the child's right to make a number of choices he or she might wish to make. Such choices might, for example, concern the finding of his or her biological parents or the recognition of a different ethnic or religious heritage.

To lie about one's infidelity (whether or not we see infidelity itself as unethical) would be unethical because it prevents the other person from making choices that might be made if this information were available. Knowing that a partner was unfaithful may lead the individual to make choices that would not be made under the assumption or belief of complete fidelity. Falsely saying, "I love you," misrepresenting your abilities in a job interview, or lying about the cleaning power of a soap are all examples of preventing people from making certain choices that they might make if they knew our actual romantic feelings, our true abilities, or the real power of the soap.

Communications designed to influence our attitudes or behaviors—whether the interpersonal interactions of a car dealer or the mass media's 60-second commercial produced by an advertising company—almost invariably presents one-sided arguments. Our task is to fill in the other sides, weigh all sides carefully, and then make our decision.

Each person has the right to make his or her own choices; thus, if we misrepresent or hide certain facts, we prevent that person from making choices he or she has a right to make. If we take the position that the truth is manipulated for the person's own good, we are in effect saying that we—and not the individual—have the right to make the choice. I like to think that we each have the right to hear all the messages that bear our names.

Individuals may, of course, give up their right to such information. The patient may have made it known that he or she does not want to know when death will occur. Marital partners may make an agreement not to reveal their affairs. When this is the case, there is no lying, no deceit, and hence no unethical behavior in not revealing this information.

WHEN A ''LIE'' IS NOT A LIE

Consider the person who arrives in a new outfit, looking pretty awful. The person asks you what you think of the new look. There seem to be a number of options. First, you can say something to the effect that it sure is different—unique, even— something quite unlike anything you have ever seen before. Second, you might, in a burst of total honesty, say that it is the worst outfit you have ever seen: "It makes you look old and sickly." Third, you might say that the outfit is really becoming— attractive, even—and suits the person's personality and body structure really well.

The first response, although technically and literally evasive and noncommittal, actually leads the other person to conclude the opposite of what you mean, and this seems to me to be lying. The second response is truthful but insensitive and cruel. And the third is dishonest, although at the time you make the comment it may seem kind. But on future occasions—when, for example, the person shows up for an important job interview or date dressed in this way—it may turn out to be the cruelest of all responses.

If our primary concern is for the person asking us the question, we must consider what that person is really seeking. If the question really asks us to evaluate the new outfit, we should focus on this and give our honest opinion in as kind and responsive (but truthful) a manner as possible. Thus, instead of saying, "It makes you look old and sickly," we can more appropriately say, "I think you would look much better in something different, something more colorful, something with a lively pattern." If, on the other hand, the question asks us to say something nice about the person (and the question about the outfit is just an excuse to get some positive stroking), we should address that question and say something that will provide the positive strokes the person is seeking. Here is one of the many instances in which specific content is not important; the psychological need of the person must be addressed. We are therefore not lying when we address this need and say, for example, "You look good," because the real question asked us to say something positive, and this is what we have done with our compliment.

Fear and Emotional Appeals

One of the most widely discussed ethical issues in communication is the legitimacy of fear and emotional appeals. Although this topic is frequently focused on public and mass communication situations, it is even more applicable to interpersonal encounters.

Consider the mother and father who are afraid that their child will be molested by some stranger. They warn the child to stay away from strangers, not to take candy or money from anyone the child does not know, and to stay out of cars, hallways, and dark alleys where strangers might loiter. They attempt to gain compliance by instilling fear in the child. In response to the child's natural question, "Why," they build elaborate stories about what strangers do to little boys and girls. Depending on their originality, such stories could range from the imposition of slavery to starvation, beating, and death. The real reason, that they might be sexually molested, is probably never mentioned.

In this type of situation, many people would side with the parents. The young child, it would be argued, is not knowledgeable enough to understand about sexual molestation, and yet some means is needed to persuade the child to keep his or her distance from strangers. The use of fear, then, serves the parents well and protects the child from various dangers.

This same type of appeal is used frequently in interpersonal situations. Take, for example, the mother who does not want her teenage son or daughter of 18 or 19 to move out of the house. Again, depending on her creativity, her method might focus on instilling fear in the teenager for his or her own well-being ("Who'll care for you? You won't eat right. You'll get sick") or, more frequently, for the mother's well-being. The caricature of a mother having a heart attack at the first sign of the child's leaving is probably played out every day, in various forms, throughout the world. But whether a heart attack is invoked or some other gross difficulty, the appeal is built on fear. Obviously, no child wants to be the cause of his or her mother's suffering. It is interesting to note that in our culture the father is not permitted to use his own suffering as an argument. Rather, his task is to show the children how much their leaving home will hurt their mother. Together, parents can make a most effective team.

Parents are actually quite adept at using fear appeals and will use them to discourage anything from smoking to premarital sex to interracial dating. The list— as any young person knows, or, indeed, as any person who has ever been young knows—is endless. Similar issues are raised when we consider the use of emotional appeal in attempting to change attitudes, beliefs, and behaviors. The case of the real estate broker appealing to our desire for status, the friend who wants a favor appealing to our desire for social approval, and the salesperson appealing to our desire for sexual rewards are all familiar examples. The question they all raise is simply, "Is this type of appeal justified?"

Many arguments can be advanced on both sides of the issue. The "everyone is doing it" argument is perhaps the most familiar but does not really answer the question of whether or not such appeals are justified. We are a combination of logic and emotion; consequently, we are persuaded by both types of appeals. To be effective, one would thus have to use both types of appeals. Again, however, this does not answer the question of whether or not such emotional appeals are ethical; it merely states that they are effective.

At times we consider the extent of the appeals and their effect on the individuals. One argument says that emotional appeals are justified as long as individuals retain their powers of reasoning. Emotional appeals become unjustified when they short-circuit the reasoning processes. Exactly when people are in possession of such "powers" or when their reasoning is "short-circuited" is, unfortunately, not made clear.

The question of fear and emotional appeals is not as easy to fit into the issue of freedom of choice as is lying. The reason is that it is difficult to determine at what point the use of fear or emotion prevents certain choices from being selected. Furthermore, we must recognize that both parties have the right to free choice. Some people might argue that the parents of the teenager who wishes to leave home are unethical when they force the teenager to choose between leaving home and hurting them, on the one hand, and staying home and pleasing them, on the other. To many this would not be *free* choice. Similarly, a group of individuals who withdraw social support from an individual unless he or she does as they wish may be charged by some with unethically limiting the individual's freedom of choice. Although it is true that the teenager and the deviant group member are physically free to do as they wish, they may be emotionally pressured to the point where they may not be free in any meaningful sense of the term.

On the other hand, it might be argued that the parents of the teenager also have rights and that they have the specific right to display their emotional hurt should the child wish to leave home. Similarly, it might be argued that the group members have the right to withdraw their social support from an individual if they so wish.

Clearly this is a difficult situation to resolve. To preserve the freedom of choice for both sides of a conflict and at the same time not allow the freedoms of one side to restrict unduly the freedoms of the other side is not easy. Part of the difficulty, I think, is due to the fact that we are on the outside looking in rather than actually participating in the conflict. My own feeling is that the parents have the right to display their hurt if this is their honest emotional response to the child's leaving home. However, if it is a technique designed to develop guilt in the child and to prevent the child from exercising certain options, their behavior must be judged unethical. Similarly, the group members who withdraw their support from the individual have a right to do so if they decide that because of these deviant behaviors they do not wish to associate or interact with this individual any longer. However, if they are using the withdrawal of social support to "force" the individual to conform and consequently to limit the individual's freedom of choice to select certain options rather than others, the group members, I think, are behaving unethically. In these situations, it is only the participants (the parents and the group members, in these examples) who can decide if they are acting fairly or unfairly, ethically or unethically.

The Prevention of Interaction

Among the most obvious instances where interactions are prevented are those concerning interracial marriage and homosexual relations. These prohibitions prevent certain groups of persons from interacting in the manner in which they wish. If an interracial couple wish to get married, the places in which such a marriage is performed and where they settle must be chosen carefully. Interracial couples will run into difficulty in finding housing, employment, and, most significant, acceptance into a community. Likewise, homosexuals will have difficulty in much the same way, and consequently many of them are forced to live "straight" lives—at least on the surface.

If you run a business, for example, should you have the right to refuse a job to a person because that person is married to an individual of another race or because that person has an affectional orientation different from yours? And if you do have the right to choose your employees on the basis of such preferences, do you still retain the rights to protection of the law that the society as a whole has granted to everyone?

Lesbians and gay men are currently prevented from holding jobs as teachers, police officers, fire fighters, and so forth in many states. These discriminatory laws are not terribly effective, but this is not the issue. The relative ineffectiveness of such prohibitions should not blind us to the social realities that these laws incorporate. What should be considered is that the homosexual cannot work as a homosexual but only as a heterosexual. We do not ask that a black act white—although society once did demand this in often subtle ways. We do not ask a Jew to act like a Christian or a Christian to act like a Jew if he or she wants a job—although, again, some persons do. Yet we do ask lesbians and gay men that they not reveal their true identities. These persons are accepted only if they act like the majority. Are we being ethical when we require such concealment of identity?

There are, of course, many different issues that such prohibitions of interactions raise. But I think the central issue is whether any one group—however large and however sanctioned by state or church—has the right to set down rules of behavior for others and literally to prevent them from exercising their right of free choice. Lest we all ease our consciences too easily, let us recognize that it is we who constitute this society, and it is we who give it the power it has—the very power we may deplore as we sit comfortably in the camp of the sanctioned majority.

If we wish to retain for ourselves the freedom to make the choices we think best, we must grant this same right to others. If we do not wish to be lied to, to have the information we receive misrepresented, or to have our own interpersonal interactions restricted, we must grant others nothing less than what we demand for ourselves. Looked at in this way, the decisions as to what is or is not ethical should not be difficult to make.

Summary: Contents in Brief

Ethics in Communication	Ethical Communications	Unethical Communications
The moral principles governing communication; the right-wrong, moral-immoral dimension of communication	Communications that facilitate the individual's freedom of choice by presenting the other person with accurate bases for choice	Communications that interfere with the individual's freedom of choice by preventing the other person from securing information relevant to the choices to be made, for example, lying, extreme fear and emotional appeal, and prevention of interaction

Sources

My primary debt for this unit is to Sissela Bok, *Lying: Moral Choice in Public and Private Life* (New York: Pantheon Books, 1978). I have relied on this work for numerous concepts developed throughout the unit, although Bok should not be held responsible for any liberties I have taken or for any of the applications to communication with which she might not agree. Another useful source is Charles Fried, *Right and Wrong* (Cambridge, Mass.: Harvard University Press, 1978). For an overview of ethics in communication, see Richard L. Johannesen, *Ethics in Human Communication*, 2d ed. (Prospect Heights, Ill.: Waveland Press, 1983). The first two ethical positions may be found in Karl Wallace, "An Ethical Basis of Communication," *Communication Education* 4 (1955): 1–9, and Paul W. Keller and Charles T. Brown, "An Interpersonal Ethic for Communication," *Journal of Communication* 18 (1968): 73–81. For an application to Wallace's system to communication evaluation see Rebecca B. Rubin and Jess Yoder, "Ethical Issues in the Evaluation of Communication Behavior," *Communication Education* 34 (January 1985): 13–17. For a scientific study on lying and its effect on communication, see Henry D. O'Hair, Michael J. Cody, and Margaret L. McLaughlin, "Prepared Lies, Spontaneous Lies, Machiavellianism, and Nonverbal Communication," *Human Communication Research* 7 (Summer 1981): 325–339.

For communication as dialogue and its ethical implications, see, for example, Richard L. Johannesen, "The Emerging Concept of Communication as Dialogue," *Quarterly Journal of Speech* 57 (1971): 373–382, and Charles T. Brown and Paul W. Keller, *Monologue to Dialogue: An Exploration of Interpersonal Communication*, 2d ed. (Englewood Cliffs, N.J.: Prentice-Hall, 1979), pp. 294–310. The concept of dialogue, of course, was most insightfully explained by Martin Buber, *I and Thou*, 2d ed. (New York: Scribner's, 1958), and *Between Man and Man*, trans. Ronald Gregor Smith (New York: Macmillan, 1972). The dialogic approach to interpersonal communication is perhaps best outlined in T. Dean Thomlison, *Toward Interpersonal Dialogue* (New York: Longman, 1982).

UNIT 6

Effectiveness in Interpersonal Communication

OBJECTIVES

Upon completion of this unit, you should be able to:

1. explain the concept of effectiveness in interpersonal communication
2. define *openness* and identify the three aspects of interpersonal communication to which it refers
3. define *empathy* and distinguish it from sympathy
4. define *supportiveness*
5. define *positiveness* and explain the three aspects of interpersonal communication to which it refers
6. explain the concept of stroking and its relevance to positiveness
7. define *equality* as it relates to interpersonal communication
8. explain *confidence* as a quality of pragmatic effectiveness and identify at least two specific behaviors through which this is evidenced
9. define *immediacy* and explain how it is communicated verbally and nonverbally
10. explain *interaction management* as a quality of interpersonal effectiveness
11. define *self-monitoring* and identify at least three differences between the high and the low self-monitor
12. explain the role of *expressiveness* in effective interpersonal interaction
13. explain the quality of *other-orientation* and how it contributes to interpersonal effectiveness

Interpersonal communication, like any form of behavior, can vary from extremely effective to extremely ineffective. No interpersonal encounter is a total failure or a total success; each could have been worse, but each could have been better. In this unit we review the characteristics of effective interpersonal communication while emphasizing that each communicative act is different and that any principle or rule must be applied judiciously with full recognition of the uniqueness of each communication event.

These characteristics of effectiveness are considered from two perspectives. The first is the humanistic perspective, which stresses openness, empathy, supportiveness, and, in general, qualities that foster meaningful, honest, and satisfying interactions. This approach is in the tradition of humanistic psychology articulated by Abraham Maslow, Gordon Allport, Carl Rogers, and numerous others.

This approach begins with the general qualities that philosophers and humanists feel define superior human relationships (for example, honesty, openness, positiveness). From these general qualities, we then deduce specific behaviors that should characterize effective interpersonal communication.

The second is the pragmatic or behavioral perspective, which stresses interaction management, immediacy, and, in general, qualities that contribute to achieving a variety of desired goals. This approach derives from the more recent pragmatic approach to communication articulated by such writers as Paul Watzlawick, William Lederer, Don Jackson, and others. (Some of the basic axioms of this pragmatic approach were identified in Unit 2.) This approach starts from specific skills that research finds effective in interpersonal communication. We then group these specific skills into general classes of behavior (for example, interaction management skills, other-orientation skills).

These two approaches, visualized in Figure 6.1, are not contradictory but actually complement each other. Each approach has much to recommend it; each contributes substantially to our understanding of interpersonal communication effectiveness. Each provides a clarification of qualities that, taken together, will improve interpersonal communication considerably. In order to present these two approaches fairly, some redundancy is inevitable. Thus, for example, empathy and empathic responses are included in the humanistic model under "empathy" but also in the pragmatic model under "other-orientation." My goal here is to provide you with a number of insights into interpersonal communication effectiveness so that you may select the

FIGURE 6.1: Effective Interpersonal Communication.

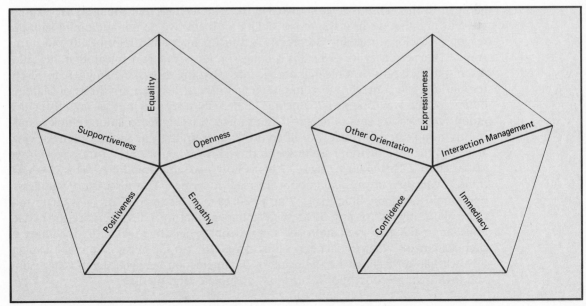

guides and insights that seem most helpful in any specific situation. Put differently, my aim is to provide a readily available arsenal of communication guides and principles that will prove useful in a wide variety of communication settings.

A HUMANISTIC MODEL OF INTERPERSONAL EFFECTIVENESS

In this humanistic (sometimes referred to metaphorically as "soft") approach to interpersonal effectiveness, five general qualities are considered: openness, empathy, supportiveness, positiveness, and equality.

Openness

The quality of *openness* refers to at least three aspects of interpersonal communication. First, and perhaps most obvious, is that effective interpersonal communicators must be open to the people with whom they interact. This does not mean that one should immediately pour out one's entire life history. Interesting as that may be, it is not usually very helpful to the communication or interesting to the other individuals. Rather, there should be a willingness to "self-disclose," to reveal information about oneself that might normally be kept hidden, provided that such disclosures are appropriate (see Unit 8).

A second aspect of openness refers to the willingness of a communicator to react honestly to incoming stimuli. Silent, uncritical, and immovable psychiatrists may be of some help in a clinical situation, but they are generally boring conversationalists. We want people to react openly to what we say, and we have a right to expect this. Nothing seems worse than indifference; even disagreement seems more welcome. Of course, there are extremes here too. We demonstrate openness by responding spontaneously and without subterfuge to the communications and the feedback of others.

A third aspect of openness concerns the "owning" of feelings and thoughts. To be open in this sense is to acknowledge that the feelings and thoughts we express are ours and that we bear the responsibility for them; we do not attempt to shift the responsibility for our feelings to others. Arthur Bochner and Clifford Kelly put it this way: "The person who owns his feelings or ideas makes it clear that he takes responsibility for his own feelings and actions. Owning shows a willingness to accept responsibility for oneself and commitment to others. It is the antithesis of blaming others for the way one feels." Bochner and Kelly advise us not to say, "Isn't this group supposed to listen to people?" but rather, "I feel ignored. I don't think people in this group listen to me." This difference is interesting from another point of view as well. When we own our feelings and thoughts—when we use "I-messages"—we say in effect, "This is how *I* feel," "This is how *I* see the situation," "This is what *I* think," with the *I* always paramount. Instead of saying, "This discussion is useless," one would say something like, "*I'm* bored by this discussion" or "*I* want to talk more about myself" or any other such statement that includes reference to the fact that *I* am making an evaluation and not describing objective reality. By including in such statements what the general semanticists call "to me–ness," we make explicit the fact that our feelings are the result of the interaction between the outside reality and own own preconceptions, attitudes, prejudices, and the like.

Empathy

Perhaps the most difficult of all communication qualities to achieve is the ability to experience *empathy* for another individual. *Empathy* was created from Greek roots to translate the German word *Einfühlung*, meaning "feeling with." To empathize with someone is to feel as that person does. As Henry Backrack puts it, empathy refers to "the ability of one person to experientially 'know' what another is experiencing at any given moment, from the latter's frame of reference, through the latter's eyes." To sympathize, on the other hand, is to feel *for* the individual—to feel sorry for the person, for example. To empathize is to feel *as* the individual feels, to be in the same shoes, to feel the same feelings in the same way.

If we are able to empathize with people, we are in a better position to understand, for example, their motivations and past experiences, their present feelings and attitudes, their hopes and expectations for the future. "One cannot grasp subtle and complicated feelings of people," notes R. Greenson, "except by this emotional knowing, the experiencing of another's feeling that is meant by the term *empathy*. It is a very special model of perceiving." Empathy, then, enables one to understand, emotionally and intellectually, what the other person is experiencing. This empathic understanding in turn enables the individual better to adjust his or her communications—what is said, how it is said, what is to be avoided, if and when silence is to be preferred, if self-disclosures should be made, and so on. In fact, C. Truax includes one's communication ability as part of the definition of empathy. "Accurate empathy," says Truax, writing from the point of view of the psychotherapist, "involves both the sensitivity to current feelings and the verbal facility to communicate this understanding in a language attuned to the client's own feelings."

More difficult than defining empathy is describing or advancing ways to increase our empathic abilities. Perhaps the first step is to avoid evaluating the other person's behaviors. If we evaluate them as right or wrong, good or bad, we will see their behaviors through these labels and will fail to see a great deal that might not be consistent with these labels. Therefore, resist the temptation to evaluate, to judge, to interpret, to criticize. It is not that these responses are "wrong," but merely that they often get in the way of understanding. Focus on understanding. Second, the more we know about a person—her or his desires, experiences, abilities, fears, and so on— the more we will be able to see what that person sees and feel as that person feels. Try to understand the reasons and the motivations that contribute to making the person feel as he or she does. Even if these reasons and motivations may appear illogical or self-destructive to you, they need to be understood if you are to achieve a meaningful degree of empathy with the other person. If you have difficulty understanding the perspective of the other, ask questions, seek clarification, encourage the person to talk. Third, try to experience what the other person is feeling from his or her point of view. Playing the role of the other person in your mind (or even out loud) can help you see the world a little more as the other person does.

Supportiveness

An effective interpersonal relationship is one in which there is supportiveness, a concept that owes much of its formulation to the work of Jack Gibb. Open and empathic communication cannot survive in an unsupportive atmosphere. Supportiveness is demonstrated and fostered by our being (1) descriptive rather than evaluative, (2) spontaneous rather than strategic, and (3) provisional rather than certain.

DESCRIPTIVENESS

An atmosphere that is descriptive rather than evaluative leads to supportiveness. When we perceive a communication as being a request for information or a description of some event, we generally do not perceive it as threatening. We are not being challenged and have no need to defend ourselves. On the other hand, a communication that is judgmental or evaluative often leads us to become defensive, to back off, and to erect some kind of barrier between ourselves and the evaluator. This is not to imply that all evaluative communications elicit a defensive response. Positive evaluations are often responded to without defensiveness and in fact with all sorts of positive reactions. Even here, however, it must be recalled that the very fact that someone has the power or the knowledge or the "right" to evaluate us in any way (even if positively) may lead us to feel uneasy and perhaps defensive. Perhaps we anticipate that the next evaluation may not be so positive. In a similar way, negative evaluations do not always elicit a defensive response. The would-be actor who wants to improve and perfect technique often welcomes negative evaluations. Similarly, many students welcome negative evaluations when they feel they are constructive and lead to substantial improvement in their ability to communicate, to calculate appropriate statistical tests, or to construct valid and reliable experimental designs.

Generally, however, an evaluative atmosphere leads people to become more defensive than would a descriptive atmosphere. Maybe we feel that whatever we do or say is going to be evaluated, and so we shy away from expressing ourselves freely, fearing that we will be criticized. Despite the usefulness of some criticism, it is still threatening, and expressing ourselves openly can be difficult when there is a strong possibility of evaluation.

In being descriptive, Toni Brougher, in *A Way with Words,* advises that we (1) describe what happened ("I lost the promotion"), (2) how we feel ("I feel miserable' I feel I've failed"), and (3) how this relates to the other person ("Would you mind if we went to the city tonight? I need to forget the job and everything about it"). Further, Brougher advises us to avoid accusations or blame ("Those Martians, they always stick together; I should have stayed with my old job and not listened to your brother's lousy advice"), evaluative terms ("Didn't your sister look *horrible* in that red dress?"), and "preaching" ("Why can't you ever cook steak like I like it?" "Why don't you learn something about word processing before you open your mouth?").

SPONTANEITY

A spontaneous as opposed to a strategic style also helps create supportiveness. Individuals who are spontaneous in their communications, who are straightforward and open about what they think, are usually responded to in the same manner—straightforwardly and openly. But in some situations we feel that certain people are hiding their true feelings—that they have some hidden plan or strategy that they are attempting to implement for some unrevealed purpose.

Most people employ some kind of strategy in their communications. For example, you may preface your remarks in such a way as to get the listener into a more receptive mood, or you may say over and over that you are doing something for the good of someone else and are not concerned with the benefits you yourself might receive. That is, you might do things to gain the favor of the individuals with whom you interact. This is a rather common approach in communicating. Often, of course, it is clear to the listener that you are in fact employing a strategy. You clearly recognize it in the salesperson who tells you that you look just great in that new jacket. What we all forget is that our own strategies are often just as apparent (and transparent) and are just as often met with resistance and resentment.

PROVISIONALISM

Being provisional means having a tentative, open-minded attitude, a willingness to hear opposing points of view and to change one's position if warranted. Such provisionalism, rather than unwavering certainty, assists in creating a supportive atmosphere.

We resist people who "know everything" and who always have a definite answer to any question. Such people are set in their ways and will tolerate no differences. They have arguments ready for any possible alternative attitude or belief. After a very short time, we become defensive with such people, and we hold back our own attitudes rather than subject them to attack. But we open up with people who take a more provisional position, who are willing to change their minds should reasonable arguments be presented. With such people we feel equal.

Closed-minded people are heavily dependent on being reinforced for their reactions to information. They evaluate information on the basis of the rewards and the punishments they receive. We all do this to some extent; the closed-minded person, however, does this to a greater degree than most people. The open-minded person is better able to resist the reinforcements of other people and outside situations.

In terms of interpersonal relationships, certain, or closed-minded, people evaluate others according to the similarity-dissimilarity of others' belief systems with their own. They evaluate positively people who have similar belief systems and negatively people who have dissimilar belief systems. Provisional, or open-minded, individuals do not use similarity of belief systems or homophily as the measure of interpersonal relationships. The certain and the provisional individuals are extreme types. Few people are completely closed or completely open. The vast majority exist somewhere between these extremes. What is most important to understand is that to the extent that we act certain and closed-minded, we encourage defensive behavior in the listener. To the extent that we act in a provisional manner, with an open mind, with a full recognition that we might be wrong, and with a willingness to revise our attitudes and opinions, we encourage supportiveness.

Positiveness

We communicate positiveness in interpersonal communication in at least two ways: (1) stating positive attitudes and (2) stroking the person with whom we interact.

ATTITUDES

Attitudinal positiveness in interpersonal communication refers to at least two aspects or elements. First, interpersonal communication is fostered if there is a positive regard for the self. People who feel negatively about themselves invariably communicate these feelings to others, who in turn probably develop similar negative feelings.

On the other hand, people who feel positively about themselves convey this feeling about themselves to others, who in turn are likely to return the positive regard.

Second, a positive feeling for the general communication situation is important for effective interaction. Nothing is more unpleasant than communicating with someone who does not enjoy the exchange or does not respond favorably to the situation or context. A negative response to the situation makes one feel almost as if one is intruding, and communication seems sure to break down quickly.

STROKING

Positiveness may be further explained by reference to the concept of stroking. *Stroking* is a term that is creeping into the general vocabulary, no doubt because of its central importance in transactional analysis and in human interaction generally. Stroking behavior acknowledges the existence, and in fact the importance, of the other person; it is the antithesis of indifference. When we stroke someone, whether positively or negatively, we are acknowledging him or her as a person, as a significant human being.

Stroking may be verbal, as in "I like you," "I enjoy being with you," or "You're a pig," or nonverbal, such as a smile, a wink, a pat on the back, a hug, or a punch in the mouth. As these examples illustrate, stroking may be positive or negative. Positive stroking generally takes the form of compliments or rewards and consists of behaviors we would normally look forward to, enjoy, and take pride in. They would bolster our self-image and make us feel a little bit better than we did before we received them. Negative strokes, on the other hand, are punishing; they are aversive. Sometimes, like cruel remarks, they hurt us emotionally or psychologically; sometimes, like a punch in the mouth, they hurt us physically.

Transactional analysts argue that people *need* to be stroked; otherwise, they will shrivel up and die. And, of course, it is positive stroking that most people are after. But if they cannot secure positive stroking, they will settle for negative stroking. The assumption is that indifference is the worst fate anyone could suffer and that anything short of that is welcomed. If positive stroking cannot be had, and if the only alternatives are negative stroking or indifference, the individual will choose the negative stroking. I should add that other theorists, most notably the rational-emotive theorists such as Albert Ellis, argue that people may *want* to be stroked but they do not *need* it; they can and do function without stroking. Personal difficulties arise, Ellis argues, when people assume that they *need* to be stroked and then are not. If, on the other hand, they recognize that they may *want* to be stroked but do not *need* it, they can be quite productive and happy even when they are not stroked. I agree with Ellis, but you may wish to explore the issue in more detail yourselves in Ellis's *A New Guide to Rational Living* or any of the numerous works on transactional analysis. Despite this interesting and important difference between the two theories, all theorists seem to agree that stroking is significant and that it has a great effect on interpersonal interactions of all types.

Many interpersonal encounters are structured by one or even both participants almost solely to get stroked. People buy new clothes to get stroked, compliment associates so that they stroke back, do favors for people in order to get stroked in return, associate with certain people because they are generous with their strokes, and so on. Marriages and other primary relationships are often entered into because they hold the promise of frequent stroking. We all do these things for the same basic reason—to receive strokes, to be acknowledged as people, to ward off any possibility of indifference. Stroking leads to more effective interpersonal communication when it helps to reinforce productive and satisfying behavior patterns or, alternatively, when it functions to decrease unproductive and unsatisfying patterns.

Equality

Equality is a peculiar characteristic. In any situation, there is probably some inequality. One person will be smarter, richer, better looking, or more athletic. Never are two people absolutely equal in all respects. Even identical twins would be unequal in some ways. Despite this inequality, interpersonal communication is generally more effective when the atmosphere is one of equality. This does not mean that unequals cannot communicate. Certainly they can. Yet their communication, if it is to be effective, should recognize the equality of personalities; that is, there should be a tacit recognition that both parties are valuable and worthwhile human beings and that each has something important to contribute.

One of the most frequent ways we violate the equality characteristic is in the way we ask questions. Compare these examples:

1. "When will you learn to phone for reservations? Must I do everything?"
2. "One of us should phone for reservations. Do you want me to do it, or do you want to do it?"

1. "When the hell are you going to fix this wallpaper? It's coming down on my head!"
2. "This wallpaper is coming down on my head. How about we stay home tonight and try to fix it together?"

In each example, in sentence 1 there is no equality; one person demands compliance and the other is ordered to do something. Questions such as these encourage defensiveness, resentment, and hostility. They provoke arguments rather than solve problems. In sentence 2 in each example, there is equality—an explicitly stated desire to cooperate, to work together to address a specific problem. As a general rule, requests (especially courteous ones) communicate equality; demands (especially discourteous ones) communicate superiority.

Equality should also characterize interpersonal communication in terms of speaking versus listening. If one person speaks all the time and the other listens all the time, effective interpersonal communication becomes difficult if not impossible. There should be an equality of sending versus receiving. Depending on the situation, one person may speak more than the other person, but this should be a function of the situation and not of the fact that one person is a "talker" and another person is a "listener."

In an interpersonal relationship characterized by equality, disagreement and conflict are seen as attempts to understand inevitable differences rather than as opportunities to put the other person down. Disagreements are viewed as ways of solving problems rather than of winning points, getting one's way, or proving oneself superior to the other. Equality does not require that we accept and approve of all the verbal and nonverbal behaviors of the other person. Some behaviors are self-destructive or have negative consequences for others and should be challenged—not out of a desire to win an argument or prove a point but out of concern for the other person and for the interpersonal relationship. Equality means acceptance and approval of the person, or, to use Carl Rogers's terms, equality asks that we give the other person "unconditional positive regard."

A PRAGMATIC MODEL OF INTERPERSONAL EFFECTIVENESS

A pragmatic or behavioral (sometimes referred to metaphorically as "hard") approach to interpersonal effectiveness, sometimes called a competence model, focuses on specific behaviors that a speaker or listener should use to gain his or her desired outcome. This model too offers five qualities of effectiveness: confidence, immediacy, interaction management, expressiveness, and other-orientation.

Confidence

The effective communicator has social confidence; any anxiety that is present is not readily perceived by others. There is instead a comfortableness with the other person and with the communication situation generally.

Openness, empathy, supportiveness, positiveness, and equality—those characteristics derived from a humanistic model—and confidence, immediacy, interaction management, expressiveness, and other-orientation—those characteristics derived from a pragmatic model—all contribute to interpersonal communication effectiveness and satisfaction.

We all have some communication apprehension or shyness (see Unit 9), but the effective interpersonal communicator controls it to the extent that it is not a source of discomfort and does not interfere with communication. Further, this quality also enables the speaker to deal effectively with people who are anxious, shy, or apprehensive and to make them feel more comfortable.

The socially confident communicator is relaxed (rather than rigid), flexible in voice and body (rather than locked into one or two ranges of voice or body movement), and controlled (rather than shaky or awkward).

A relaxed posture, researchers find, communicates a sense of control, status, and power. Tenseness, rigidity, and discomfort, on the other hand, signal a lack of self-control, which in turn signals general inability to control one's environment or fellow workers and an impression of being under the power and control of some outside force or other person.

Immediacy

The effective interpersonal communicator conveys a sense of immediacy, of contact, of togetherness. This person communicates to others a feeling of interest, an attentive attitude, a liking for and attraction toward the other person.

Immediacy is communicated both verbally and nonverbally. Verbally we communicate immediacy by joining ourselves with the other person with terms such as *we, our,* and *us,* by using the other person's name, by focusing on the other person's remarks, by providing relevant and immediate feedback, and, of course, by reinforcing or rewarding the other person. Nonverbally we communicate immediacy by maintaining appropriate eye contact, a physical closeness that echoes a psychological closeness, and a direct and open body posture. This involves arranging the body to keep others out, limiting looking around at others, smiling, and similar behaviors that say, "I'm interested in you."

Interaction Management

The effective communicator controls the interaction to the satisfaction of both parties. In effective interaction management, neither person feels ignored or on stage; each contributes to the total communication interchange.

Maintaining one's role as speaker or listener and passing back and forth—through appropriate eye movements, vocal expressions, and body and facial gestures—the opportunity to speak are interaction management skills. Similarly, keeping the conversation flowing and relatively fluent without long and awkward pauses that make everyone uncomfortable are signs of effective interaction management.

The effective interaction manager presents verbal and nonverbal messages that are consistent and reinforce each other. Contradictory signals—where, for example, the nonverbal message contradicts the verbal message—are rarely in evidence. It is relevant to note here that women generally use more positive or pleasant nonverbal expressions than men. For example, they smile more, nod in agreement more, and more openly verbalize positive feelings. When expressing anger or power, however, many women (though surely not all) continue using these positive nonverbal signals, which dilute the verbally expressed anger or power. The net result is that we see such women as being uncomfortable with strong negative emotions and expressions of power, and we are therefore less likely to believe them or feel threatened by them.

SELF-MONITORING

Integrally related to interpersonal interaction management is *self-monitoring;* the manipulation of the image that we present to others in our interpersonal interactions. High self-monitors carefully adjust their behaviors on the basis of feedback from others so that they produce the most desirable effect. Their interpersonal interactions are manipulated in an attempt to give the best and most effective interpersonal impression. Low self-monitors, on the other hand, are not concerned with the image they present to others. Rather, their interactions are characterized by an openness in which they communicate their thoughts and feelings with no attempt to manipulate the impressions they create. Most of us lie somewhere between the two extremes. (You may wish at this point to take the brief self-monitoring test on page 79.)

When high and low self-monitors are compared, a number of interesting differences are noted. For example, high self-monitors are more apt to take charge of a situation, are more sensitive to the deceptive techniques of others, and are better able to detect self-monitoring or impression management techniques when used by others. High self-monitors prefer to interact with low self-monitors. They prefer to live in a relatively stable world with people who will not be able to detect their self-monitoring techniques. By interacting with low self-monitors, the high self-monitors are more likely to be able to assume positions of influence and power. High self-monitors also seem better able to present their true selves than are low self-monitors. For example, if an innocent person is charged with a crime, to use the example cited by Mark Snyder (on whose research this discussion is based), a high self-monitor would be able to present his or her innocence more effectively than would a low self-monitor.

Although there seem to be two relatively clear-cut types of persons—high and low self-monitors—we all engage in selective-monitoring, depending on the situation. If we go for a job interview, we are likely to monitor our behaviors very carefully. On the other hand, if we are interacting with a group of friends, we are less likely to monitor our performance; we are more apt to express our feelings and thoughts openly without any great attempt at impression management.

A careful reading of the research and theory on self-monitoring, on openness, and on self-disclosure (a topic reviewed in detail in Unit 8) supports the conclusion that our effectiveness is ordinarily increased if we are selectively self-disclosing, are selectively open, and engage in selective self-monitoring. To be totally open, to disclose everything to everyone, to ignore the feedback of others, and to refuse to engage in any self-monitoring seems absurd. The opposite extreme of the closed, never-disclosing individual who monitors each and every utterance is equally absurd and should likewise be avoided.

There are no easy and simple answers to such questions as, "To what degree should we be open?" "How much and to whom should we self-disclose?" and "To what extent should we attempt to self-monitor our communication behaviors?" Fortunately, however, there are competencies that we can develop to guide us and enable us to function more effectively interpersonally. It is to the development of these competencies that the study of interpersonal communication is directed.

SELF-MONITORING TEST

These statements concern personal reactions to a number of different situations. No two statements are exactly alike, so consider each statement carefully before answering. If a statement is true, or mostly true, as applied to you, circle the T. If a statement is false, or not usually true, as applied to you, circle the F.

1. I find it hard to imitate the behavior of other people. T F

2. I guess I do put on a show to impress or entertain people. T F

3. I would probably make a good actor. T F

4. I sometimes appear to others to be experiencing deeper emotions T F
than I actually am.

5. In a group of people, I am rarely the center of attention. T F

6. In different situations and with different people, I often act like T F
very different persons.

7. I can only argue for ideas I already believe. T F

8. In order to get along and be liked, I tend to be what people expect T F
me to be rather than who I really am.

9. I may deceive people by being friendly when I really dislike them. T F

10. I am always the person I appear to be. T F

SCORING

Give yourself one point for each of questions 1, 5, and 7 that you answered F. Give yourself one point for each of the remaining questions that you answered T. Add up your points. If you are a good judge of yourself and scored 7 or above, you are probably a high self-monitoring individual; 3 or below, you are probably a low self-monitoring individual.

SOURCE: This test appeared in Mark Snyder, "The Many Me's of the Self-Monitor," *Psychology Today* 13 (March 1980), p. 34, and is reprinted here by permission of Mark Snyder.

Expressiveness

Expressiveness refers to the skill of communicating genuine involvement in the interpersonal interaction. It is playing the game instead of just watching it as a spectator. Expressiveness is similar to openness in its emphasis on involvement and includes, for example, expressing responsibility for one's thoughts and feelings, encouraging expressiveness or openness in others, and providing feedback that is relevant and appropriate.

This quality also includes taking responsibility for both talking and listening and in this way is similar to equality. In conflict situations (see Unit 21), expressiveness involves fighting actively and stating disagreement directly and with I-messages rather than fighting passively, withdrawing from the encounter, or attributing responsibility to others.

We demonstrate expressiveness by using appropriate variations in vocal rate, pitch, volume, and rhythm to convey involvement and interest and by allowing our facial muscles to reflect and echo this inner involvement.

Similarly, the use of gestures (appropriate in style and frequency) communicates involvement. Too few gestures signal disinterest, while too many may communicate discomfort, uneasiness, and awkwardness.

The monotone and motionless speaker who talks about sex, winning the lottery, and fatal illnesses all in the same tone of voice, with a static posture and an expressionless face, is the stereotype of the ineffective interaction manager.

Other-orientation

Too often we are self-oriented; that is, we focus almost exclusively on ourselves. In interpersonal interaction, this takes the form of talking about ourselves, our experiences, our interests, and our desires, doing most if not all of the talking, and paying little or no attention to verbal and nonverbal feedback from the other person.

Other-orientation is the opposite of self-orientation. It refers to one's ability to adapt to the other person during the interpersonal encounter. It involves communicating attentiveness and interest in the other person and in what is being said.

We communicate our orientation toward the other nonverbally through focused eye contact, smiles, head nods, leaning toward the other person, and displaying feelings and emotions through appropriate facial expression. Verbally we show interest through such comments as "I see," "Really," through requests for further information ("What else did you do in Vegas?"), and through expressions of empathy ("I can understand what you're going through; my parents divorced recently too").

An other-oriented communicator perceives the situation and the interaction from the viewpoint of the other person and appreciates the different ways in which this other person punctuates the sequence of events. Similarly, the other-oriented person communicates empathic understanding, at times by echoing the feelings of the other, at times by disclosing similar experiences or feelings. To achieve empathy, the other-oriented person listens attentively—demonstrating this attention verbally and non-verbally—and provides appropriate, immediate feedback that demonstrates in-depth understanding and sharing of thoughts and feelings.

Other-orientation demonstrates consideration and respect—for example, asking if its all right to dump your troubles on someone before doing so or asking if your phone call comes at an inopportune time before launching into your conversation. Other-orientation involves acknowledging others' feelings as legitimate: "I can understand why you're so angry; I would be too."

These ten qualities, presented in brief here, are returned to throughout the text. These qualities should serve as general headings under which the additional and more detailed discussions that follow may be subsumed.

Summary: Contents in Brief

A HUMANISTIC MODEL OF EFFECTIVENESS		A PRAGMATIC MODEL OF EFFECTIVENESS	
Characteristics	**Definitions**	**Characteristics**	**Definitions**
Openness	Self-disclosure regulation; reactions to others; owning one's thoughts and feelings	*Confidence*	Comfortable, at-ease feeling; control of shyness
Empathy	Feeling as the other feels	*Immediacy*	A sense of contact and togetherness; a feeling of interest and liking
Supportiveness	Descriptions, spontaneity, and provisionalism encourage a supportive atmosphere	*Interaction management*	Control of interaction to the satisfaction of both parties; managing conversational turns, fluency, and message consistency; self-monitoring as appropriate
Positiveness	Expression of positive attitudes toward self, other, and situation; stroking to acknowledge and reinforce the other person	*Expressiveness*	Genuine involvement in speaking and listening, expressed verbally and nonverbally
Equality	Recognition that both parties are important; an equal sharing of the several communication functions	*Other-orientation*	Attentiveness, interest, and concern for the other

Sources

For this unit I relied on the work of Jack Gibb, particularly his insightful "Defensive Communication," *Journal of Communication* 11 (1961): 141–148, reprinted in Joseph A. DeVito, *Communication: Concepts and Processes,* 3d ed. (Englewood Cliffs, N.J.: Prentice-Hall, 1981). For an experimental investigation of defensiveness and supportiveness, see William F. Eadie, "Defensive Communication Revisited: A Critical Examination of Gibb's Theory," *Southern Speech Communication Journal* 47 (Winter 1982): 163–177.

On empathy, see R. Greenson, "Empathy and Its Vicissitudes," *International Journal of Psychoanalysis* 41 (1960): 418–424, and C. Truax. *A Scale for the Measurement of Accurate Empathy,* Wisconsin Psychiatric Institute Discussion Paper No. 20 (Madison, 1961). These and various other contributions to the study of empathy are discussed in Henry M. Backrack, "Empathy," *Archives of General Psychiatry* 33 (1976): 35–38. William S. Howell, in *The Empathic Communicator* (Belmont, Calif.: Wadsworth, 1982), has built his entire introduction to communication around the concept of empathy. The concept of owning thoughts was taken from Arthur P. Bochner and Clifford W. Kelly, "Interpersonal competence: Rationale, Philosophy, and Implementation of a Conceptual Framework," *Communication Education* 23 (November 1974):

279–301. Also see Arthur P. Bochner and Janet Yerby, "Factors Affecting Instruction in Interpersonal Competence," *Communication Education* 26 (March 1977): 91–103. Two useful works that provide interesting perspectives on interpersonal skills are Albert Ellis and Robert A. Harper, *A New Guide to Rational Living* (Hollywood, Calif.: Wilshire Books, 1975) and Toni Brougher, *A Way With Words* (Chicago, Ill.: Nelson-Hall, 1982).

On satisfaction, see Michael L. Hecht, "The Conceptualization and Measurement of Interpersonal Communication Satisfaction," *Human Communication Research* 4 (Spring 1978): 253–264, and "Toward a Conceptualization of Communication Satisfaction," *Quarterly Journal of Speech* 64 (February 1978): 47–62.

On the pragmatic model of effectiveness, see John M. Wiemann, "Explication and Test of a Model of Communicative Competence," *Human Communication Research* 3 (1977): 195–213 and John M. Wiemann and P. Backlund, "Current Theory and Research in Communicative competence," *Review of Educational Research* 50 (1980): 185–199; Brian H. Spitzberg and Michael L. Hecht, "A Component Model of Relational Competence," *Human Communication Research* 10 (Summer 1984): 575–599, and Brain H. Spitzberg and William R. Cupach, *Interpersonal Communication Competence* (Beverly Hills, Calif.: Sage, 1984).

Part 1: Skills in Brief

Noise
Combat the effects of physical, semantic, and psychological noise by eliminating or lessening the sources of physical noise, securing agreement on meanings, and interacting with an open mind in order to increase communication accuracy.

Feedback
Give clear and immediate feedback to others and respond to the feedback of others through corrective measures or continued current performance to increase communication efficiency and satisfaction.

Irreversibility
Avoid saying things (for example, in anger or in commitment) that you may wish to (but will not be able to) retract in order to prevent resentment and ill feeling.

Relational Messages
Recognize and respond to relational as well as content messages in order to ensure a more complete understanding of the messages intended.

Inevitability
Remember that all behavior communicates; seek out nonobvious messages and meanings.

Adjustment
Expand the common areas between you and significant others; learn each other's system of communication signals and meanings in order to increase understanding and interpersonal communication effectiveness.

Punctuation
See the sequence of events punctuated from perspectives other than your own in order to increase empathy and mutual understanding.

Progressive Differentiation, Rigid Complementarity
Recognize instances of progressive differentiation and rigid complementarity in order to assess their effects and take appropriate action.

Attribution
In attempting to identify the motivation for behaviors, examine consensus, consistency, and distinctiveness. Generally, low consensus, high consistency, and low

distinctiveness identify internally motivated behavior; high consensus, low consistency, and high distinctiveness identify externally motivated behavior.

Self-serving Bias

In examining the causes of your own behavior, beware of the self-serving bias, the tendency to attribute negative behaviors to external factors and positive behaviors to internal factors. In self-examinations of your behaviors, ask yourself if and how the self-serving bias might be operating.

Mirroring Destructive Behavior

Beware of mirroring destructive behavior and creating a spiral wherein the unproductive behavior of one person stimulates similarly unproductive behavior in the other, with the result that conflict and differences are maximized and agreements and similarities are minimized.

Implicit Personality Theory

Bring your implicit personality theories to consciousness; avoid drawing firm conclusions about others on the basis of these implicit personality theories.

Self-fulfilling Prophecy

Avoid fulfilling your own negative prophecies and seeing only what you want to see. Be especially careful to examine your perceptions when they conform too closely to your expectations; check to make sure that you are seeing what exists in real life, not just in your expectations or predictions.

Primacy and Recency

Beware of first impressions serving as filters that prevent you from perceiving other and perhaps contradictory behaviors and changes in situations and especially in people. Recognize the normal tendency for first impressions to leave lasting impressions and to color what we see and the conclusions we draw. Be at your very special best in first encounters. Also, take the time and effort to revise your impressions of others on the basis of new information.

Consistency

Recognize the human tendency to seek and see consistency even where it does not exist—to see our friends as all positive and our enemies as all negative.

Perceptual Accentuation

Be aware of the influence that your own needs, wants, and expectations have on your perceptions. Recognize that what you perceive is a function of what exists in reality and what is going on inside your own head. Distinguish the two.

Stereotyping

Avoid stereotyping others; instead, see and respond to each individual as a unique individual. Discriminating among individuals prevents discrimination against individuals.

Listening

Adjust your listening perspective as the situation warrants, between active and passive, judgmental and nonjudgmental, surface and deep, and empathic and objective listening in order to derive maximum benefits from the interpersonal interaction.

Active Listening

Listen actively by paraphrasing the speaker's meanings, expressing an understanding of the speaker's feelings, and asking questions to enable you to check on the accuracy of your understanding of the speaker, express acceptance of the speaker's feelings, and stimulate the speaker to explore further his or her feelings and thoughts and thereby increase meaningful sharing.

Ownership of Feelings

Own your own feelings; use I-messages; acknowledge responsibility for your own thoughts and feelings to increase honest sharing.

Empathy

Empathize with the feelings of others and express this empathic understanding verbally and nonverbally.

Supportiveness

Encourage supportiveness in others by being descriptive rather than evaluative, spontaneous rather than strategic, and provisional rather than certain.

Positiveness

Verbally and nonverbally, communicate a positive attitude toward yourself, others, and situation by smiles, positive facial expressions, attentive gestures, positive verbal expressions, and the elimination or reduction of negative appraisals.

Stroking

Stroke or positively reinforce others to express acknowledgment and validation and thus encourage increased positiveness and interpersonal satisfaction.

Confidence

Communicate a comfortable, at-ease feeling with the interaction through appropriate verbal and nonverbal signals.

Immediacy

Communicate immediacy through appropriate word choice, feedback, eye contact, body posture, and physical closeness.

Interaction Management

Manage the interaction to the satisfaction of both parties by sharing the roles of speaker and listener, avoiding long and awkward silences, and being consistent in your verbal and nonverbal messages.

Self-monitoring

Self-monitor your verbal and nonverbal behavior as appropriate in order to communicate the desired impression.

Expressiveness

Communicate involvement and interest in the interaction by providing appropriate feedback, by assuming responsibility for your thoughts and feelings and for your role as speaker and listener, and by appropriate expressiveness, variety, and flexibility in voice and bodily action.

Other-orientation

Convey concern for and interest in the other person by empathic responses, appropriate feedback, and attentive listening responses.

The Self in Interpersonal Communication

In this second part we focus on the self in interpersonal communication and consider self-awareness, what it is, and how it might be increased. Next we consider one of the most important forms of interpersonal communication, self-disclosure—the process whereby we reveal our hidden selves to another person. Some of the advantages and some of the cautions to be observed in this type of communication are identified. We then consider apprehension (or shyness), what it is, and how we might effectively deal with it, as well as assertiveness.

In this discussion of the self, we consider questions such as these:

What is the self? ■ What is self-awareness? ■ How can we increase self-awareness? ■ How will increased self-awareness improve our interpersonal communication abilities? ■ What is self-disclosure? ■ Why do we resist disclosing so many of our secrets? ■ How do women and men differ in their self-disclosing behavior? ■ What guidelines might we use in deciding what, when, to whom, and whether to self-disclose? ■ How does communication apprehension develop? ■ How can we reduce our own anxiety in communication situations? ■ How can we increase our assertiveness? ■ What skills can you master that will enable you to achieve greater self-awareness, regulate your self-disclosing behaviors, reduce your apprehension, and increase your assertiveness in interpersonal encounters?

UNIT OUTLINE

Universals of the Self and Self-awareness

Self-disclosure

Apprehension and Assertiveness

Skills in Brief

Universals of the Self and Self-awareness

OBJECTIVES

Upon completion of this unit, you should be able to:

1. explain the structure and general function of the Johari window
2. define the open, blind, hidden, and unknown selves
3. provide examples of information that might be contained in each of the four selves
4. explain the concept of life positions or "scripts"
5. identify and explain the ways in which people in the four different life positions see themselves and others
6. explain at least five specific suggestions for increasing self-awareness

If we had to list some of the qualities we would like to possess, that of self-awareness would surely rank high. Most of us wish to know ourselves better. The reason is logical enough: We are in control of our thoughts and our behaviors only to the extent that we understand ourselves, that we are aware of our strengths and our weaknesses, our wants and our needs. Likewise, self-improvement is dependent on self-awareness; we need first to know where we are and who we are effectively to improve our abilities and competencies, effectively to chart and guide our futures.

Self-awareness is central to an understanding of interpersonal communication and seems best explained by reference to two insightful theoretical models. The first is a model of the Johari window, which explains the four different selves of which we are each composed. The second is the model of transactional analysis, particularly the portion dealing with the four major life positions, the four scripts or attitudes we maintain about ourselves and about others. With these as a foundation, we will then examine some of the ways we might increase our own self-awareness.

THE FOUR SELVES

Basic to an understanding of both intrapersonal and interpersonal communication is the model of the four selves, the Johari window, presented in Figure 7.1. The model

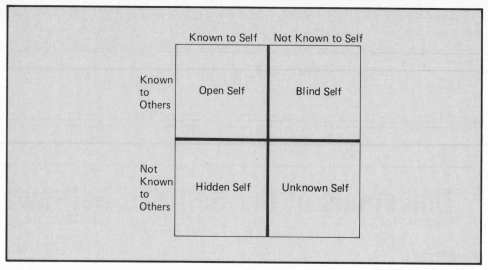

FIGURE 7.1: The Johari Window. The name *Johari* was derived from the first names of the two persons who developed the model, Joseph Luft and Harry Ingham. [*Source:* Joseph Luft, *Group Processes: An Introduction to Group Dynamics* (Palo Alto, Calif.: National Press Books, 1970), p. 11.]

is broken up into four basic areas, or quadrants, each of which contains a somewhat different self.

The Open Self

The open self represents all the information, behaviors, attitudes, feelings, desires, motivations, and ideas that are known to the self and also known to others. The type of information included here might vary from one's name, skin color, and sex to one's age, political and religious affiliations, and batting average. Each individual's open self varies in size, depending on the situation and the individuals the person is dealing with. Some people, for example, make us feel confortable and support us; to them, we open ourselves wide, but to others we prefer to leave most of ourselves closed.

"The smaller the first quadrant," says Joseph Luft, "the poorer the communication." Communication depends on the degree to which we open ourselves to others and to ourself. If we do not allow others to know us (that is, if we keep the open self small), communication between them and us becomes difficult, if not impossible. We can communicate meaningfully only to the extent that we know each other and know ourselves. To improve communication, we have to work first on enlarging the open self.

Note that a change in the open area—or in any of the quadrants—brings about a change in the other quadrants. Visualize the entire model as of constant size but each section as variable, sometimes small, sometimes large. As one section becomes smaller, one or more of the others must become larger. Similarly, as one section becomes larger, one or more of the others must become smaller. For example, if we enlarge the open self, this shrinks the hidden self. Further, this revelation or disclosure in turn leads others to decrease the size of our blind selves by revealing to us what they know and we do not know.

The Johari model emphasizes that the several aspects or dimensions of the self are not separate and distinct pieces but are parts of a whole that interact with each other; each part is intimately dependent on each other part. Like our model of interpersonal communication, this model of the self is a transactional one.

In Figure 7.2 two models of the self are presented to illustrate the different sizes of the four selves, depending on the particular interpersonal situation. In Figure 7.2(left) let us assume that we are with a friend to whom we have opened up a great deal. Consequently, our open self is large and our hidden self is small. In Figure 7.2(right) let us assume that we are with a new employer whom we do not know very well and with whom we are still a bit uncomfortable. Thus our open self is relatively small and our hidden self is large. These models are, of course, hypothetical illustrations designed to explain how the different selves may change from one situation to another. We have no measuring instrument which would allow us to measure accurately the relative sizes of these four selves.

The Blind Self

The blind self represents all the things about ourselves that others know but of which we are ignorant. This may vary from the relatively insignificant habit of saying "you know" or rubbing your nose when you get angry or having a peculiar body odor to something as significant as defense mechanisms or fight strategies or repressed past experiences.

Some people have a very large blind self and seem to be totally oblivious to their own faults and sometimes (though not as often) their own virtues. Others seem overly concerned with having a small blind self. They seek therapy at every turn and join every encounter group. Some are even convinced that they know everything

FIGURE 7.2: Two Models of the Four Selves.

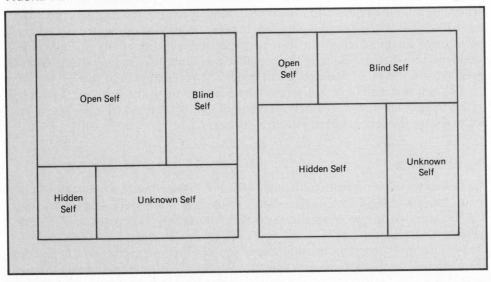

there is to know about themselves, that they have reduced the blind self to zero. Most of us lie between these extremes.

Interpersonal communication depends in great part on both parties' sharing the same basic information about each other. To the extent that blind areas exist, communication will be made difficult. Yet blind areas always exist for each of us. We may be able to shrink our blind areas, but we can never totally eliminate them.

Although communication and interpersonal relations are generally enhanced as the blind area becomes smaller, do not assume that people should therefore be forced to see themselves as we see them. Forcing people to see what we see may cause serious trauma. Such a revelation might cause a breakdown in defenses; it might force people to see their own masochism or jealousy or prejudice when they are not psychologically ready to deal with such information. Such revelations are best dealt with in the company of trained personnel.

The Hidden Self

The hidden self contains all that you know of yourself and of others but that you keep to yourself. This area includes all your successfully kept secrets about yourself and others. In any interaction, this area includes all that is relevant or irrelevant to the conversation but that you do not want to reveal.

At the extremes we have the overdisclosers and the underdisclosers. The overdisclosers tell all. They keep nothing hidden about themselves or others. They tell you their family history, their sexual problems, their marital difficulties, their children's problems, their financial status, their strategies for rising to the top, their goals, their failures and successes, and just about everything else. For them this area is very small, and had they sufficient time and others sufficient patience, it would be reduced to near zero. The problem with these overdisclosers is that they do not discriminate. They do not distinguish between those to whom such information should be disclosed and those to whom it should not be disclosed. Nor do they distinguish among the various types of information that should or should not be disclosed.

The underdisclosers tell nothing. They talk about you but not about themselves. Depending on one's relationship with these underdisclosers, we might feel that they are afraid to tell anyone anything for fear of being laughed at or rejected. Or we may feel rejected for their refusal to trust us. Never to reveal anything about yourself comments on what you think of the people with whom you are interacting. On one level, at least, it says, "I don't trust you enough to reveal myself to you."

The vast majority of us are somewhere between these two extremes. We keep certain things hidden and we disclose certain things. We disclose to some people and not to others. We are, in effect, selective disclosers.

The Unknown Self

The unknown self represents truths that exist but that neither we nor others know about. One could legitimately argue that if neither we nor anyone else knows what is in this area, we cannot know that it exists at all. Actually, we do not *know* it exists; rather, we *infer* it exists.

We infer its existence from a number of sources. Sometimes this area is revealed to us through temporary changes brought about by drug experiences or through special experimental conditions such as hypnosis or sensory deprivation. Sometimes this area is revealed by various projective tests or dreams. There seem to be sufficient instances of such revelations to justify our including this unknown area as part of the self.

Although we cannot easily manipulate this area, recognize that it does exist and that there are things about ourselves and about others that we simply do not know and may never know.

THE FOUR LIFE POSITIONS

One of the basic tenets of transactional analysis is that we live our lives largely according to "scripts." These scripts are similar to dramatic scripts, complete with a list of characters and roles, stage directions, dialogue, and plot.

Our culture provides us with one kind of script. This cultural script provides us with guides to proper dress; rules for sexual conduct; roles for men and women; a value system pertaining to marriage, children, money, and education; the concepts of success and failure; and so on. Families provide another kind of script. Family scripts contain more specific instructions for each of the family members—the boys should go into politics, the girls should get involved in social work; this family will always have its own business; this family may not earn much money but will always have adequate insurance; the oldest son takes over the father's business; the oldest daughter gets married first; and so on.

From our early experiences, particularly from the messages received from our parents (both verbal and nonverbal), we develop a psychological script for ourselves and, for the most part, follow this throughout our lives. Individual scripts are generally "written" by the age of three and provide us with specific directions for functioning within the larger cultural script. Should we play the victim or the persecutor, the slave or the master, the clown or the intellectual?

Some children, for example, are told they will be successes. Nonverbally, they are given love and affection; verbally, they are reinforced for numerous actions. Other children have been told they will never succeed. Statements such as "No matter what you do, you'll be a success" and "You'll never amount to anything" are extremely important in determining the script the child assumes in later life. Generally, people follow the scripts their parents have written for them. But such scripts can be broken—we do not *have* to follow the script written for us by our parents. One of the major purposes of transactional analysis is to break the negative and unproductive scripts, to substitute positive and productive scripts in their places, and to prevent destructive messages from getting written into the script.

These scripts, which we all have, are the bases on which we develop what are called "life positions." In transactional analysis there are four basic life positions.

I'm Not OK, You're OK

This person sees others as well-adjusted and effective (you're OK) but sees himself or herself as maladjusted and ineffective (I'm not OK). This is, according to Thomas A. Harris, the first position we develop as very young children. This is the position of the child who sees himself or herself as helpless and dirty and sees the adult as all-powerful and all-knowing. This person feels helpless and powerless in comparison to others and withdraws from confrontations rather than competing. This life position leads one to live off others, to make others pay for their being OK (and for oneself's being not OK). Such people are frequently depressed; at times they isolate themselves, lamenting, "If only . . ." or "I should have . . ."

I'm Not OK, You're Not OK

People in this category think badly of themselves (I'm not OK) as well as of other people (you're not OK). They have no real acceptance of either themselves or others. They give themselves no support (because they are not OK), and they accept no support from others (because others are not OK). These people have given up. To them, nothing seems worthwhile, and so they withdraw. Interpersonal communication is extremely difficult since they put down both themselves and others, and intrapersonal communication does not seem particularly satisfying either. Attempts to give such people help are generally met with refusals since the would-be helpers are seen as being not OK.

Such people seem to have lost interest in themselves, in others, and in the world generally. Living seems a drag. In the extreme, argue Eric Berne and other transactional analysts, they are the suicides and homicides, the autistics and pathologicals.

I'm OK, You're Not OK

Persons in this position view themselves as effective (I'm OK) but see others as ineffective (you're not OK): "I am good; you are bad." These people have little or no respect for others and easily and frequently find fault with both friends and enemies. They are supportive of themselves but do not accept support from others. They are independent and seem to derive some satisfaction from *intra*personal communication but reject *inter*personal interaction and involvement. Literally and figuratively they need space, elbow room; they resent being crowded by people who are "not OK." Criminals come with disproportional frequency from this class, as do paranoids, who feel persecuted and blame others for their problems.

I'm OK, You're OK

This is the adult, normal, healthy position. This, says Eric Berne in *What Do You Say After You Say Hello?*, is "the position of genuine heroes and princes, and heroines and princesses." These people approach and solve problems constructively. They have valid expectations about themselves and others and accept themselves and others as good, worthy, and significant human beings. These people feel free to develop and progress as individuals. They enter freely into meaningful relationships with other people and do not fear involvements. They feel neither inferior nor superior to others. Rather, they feel worthy and feel others are worthy. This is the position of winners.

This is the position of the effective communicator, the one who views oneself and others positively, equally, supportively, empathically, and openly. This is the person who communicates with confidence, with a connectedness that is evidenced both verbally and nonverbally, with specific goals and relevant strategies for achieving these goals, expressively and with a view of and a focus on the other person.

Depending on the specifics of the situation (source, receiver, message, channel, context), each of the other positions lack several or all of these qualities of effective interpersonal interaction.

It is impossible to say how many people are in each class. Many pass through the "I'm not OK, you're OK" position. Few arrive at the "I'm Ok, you're OK" position; few people are winners in this sense. Very probably the vast majority of people are in the "I'm not OK, you're OK" and "I'm OK, you're not OK" positions. These are, of course, general classes, and human beings resist each classification. Thus these four positions should be seen as areas on a continuum, none of which have clear-cut boundaries and yet all of which are different.

INCREASING SELF-AWARENESS

Embedded in the foregoing discussion were suggestions on how to increase your own self-awareness. Some of these may now be made explicit.

Ask Yourself About Yourself

No one knows you better than you do; the problem is that we seldom, if ever, ask ourselves about ourselves. It can be interesting and revealing. There are a number of ways to do this. One way is to take a "Who Am I?" test informally. Take a piece of paper, head it "Who Am I?" and write 10 or 15 or 20 times, "I am . . . ." Then complete the sentence each time. Try not to give only positive or socially acceptable responses; just respond with what comes to mind first. Second, take another piece of paper and divide it into two columns. Head one column "Strengths" or "Virtues" and the other column "weaknesses" or "vices." Fill in each column as quickly as possible. Third, using these first two "tests" as a base, take a third piece of paper, head it "Self-improvement Goals," and complete the statement "I want to improve my . . ." as many times as you can in, say, five minutes. Whether or not these particular methods are used is not important; what is important is that you begin a dialogue with yourself about yourself.

Further, remember that you are constantly changing; consequently, these self-perceptions and goals also change rapidly, and often in drastic ways; they therefore need to be updated at regular and frequent intervals.

Listen to Others

We can learn a great deal about ourselves from seeing ourselves as others do. Conveniently, others are constantly giving us the very feedback we need to increase self-awareness. In every interpersonal interaction, people comment on us in some way—on what we do, what we say, how we look. Sometimes these comments are explicit; most often they are only implicit. Often they are "hidden" in the way in which others look at us, in what they talk about, in their interest in what we say. We need to pay close attention to this kind of information (both verbal and nonverbal) and use it to increase our own self-awareness. In the discussions of verbal and nonverbal communication that follow, suggestions and insights for reading these hidden messages are offered.

One of the best ways to learn about ourselves and to increase self-awareness is to actively seek out information about the self. A trained counselor, a sensitive friend, or a family member can often add considerably to our self-awareness, self-understanding, and ultimately our interpersonal effectiveness.

Actively Seek Information About Yourself

Actively seek out information to reduce your blind self. Generally, people will reveal more when they are encouraged to do so. You need not be so blatant as to say, "Tell me about yourself" or "What do you think of me?" But you can use some of the situations that arise every day to gain self-information: "Do you think I came down too hard on the instructor today?" or "Do you think I was assertive enough when asking for the raise?" or "Do you think I'd be thought too forward if I invited myself to their house for dinner?" Do not, of course, seek this information constantly; your friends would then surely and quickly find others with whom to interact. But you can make use of some situations—perhaps those in which you are particularly unsure of what to do or how you appear—to reduce your blind self and increase self-awareness.

See Yourself from Different Perspectives

Each of us is viewed differently by each of our friends and relatives; to each we are a somewhat different person. Yet we are really *all* of these. Practice seeing yourself as do the people with whom you interact. For starters, visualize how you are seen by your mother, your father, your teachers, your best friend, the stranger you sat next to on the bus, your employer, your neighbor's child. Each of these people sees you differently. Because you are, in fact, a composite of all of these views, it is important that you for a moment see yourself through the eyes of these others. The experience will surely give you new and valuable perspectives on yourself.

Increase Your Open Self

The extent to which you reveal yourself to others—the degree to which you increase your open self—influences at least two dimensions of self-awareness. First, when you reveal yourself to others, you reveal yourself to yourself at the same time. At the very least, you bring into consciousness or into clearer focus what you may have buried within. As you discuss yourself, you may see connections that you had previously missed, and with the aid of feedback from others, you may gain still more insight. All this helps to increase your self-awareness. Second, by increasing the open self, you increase the likelihood that a meaningful and intimate dialogue will develop, and it is through such interactions that you best get to know yourself.

There are risks involved in revealing yourself, and these need to be taken into consideration. The risks (and advantages) of self-disclosure are considered in the next unit.

Be Conscious of Your Life Position

Recognize when you are functioning with an inappropriate and self-destructive script. Recognize that a negative self-image (the "I'm not OK" position) may have been internalized when you were very young and may be a totally inadequate reflection of what you are now. Further, a negative self-image will invariably impair your general effectiveness; it often makes one frightened to take risks, to see accomplishments as less important than they really are, to see in many situations failure when it would be just as easy to see success. Realize that these scripts can be changed, rewritten. Substitute the productive "I'm OK"–position script for the unproductive, self-destructive "I'm not OK" script.

Similarly, realize that other people, too, are "OK" and have a great deal to contribute to society in general and to each of us in particular. There *is* strength in unity, and we will profit a great deal from learning and using the insights and talents of others.

Remember, the "I'm OK, you're OK" position frees us to think positively about ourselves and about others, to open ourselves to new experiences, and to interact openly with other people. When we do this, self-awareness is sure to follow.

Summary: Contents in Brief

Four Selves	Four Life Positions	Increasing Self-awareness
Open self: known to self and others	I'm not OK, you're OK (sees self as powerless and inadequate; sees others as competent and capable)	Ask yourself about yourself
Blind self: known to others, unknown to self		Listen to others
Hidden self: known to self, unknown to others	I'm not OK, you're not OK (sees both self and others as losers)	Actively seek information about yourself
		See yourself from different perspectives

Summary: Contents in Brief (continued)

Four Selves	Four Life Positions	Increasing Self-awareness
Unknown self: unknown to self and others	I'm OK, you're not OK (sees self as independent and others as inadequate and undeserving of respect)	Increase your open self Be conscious of your life position
	I'm OK, you're OK (sees both self and others as accepting, worthy, significant, and competent, as winners)	

Sources

The model of the four selves is based on the Johari window, thoroughly discussed in the works of Joseph Luft, particularly *Group Processes: An Introduction to Group Dynamics*, 2d ed. (Palo Alto, Calif.: Mayfield Publishing Company, 1970) and *Of Human Interaction* (Palo Alto, Calif.: Mayfield Publishing Company, 1969). John Powell's *Why Am I Afraid to Tell You Who I Am?* (Niles, Ill.: Argus Communications, 1969), *Why Am I Afraid to Love?* (Niles, Ill: Argus Communications, 1972), and *The Secret of Staying in Love* (Niles, Ill.: Argus Communications, 1974) are three of the most interesting and perceptive works in this area. They are deceptively simple, so do not dismiss them if they appear too elementary.

George Weinberg, in *Self-Creation* (New York: St. Martin's Press, 1978), provides numerous insights into the self that relate directly to many of the issues raised in the discussions of relationships (Units 18–26). A useful compendium of techniques for increasing self-awareness and for dealing with various psychological problems is provided by Salvatore V. Didato, *Psychotechniques* (New York: Playboy Paperbacks, 1980).

The discussion of the life positions is based on the work of the transactional analysts. Most of the popular works on transactional analysis cover essentially the same basics but apply them to different areas. In writing this section, I made most use of Thomas A. Harris, *I'm O.K., You're O.K.* (New York: Harper & Row, 1969), which I wholeheartedly recommend to any college student. Also useful are Muriel James and Dorothy Jongeward, *Born to Win: Transactional Analysis with Gestalt Experiments* (Reading, Mass.: Addison-Wesley, 1971), and Eric Berne, *Games People Play* (New York: Grove Press, 1964). An excellent overview may be found in General M. Goldhaber and Marylynn B. Goldhaber, *Transactional Analysis: Principles and Applications* (Boston: Allyn & Bacon, 1976). A recent and excellent discussion of transactional analysis is provided by Amy Bjork Harris and Thomas A. Harris, *Staying OK* (New York: Harper & Row, 1985).

UNIT 8

Self-disclosure

OBJECTIVES

Upon completion of this unit, you should be able to:

1. define *self-disclosure*
2. identify and define at least four dimensions of self-disclosure
3. explain at least five factors influencing self-disclosure
4. explain at least three sources of resistance to self-disclosure
5. explain at least three rewards of self-disclosure
6. explain the dangers of self-disclosure
7. identify at least four guidelines for use in self-disclosing
8. identify at least four guidelines recommended for responding to the disclosures of others

Probably the most important form of interpersonal communication is that of self-disclosure. Here we consider the nature of self-disclosure, some of the factors influencing self-disclosure, the sources of resistance to self-disclosure, the rewards to be derived from self-disclosing, the dangers of self-disclosing, and, last, guidelines that may prove useful in your decisions concerning you own self-disclosures and your responses to the disclosures of others.

THE NATURE OF SELF-DISCLOSURE

Because self-disclosure is such a significant form of interpersonal communication, we need to inquire into its nature and consider, first, the definition of self-disclosure and how it differs from all other forms of interpersonal interaction and, second, its dimensions, ways in which self-disclosures may vary.

A Definition of Self-disclosure

Self-disclosure is a type of communication in which information about the self that is normally kept hidden is communicated to another person. Special note should be taken of several aspects of this elementary definition. Because self-disclosure is a type of communication, overt statements pertaining to the self as well as slips of the tongue, unconscious nonverbal movements, written confessions, and public confessions would all be classified as self-disclosing communications. Only new knowledge is useful. To tell someone something he or she already knows would not be self-disclosure; some new knowledge would have to be communicated. Further, to be self-disclosure, the information must be something that is normally kept hidden. To tell someone your age, religion, or political leanings would be self-disclosure only if you normally keep these data secret or hidden from most people.

Self-disclosure involves at least one other individual; it cannot be an *intra*personal communication act. Nor may we "disclose" in a manner that makes it impossible for another person to understand. This is not a disclosure at all. Nor can we write in diaries that no one reads and call this self-disclosure. To be self-disclosure, the information must be received and understood by another individual.

HISTORY AND STORY

Gerard Egan, in *Encounter,* makes another distinction that may prove useful. He distinguishes between *history,* "the mode of noninvolvement," and *story,* "the mode of involvement." History is a manner of revealing the self that is only pseudo-self-disclosure. It is an approach that details some facts of the individual's life but does not really invite involvement from listeners. From a person's history we may learn what the individual did or what happened throughout that person's life, but somehow we really do not get to know the person. Story, on the other hand, is authentic self-disclosure. In story, individuals communicate their inner selves and look for some human response rather than just simple feedback. The speaker takes a risk and reveals something significant about who she or he is and not merely what she or he has done.

Dimensions of Self-disclosure

Self-disclosures may differ from one another in terms of five basic dimensions or qualities. Perhaps the most obvious is the *amount* of self-disclosure that takes place. The amount of self-disclosure may be gauged by examining the frequency with which one self-discloses and the duration of the self-disclosing messages, that is, the time taken up with self-disclosing statements. A second factor is *valence,* the positiveness or negativeness of the self-disclosure. We can self-disclose favorable and flattering things about ourselves as well as unfavorable and unflattering things, and, as can easily be appreciated, the resultant self-disclosures will be drastically different in their effect on the self-discloser as well as on the listener. As explained in the next section, this valence factor also influences the nature and extent of our self-disclosures.

A third factor is the *accuracy* and *honesty* with which one self-discloses. The accuracy of our self-disclosures will be limited by the extent to which we know ourselves; some of us know ourselves quite thoroughly and therefore may make extremely accurate self-disclosures. Others of us seem totally out of touch with what is going on inside our skins, and there is little chance of these persons' self-disclosures being accurate. Further, our self-disclosures may vary in terms of honesty. We may be totally honest or we may exaggerate, omit crucial details, or simply lie. The fourth factor is *intention,* the extent to which we disclose what we intend to disclose, the extent to which we are in conscious control of the self-disclosures we make. Some people reveal a great deal but rarely intend to be so revealing; others may wish to reveal a great deal but, for one reason or another, make statements that are difficult to interpret. Fifth, self-disclosures may vary in terms of *intimacy*. We can disclose the most intimate details of our lives, items we regard as peripheral or impersonal, or items that lie anywhere in between these extremes.

FACTORS INFLUENCING SELF-DISCLOSURE

Self-disclosure occurs more readily under certain circumstances than under others. A few of the more significant factors influencing self-disclosure are identified here.

The Disclosures of Others: The Dyadic Effect

Generally, self-disclosure is reciprocal. In any interaction, self-disclosure is more likely to occur if the other person has previously self-disclosed. Self-disclosure follows self-disclosure. This is the dyadic effect; what one person in a dyad does, the other person does as a response. This dyadic affect in self-disclosure implies that a kind of spiral effect operates here, with each person's self-disclosures serving as the stimulus for additional self-disclosures by the other person. These in turn serve as the stimulus for still more self-disclosures, and so on.

When the receiver is positive and reinforcing, there is naturally a greater tendency to self-disclose than when the receiver is negative and punishing. Generally, people tend to like others who disclose about the same amount as they do. If you disclose much more or much less than do the people with whom you are interacting, you may be in line for a negative evaluation.

Audience Size

Self-disclosure, perhaps because of the numerous fears we have about revealing ourselves, is more likely to occur in small groups than in large groups. Dyads are perhaps the most common situations in which self-disclosure takes place. A dyad seems more suitable because it is easier for the self-discloser to deal with one person's reactions and responses than with the reactions of a group of three or four or five. The self-discloser can attend to the responses quite carefully and, on the basis of the support or lack of support, monitor the disclosures, continuing if the situation is supportive and stopping if it is not. With more than one listener such monitoring is impossible since the responses are sure to vary among the listeners. Another reason is that when the group is larger than two, the self-disclosure takes on aspects of exhibitionism and public exposure. It is no longer a confidential matter; now it is one about which many people know. From a more practical point of view, it is often difficult to assemble in one place at one time only those people to whom we would want to self-disclose.

Topic

The topic influences the amount and type of self-disclosure. Certain areas of the self are more likely to be self-disclosed than others. We would more likely self-disclose information about our job or hobbies, for example, than about our sex life or financial situation. Sidney M. Jourard found that self-disclosures about money (for example, the amount of money one owes), personality (for example, the things about which one experiences guilt), and body (for example, one's feelings of sexual adequacy) were less frequent than disclosures about tastes and interests, attitudes and opinions, and work. Clearly, the first three topics are more closely related to one's self-concept, and disclosures about these are therefore potentially more threatening than are disclosures about tastes in clothing, views on religion, or pressures at work.

Valence

The valence (the positive or negative quality) of the self-disclosure is also significant. Positive self-disclosures are more likely than negative self-disclosures and may be made to nonintimates as well as to intimates. Negative self-disclosures, on the other hand, take place most often with close intimates and usually after considerable time has elapsed in a relationship. This finding is consistent with the evidence that shows that self-disclosure and trust are positively related.

Research indicates that we develop greater attraction for people who engage in positive self-disclosure than for those who engage in negative self-disclosure. This is particularly significant in the early stages of a relationship. Negative self-disclosures to a stranger or even a casual acquaintance are perceived as inappropriate, no doubt because such self-disclosures violate our culture's norms for such communications. This may suggest a warning: If your aim is to be perceived as attractive, consider curtailing negative self-disclosures, at least in the early stages of relationships.

Sex

Most research indicates, generally, that women disclose more than men but that both men and women make negative disclosures about equally. Commenting on the male reluctance to self-disclose that most researchers have found, Patricia Middlebrook notes that "part of the male role in our society may involve not discussing the self, which, in turn, may add to the level of stress experienced by males and to their early death." Although we may not wish to accept so extreme a relationship as Middlebrook suggests, it does seem that the need or pressure not to self-disclose creates stress and discomfort for males.

Men and women give different reasons for avoiding self-disclosure. The main reason for avoiding self-disclosure, however, is common to both men and women: "If I disclose, I might project an image I do not want to project." In a society where image is so important—where one's image is often the basis for success or failure—this reason for avoiding self-disclosure is expected. Other reasons for avoiding self-disclosure, however, are unique for men and women. For men the reasons reported are "If I self-disclose, I might give information that makes me appear inconsistent," "If I self-disclose, I might lose control over the other person," and "Self-disclosure might threaten relationships I have with people other than close acquaintances." Lawrence Rosenfeld sums up the male reasons for self-disclosure avoidance as "If I disclose to you, I might project an image I do not want to project, which could make me look bad and cause me to lose control over you. This might go so far as to affect relationships I have with people other than you." The principal objective of men is to avoid self-disclosure so that control can be maintained.

In addition to fearing the projection of an unfavorable image, women avoid self-disclosure for the following reasons: "Self-disclosure would give the other person information that he or she might use against me at some time," "Self-disclosure is a sign of some emotional disturbance," and "Self-disclosure might hurt our relationship." The general reason women avoid self-disclosure, says Rosenfeld, is "If I disclose to you, I might project an image I do not want to project, such as my being emotionally ill, which you might use against me and which might hurt our relationship." The principal objective for avoiding self-disclosure for women is "to avoid personal hurt and problems with the relationship."

Rosenfeld summarizes the results of his investigation by observing, "The stereotyped male role—independent, competitive, and unsympathetic—and the stereotyped female role—dependent, nonaggressive, and interpersonally oriented—were evident in the reasons indicated for avoiding self-disclosure. Seeking different rewards from their interpersonal relationships, many males and females go about the business of self-disclosing, and *not* self-disclosing, differently." You might wish to test some of these findings yourself by talking with your peers about the reasons they avoid self-disclosure and about the reasons for their reasons. Why do men and women have different reasons for avoiding self-disclosure? What is there in the learning histories of the two sexes that might account for such differences?

Race, Nationality, and Age

There are racial and national differences in self-disclosure as well. Black students disclose significantly less than do white students, and students in the United States disclose more than similar groups in Puerto Rico, Germany, Great Britain, and the Middle East. There are even differences in the amount of self-disclosure in different age groups. Self-disclosure to a spouse or to an opposite-sex friend increases from the age of about 17 to about 50 and then drops off.

Receiver Relationship

The person to whom the disclosures are made influences the frequency and the likelihood of self-disclosure. Research has not been able to identify fully the specific characteristics of the person with whom self-disclosure is most likely to take place. Most studies have found that we disclose more often to people who are close to us— our spouses, our family, our close friends. Some studies claim that we disclose most to persons we like and do not disclose to persons we dislike regardless of how close they are to us. Thus we may disclose to a well-liked teacher even though this teacher is not particularly close and yet not disclose to a brother or sister who is close but whom we may not like very much.

We are more apt to disclose to people we see as accepting, understanding, warm, and supportive. Generally, of course, these are people we are close to and like. Still other studies claim that a lasting relationship between people increases the likelihood of self-disclosure, while others find that self-disclosure is heightened in temporary relationships, for example, between strangers on a train.

Male college students are more likely to disclose to a close friend than to either of their parents. But female college students disclose about equally to their mothers and to their best friends but do not disclose very much to their fathers or to their boyfriends.

As might be expected, husbands and wives self-disclose to each other more than they do to any other person or group of persons. "This confirms the view," says

Jourard in *The Transparent Self,* "that marriage is the 'closest' relationship one can enter, and it may help us the better to understand why some people avoid it like the plague. Anyone who is reluctant to be known by another person and to know another person—sexually and cognitively—will find the prospective intimacy of marriage somewhat terrifying." There is some evidence to suggest, however, that wives from the lower social classes disclose most not to their husbands but to their women friends.

SOURCES OF RESISTANCE TO SELF-DISCLOSURE

For all its advantages and importance, self-disclosure is a form of communication that is often fiercely resisted. Some of the reasons for its resistance should be examined so that we may better understand our own reluctance to enter into this type of communication experience.

Societal Bias

Perhaps the most obvious reasons for our reluctance to self-disclose, according to Gerard Egan, is that we have internalized the societal bias against it; that is, we have been conditioned against self-disclosure by the society in which we live. The hero in folklore is strong but silent; he bears responsibilities, burdens, and problems without letting others even be aware of them. He is self-reliant and does not need the assistance of anyone. Men have internalized this folk hero. Women are a bit more fortunate in this respect. They are allowed the luxury of some self-disclosure; they are allowed to tell their troubles to someone, to pour out their feelings, to talk about themselves. Women are allowed great freedom in expressing emotions, in verbalizing love and affection. Men are more restricted; they are conditioned to avoid such expressions. These, men have been taught, are signs of weakness rather than strength. This societal bias is reflected even in our evaluations of self-disclosing men and women. For example, women who disclose a great deal are generally evaluated positively, but men who disclose a great deal, regardless of the subjects they disclose, are evaluated negatively.

Fear of Punishment

Many people resist self-disclosing because of a fear of punishment, generally in the form of rejection. We may picture other people laughing at us or whispering about us or condemning us if we self-disclose. These mental pictures help to convince us that self-disclosure is not the most expedient course of action.

We may also fear punishment in the form of tangible or concrete manifestations, such as the loss of a job or of friends. At times this happens. The ex-convict who self-discloses a past record may end up without a job or out of a political office. Generally, however, these fears are overblown. These fears are often excuses that allow us to rest contentedly without self-disclosing.

Gerard Egan, in *Encounter,* points out that this fear of rejection operates like a reverse halo effect. *Halo effect* refers to the generalizing of virtue from one area to another. For example, your communication teacher may know a great deal about communication and may be perceived as highly credible in that field. The halo effect operates to generalize that perceived credibility to other fields as well, so when she or he talks about politics or economics or psychology, we are more apt to see her or him as credible and knowledgeable in these areas, too. The reverse halo effect operates in a similar manner. We assume that if we tell others something negative about ourselves, their negative responses will generalize to other aspects of our behavior and they will see us as negative generally.

Fear of Self-knowledge

Another possible reason we resist self-disclosure is what Egan calls fear of self-knowledge. We may have built up a beautiful, rationalized picture of ourselves, emphasizing the positive and eliminating or minimizing the negative. Self-disclosure often forces us to see through the rationalizations. We see the positive aspects for what they are, and we see the negative aspects that were previously hidden.

REWARDS OF SELF-DISCLOSURE

The obvious question when the topic of self-disclosure arises is ''Why?'' Why should anyone self-disclose to anyone else? What is it about this type of communication that merits its being singled out and discussed at length? There is no clear-cut answer to these very legitimate questions. No statistical research findings prove the usefulness or importance of self-disclosure. Yet evidence in the form of testimony, observational reports, and some experimental research has led a number of researchers and theorists to argue that self-disclosure is perhaps the most important form of communication anyone can engage in. This is not to imply that no risks are involved; there are dangers in self-disclosing, and we will consider some of these later. Here, however, we focus on the rewards or advantages of this form of interpersonal communication.

Knowledge of Self

One argument in favor of self-disclosure is that we cannot know ourselves as fully as possible if we do not self-disclose to at least one other individual. By self-disclosing we gain a new perspective on ourselves, a deeper understanding of our own behavior. In therapy, for example, very often the insight does not come directly from the therapist; while the individual is self-disclosing, she or he recognizes some facet of behavior or some relationship that was not known before. Through self-disclosure, then, we may come to understand ourselves more thoroughly. Sidney M. Jourard, in *The Transparent Self*, notes that self-disclosure is an important factor in counseling and psychotherapy and argues that people may need such help because they have not disclosed significantly to other people. This relationship between self-disclosure and mental health is frequently discussed, and not everyone would agree with Jourard's rather strong claim. A more reasoned hypothesis, I think, is offered by Paul Cozby, who after a thorough review of the self-disclosure and mental-adjustment literature concluded that ''persons with positive mental health . . . are characterized by high disclosure to a few significant others and medium disclosure to others in the social environment. Individuals who are poorly adjusted . . . are characterized by either high or low self-disclosure to virtually everyone in the social environment.'' It is selective self-disclosure, or self-disclosure in moderation, then, that seems to characterize the well-adjusted personality.

Ability to Cope

Improved ability to deal with our problems, especially our guilt, frequently comes through self-disclosure. One of the great fears that many people have is that they will not be accepted because of some deep, dark secret, because of something they have done, or because of some feeling or attitude they might have. Because we feel these things as a basis for rejection, we develop guilt. If, for example, you do not love one of your parents, you might fear being rejected if you were to self-disclose such a feeling; thus a sense of guilt develops. By self-disclosing such feelings and being supported rather than rejected, we are better prepared to deal with the guilt and perhaps reduce or even eliminate it. Even self-acceptance is difficult without self-disclosure. We accept ourselves largely through the eyes of others. If we feel that others will reject us, we are apt to reject ourselves as well. Through self-disclosure and subsequent support, we are in a better position to see the positive responses to us and are more likely to respond by developing a positive self-concept.

Energy Release

Keeping our secrets to ourselves and not revealing who we are to others takes a great deal of energy and leaves us with that much less energy for other things. We must be constantly on guard, for example, lest someone see in our behavior what we

Perhaps the most frequently discussed topic in the college cafeteria is the self. At college, probably as in no other place, we attempt to learn who we are and what we ought to be doing. Self-disclosing these feelings teaches us a great deal about ourselves and very likely influences our subsequent choices at least as much as do the formal learnings that take place in the classrooms.

consider to be a deviant orientation, attitude, or behavior pattern. We might avoid certain people for fear they will tell this awful thing about us, or avoid situations or places because if we are seen there, others will know how terrible we really are. By self-disclosing, we rid ourselves of the false masks that otherwise must be worn. Jourard puts this most clearly:

> *Every maladjusted person is a person who has not made himself known to another human being and in consequence does not know himself. Nor can he be himself. More than that, he struggles actively to avoid becoming known by another human being. He works at it ceaselessly, twenty-four hours daily, and it is work! In the effort to avoid becoming known, a person provides for himself a cancerous kind of stress which is subtle and unrecognized, but none the less effective in producing not only the assorted patterns of unhealthy personality which psychiatry talks about, but also the wide array of physical ills that have come to be recognized as the province of psychosomatic medicine.*

Communication Effectiveness

Self-disclosure is also helpful in improving communication efficiency. Since we understand the messages of others largely to the extent that we understand the other individuals, we can better understand what a person means if we know that person well. We can tell what certain nuances mean, when the person is serious and when she or he is joking, when the person is being sarcastic out of fear and when out of resentment, and so on. Self-disclosure is an essential condition for getting to know another individual. You might study a person's behavior or even live with a person for years, but if that person never self-discloses, you are far from understanding that individual as a complete person.

Meaningfulness of Relationships

Self-disclosure is necessary if a meaningful relationship between two people is to be established. Without self-disclosure, meaningful relationships seem impossible to develop. There are, it is true, relationships that have lasted for as long as 30 or 40 years without self-disclosure. Many married couples would fall into this category, as would colleagues working in the same office or factory or people living in the same neighborhood or apartment house. Without self-disclosure, however, these relationships are probably not terribly meaningful, or at least not as meaningful as they might be. By self-disclosing, we are in effect saying to other individuals that we trust them, that we respect them, that we care enough about them and about our relationship to reveal ourselves to them. This leads the other individual to self-disclose in return. This is at least the start of a meaningful relationship, a relationship that is honest and open and goes beyond surface trivialities.

Physiological Health

Recent research by psychologist James Pennebacker demonstrates that people who self-disclose are less vulnerable to illnesses. Self-disclosures seem to protect the body from the damaging stresses that accompany nondisclosure. For example, bereavement over the death of someone very close is linked to physical illness for those who bear this alone and in silence but is unrelated to any physical problems for those who share their grief with others. Similarly, women who suffered sexual trauma experience a variety of illnesses (for example, headaches and stomach problems). Women who kept these experiences to themselves, however, suffer these illnesses to a much greater extent than do those who talked with others about these traumas. Persons who do not self-disclose have also been found to have less effective immune systems than those who self-disclose. The physiological effort required to keep one's burdens to oneself seems to interact with the effects of the burden or trauma to create a combined stress that can lead to a variety of diseases and illnesses.

DANGERS OF SELF-DISCLOSURE: RISKS AHEAD

Undoubtedly, there are numerous advantages to be gained from self-disclosure. Yet these should not blind us to the fact that self-disclosure often involves very real risks. An investment analogy may prove useful: When the payoffs or potential gains are great, so are the risks. When the payoffs are small, so are the risks. The same seems true of self-disclosure. When the potential rewards of self-disclosure are great, so are the risks. These potential rewards and risks need to be weighed carefully before engaging in significant self-disclosure. The risks may be of various types—risks to one's job, to one's professional advancement, to one's social and family life, and to just about any and every aspect of one's life. Politicians who disclose that they have been seeing a psychiatrist may later face a loss of party and voter support. Men and women in law enforcement agencies who disclose that they are homosexual may find themselves confined to desk jobs, prevented from further advancement, or charged with criminal behavior and fired. Teachers who disclose former or present drug behavior or cohabitation with students may find themselves denied tenure, teaching undesirable courses at undesirable hours, and eventually being victims of "budget cuts." And teachers or students who, in the supportive atmosphere in their interpersonal communication course, disclose about their sex lives, financial conditions, or self-doubts, anxieties, or fantasies may find that some less sympathetic listeners may later use that information against them.

Even in close and long-lasting relationships, self-disclosure can cause problems. After reviewing the self-disclosure research, Arthur Bochner concluded that "uncensored candor is a bad idea." In cases where the individuals desire to maintain a relationship, total self-disclosure may prove threatening and may, in fact, lead to a decrease in mutual attraction, trust, or any of the bonds holding the individuals together. It is easy to visualize for such cases how self-disclosures concerning, for example, infidelity, romantic fantasies, past indiscretions or crimes, lies, or hidden weaknesses and fears could have such negative effects.

All communication revolves around questions of choice. With self-disclosure, the choices are particularly difficult to make, largely because the advantages and disadvantages are so significant and cannot be predicted easily. To one person, self-disclosures may bring only rewards; to another, the same self-disclosures may bring only punishments. One may receive a promotion for demonstrated self-confidence; the other may be fired for unbecoming behavior.

In making your choice between disclosing and not disclosing, keep in mind—in addition to the advantages and dangers already noted—the irreversible nature of communication that was noted in Unit 2. Regardless of how many times we may attempt to qualify something, "take it back," or deny it, once something is said, it cannot be withdrawn. We cannot erase the conclusions and inferences listeners have made on the basis of our disclosures. I am not advocating that you therefore refrain from self-disclosing, only reminding you to consider the irreversible nature of communication as one additional factor in your choices.

SELF-DISCLOSURE GUIDELINES

Self-disclosure involves both potential rewards and dangers. Therefore, examine carefully the predicted consequences before deciding whether or not to self-disclose. Almost equally difficult is responding appropriately to the disclosures of others. Because self-disclosure is so important and so delicate a matter, guidelines are offered here for (1) deciding whether to self-disclose and how and (2) responding to the disclosures of others.

Guidelines for Self-disclosing

Each person has to make her or his own decisions concerning self-disclosure; there is no universal answer. Further, your decision will be based on numerous variables, many of which were considered in the foregoing discussion. The following guidelines will help you raise the right questions before making what must be *your* decision.

CONSIDER THE MOTIVATION FOR THE SELF-DISCLOSURE
Self-disclosure should be motivated out of a concern for the relationship, for the others involved, and for oneself. Some people self-disclose out of a desire to hurt the listener. Persons who tell their parents that they never did love them or that they hindered rather than helped their emotional development may be disclosing out of a desire to hurt and perhaps to punish rather than out of a desire to improve the relationship. Nor, of course, should self-disclosure be used to punish oneself (perhaps because of some guilt feeling or unresolved conflict). Self-disclosure should not be an exercise in exhibitionism or an opportunity to parade one's sexual fantasies, past indiscretions, or psychological problems. Self-disclosure should serve a useful and productive function for all persons involved.

CONSIDER THE APPROPRIATENESS OF THE SELF-DISCLOSURE
Self-disclosure should be appropriate to the context and to the relationship between speaker and listener. Before making any significant self-disclosure, ask if this is the right time and place. Could a better time and place be arranged? Ideally, self-disclosures should grow naturally out of the developing situation and relationship. Is this self-disclosure appropriate to the relationship? Generally, the more intimate the disclosures, the closer the relationship should be. It is probably best to resist intimate disclosures with nonintimates or casual acquaintances or in the early stages of a relationship. This suggestion is especially applicable to intimate negative disclosures. Is it important that this particular listener hear this particular self-disclosure? Is this self-disclosure something that will help the relationship grow and prosper? Will the listener be better able to understand you as a result of this disclosure?

CONSIDER THE OPPORTUNITY AVAILABLE FOR OPEN AND HONEST RESPONSES

Self-disclosure should occur in an atmosphere where open and honest responses can be made. Don't hit and run. Avoid self-disclosure when the people involved are under pressures of time or when they are in a situation that will not allow them to respond as they might wish. Ask yourself, then, if there is sufficient time and if the atmosphere is such that the individual can respond at length to your self-disclosures if she or he wishes. If the answer is no, wait for another time and another place.

CONSIDER THE CLARITY AND DIRECTNESS OF THE SELF-DISCLOSURE

The goal of self-disclosure is to inform, not to confuse, the other person. Often, however, we self-disclose only partially or self-disclose in such an oblique and round-about way that the listener walks away more confused than before the disclosure. If you are going to self-disclose, consider the extent of the disclosure and be prepared to disclose enough to ensure the necessary understanding, or perhaps reconsider whether you should self-disclose at all. This does not mean that you have to disclose everything you have hidden concerning the matter, only that you need to consider whether the omitted information is going to prevent the achievement of the under-standing you seek. One of the ill effects that too sketchy a disclosure often has is that the other person fills in the omitted portions incorrectly, with the result that you are more misunderstood afterward than before. This defeats the very purpose of self-disclosure.

The most important suggestion in this regard is to disclose gradually. Disclose in small increments. When disclosures are made too rapidly and all at once, it is impossible to monitor your listener's responses and to retreat if the responses are not positive enough. Further, you prevent the listener from responding with his or her own disclosures and thereby upset the natural balance so helpful in this kind of communication exchange.

CONSIDER THE DISCLOSURES OF THE OTHER PERSON

During your disclosures, give the other person a chance to reciprocate with his or her own disclosures. If such reciprocal disclosures are not made, reassess your own self-disclosures. The lack of reciprocity may be a signal that for this person at this time and in this context, your disclosures are not welcomed or appropriate.

CONSIDER THE POSSIBLE BURDENS SELF-DISCLOSURE MIGHT ENTAIL

Any potential self-discloser should carefully weigh the potential problems that may be incurred as a result of a disclosure. Can you afford to lose your job should you disclose your previous prison record? Are you willing to risk failing the course should you confess to having plagiarized your term paper?

Ask yourself whether you are making unreasonable demands on the listener. For example, consider the person who swears his or her mother-in-law to secrecy and then self-discloses to having an affair with a neighbor. This type of situation, it seems, places an unfair burden on the mother-in-law, who is now in a bind either to break her promise of secrecy or to allow her child to believe a lie. Parents often place unreasonable burdens on their children by self-disclosing marital problems or infi-delities or self-doubts without realizing that the children may be too young or too emotionally involved to deal effectively with this information. Often such disclosures do not make the relationship a better one but instead add tension and friction, something we can all do without. Often such disclosures are made to ease one's own guilt without considering the burden this places on the other person.

Guidelines for Responding to Self-disclosures

When someone discloses to you, it is usually a sign of trust and affection. In serving this most important receiver function, keep the following in mind.

PRACTICE THE SKILLS OF EFFECTIVE AND ACTIVE LISTENING

In Unit 4, we identified the skills of effective listening. These are especially important when listening to self-disclosures. So listen actively, listen for different levels of meaning, listen with empathy, and listen with an open mind. Paraphrase the speaker so that you can be sure you understand both the thoughts and the feelings communicated. Express understanding of the speaker's feelings to allow the speaker the opportunity to see these more objectively and through the eyes of another individual. Ask questions to ensure your own understanding and to signal your own interest and attention.

SUPPORT THE DISCLOSER

Express support for the person during and after the disclosures. Refrain from evaluation during the disclosures; concentrate on understanding and empathizing with the discloser. Allow the discloser to choose her or his own pace; don't rush the discloser with the too-frequent "So how did it all end?" type of response. Make your supportiveness clear to the discloser through your verbal and nonverbal responses.

REINFORCE THE DISCLOSING BEHAVIORS

The difficulty of self-disclosure makes it important that you reinforce the disclosing behavior throughout the experience. No reinforcement or too little reinforcement is likely to be interpreted as indifference or disapproval, with the result that the self-disclosing stops short. Nod your understanding, echo the feelings and thoughts of the person, maintain appropriate eye contact, and otherwise indicate your positive attitudes toward the discloser and the act of disclosing.

KEEP THE DISCLOSURES CONFIDENTIAL

When a person discloses to you, it is because she or he wants you to know these feelings and thoughts. If the discloser wishes others to share these, then it is up to her or him to disclose them. If you reveal these disclosures to others, all sorts of negative effects are bound to occur. It will likely inhibit future disclosures of this individual in general and to you in particular, and it is probable that your relationship will suffer considerably. Those to whom you reveal these disclosures will likely feel that since you have betrayed a confidence this time, you will do so again, perhaps with their own self-disclosures. A general climate of distrust is easily established. But most important, betraying a confidence is unfair; it debases what could be and should be a significant and meaningful interpersonal experience.

DON'T USE THE DISCLOSURES AGAINST THE PERSON

This is one of the most often abused rules concerning self-disclosures. Many self-disclosures expose some kind of vulnerability, some weakness. If we later turn around and use these against the person, as we might in beltlining (see Unit 21), we betray the confidence and trust invested in us. Regardless of how angry we might get, we need to resist the temptation to use self-disclosures as weapons. If we do use disclosures against the person, the relationship is sure to suffer and may, in fact, never fully recover. And remember always, we can never uncommunicate.

Summary: Contents in Brief

Self-Disclosure: communication in which information about the self that is normally kept hidden is communication to another person

Dimensions	Influencing Factors	Sources of Resistance	Rewards and Dangers	Guidelines
Amount	Disclosures of others	Societal bias	*Rewards*	*In self-disclosure consider:*
Valence		Fear of punishment	Self-knowledge	• motivation
Accuracy/ honesty	Audience size	Fear of self-knowledge	Ability to cope	• appropriateness
Intention	Topic		Energy release	• opportunity for open and honest responses
Intimacy	Valence		Communication effectiveness	• clarity and directness
	Sex		Meaningfulness of relationships	• disclosures of other person
	Race		Physiological health	• possible burdens imposed
	Nationality			
	Age		*Dangers*	
	Receiver relationship		Professional loss	*In responding to disclosures of others:*
			Social loss	• listen effectively
			Interpersonal loss	• express support
			Decrease in interpersonal bonds	• reinforce disclosing behaviors
			Remember, communication is irreversible.	• keep disclosures confidential
				• don't use disclosures as weapons

Sources

On self-disclosure, see Sidney M. Jourard, *Disclosing Man to Himself* (New York: Van Nostrand Reinhold, 1968) and *The Transparent Self*, rev. ed. (New York: Van Nostrand Reinhold, 1971). In writing this unit I relied heavily on the insights of Gerard Egan; see especially his *Encounter: Group Processes for Interpersonal Growth* (Belmont, Calif.: Brooks/Cole, 1970), or, if you prefer a shorter version, *Face to Face: The Small-Group Experience and Interpersonal Growth* (Belmont, Calif.: Brooks/Cole, 1973). An overview of self-disclosure in communication is provided by W. Barnett Pearce and Stewart M. Sharp, "Self-disclosing Communication," *Journal of Communication* 23 (December 1973): 409–425. This article also provides an excellent review of the research on self-disclosure and communication. Another excellent review is by Paul Cozby, "Self-disclosure: A Literature Review," *Psychological Bulletin* 79 (1973): 73–91.

A great deal of research is currently being conducted on self-disclosure. For example, for the five dimensions of self-disclosure, see Lawrence R. Wheeless and Janis Grotz, "Conceptualization and Measurement of Reported Self-disclosure," *Human Communication Research* 2 (Summer 1976): 338–346. On sex differences, see Shirley J. Gilbert and Gale G. Whiteneck, "Toward a Multidimensional Approach to the Study of Self-disclosure," *Human Communication Research* 2 (Summer 1976): 347–355. On valence, see Shirley J. Gilbert and David Horenstein, "The Communication of Self-disclosure: Level Versus Valence," *Human Communication Research* 1 (Summer 1975): 316–322. On the relationship between trust and self-disclosure, see Lawrence R. Wheeless and Janis Grotz, "The Measurement of Trust and Its Relationship to Self-disclosure," *Human Communication Research* 3 (Spring 1977): 250–257. For the study on self-disclosure avoidance, see Lawrence Rosenfeld, "Self-disclosure Avoidance: Why I Am Afraid to Tell You Who I Am," *Communication Monographs* 46 (March 1979): 63–74. James Pennebacker's research was reported in the *New York Times* (September 18, 1984). Patricia Middlebrook, in *Social Psychology and Modern Life* (New York: Knopf, 1974), provides a useful overview of the social-psychological dimensions of the self and some interesting insights on self-disclosure.

An interesting and popular presentation of self-disclosure is provided by Steven Naifeh and Gregory White Smith, *Why Can't Men Open Up?* (New York: Clarkson N. Potter, 1984). A perceptive review of the literature and some interesting conclusions are offered by Arthur Bochner, "The Functions of Human Communication in Interpersonal Bonding," in *Handbook of Rhetorical and Communication Theory*, ed. Carroll C. Arnold and John Waite Bowers (Boston: Allyn & Bacon, 1984), pp. 601–608.

A comprehensive and insightful discussion of the relationship between communication and psychological and physiological reactions is provided by James J. Lynch, *The Language of the Heart: The Body's Response to Human Dialogue* (New York: Basic Books, 1985).

UNIT 9

Apprehension and Assertiveness

OBJECTIVES

Upon completion of this unit, you should be able to:

1. identify and explain the three positions on how apprehension and nonassertiveness develop
2. define *communication apprehension*
3. distinguish between trait and state apprehension
4. identify at least four specific apprehensive behaviors
5. identify at least four causes of communication apprehension
6. identify at least four specific suggestions advanced for managing communication apprehension
7. define and give examples of assertive behavior
8. distinguish among assertiveness, nonassertiveness, and aggressiveness
9. identify at least two types of situations in which a person may logically choose not to be assertive
10. state and explain the five principles for increasing assertiveness
11. explain why feedback is important in increasing assertive behaviors
12. identify the cautions that should be observed in adopting new assertive behaviors

Among the most important communication skills are those concerned with reducing communication apprehension and increasing assertiveness. Many of us are apprehensive (or shy or reticent) in different communication situations and to different degrees; similarly, many of us are reluctant to assert ourselves, to speak up for our rights. In this unit we address these related issues of apprehension and assertiveness with a view to increasing our understanding of these qualities and to enabling us to manage our own apprehension and assertiveness more effectively.

HOW APPREHENSION AND NONASSERTIVENESS BEGIN

There are a number of explanations of the origins of apprehension and nonassertiveness. Three of the most popular are the theories of innateness, personal inadequacy, and learned behavior.

Innateness

The innateness theory holds that people are born apprehensive or nonassertive; an innate factor determines whether a person will be apprehensive or nonapprehensive, assertive or nonassertive. If, as it seems, people are born with different sensitivities to sound or pain, for example, it seems not too great a leap to argue that people are also born with different sensitivities to strangers or to new situations or to interpersonal encounters that call for assertiveness.

Personal Inadequacy

The personal inadequacy theory has its foundation in the approach of clinical psychology and psychiatry. It is argued that one's apprehension or lack of assertiveness is a symptom of personal inadequacy, of some problem or conflict. This symptom may be the result of some early traumatic experience or rejection by one's mother, for example, or of some later problem, such as repeated failure in athletic activities or rejection by peers. In a more Freudian interpretation, apprehension would be seen as a symptom of unfulfilled desires, primarily sexual. There are probably hundreds of variations on this same basic theme, but all seem to agree that both nonassertive and apprehensive behaviors are symptoms of some problem or inadequacy. All such approaches also agree that the remedy for apprehensive and nonassertive behavior is to be found in early experiences and in the problems and inadequacies they generated. According to this position, to reduce apprehension or increase assertiveness, one would need intensive therapy.

Learned Behavior

A more satisfying explanation, I feel, is that apprehension and nonapprehension, nonassertiveness and assertiveness are learned behaviors and that somewhere in our personal history we have learned to act as we do. Some people, because of their unique set of experiences, learned assertive behaviors, while others, because of their unique set of experiences, learned nonassertive behaviors. But we all learned the behaviors, whatever they are, in essentially the same way. Here, too, there are a number of explanations concerning how the specific learning took place.

REINFORCEMENT

A reinforcement or conditioning position would argue that we learned behaviors, whether assertive or apprehensive, that were followed by reinforcement (the presentation of a rewarding stimulus or the removal of an aversive or painful stimulus) and failed to learn (or, if already learned, unlearned) behaviors that were followed by punishment. Thus, if our attempts at being assertive were rewarded, we learned to repeat assertive behaviors on further occasions. If, on the other hand, our assertive behaviors were punished, socially or physically, we learned not to engage in such behaviors in other situations; that is, we learned nonassertive behaviors.

LABELING

Another type of learning position, often referred to as *semantogenic* or labeling theory, argues that we learned apprehension because we were labeled "shy" and we conformed to the label that people placed on us. An awkward person, for example, can often trace the awkwardness back to being called "awkward" by family and friends. Stutterers, according to some theories, were developed or "created" from normal speakers who experienced normal speech hesitations but who were labeled "stutterer" by their parents. They then attempted not to hesitate (which is impossible at certain early ages) and as a result hesitated all the more. These increased hesitations are the essence of what we consider stuttering.

Whether by reinforcement, labeling, or some other learning process, the evidence clearly favors the notion that such behaviors are learned rather than inborn or symptoms of some psychological trauma or conflict. The important implication of this learning position is that if the behaviors were learned, they can be unlearned. We can, for example, rearrange the reinforcement contingencies and thus alter our behavior, or we can focus attention on the labels and substitute more appropriate ones. All this is not to say that such change will therefore be easily effected, only that such change is possible without rearranging our innate structure (even if that were possible) or solving all our early psychological problems (even if that were possible).

APPREHENSION

This discussion will prove more valuable if you first take the brief test provided in Table 9.1. This test, developed by James McCroskey, is a measure of your apprehension in a variety of communication situations. Take this test and score it according to the directions provided on page 118.

Now that you have a general idea of your own communication apprehension, it might be of interest to note that according to James McCroskey and Lawrence Wheeless, "communication apprehension is probably the most common handicap . . . suffered by people in contemporary American society." According to surveys of college students, between 10 and 20 percent suffer "severe, debilitating communication apprehension," while another 20 percent suffer from "communication apprehension to a degree substantial enough to interfere to some extent with their normal functioning."

In related research—on shyness, psychologist Philip Zimbardo noted that of the college students who indicated that they were shy with certain people, 70 percent specified that they were especially shy with strangers; whereas, 64 percent said "opposite sex persons," 55 percent said "authorities by virtue of their knowledge," 40 percent said "authorities by virtue of their role," and 21 percent said "relatives."

Among the contexts that generate shyness, being the focus of attention in a large group—as in giving a speech—was noted by 73 percent of the shy students, while 68 percent noted that they were shy in large groups generally. Other contexts noted for inducing shyness were general social situations, new social situations, situations calling for assertiveness, situations in which the person is being evaluated, situations in which the individual needs help, and small task-oriented groups.

Here we examine the nature of communication apprehension, the characteristics of communication apprehensives, some of the causes of apprehension, and some of the ways to manage apprehension more effectively.

What Is Communication Apprehension?

Although there are many alternative terms (shyness, unwillingness to communicate, stage fright, reticence), and each theorist defines the concept in slightly different ways, all terms refer, at least generally, to a state of fear or anxiety about communication interaction. People develop negative feelings and predict negative results as a function of engaging in communication interactions. They feel that whatever gain would accrue from engaging in communication would be outweighed by the fear. To high communication apprehensives, the communication interaction just isn't worth the fear it engenders.

TABLE 9.1: Apprehension Questionnaire

Directions: This questionnaire is composed of 24 statements concerning your feelings about communication with other people. Please indicate in the space provided the degree to which each statement applies to you by marking whether you (1) strongly agree, (2) agree, (3) are undecided, (4) disagree, or (5) strongly disagree with each statement. There are no right or wrong answers. Many of the statements are similar to other statements; do not be concerned about this. Work quickly; record your first impression.

_____ 1. I dislike participating in group discussions.

_____ 2. Generally, I am comfortable while participating in group discussions.

_____ 3. I am tense and nervous while participating in group discussions.

_____ 4. I like to get involved in group discussions.

_____ 5. Engaging in a group discussion with new people makes me tense and nervous.

_____ 6. I am calm and relaxed while participating in group discussions.

_____ 7. Generally, I am nervous when I have to participate in a meeting.

_____ 8. Usually, I am calm and relaxed while participating in meetings.

_____ 9. I am very calm and relaxed when I am called upon to express an opinion at a meeting.

_____ 10. I am afraid to express myself at meetings.

_____ 11. Communicating at meetings usually makes me uncomfortable.

_____ 12. I am very relaxed when answering questions at a meeting.

_____ 13. While participating in a conversation with a new acquaintance, I feel very nervous.

_____ 14. I have no fear of speaking up in conversations.

_____ 15. Ordinarily I am very tense and nervous in conversations.

_____ 16. Ordinarily I am very calm and relaxed in conversations.

_____ 17. While conversing with a new acquaintance, I feel very relaxed.

_____ 18. I'm afraid to speak up in conversations.

_____ 19. I have no fear of giving a speech.

_____ 20. Certain parts of my body feel very tense and rigid while giving a speech.

_____ 21. I feel relaxed while giving a speech.

_____ 22. My thoughts become confused and jumbled when I am giving a speech.

_____ 23. I face the prospect of giving a speech with confidence.

_____ 24. While giving a speech, I get so nervous that I forget facts I really know.

Scoring

To obtain your apprehension score, follow these instructions.

The questionnaire permits computation of one total score and four subscores. The subscores relate to communication apprehension in each of four common communication contexts: group discussions, meetings, interpersonal conversations, and public speaking. To compute your scores, merely add or subtract your scores for each item as indicated below.

Subscore Desired	Scoring Formula
Group discussions	18 + scores for items 2, 4, and 6; − scores for items 1, 3, and 5.
Meetings	18 + scores for items 8, 9, and 12; − scores for items 7, 10, and 11.
Interpersonal conversations	18 + scores for items 14, 16, and 17; − scores for items 13, 15, and 18.
Public speaking	18 + scores for items 19, 21, and 23; − scores for items 20, 22, and 24.

To obtain your total score, simply add your four subscores together.

Each subscore should range from 6 to 30; the higher the score, the greater the apprehension. Any score above 18 indicates some degree of apprehension. Most people score above 18 for the public speaking context, so if you scored relatively high in this subdivision, you are among the vast majority of people. Most people also scored higher on public speaking than on any of the other subdivisions.

TRAIT AND STATE APPREHENSION

Trait apprehension refers to fear of communication generally, regardless of the specific situation. It appears in dyadic, small group, public speaking, and mass communication situations. *State apprehension,* on the other hand, is a fear that is specific to a given communication situation. For example, a speaker may fear public speaking but have no difficulty with dyadic communication, or a speaker may fear job interviews but have no fear of public speaking. State apprehension is extremely common; it is experienced by most persons for some situations.

DIFFERENCES IN DEGREE

Speaker apprehension exists on a continuum. People cannot be considered either apprehensive or not apprehensive; we all experience some degree of apprehension. Some people are extremely apprehensive and become incapacitated in a communication situation. They suffer a great deal in a society oriented, as is ours, around communication and in which success depends on one's ability to communicate effectively. Others are so mildly apprehensive that they appear to experience no fear at all when confronted by communication situations; they actively seek out communication experiences and rarely experience even the slightest apprehension. Most of us fall between these two extremes: We fear some situations more than others. For some of us this apprehension is debilitating and hinders personal effectiveness in dealing with people. On the other hand, apprehension energizes and makes others of us more alert, active, and responsive and aids us in achieving our goals.

APPREHENSIVE BEHAVIORS

Apprehension may also be examined in more behavioral terms. Generally, we see a decrease in the frequency, strength, and likelihood of engaging in communication transactions. Apprehensives avoid communication situations and, when forced to participate, participate as little as possible. This reluctance to communicate manifests itself in a variety of forms. For example, in small group situations, apprehensives will not only talk less but will also avoid the seats of influence, for example, those in the direct line of sight of the group leader. Even in classrooms, they avoid seats where they can be easily called on, and they maintain little direct eye contact with the instructor, especially when a question is likely to be asked. Probably not unrelated to this is the finding that apprehensives have more negative attitudes toward school, earn poorer grades, and are considered less desirable social choices by both teachers and fellow students.

Apprehensives disclose little and avoid occupations with heavy communication demands (for example, teaching or public relations). Within their occupation, they are less desirous of advancement, largely because with advancement there is a corresponding increase in communication.

Apprehensives also engage in more steady dating, a finding that is not unexpected. One of the most difficult communication situations is asking for a date (especially a first date) and developing a new relationship. Consequently, once a dating relationship has been established, the apprehensive is reluctant to give this up and go through the anxiety of another first date and another get-acquainted period.

All this is not to say that apprehensives are ineffective or unhappy people. Most apprehensives have learned or can learn to deal with their communication anxiety or fear.

Some Causes of Apprehension

James McCroskey, the leading researcher in apprehension, has identified a number of factors leading to communication apprehension. Here we consider five of the major causes.

LACK OF COMMUNICATION SKILLS AND EXPERIENCE

If we lack skills in typing, we can hardly expect to type very well. Yet we rarely assume that a lack of communication skills and experience can cause difficulty with communication and create apprehension. It can. If we have never spoken to a large group and have no idea of how to construct a public speech, for example, it is perfectly reasonable that we will feel apprehension.

DEGREE OF EVALUATION

The more we perceive the situation as one in which we will be evaluated, the greater is our apprehension. Employment interviews, for example, are anxiety-provoking largely because they are highly evaluative. Similarly, in asking for that first date, we know we are being evaluated and consequently experience apprehension.

DEGREE OF CONSPICUOUSNESS

The more conspicuous we are, the more likely we are to feel apprehensive. This is why delivering a public speech to a large audience is more anxiety-provoking than speaking in a small group communication situation; we are more conspicuous before the large group; we stand out, and all attention is on us. But in a small group that attention is spread over a number of people and, of course, the time we are in focus is much less. Should we get too nervous, we can stop or cut short our comment; we cannot do that when speaking to an audience of several hundred people.

DEGREE OF UNPREDICTABILITY

The more unpredictable the situation, the greater our apprehension. Ambiguous situations and new situations are unpredictable; we cannot know beforehand what the situation will be like; hence we become anxious.

PRIOR SUCCESSES AND FAILURES

Our prior history in similar situations greatly influences how we respond to new ones. Prior success generally (though not always) reduces apprehension, whereas prior failure generally (though not always) increases apprehension. There is no mystery here: Prior success tells us that we can succeed this time as well; prior failure warns us that we may fail again.

Managing Communication Apprehension

It is probably impossible to eliminate communication apprehension. However, we can manage apprehension effectively so that it does not debilitate us or prevent us from achieving goals that require us to communicate in a variety of situations.

ACQUIRE COMMUNICATION SKILLS AND EXPERIENCE

As already noted, one of the major causes of apprehension is a lack of skills and experience; the remedy (at least for this cause) is to acquire the requisite skills and experience. In this course you are acquiring the skills of effective interpersonal interaction. Additional courses and experiences should be selected to enable you to acquire the skills you need most. Refer to your communication apprehension test to see in which areas you are most apprehensive and then consider selecting courses and experiences to meet the most obvious needs.

PREPARE AND PRACTICE

The more preparation and practice you put into something, the more comfortable you feel with it and, consequently, the less apprehension you feel.

FOCUS ON SUCCESS

Think positively. Concentrate your energies on doing the very best job you can in whatever situation you are in. Put negative thoughts and thoughts of failure out of your mind. If you visualize yourself failing, you very likely will fail. Fortunately, the reverse also seems true; visualize yourself succeeding and you stand a good chance of doing just that. Remember that having failed in the past does not mean that you must fail again in the future. You now have new skills and new experiences, and these increase your chances for success.

FAMILIARIZE YOURSELF WITH THE SITUATION

The more you familiarize yourself with the situation, the better. The reason is simple: When you are familiar with the situation and with what will be expected of you, you are better able to predict what will happen. This will reduce the ambiguity and the perceived newness of the situation.

PHYSICAL RELAXATION HELPS

Apprehension is reduced when you are physically relaxed. Breathing deeply and engaging in some kind of physical activity (for example, walking or writing on a chalkboard) help reduce tension and lessen the apprehension and anxiety you feel.

PUT COMMUNICATION APPREHENSION IN PERSPECTIVE

In engaging in any communication experience, remember that the world will not cave in if you do not succeed. Also remember that other people are not able to perceive your apprehension in the same way you do. You may feel a dryness in your throat and a rapid heartbeat, but others do not.

ASSERTIVENESS

Thomas Moriarty has conducted a number of interesting experiments to illustrate just how passive we have learned to become. For example, in one experiment, subjects taking a psychological test were placed near a confederate of the experimenter who played loud rock-and-roll music during the test. Of the 20 subjects, 16 made no comment at all. Even when the students were told that they would receive mild electric shocks for wrong answers, 16 of the 20 subjects still said nothing to the music player. Similar experiments were repeated in natural settings like the library and the movies, both with loud talking. Rarely did anyone object.

In perhaps the most clever variation, subjects approached people after they had left a phone booth, saying that they had lost a ring and would the person mind emptying his pockets to see if he had perhaps picked up the ring. Of the 20 adult males who were approached, 16 emptied their pockets (80 percent). When the experiment was repeated using graduate students, 20 of 24 men (83 percent) emptied their pockets. "I believe," concludes Moriarty, "that many of us have accepted the idea that few things are worth getting into a hassle about, especially with strangers. And I believe this is particularly true of younger people."

The aims of assertiveness training are to convince us that we would be happier if we were more assertive and to show us how we might increase our own assertive behaviors.

Assertiveness is, as I see it, largely an interpersonal communication characteristic. It is mainly in interpersonal situations (though also in small groups and at times in large group situations) that the occasion and the need to assert ourselves arises. Our own assertiveness, or lack of it, greatly influences our interpersonal interactions—a premise that will be demonstrated in this unit and in Experiential Vehicles 16 and 17. It is also interesting to note that the qualities that assertiveness theorists consider characteristic of the assertive individual are also the qualities that communicologists consider characteristic of the effective interpersonal communicator.

Nonassertiveness, Aggressiveness, and Assertiveness

The relevance of assertiveness to interpersonal communication may be further clarified by examining the distinctions among assertiveness, nonassertiveness, and aggressiveness.

NONASSERTIVENESS

Nonassertiveness comes in two forms: situational and generalized. *Situational nonassertiveness* refers to a lack of assertiveness in only certain kinds of situations, for example, situations that create a great deal of anxiety or situations in which authority must be exercised. *Generalized nonassertiveness* is, as the term implies, behavior that is normally or typically nonassertive. People who exhibit these behaviors are timid and reserved and are unable to assert their rights regardless of the specifics of the situation. These people do what others tell them to do—parents, employers, and the like—without questioning and without concern for what is best for them. When these persons' rights are infringed upon, they do nothing about it and even at times accuse themselves of being nonaccepting. Generalized nonassertive persons often ask permission from others to do what is their perfect right. Social situations create anxiety for these individuals, and their self-esteem is generally low. In the extreme, a generalized nonassertive person would be characterized as inhibited and emotionally unresponsive, with feelings of personal inadequacy.

AGGRESSIVENESS

Aggressiveness may also be considered as being of two types: situational and generalized. *Situationally aggressive* people are aggressive only under certain conditions or in certain situations. For example, they may become aggressive after being taken advantage of over a long period of time or after being taken advantage of by someone for whom they have done a great deal. Or perhaps these people would be aggressive in dealing with teachers or fellow classmates or parents or older people. The important characteristic is that these people are usually not aggressive; only in certain situations do they behave aggressively.

Generally aggressive people, on the other hand, meet all or at least most situations with aggressive behavior. These persons seem in charge of almost all situations; regardless of what is going on, they take over. These individuals appear to think little of the opinions, values, or beliefs of others and yet are extremely sensitive to others' criticisms of their own behavior. Consequently, they frequently get into arguments with others and find that they have few friends. They think little of others, and others think little of them.

ASSERTIVENESS

Assertive behavior is the desired alternative and has been characterized in various ways by various writers. Basically, assertive individuals are willing to assert their own rights, but unlike their aggressive counterparts, they do not hurt others in the process. Assertive individuals speak their minds and welcome others' doing likewise. Robert Alberti and Michael Emmons, in *Your Perfect Right*, the first book on assertiveness training, note that "behavior which enables a person to act in his own best interest, to stand up for himself without undue anxiety, to express his honest feelings comfortably, or to exercise his own rights without denying the rights of others we call *assertive behavior.*" Furthermore, "the assertive individual is fully in charge of himself in interpersonal relationships, feels confident and capable without cockiness or hostility, is basically spontaneous in the expression of feelings and emotions, and is generally looked up to and admired by others." Surely this is the picture of an effective individual.

In an exploration of assertiveness as a communication variable, Robert Norton

Sometimes—for example, when there are great status or age differences—it is difficult to assert one's rights. There is a presumption of right in favor of the higher status or older individual that probably contributes to the difficulty many people have in asserting their own rights in family as well as in professional situations.

and Barbara Warnick found that four characteristics may be identified as describing and defining assertiveness in interpersonal communication. Assertive individuals are, first, *open* persons. They engage in frank and open expression of their feelings to people in general as well as to those for whom there may be some sexual interest. Second, assertive individuals are *not anxious;* they readily volunteer opinions and beliefs, deal directly with interpersonal communication situations that may be stressful, and question others without fear. Their communications are dominant, frequent, and of high intensity. They have a positive view of their own communication performance, and this view seems to be shared by those with whom they communicate. Third, assertive interpersonal communicators are *contentious;* they stand up and argue for their rights, even if this entails a certain degree of unpleasantness with relatives or close friends. Fourth, assertive persons are *not intimidated* and are not easily persuaded.

Assertive people are assertive when they want to be but can be nonassertive if the situation seems to call for it. For example, we might wish to be nonassertive in a situation in which our assertiveness might emotionally hurt the other person. Let us say that an older relative wishes us to do something for her or him. We could assert our rights and say no, but in doing so we would probably hurt this person, so it might be better simply to do as was asked. Of course, there are limits that should be observed. The individual should be careful, in such a situation, that she or he is not hurt instead. For example, the parents who wish their child to remain living at home until marriage may be hurt by the child's assertive behavior, yet the alternative is to hurt oneself. So here assertive behavior seems the better choice, even though someone may be hurt in the process.

Principles for Increasing Assertiveness

The general assumption made by most assertiveness trainers is that the majority of people are situationally nonassertive. Most people are able to modify their behavior, with a resultant increase in general interpersonal effectiveness and in self-esteem.

Those who are generally nonassertive, however, probably need extensive training with a therapist. Those who are only moderately nonassertive and who wish to understand their assertiveness—and perhaps behave differently in certain situations—should find the following principles of value. The rationale and the specific principles derive from the behavior modification techniques of B. F. Skinner and the systematic desensitization techniques of Joseph Wolpe and others. In formulating these five principles, the techniques of these theorists, as well as the specific assertiveness training manuals noted in the Sources, were most helpful.

It should be said at the outset that this training or retraining deals with behavior and not with abstract or repressed needs and desires. The emphasis is on behavior, and it is assumed that if one behaves in assertive ways, one will in fact become more assertive. Further, it is assumed that these behaviors will reflect on the way in which these people think of themselves. For example, if we act assertively, we will soon think of ourselves as assertive individuals, and, more important, our self-concepts in general will be improved.

1. ANALYZE THE ASSERTIVE BEHAVIOR OF OTHERS

The first step in increasing assertiveness is to understand the nature of this behavior. On an intellectual level this understanding should already have been achieved. What is necessary and more important than an intellectual understanding, however, is to understand actual assertive and nonshy behavior, and the best way to start is to observe and analyze the behaviors of others. We should become able to distinguish the differences among assertive, aggressive, and nonassertive behaviors. Focus on what makes one behavior assertive and another behavior shy or aggressive or nonassertive. Listen to what is said and how it is said. Recall the nonverbal behaviors and try to categorize nonverbal behaviors as assertive, aggressive, or nonassertive.

2. ANALYZE YOUR OWN BEHAVIORS

It is generally easier to analyze the behaviors of others than our own. We find it difficult to be objective with ourselves. After we have acquired some skills in observing the behaviors of others, we can turn our analysis to ourselves. Analyze situations in which you are normally assertive, nonassertive, and aggressive. What characterizes these situations? What do the situations in which you are normally aggressive have in common? How do these situations differ from the situations in which you are normally nonassertive?

We should also be able to analyze our nonverbal behaviors. How do we stand when we are assertive? Aggressive? Nonassertive? What tone of voice do we use? What kind of eye contact do we maintain? What do we do with our hands? Our nonverbal behaviors are probably different for each type of behavior.

3. RECORD YOUR BEHAVIORS

It is essential in any training program that you record your behaviors as accurately as possible. The advantages of this practice are many. First, it will force you to pay special attention to all your behaviors and to determine whether they are assertive or nonassertive. Second, it will enable you to see if improvements have been made, and, assuming they have been, this will provide reinforcement and encourage you to continue your efforts. Third, this record will spotlight where improvement is particularly needed and will then serve as a guide for future behaviors.

A simple three-part form with space for recording assertive, aggressive, and nonaggressive behaviors will suffice. Be as specific as possible in recording your behaviors, and give as many details of the actual situation as seems reasonable.

4. REHEARSE ASSERTIVE BEHAVIORS

A number of systems have been proposed for effective rehearsal of assertive behaviors. One of the most popular is to select a situation in which you are normally nonassertive and build a hierarchy that begins with a relatively nonthreatening behavior and ends with the desired behavior. For example, let us say that you have difficulty speaking in class and that the desired behavior is to speak your mind in class. You might construct a hierarchy of situations that lead up to speaking in class. Such a hierarchy might begin with something like simply visualizing yourself sitting in class. You might then visualize yourself sitting in class while you are in a state of relaxation. Once you have mastered this visualization you may proceed to the next step, visualizing the instructor asking a question. Once you are able to visualize this situation and remain relaxed throughout, visualize the instructor asking you the question. Visualize this situation until you can do so while relaxed. Then try visualizing yourself answering the question. Again, do this until you can do it while fully relaxed. Next you might rehearse visualizing volunteering your opinion in class—the desired behavior. Do this until you can do it while totally relaxed.

This is the mental rehearsal. You might add an actual vocal dimension to this by actually answering the question you imagine the teacher asking you and vocalizing your opinion. Again, do this until you have no difficulty. Next, try doing this in front of a supportive friend or group of friends. After this rehearsal, you are probably ready for the next step.

5. DO IT

This step is naturally the most difficult but obviously the most important. You can increase assertiveness only by acting out these behaviors; you cannot become assertive by acting nonassertively.

Again, do this in small steps. Staying with the previous example, attempt to answer a question that you are sure of before attempting to volunteer an opinion or argue with the position of the instructor. Once you have done this, it is essential (and pleasant) to *reward yourself* in some way. Give yourself something you want—an ice cream cone, a record, a new jacket. The desired behavior will be more easily and permanently learned if you reward yourself immediately after engaging in the behavior. Try not to delay the reward too long: Rewards work best when they are immediate.

After performing the behavior, get feedback from others. Start with people who are generally supportive. They should provide you with the social reinforcement so helpful in learning new behavior patterns. This feedback is particularly important because your intention and the perception of your behavior by a receiver may be totally different. For example, you may behave in certain ways with the intention of communicating confidence or determination, but the receiver may perceive them as arrogance or stubbornness. Thus another person's perception of your behavior can often help a great deal in allowing you to see yourself from the outside.

In all behaviors, but especially with new behaviors, recognize that we may initially fail in what we attempt to do. We might attempt to assert ourselves only to find that we have been unsuccessful. You might, for example, try to answer the teacher's question and find that not only do you have the wrong answer, but you did not even understand the question. Or you might raise your hand and find yourself at a loss for words when you are recognized. Such incidents should not discourage us; recognize that in all attempts to change behaviors, we will experience both failure and success. Naturally, we should try to develop these behaviors in situations that are likely to result in success, but failures should not discourage us. They are only momentary setbacks, not insurmountable problems.

A note of caution should be added to this discussion. It is easy to visualize a situation in which people are talking behind us in a movie and, with our newfound enthusiasm for assertiveness, we tell these people to be quiet. It is also easy to visualize our getting smashed in the teeth as a result. Equally easy to visualize is asserting ourselves with someone we care for only to find that as a result this person bursts into tears, unable to handle our new behavior.

In applying these principles, be careful that you do not go beyond what you can handle, physically and emotionally. Do not, for example, assert yourself out of a job. It is wise to be careful when changing any behavior, especially assertiveness.

Summary: Contents in Brief

Definitions	Management Principles
Apprehension: a state of fear or anxiety about communication situations	*Managing communication apprehension*
Trait apprehension: a fear of communication generally	1. Acquire communication skills and experience
State apprehension: a fear of communication that is specific to a situation (for example, an interview or public speaking situation)	2. Prepare and practice
	3. Focus on success
	4. Familiarize yourself with the situation
	5. Physical relaxation helps
	6. Put communication apprehension in perspective

Summary: Contents in Brief (continued)

Definitions	Management Principles
Assertiveness: behavior that enables a person to act in her or his own best interests without denying the rights of others	*Principles for increasing assertiveness* 1. Analyze the assertive behaviors of others 2. Analyze your own behaviors 3. Record your behaviors 4. Rehearse assertive behaviors 5. Do it

Nonassertiveness:
   Situational: inability to assert oneself in certain situations
   Generalized: inability to assert oneself in most or all situations	

Aggressiveness: behavior that serves self-interests without any consideration for the rights of others.	

Sources

The area of apprehension owes much to the theoretical and experimental research of James C. McCroskey. For general overviews, I would suggest his "Oral Communication Apprehension: A Summary of Recent Theory and Research," *Human Communication Research* 4 (Fall 1977): 78–96 and "Classroom Consequences of Communication Apprehension," *Communication Education* 26 (January 1977): 27–33. Another useful survey is contained in James C. McCroskey and Lawrence R. Wheeless, *Introduction to Human Communication* (Boston: Allyn & Bacon, 1976). Specific studies dealing with issues relevant to this unit include James C. McCroskey, John A. Daly, and Gail Sorensen, "Personality Correlates of Communication Apprehension: A Research Note," *Human Communication Research* 2 (Summer 1979): 376–380; James C. McCroskey, John A. Daly, Virginia P. Richmond, and Raymond Falcione, "Communication Apprehension and Self-esteem," *Human Communication Research* 3 (Spring 1977): 269–277; John A. Daly, "Communication Apprehension and Behavior: Applying a Multiple Act Criteria," *Human Communication Research* 4 (Spring 1978): 208–216; H. Thomas Hurt and Raymond Preiss, "Silence Isn't Necessarily Golden: Communication Apprehension, Desired Social Choice, and Academic Success Among Middle-School Students," *Human Communication Research* 4 (Summer 1978): 315–328. On shyness see Philip Zimbardo, *Shyness* (Reading, Mass.: Addison-Wesley, 1977).

For a report on the treatment of apprehension, see Susan R. Glaser, "Oral Communication Apprehension and Avoidance: The Current Status of Treatment Research," *Communication Education* 30 (October 1981): 321–341. For a thorough discussion of apprehension and how it relates to other similar behaviors, see Lynne Kelly, "A Rose by Any Other Name Is Still a Rose: A Comparative Analysis of Reticence, Communication Apprehension, Unwillingness to Communicate, and Shyness," *Human Communication Research* 8 (Winter 1982): 99–113. The apprehension questionnaire is reprinted with the permission of James McCroskey from his *Introduction to Rhetorical Communication*, 4th ed. (Englewood Cliffs, N.J.: Prentice-Hall, 1982).

On assertiveness, two books by Robert E. Alberti and Michael L. Emmons are perhaps the best starting places: *Your Perfect Right: A Guide to Assertive Behavior* (San Luis Obispo, Calif.: Impact, 1970) and *Stand Up, Speak Out, Talk Back: The Key to Self-assertive Behavior* (New York: Pocket Books, 1970). For research and theory see Robert Alberti, ed. *Assertiveness: Innovations, Applications, Issues* (San Luis Obispo, Calif.: Impact, 1977). Robert J. Ringer, *Winning Through Intimidation* New York: Fawcett, 1973) presents many ideas from the point of view of a real estate salesperson, but they are applicable to everyone. S. Phelps and N. Austin, *The Assertive Woman* (San Luis Obispo, Calif.: Impact, 1975) addresses assertive behavior in relation to the particular problems women face. The experiments of Thomas Moriarty are reported in his "A Nation of Willing Victims," *Psychology Today* 8 (April 1975): 43–50. Perhaps the most thorough discussion of assertiveness as communication is Ronald B. Adler, *Confidence in Communication: A Guide to Assertive and Social Skills* (New York: Holt, Rinehart and Winston, 1977). This book contains numerous exercises that may be used individually or in groups. The relationship between assertiveness and communication is examined in Robert Norton and Barbara Warnick, "Assertiveness as a Communication Construct," *Human Communication Research* 3 (Fall 1976): 62–66.

Part 2: Skills in Brief

Self-awareness
Increase self-awareness by asking yourself about yourself, listening to others, actively seeking information about yourself that others have by carefully observing their interactions with you and by asking relevant questions, seeing yourself from different perspectives, increasing your open self, and being conscious of your life position.

Open Self
Adjust your open self in light of the total context, disclosing or not disclosing yourself to others as appropriate.

Self-appreciation
Self-appreciate; identify your positive (OK) qualities; thinking positively about yourself.

Life Position
Identify your life position or script by examining your self-perceptions and your perceptions of others.

Negative Scripts
Rewrite negative scripts to unleash your potential and to eliminate or reduce the internalized negative and unproductive directions now written into your life position.

I'm OK, You're OK
Strive for the "I'm OK, you're OK" position by focusing on both self and others as winners—as good, worthy, productive, and significant individuals.

Self-disclosure Regulation
Self-disclose selectively; regulate your self-disclosures as appropriate to the context, topic, audience, potential rewards, and risks to secure the maximum advantage and reduce the possibility of negative effects of the disclosing experience.

Self-disclosure Conditions
Self-disclose when the motivation is to improve the relationship, when the context and the relationship are appropriate for the self-disclosure, when there is an opportunity for open and honest responses, when the self-disclosures will be made with clarity and directness, when there are appropriate reciprocal disclosures, and

when you have examined and are willing to risk the possible burdens that self-disclosure might entail.

Premature Self-disclosures

Resist too intimate or too negative self-disclosures early in the development of a relationship.

Disclosure Responses

In responding to the disclosures of others, demonstrate the skills of effective listening, express support (but resist evaluation) for the discloser, reinforce the disclosing behavior, keep the disclosures confidential, and avoid using the disclosures against the person.

Active Listening and Self-disclosure

In responding to the disclosures of others, listen actively: Paraphrase the speaker's thoughts *and* feelings, express understanding of the speaker's feelings, and ask relevant questions to ensure understanding and to signal attention and interest.

Listening and Self-disclosure

Demonstrate the skills of effective listening by listening for different levels of meaning, with empathy and empathic responses and with an openness to the other person.

Supportiveness

Express support for the discloser. Resist evaluation. Do not rush the discloser. Express support verbally and nonverbally: nod in agreement, maintain appropriate eye contact, smile, ask for relevant elaboration, maintain physical closeness and directness.

Apprehension Causes

Identify the causes of your own apprehension, considering, for example, lack of communication skills and experience, fear of evaluation, conspicuousness, unpredictability of the situation (ambiguity, newness), and your history of prior successes or failures in similar and related situations.

Apprehension Management

Manage your own communication apprehension by acquiring the necessary communication skills and experience, prepare and practice for relevant communication situations, focus on success, familiarize yourself with the communication situations important to you, use physical activity and deep breathing to relax, and put communication apprehension in perspective. In cases of extreme communication apprehension, seek professional help.

Assertiveness

Increase assertiveness (if desired) by analyzing the assertive and nonassertive behaviors of others, analyzing your own behaviors in terms of assertiveness, recording your behaviors, rehearsing assertive behaviors, and acting assertively in appropriate situations. Secure feedback from others for further guidelines in developing increased assertiveness.

PART 3

Verbal Messages

In Part Three we focus on verbal messages and consider the nature of language and meaning and, especially, the way in which meaning is communicated from one person to another. The social dimension of language, especially sublanguages and taboo, are discussed to emphasize the fact that language is a social tool, used in a social context, for social ends. Racism and sexism in language are also considered here. Some principles for using language more effectively and for avoiding the common barriers to meaningful interaction are also discussed.

In this consideration of verbal messages we focus on questions such as the following:

What is language? ■ What is meaning? ■ How do different subcultures communicate? ■ Do men and women speak the same language? ■ When is language racist? ■ Sexist? ■ What is taboo? ■ What are its effects? ■ Why do we lie? ■ What effects does lying have? ■ What about gossip? ■ Should we eliminate gossip? ■ When is gossip unethical? ■ How can we make our language behavior more "sane" and less "unhealthy"? ■ What skills can you master to enable you to use language more effectively?

UNIT OUTLINE

Universals of Verbal Messages

Language, Sublanguage, and Culture

Seven Pitfalls and Principles of Language and Verbal Interaction

Barriers to Verbal Interaction

Skills in Brief

UNIT 10

Universals of Verbal Messages

OBJECTIVES

Upon completion of this unit, you should be able to:

1. define *language* and each of its six essential characteristics
2. diagram and explain Wendell Johnson's model of meaning
3. identify and explain three implications of Johnson's view of meaning
4. distinguish between directive and nondirective language and identify at least two implications of this distinction for interpersonal communication
5. distinguish between direct and indirect speech
6. identify at least two functions and two problems of indirect speech
7. define *denotation* and *connotation* and provide examples of each type of meaning
8. explain the nature and operation of the semantic differential
9. identify at least two practical implications to be drawn from the distinction between denotative and connotative meaning

The verbal message system is extremely complex. Perhaps the best way to understand this system of language and meaning is to focus on the features that are universal, that are present in any and all verbal message exchanges. In this unit, then, some general characteristics of language and meaning are considered.

LANGUAGE AND MEANING

In this first part of this unit we discuss (1) a definition of language and its essential characteristics and (2) a definition and model of meaning.

The Nature of Language

The human language system is a specialized, productive system capable of displacement and composed of rapidly fading, arbitrary, culturally transmitted symbols. Contained in this definition are six universal characteristics of all human language sys-

133

tems: specialization, productivity, displacement, rapid fading, arbitrariness, and cultural transmission.

SPECIALIZATION

When a human speaks, the speech process serves no biological function; it is, instead, specialized for communication. A specialized communication system, according to Charles Hockett, is one whose "direct energetic consequences are biologically irrelevant." Human language serves only one major purpose—to communicate. It aids no biological function. On the other hand, while a panting dog communicates information about its presence and perhaps about its internal state, the panting serves first and foremost the biological function of temperature regulation. The fact that communication accompanies or results from this behavior is only incidental.

DISPLACEMENT

Human language can be used to talk about things that are remote in both time and space; one can talk about the past and the future as easily as the present. And one can talk about things that one has never and will never perceive—about mermaids and unicorns, about supernatural beings from other planets, about talking animals. One can talk about the unreal as well as the real, the imaginary as well as the actual. This characteristic is known as *displacement* and refers to the fact that messages may have effects or consequences that are independent of their context. Thus, for example, statements uttered in one place today may have effects elsewhere tomorrow. That is, both the referents (what is talked about) and the effects of messages may be displaced.

PRODUCTIVITY

Human verbal messages evidence productivity—sometimes referred to as openness or creativity. Our verbal messages are novel utterances; each utterance is generated anew. There are exceptions to this general rule, but these are few and trivial. For example, sentences such as, "How are you?," "What's new?," "Good luck," and similar expressions do not evidence productivity; they are not newly created each time they are uttered. Except for sentences such as these, all other verbal messages are created at the time of utterance. When you speak, you are not repeating memorized sentences but rather creating your own sentences. Similarly, your understanding of verbal messages evidences productivity in that you can understand new utterances as they are uttered. Your ability to comprehend verbal messages is not limited to previously heard and learned utterances.

Another dimension of productivity is that human message systems allow the introduction of new words. When something is discovered or invented, we can create new words to describe it. When new ideas or new theoretical concepts are developed, we can create words to describe them. And it does not seem to matter whether we create the new word by joining together old words or parts of old words or create it from scratch. What does matter is that the language system is open to expansion—a feature that seems absent from just about all known animal communication systems.

RAPID FADING

Speech sounds fade rapidly; they are evanescent. They must be received immediately after they are emitted, or else they will not be received at all. Although mechanical devices now enable sound to be preserved much as writing is preserved, this is not a characteristic of human language. Rather, these are nonlanguage or extralinguistic means of storing information and aiding memory. Of course, all signals fade; written symbols and even symbols carved in rock are not permanent. In relative terms, however, speech signals are probably the least permanent of all communicative media.

ARBITRARINESS

Language signals are arbitrary; they do not possess any of the physical properties or characteristics of the things for which they stand. The word *wine* is no more tasty than the word *sand,* nor is the latter any less wet.

Opposed to arbitrariness is *iconicity.* Iconic signals do bear a resemblance to their referents. A line drawing of a person is iconic in representing the body parts in proper relation to each other. But it is arbitrary in representing the texture and thickness of the anatomical structures.

Both arbitrariness and iconicity are relative. For example, a line drawing is more arbitrary than a black-and-white photograph, which is more arbitrary than a color photograph. Paralinguistic features (volume, rate, rhythm) are more iconic than the features normally classified as belonging to language. Rate, for example, may vary directly with emotional arousal and hence would be iconic. But the sound of the word *fast* is not actually fast. (See Unit 17 for discussions on paralanguage.)

CULTURAL TRANSMISSION

The form of any particular human language is culturally or traditionally transmitted. The child raised by English speakers learns English as a native speaker, regardless of the language of his or her biological parents. The genetic endowment pertains to human ability to use language in general rather than to any specific human language.

One of the consequences of cultural transmission is that any human language can be learned by any normal human being. All human languages—English, Chinese, Italian, Russian, Bantu, or any of the other approximately 3,000 languages—are equally learnable; no one language should present any greater difficulty for a child than any other language. It should be added, however, that this ability to learn any language is true only at particular times in the life of the individual. One generally cannot learn to speak a language as fluently as a native after passing a certain age, usually around puberty.

The Nature of Meaning

Meaning is an active process created in cooperation between source and receiver, speaker and listener, writer and reader. This is illustrated in the model developed by Wendell Johnson, depicted in Figure 10.1. Although it may seem complex, the model is actually rather simple when compared to the truly complex process of transferring meaning from one person to another. The surrounding rectangle indicates that communication takes place in a context that is external to both speaker and listener and to the communication process as well. The twisted loop indicates that the various stages of communication are actually interrelated and interdependent.

The actual process begins at 1, which represents the occurrence of an event—anything that can be perceived. This event is the stimulus. At stage 2 the observer is

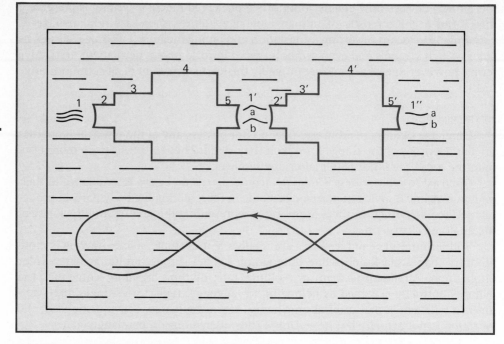

FIGURE 10.1: Johnson's Model of Communication. [*Source:* Wendell Johnson, "The Spoken Word and the Great Unsaid," *Quarterly Journal of Speech* 37 (1951): 421.]

stimulated through one or more sensory channels. The opening at 2 is purposely illustrated as being relatively small to emphasize that out of all the possible stimuli in the world, only a small number of these actually stimulate the observer. At stage 3 organismic evaluations occur. Nerve impulses travel from the sense organs to the brain, causing certain bodily changes, for example, in muscular tension. At 4 the feelings aroused at 3 are beginning to be translated into words—a process that takes place in accordance with the individual's unique language habits. At stage 5, from all the possible linguistic symbols, certain ones are selected and arranged into some pattern.

At 1' the words that the speaker utters, by means of sound waves, or the words that are written, by means of light waves, serve as stimulation for the hearer, much as the outside event at 1 served as stimulation for the speaker. At 2' the hearer is stimulated, at 3' there are organismic evaluations, at 4' feelings are beginning to be translated into words, at 5' certain of these symbols are selected and arranged, and at 1" these symbols, in the form of sound or light waves, are emitted and serve as stimulation for another hearer. The process is a continuous one.

A few of the implications this model has for meaning and effective interpersonal interaction may be identified here.

MEANINGS ARE IN PEOPLE

Meaning is a function not only of messages (whether verbal, nonverbal, or both) but of the interaction of these messages and the receiver's own thoughts and feelings. We do not "receive" meaning; we create meaning. Words do not mean; people mean. Consequently, to uncover meaning, we need to look into people and not merely into words.

An example of the confusion that can result when this relatively simple fact is not taken into consideration is provided by Ronald D. Laing, H. Phillipson, and A. Russell Lee in *Interpersonal Perception* and analyzed with insight by Paul Watzlawick in *How Real Is Real?* A couple on the second night of their honeymoon were sitting at a hotel bar. The woman struck up a conversation with the couple next to her. The husband refused to communicate with the couple and became antagonistic to his wife as well as to the couple. The wife then became angry because he created such an awkward and unpleasant situation. Each became increasingly disturbed, and the evening ended in a bitter conflict in which each was convinced of the other's lack of consideration. Eight years later, they analyzed this argument. Apparently "honeymoon" had meant very different things to each of them; to the husband it had meant a "golden opportunity to ignore the rest of the world and simply explore each other." His wife's interaction with the other couple implied to him that there was something lacking in him to make her seek out additional people with whom to interact. To the wife "honeymoon" had meant an opportunity to try out her new role as wife. "I have never had a conversation with another couple as a wife before," she said. "Previous to this I had always been a 'girl friend' or 'fiancée' or 'daughter' or 'sister.' "

MEANINGS ARE MORE THAN WORDS

When we experience something or have an idea or feel an emotion and want to communicate this to another person, we do so with relatively few words. These few words symbolize just a small part of our experience or feeling. There is much more that we feel or think that remains unspoken. If we were to attempt to describe every feeling in detail, we would never get on with the job of living. The meanings we feel and attempt to communicate are more than the words, and the two should never be confused.

As a result, we can never know fully what another person is thinking or feeling; we can only approximate it on the basis of the meanings we receive (which, as already noted, are greatly influenced by who *we* are and what *we* are feeling). Conversely, another can never know us fully; they too can only approximate what we are feeling. Failure to understand another person or to be understood are not abnormal situations; they are inevitable and should make us realize that we can always understand each other a little better than we do now.

MEANINGS ARE UNIQUE

Because meanings are derived from both the messages communicated and the receiver's own thoughts and feelings, no two people ever derive the same meanings. Similarly, because people change constantly, no one person can derive the same meanings on two separate occasions. Who we are can never be separated from the meanings we create. As a result, we need to check our perceptions of another's meanings by asking questions, echoing what we perceive to be the other person's feelings or thoughts, seeking elaboration and clarification, and, in general, practicing all the skills identified in our consideration of effective listening.

Also recognize that as we change, we also change the meanings we created out of past messages. Thus, although the message sent may not have changed, the meanings we created from it yesterday and the meanings we created from it today may be quite different. Yesterday, when a special someone said "I love you," we created certain meanings; but today, when we learn that same "I love you" was said to three other people or when we fall in love with someone else, we quickly and drastically change the meanings we created from those three words.

Phatic Communion

No discussion of language and meaning can omit phatic communion—the small talk that precedes the big talk, the talk that opens the channels of communication so that the important and significant issues may be discussed.

In terms of content, phatic communion is trivial: "Hello," "How are you?," "Fine weather, isn't it?," "Have a nice day," and the like. But in terms of establishing and maintaining relationships, phatic talk is extremely important.

For one thing, phatic communication assures us that the social customs are in effect; the general rules of communication that we expect to operate will operate here also. The teacher who says, "Turn to Chapter Three" before saying "Hello" clues us in to a situation in which the normal rules may not operate.

In first encounters, phatic communion enables us to reveal something of ourselves and at the same time to gain some preliminary information about the other person. Even if it is only to hear the tone or quality of voice, something is gained. Sometimes the important benefit is that phatic talk allows us time to look each other over and to decide on our next move. Phatic communion also shows us that the other person is willing to communicate, that in fact the channels of communication are open, that there is some willingness to pursue the interaction.

The person who says, "Haven't I seen you here before?" is probably asking not if you have been here before but rather "Would you like to talk with me?" To answer the literal question and fail to respond to the underlying and more significant question is a clear example of miscommunication.

Phatic communion, by its nature and because of the purposes it serves, is non-controversial; with phatic talk there is little chance for conflict or fighting. Similarly, the topics considered are unemotional and hence not ego-involving. They are neither intellectually demanding nor too personal. In phatic talk the parties avoid extreme positions; rather, they seem to engage in what appears to be rather bland, innocuous, inane chatter. But we need to see that what on the surface is shallow is actually a foundation for later and more significant communication.

THREE DIMENSIONS OF VERBAL MESSAGES

Three dimensions of verbal messages, each involving two sides or two poles, are considered here: directive and nondirective language, direct and indirect speech, and denotative and connotative meaning. These three dimensions provide essential insights and tools for using language effectively.

Directive and Nondirective Language

One of the most important dimensions of language is its directive-nondirective quality, the extent to which the language used directs us to focus on or to see certain things or to respond in certain ways.

Consider, for example, the seemingly insignificant distinction between *the* and *a*. In one experiment students were shown a film of a car crash. After the showing they were asked a series of questions about the film. One group was asked (1) "Did you see the broken headlight?" Another group was asked (2) "Did you see a broken headlight?" In the actual film there was no broken headlight. Yet, with question 1, 22 instances of a broken headlight were reported; with question 2, only 10 instances were reported. Note the important distinction. *The,* as in question 2, assumes the existence of a broken headlight; the question itself tells us that there was a broken headlight and asks if we saw it. But *a,* as in question 2, simply asks if we saw a broken headlight without assuming anything about whether there was one to see or not. *The* directs our focus and our response. *A* does not; *a* is nondirective.

In additional experiments where the object was in fact present (for example, in a film where the headlight was actually broken), the same type of results were obtained. More people respond affirmatively when their response is directed by the word *the*.

In another study the responses of observers were directed by the types of words used. Here students were shown pictures of a car crash and were asked to estimate the speed at which the cars were traveling when they crashed. But the questions the various groups of observers were asked varied in one word. Some were asked to estimate how fast the two cars were going when they "smashed." Others were asked how fast they were going when they "collided." In all, five different verbs were used. The results, in mean estimated speed, are presented in Table 10.1. Note how different the estimated speeds are solely on the basis of the verb used to describe the event.

At a later date the experimenter brought back students who had heard the word *smashed* and students who had heard the word *hit.* Both groups were asked if they had seen any broken glass. Although there was actually no broken glass in the film, 14 percent of those who had had the film described with *hit* reported seeing glass— and more than twice as many (32 percent) who had had the film described with *smashed* reported seeing broken glass.

We can also direct the responses of people by suggesting appropriate choices. For example, people were interviewed about headache remedies they tried. One group was asked the question as follows: (1) "How many other products did you try? 1, 2, 3?" Another group was asked, (2) "How many other products did you try? 1, 5, 20?" The persons asked question 1 responded with a mean of 3.3, while those asked question 2 responded with a mean of 5.2.

Similarly, the way in which doctors phrase their questions influence their patients'

TABLE 10.1: Language Intensity and Perception

Descriptive Word	Mean Estimated Speed
Smashed	40.8 mph
Collided	39.3
Bumped	38.1
Hit	34.0
Contacted	31.8

The way in which we ask questions greatly influences the answers given in response. In many cases—as, for example, with doctors—the asking of questions that encourage open and honest responses becomes an essential professional skill.

responses. When doctors asked, "Do you get headaches frequently?" the average response was 2.2 times per week. But when the question was expressed as "Do you get headaches occasionally?" the average dropped to 0.7 times per week.

IN INTERPERSONAL INTERACTIONS

All of these examples, based on research conducted by psychologist Elizabeth Loftus, illustrate the powerful influence of language in serving a directive function, of telling us what to look for and how to respond. The situation is not, of course, limited to the experimental laboratory but occurs in our everyday interpersonal interactions. Consider a student who comes to me after having done poorly on an examination covering an assigned book. Note that I can say, (1) "Obviously you did the reading assigned, didn't you?" Or I can say something like, (2) "Did you have the opportunity to get the assigned reading done?"

In 1 I am influencing the student's response and making it difficult for the student to answer with anything but, "Yes, of course." But in 2 I am giving the student the opportunity to say either yes or no and am at least opening the channels for meaningful and honest communication. Questions like 1 seem to encourage lying and deceit when they occur between teacher and student, parent and child ("You didn't drink while you were driving, did you?"), two friends ("Didn't you try to call me to come to the party?"), or two lovers ("You do want to make love with me, don't you?").

If you want honest responses, ask questions that are nondirective, that provide the other person with the opportunity to respond as he or she sees fit and not with directives to respond in a specific way. As a listener (or a responder), be especially careful when confronted with directive questions; it is perhaps wise to respond by saying something like, "You seem to want me to say yes" or "Your question doesn't give me much freedom to respond as I want." Perhaps you might ask the person to rephrase the question: "I'm not sure what you mean by that question."

The most important implication to be learned is that language can fool us; it can make us think we saw broken glass, for example. And it can lead us to think that lying and deception are expected and appropriate ways of responding. Language is an instrument, a tool, for effective and meaningful communication. We need to learn to control language and not have it control us.

Direct and Indirect Speech

Another important language distinction to observe is that between direct and indirect speech. Consider the following pairs of sentences:

(1) I'm so bored; I have nothing to do tonight.
(2) I'd like to go to the movies. Would you like to come?

(1) Do you feel like hamburgers tonight?
(2) I'd like hamburgers tonight. How about you?

The statements numbered 1 are indirect; they are attempts to get the listener to say or do something without committing the speaker. Number 2 statements, however, clearly state the speaker's preferences and then ask the listeners if they agree. A more obvious example is the frequent comment on the temperature of a room, said in order to get the other person to do something about it: "Isn't it hot in here?" is an indirect request to open the windows or to turn on the air conditioner.

Indirect speech serves a number of important and useful functions, but it can also cause difficulties in interpersonal communication.

FUNCTIONS OF INDIRECT SPEECH

One obvious function is *to express a desire without insulting or offending anyone.* Indirect speech allows us to observe the rules of polite interaction. So instead of saying, "I'm bored with this group," we say, "It's getting late and I have to get up early tomorrow." Instead of saying, "This food tastes like cardboard," we say, "I just started my diet" or "I'm stuffed." In each instance we are stating a preference but are saying it indirectly so as to avoid offending.

Sometimes indirect speech allows us *to ask for compliments in a socially acceptable manner,* and so we say, "I was thinking of getting a nose job," hoping to get the desired compliment, "A nose job? You? Your nose is perfect."

Indirect speech also enables us *to disagree without being disagreeable.* So when someone says that veal comes from a lamb, we can say, "Does it really? I thought veal came from a calf" instead of "No, it doesn't; lamb comes from lambs, and veal comes from calves." Similarly, we often use indirect speech to respond to a person's prejudices: "Do Martians really kill their firstborn child? I always thought they were devoted to all their children." This is surely more polite than stating what we're really thinking: "That's absurb," "You're ignorant," or simply "Shut your mouth."

Consider the following dialogue:

Pat: You wouldn't like to have my parents over for dinner this weekend, would you?

Chris: I really wanted to go to the shore and just relax.

Pat: Well, if you feel you have to go to the shore, I'll make the dinner myself. You go to the shore. I really hate having them over and doing all the work myself. It's such a drag doing all the shopping, cooking, and cleaning all by myself.

Win–Lose and Win–Win Situations. Given this situation, Chris has two basic alternatives. One is to stick with the plans to go to the shore and relax. In this case Pat is going to be upset and Chris is going to be made to feel guilty for not helping with the dinner. A second alternative is to give in to Pat, help with the dinner, and not go to the shore. In this case Chris is going to have to give up some much desired plan and is sure to resent Pat's manipulative tactics. Regardless of which decision is made, one person wins and one person loses. We have what is called a win-lose situation—a situation that creates resentment, competition, and, often, an "I'll get even" mental set.

With direct requests, this type of situation is much less likely to develop. Consider:

Pat: I'd like to have my parents over for dinner this weekend. What do you think?

Chris: Well, I really wanted to go to the shore and just relax.

Regardless of what develops next, both individuals are starting out on relatively equal footing. Each has clearly and directly stated a preference. In this case, these preferences are mutually exclusive. Someone has to give in or be disappointed. But, observe that there is room for compromise. For example, Chris might say, "How about going to the shore this weekend and having your parents over next weekend? I'm really exhausted; I could use the rest." Here is a direct response to a direct request. Unless there is some pressing need to have Pat's parents over for dinner this weekend, this response seems like a workable compromise.

With the use of indirect requests, compromises are difficult to propose and difficult to accept largely because there is a stated inequality and an attempt to manipulate the other person. With direct requests, on the other hand, there is no manipulation. The result is that compromises readily suggest themselves, and there is little or no defensiveness to make the acceptance of a compromise difficult or ego-threatening. Here both parties can get what they want; it is a win-win situation—a situation that creates supportiveness and a willingness to cooperate and compromise.

Responsibility and Honesty. There are other problems with indirect requests. In indirect requests, the questionner attempts to shift the burden of responsibility to the other person. With direct requests, the individual assumes the burden of responsibility for his or her own requests and desires. Note that in "You don't really want to have my parents over for dinner this weekend," the questionner is attempting to shift the responsibility for the decision to the other person. With "I'd like to have my parents over for dinner this weekend," the questionner owns his or her own statements, thoughts, and feelings.

Perhaps the most obvious difference between direct and indirect requests is that direct requests are honest and open; indirect requests are often (though surely not always) dishonest and manipulative. Direct questions encourage responses that are open, honest, and supportive; indirect questions encourage responses that are manipulative, dishonest, and defensive.

Denotative and Connotative Language

To explain denotative and connotative meaning, let us take as an example the word *death*. To a doctor this word might mean, or denote, simply the time when the heart stops beating. Thus to a doctor this word may be an objective description of a particular event. On the other hand, to a mother whose son has just died, the word means much more. It recalls to her the son's youth, his ambitions, his family, his illness, and so on. To her it is a highly emotional word, a highly subjective word, a highly personal word. These emotional or subjective or personal reactions are the word's connotative meaning. The *denotation* of a word is its objective definition; the *connotation* of a word is its subjective or emotional meaning.

Some words are primarily, perhaps even completely, denotative. Words like *the*, *of*, *a*, and the like are perhaps purely denotative; no one seems to have emotional reactions to such words. Other words are primarily denotative, such as *perpendicular*, *parallel*, *cosine*, *adjacent*, and the like. Of course, even these words might have strong connotative meanings for some people. Words such as *geometry, north*, and *south, up* and *down*, and *east* and *west*—words that denote rather specific directions or areas—can produce strong emotional reactions from some people. For example, the student who failed geometry might have a very strong emotional reaction to the word, even though to most people it seems a rather unemotional, objective kind of word. Other words, such as derogatory racial names and curse words, are primarily connotative and often have little denotative meaning. Very simply, words may vary from highly denotative to highly connotative. A good way to determine a word's connotative meaning is to ask where it would fall on a good–bad scale. If "good" and "bad" do not seem to apply to the word, then it has little, if any, connotative meaning for you. If, however, the term can be placed on the good–bad scale with some degree of conviction, it has connotative meaning for you.

Another distinction between the two types of meaning has already been implied. The denotative meaning of a word is more general or universal; that is, most people agree with the denotative meanings of words and would give similar definitions. Connotative meanings, however, are extremely personal, and few people would agree on the precise connotative meaning of a word. If this does not seem correct, try to get a group of people to agree on the connotative meaning of words such as *religion, God, democracy, wealth*, and *freedom*. Chances are very good that it will be impossible to reach an agreement about such words.

The denotative meaning of a term can be learned from any dictionary. When we consult a dictionary, it is the denotative meaning for which we are looking. The dictionary would tell us, for example, that *south* means "a cardinal point of the compass directly opposite to the north; the direction in which this point lies," and so on. Connotative meaning, on the other hand, cannot be found in a dictionary. Instead it must be found in each person's reactions to or associations with the word. To some people, for example, *south* might mean poverty; to others it might mean wealth and good land investment; to still others it might recall the Civil War, or perhaps warmth and friendliness. Obviously, no dictionary could be compiled for connotative meanings, simply because each person's connotative meaning for a word would be different.

Denotative meaning differs from connotative meaning in yet another way. Denotative meanings are relatively unchanging and static. Although definitions of all words change over time, denotative meanings generally change very slowly. The word *south,* for example, meant denotatively the same thing 1,000 years ago that it does now. But connotative meanings change rapidly. A single favorable experience in the South, for example, might change completely one's connotative meaning for the word.

NAMES AND NAMING

Very often we are not aware of the connotative meanings of terms and naively assume them to be purely denotative. First names are one of the clearest examples. Through various associations, some recent and some long past, names have acquired strong connotative meanings, which have been the object of considerable research in the past 20 years. It has been found, for example, that *Michael, James,* and *Wendy* are perceived as active, whereas *Alfreda, Percival,* and *Isadore* are perceived as passive. *Michael* and *James* are seen as masculine, but *Percival* and *Isadore* are not; *Wendy* is perceived as feminine, but *Alfreda* is not. Common names, such as *James, John, Joseph, Michael,* and *Paul,* are perceived as designating individuals who are better, stronger, and more active than those who have more unusual names, such as *Dale, Edmond, Raymond, Stanley,* and *Lawrence.* It has also been shown, for example, that male students with unusual names were more likely to flunk out of Harvard, were more likely to be neurotic, and had a higher incidence of psychosis than those with common names. Interestingly enough, this relationship did not hold for female names.

In other studies it has been found that teachers gave essays supposedly written by students with unpopular names (for example, *Elmer* and *Bertha*) lower grades than those supposedly written by students with popular names (for example, *Karen* and *Michael*).

Although this research is in many ways in its infancy, it seems to be demonstrating that few terms, if any, are purely denotative and that the connotative value of names in particular influences a wide variety of perceptions in a wide variety of people.

SEMANTIC DIFFERENTIATION

Perhaps the most popular and most insightful approach to connotative meaning is that of semantic differentiation—a procedure in which a word is rated on selected bipolar seven-point scales to tap an individual's connotative meaning.

The scales are of three types or meaning dimensions. The evaluative dimension uses such scales as good–bad, sad–happy, valuable–worthless, and bitter–sweet. The potency dimension uses such scales as strong–weak and light–heavy. The activity dimension uses such scales as hot–cold, active–passive, and fast–slow. By using such scales, meanings may be indexed for (1) different concepts by the same subject, (2) the same concepts by different subjects, or (3) various concepts by the same subjects at different times (for example, before and after therapy, before and after taking a specific course, or before and after hearing a specific communication).

As an example, take the concept of a "college education" as rated by the typical college graduate. It might look something like Figure 10.2.

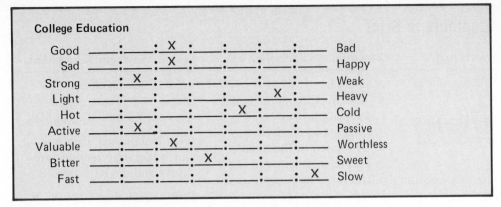

FIGURE 10.2: An Example of Semantic Differential Scales.

If we number the scales, using 7 for the positive end and 1 for the negative end, we can add the various judgments and get summary figures. Taking the evaluative dimension as an example, we have the scales good–bad, sad–happy, valuable–worthless, and bitter–sweet. On the good–bad scale this subject rated "college education" 5, on the sad–happy scale 3, on the valuable–worthless scale 5, and on the bitter–sweet scale 4 (note that we are considering the positive ends, good and happy, as 7 and the negative ends, bad and sad, as 1). This totals 17 on the evaluative dimension. This score means little unless we compare it to something else. We might, for example, compare it with the ratings of other students or the ratings of students in different colleges or those studying different majors. Or we might test the difference between males and females or study changes in one individual from freshman to senior year.

SOME PRACTICAL IMPLICATIONS

The distinction between denotative and connotative meaning has a number of important practical implications for interpersonal communication.

Meanings Change. First, meanings, especially connotative meanings, differ from one moment to the next and, most important, from one person to another. Do not assume that the meanings you attributed are the same as the meanings another person attributes to a word, even though you both may use the exact same words. Before agreeing or disagreeing, check to make certain that you understand each other's meanings. Words such as *love, wealth, happiness,* and thousands of others are given drastically different meanings by different people and by the same person at different times.

Meanings Are Composites. Second, meanings are a combination or composite of thoughts and feelings. The symbols we use do not refer objectively to things but only indirectly through our feelings and thoughts. Therefore, we always talk about ourselves, and an appropriate response addresses both the things talked about and the speaker's feelings, which are inevitably reflected in the verbal messages.

Meanings Are Multidimensional. Third, by understanding how connotative meanings may be dissected (into, for example, evaluative, potency, and activity dimensions), we are in a better position to remember that an individual's meaning for a term is multifaceted and that effective communication depends on understanding what the other person means, not only on what the word means. Listen, then, not only to what is said but also to what is meant.

Summary: Contents in Brief

Language Characteristics	Meaning Characteristics	Verbal Message Dimensions
Specialization: serves only to communicate	*Meaning is:* • an active process created in cooperation between source and receiver • a function of the interaction of messages and the receiver's own nervous system	*Directive and nondirective:* extent to which language directs our focus and responses
Displacement: able to refer to matters remote in time and space		*Direct and indirect:* extent to which language requests are clearly and directly stated
Productivity: new messages are created regularly		*Denotation and connotation:* extent to which the language is objective or subjective in meaning
Rapid fading: speech signals fade rapidly	*Meanings are:* • in people • more than words • unique • ever changing • composites of thoughts and feelings • multidimensional	
Arbitrariness: language signals bear an arbitrary connection to the referents		
Cultural transmission: the language we acquire is learned through the culture		

Sources

For the characteristics of language, I relied on the work of Charles F. Hockett. See his *The View From Language* (Athens: University of Georgia Press, 1977). The concepts of language universals are thoroughly surveyed in Joseph Greenberg's *Universals of Language* (Cambridge, Mass.: M.I.T. Press, 1963). Most of the material, however, presumes a rather thorough knowledge of linguistics. The discussion of directive and nondirective and direct and indirect language owes much to the research and theory of Elizabeth Loftus. See, for example, *Eyewitness Testimony* (Cambridge, Mass.: Harvard University Press, 1979) and Elizabeth Loftus and J. Monahan, "Trial by Data: Psychological Research as Legal Evidence," *American Psychologist* 35 (1980): 270–283. An excellent introduction to this area is provided by Loftus in *The Manipulative Uses of Language,* a Psychology Today Cassette (New York: Ziff-Davis, 1979).

The concept of meaning is covered in the works on semantics and general semantics. Articles in Paul A. Eschholz, Alfred F. Rosa, and Virginia P. Clark, *Language Awareness* (New York: St. Martin's Press, 1974) and Joseph A. DeVito, *Language: Concepts and Processes* (Englewood Cliffs, N.J.: Prentice-Hall, 1973) provide an excellent overview of this area.

Numerous examples of meaning confusion as well as insightful analyses may be found in Ronald D. Laing, H. Phillipson, and A. Russell Lee, *Interpersonal Perception* (New York: Springer-Verlag, 1966) and Paul Watzlawick, *How Real Is Real? Confusion, Disinformation, Communication* (New York: Random House [Vintage Books], 1977). On names, see Muriel Beadle, "The Game of the Name," *New York Times Magazine*

(October 21, 1973): 38ff., and Mary G. Marcus. "The Power of a Name," *Psychology Today* 10 (October 1976): 75–76, 108. Both articles provide extensive lists of common names. For an interesting discussion of names and our treatment of them as more than just labels, see Myrna Frommer, "Names," *et cetera* 39 (Summer 1982): 106–108.

UNIT 11

Language, Sublanguage, and Culture

OBJECTIVES

Upon completion of this unit, you should be able to:

1. explain language as a social institution
2. explain the functions of sublanguages
3. define *sublanguage*, *subculture*, *argot*, *cant*, *jargon*, *slang*, *taboo*, and *euphemism*
4. identify the three general origins of taboos and provide at least one example of each
5. explain at least four variables that influence the usage of taboo expressions
6. explain the concept of language racism and sexism

One of the features shared by all human languages is the existence within the language of *sublanguages*—languages used by subcultures or subgroups for communication among their members. In order to explore the concept of sublanguages in depth, the nature of language as a social institution must first be understood.

LANGUAGE AS A SOCIAL INSTITUTION

Language is a social institution designed, modified, and extended (some purists might even say distorted) to meet the ever-changing needs of the culture or subculture. As such, language differs greatly from one culture to another and, equally important, though perhaps less obvious, from one subculture to another.

Subcultures are cultures within a larger culture and may be formed on the basis of religion, geographical area, occupation, affectional orientation, race, nationality, living conditions, interests, needs, and so on. Catholics, Protestants, and Jews; New Yorkers, Californians, and mountain folk; teachers, plumbers, and musicians; blacks, Chinese, and Native Americans; prisoners, suburbanites, and drug addicts; diabetics, the blind, and ex-convicts may all be viewed as subcultures, depending, of course, on the context on which we focus. In the United States as a whole, Protestants would not constitute a subculture (though Catholics and Jews would). In New York City, on the other hand, Protestants would constitute a subculture. Blacks and Chinese would be subcultures only outside of Africa and China. The majority generally constitutes the culture, and the various minorities generally constitute the subcultures. Yet this is not always the case. Women, although the majority in our culture, may be viewed as a subculture primarily because society as a whole is male-oriented. Whether a group should be regarded as a subculture or a culture, then, depends on the context being considered and the orientation of the society of which these groups are a part.

Each individual belongs to several subcultures. At the very least he or she belongs to a national, a religious, and an occupational subculture. The importance of the subcultural affiliation varies greatly from one individual to another, from one context to another, and from one time or circumstance to another. To some people in some contexts, an individual's religious affiliation may be inconsequential and his or her membership in this subculture hardly considered. If, on the other hand, the individual wishes to marry into a particular family, this once inconsequential membership may take on greater significance.

Because of the common interests, needs, or conditions of individuals constituting a subculture, sublanguages come into being. Like language in general, sublanguages exist to enable members of the group to communicate with each other. And again like language in general, there are regional differences, changes over time, and other variations. Sublanguages also serve other functions, which constitute their reason for existence. If they did not serve these several functions, they would soon disappear.

KINDS OF SUBLANGUAGES

Sublanguage is used here as a general term to denote a variation from the general language that is used by a particular group or subculture existing within the broader, more general culture. There are four major types of sublanguages.

Argot

Argot is the specialized vocabulary of some disreputable or underworld subcultures. It is the sublanguage of pickpockets, murderers, drug dealers, and prostitutes. Expressions such as *college* (meaning prison), *stretch* (jail sentence), *to mouse* (to escape from prison), and *lifeboat* (a pardon) are examples of argot. In its true form argot is not understood by outsiders. Today, with television and movies so much a part of our lives, it is difficult for any group, however specialized and "underground," to hide its specialized language. Consequently, many people know some argot expressions.

Cant

Cant designates the specialized vocabulary of any nonprofessional (usually noncriminal) group and would include, for example, the specialized sublanguage of the taxi driver, the truck driver, the CB operator, and the soldier. Often cant is used to denote the speech of such groups as peddlers and tramps. As is the case with argot, these vocabularies would ideally not be understood by nonmembers were it not for television and film. Expressions such as *dog* (meaning a motor vehicle inspector), *kidney buster* (hard-riding truck), and *sweatshop* (bulletproof cab with poor ventilation) are examples of cant.

Jargon

Jargon is the technical language of a professional class, for example, college professors, writers, medical doctors, and lawyers. Terms such as *perceptual accentuation, inflationary spiral, behavioral objectives,* and others used throughout your college experience are examples of professional academic jargon, as are the technical terms for the proofreading and editing of a writer, for the diseases and medications of a doctor, and for the legal documents and criminal offenses of the lawyer.

Slang

Slang is the most general sublanguage, consisting of vocabulary terms derived particularly from cant and argot that are understood by most persons but would not necessarily be used in "polite society" or in formal written communications. Terms such as *skirt* (meaning woman), *skiddoo* (leave fast), *goo goo eyes, hush money, booze, brass* (impudence), and *to knock off* (to quit working) are examples of slang. Slang is usually short-lived. *Skirt, skiddoo,* and *goo goo eyes* are rarely used today, and when they are used, they conjure up an image of an antiquated, out-of-touch-with-reality type of person. There are, of course, exceptions to this short life; some slang terms have been around for decades and remain classified as slang. For example, according to famed lexicographer H. L. Mencken, *booze* dates back to the fourteenth century, *brass* to 1594, and *knock off* to 1662.

   With the passage of time and increased frequency of usage, slang terms enter the general language as socially acceptable expressions. As this happens, new terms are coined by the subcultures. The old terms are dropped from the sublanguage, since they no longer serve the functions for which they were originally developed. This is just one of the ways in which new words enter the language and in which sublanguages are kept distinct from the general language.

FUNCTIONS OF SUBLANGUAGES

Sublanguages serve numerous functions, depending on the particular subculture, the communication context, and a host of linguistic and nonlinguistic variables. Here we identify a few of the more pervasive functions.

To Facilitate Subcultural Communication

One of the most obvious facts about language and its relation to culture is that concepts that are important to a given culture are given a large number of terms. For example, in our culture money is extremely important; consequently, we have numerous terms denoting this concept: *finances, funds, capital, assets, cash, pocket money, spending money, pin money, change, bread, loot, swag,* and various others. Transportation and communication are other concepts for which numerous terms exist in our language. Without knowing anything about a given culture, we could probably make

Each subculture has its own sublanguage designed to facilitate subcultural communication, to serve as a means of identification, to ensure communication privacy, and, unfortunately, in some cases, to impress and confuse nonmembers.

some pretty good guesses as to the important concepts in that culture simply by examining one of its dictionaries or thesauruses. With sublanguages, the same principle holds. Concepts that are of special importance to a particular subculture are given a large number of terms. Thus one function of sublanguages is to provide the subculture with convenient synonyms for concepts that are of great importance and hence are spoken about frequently. To prisoners, for example, a prison guard—clearly a significant concept and one spoken about a great deal—may be denoted by *screw, roach, hack, slave driver, shield, holligan,* and various other terms. Heroin, in the drug subculture, may be called *H, Harry, smack, Carga, joy powder, skag, stuff,* or *shit.*

Sublanguages provide the subculture with convenient distinctions that are important to the subculture but generally not to the culture at large—and thus distinctions that the general language does not make. This function is clearly seen in the technical jargon of the academic world. Whereas the term *learning* may be sufficient for the general population, the psychologist needs to distinguish between classical and instrumental learning, incidental and instructed learning, response and stimulus learning, and so on. In the field of communication, instead of the general term *message* we distinguish between digital and analogic messages, verbal and nonverbal messages, content and relational messages, content and metamessages, and so on. These distinctions are all helpful in conceptualizing and communicating the data and theories of a discipline.

To Serve as a Means of Identification

By using a particular sublanguage, speakers identify themselves to hearers as members of that subculture—assuming, of course, that the listeners know the language being used. Individuals belonging to various nationality-based subcultures frequently drop a foreign word or phrase in the conversation to identify themselves to their audience. Similarly, homosexuals and ex-convicts at times identify themselves by using the sublanguage of their subculture. When the subcultural membership is one that is normally hidden, as in the case of homosexuals and ex-convicts, these clues to self-identification are subtle. Generally, they are given only after the individuals themselves receive some kind of positive feedback that leads them to suspect that the hearer also belongs to the subculture in question or that the hearer is at least sympathetic. In a similar vein, sublanguages also function to express to others one's felt identification with that subculture, as when blacks address each other as *brother* and *sister* when meeting for the first time. The use of these terms by blacks as well as the frequent use of foreign expressions by members of various national groups communicate to others that the speaker feels a strong identification with the group.

Sublanguages, then, provide the group with an identity and a sense of fraternity. Because ex-convicts all over the country know the same sublanguage, they are, in a sense, bound together. The more the subculture has a need to band together, the greater the importance of a specialized language.

To Ensure Communication Privacy

Sublanguages enable members of the subculture to communicate with one another while in the presence of nonmembers without having their conversation completely understood. A common example of this, which many of us may have heard but been unaware of, occurs in stores that attempt to take unfair advantage of customers. Salespersons will describe arriving customers as *J.L.* (just looking), *skank* (cheap individual), *T.O.* (turn over to an experienced salesperson), or *palooka* (one who is on a buying binge).

In certain situations, of course, the sublanguage may reveal the individual as a member of a particular subculture, and so he or she will refrain from using the sublanguage. This is often the case among criminals in a noncriminal environment. At other times, however, the use of a sublanguage does not lead to an individual's identification as a subculture member, and the sublanguage serves the useful purpose of excluding nonmembers from the class of decoders.

To Impress and Confuse

One of the less noble functions of sublanguages—capitalized on by numerous professionals—is to impress and at times confuse outsiders. The two functions, I think, often go hand in hand; many people are impressed in direct proportion to their confusion. Insurance policies and legal documents are perhaps the best examples. I suspect that in many instances this technical language is used to impress and confuse people. Then, when there is doubt about something, the insurance adjuster and lawyer begin with an advantage—they understand the language, whereas you and I do not. Similarly, in evaluating and in signing such documents, we are unable even to ask the right questions because there is so much we do not understand. Fortunately, as *Time* magazine has reported, "the forces of hereinafter, *res ipsa loquitur* and party of the first part are now clearly on the defensive." In recent years certain government agencies have enlisted the aid of communication experts to rewrite much of their incomprehensible prose.

Physicians and many academicians are also in this class. We are easily impressed by the physician's facile use of technical terms and are more apt to pay for the services of those who—like the witch doctors of primitive societies—know the language. To talk of a *singultus spasm* or *bilateral periorbital hematoma* instead of hiccups or a black eye does little to aid meaningful communication. From an analysis of this "medicalese," sociolinguist Joyce Hertzler notes (and I fully agree): "The conclusion must be that the effort is being made to mystify the public with respect to the highly technical and esoteric nature of their knowledge and performance, and to create an aura about their profession."

LANGUAGE TABOO AND EUPHEMISM

One of the best ways of examining language in general, and the social dimension of language in particular, is to focus on taboo and euphemism. *Language taboo* refers to verbal behavior that is forbidden by the society for reasons that are not always clear; generally it is for some vague and seemingly irrational reason. When we think of taboo, we often think of primitive societies with elaborate precautions against and punishments for uttering particular words and phrases. But language taboo is actually universal; all languages and all societies have language taboos built into their social structure.

Taboo Origins

Stephen Ullmann, in *Semantics*, notes that there are three general origins of language taboo. The first are taboos rooted in fear. We may fear being punished by God, for example, so we avoid naming the dead or avoid using the name of God or of the Devil. Similarly, fear perhaps motivates our not taking the name of God in vain. The second is the taboo of delicacy. This taboo centers on an avoidance of unpleasant topics and leads us to avoid talking of death, illness, and disease. A familiar example occurs when referring to someone who has a mental deficiency and avoiding such expressions as *idiot* or *imbecile,* using instead such expressions as *mentally retarded* or *intellectually impaired.* The third is the taboo of propriety. This leads us to avoid certain sexual references and swear words and naming certain parts and functions of the body. Although it is true that we no longer say *limbs* or *benders* instead of *legs,* there are many parts of the body for which we avoid speaking the terms we think and instead employ some other term that is more socially acceptable.

Taboo Variations

Although taboo is a language universal, its form varies from one language to another and from one culture or subculture to another. Thus the terms under taboo in our culture may not be under a taboo in other cultures. Even within any culture or subculture, what is and what is not taboo varies on the basis of a number of factors. Taboo varies greatly with age, for example. Young people are more restricted in their language usage than are adults. Adults are allowed to talk about topics that are forbidden to children and in language that children would be punished for using. Taboo also varies on the basis of sex. Our society—and, in fact, most societies—allows men greater freedom. That these different taboos still operate is seen when the speech of men and women is analyzed; male speech contains a far greater number of taboo expressions than does female speech.

Taboo also varies with the educational and intellectual level of the individual. Uneducated persons generally demonstrate greater freedom of expression—in part because they do not have alternative expressions. The educated do have these alternatives and, at least when in "polite society," use these rather than the taboo expressions. The communication context also influences the frequency and strength of taboo expressions. Generally, as the formality of a situation increases, so do the linguistic restrictions. There are, for example, greater restrictions in a classroom than there are in the cafeteria. Perhaps the most important variable influencing taboo is the speaker-listener relationship. If the speaker and listener are equals, there are usually fewer restrictions on their speech than if they are of widely differing statuses. There is less restriction between two teachers than between either a student and a teacher or a teacher and a dean. You know from your own experiences that you monitor your speech when talking to persons who are higher than you in status or people you may be trying to impress, for example, a new date or a potential employer. In talking with equals, you are less likely to monitor and censor your expression.

Taboo Effects

Some people use taboo expressions because this is their natural mode of communication, and they do not monitor or censor any of it before speaking—"They call it as they see it." To these people, these expressions are natural rather than taboo. Others use taboo expressions because they are not aware of their inappropriateness; they are not sensitive to the communication context or to the differences in speaker-listener status. Often, however, the other person is aware and the focus shifts from the content of the communication to the taboo expression and, for a while at least, real and meaningful communication breaks down. This is seen frequently when people talk about throwing up or some particularly gory accident during dinner or when one of two people who do not know each other well uses expressions that prove offensive, crude, or gross to the other. Some persons use taboo expressions for their shock value. They want to shock other people or present particular images of themselves that taboo expressions help achieve.

When the language taboo is broken, various forms of punishment may be meted out. For the most part, we no longer have legal punishments, although taboo expressions uttered in court, for example, often result in a fine, and the use of taboo expressions in print may in some cases bring similar penalties. But for the most part such penalties have been removed. Nevertheless, there are still punishments that are administered. Persons who frequently use taboo expressions often find themselves laughed with over coffee but then not invited to more sophisticated functions; they may find themselves popular in the mail room while corporate advancement eludes them.

Taboo Alternatives: Euphemisms

In all languages there are alternative expressions that are used instead of taboo expressions, and these are called *euphemisms*. They are the nice words designed to replace taboo expressions and to sweeten topics that may be unpleasant or less than desirable—and so we say *mortician* instead of *undertaker*, and instead of *toilet* we say *restroom* (though few really rest there) or *bathroom* (though we are not going to bathe) or *little boy's* or *little girl's room* (though we are grown men and women). H. L. Mencken, in *The American Language*, identifies hundreds of such euphemistic substitutions: *collection correspondent* for *bill collector*; *section manager* for *floor walker*; *superintendent* for *janitor*; and *sanitary officer* for *garbage man*. A friend of mine who works for the Department of Sanitation actually refers to himself as a "garbologist."

LANGUAGE RACISM AND SEXISM

No discussion of sublanguages would be complete without consideration of the terms and phrases used to denigrate various subcultures. These are not themselves sublanguages but are terms and phrases used to refer to the various subcultures, usually negatively.

Racism

Perhaps the most obvious examples are those that refer to a person's race. We all know these terms, and listing them here would serve no purpose. In fact, I suspect that part of the reason these terms persist is because academicians and the media use them to illustrate how "liberal" they are and feel that in doing so they are really putting down such prejudice. I think that the use of such terms, for example, on "All in the Family," did not work against their increased popular use but rather seemed to make them appear more acceptable and more harmless than they really are. We do not have to tell a racist joke to illustrate how racist jokes foster racial prejudice.

These derogatory terms are used by the principal culture to disparage subculture members, their customs, or their accomplishments. Every subgroup has such negative terms, whose main function is to separate the majority from the minority group and to create a sociological and linguistic hierarchy, with the majority members on the top and the minority members on the bottom. The social consequences of such hierarchies in terms of employment, education, housing opportunities, and general community acceptance seem well known.

One of the qualifications frequently made in this connection is that it is permissible for members of the subculture to refer to themselves with these negative terms without any problems being created. That is, Italians may use the negative terms referring to Italians, blacks may use the negative terms referring to blacks, and so on. The reasoning seems to be that groups should be able to laugh at themselves. I am not sure we should accept this position. In fact, it seems likely that such personal usage is even more damaging, because the negative connotations of these terms feed back to the individual and may well function to reinforce the negative stereotypes that society has already assigned this group. The use of such terms in effect tells the individual that his or her subcultural affiliation is somehow not as good as that of the majority culture.

This is seen clearly when gay men and lesbians use the negative terms of heterosexual society to refer to themselves. By using these terms, they seem to be in effect confirming, at least in part and perhaps subconsciously, the connotations that the heterosexual culture has included in these terms. This is not to imply that the connotations in the minds of the subculture member and the majority member will be the same, only to suggest that the connotations both persons have may have negative aspects that may not necessarily or always be conscious.

Sexism

Consider some of the language used to refer to women. A woman loses her last name when she marries and in certain instances loses her first name as well. She changes from "Ann Smith" to "Mrs. John Jones." On a recent talk show, Gary Morton, for example, noted that when his wife, Lucille Ball, comes home from work, she becomes "Mrs. Morton."

We say that a woman "marries into" a man's family and that a family "dies out" if there are no male children. We do not speak of a man marrying into a woman's family (unless that family is extremely prestigious or wealthy or members of royalty), and a family can still "die out" even if there are ten female children. In the traditional marriage ceremony, we hear "I now pronounce you man and wife," not "man and woman" or "husband and wife." The man retains his status as man, but the woman changes hers from woman to wife.

Many of the terms used for women are used to define them sexually. Consider, for example, the once parallel terms *master* and *mistress*. These terms at one time designated persons who had power and privilege over others. Now, however, *master* refers not to a man who has power over other people but to a man who has power over things, as in, for example, "He is a master craftsman" or "He is a master teacher." But note that *mistress* did not develop in a parallel way; the term now denotes a sexual relationship, particularly one in which the woman is possessed by and subordinated to the man, as in "She is the senator's mistress." The term *professional,* when applied to a man, refers to his high-status occupation. When applied to a woman, it often has a sexual connotation. The same is true for the expression "in business" in certain parts of the country.

Another interesting lack of parallelism between the sexes is found in the terms *bachelor* and *spinster. Bachelor* varies from neutral to positive in connotation, but *spinster* is always negative. We would say, "Margaret is dating an eligible bachelor," but would not say, "Joe is dating an eligible spinster." The term *spinster* seems to preclude eligibility. Even when the terms are used metaphorically, this same lack of parallelism can be seen. When we say that "Joe is a regular bachelor," we imply that he is free and is living an exciting and sexually fulfilling life. But when we say, "Margaret is a regular spinster," we imply that she is living an uninteresting and sexually unfulfilling life.

The use of *man* to designate "human being" and the use of the masculine pronoun to refer to any individual regardless of sex further illustrate the extent of linguistic sexism. There seems to me no legitimate reason why the feminine pronoun could not alternate with the masculine pronoun in referring to hypothetical individuals or why such terms as *he and she* or *her and him* could not be used instead of just *he* or *him.*

Summary: Contents in Brief

	Sublanguage	Taboo
Definition	Specialized vocabularies established by subcultures	Verbal behavior that is forbidden by the society
Functions	To facilitate subcultural communication	To gain attention
		To shock
	To serve as a means of identification and provide a sense of fraternity	To communicate feelings
	To ensure communication privacy	
	To impress and confuse outsiders	
Kinds	*Argot:* disreputable subculture language	Fear taboo leading to avoidance of names of dead or of God
	Cant: nonprofessional group's language	Delicacy taboo leading to avoidance of topics such as death, illness, disease
	Jargon: professional group's language	Propriety taboo leading to avoidance of sex, swearing, and certain body parts and functions.
	Slang: once specialized vocabularies now publicly understood	

Sources

On sublanguages, see H. L. Mencken, *The American Language* (New York: Knopf, 1971). The chapter "American Slang" is a classic work and a most interesting one. Much interesting research relevant to sublanguages is reported in the various works on sociolinguistics, for example, Dell Hymes, *Foundations in Sociolinguistics: An Ethnographic Approach* (Philadelphia: University of Pennsylvania Press, 1974), Joyce Hertzler, *The Sociology of Language* (New York: Random House, 1965), and Ralph Fasold, *The Sociolinguistics of Society* (New York: Basil Blackwell, 1984). One of the most insightful essays is Paul Goodman, "Sublanguages," in *Speaking and Language: Defence of Poetry* (New York: Random House, 1971). Stephen Ullmann's classic *Semantics* (New York: Barnes & Noble, 1962) presents much that is of interest to taboo. Many of the insights and examples concerning language sexism came from Casey Miller and Kate Swift, *Words and Women: New Language in New Times* (Garden City, N.Y.: Doubleday, 1976) and Robin Lakoff, *Language and Woman's Place* (New York: Harper & Row, 1975). I recommend both of these books highly. In this connection, see also Cheris Kramer, "Women's Speech: Separate but Unequal?" *Quarterly Journal of Speech* 60 (February 1974): 14–24. The broad area of sex differences in communication is surveyed in Barbara Eakins and R. Gene Eakins, *Sex Differences in Communication* (Boston: Houghton Mifflin, 1978) and Judy Cornelia Pearson, *Gender and Communication* (Dubuque, Iowa: Brown, 1985). For an examination of the effects of qualifying phrases used by men and women, see Patricia Hayes Bradley, "The Folk-Linguistics of Women's Speech: An Empirical Examination," *Communication Monographs* 48 (March 1981): 73–90. Richard W. Brislin, in *Cross-Cultural Encounters: Face-to-Face Interaction* (New York: Pergamon Press, 1981) discusses much of relevance to this discussion of sublanguages. For a comprehensive introduction to jargon see Don Ethan Miller, *The Book of Jargon* (New York: Macmillan, 1981).

UNIT 12

Seven Pitfalls and Principles of Language and Verbal Interaction

OBJECTIVES

Upon completion of this unit, you should be able to:

1. define *downward* and *upward talk* and the principle of *equality* and provide examples of each
2. explain the major reasons people lie
3. explain some of the disadvantages of lying from a communication point of view
4. define *in-group talk* and the principle of *inclusion* and provide examples of each
5. define *self-talk, other talk,* and the principle of *balance* and provide examples of each
6. define *gossip* and explain how the principle of *confidentiality* should operate
7. explain the three conditions that, according to Sissela Bok, make gossip unethical
8. explain how criticism and praising can be verbal turnoffs and how the principle of honesty can be used in this connection
9. explain the varieties of offending talk and the principle of fairness and provide examples of each

The effects that people have on us and that we have on them are largely due to the verbal messages sent and received—the way we talk, the way we express our ideas and our feelings, the way we verbalize our relationship to the other person. In this unit, we consider seven pitfalls, seven ways in which we may create negative effects, and their corresponding opposites—the principles that should be followed to avoid such negative reactions. At the same time, these principles should enable us to create a more positive environment for communication in all its forms.

TALKING DOWN AND UP

In communication theory, particularly in the area of communication concerned with organizations, downward and upward communication have very specific meanings. Downward communication refers to communication originating from a high-level source (for example, a manager or executive) and directed at a lower-level receiver (for example, a line worker). Upward communication is the reverse and refers to communication originating from an individual who is low on the organizational hierarchy and directed to someone higher up. As used here, however, the terms refer to that irksome habit of people talking down or talking up to others.

Talking Down

Here we feel that the speaker for some unknown reason has "the" word and is passing it on to the masses. It is the teacher who says, "This may be beyond your reach, but try to grasp it anyway," or the film buff who says, "I realize that the movie was complex and that you didn't enjoy it," or the doctor who talks to lay people in medicalese, or the "friend" who puts himself or herself above others by using phrases such as "you probably didn't realize this but . . ." or "I know you don't keep up with the computer literature but . . ." Regardless of who is doing the talking, we get the distinct feeling that somehow the speaker is above us for a multitude of reasons—intelligence, experience, knowledge, position, wealth, whatever. We are put into a position of learner, of subordinate.

Another way in which some people talk down is in telling others how to feel and how to act. Consider this scene. You are at a party with a group of people who are singing along with a record. One individual, perhaps because of shyness, perhaps for some other reason, does not join in. The individual remains social but doesn't participate in the sing-along. Enter the problem communicator: "Come on, loosen up, sing with us." The person no doubt means well but at the same time displays a total lack of respect for the other person's behaviors and feelings. If one member chooses not to sing along, that is his or her choice, and as friends and associates, we need to respect that choice. To insist that the individual sing along (or change his or her behavior in some other way) only creates further problems by throwing the spotlight on this individual, who probably didn't sing to escape such attention in the first place.

There is usually little point in attempting to take on the responsibility for another person's feelings. It is far better to assume that each person can and prefers to make his or her own decisions. Few persons need us to tell them to loosen up, to have fun, or to do this or that.

Talking down is also seen in the individual who plays power games with us. Games of interruption, increasing one's volume to overpower the other, and verbal put-down such as "you can't be serious" are popular forms of talking down, which we cover in our discussion of power (Unit 20).

PRONOUNCEMENTS

Another popular type of talking down occurs in the making of what John Sanford, in *Between People: Communicating One-to-One,* calls "pronouncements." Pronouncements are especially popular with persons in authority—teachers, religious leaders, doctors, and parents. Because they are in positions of authority, it is easy for them to assume a superior stance and to approach and "resolve" problems by making pronouncements rather than through authentic communication. Differences of opinion or disagreements are "settled" by mandate rather than by compromise and cooperation.

Notice that pronouncements not only "establish" the speaker as the authority but also put the listener into a childlike role where he or she must be told what to do and how to do it. The common results of communication by pronouncement are resentment, defensiveness, and a general breakdown in meaningful and equal interaction.

Talking Up

An equally difficult type of communication to deal with is the communication that always approaches you as if you have the answer, as if you are the authority. As anyone who has been in this position knows (teachers are often put into this position), it is tiresome and it is difficult. You have to be at your best at all times.

Sometimes the individual talks upward in an attempt to manipulate you, to flatter you so that you will treat what is to be said kindly. In many instances, these people begin their communications with what are called disqualifiers: "I'm not sure of this but . . ." or "I'm probably wrong, but I was wondering . . ." or "You know

Giving directions to a subordinate, which in organizational communication is called "downward communication," is not comparable to talking down to another where we belittle or act condescendingly toward the person. Talking down impedes effective interpersonal communication, encourages defensiveness, and maximizes rather than minimizes interpersonal differences.

this better than I do, but would it be possible to . . . ?'' These disqualifiers appear to put the speaker one down and the listener one up. At times these disqualifiers are genuine expressions of doubt and uncertainty, in which case there is no problem. At other times, however, they are just verbal manipulations to throw the other person off guard or to create an impression of the individual as totally without power. At still other times they are reflections of an inferiority complex that manifests itself in constant attempts to put oneself down.

The Principle of Equality

Both downward and upward talk, when used unfairly to intimidate or to manipulate, create problems for all involved. Although there are a number of ways of dealing with these attempts, perhaps the most helpful is the principle of equality. As a receiver of messages that talk down to us or attempt to strip us of any power, we need to recognize that all parties in the communication act are equal in the sense that each person's communications are worthwhile and each person has something to contribute. Some of you may be using these power plays and manipulations without even being aware that you have been doing so (hopefully, only until now). Perhaps keeping the principle of equality in mind will lessen the likelihood of your doing this in the future. As a receiver, recognize your own responsibility in these situations; when you allow people to interrupt you or to treat your communications as of lesser importance, you are in effect encouraging and reinforcing this behavior. Demand communication equality.

LYING

According to the *Random House Dictionary,* a lie is ''a false statement made with deliberate intent to deceive; a falsehood; something intended or serving to convey a false impression.'' As these definitions make clear, lying may be both overt and covert. Although usually involving overt statements, lying may also be committed by omission. When we omit something relevant, leading others to draw incorrect inferences, we are lying just as surely as if we had stated an untruth. Most of us can appreciate this by recalling when we were very young and our parents, suspicious for various reasons about what went on last night, asked us what happened. Many of us probably recited all the innocent things and conveniently omitted what our parents were really asking us. We were lying, and we knew it.

Similarly, although most lies are verbal, some are nonverbal, and most seem to involve at least some nonverbal elements. The innocent facial expression—despite the commission of some punishable act—and the ''knowing'' nod instead of the honest expression of ignorance are common examples of nonverbal lying.

Lies may range from the ''white'' lie, ''stretching'' the truth, to the big lie, formulating falsehoods that are so enormous that everyone comes to believe they are true.

Why We Lie

There are probably as many reasons for lying as there are lies; each situation is different, and each seems to be governed by a different reason or set of reasons. But if we boiled it down, we would probably find that people lie for two main reasons: to gain some reward or to avoid some punishment. Carl Camden, Michael Motley, and Ann Wilson, in their study of white lies in interpersonal communication, have identified four major reward categories that seem to motivate lying behavior:

1. *Basic needs:* lies told to gain or retain objects that fulfill basic needs, for example, money or various material possessions
2. *Affiliation:* lies told to increase desired affiliations or decrease undesired affiliations, for example, lies told to prolong desirable social interactions, to avoid interpersonal conflicts, to avoid granting some request, to avoid prolonged interaction; also, lies told to gain or maintain conservational control during interpersonal interaction, for example, lies told to avoid certain self-disclosures or to manipulate the conversation in a desired direction
3. *Self-esteem:* lies told to protect or increase the self-esteem of oneself, the person with whom one is interacting, or some third party, for example, lies told to increase one's perceived competence, taste, or social desirability
4. *Self-gratification:* lies told to achieve some personal satisfaction, for example, lies told for the sake of humor or to exaggerate for some desired effect

Very likely an in-depth analysis of the avoidance of punishment would yield categories similar to those identified for gaining rewards. That is, we probably lie *to avoid* such punishments as having our basic needs taken away (losing money, for example), decreasing desired affiliations and increasing undesirable affiliations, decreasing self-esteem, and losing or decreasing personal satisfaction.

Generally, people lie in order to achieve some reward or avoid some punishment for themselves, although some lies are motivated out of a desire to benefit the person with whom one is interacting or some third party. From an analysis of 322 lies, Camden, Motley, and Wilson found that 75.8 percent benefited the liar, 21.7 percent benefited the other interactant, and 2.5 percent benefited some third party.

The (In)effectiveness of Lying

Lies have both ethical and effectiveness dimensions; both need to be considered. The ethical dimensions concerns what is right and what is wrong. Lying is unethical simply because each person has a right to base his or her choices on the best information available. By lying we withhold at least part of that information and contribute to decisions based on incorrect assumptions, falsehoods, and the like. (See Unit 5 for more on the ethical dimension of lying.)

The effectiveness dimension concerns whether the lie succeeds or fails in gaining the reward or avoiding the punishment. Many lies are effective; people have risen to the top of their professions and have amassed fortunes built on lies and deceit. There can be little doubt that in many instances lying works. Yet the problems and disadvantages of lying should, nevertheless, be considered.

As already noted, communication messages are sent and received as packages. Lies are no exception. But it is often difficult to lie nonverbally with any degree of conviction. Often our lies are betrayed nonverbally. It is far easier to lie with our mouths than with our faces and bodies. And when the contradiction is observed, it is the nonverbal that is generally believed. The end result is that we have lied to no avail. Our reputation may suffer without our having achieved the reward or avoided the punishment. Perhaps the main disadvantage of lying is that it influences who we are and what we think of ourselves. When we have the internalized belief that lying is wrong and lie anyway, we create a psychological imbalance and an intrapersonal conflict, neither of which is healthy. We humans seem to be designed to function as a consistent whole, with thinking and behavior echoing each other. When we believe one thing and do something else, we develop internal conflicts.

One has to expend a considerable amount of energy to maintain a lie. As F. M. Knowles wrote in *A Cheerful Year Book,* "There is nothing so pathetic as a forgetful liar." The more people we lie to, and the more complex the lie, the more energy we have to devote to keeping things straight to preserve that lie. Expending this energy leaves us with that much less for other matters. This is similar to the case of self-disclosure; the more secrets we keep, the more energy we must exert to maintain those secrets.

Perhaps the most obvious disadvantage is that there will be social disapproval when the lie is discovered. Although the vast majority of people lie at some times and on some issues, the vast majority dislike lying and condemn it. Consequently, when our lie is discovered, we incur social disapproval, which may range from mild disapproval to total ostracism from the group or organization.

The upshot of all this is that the liar's communication effectiveness is drastically impaired. "The principle difference between a cat and a lie," observed Mark Twain, "is that a cat has only nine lives." An individual known to have lied or to be a liar is seldom believed, even when telling the truth. We not only disbelieve the information that this individual might wish to communicate, but we give no persuasive force to his or her arguments, frequently discounting them as lies. But even more important, it seems, is that one's relational messages and relational interactions generally become less meaningful. The most important messages an individual can communicate—the "I love you," "I enjoy being with you" messages—are discounted since we can no longer ascertain whether or not they are true.

Although some lies may have short-term benefits, in the long run, even trivial lies—or lies we think are trivial—have an effect on our perceptions and evaluations of an individual. A person who develops a reputation as a liar almost invariably becomes ineffective and virtually powerless in a wide variety of communication encounters.

The Principle of Honesty

Honesty, of course, is never license to hurt another person, to destroy their illusions, or to make fun of their inadequacies and problems. Honesty can only serve effectively as a means for relating more closely, for exchanging feelings, for sharing, for responding to the deeper levels of communication. When viewed in this way, there is little chance that honesty will be confused with forcing others to see what they may not wish to see or what they may not be ready to see.

EXCLUDING TALK

One of the most annoying and destructive verbal habits is the use of in-group talk in the presence of someone who is not a member of the in-group. When doctors get together and discuss medicine, there is no problem. But when one of their number is not a doctor, the doctors often fail to adjust to this new person. Instead, they continue with discussions of prescriptions, symptoms, medication, and all the in-group talk that could interest only another doctor. Many professionals do the same thing; teachers talk teaching, lawyers talk lawyering, and so on. In-grouping makes for pretty boring conversation, even among in-group members. But when nonmembers are involved, it makes for communication that is both ineffective and insulting.

A variant of this habit occurs when a group of people, most of whom belong to the same national group, get together and use their national language, sometimes just isolated words, sometimes sentences, sometimes even entire conversations in a language totally foreign to some of the members. This is not merely a question of understandability. The use of these terms in the presence of a nonmember emphasizes that person's status as an outsider. In almost every instance, the foreign term could be easily translated. The use of the foreign expression does not aid communication; it serves no other purpose than to mark the in-group members as united and the other member as an outsider.

165

Unit 12: Seven
Pitfalls and
Principles of
Language and
Verbal Interaction

In its more exaggerated form, in-grouping can be seen in children's play behavior when several children have a secret and refuse to tell one of their number what it is. The ''we know something you don't know'' type of behavior of children, it seems, is best left in the sandbox.

The Principle of Inclusion

Instead of trying to emphasize the exclusion of one or more members, consider the principle of inclusion. Regardless of the type of communication situation we are in, everyone needs to be included in the interaction. Even if job-related issues have to be discussed in the presence of a nonmember, that person can be included in a variety of ways, for example by seeking a nonmember's perspective or drawing an analogy with that person's field.

Another way to practice inclusion is to fill in relevant details discussed by the group for those who may be unaware. For example, when in a group and people or places or events are referred to, briefly identify these for those to whom these people or events may be unfamiliar. Brief parenthetical identifying phrases are usually sufficient: ''But Margo—she's Jeff's youngest daughter—loved San Francisco State.''

When someone asks a question or makes a comment requiring some response, be sure to respond in some way. Even if you are talking, attending to someone else, or otherwise engaged, respond in some way to indicate your acknowledgment of the comment—verbally, if possible, or nonverbally with a nod or smile, for example.

Practicing inclusion is so easy that I am amazed when I see it violated so blatantly and so often. When inclusion is practiced, everyone gains a great deal more satisfaction from the interaction.

TALKING ABOUT SELF OR OTHERS

Many people—some of our friends and acquaintances are surely among them—act and talk as if they were the center of the universe. They talk constantly about themselves—about their jobs, their accomplishments, their plans, their families, their love lives, their problems, their successes, and sometimes even their failures. Rarely do they ask how we are, what we think (except perhaps when it is about them), or what our plans are.

Other people go to the other extreme and never talk about themselves. These are the underdisclosers we discussed in Units 7 and 8, the people who want to learn everything about you but are not willing to share themselves. They do not want to reveal anything about themselves that might make them vulnerable. As a result, we go away from the interaction with the feeling that they either did not like us very much or did not trust us. Otherwise, we feel, they would have revealed something of themselves.

The Principle of Balance

Admittedly, it is not easy to steer a comfortable course between too much and too little self-talk. And there are certainly times when we just cannot stop talking about a new job or new romantic partner. But under most circumstances we should strive for interactions governed by the principle of balance—some self-talk, some other-talk, never all one or the other. Communication is a two-way process; each person needs to function as source and as receiver; each person should have a chance to function as subject. Balanced communication interactions are more satisfying and more interesting. We all get bored with too much about the other person, and, let's face it, the others get bored with too much about us. The principle of balance is a guide to protect both us and others.

GOSSIPING

There can be no doubt that we spend a great deal of time in gossiping. According to the *Random House Dictionary, gossip* is defined as "idle talk or rumor, esp. about the personal or private affairs of others." A *gossiper,* then, is a person who engages in this idle talk, and a *gossipmonger* is one who is particularly addicted to this type of interpersonal interchange.

Gossip is an inevitable part of our daily interactions, and to advise anyone to refrain from gossiping would be absurd—no one would listen, and even if people did listen, it would eliminate one of the most frequently employed and enjoyed forms of communication. Clearly, we are not going to stop talking about the personal and private affairs of others. And, let us be equally clear, others are not going to stop talking about our personal and private affairs. I doubt that many of us would actually want others to do so; it would be testimony that our lives were too dull for gossip and that our friends and associates were indifferent to our feelings, thoughts, and behaviors.

Nevertheless, gossip does create serious problems when not managed correctly or fairly, and it is to this management that our attention should be directed. When we tell someone something about our feelings about some third party, we normally expect that the conversation will be held in confidence; we do not expect this to be relayed to others, especially not to the individual talked about. If we wanted it relayed, we probably would have done so ourselves. When such a conversation is relayed without our knowledge or approval, we feel, and rightly so, that our confidence has been betrayed. Consider the following fairly typical incident. You're talking with a friend and mention that a mutual friend, Pat, should really devote more attention to dressing properly. You might further continue to note that you would like to invite Pat to your home to meet your parents but the constant use of vulgar language might embarrass your parents and make the evening difficult. Surely this is not a savage attack on Pat and may even have been said with a certain degree of kindness. But consider what happens when our "friend" relays that you said that Pat doesn't know how to dress and is embarrassing because Pat has such a filthy mouth. The effect of such an exchange is to create hostility toward all—toward you for making the original observations and to the person who repeated them. The person talked about is probably going to act in a less friendly manner or perhaps respond in kind by repeating personal conversations to others. The net result is that the entire situation snowballs and what may have been an innocent remark becomes the cause of a friendship breakdown.

Quite often the person who repeats such remarks is, perhaps subconsciously, seeking to create friction between the two individuals. And this motivation is usually recognized, sooner or later, by all parties involved.

To claim, as some people do, that they did not realize you didn't want anything repeated is absurd. It is usually obvious from the context what should and what should not be held in confidence. We have little trouble in deciding when something is said in confidence, and it does not seem unreasonable to expect others to be equally discerning.

Gossip and Ethics

Gossip also has an ethical dimension. In some instances gossip is immoral. Sissela Bok, in *Secrets,* identifies three kinds of gossip that she considers unethical. First, it is unethical to reveal information that you have promised to keep secret. When we promise to keep something confidential, we should do so. In situations where that is impossible (Bok offers the example of the teenager who confides a suicide plan), the information should be revealed only to those required to know it and not to the world at large.

Second, gossip is unethical when we know it to be false and nevertheless pass it on. When we attempt to deceive our listeners by spreading gossip we know to be false, our communications are unethical.

Third, gossip is unethical when it is invasive, when it invades the privacy that everyone has a right to. More specifically, invasive gossip is unethical when it concerns matters that are properly considered private and when the gossip can hurt the individual involved.

Bok does not argue that these conditions are easy to identify in any given instance of gossip. But, they do provide us with excellent starting points for asking ourselves, "Is this talk about another person ethical?"

The Principle of Confidentiality

I think the principle of confidentiality is a good one to begin with: Keep confidential all private conversations about third parties. Messages that begin with "He said . . ." or "She thinks that you . . ." should be automatically suspect as potential violators of the principle of confidentiality. Remember too the principle of irreversibility—we cannot take messages back; once we say something, we cannot uncommunicate it.

CRITICIZING AND PRAISING

Throughout our communication experiences we are expected to criticize, to evaluate, and to otherwise render some kind of judgment. Especially in a helping profession like teaching, nursing, or counseling, criticism becomes an important and frequently used skill. In short, criticism is a most useful and important part of our interactions and our communications generally. The language turnoff develops when criticism is used outside of its helping function, when it is used inappropriately, or when it is used to excess. We need to develop a facility for detecting when a person we are interacting with is asking for our criticism and when that person is simply asking for a compliment. Thus when a friend asks how you like the new apartment, he or she may be searching for a compliment and not really be interested in your itemizing all the things wrong with it. Often, too, we use such opportunities to hurt other people, sometimes even people we care for or love.

Sometimes the desire to be liked (or perhaps the need to be appreciated) is so strong that we go to the other extreme and paint everything with praise. I'm sure you know people who do this. The most average jacket, the most ordinary thought, the most common meal are given extraordinary praise, way beyond their merits.

The overly critical and the overly complimentary soon find that their comments are no longer responded to with concern or interest.

The Principle of Honest Appraisal

As an alternative consider the principle of honest appraisal. Tell the truth. But note that there is an art to truth telling, just as there is an art to all other forms of communication effectiveness. First, distinguish between instances where an honest appraisal or evaluation is asked for and one where the individual is in need of a compliment. Respond to the appropriate level of meaning. Second, if an honest appraisal is desired and if your honest appraisal is a negative one, give some consideration to how you should phrase your criticism. Begin positively and proceed gently and always with a concern for the other person and for your relationship.

OFFENDING TALK

No group is immune to being offended in language. Jokes and put-downs abound for just about every national, racial, religious, age, and sexual group. We are all victims in one way or another.

Perhaps the most obvious instances are verbal attacks on a person's race. The derogatory terms for the various races serve little purpose other than to offend certain people. Similarly, using the popular stereotypes for women and at the same time not according women equality in language does nothing but offend. To imply in our verbalizations that all doctors are men (by automatically referring to "a doctor" as "he" or by using such qualifiers as "woman doctor") or that all secretaries are women merely perpetuates the stereotypes and makes it more difficult for men and women to interact as equals. Even though women do not yet enjoy equal status in many fields, it is becoming fashionable to verbalize a certain equality, and that is a step in the right direction.

Public criticism against women, as well as against many other groups, is often fiercely resisted and refuted by the general society. In some cases, legal action is taken against the offending individuals. Lesbians and gay men, on the other hand, are still criticized without any serious rebuttal. Thus, Eddie Murphy may do an entire routine satirizing lesbians and gay men without any apparent repercussions, and a nationally known theatre critic, at least as quoted in the *Daily News* (March 11, 1985), is "allowed" to say, "Homosexuals in the theatre. My God, I can't wait until AIDS gets all of them!" without any apparent repercussions. And so, while we have come a long way in eliminating offending talk, there is still more to accomplish.

But, the fact that offenses against women or blacks or Hispanics, for example, are dealt with harshly by the system and that offenses against lesbians and gay men are not, should not lead us to assume that other minority groups are, therefore, dealt with fairly and equally. Unfortunately, public censure of discrimination often tells us little of people's private feelings and attitudes, as well as of their intrapersonal and interpersonal messages. Observe that despite a public display of equality, women and blacks still earn less than their white male counterparts and that some lesbians and gay men still do not enjoy freedom from discrimination in employment and in housing.

The Principle of Fairness

As an antidote to offensive talk, try the simple principle of fairness. Treat each person as you would want to be treated—an old rule but a badly neglected one. A good guide to follow might be to imagine that the person whose group you might disparage is in a position to offer you just the job you have been looking for at just the right salary. With that in mind, it might be a little more difficult to use language that others might find offensive or degrading.

These seven principles will not correct all verbal message problems; but when conscientiously applied, they should go a long way in reducing the frequency of some annoying and destructive habits and in making verbal interaction more pleasant and more productive.

Summary: Contents in Brief

Avoid These Patterns	Practice These Principles
1. Talking down and up	The principle of equality: talk across; demand communication equality
2. Lying	The principle of honesty: tell the truth as you know it

Summary: Contents in Brief (continued)

Avoid These Patterns	Practice These Principles
3. Excluding others; in-group talk	The principle of inclusion: include all members present in the interaction
4. Excessive self-talk; excessive other-talk	The principle of balance: talk about yourself and about the other in balance
5. Gossip	The principle of confidentiality: keep confidential what others have revealed to you about others
6. Excessive criticism; undeserved praise	The principle of honest appraisal: say what you feel, but gently
7. Offending talk	The principle of fairness: use language that neither offends nor demeans

Sources

There are a number of excellent sources for eliminating problems in communication. Edmond G. Addeo and Robert E. Burger, *Egospeak: Why No One Listens to You* (New York: Bantam, 1973) covers a wide variety of verbal turnoffs. J. Dan Rothwell, *Telling It Like It Isn't* (Englewood Cliffs, N.J.: Prentice-Hall [Spectrum], 1982) likewise covers a variety of barriers and their corrections. Theodore Isaac Rubin, *One to One: Understanding Personal Relationships* (New York: Viking Press, 1983) discusses the relationship process and offers considerable insight into language and effective communication. On pronouncements see John A. Sanford, *Between People* (New York: Paulist Press, 1982). On lying see Sissela Bok, *Lying: Moral Choice in Public and Private Life* (New York: Pantheon Books, 1978) and *Secrets* (New York: Vintage, 1983). The analysis of rewards for lying is taken from Carl Camden, Michael T. Motley, and Ann Wilson, *White Lies in Interpersonal Communication: A Taxonomy and (Preliminary) Investigation of Social Motivations*, paper delivered at the International Communication Association convention (Dallas, Texas, 1983). The insightful and comprehensive *Excuses: Masquerades in Search of Grace* by C. R. Snyder, Raymond L. Higgins, and Rita J. Stucky (New York: Wiley/Interscience, 1983) contains much that is relevant to this unit. On lying and deception clues see Paul Ekman, *Telling Lies: Clues to Deceit in the Marketplace, Politics, and Marriage* (New York: Norton, 1985).

Barriers to Verbal Interaction

OBJECTIVES

Upon completion of this unit, you should be able to:

1. explain the concept of *barriers* to interpersonal communication
2. define *polarization* and identify instances of polarization in the media and in your own communications
3. define *intensional orientation* and *extensional orientation* and identify instances of intensional orientation in the media and in your own communications
4. define *fact-inference confusion* and identify instances of fact-inference confusion in the media and in your own communications
5. explain the concept of *pragmatic implication* and its relationship to fact-inference confusion
6. define *allness* and identify instances of allness in the media and in your own communications
7. define *static evaluation* and identify instances of static evaluation in the media and in your own communications
8. define *indiscrimination* and identify instances of indiscrimination in the media and in your own communications

Throughout this book I have stressed the complexity of interpersonal communication. It is also quite fragile—in part because of its complexity and in part because it is a human process, subject to all the failings and problems of fallible people. Chief among these problems are what are generally called *barriers*. In using this term I do not mean to imply that interpersonal communication is a mechanical process and that somewhere along the communication chain of events, barriers, like roadblocks, are erected that stop or hinder the flow. The alternative terms *breakdown* and *obstacle* seem to suffer from the same misleading mechanistic connotations.

I use the term *barriers*, then, not to convey the idea that communicators function as machines or that communication is a mechanical process, but rather to convey that effective and meaningful interpersonal communication—the kind that we have been talking about throughout this book—may lose some of its effectiveness and meaningfulness when certain factors are present, or rather when communicators think or behave in certain ways. Recognize that these barriers are of human origin and development; it is the communicators who, for one reason or another, create and maintain these barriers.

All six barriers discussed here—polarization, intensional orientation, fact-inference confusion, allness, static evaluation, and indiscrimination—are ways in which our verbal messages describe the world in illogical, distorted, or unscientific ways. An analogy can be made between verbal messages and geographic maps. Maps that accurately describe the world assist the traveler in getting from one place to another. To the extent that such maps inaccurately describe the world, they hinder the traveler in getting from one place to another. Our verbal messages are like maps. To the extent that they accurately represent reality, they are helpful and aid effective and meaningful interpersonal communication. To the extent that they distort reality, they are hindrances and prevent effective and meaningful interpersonal communication.

An examination of these barriers will enable us (1) to detect distortions when they are present in our own or in others' communications and (2) to improve our verbal message making so that these distortions will be kept to a minimum or even eliminated entirely. Interpersonal communication will be enhanced to the degree that we achieve either or both of these purposes.

POLARIZATION

Polarization refers to the tendency to look at the world and to describe it in terms of extremes—good or bad, positive or negative, healthy or sick, intelligent or stupid, rich or poor, and so on. It is often referred to as the fallacy of "either–or" or "black and white." Although it is true that magnetic poles may be described as positive or negative and that certain people are extremely rich while others are extremely poor, the vast majority of cases are clearly in the middle, between the two extremes. Most people exist somewhere between the extremes of good and bad, healthy or sick, intelligent or stupid, rich or poor. Yet there seems to be a strong tendency to view only the extremes and to categorize people, objects, and events in terms of these polar opposites.

This tendency may be easily illustrated by attempting to fill in the polar opposites for the following words:

tall	→	_____
heavy	→	_____
strong	→	_____
happy	→	_____
legal	→	_____

Filling in these opposites should have been relatively easy and quick. The words should also have been fairly short. Further, if a number of people supplied opposites, we would find a high degree of agreement among them.

Now attempt to fill in the middle positions with words meaning, for example, "midway between tall and short," "midway between heavy and light," and so on. These midway responses (compared to the opposites) were probably more difficult to think of and took more time. The words should also have been fairly long or phrases of two, three, four, or more words. Further, we would probably find rather low agreement among different people completing this same task.

It might be helpful to visualize the familiar bell-shaped curve. Few items exist at either of the two extremes, but as we move closer to the center, more and more items are included. This is true of any random sample. If we selected 100 people at random, we would find that their intelligence, height, weight, income, age, health, and so on would, if plotted, fall into a bell-shaped or "normal" distribution. Yet our tendency seems to be to concentrate on the extremes, the ends of this curve, and ignore the middle, which contains the vast majority of cases.

It is legitimate to phrase certain statements in terms of two values. For example, this thing that you are holding is either a book or it is not. Clearly the classes of book and not-book include all possibilities. There is no problem with this kind of statement. Similarly, we may say that a student will either pass this course or will not pass it, as these two categories include all the possibilities.

We create problems, however, when we use this basic form in situations in which it is inappropriate; for example, "The politician is either for us or against us." Note that these two possibilities do not include all possibilities; the politician may be for us in some things and against us in other things, or may be neutral. During the Vietnam War there was a tendency to categorize people as either hawk or dove, but clearly there were many people who were neither and many who were probably both—hawks on certain issues and doves on others.

We need to beware of implying and believing that two extreme classes include all possible classes—that an individual must be a hawk or a dove and that there are no other alternatives. "Life is either a daring adventure or nothing," said Helen Keller. But for most people it is neither a daring adventure nor nothing but rather something somewhere between these two extremes.

INTENSIONAL ORIENTATION

Intensional orientation refers to the tendency to view people, objects, and events in terms of the way in which they are talked about or labeled rather than in terms of the way in which they actually exist and operate. *Extensional orientation*, on the other hand, is the tendency to look first at the actual people, objects, and events and only then at their labels. It is the tendency to be guided by what we see happening rather than by the label used for what is happening.

Intensional orientation is seen when we act as if the words and labels were more important than the things they represent—as if the map were more important than the territory. In its extreme form, intensional orientation is seen in the person who is afraid of dogs and begins to sweat when shown a picture of a dog or when hearing people talk about dogs. Here the person is responding to the labels as if they were the actual thing.

Intensional orientation may be seen clearly in the results of the numerous studies on prestige suggestion. Basically, these studies demonstrate that we are influenced more when we assume that the message comes from a prestigious personality than when it comes from an average individual. Such studies have shown that if given a painting, we will evaluate it highly if we think it was painted by a famous artist, but we will give it a low evaluation if we think it was produced by a little-known artist. Other studies have focused on our agreement with dogmatic statements, our judgments on literary merit, our perceptions of musical ability, and so on. In all of these studies, the influencing factor was not the message itself—the painting, the literature, the music—but the name attached to it. Advertisers, of course, have long known the value of this type of appeal and have capitalized on it quite profitably.

One of the most ingenious examples of intensional orientation requires that you role-play for a minute. Picture yourself seated with a packet of photographs before you. Each of the photographs is of a person you have never seen. You are asked to scratch out the eyes in each photograph. You are further told that this is simply an experiment and that the individuals whose pictures you have will not be aware of anything that has transpired here. As you are scratching out the eyes, you come upon a photograph of your mother. What do you do? Are you able to scratch out the eyes as you have done with the pictures of the strangers, or have you somehow lost your ability to scratch out eyes? If, as with many others, you are unable to scratch out the eyes, you are responding intensionally. You are, in effect, responding to the map (in this case the picture) as if it were the territory (your mother).

In a recent study, Philip Goldberg claimed that women were prejudiced against women. Specifically, he found that women felt that articles written by men were more authoritative and more valuable than identical articles with feminine by-lines. This result was found for messages in "traditionally masculine fields," such as law and city planning, as well as in "traditionally feminine fields," such as elementary school teaching and dietetics. Again this is a clear example of intensional orientation, of our tendency to look at the label (in this case the by-line) and to evaluate the territory (in this case the actual article) only through the label.

An experiment conducted with stutterers further illustrates the notion of intensional orientation. Research has found that stutterers stutter more when talking with persons in authority than with subordinates. Stutterers stutter very little when talking with children or when addressing animals, for example, but when it comes to teachers or employers, they stutter a great deal. Another finding on stuttering concerns adaptation. This refers to the fact that as a stutterer reads a particular passage, he or she will stutter less and less on each successive reading. In this experiment the researcher obtained from the stutterers the names of the persons to whom they had most difficulty speaking. At a later date the researchers had each stutterer read a passage five times. As predicted, the stuttering decreased on each reading to the point where it was almost entirely absent on the fifth reading. Before the sixth reading the experimenter placed in front of the stutterer a photograph of the person the stutterer had named as the most difficult to speak to. On the sixth reading the stuttering increased approximately to the level during the first reading of the passage. Again, the individual was responding to the photograph—the label or the map—as if it were the actual thing.

Labels are certainly helpful guides, but they are not the things themselves and should not be confused with the things for which they are only symbols.

FACT–INFERENCE CONFUSION

We can make statements about the world that we observe, and we can make statements about what we have not observed. In form or structure these statements are similar and could not be distinguished from each other by any grammatical analysis. For example, we can say, "She is wearing a blue jacket" as well as "He is harboring an illogical hatred." If we diagramed these sentences, they would yield identical structures, and yet we know quite clearly that they are very different types of statements. In the first one we can observe the jacket and the blue color. But how do we observe "illogical hatred"? Obviously, this is not a descriptive statement but an inferential statement. It is a statement that we make not solely on the basis of what we observe but on the basis of what we observe plus our own conclusions.

There is no problem with making inferential statements; we must make them if we are to talk about much that is meaningful to us. The problem arises when we act as if those inferential statements were factual statements.

Consider, for example, the following anecdote: A woman went for a walk one day and met her friend, whom she had not seen or heard from or heard of in ten years. After an exchange of greetings, the woman said, "Is this your little boy?" and her friend replied, "Yes, I got married about 6 years ago." The woman then asked the child, "What is your name?" and the little boy replied, "Same as my father's." "Oh," said the woman, "then it must be Peter."

The question, of course, is how did the woman know the boy's father's name if she had not seen or heard from or heard of her friend in the last ten years? The answer, of course, is obvious. But it is obvious only after we recognize that in reading this short passage we have, quite unaware, made an inference that is preventing us from answering. We have inferred that the woman's friend is a woman. Actually, the friend is a man named Peter.

Perhaps the classic example of this type of fact-inference confusion concerns the case of the "empty" gun that unfortunately proves to be loaded. With amazing frequency we find in the newspapers examples of people being so sure that the guns are empty that they point them at another individual and fire. Many times, of course, they are empty. But, unfortunately, many times they are not. Here one makes an inference (that the gun is empty) but acts on the inference as if it were a fact and fires the gun.

Pragmatic Implications

A related communication barrier is raised by what linguistic philosophers call *pragmatic implication*. Consider the following: We hear that our biology teacher has been replaced for next year. Further, we know that our biology class has not been very exciting and that many students complained about the poor instruction. On the basis of this knowledge, we draw a pragmatic implication. Unlike a logical implication, which must be true, a pragmatic implication is an inference that is probably but not necessarily true. In this example we infer that the teacher was fired for ineffective teaching. Note that here we have two pragmatic implications: (1) The teacher was fired; (2) the reason for the firing was ineffective teaching. Again, there is nothing wrong with drawing pragmatic implications; we all do it. The problem is created, in a way, by our memory systems. After making such pragmatic implications, we forget that they are in fact inferences and not observed facts. We remember these implications or inferences just as we remember the fact that the biology teacher has been replaced.

This type of situation happens every day. We see two friends in a quiet romantic restaurant. We draw the pragmatic implication that they are dating or that they are somehow romantically involved. We forget that this is only an implication and remember it as observed fact. When, on subsequent occasions, we see these same friends with different partners, the plot thickens and we begin to draw pragmatic implications on top of pragmatic implications and, again, fail to distinguish between what was actually observed fact and what was inference. In the process we move further and further away from facts and observations without ever realizing that we are doing so.

Distinguishing Between Facts and Inferences

Some of the essential differences between factual and inferential statements are summarized in Table 13.1. Distinguishing between these two types of statements does not imply that one type is better than the other. We need both types of statements; both are useful, both important. The problem arises when we treat one type of statement as if it were the other. Specifically, the problem arises when we treat an inferential statement as if it were a factual statement.

Inferential statements (and pragmatic implications) need to be accompanied by tentativeness. We need to recognize that such statements may prove to be wrong, and we should be aware of that possibility. Inferential statements should leave open the possibility of other alternatives. If, for example, we treat the statements ''Pat and Chris are dating'' or ''Higgins was fired'' as factual, we eliminate the possibility of other alternatives. When making inferential statements, we should be psychologically prepared to be proved wrong. This requires a great deal of effort, but it is probably effort well spent. If we are psychologically prepared to be proved wrong, we will be less hurt if and when we are shown to be incorrect.

ALLNESS

The world is infinitely complex, and because of this we can never say all there is to say about anything—at least not logically. This is particularly true in dealing with people. We may *think* we know all there is to know about individuals or about why they did what they did, yet clearly we do not know all. We can never know all the reasons we ourselves do something, yet we often think that we know all the reasons why our parents or our friends or our enemies did something. And because we are so convinced that we know all the reasons, we are quick to judge and evaluate the actions of others with great confidence that what we are doing is justified.

TABLE 13.1: Differences Between Factual and Inferential Statements

Factual Statements	Inferential Statements
1. may be made only after observation	1. may be made at any time
2. are limited to what has been observed	2. go beyond what has been observed
3. may be made only by the observer	3. may be made by anyone
4. may only be about the past or the present	4. may be about any time—past, present, or future
5. approach certainty	5. involve varying degrees of probability
6. are subject to verifiable standards	6. are not subject to verifiable standards

We may, for example, be assigned a textbook to read and because previous texts have been dull and perhaps the first chapter is dull, we infer that all the rest of the book will likewise be dull. Of course, it often turns out that the rest of the book is even worse than the beginning. Yet it could be that the rest of the book would have proved exciting had it been read with an open mind. The problem here is that we run the risk of defining an entire text (on the basis of previous texts or a single chapter) in such a way as to preclude any other possibilities. If we tell ourselves that the book is dull, it probably will seem dull. If we say a course will be useless ("all required courses are useless"), it will be extremely difficult for the instructor to make the course anything but what we have defined it to be. Only occasionally do we allow ourselves to be proved wrong; for the most part we resist rather fiercely.

The parable of the six blind men and the elephant is an excellent example of an allness orientation and its attendant problems. You may recall from elementary school the poem by John Saxe that concerns six blind men of Indostan who came to examine an elephant, an animal they had only heard about. The first blind man touched the elephant's side and concluded that the elephant was like a wall. The second felt the tusk and said the elephant must be like a spear. The third held the trunk and concluded that the elephant was much like a snake. The fourth touched the knee and knew the elephant was like a tree. The fifth felt the ear and said the elephant was like a fan. And the sixth grabbed the tail and concluded that the elephant was like a rope. Each of these learned men reached his own conclusion regarding what the elephant was really like. Each argued that he was correct and that the others were wrong. Each, of course, was correct; but at the same time, each was wrong. The point this poem illustrates is that we are all in the position of the six blind men. We never see all of something; we never experience anything fully. We see part of an object, an event, a person—and on that limited basis conclude what the whole is like. This procedure is a universal one; we have to do this, since it is impossible to observe everything. Yet we must recognize that when we make judgments of the whole based on only a part, we are actually making inferences that can later be proved wrong. If we assume that we know all of anything, we fall into the pattern of misevaluation called *allness*.

Disraeli once said that "to be conscious that you are ignorant is a great step toward knowledge." That observation is an excellent example of a nonallness attitude. If we recognize that there is more to learn, more to see, more to hear, we leave ourselves open to this additional information and are better prepared to assimilate it into our existing structures.

Allness and Conflict

In conflict situations, negative allness statements—especially those containing *always* and *never*—are particularly troublesome. Allness statements ("You *always* criticize me in front of your friends," "You *never* do what I want," "You're *always* nagging," "You *never* want to visit my family") encourage defensiveness and are more in the nature of attacks than attempts to pinpoint and resolve problems.

It would be just as easy and much more constructive to say, for example, "At Pat's party, you talked about my being a terrible cook. That really embarrassed me. I don't know if you realized it, but I felt hurt. If you want to criticize something, I think it should be kept private and said when we're alone." Expressed in this way, there is no attack, no encouragement of defensiveness. Instead, there is a clear and descriptive statement of the problem and a proposed solution that can be discussed reasonably.

ETC.

A useful device to help us remember our nonallness orientation is to end each statement, verbally or mentally, with an *etc.*, a reminder that there is more to learn, more to know, more to say—a reminder that every statement is inevitably incomplete.

STATIC EVALUATION

To understand the concept of static evaluation, try to write down a statement or two that makes no reference to time—that is, we must not be able to tell whether the statement refers to the past, present, or future. Write this statement down before reading on. Next, attempt to date the following quotation. Approximately when was it written?

When in anger, we are most likely to say things for which we may be sorry. In conflict situations, therefore, it is especially important to remember the irreversibility of communication and to withhold negative statements (especially negative allness statements) that we may regret saying later.

Those states are likely to be well administered in which the middle class is large, and larger if possible than both the other classes or at any rate than either singly; for the addition of the middle class turns the scale and prevents either of the extremes from being dominant.

These two brief exercises should illustrate an interesting dimension of the English language. It was probably extremely difficult, if not impossible, for you to produce a sentence that made no reference to time whatsoever. Time, in English, is an obligatory category, which means that all sentences must contain some reference to past, present, or future. Our verb system is constructed in such a way that it is impossible to produce a sentence without including a reference to time in the verb. This is not true in all languages. In dating the quotation, most persons would find themselves missing the actual date by at least a few hundred years. The statement was actually written by Aristotle in his *Politics* approximately 2,300 years ago.

Thus while it is impossible to make statements without reference to the past, present, or future, it is almost impossible to tell when statements were produced. These, of course, are obvious facts about language. Yet their consequences are often not so obvious.

Often when we formulate a verbal statement about an event or a person, that statement has a tendency to remain static and unchanging, while the object or person to whom it originally referred may change enormously. Alfred Korzybski used an interesting illustration in this connection. In a tank we have a large fish and many small fish that are the natural food for the large fish. Given freedom in the tank, the large fish will eat the small fish. After some time we partition the tank, with the large fish on one side and the small fish on the other, divided only by a clear piece of glass. For a considerable time the large fish will attempt to eat the small fish but will fail each time; each time it will knock into the glass partition. After some time it will "learn" that attempting to eat the small fish means difficulty and will no longer go after them. Now, however, we remove the partition, and the small fish swim all around the big fish. But the big fish does not eat them and in fact will die of starvation while its natural food swims all around. The large fish has learned a pattern of behavior, and even though the actual territory has changed, the map remains static.

While we would probably all agree that everything is in a constant state of flux, the relevant question is whether we act as if we know this. Put differently, do we act in accordance with the notion of change, instead of just accepting it intellectually? Do we realize, for example, that just because we have failed at something once, we need not fail again? Do we realize that if someone has done something particularly poorly or particularly well, he or she is also in a constant state of change? Our evaluations of ourselves and of others must keep pace with the rapidly changing real world; otherwise we will be left with attitudes and beliefs about a world that no longer exists.

THE DATE

To guard against static evaluation, date your statements and especially your evaluations. Remember that Pat Smith$_{1984}$ is not Pat Smith$_{1986}$; academic abilities$_{1985}$ are not academic abilities$_{1987}$. T. S. Eliot, in *The Cocktail Party*, said that "what we know of other people is only our memory of the moments during which we knew them. And they have changed since then . . . at every meeting we are meeting a stranger."

INDISCRIMINATION

Nature seems to abhor sameness at least as much as vacuums, for nowhere in the universe can we find identical entities. Everything is unique, unlike everything else.

Our language, however, provides us with common nouns, such as *teacher, student, friend, enemy, war, politician, liberal,* and the like, which lead us to focus on similarities. Such nouns lead us to group together all teachers, all students, all friends, and perhaps divert attention from the uniqueness of each individual, object, and event.

The misevaluation of *indiscrimination,* then, occurs when we focus on classes of individuals or objects or events and fail to see that each is unique, each is different, and each needs to be looked at individually.

This misevaluation is at the heart of the common practice of stereotyping national, racial, and religious groups. A stereotype is a relatively fixed mental picture of some group that is applied to each individual of the group without regard to his or her unique qualities. It is important to note that although stereotypes are usually thought of as negative, they may also be positive. We can, for example, consider certain national groups as lazy or superstitious or mercenary or criminal, but we can also consider them as intelligent, progressive, honest, hardworking, and so on. Regardless of whether such stereotypes are positive or negative, however, the problems they create are the same. They provide us with shortcuts that are most often inappropriate. For example, when we meet an individual, we invariably fail to devote sufficient attention to his or her unique characteristics.

It should be emphasized that there is nothing wrong with classifying. No one would argue that classifying is unhealthy or immoral. It is, on the contrary, an extremely useful method of dealing with any complex matter; it puts order into our thinking. The problem arises not from classification in itself but from our classifying, then applying some evaluative label to that class, and then using that label as an "adequate" map for each individual in the group. Indiscrimination is a denial of another's uniqueness.

THE INDEX

A useful antidote to indiscrimination is the *index,* a verbal or mental subscript that identifies each individual as an individual even though both may be covered by the same label: politician$_1$ is not politician$_2$, teacher$_1$ is not teacher$_2$. The index helps us to discriminate among without discriminating against.

Summary: Contents in Brief

Barrier	Communication Problem	Corrective
Polarization	Tendency to describe the world in terms of extremes or polar opposites	Use middle terms and qualifiers
Intensional orientation	Tendency to view the world in the way it is talked about or labeled.	Respond to things first; look for the labels second
Fact-inference confusion	Tendency to confuse factual and inferential statements and to respond to inferences as if they were facts	Distinguish facts from inferences and respond to inferences as inferences, not as facts
Allness	Tendency to describe the world in extreme terms that imply one knows all or is saying all there is to say	Avoid allness terms; recognize that one can never know all or say all about anything; use *etc.*
Static evaluation	Tendency to describe the world in static terms, denying constant change	Recognize the inevitability of change; date statements
Indiscrimination	Tendency to group unique individuals or items because they are covered by the same term or phrase	Recognize that sameness does not exist; index terms and statements

Sources

The barriers to verbal interaction owe their formulation to the work of the general semanticists, the definitive work of which is Alfred Korzybski, *Science and Sanity: An Introduction to Non-Aristotelian Systems and General Semantics* (Lakeville, Conn.: International Non-Aristotelian Library Publishing Co., 1933). I would especially recommend for beginners John C. Condon, Jr., *Semantics and Communication,* 2d ed. (New York: Macmillan, 1974); William V. Haney, *Communication and Organizational Behavior: Text and Cases,* 3d ed. (Homewood, Ill.: Irwin, 1973); and S. I. Hayakawa, *Language in Thought and Action,* 4th ed. (Orlando, Fla.: Harcourt Brace Jovanovich, 1978). Goldberg's study may be found in "Are Women Prejudiced Against Women?" *Trans-action* 5 (1968):28–30.

Much that appears in this unit appears in more detail in my *General Semantics: Guide and Workbook,* rev. ed. (DeLand, Fla.: Everett/Edwards, 1974). My cassette tape series *General Semantics: Nine Lectures* (DeLand, Fla.: Everett/Edwards, 1971) also covers this material. Perhaps the most useful introduction to the barriers to verbal interaction is J. Dan Rothwell, *Telling It Like It Isn't* (Englewood Cliffs, N.J.: Prentice-Hall [Spectrum], 1982).

Part 3: Skills in Brief

Meaning Interpretation

Assess meaning as a function of the messages sent and the receiver's own nervous system to account for the influence of personality, past experiences, attitudes, and the like on meaning so as to secure a more accurate interpretation of meaning.

Directive Language

Use language to direct the focus of the receiver to increase comprehension and persuasiveness.

Nondirective Language

To encourage open and honest responses and to avoid leading the receiver to feed back what is thought to be wanted, ask questions in a nondirective manner.

Indirect Speech

Use indirect speech (1) to express a desire without insulting or offending anyone, (2) to ask for compliments in a socially acceptable manner, and (3) to disagree without being disagreeable.

Direct Speech

Use direct requests and responses (1) to encourage compromise, (2) to acknowledge responsibility for your own feelings and desires, and (3) to state your own desires honestly so as to encourage honesty, openness, and supportiveness in others.

Self-references

Recognize and respond to the inevitable self-references in the messages of others in order to respond more fully to the meanings communicated.

Sublanguage Confusion

Avoid being impressed or confused by technical sublanguages by learning relevant sublanguage vocabulary and asking questions where meanings are hidden by jargon.

Sublanguage Communication

Use your own sublanguages to facilitate subcultural communication, to identify yourselves to other members, and to ensure communication privacy; avoid sublanguages when inappropriate, for example, when interacting with nonmembers.

Taboo

Avoid taboo expressions in order to avoid negative evaluations by others; substitute more socially acceptable expressions or euphemisms where and when appropriate.

Racist and Sexist Language

Avoid racist and sexist terms so as not to offend or alienate others.

Equal Communication

Talk to others as equals, neither down nor up, to increase interpersonal satisfaction and efficiency.

Truth and Deception

State the truth as you know it with gentleness.

Inclusion

Include all members present in the interaction (both verbally and nonverbally) so as not to exclude and offend or fail to profit from the contributions of others.

Self-talk and Other-talk

Balance talk about yourself with talk about the other; avoid excessive self-talk or extreme avoidance of self-talk to encourage equal sharing and interpersonal satisfaction.

Gossip

Avoid gossip that breaches confidentiality, that is known to be false, and that is unnecessarily invasive.

Confidentiality

Keep confidential the disclosures of others; resist the temptation to reveal others' disclosures.

Praise and Criticism

Say what you feel without excessive and unjustified praising or criticizing.

Language Fairness

Use language fairly; avoid language that offends or demeans.

Polarization

Use middle terms and qualifiers when describing the world; avoid talking in terms of polar opposites (black and white, good and bad) in order to describe reality more accurately.

Intentional Orientation

Respond first to things; avoid responding to labels as if they were things; do not let labels distort your perception of the world.

Pragmatic Implication

Distinguish between pragmatic and logical implications and recognize that our memories often confuse the two. In recalling situations and events, ask yourself if your conclusions are based on pragmatic or logical implications.

Fact–Inference Differentiation

Distinguish facts from inferences; respond to inferences as inferences and not as facts; avoid confusing facts and inferences and responding to inferences as if they were facts.

Allness

End statements with an implicit *etc.* to indicate that more could be known and said; avoid allness terms and statements.

Negative Allness and Conflict

Avoid negative allness terms and statements in conflict situations.

Constant Change

Date your statements to emphasize constant change; avoid the tendency to think of and describe things as static and unchanging.

Indiscrimination

Index your terms and statements to emphasize that each person and event is unique; avoid indiscrimination or treating all individuals the same because they are covered by the same label or term.

Nonverbal Messages

In this fourth part we focus on nonverbal messages. Here we consider the wide variety of nonverbal messages that we send and receive every minute: gestural messages, facial and eye expressions, touching, the closeness with which we stand or sit next to another person, silence, time, and a number of other forms that nonverbal communication may take.

In this focus on nonverbal communication, we consider a variety of questions:

How believable is nonverbal communication? ■ Can we tell if someone is lying? ■ How do the gifts we give communicate? ■ What do our eyes communicate? ■ How accurate are we at judging emotions on the basis of facial expression? ■ Who touches whom where? ■ How do men and women differ in their touching behavior? ■ Do colors communicate? ■ How do we signal ownership of a territory? ■ What messages does silence communicate? ■ Is the "fast talker" really effective? ■ How does time talk? ■ What skills can you master that will enable you to respond more appropriately and more effectively to the nonverbal messages of others? ■ What skills can you master that will enable you to communicate nonverbally more effectively?

UNIT OUTLINE

Universals of Nonverbal Messages

Body Communication

Space Communication

Silence, Paralanguage, and Temporal Communication

Skills in Brief

UNIT 14

Universals of Nonverbal Messages

OBJECTIVES

Upon completion of this unit, you should be able to:

1. identify the goals of studying nonverbal communication
2. explain the principle that nonverbal communication occurs in a context
3. explain the reasons why nonverbal behaviors in an interactional situation always communicate
4. explain the rule-governed nature of nonverbal communication
5. explain why nonverbal communication is purposeful
6. explain the packaged nature of nonverbal behaviors
7. define and give examples of double-bind messages
8. identify the reasons for assuming that nonverbal communication is highly believable
9. identify some of the nonverbal signals that have been observed to accompany lying
10. define *metacommunication*
11. provide at least three examples of the ways in which nonverbal behavior is frequently metacommunicational
12. cite at least three examples of unwritten nonverbal rules of behavior

The gimmick used in selling books or articles on nonverbal communication is the promise that you can learn to decipher what other people are thinking by observing their "body language." The cover of Julius Fast's *Body Language*, for example, shows the picture of a woman sitting in a chair with her arms folded and her legs crossed. Surrounding the woman are such questions as "Does her body say that she's a loose woman?," "Does your body say that you're hung up?," "Does his body say that he's a manipulator?," and so on. Who could resist learning this kind of information? It would be indispensable at parties and social gatherings, and success in one's business and social life would almost be assured.

But, as anyone who has read such works knows, such significant insight is not so easy to attain. Perhaps the primary reason is simply that we do not know enough about nonverbal communication to enable the layperson to make instant and accurate readings of the inner workings of the mind. And yet we have learned a great deal about nonverbal communication, especially in the past decade.

This unit identifies universals pertaining to nonverbal communication. The goal of such a discussion is not to provide the means for personality diagnosis, for dating success, or for determining when someone is bluffing in a poker game, but rather to enable us (1) to understand better our own nonverbal communication system, (2) to understand better the nonverbal systems of others, and (3) to communicate more effectively as sender and receiver of nonverbal messages.

NONVERBAL COMMUNICATION OCCURS IN A CONTEXT

Like verbal communication, nonverbal communication exists in a context, and that context determines to a large extent the meanings of any nonverbal behaviors. The same nonverbal behavior may have a totally different meaning when it occurs in another context. A wink of the eye to an attractive person on a bus means something completely different from a wink of the eye to signify a put-on or a lie. Similarly, the meaning of a given bit of nonverbal behavior depends on the verbal behavior it accompanies or is close to in time. Pounding the fist on the table during a speech in support of a politician means something quite different from that same fist pounding in response to news of a friend's death. Divorced from the context, it is impossible to tell why any given bit of nonverbal behavior may mean. Of course, even if we know the context in detail, we still might not be able to decipher the meaning of the nonverbal behavior. In attempting to understand and analyze nonverbal communication, however, it is essential that full recognition be taken of the context.

NONVERBAL BEHAVIORS ARE NORMALLY PACKAGED

Nonverbal behaviors, whether they involve the hands, the eyes, or the muscle tone of the body, normally occur in "packages" or "clusters," where the various verbal and nonverbal behaviors reinforce each other, a condition referred to as *congruence*.

Nonverbal Packages

All parts of the body normally work together to communicate a particular meaning. We do not express fear with our eyes while the rest of our body relaxes as if sleeping. Rather, the entire body expresses the emotion. We may, for purposes of analysis, focus primarily on the eyes, the facial muscles, or the hand movements, but in everyday communication, these do not occur in isolation from other nonverbal behaviors. In fact, it is physically difficult to express an intense emotion with only one part of the body. Try to express an emotion with your face only. You will probably find that the rest of your body takes on the qualities of that emotion as well.

In this packaged nature of nonverbal communication, then, we find yet another warning against the too-easy reading of nonverbal behaviors. Before the meaning of any bit of nonverbal behavior can be identified or guessed, we need to take into consideration the entire package or cluster of which it is a part, the way in which the cluster is a response to the context, and the role of the specific nonverbal behavior within that cluster. That attractive person winking in your direction may be giving you the come-on; on the other hand, do not too quickly rule out ill-fitting contact lenses.

Without knowing the context, it is difficult to tell what any nonverbal behavior means. We may, for example, cover our face when embarrassed, when horrified, when laughing, when crying, and when playing with a child. Interpreting the meaning of any such nonverbal behavior, then, must take into consideration the entire context in which the behavior occurs as well as the other nonverbal and verbal messages.

It is even more difficult to express widely different or contradictory emotions with different parts of the body. For example, when you are afraid of something and your body tenses up, it becomes very difficult to relax your facial muscles and smile. In fact, it has been argued that even our graphic gestures (handwriting) are correlated with and echo or imitate our habitual body-gesture style. For example, a person whose body is normally curled up and closed, who avoids direct eye contact, and who constantly turns away when addressed seems to evidence similar graphic movements in handwriting; the writing will be small and the letters tightly packed. People who take up more physical space—for example, those who want or need more room between themselves and others than do most people and who literally spread themselves all over—also seem to take up more room with their handwriting. Their signatures, in particular, take up a great deal of space in a manner similar to the signatures of high-status persons, which normally take up more space than those of lower-status persons.

We generally do not pay much attention to the packaged nature of nonverbal communication; it is so expected that it goes unnoticed. But when there is an incongruity—when the weak handshake belies the smile, when the nervous posture belies the focused stare, when the constant preening belies the relaxed whistling or humming—we take notice. Invariably we are led to question the credibility, the sincerity, the honesty of the individual. Research tells us that our instincts serve us well in this type of situation. When nonverbal behaviors contradict each other, there seems good reason to question the believability of the communicator.

Verbal and Nonverbal Packages

Nonverbal communications also evidence this packaged quality with their accompanying verbal messages. When we express anger verbally, our body and face also express anger by tensing, scowling, perhaps assuming a fighting posture. Again, we often fail to notice this because it seems so natural, so expected. But when the nonverbal messages of one's posture or face contradict what one says verbally, we take special notice. For example, a person who says, "I'm so glad to see you," but who avoids direct eye contact and who looks around as if to see who else is present is sending contradictory messages. Contradictory messages (also called "mixed messages" by some writers) are seen frequently in couples (whether newly dating or long married) who say they love each other but who seem to go out of their way to hurt each other nonverbally—for example, by being late for important dates, by dressing in ways the other person dislikes, by flirting with others, by avoiding direct eye contact, or by not touching each other. In the film *The Graduate* there is a particularly interesting example of contradictory messages. Dustin Hoffman (Benjamin Braddock, the graduate) and Anne Bancroft (Mrs. Robinson) are having an affair, which under normal circumstances would indicate a fair degree of intimacy. But Benjamin repeatedly and consistently calls his partner "Mrs. Robinson," which seems to indicate that he was uncomfortable with the relationship, that he felt unequal in the partnership (he was still a boy, while Mrs. Robinson was a mature woman), that she was married, and that he felt the relationship would not progress or develop further.

Double–Bind Messages

A particular type of contradictory message that deserves special mention is the *double-bind* message. Consider the following interpersonal interaction:

Pat: Love me.
Chris: (Makes advances of a loving nature.)
Pat: (Nonverbal tenseness, failure to maintain eye contact, and, in general, nonverbal messages that say, "Don't love me.")
Chris: (Withdraws.)
Pat: See, you don't love me.

Notice the elements involved for an interaction to constitute a double-bind.
Intense Relationship. The two persons interacting must share a relatively intense relationship in which the messages and demands of one and the responses of the other are important. Lovers clearly meet this first condition. If the relationship is not intense, the various demands and counterdemands will have little effect. Examples of such intense relationships are many and include relationships between various family members, between husband and wife, and in some instances between employer and employee.
Incompatible Responses. There must be two messages that demand different

and incompatible responses. That is, the messages must be such that both cannot logically be verbalized. Usually, the positive message is communicated verbally, for example, "Love me." The accompanying message, usually communicated nonverbally, contradicts the first message, for example, withdrawal and a general tenseness that communicates "Stay away," "Don't love me." Both parties in a double-bind relationship are likely to engage in sending such messages, either both in the same conversation or separately on different occasions.

Inability to Escape. At least one or both of the individuals in a double-bind situation must be unable to escape from the contradictory messages. The individual or individuals lack the opportunities to meet their needs elsewhere or have been in their roles or positions so long that alternatives no longer seem available. People in double-bind situations feel trapped. Preventing an individual's escape from the contradictory message may be a legal commitment (like a marriage license) or, in the case of lovers, an understood but unwritten agreement that implies that each loves the other and cares about meeting mutual needs. No matter what response is made, the person receiving the message is failing to comply with at least one of the demands. If, for example, Chris makes loving advances, the nonverbal injunction "Don't love me" is violated. If Chris does not make any loving advances, the verbal injunction "Love me" is violated.

Threat of Punishment. There must be a threat of punishment of some sort for the failure of the message receiver to comply with the sender's verbal or nonverbal demands. In our example, there is an implied threat of punishment for the failure to make loving advances but also for the failure to comply with the demand not to love. Regardless of how the lover responds—by making loving advances or not making such advances—some form of punishment will follow. This is one reason why the relationship between the people must be relatively intense; otherwise, the threat of punishment would not be significant.

Frequent Occurrences. For double-binding to be a serious communication problem, it must occur frequently. Such frequent exposure has the effect of setting up a response pattern in the individual such that she or he comes to anticipate that whatever is done will be incorrect, that there is no escape from these confused and confusing communications, and that punishment will follow noncompliance (and since noncompliance is inevitable, punishment is inevitable).

Double-bind messages are particularly significant to children because they can neither escape from such situations, nor can they communicate about the communications. They cannot talk about the lack of correspondence between the verbal and the nonverbal. They cannot ask their parents why they do not hold them or hug them when they say they love them.

Sometimes there are different rules for, say, adults and children, but because these rules are never stated explicitly, they create conflicts for the child. On one occasion I observed a group of adults playing poker for small change. In the next room two young girls—children of these adults—were also playing cards. After an hour or so the young girls asked their parents for some change so that they too could play cards for money. Almost with one voice, the parents began shouting that the girls should not gamble, gambling was wrong, and that they could have just as much fun without money. On previous occasions the children were taught to emulate their parents, to act grown up. Now they were told not to act like their parents. Some researchers call contradictory messages and double binds like these "crazy makers."

Ernst Beier has argued that these double-bind messages—which he refers to as "discordance"—are the result of the desire of the individual to communicate two different emotions or feelings. For example, we may like a person and want to communicate this positive feeling, but we may also feel resentment toward this person and want to communicate this negative feeling as well. The result is that we communicate both feelings, one verbally and one nonverbally.

NONVERBAL BEHAVIOR ALWAYS COMMUNICATES

The observation that all behavior in an interactional situation is communicative is particularly important in regard to nonverbal communication. It is impossible not to behave; consequently, it is impossible not to communicate. Regardless of what one does or does not do, one's nonverbal behavior communicates something to someone (assuming that it occurs in an interactional setting).

Sitting silently in a corner and reading a book communicates to others just as surely as would verbalization. Staring out the window during class communicates something to the teacher just as surely as would your saying, "I'm bored." Notice, however, an important difference between the nonverbal and the verbal statements. The student looking out the window, when confronted by the teacher asking, "Why are you bored?" can always claim to have been momentarily distracted by something outside. Saying, "I'm bored," on the other hand, prevents the student from backing off and giving a more socially acceptable meaning to the statement. The nonverbal communication, however, is also more convenient from the point of view of the teacher. The teacher, if confronted with the student's "I'm bored," must act on that in some way. Some of the possibilities include saying, "See me after class," "I'm just as bored as you are," "Who cares?," "Why are you bored?," and so on. All of them, however, are confrontations of a kind. The teacher is in a sense forced to do something even though she or he might prefer to ignore it. The nonverbal staring out the window allows the teacher to ignore it. This does not mean that the teacher is not aware of it or that the staring is not communicating. Rather, nonverbal communication allows the "listener" an opportunity to feign a lack of awareness.

There are, however, exceptions to this general rule. Consider, for example, if the student, instead of looking out the window, gave the teacher some unmistakable nonverbal signal, such as the thumbs-down gesture. This type of nonverbal communication is not so easy to feign ignorance of. Here the teacher must confront this comment just as surely as she or he would have to confront the comment "I'm bored."

Even the less obvious and less easily observed behaviors communicate. The smaller movements of the eyes, hands, facial muscles, and other parts also communicate, just as the gross movements of gesturing, sitting in a corner, or staring out a window do.

These small movements are extremely important in interpersonal relationships. We can often tell, for example, when two people genuinely like each other and when they are merely being polite. If we had to state how we know this, we would probably have considerable difficulty. These inferences, many of which are correct, are based primarily on these small nonverbal behaviors of the participants—the muscles around the eyes, the degree of eye contact, the way in which the individuals face each other, and so on. All nonverbal behavior, however small or transitory, is significant; all of it communicates.

Gifts as Nonverbal Messages

A number of theorists have recently pointed out how we communicate even in our gift giving. Aside from the obvious messages—remembering one's birthday or celebrating Christmas, for example—gifts often communicate less noble motives. For example, giving candy or chocolates to a diabetic or to someone who wants to lose weight or a bottle of liquor to someone with a drinking problem are examples of destructive gifts. Their selection seems to communicate an underlying hostility. One type of gift has been referred to as the "Pygmalion gift," the gift that is designed to change the person into what the donor wants that person to become. The husband who buys his wife sexy lingerie may be asking his wife to be sexy; the wife who buys her husband a weight-lifting machine or tight-fitting underwear may well be asking the same thing. The parent who repeatedly gives a child books or science equipment may be asking the child to be a scholar. The problem with some of these gifts is that the underlying motives—the underlying displeasures—may never be talked about and hence never resolved. When a parent gives a child a nonplay gift— for example, practical gifts of clothes or books—the parent may be responding to her or his own inability to play, to enjoy spontaneous and seemingly impractical pleasures.

This is not to say that all such gifts are motivated by the more negative aspects of our personalities, only to suggest that even in gift giving there are messages communicated that are often overlooked and that often function below the level of conscious awareness. Nevertheless, such messages may have considerable impact on the recipient, the donor, and the relationship itself.

NONVERBAL COMMUNICATION IS GOVERNED BY RULES

The characteristic of rule-governed behavior is easily appreciated when applied to verbal communication. In fact, the entire field of linguistics is devoted to explaining the rule-governed nature of language. The formulation of rules governing the sound, meaning, and structural systems of language occupies the bulk of the contemporary linguist's time. These are the rules that native speakers of the language follow in producing and in understanding sentences—rules that they may be unable to state explicitly.

Nonverbal communication is also rule-governed; it is regulated by a system of rules or norms that state what is and what is not appropriate, expected, and permissible in specific social situations. We learned both the ways to communicate nonverbally *and* the rules of appropriateness at the same time from observing the behaviors of the adult community. For example, we learn how to express sympathy along with the rules that our culture has established for appropriately communicating sympathy. We learn that touch is permissible under certain circumstances but not others, and we learn which type of touching is permissible and which is not; in short, we learn the rules governing touching behavior. We learn that women may touch each other in public; for example, they may hold hands, walk arm in arm, engage in prolonged hugging, and even dance together. We also learn that men may not do this, at least not without social criticism. And, perhaps most obvious, we learn that there are certain parts of the body that may not be touched and certain parts that may. As a relationship changes, so do the rules of touching. As we become more intimate, the rules for touching become less restrictive.

We learn rules for sitting and walking behavior. Boys sit with their legs open and girls sit with their legs closed. Men take big steps when they walk; women take small steps. Men sit with their arms stretched out; women sit with their arms close to their bodies.

In the United States, direct eye contact signals openness and honesty. But in various countries of Latin America and among some Native Americans, direct eye contact between, say, a teacher and a student would be considered inappropriate, perhaps aggressive. Appropriate student behavior would be to avoid eye contact with the teacher. From even this simple example it is easy to see how miscommunication can easily take place. To a teacher in the United States, avoidance of eye contact by a Latin American or Native American could easily be taken to mean guilt, disinterest, or disrespect, when in fact the child was following her or his own culturally established rules for eye contact.

Like the nonverbal behaviors themselves, these rules are learned without conscious awareness. We learn them largely from observing others. The rules are brought to our attention only in formal discussions of nonverbal communication, such as this one, and when the rules are violated and the violations are called to our attention—either directly by some tactless snob or indirectly through the examples of others. While linguists are attempting to formulate the rules for verbal messages, nonverbal researchers are attempting to formulate the rules for nonverbal messages—rules that native communicators know and use every day but cannot necessarily verbalize. A major function of the following units on nonverbal communication is to bring to consciousness some of these implicit rules and the meanings and implications behind their appropriate and inappropriate use.

NONVERBAL COMMUNICATION IS DETERMINED

Like verbal messages, nonverbal messages evidence the quality of determinism. All messages (verbal and nonverbal alike) are motivated in some way; all are determined. The smile or frown, the forward or backward glance, the strong or mild hug, the long or short kiss—all are motivated in different ways. Much as the smile and the frown, for example, communicate different meanings to receivers, they are also reflections of different meanings in the source. Smiling seems obviously motivated by a different set of factors than frowning. From this rather weak claim, many will make the further assumption that we can therefore learn a person's motives (or subconscious desires or repressed fears or strengths and weaknesses) by analyzing her or his nonverbal behaviors. As we noted, such significant insight into a person's personality and motivation does not come easily. We cannot tell what is going on inside a person's skin by focusing solely on what is going on nonverbally.

This is illustrated in an experiment in which analysts looked for various nonverbal cues in videotapes of happily and unhappily married couples who were experiencing interpersonal conflict. The happy couples sat closer together, looked more frequently into each other's eyes, and touched each other more than they touched themselves. The unhappy couples, on the other hand, crossed their arms and legs, made less direct eye contact with each other, and touched themselves more than they touched each other. Clearly, then, happy and unhappy couples behave differently nonverbally. But this is not the same as saying that couples who touch themselves more than they touch each other are unhappy or are experiencing interpersonal conflict. Their touching means something, but exactly what it means for the specific person cannot be accurately determined from the nonverbal behavior alone.

Our assumption of determinism may assist us in suggesting possible hypotheses about what is going on inside the person. But that is about as far as we can legitimately go with our present level of knowledge of nonverbal communication. One of the reasons for this is simply that people are different; one person's smile may mean ''I'm happy,'' whereas another person's smile may cover up seething hostility. Also, there are contextual factors that influence nonverbal behaviors; a smile with one person in one place may mean something totally different from a smile with someone else in another place. Social and cultural factors also influence what a person means when she or he engages in various nonverbal behaviors; while one culture may encourage direct eye contact in interpersonal interaction, another culture may discourage it.

NONVERBAL BEHAVIOR IS HIGHLY BELIEVABLE

For some reasons, not all of which are clear to researchers, we are quick to believe nonverbal behaviors even when these behaviors contradict verbal behaviors. Consider, for example, a conversation between an employer and an employee. The employee is attempting to get a higher salary and is in the process of telling the employer how much hard work she or he put into the job. Throughout the discussion, however, the employee betrays her or his real intentions with various small muscle movements, inconsistent smiles, a lack of direct eye contact, and so on. Somehow, the employer goes away with the feeling, based on the nonverbal behavior, that the employee is lying. For the most part, research has shown that when the verbal and nonverbal messages differ, we believe the nonverbal. In fact, Albert Mehrabian argues that the total impact of a message is a function of the following formula:

$$Total\ impact\ =\ .07\ verbal\ +\ .38\ vocal\ +\ .55\ facial$$

This formula leaves very little influence to verbal messages. Only one-third of the impact is vocal (that is, paralanguage elements such as rate, pitch, and rhythm), and over half of the message is communicated by the face. The formula, developed by Mehrabian and his colleagues from their studies on the emotional impact of messages, is not applicable to all messages; it is applicable only to the expression of feelings. Although it is interesting to speculate on what percentage of message impact is due to nonverbal elements, there is no valid and reliable answer at this time.

Why we believe the nonverbal message over the verbal message is not clear. It may be that we feel verbal messages are easier to fake. Consequently, when there is a contradiction, we distrust the verbal and accept the nonverbal. Or it may be that the nonverbal messages often function below the level of conscious awareness. We learned them without being aware of any such learning, and we perceive them without conscious awareness. Thus, when such a conflict arises, we somehow get this "feeling" from the nonverbal messages. Since we cannot isolate its source, we assume that it is somehow correct.

Believability and Deception

Usually our verbal and nonverbal behavior is consistent; it is packaged, as already noted. Thus when we lie verbally, we also try to lie nonverbally; we strive always for consistency. Yet both our verbal and our nonverbal behaviors often (though surely not always) betray us. Nonverbal researchers have identified a number of behaviors that often accompany deception. Generally, a liar moves less than a person who is telling the truth, talks more slowly (perhaps to give herself or himself the time needed to create the fabrication or mentally check on the consistency of the story), and makes more speech errors. The best indicator of lying, according to Albert Mehrabian, is that the liar uses fewer words, particularly in answering questions. The liar gives monosyllabic answers and generally does not elaborate on them.

In an investigation of paralinguistic and verbal leakage, Michael Cody, Peter Marston, and Myrna Foster discovered a number of other clues to deception. When compared with truth-tellers, liars paused longer before answering questions and used longer pauses throughout their communications; they also used fewer words. These findings support those by Mehrabian noted above. Further, liars used more "generalizing terms" (for example, "you know what I mean," "stuff like that," and "you know" at the ends of sentences). Liars also used less concrete and specific terms. For example, they spoke of nonspecific activities ("hung out," "had fun") more often than truth-tellers. They also referred less frequently than did truth-tellers to specific persons and specific places.

Allan Pease, in *Signals,* and Desmond Morris, in *Manwatching,* note a number of gestures that seem to indicate lying. Most prominent among these are the mouth guard (hand over mouth and thumb on cheek), nose touching, and eye rubbing. Rubbing the ear, notes Pease, seems to indicate that the listener doubts the truthfulness of the speaker.

Do not forget that nonverbal (and verbal) behaviors must be interpreted as part of the context in which they occur; the ones just cited should be used to suggest hypotheses concerning deceit rather than firm conclusions. After reviewing the extensive literature on deception, Paul Ekman, in *Telling Lies,* cautions: "Evaluating behavioral clues to deceit is hazardous. . . . The lie catcher must always estimate the *likelihood* that a gesture or expression indicates lying or truthfulness; rarely is it absolutely certain."

NONVERBAL BEHAVIOR IS OFTEN METACOMMUNICATIONAL

Metacommunication is communication that refers to other communications; it is communication about communication. All behavior, verbal as well as nonverbal, can be metacommunicational. We can say, for example, "This statement is false" or "Do you understand what I am trying to tell you?" Such statements that make reference to communication are called *metacommunicational statements.*

Nonverbal behavior is often metacommunicational. Obvious examples include crossing one's finger behind one's back or winking when telling a lie. But the more subtle instances of metacommunication are the more interesting. Take the first day of class as an example. The teacher walks in and says that she or he is the instructor for the course and might then say how the course will be conducted, what will be required, what the goals of the course will be, and so on. But much metacommunication is also going on. The clothes the teacher wears and how she or he wears them, the length and style of hair, the general physical appearance, the style of walking, the tone of voice, and so on, all communicate about the communication—in addition to communicating in and of themselves. These nonverbal messages comment on the verbal messages the instructor is trying to communicate. On the basis of these cues, students will come to various conclusions. They might conclude that this teacher is going to be easy even though a long reading list was given or that the class is going to be enjoyable or boring or too advanced or irrelevant.

The metacommunicational function of nonverbal communication is not limited to its role as an adjunct to verbal communication; nonverbal communication frequently comments on other nonverbal communication. The individual who when meeting a stranger both smiles and presents a totally lifeless hand for shaking is a good example of how one nonverbal behavior may refer to another nonverbal behavior.

But most often when nonverbal behavior is metacommunicational, it functions to reinforce (rather than to contradict) other verbal or nonverbal behavior. You may literally roll up your sleeves when talking about cleaning up the room, smile when greeting someone, run to meet someone you say you are eager to see, or arrive early for a party you verbally express pleasure in attending. On the negative (though still consistent) side, you may arrive late for a dental appointment (presumably with a less-than-pleasant facial expression) or grind your teeth when telling off your boss. Clearly, much nonverbal communication is metacommunicational. This does not mean that nonverbal communication may not refer to people, events, things, relationships, and so on (that is, *object* communication), nor does it mean that verbal communication may not be metacommunication. I merely stress here the role of nonverbal communication as metacommunication because of its frequent use in this function.

Summary: Contents in Brief

Nonverbal Universal	Precept
Contextual	Nonverbal communication cannot be understood apart from the context in which it occurs.
Packaged	Nonverbal behaviors occur in clusters and are usually consistent with other nonverbal and verbal messages; double-bind messages contain contradictory messages.

Summary: Contents in Brief (continued)

Nonverbal Universal	Precept
Communicative	All nonverbal behaviors have message value.
Rule-governed	Nonverbal communication, like verbal communication, follows rules that are culture-specific.
Determined	All nonverbal behaviors are motivated in some way; all are emitted for some reason, which may or may not be identifiable.
Believable	Nonverbal messages are highly believable; nonverbal channels (especially the face and the voice) reportedly communicate over 90 percent of the total expression of *feelings*.
Metacommunicational	Nonverbal behavior frequently serves a metacommunication function, for example, to reinforce or contradict other verbal or nonverbal messages.

Sources

General introductions to the area of nonverbal communication are plentiful and make interesting reading. Perhaps the most entertaining is Desmond Morris, *Manwatching* (New York: Abrams, 1977). This work contains numerous photographs that help greatly in explaining the various aspects of nonverbal behaviors. Three excellent works that thoroughly review the research on nonverbal communication are Dale G. Leathers, *Nonverbal Communication Systems* (Boston: Allyn & Bacon, 1976); Mark L. Knapp, *Nonverbal Communication in Human Interaction*, 2d ed. (New York: Holt, Rinehart and Winston, 1978); and Loretta A. Malandro and Larry Barker, *Nonverbal Communication* (Reading, Mass.: Addison-Wesley, 1983). Also see Allan Pease, *Signals* (New York: Bantam, 1984) for additional insights. For Ernst Beier's analysis of discordance, see his "How We Send Emotional Messages," *Psychology Today* 8 (October 1974): 53–56. Mehrabian's formula has been presented in a number of places but was first introduced, I believe, in his "Communication Without Words," *Psychology Today* 2 (September 1968): 53–55. In this connection also see Timothy Hegstrom, "Message Impact: What Percentage is Nonverbal?" *Western Journal of Speech Communication* 43 (Spring 1979): 134–142. On handwriting, see Rhoda Riddell, "Writing Personalities," *Human Behavior* 7 (July 1978): 18–23. Some of the issues central to the study of nonverbal communication are considered in a thoughtful essay by Mark

L. Knapp, John M. Wiemann, and John A. Daly, "Nonverbal Communication: Issues and Appraisal," *Human Communication Research* 4 (Spring 1978): 271–280. An excellent collection of articles on nonverbal communication is contained in Shirley Weitz, ed., *Nonverbal Communication: Readings with Commentary,* 2d ed. (New York: Oxford University Press, 1979). For the insights on gift giving I relied on Georgia Dullea, "Presents: Hidden Messages," *New York Times,* December 14, 1981, p. D12.

Much research is currently being conducted in the area of deception. The communication literature is well surveyed in Mark Knapp and Mark Comadena, "Telling It Like It Isn't: A Review of Theory and Research on Deceptive Communication," *Human Communication Research* 5 (1979): 270–285 and Michael Cody, Peter Marston, and Myrna Foster, "Deception: Paralinguistic and Verbal Leakage," *Communication Yearbook 8,* ed. Robert N. Bostrom (Beverly Hills, Calif.: Sage, 1984), pp. 464–490. The psychological literature is surveyed by Paul Ekman, *Telling Lies: Clues to Deceit in the Marketplace, Politics, and Marriage* (New York: Norton, 1985).

UNIT 15

Body Communication

OBJECTIVES

Upon completion of this unit, you should be able to:

1. define and provide at least two examples of emblems, illustrators, affect displays, regulators, and adaptors
2. identify instances of the five types of movements in the behaviors of others and in your own behaviors
3. identify the types of information communicated by facial expressions
4. identify at least two problems in determining the accuracy of judging facial expressions
5. explain the role of context and culture in influencing facial expressions and their decoding
6. explain *micromomentary expressions*
7. identify at least three functions of eye contact
8. identify at least two functions of eye avoidance
9. explain the types of information communicated by pupil dilatation and constriction
10. define *tactile communication* and explain at least three functions served by tactile communication
11. explain and provide specific examples of how gender influences touch communication
12. explain and provide specific examples of how culture influences touch communication

Of all the nonverbal communication systems, the body is surely the most important. With the body we communicate a wide variety of messages through gestures, facial expressions, eye movements, and touching behavior. Each of these four major areas of body communication is examined in this unit.

GESTURAL COMMUNICATION

In dealing with nonverbal body gestures, a classification offered by Paul Ekman and Wallace V. Friesen seems the most useful. These researchers distinguish five classes of nonverbal movements based on the origins, functions, and coding of the behavior: emblems, illustrators, affect displays, regulators, and adaptors.

Emblems

Emblems are nonverbal behaviors that translate words or phrases rather directly. Emblems include, for example, the OK sign, the peace sign, the come-here sign, the hitchhiker's sign, the "up yours" sign, and so on. Emblems are nonverbal substitutes for specific verbal words or phrases and are probably learned in essentially the same way as are specific words and phrases—without conscious awareness or explicit teaching and largely through imitation.

Although emblems seem rather natural to us and almost inherently meaningful, they are as arbitrary as any word in any language. Consequently, our present culture's emblems are not necessarily the same as our culture's emblems of 300 years ago or the same as the emblems of other cultures. For example, the OK sign may mean "nothing" or "zero" in France, "money" in Japan, and something sexual in certain southern European cultures. Just as the English language is spreading throughout the world, so too is the English nonverbal language. The meaning of the thumb and index finger forming a circle meaning "OK" is spreading just as fast as, for example, English technical and scientific terms.

Emblems are often used to supplement the verbal message or as a kind of reinforcement. At times they are used in place of verbalization, for example, when there is a considerable distance between the individuals and shouting would be inappropriate or when we wish to communicate something behind someone's back.

Illustrators

Illustrators are nonverbal behaviors that accompany and literally illustrate the verbal messages. In saying, "Let's go up," for example, there will be movements of the head and perhaps hands going in an upward direction. In describing a circle or a square, you are more than likely to make circular or square movements with your hands.

We are aware of illustrators only part of the time; at times they may have to be brought to our attention and our awareness. Illustrators seem more natural and less arbitrary than emblems. They are partly a function of learning and partly innate. Illustrators are more universal; they are more common throughout the world and throughout time than emblems. Consequently, it is likely that there is some innate component to illustrators, contrary to what many researchers might argue.

Affect Displays

Affect displays are the movements of the facial area that convey emotional meaning—the facial expressions that show anger and fear, happiness and surprise, eagerness and fatigue. They are the facial expressions that "give us away" when we attempt to present a false image and that lead people to say, "You look angry. What's wrong?" We can, however, also consciously control affect displays, as actors do when they play a role. Affect displays are more independent of verbal messages than illustrators and less under conscious control than either emblems or illustrators.

Affect displays may be unintentional—as when they give us away—but they may also be intentional. We may want to show anger or love or hate or surprise, and, for the most part, we do a creditable job. Actors are often rated by the public for their ability to portray affect accurately by movements of their facial muscles.

As we talk with our mouths, we also communicate with our bodies. This speaker's gestures are illustrators and seem to be describing or illustrating what is being discussed.

Regulators

Regulators are nonverbal behaviors that "regulate" (monitor, maintain, or control) the speaking of another individual. When we listen to another, we are not passive; we nod our heads, purse our lips, adjust our eye focus, and make various paralinguistic sounds such as "mm-mm" or "tsk." Regulators are clearly culture-bound and are not universal.

Regulators in effect tell speakers what we expect or want them to do as they are talking—"Keep going," "What else happened?," "I don't believe that," "Speed up," "Slow down," and any number of other directions. Speakers often receive these nonverbal behaviors without being consciously aware of them. Depending on their degree of sensitivity, they modify their speaking behavior in line with the directions supplied by the regulators. Regulators would also include such gross movements as turning one's head, leaning forward in one's chair, and walking away.

Adaptors

Adaptors are nonverbal behaviors designed to satisfy some need. Sometimes the need is physical, as when we scratch to satisfy an itch or when we push our hair out of our eyes. Sometimes the need is psychological, as when we bite our lip when anxious.

Sometimes adaptors are directed at increasing comfort, as when we moisten dry lips.

When these adaptors occur in private, they occur in their entirety: We scratch our head until the itch is gone; we pick our nose until we're satisfied. But in public these adaptors usually occur in abbreviated form. For example, when people are watching us, we might put our fingers to our head and move them around a bit but probably not scratch with the same vigor as when in private. Similarly, we might put our finger to our nose but would probably not pursue this simple act to completion.

Because publicly emitted adaptors usually occur in abbreviated form, it is often difficult for an observer to tell what this partial behavior was intended to accomplish. For example, observing someone's finger near the nose, we cannot be certain that this behavior was intended to pick it, scratch it, or whatever.

Adaptors usually occur without conscious awareness; they are unintentional movements that usually go unnoticed. Generally, researchers report, adaptors are signs of negative feelings. For example, we emit more adaptors when we feel hostile than when we feel friendly. Further, as anxiety and uneasiness increase, so does the frequency of adaptors.

FACIAL COMMUNICATION

Throughout our interpersonal interactions, our faces communicate, especially our emotions. For example, Paul Ekman, Wallace V. Friesen, and Phoebe Ellsworth claim that facial messages may communicate at least the following eight emotion categories: happiness, surprise, fear, anger, sadness, disgust, contempt, and interest. Dale Leathers has proposed that in addition to these eight, facial movements may also communicate bewilderment and determination.

A somewhat different approach has been offered by nonverbal researcher Albert Mehrabian, who classifies the types of feelings communicated nonverbally into three major categories: (1) pleasure–displeasure, (2) arousal (physical activity and mental alertness), and (3) dominance—submissiveness. These three dimensions, in various combinations, account for all the emotions and feelings we might express. For example, pleasure, positive arousal, and submissiveness (indicating that the situation controls the individual rather than the individual controlling the situation) would include such emotions as amazement, being impressed, being loved, and surprise. Displeasure, positive arousal, and dominance would include hatred, scorn, hostility, and disgust.

Each of these three major dimensions is communicated nonverbally through various means. For example, we communicate pleasure through laughter, smiling, and a lively and elated quality in our speech and in our body movements generally. Dominance is expressed nonverbally through a relaxed posture, taking control of the initiation of interaction, loudness of voice, controlling a larger portion of the conversation, maintaining larger spaces (for example, a large office or a large home). Arousal is communicated through three major means: rate of speech, vocal expressiveness, and speech volume. The faster, the more expressive, and the louder the speech, the greater the arousal communicated.

Try to communicate surprise using only facial movements. Do this in front of a mirror and attempt to describe in as much detail as possible the specific movements of the face that make up surprise. If you signal surprise like most people, you probably employ raised and curved eyebrows, long horizontal forehead wrinkles, wide-open eyes, a dropped-open mouth, and lips parted with no tension. Even if there were differences—and clearly there would be from one person to another—you could probably recognize the movements listed here as indicative of surprise. In FAST (*facial affect scoring technique*) the face is broken up into three main parts: eyebrows and forehead, eyes and eyelids, and the lower face from the bridge of the nose down. Judges then attempt to identify various emotions by observing the different parts of the face and writing descriptions for the various emotions similar to the one just given for surprise. In this way we can study more effectively just how the face communicates the various emotions.

Communication Accuracy

The accuracy with which people express emotions facially and the accuracy with which receivers decode the expressions have been the object of considerable research. One problem confronting this research is that it is difficult to separate the ability of the encoder from the ability of the decoder. Thus a person may be quite adept at communicating emotions, but the receiver may prove to be insensitive. On the other hand, the receiver may be quite good at deciphering emotions, but the sender may be inept. And, of course, there are tremendous differences from one person to another and with the same person at different times.

A second problem is that accuracy seems to vary with the method of the research. In some cases still photographs are used and people are asked to judge the emotions the people pictured are experiencing. Some research uses live models or actors and actresses who have been trained to communicate the different emotions. Still others use more spontaneous methods. For example, an individual judge views a person who is herself or himself viewing and reacting to a film. The judge, without seeing the film, has to decode the emotion the viewer is experiencing. As can be appreciated, each method yields somewhat different results. Accuracy also varies with the emotions themselves. Some emotions are easier to communicate and to decode than others. Ekman, Friesen, and Carlsmith report, for example, that happiness is judged with an accuracy ranging from 55 to 100 percent, surprise from 38 to 86 percent, and sadness from 19 to 88 percent. All this is not to say that the results of these studies are of no value; it is merely to inject a note of caution in dealing with "conclusions" about facial communication.

The Influence of Context

The same facial expressions are perceived differently if people are supplied with different contexts. For example, in a study by M. G. Cline it was found that when a smiling face was presented looking at a glum face, the smiling face was judged to be vicious and taunting, but when the same smiling face was presented looking at a frowning face, it was judged to be peaceful and friendly. This is similar to the experiments done by the Russian filmmaker Kuleshev in the 1920s who "discovered" the technique of "montage" (film editing) by juxtaposing a "reaction shot" of a man's face with various different events. To the viewer, the face seemed to register different emotions depending on what scene it followed.

Universal or Relative?

It appears from cross-cultural research that facial expressions have a somewhat universal nature. For example, people in Borneo and New Guinea who have had little contact with Western cultures were able to match accurately emotions with pictures of facial expressions of Westerners. Further, their own facial expressions, posed to communicate different emotions, were accurately decoded by Americans. Similarly, studies conducted with children who were born blind and who therefore could not see how others facially expressed the various emotions seem to use the same facial expressions as their sighted peers. Studies such as these point to a universality among facial gestures. The wide variations in facial communication that we do observe in different cultures seem to reflect what is permissible and not permissible to communicate rather than a difference in the way in which emotions are expressed facially. For example, in some cultures it is permissible openly and publicly to show contempt or disgust, but in others people are taught to hide such emotions in public and to display them only in private.

Micromomentary Expressions

A frequently asked question in this regard concerns whether these emotions can really be hidden or whether they somehow manifest themselves below the level of conscious awareness. Is our contempt encoded facially without our being aware of it or even without observers' being aware of it? Although a complete answer to this question is not possible at this time, some indication that we do, in fact, communicate these emotions without awareness comes from research on micromomentary expressions. E. A. Haggard and K. S. Isaacs, for example, conducted studies in which they showed films of therapy patients in slow motion. They noted that often the patient's expression would change dramatically. For example, a frown would change to a smile and then quickly back to a frown. If the film was played at normal speed, the change to the smile would go unnoticed. Only when the film was played at slow speed was it apparent that the patient smiled between frowns. Generally, if a facial expression is of less than two-fifths of a second's duration, the expression goes unnoticed unless it is filmed and then played back at reduced speed. These extremely brief movements, called *micromomentary expressions,* seem indicative of an individual's real emotional state. Our conditioning leads us to repress such expressions.

EYE COMMUNICATION

From Ben Johnson's poetic observation, "Drink to me only with thine eyes, and I will pledge with mine," to the scientific observations of contemporary researchers, the eyes are regarded as the most important nonverbal message system.

Eye Contact Functions

Mark Knapp, as well as various other researchers, notes four major functions of eye communication.

TO MONITOR FEEDBACK

In talking with someone, we look at the person intently, as if to say, "Well, what do you think?" or "React to what I've just said." Also, we look at speakers to let them know that we are listening. In studies conducted on gazing behavior and summarized by Knapp, it has been found that listeners gaze at speakers more than speakers gaze at listeners. The percentage of interaction time spent gazing while listening, for example, has been observed in two studies to be 62 percent and 75 percent, while the percentage of time spent gazing while talking has been observed to be 38 percent and 41 percent. It is interesting to note that when these percentages are reversed—when a speaker gazes at the listener for longer than "normal" periods or when a listener gazes at the speaker for shorter than "normal" periods—the conversational interaction becomes awkward and uncomfortable. You may wish to try this with a friend; even with mutual awareness, you will note the discomfort caused by this seemingly minor communication change.

TO SIGNAL A CONVERSATIONAL TURN

A second and related function is to inform the other person that the channel of communication is open and that she or he should now speak. The clearest example of this is seen in the college classroom, where the instructor asks a question and then locks eyes with a student. Without any verbal message, it is assumed that the student should answer the question.

TO SIGNAL THE NATURE OF THE RELATIONSHIP

A third function is to signal the nature of the relationship between two people, for example, one of positive or negative regard. When we like someone, we increase our eye contact. Nonverbal researcher Michael Argyle, for example, notes that when eye contact goes beyond 60 percent, the individuals are probably more interested in each other than in the verbal messages being exchanged. Another relational message that eye contact communicates is the individual's willingness to pursue the development of a relationship. When direct eye contact is made, held for a few moments, and when each person's eyes sweep over the other's body and then return to direct eye contact, we may reasonably predict (especially if accompanied by a smile) that each would willingly pursue a get-together. If, on the other hand, after direct eye contact is made, it is broken quickly and not returned, we may reasonably predict that this is not a relationship that will blossom very quickly.

When we dislike someone, we avoid looking at that person and especially avoid direct eye contact. One obvious exception to this general rule is when we are in direct verbal combat; here we often stare at each other in an attempt to communicate our hostility and assert our superiority.

We may also signal status relationships with our eyes. This is particularly interesting because the same movements of the eyes may signal either subordination or superiority. The superior individual, for example, may stare at the subordinate or may glance away, and the subordinate may look directly at the superior or perhaps to the floor. Similarly, a direct stare may signal an amorous or a hostile relationship. Because of these contradictory meanings, we generally utilize information from other areas, particularly the face, to decode the message before making any final judgments.

Eye movements are often used to compensate for increased physical distance. By making eye contact, we overcome psychologically the physical distance between us. When we catch someone's eye at a party, for example, we become psychologically close even though we may be separated by considerable physical distance. Eye contact and other expressions of psychological closeness, such as self-disclosure and intimacy, have been found to vary in proportion to each other.

We have already noted that women engage in more expressions of intimacy than men—for example, greater self-disclosure and greater use of affectional language. Women also engage in more eye contact than men. Whether interacting with men or with other women, women maintain greater eye contact when listening as well as when speaking.

Eye Avoidance Functions

The eyes, sociologist Erving Goffman, in *Interaction Ritual,* observed, are "great intruders." When we avoid eye contact or avert our glance, we enable others to maintain their privacy. We frequently do this when a couple argues, say in the street or on a bus. We turn our eyes away (though our ears may be wide open) as if to say, "We don't mean to intrude; we respect your privacy." Goffman refers to this behavior as *civil inattention.*

Eye avoidance can signal disinterest—in a person, a conversation, or some visual stimulus. At times, like the ostrich, we hide our eyes in an attempt to cut off unpleasant stimuli. Notice, for example, how quickly people close their eyes in the face of some extreme unpleasantness. Interestingly enough, even if the unpleasantness is auditory, we tend to shut it out by closing our eyes. Sometimes we close our eyes to block out visual stimuli and thus heighten our other senses; we often listen to music with our eyes closed. Lovers often close their eyes while kissing, and many prefer to make love in a dark or dimly lit room.

Pupil Dilatation

In addition to eye movements, considerable research has been done on pupil dilatation. In the fifteenth and sixteenth centuries in Italy, women used to put drops of belladonna (which literally means "beautiful woman") into their eyes to dilate the pupils so that they would look more attractive. Contemporary research seems to support the intuitive logic of these women; dilated pupils are in fact judged to be more attractive than constricted pupils.

In one study, photographs of women were retouched. In one set the pupils were enlarged, and in another they were made smaller. Men were then shown the photographs and asked to judge the women's personalities. The photos of women with small pupils drew responses such as cold, hard, and selfish; those with dilated pupils drew responses such as feminine and soft. The male observer, however, could not verbalize the reasons for the different perceptions. Pupil dilatation and reactions to changes in pupil size of others both seem to function below our level of awareness.

Although belladonna is no longer used, the cosmetics industry has made millions selling eye enhancers—eye shadow, eye liner, false eyelashes, and glasses with rhinestones and engraved initials. These devices function (ideally, at least) to draw attention to these most powerful communicators.

Pupil size is also indicative of one's interest and level of emotional arousal. One's pupils enlarge when one is interested in something or when one is emotionally aroused. When homosexuals and heterosexuals were shown pictures of nude bodies, the homosexuals' pupils dilated more when viewing same-sex bodies, while the heterosexuals' pupils dilated more when viewing opposite-sex bodies. Perhaps we judge dilated pupils as more attractive because we judge the individual's dilated pupils to be indicative of an interest in us.

TOUCH COMMUNICATION

Of all the forms of nonverbal communication, touch, or tactile, communication is perhaps the most primitive. In terms of sense development, it is probably the first to be used; even in the womb the child is stimulated by touch. Soon after birth the child is fondled, caressed, patted, and stroked by the parents and by any other relative who happens to be around. The whole world wants to touch the new infant. Touch becomes for the child a pleasant experience, and she or he begins to touch. Everything is picked up, thoroughly fingered, and put into the mouth in an attempt to touch it as closely as possible. The child's favorite toys seem to be tactile ones—cuddly teddy bears, teething rings, even pieces of blankets. Much in the same way as children touch objects in the environment, they also touch themselves; children play with toes and fingers, nose and lips, ears and genitals. At some point, children are stopped from picking their noses and playing with their genitals. No reason is given other than the admonition "Don't do that" or a gentle slap on the hands. As children mature and become sociable, they begin to explore others through touch, though again there are certain parts that we are forbidden to touch or to have touched by others. Nonverbal researcher Lawrence Frank has observed that some of the ways in which we dress our bodies—the clothing we wear, the jewelry, even the makeup and general cosmetics—send out invitations to others to touch us. The way we adorn our bodies indicates our readiness and our willingness to be touched, though often on a subconscious level.

Functions of Touching Behavior

Touching as a form of communication can serve any number of functions. In fact, one would be hard pressed to name a general function of communication that could not be served by tactile communication. Special note, however, should be made of a few major functions frequently served by tactile communication.

SEXUAL EXPRESSION

Perhaps the most obvious is a sexual one. Touch seems to be the primary form of sexual interaction. From fondling one's genitals as a child, to kissing, to fondling another individual, to sexual intercourse, touch plays a primary role. Men shave or grow beards, women shave their legs and underarms, and both use body oils and creams to keep their skin smooth in a conscious or subconscious awareness of the powerful role of touch as a form of communication.

CONSOLATION AND SUPPORT

Touch also serves a primary role in consoling another individual. For example, we put our arms around people, hold their head in our hands, hold their hands, or hug them in an attempt to empathize with them more fully. It seems like an attempt to feel what the other person is feeling by becoming one with them—perhaps the ideal in empathic understanding. Try to console someone, even in role playing, when you are not allowed to touch them, and you will see how unnatural it seems and how difficult it is to say the appropriate words.

In almost all group encounter sessions, touch is used as a supportive gesture. Generally, we do not touch people we dislike (except in fighting with them). Otherwise, we only touch people we like, so the very act of touching says, ''I like you,'' ''I care about you,'' ''I want to be close to you.'' Touching implies a commitment to the other individual; where and how we touch seems to determine the extent of that commitment. To shake someone's hand, for example, involves a very minor commitment. Our culture has, in effect, defined handshaking as a minor social affair. But to caress someone's neck or to kiss someone's mouth implies a commitment of much greater magnitude. ''Touch is such a powerful signaling system,'' notes Desmond Morris in *Manwatching*, ''and it's so closely related to emotional feelings we have for one another that in casual encounters it's kept to a minimum. When the relationship develops, the touching follows along with it.''

In their popular and influential *One Minute Manager*, Kenneth Blanchard and Spencer Johnson offer an interesting rule for touching: ''When you touch, don't take.'' You should touch another person, these authors suggest, only when you give (for example, support, consolation, reassurance, encouragement). Never touch when you take; never touch at the same time that you criticize, admonish, or otherwise negatively respond to another.

POWER AND DOMINANCE

In *Body Politics*, Nancy Henley argues that touching behavior can be both a sign of affection, which we have already noted, and also a sign of dominance. Consider, as Henley suggests, who would touch whom—say, by putting one's arm on the other person's shoulder or by putting one's hand on the other person's back—in the following dyads: teacher and student, doctor and patient, master and servant, manager and worker, minister and parishioner, police officer and accused, executive and secretary. Most people brought up in our culture would say that the first-named person in each dyad would be more likely to touch the second-named person than the other way around. The higher-status person is permitted to touch the lower-status person; it would be a breach of etiquette for the lower-status person to touch the person of higher status.

Henley further argues that in addition to indicating relative status, touching also demonstrates the assertion of male power and dominance over women. Men may, says Henley, touch women in the course of their daily routine—in a restaurant, an office, and a school, for example—and thus indicate their ''superior status.'' When women touch men, on the other hand, the interpretation that it designates a female-dominant relationship is found not acceptable (to men), and so this touching is explained and interpreted as a sexual invitation.

Touching ourselves, of course, also communicates. We are all familiar with the individual who is constantly fixing her or his hair—to the point where we feel like screaming and perhaps sometimes do. Although we have learned somewhere that these adaptors—these ways of touching oneself—are forbidden, at least in public, there are still people who pick their noses, scratch their heads, stick their fingers in their ears, or scratch their genitals or buttocks without the least concern for those around who might not care to witness this exercise in self-gratification.

Who Touches Whom Where: Gender and Cultural Differences

A great deal of research has been directed at the question of who touches whom where. Most of it has attempted to address two basic questions: (1) Are there gender differences? Do men and women communicate through touch in the same way? Are men and women touched in the same way? (2) Are there cultural differences? Do people in widely different cultures communicate through touch in the same way?

GENDER DIFFERENCES

One of the most famous studies on gender differences was conducted by Sidney M. Jourard, a summary of whose findings is presented in Figure 15.1. In the first figure, labeled "Body for Mother," we have the areas and frequency with which these areas of a male college student's body were touched by his mother. The second figure records the areas and frequency with which these areas were touched by the student's father, and so on. The key within the figure indicates the percentage of students who reported being touched in these areas.

Jourard reports that touching and being touched differ little between men and women. Men touch and are touched as often and in the same places as women. The major exception to this is the touching behavior of mothers and fathers. Mothers touch children of both sexes and of all ages a great deal more than do fathers, who in many instances go no further than touching the hands of their children. The studies that have found differences between touching behavior in men and women seem to indicate that women touch more than men do. For example, women touch their fathers more than men do. Also, female babies are touched more than male babies. In an investigation of the wish to be held versus the wish to hold, women reported a greater desire to be held than to hold; and whereas men also report a desire to be held, it is not as intense as that of women. This, of course, fits in quite neatly with our cultural stereotypes of men being protectors (and therefore indicating a preference for holding) and women being protected (and therefore indicating a preference for being held).

A great deal more touching is reported among opposite-sex friends than among same-sex friends. Both male and female college students report that they touch and are touched more by their opposite-sex friends than by their same-sex friends. No doubt the strong societal bias against same-sex touching accounts, at least in part, for the greater prevalence of opposite-sex touching that most studies report. I suspect, however, that a great deal of touching goes on among same-sex friends but goes unreported because many people are unaware of touching same-sex partners.

The Jourard study, replicated ten years later, found support for all Jourard's

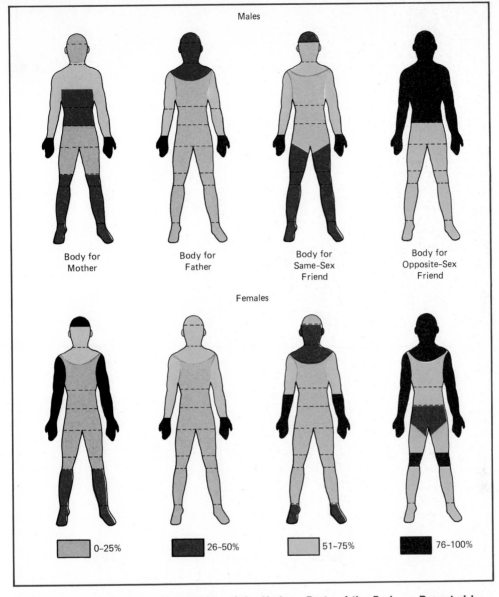

Males

Body for
Mother

Body for
Father

Body for
Same-Sex
Friend

Body for
Opposite-Sex
Friend

Females

0–25%   26–50%   51–75%   76–100%

**FIGURE 15.1: The Amount of Touching of the Various Parts of the Body as Reported by
Male and Female College Students.** [*Source:* S. M. Jourard, "An Exploratory
Study of Body Accessibility," *British Journal of Social and Clinical Psychology* 5
(1966): 221–231.]

earlier findings, except that in the later study both males and females were touched
more by opposite-sex friends than in the earlier study.

CULTURAL DIFFERENCES

In a similar study, college students in Japan and in the United States were
surveyed. The results, presented in Figure 15.2, make a particularly dramatic case
for cross-cultural differences; students from the United States reported being touched

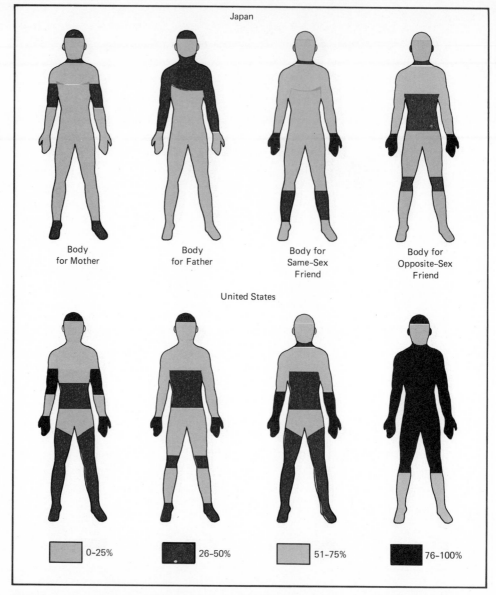

FIGURE 15.2: Areas and Frequency of Touching as Reported by Japanese and United States College Students. [*Source:* Dean C. Barnlund, "Communicative Styles in Two Cultures: Japan and the United States," in A. Kendon, R. M. Harris, and M. R. Key, eds., *Organization of Behavior in Face-to-Face Interaction* (The Hague: Mouton, 1975).]

twice as much as did students from Japan. In Japan there is a strong taboo against strangers touching, and the Japanese are therefore especially careful to maintain sufficient distance.

Another obvious cross-cultural difference is in the Middle East, where same-sex touching in public is extremely common. Men will, for example, walk with their arms on each other's shoulders—a practice that would cause many raised eyebrows in the United States. Middle Easterners, Latin Americans, and southern Europeans touch each other while talking a great deal more than do people from "noncontact cultures"—Asia and northern Europe, for example.

Even such seemingly minor nonverbal differences as these can create difficulties when members of different cultures interact. Northern Europeans or Japanese may be perceived as cold, distant, and uninvolved by southern Europeans, who in turn may be perceived as pushy, aggressive, and inappropriately intimate.

Summary: Contents in Brief

"Gestural" Communication Functions	Facial Communication Functions	Eye Communication Functions	Touch Communication Functions
Emblems translate words and phrases rather directly. *Illustrators* accompany and literally illustrate the verbal messages. *Affect displays* convey emotional meaning through facial expressions. *Regulators* monitor or control the speaking of the other person. *Adaptors* serve some need and are usually performed only partially when in public.	*Emotional expression:* happiness, surprise, fear, anger, sadness, disgust, contempt, interest; bewilderment, determination *Types of feelings:* • pleasure–displeasure • arousal (physical and mental) • dominance–submissiveness	*Eye contact:* • monitor feedback • signal conversational turns • signal nature of relationship • compensate for physical distance *Eye avoidance:* • to give others privacy • to signal disinterest • to cut off unpleasant stimuli • to heighten other senses *Pupil dilatation:* • interest and disinterest • attraction and attractiveness	Sexual interaction Consolation and support Power and dominance

Sources

Perhaps the most authoritative source on body communication is Ray L. Birdwhistell, *Kinesics and Context: Essays on Body Motion Communication* (New York: Ballantine Books, 1970). This paperback contains 28 articles by Birdwhistell on body communication plus an extensive bibliography of research and theory in this area. The discussion and classification of types of body movements is from Paul Ekman and Wallace V. Friesen, "The Repertoire of Nonverbal Behavior: Categories, Origins,

Usage, and Coding," *Semiotica* 1 (1969): 49–98. A thorough review and analysis of research and theory is provided in Peter Bull, *Body Movement and Interpersonal Communication* (New York: Wiley, 1983).

The studies referred to in this discussion of facial and eye communication are as follows: Albert Mehrabian, "Communication Without Words," in Joseph A. DeVito, ed., *Communication: Concepts and Processes,* rev. ed. (Englewood Cliffs, N.J.: Prentice-Hall, 1976); Paul Ekman, Wallace V. Friesen, and Phoebe Ellsworth, *Emotion in the Human Face: Guidelines for Research and an Integration of Findings* (New York: Pergamon Press, 1972); Paul Ekman, Wallace V. Friesen, and S. S. Tomkins, "Facial Affect Scoring Technique: A First Validity Study," *Semiotica* 3 (1971): 37–58; M. G. Cline, "The Influence of Social Context on the Perception of Faces," *Journal of Personality* 2 (1956): 142–185; E. A. Haggard and K. S. Isaacs, "Micromomentary Facial Expressions as Indicators of Ego Mechanisms in Psychotherapy," in L. A. Gottschalk and A. H. Auerbach, eds., *Methods of Research in Psychotherapy* (Englewood Cliffs, N.J.: Prentice-Hall, 1966). The Ekman, Friesen, and Carlsmith study may be found in *Emotion in the Human Face,* cited above. An interesting discussion of nonverbal communication by one of the leading researchers is available: Albert Mehrabian, *How We Communicate Feelings Nonverbally,* A Psychology Today Cassette (New York: Ziff-Davis, 1978). Other references cited in this unit include: Dale Leathers, *Nonverbal Communication Systems* (Boston, Mass.: Allyn & Bacon, 1976); Mark Knapp, *Nonverbal Communication in Human Interaction,* 2d ed. (New York: Holt, Rinehart and Winston, 1978); Desmond Morris, *Manwatching* (New York: Abrams, 1977); Erving Goffman, *Interaction Ritual: Essays in Face-to-Face Behavior* (Chicago, Ill.: Aldine, 1967); and Michael Argyle, *The Psychology of Interpersonal Behaviour* (New York: Penguin, 1967). Recent research and theory on eye communication is covered in Evan Marshall, *Eye Language: Understanding the Eloquent Eye* (New York: New Trend, 1983).

For body touching, see Ashley Montague, *Touching: The Human Significance of the Skin* (New York: Harper & Row, 1971). For Jourard's studies on touching, see Sidney M. Jourard, *Disclosing Man to Himself* (New York: Van Nostrand Reinhold, 1968) and *Self-disclosure* (New York: Wiley, 1971). Marc Hollender and Alexander Mercer conducted the study on holding: "Wish to Be Held and Wish to Hold in Men and Women," *Archives of General Psychiatry* 33 (January 1976): 49–51. On the role of touching in status and power relationships, see Nancy M. Henley, *Body Politics: Power, Sex, and Nonverbal Communication* (Englewood Cliffs, N.J.: Prentice-Hall, 1977). Also see Helen Colton, *Touch Therapy* (New York: Kensington, 1983) for the influence of touch on relationships.

Space Communication

OBJECTIVES

Upon completion of this unit, you should be able to:

1. define *proxemics*
2. identify and explain the four proxemic distances
3. give examples of the kinds of communications that would take place in each of the four proxemic distances
4. define *territoriality* and explain its role in signaling ownership and status
5. give examples of the operation of territoriality from your own experiences
6. explain how different surroundings might influence perception
7. explain the arbitrariness of color symbolism

Like verbal behavior, spatial behavior communicates; space speaks just as surely and as loudly as do words. A speaker who stands close to the listener, hands on the listener's shoulders and eyes focused directly on those of the listener, clearly communicates something very different from the speaker who sits crouched in a corner with arms folded and eyes to the floor. Like verbal and body communication, spatial behavior is learned without any conscious or direct teaching by the adult community. Children are merely exposed to certain spatial relations, which they internalize unconsciously, much as children seem to acquire the particular codes of speech and body motion.

In this unit we explore several dimensions of spatial communication. First, we discuss the general area of *proxemics*, or spatial communication—specifically, the major proxemic distances (or the physical space between people in their interpersonal interactions). Second, we look at the concept of *territoriality*—the possessive or ownership-like reaction to an area or to a particular object. Third, we consider the role of aesthetics and color, that is, some of the ways in which space may be "decorated" to communicate different meanings.

215

PROXEMICS

Edward T. Hall, in the study he calls *proxemics,* provides much new and significant insight into nonverbal communication by demonstrating how messages from these different channels may be analyzed and by relating them to the spatial dimensions of communication. More formally, in "A System for the Notation of Proxemic Behavior," Hall defines *proxemics* as the "study of how man unconsciously structures microspace—the distance between men in the conduct of their daily transactions, the organization of space in his houses and buildings, and ultimately the layout of his towns."

One of the earliest references to space as communication occurs in the Gospel of Luke (14:8–11):

> *When thou art invited to a wedding feast, do not recline in the first place, lest perhaps one more distinguished than thou have been invited by him, and he who invited thee and him come and say to thee, "Make room for this man"; and then thou begin with shame to take the last place. But when thou are invited, go and recline in the last place; that when he who invited thee comes in, he may say to thee, "Friend, go up higher!" Then thou wilt be honored in the presence of all who are at table with thee. For everyone who exalts himself shall be humbled, and he who humbles himself shall be exalted.*

This passage illustrates one of the concepts or meanings that space communicates, namely, status. We know, for example, that in a large organization, status is the basis for determining how large an office one receives, whether that office has a window or not, what floor of the building the office is on, and how close one's office is to that of the head of the company.

Space is especially important in interpersonal communication, although we seldom think about it or even consider the possibility that it might serve a communicative function. Hall distinguishes four distances that he feels define the type of relationship permitted. Each of these four distances has a close phase and a far phase, giving us a total of eight clearly identifiable distances. These four distances, according to Hall, correspond closely to the four major types of relationships: intimate, personal, social, and public.

Intimate Distance

In *intimate distance,* ranging from the close phase of actual touching to the far phase of 6 to 18 inches, the presence of the other individual is unmistakable. Each individual experiences the sound, smell, and feel of the other's breath. The close phase is used for lovemaking and wrestling, for comforting and protecting. In the close phase the muscles and the skin communicate, while actual verbalizations play a minor role. In this close phase, whispering, says Hall, has the effect of increasing the psychological distance between the two individuals. The far phase allows us to touch each other by extending our hands. The distance is so close that it is not considered proper in public, and because of the feeling of inappropriateness and discomfort (at least for some Americans), the eyes seldom meet but remain fixed on some remote object.

Personal Distance

Each of us, says Hall, carries a protective bubble defining our *personal distance,* which allows us to stay protected and untouched by others. In the close phase of personal

Intimate proxemic distance echoes and encourages interpersonal intimacy and interpersonal intimacy encourages intimate distance. Each facilitates the other.

distance ($1\frac{1}{2}$ to $2\frac{1}{2}$ feet) we can still hold or grasp each other but only by extending our arms. We can then take into our protective bubble certain individuals—for example, loved ones. In the far phase ($2\frac{1}{2}$ to 4 feet) two people can touch each other only if they both extend their arms. This far phase is the extent to which we can physically get our hands on things; hence it defines, in one sense, the limits of our physical control over others. Even at this distance we can see many of the fine details of an individual—the gray hairs, tooth stains, clothing lint, and so on. However, we can no longer detect body heat. At times we may detect breath odor, but generally at this distance etiquette demands that we direct our breath to some neutral corner so as not to offend.

This distance is particularly interesting from the point of view of body odor and the colognes designed to hide it. At this distance we cannot perceive normal cologne or perfume. Thus it has been proposed that cologne has two functions: First, it serves to disguise the body odor or hide it; and second, it serves to make clear the limits of the protective bubble around the individual. The bubble, defined by the perfume, signals that you may not enter beyond the point at which you can smell me.

Social Distance

At the *social distance* we lose the visual detail we had in the personal distance. The close phase (4 to 7 feet) is the distance at which we conduct impersonal business, the distance at which we interact at a social gathering. The far phase (7 to 12 feet) is the distance we stand when someone says, "Stand away so I can look at you." At this level business transactions have more formal tone than when conducted in the close phase. In offices of high officials, the desks are positioned so that the individual is assured of at least this distance when dealing with clients. Unlike the intimate distance, where eye contact is awkward, the far phase of the social distance makes eye contact essential—otherwise communication is lost. The voice is generally louder than normal at this level, but shouting or raising the voice has the effect of reducing the social distance to a personal distance. It is at this distance that we can work with people and yet not constantly interact with them and not appear rude.

This social distance requires that a certain amount of space be available. In many instances, however, such distances are not available; yet it is necessary to keep social distance, psychologically if not physically. For this we attempt different arrangements with the furniture. In a small office, for example, people sharing an office might have their desks face in different directions so that each worker may stay separated from the other. Or they may position their desks against opposite walls so that each will feel psychologically alone in the office and thus be able effectively to maintain a social rather than a personal distance.

Public Distance

In the close phase of *public distance* (12 to 15 feet) an individual seems protected by space. At this distance one is able to take defensive action should one be threatened. On a public bus or train, for example, we might keep at least this distance from a drunkard so that should anything come up (literally or figuratively), we could get away in time. Although at this distance we lose the fine details of the face and eyes, we are still close enough to see what is happening should we need to take defensive action.

At the far phase (more than 25 feet) we see individuals not as separate individuals but as part of the whole setting. We automatically set approximately 30 feet around public figures who are of considerable importance, and we seem to do this whether or not there are guards preventing us from entering this distance. This far phase is, of course, the distance from which actors perform on stage; consequently, their actions and voices have to be somewhat exaggerated.

TERRITORIALITY

One of the most interesting concepts in ethology—the study of animals in their natural surroundings—is *territoriality,* the possessive or ownership-like reaction to an area of space or to particular objects.

Signaling Ownership

Many male animals stake out a particular territory and signal their ownership to all others. They allow prospective mates to enter but defend the territory against entrance by other males of the same species. Among deer, for example, the size of the territory signifies the power of the buck, which in turn determines how many females he will mate with. Less powerful bucks will be able to hold on to only small parcels of land and consequently will mate with only one or two females. This adaptive measure ensures that the strongest members of the society produce most of the offspring. When the "landowner" takes possession of an area—either because it is vacant or because he gains it through battle—he marks it, for example, by urinating around the boundaries.

These same general patterns are felt by many to be integral parts of human behavior. Some researchers claim that this form of behavior is instinctive and is a symptom of the innate aggressiveness of humans. Others claim that territoriality is learned behavior and is culturally based. Most, however, seem to agree that a great deal of human behavior can be understood and described as territoriality regardless of its possible origin or development.

If we look around at our homes, we would probably find certain territories that different people have staked out and where invasions are cause for at least mild defensive action. This is perhaps seen most clearly with siblings who each have (or "own") a specific chair, room, radio, and so on. Father has his chair and mother has her chair. Archie and Edith Bunker always sat in the same chairs, and great uproars occurred when Archie's territory was invaded. Similarly, the rooms of the house may be divided among members of the family. The kitchen, traditionally at least, has been the mother's territory. Invasions from other family members may be tolerated but are often not welcomed, and at times they are resisted. Invasions by members not of the immediate family—brother-in-law, mother-in-law, or neighbor, for example— are generally resented much more.

In the classroom, where seats are not assigned, territoriality can also be observed. When a student sits in a seat that has normally been occupied by another student, the regular occupant will often become disturbed and resentful and might even say something about it being "my" seat. Like animals, humans also mark their territory. In a library, for example, you mark your territory with a jacket or some books when you leave the room. You expect this marker to function to keep others away from your seat and table area. Most of the time it works. When it does not work, there is cause for conflict.

Signaling Status

Like that of animals, the territory of humans communicates status in various ways. Clearly the size and location of the territory indicates something about status. A town house on Manhattan's East Side, for example, is perhaps the highest-status territory for living in the country; it is large and at the same time located on the world's most expensive real estate. Status is also signaled by the unwritten law granting the right of invasion. High-status individuals have a right (or at least more of a right) to invade the territory of others than vice versa. The boss of a large company, for example, can invade the territory of a junior executive by barging into her or his office, but the reverse would be unthinkable. Similarly, a teacher may invade the personal space of a student by looking over her or his shoulder as the student writes. But the student cannot do the same in return.

AESTHETICS AND COLORS

The aesthetics and color treatment of space communicate a great deal. On the basis of the ways in which space is "decorated," we make inferences about the individuals who occupy the space. Thus, oriental rugs, eighteenth-century oil paintings, and antique furniture communicate something very different from bare floors, unframed posters, and inflatable furniture. Similarly, a room painted bright red with a black ceiling and floor and all-white furniture communicates something quite different from a room painted beige with earth-tone furniture. In addition, the aesthetic and color variations influence our behaviors within these spaces; we function differently in differently decorated spaces.

Aesthetics

That the decorations or surroundings of a particular place exert influence on us should be obvious to anyone who has ever entered a hospital, with its sterile walls and furniture, or a museum, with its imposing columns, glass-encased exhibits, and brass plaques.

Even the way in which a relatively ordinary room is furnished exerts considerable influence on us. In an insightful study on this question, Abraham Maslow and Norbett Mintz attempted to determine if the aesthetic conditions or surroundings of a room would influence the judgments people made in these rooms. Three rooms were used; one was beautiful, one average, and one ugly.

The beautiful room had large windows, beige walls, indirect lighting, and furnishings that made the room seem attractive and comfortable. Paintings were on the walls, a large Navajo rug covered the floor, and drapes were on the windows. The average room was a professor's office with two mahogany desks and chairs, a metal bookcase, metal filing cabinets, and shades on the windows. The ugly room was painted battleship gray; lighting was provided by an overhead bulb with a dirty, torn shade. The room was furnished to give the impression of a janitor's storeroom in horrible condition. The ashtrays were filled and the window shades torn.

In the three different rooms, students rated ten art prints in terms of the fatigue–energy and displeasure–well-being depicted in them. As predicted, the students rated the prints in the beautiful room to be more energetic and to evidence more well-being. Those judged in the ugly room were rated as evidencing fatigue and displeasure, while those judged in the average room were perceived as somewhere between those two extremes.

In a follow-up study Mintz selected two of the subjects from the previous experiment and used them as "examiners." For a period of three weeks these two subjects tested other subjects for one hour per day, each alternating every day between the beautiful and the ugly room. After each hour the "examiners" were asked to rate the prints again, supposedly for measures of reliability.

It was found that the ratings of the prints were similar to that found in the first experiment. The subjects still rated the prints as more energetic and evidencing more well-being when in the beautiful room than when in the ugly room. Further, these results were consistent over the three weeks. The subjects did not adjust to the surroundings over time. The experimenter also tested the time spent by the "examiners" in testing their subjects. It was found that the testing in the ugly room was completed faster than that in the beautiful room 27 out of 32 times.

General observational conclusions show that the subjects did not want to test in the ugly room, became irritable and aggressive when they had to test in that room, and felt that time seemed to move more slowly when in the ugly room.

The implications of this type of finding seem extremely important. We are forced to wonder if a ghetto child studying in a crowded tenement is able to derive the same benefits as a middle-class student studying in her or his own room. Can workers in an unappealing factory ever enjoy their job as much as workers in a pleasant office? What about prisons? Is aggressive behavior in prisons partly a function of the horrible surroundings prisoners are forced to live in? Is the higher crime rate in depressed areas, in part at least, a function of the ugliness of the surroundings? Questions such as these are not easy to answer, but they should be considered by any student of nonverbal communication.

Color Communication

When we are in debt, we speak of being "in the red"; when we make a profit, we are "in the black." When we are sad, we are "blue"; when we are healthy, we are "in the pink"; when we are jealous, we are "green with envy"; and when we are happy, we are "tickled pink." To be a coward is to be "yellow," and to be inexperienced is to be "green." When we talk a great deal, we talk "a blue streak," and when we talk to no avail, we talk until we are "blue in the face." When we go out on the town, we "paint it red," and when we are angry, we "see red." Our language, especially well revealed through these time-worn clichés, abounds in color symbolism.

THE MEANINGS OF COLORS

Henry Dreyfuss, in his *Symbol Sourcebook*, reminds us of some of the positive and negative meanings associated with various colors. Some of these are presented in Table 16.1. Dreyfuss also notes some cultural comparisons for some of these colors.

TABLE 16.1: Some Positive and Negative Messages of Colors

Color	Positive Messages	Negative Messages
red	warmth passion life liberty patriotism	death war revolution devil danger
blue	religious feeling devotion truth justice	doubt discouragement
yellow	intuition wisdom divinity	cowardice malevolence impure love
green	nature hope freshness prosperity	envy jealousy opposition disgrace
purple	power royalty love of truth nostalgia	mourning regret penitence resignation

SOURCE: Adapted from Henry Dreyfuss, *Symbol Sourcebook* (New York: McGraw-Hill, 1971).

For example, red in China is a color for joyous and festive occasions, whereas in Japan it is used to signify anger and danger. Blue for the Cherokee Indian signifies defeat, but for the Egyptian it signifies virtue and truth. In the Japanese theater blue is the color for villains. Yellow signifies happiness and prosperity in Egypt, but in tenth-century France yellow colored the doors of criminals. Green communicates femininity to certain American Indians, fertility and strength to Egyptians, and youth and energy to the Japanese. Purple signifies virtue and faith in Egypt, grace and nobility in Japan.

In English our connotative meanings for colors vary considerably. In Table 16.2 five color terms are presented with their average ratings on evaluation (for example, the good–bad, positive–negative dimension of language), potency (for example, the strong–weak, large–small dimension of language), and activity (for example, the active–passive, fast–slow dimension of language). The numbers are based on a seven-point scale ranging from + 3 for the good, strong, and active sides of the scales through 0, the neutral position, to − 3 for the bad, weak, and passive sides of the scale. As can be seen, red and blue are the most positive in terms of evaluation; gray is the most negative. Red is the most potent and gray is the least potent. Red is the most active and gray the least active.

There is also some scientific evidence that colors affect us physiologically. For example, respiratory movements increase with red light and decrease with blue light. Similarly, the frequency of eye blinks increases when eyes are exposed to red light and decreases when exposed to blue light. This seems consistent with our intuitive feelings about blue being more soothing and red being more active and also with the ratings noted in Table 16.2. In *Gone With the Wind,* Rhett Butler, upon hearing of Scarlett O'Hara's indiscretion with Ashley Wilkes and knowing that everyone at the upcoming ball would be talking about Scarlett's behavior, makes her wear a red dress—a color symbolic of her supposedly shameless and immoral behavior. Even the name Scarlett foretells something of her temperament and her future behavior. And in Nathaniel Hawthorne's *The Scarlet Letter,* Hester Prynne is forced to wear the letter *A* for "adultress," and it is no accident that the *A* is red.

COLORS AND PERSONALITY

Perhaps the most talked about (but least documented) communicative function of color is its supposed reflection of personality. Faber Birren argues that if you like red, your life is directed outward and you are impulsive, active, aggressive, vigorous, sympathetic, quick to judge people, impatient, optimistic, and strongly driven by sex.

TABLE 16.2: Evaluation, Potency, and Activity Ratings
for Five Color Terms

	Evaluation	Potency	Activity
yellow	.544	.212	− .637
red	1.256	1.012	− .050
green	.969	.706	− .619
gray	− .200	− .394	− 1.362
blue	1.255	.812	− .375

SOURCE: Adapted from James Snider and Charles E. Osgood, eds., "Semantic Atlas for 550 Concepts," in *Semantic Differential Technique: A Sourcebook* (Chicago: Aldine, 1969), pp. 625–636.

If, on the other hand, you dislike red, you also dislike the qualities in people who like red. You feel that others have gotten the better deal in life, and you never feel really secure. Sexually, you are unsatisfied.

If you like blue, you are probably conservative, introspective, and deliberate. You are sensitive to yourself and to others and have your passions under control. In your own communications you are cautious, your opinions and beliefs seldom change, and you question just about everything you do not understand. If you dislike blue, you resent the success of others and in fact enjoy their failures. You feel that your emotional and intellectual lives are not fulfilled. You get irritated and are somewhat erratic in your own behavior.

This analysis was drawn from the many comments of Faber Birren in *Color in Your World*. Analyses of your personality based on your likes and dislikes of 11 colors as well as on conflicts (liking one color and disliking another color) are readily supplied by Birren and by various other writers, though there seems to be no hard evidence for these claims. The idea of analyzing someone's personality on the basis of color preferences seems intriguing, yet the validity of such analyses remains to be demonstrated.

The messages that colors communicate about a culture are easily determined, while the personality traits that colors supposedly reveal are quite difficult and perhaps impossible to determine. As is true of so many aspects of nonverbal communication, we should be cautious in drawing conclusions about people on the basis of their color preferences.

Summary: Contents in Brief

Proxemic Distances	Territoriality	Aesthetics	Colors
Intimate (touching to 18 inches) Personal ($1\frac{1}{2}$ to 4 feet) Social (4 to 12 feet) Public (12 to 25 feet)	Signals ownership (permanent or temporary) Signals status	Attractiveness of surroundings influence: • energy level • time perception • aggressiveness • irritability level • perceptions of energy and well-being	Communicate different meanings Vary in meaning from one culture to another Affect us physiologically Color preferences have been used (with little evidence) to infer personality characteristics

Sources

For spatial communication, the work of Edward T. Hall is perhaps the best known and the most insightful. Proxemic dimensions are discussed in his "A System for the

Notation of Proxemic Behavior," *American Anthropologist* 65 (1963): 1003–1026. The discussion of proxemic distances comes from his *The Hidden Dimension* (New York: Doubleday, 1966). Hall's first popular work on spatial communication and still one of the most famous is *The Silent Language* (New York: Doubleday, 1959). Robert Sommer also deals with spatial communication, but from a somewhat different point of view. Particularly interesting are his *Personal Space: The Behavioral Basis of Design* (Englewood Cliffs, N.J.: Prentice-Hall, 1969) and *Design Awareness* (San Francisco: Rinehart Press, 1972). On territoriality, see Robert Ardrey, *The Territorial Imperative* (New York: Atheneum, 1966), a fascinating book on human territorial behavior. Also relevant here is the work of Edward Hall cited above.

The effects of surroundings are perhaps best explained in the work of Sommer cited above. The experiment on aesthetic surroundings is described in A. H. Maslow and N. L. Mintz, "Effects of Esthetic Surroundings: I. Initial Effects of Three Esthetic Conditions upon Perceiving 'Energy' and 'Well-Being' in Faces." *Journal of Psychology* 41 (1956): 247–254. Also relevant here is N. L. Mintz, "Effects of Esthetic Surroundings: II. Prolonged and Repeated Experience in a 'Beautiful' and 'Ugly' Room," *Journal of Psychology* 41 (1956): 459–466. I. A. Scott, ed. and trans., *The Lüscher Color Test* (New York: Pocket Books, 1971); Faber Birren, *Color in Your World* (New York: Collier Books, 1962); and Linda Clark, *The Ancient Art of Color Therapy* (New York: Pocket Books, 1975) are interesting attempts to relate color and personality and are useful for raising rather than answering questions.

Loretta A. Malandro and Larry Barker, *Nonverbal Communication* (New York: Random House, 1983) provide a useful review of space communication.

Silence, Paralanguage, and Temporal Communication

OBJECTIVES

Upon completion of this unit, you should be able to:

1. identify at least five functions of silence
2. define *paralanguage*
3. explain at least three messages that variations in paralinguistic phenomena might communicate
4. explain the communicative function of time
5. explain the relationship of time to culture, status, and appropriateness

We have seen how we can communicate by manipulating words and gestures. But we can also communicate with silence; by manipulating such paralinguistic factors as volume, rate, and pitch; and by our treatment of time. These three areas of nonverbal communication are the focus of this unit.

SILENCE

Don Fabun noted that "the world of silence may be a cold and bitter one; like the deep wastes of the Arctic regions, it is fit for neither man nor beast. Holding one's tongue may be prudent, but it is an act of rejection; silence builds walls—and walls are the symbols of failure." Thomas Mann, in one of the most often quoted observations on silence, said, "Speech is civilization itself. The word, even the most contradictory word, preserves contact; it is silence which isolates." On the other hand, philosopher Karl Jaspers observed that "the ultimate in thinking as in communication is silence," and Max Picard noted that "silence is nothing merely negative; it is not the mere absence of speech. It is a positive, a complete world in itself."

   All of these are rather extreme statements on the nature and function of silence. Actually, I think all are correct—for some occasions and for some people. The one thing on which all observations are clearly in agreement, and that needs to be stressed here, is that silence communicates. As we have seen, one of the universals of nonverbal behaviors is that they always communicate, and this is no less true of silence. Our silence communicates just as intensely as anything we might verbalize.

Functions of Silence

Perhaps the best way to approach silence is to consider some of the functions it might serve or the meanings it may communicate.

TO PROVIDE THINKING TIME

One of the most frequent functions of silence is to allow the speaker time to think. In some cases, silence allows the speaker the opportunity to integrate previous communications in order to make the necessary connections before the verbal communications may logically continue. In other instances it gives the speaker or listener time for previous messages to sink in. This is seen most clearly after someone makes what she or he thinks is a profound statement, almost as if to proclaim that this message should not be contaminated by other, less significant and less insightful messages. At still other times silence allows the individual to think of future messages. Lecturers often remain silent for short periods—though these might seem inordinately long to the lecturer as well as to the listeners—in order to think of what is to come next or perhaps to recall some fact or reference. In many instances people remain silent to prepare themselves for the intense communications that are to follow, rather like the calm before the storm. Before messages of intense conflict, as well as before messages confessing undying love, there is often silence. Again, silence seems to prepare the receiver for the importance of these future messages.

TO HURT

Some people use silence as a weapon to hurt others. We often speak here of giving someone "the silent treatment." After a conflict, for example, one or both individuals might remain silent as a kind of punishment. Children often imitate their parents in this and refuse to talk to playmates when they are angry with them. Silence to hurt others may also take the form of refusing to acknowledge the presence of another person; here silence is a dramatic demonstration of the total indifference one person feels toward the other. It is a refusal to recognize the person as a person, a refusal to treat the person any differently than one would treat an inanimate object. Such silence is most often accompanied by blank stares into space or a preoccupation with a magazine or some manual task or perhaps by feigning resting or sleeping. Here the nonverbal movements reinforce silence as a refusal to acknowledge the individual as a person.

TO ISOLATE ONESELF

Sometimes silence is used as a response to personal anxiety, shyness, or threats. One might feel anxious or shy among new people and prefer to remain silent. By remaining silent the individual precludes the chance of rejection. Only when the silence is broken and an attempt to communicate with another person is made does one risk rejection. At other times silence may be a kind of flight response made to threats by another individual or group of individuals. A street gang that makes

In good times silence can communicate affection, caring, and love; in bad times it often insults, intensifies conflicts, and delays resolution of interpersonal difficulties.

remarks as one passes is one example. By remaining silent, by refusing to engage in verbal contact, we attempt to remove ourselves psychologically from the situation.

TO PREVENT COMMUNICATION

Silence may be used to prevent the verbal communication of certain messages. In conflict situations silence is sometimes used to prevent certain topics from surfacing and to prevent one or both parties from saying things they may later regret. We made the point earlier that verbal expressions can never be reversed; once said, something cannot be unsaid. In conflict situations silence often allows us time to cool off before uttering expressions of hatred, severe criticism, or personal attacks, and here it serves us to good advantage.

Silence may be used to prevent one from saying the wrong thing or from making a fool of oneself. "Keep quiet and people will think you a philosopher," a Latin proverb advises. The alternative, though, is perhaps what most people have in mind when they remain silent: "Talk and people will think you a fool."

TO COMMUNICATE FEELINGS

Like the eyes, face, or hands, silence can also be used to communicate emotional responses. Sometimes silence communicates a determination to be uncooperative or defiant; by refusing to engage in verbal communication, we defy the authority or the legitimacy of the other person's position. In most pleasant situations silence might be used to express affection or love, especially when coupled with long and longing stares into each other's eyes. In many religious ceremonies, for example, reverence is signaled by silence. Often the congregation remains silent throughout a religious ritual or verbalizes only formal responses. Silence is often used to communicate annoyance, usually coupled with a pouting expression, arms crossed in front of the chest, and nostrils flared. In some of these situations silence is used because talk is perceived as superfluous or perhaps as less effective.

TO COMMUNICATE "NOTHING"

Of course, silence is often used when there is simply nothing to say, when nothing occurs to one to say, or when one does not want to say anything. James Russell Lowell expressed this best, I think: "Blessed are they who have nothing to say, and who cannot be persuaded to say it."

Cultural Differences

The communicative functions of silence in the situations just cited are not universal. The Apache, for example, regard silence very differently. Among the Apache, mutual friends do not feel the need to introduce strangers who may be working in the same area or on the same project. The strangers may remain silent for several days. During this time they are looking each other over, attempting to determine if the other person is all right. Only after this period would the individuals talk. When courting, especially during the initial stages, Apache individuals remain silent for hours; if they do talk, they generally talk very little. Only after a couple has been dating for several months will they have lengthy conversations. These periods of silence are generally attributed to shyness or self-consciousness. The use of silence is explicitly taught to Apache women, who are especially discouraged from engaging in long discussions with their dates. Silence during courtship is to many Apache a sign of modesty. If a young woman speaks a great deal, she is thought to be betraying prior experience with men, and in some instances it is seen as a sign of the woman's willingness to engage in sexual relations.

PARALANGUAGE

An old exercise to increase a student's ability to express different emotions, feelings, and attitudes was to have the student say the following sentences while accenting or stressing different words: "Is this the face that launched a thousand ships?" Significant differences in meaning are easily communicated depending on where the stress is placed. Consider, for example, the following variations:

1. *Is* this the face that launched a thousand ships?
2. Is *this* the face that launched a thousand ships?
3. Is this the *face* that launched a thousand ships?
4. Is this the face that *launched* a thousand ships?
5. Is this the face that launched a *thousand ships?*

Each of these five sentences communicates something different. Each, in fact, asks a totally different question, even though the words used are identical. All that distinguishes the sentences is stress, one of the aspects of what is called paralanguage. *Paralanguage* may be defined as the vocal (but nonverbal) dimension of speech. Paralanguage refers to the manner in which something is said rather than to what is said, to such vocal qualities as rate of speech, volume, rhythm, resonance; vocalizations such as laughing, yelling, moaning, whining, and belching; vocal segregates such as "un-uh" and "shh"; and pitch, the highness or lowness of vocal tone.

On the basis of these vocal qualities, what we call "paralinguistic cues," we form opinions about people (about their emotional states as well as about their status, sex, and various other characteristics), about potential conversational exchanges (when to talk and when to keep silent, for example), and about whether to believe or not to believe the speaker. Each of these three issues is examined here.

Paralanguage and People Perception

We are a diagnostically oriented people, quick to make judgments about another's personality based on various paralinguistic cues. At times our judgments turn out to be correct, at other times incorrect. We may, for example, conclude that speakers who speak so softly that we can hardly hear them have some kind of problem. Perhaps they feel inferior—they "know" that no one really wants to listen, that nothing they say is significant, so they speak softly. Other speakers speak at an extremely loud volume, perhaps because of an overinflated ego and the belief that everyone in the world wants to hear them, that no one can risk not hearing every word. Speakers who speak with no variation, in a complete monotone, seem uninterested in what they are saying and seem to encourage a similar lack of interest from their listeners—if any are still around. We might perceive such people as having a lack of interest in life in general, as being bland individuals. All of these conclusions are, at best, based on little evidence. Yet this does not stop us from reaching such conclusions.

IMPRESSION FORMATION

It is important for us to inquire into the relationship between paralanguage and impression formation. It does seem that certain voices are symptomatic of certain personality types, of certain problems, and specifically that the personality orientation gives rise to the vocal qualities. When listening to people speak—regardless of what they are saying—we form impressions based on their paralanguage as to what kind of people they are. Our impressions seem to consist of physical impressions (perhaps about body type and certainly about sex and age), personality impressions (they seem outgoing, they sound shy, they appear aggressive), and evaluative impressions (they sound like good people, they sound evil and menacing, they sound lovable, they have vicious laughs).

Much research has been directed to the question of the accuracy of these judgments—that is, how accurately we may judge a person on the basis of voice alone. One of the earliest studies on this question was conducted by T. H. Pear, who had over 4,000 listeners make guesses about nine speakers. The sex and age of the speaker were guessed with considerable accuracy. However, the listeners were able to guess the occupations of only the clergyman and the actor.

Other studies pursued the investigation of the relationship between vocal characteristics and personal characteristics. Most studies suggest, in agreement with Pear, that sex and age can be guessed accurately on the basis of the voice alone. This is not to say that complete accuracy is possible, but age does seem capable of being guessed within relatively small ranges.

One of the most interesting findings on voice and personal characteristics is that listeners can accurately judge the status (high, middle, or low) of speakers after hearing a 60-second voice sample. In fact, many listeners reported that they made their judgments in less than 15 seconds. It has also been found that the speakers judged to be of high status were rated as being of higher credibility than those rated of middle or low status.

One important finding reported in a number of studies is that on the basis of paralinguistic information, listeners agree about the personality of the speaker. The listeners' judgments, however, are very often in error. Listeners seem to have stereotyped ideas about how vocal characteristics and personality characteristics are related and use these stereotypes in their judgments. Sometimes the stereotypes are of the groups to which the listeners themselves belong. For example, in a study of Scottish and English speakers, Scottish listeners judged the Scottish voices as belonging to persons of greater generosity, friendliness, good-heartedness, and likability. English listeners, on the other hand, judged the English voices as belonging to persons who were more intelligent, ambitious, self-confident, and apt to serve as leaders.

IDENTIFYING EMOTIONAL STATES

There is much greater agreement in the literature on the question of identifying the emotional states of speakers from their vocal expression. Generally, in these studies the content of the speech is nonexistent or is held constant. In a content-free situation the speakers might recite the alphabet or count to 100. In the situation where the content is held constant, the speakers say the same sentences (generally rather unemotional ones) for all the emotions they are to communicate. Speakers *can* communicate or encode emotions through content-free speech or through content that is unrelated to the emotions, and listeners *are* able to decode these emotions. A typical study might involve speakers using numbers to communicate different emotions. Listeners would have to select the emotion being communicated from a list of ten possible emotions. In situations like this listeners are generally effective in guessing the motions.

But there is still variation: Listeners vary in their ability to decode the emotions, speakers vary in their ability to encode the emotions, and the accuracy with which emotions are guessed depends on the emotions themselves. For example, while it may be easy to distinguish between hate and sympathy, it may not be so easy to distinguish between fear and anxiety.

Testing Your Decoding Ability. To test your ability to decode emotions on the basis of verbal descriptions, try to "hear" the following voices and to identify the emotions being communicated. Do you hear affection, anger, boredom, or joy?

1. This voice is soft, with a low pitch, a resonant quality, a slow rate, and a steady and slightly upward inflection. The rhythm is regular, and the enunciation is slurred.
2. This voice is loud, with a high pitch, a moderately blaring quality, a fast rate, an upward inflection, and a regular rhythm.

3. This voice is loud, with a high pitch, a blaring quality, a fast rate, and an irregular up-and-down inflection. The rhythm is irregular, and the enunciation is clipped.
4. This voice is moderate to low in volume, with a moderate-to-low pitch, a moderately resonant quality, a moderately slow rate, and a monotonous or gradually falling inflection. The enunciation is somewhat slurred.

According to research by Joel Davitz, the first voice would communicate affection, the second joy, the third anger, and the fourth boredom.

Paralanguage and Conversational Turns

Paralinguistic cues are widely used to signal conversational turns, the maintaining or changing of the speaker or listener role during the conversation.

MAINTAINING THE SPEAKER OR LISTENER ROLE

Perhaps the most obvious way in which paralinguistic cues are used in conversational turns is a speaker's using them to maintain her or his speaking position. The speaker may in the course of conversation pause while vocalizing "um," "er," and the like. These vocalized pauses are insurance that no one else will jump in and take over the role of speaker; they announce to others in the conversation that this speaker is not finished but has more to say.

The absence of vocalized pauses, especially when accompanied by a falling intonation at the end of the sentence, often invites others to interject or assume their conversational turn, even when the speaker is not ready to relinquish the speaking role. Some people, especially those from relatively fast-paced cultures (New Yorkers are a good example), have a tendency to read all such pauses and falling intonations as invitations to speak, while the speakers, who may simply be thinking of their next thought, may consider this rude.

In a somewhat more oblique way, paralinguistic cues are used to maintain one's role as listener. This takes the form of vocalizing some reinforcing or approving type of sound while someone else is talking. This kind of positive feedback tells the speaker to keep going, to say more—and, perhaps most important, it tells the speaker that this listener approves of what is being said.

SIGNALING CHANGE OF ROLE

One of the most important conversational functions paralinguistic cues serve is to announce to others in the conversation that the speaker has finished and that it is now someone else's turn to speak. The speaker may add at the end of a statement some paralinguistic cue such as "eh?" which asks the others in the conversation to speak now. But such paralinguistic cues do not give the new speaker carte blanche; they signal relinquishing of the speaker's position with specific stipulations. For example, the speaker who says, "Schmedly gave me the F unfairly, eh?" is actually making three statements with this simple *eh?* First, the speaker is asking the other person to speak. Second, the speaker is asking that the other person speak specifically on the topic of the F grade. And third, the speaker is asking the new speaker to agree that the F was unfair. Of course, not all paralinguistic invitations to speak ask that the listener speak so specifically. Often, speakers indicate that they have finished speaking by dropping their intonation, by a prolonged silence, or by asking some general type of question. In these cases the new speaker has considerably more freedom.

Still another function of paralinguistic cues is to indicate to the speaker that a listener would like to say something, that the listener would like to take a turn as speaker. Sometimes listeners do this by simply saying, "I would like to say something," but often it is done paralinguistically by uttering some vocalized "er" or "um" that tells the speaker (at least the sensitive speaker) that someone else would like to speak. (These vocalizations are in many instances indistinguishable from those the speaker uses to maintain the speaking position.) This request to speak is also often done with facial and mouth gestures. Frequently, a listener will indicate a desire to speak by opening her or his eyes and mouth wide as if to say something or just begin to gesture with a hand.

Paralanguage and Persuasion

The rate of speed at which people speak is the aspect of paralanguage that has received the most attention. It is of interest to the advertiser, the politician, and, in fact, anyone who attempts to convey information or to influence others. This is especially so when time is limited or expensive. The research conducted on rate shows that in one-way communication situations (where one person is doing all or most of the speaking and the other person is doing all or most of the listening), persons who talk fast are more persuasive and are evaluated more highly than are persons who talk at or below normal speeds. This greater persuasiveness and higher regard holds true regardless of whether the individual talks fast naturally or if the speech is speeded up electronically (as in time-compressed speech).

In one experiment, for example, subjects were asked to listen to taped messages and then to indicate the degree to which they agreed with the message and their opinions as to how intelligent and objective they thought the speaker was. Rates of 111, 140, and 191 words a minute were used. (The average speaking rate is about 130 to 150 words per minute.) Subjects agreed most with the fastest speech and least with the slowest speech. Further, they rated the fastest speaker as the most intelligent and the most objective and rated the slowest speaker as the least intelligent and the least objective. Even in experiments in which the speaker was demonstrated to have something to gain personally from persuasion (as would, say, a used-car dealer), the speaker who spoke at the fastest rate was the most persuasive.

In terms of comprehension, rapid speech also has the advantage. The comprehension of subjects who listened to speeches at different speeds was measured by means of multiple-choice tests. Using 141 words per minute as the average and considering comprehension at this rate as 100 percent, comprehension was 95 percent when the rate was increased to 201 words per minute, and when the rate was further increased to 282 words per minute (that is, double the normal rate), comprehension was still 90 percent. Even though the rates increased dramatically, the comprehension rates fell only slightly. These 5 percent and 10 percent losses are more than offset by the increased speed and thus make the faster rates much more efficient in communicating information. If the speech speeds are increased more than 100 percent, however, comprehension falls dramatically.

A faster-than-normal speed is also preferred by most listeners. For example, when subjects were able to adjust the speed at which they heard a message, they adjusted it to approximately 25 percent faster than normal speed. Similarly, persons find commercials presented at approximately 25 percent faster than normal more interesting than commercials presented at normal speeds, and the level of attention (indexed by the amount of electrical activity measured by electrodes attached to the subjects' frontalis muscle of the forehead) is greater for fast speeds than for normal or slow speeds.

CAUTION

We need to be cautious, however, in applying this research to the interpersonal communication situation. As John MacLachlan points out, during the time the speaker is speaking, the listener is generating and framing a reply. If the speaker talks too rapidly, there may not be enough time to compose this reply, and resentment may therefore be generated. Furthermore, the increased rate may seem so unnatural that the listener may come to focus on the speed of speech rather than the thought expressed. But in one-way communication situations, especially mass communication ones, it is clear that increased rates will become more and more popular. Already, increased speech rates are used extensively in direct-selling commercials, which seem to be increasing almost daily. Their popularity will, it seems, influence other forms of mass-media advertising and electronic communication in general.

TEMPORAL COMMUNICATION

In a manner analogous to space, time communicates. Consider, for example, students who repeatedly arrive late for biology class. Their previous class is next door, so difficulty in getting to the class is not the problem. Yet they consistently come late. (Consider what you would think if the biology teacher were always late for class.) For some reason they find themselves engaged in something else that invariably consumes more time than anticipated. These same students, however, are always early for their interpersonal communication class. Regardless of the reasons for being late and early, they communicate something to the instructors of both courses. To the biology teacher it might be that the students hate the class, that they are somehow disorganized, or that they have weak kidneys. To the communication teacher it might mean that they are eager to get better acquainted with the other students, that they are interested in the course, or perhaps that they have nothing else to do. Regardless of what impression the teachers get, they do get impressions.

Time and Culture

The sense of time varies with different cultures and even with different subcultures. In different parts of the United States and in different parts of the world, there are wide variations in the treatment of time. In New York City, for example, time is treated reverently; being late is serious and is looked upon with considerable disdain. In San Francisco, on the other hand, people do not seem to worry so much about being "on time"; being late is seldom interpreted as a social catastrophe. Northern Europe operates on a clock that is relatively exact, whereas southern Europe operates on a clock that is more approximate. And, as in the United States, there are variations within each of these countries.

In our society, generally, it is permissible to be five or ten minutes early or late for most appointments. For the most part our culture demands considerable clock-watching. In other societies time is not regarded in the same way, and there is nothing wrong with being one or even two hours "late." Appointments are not made so that a specific block of time is set aside for you (as in our culture); rather, you are expected to arrive sometime in the evening, for example, and the business or socializing will take place when you get there. This may cause considerable problems for persons from the United States working in foreign countries and for foreigners working in the United States. Consider, for example, someone being one or two hours late for dinner and then entering without even attempting to make an apology. Surely we would assume that we have a right to be angry. Yet to this particular foreigner, nothing inappropriate—and certainly nothing to offend the host—has occurred.

In our culture, for example, consider what arriving at or leaving a party early or late might mean. On one level the time of arrival and departure might communicate something about interest or enjoyment. But such messages also communicate something about our willingness to socialize, our concern for the host, our level of frustration tolerance, our need to make a grand entrance or exit, and so on. Some persons seem particularly sensitive to the appropriateness of time, while others seem totally oblivious. Some persons consistently arrive late for dinner, for example, and then wonder why they are seldom invited back. Some seem totally unaware of when to leave. The host may look at a watch or clock several times, yawn repeatedly at strategic places in the conversation, mention that there is a full day of work tomorrow, and give any number of other cues, yet some people still do not realize that it is time to leave.

Time and Status

Time is especially linked to status considerations. For example, the importance of being on time varies directly with the status of the individual we are visiting. If the person is extremely important, we had better be there on time; in fact, we had better be there early just in case the person is able to see us before schedule. The lower the individual's status, the less important it is for us to be on time. Students, for example, must be on time for conferences with teachers, but it is more important to be on time for deans and still more important to be on time for the president of the college. Teachers, on the other hand, may be late for conferences with students but not for conferences with deans or the president. Deans, in turn may be late for teachers but not for the president. Within any hierarchy, similar unwritten rules are followed. This is not to imply that these "rules" are just or fair, only that they exist.

Even the time of dinner and the time from the arrival of guests to eating varies on the basis of status. Among lower-status individuals, dinner is served relatively early; if there are guests, they eat soon after they arrive. For higher-status people, dinner is relatively late, and a longer period of time elapses between arriving and eating—usually the time it takes to consume two cocktails.

Time and Appropriateness

Promptness or lateness in responding to letters, in returning telephone calls, in acknowledging gifts, and in returning invitations all communicate significant messages to other individuals. Such messages may be indexed on such scales as interest–disinterest, organized–disorganized, considerate–inconsiderate, and sociable–unsociable.

The amount of time people live in one place, the time a professor stays at one school, or the time an individual remains with a particular doctor, lawyer, or therapist also communicates something about the individual and the relationship.

There are times during which certain activities are considered appropriate and other times during which they are considered inappropriate. Thus it is permissible to make a social phone call during the late morning, afternoon, and early evening, but it is not permissible to call before eight or nine in the morning, during dinner time, or after 11 at night. Similarly, in making dates, an appropriate amount of notice is customary. When that acceptable amount of time is given, it communicates recognition of the accepted standards, perhaps respect for the individual, perhaps a certain social awareness. Should any of these time conventions be violated, however, other meanings are perceived. For example, a phone call at an abnormal hour almost always communicates urgency; we begin to worry what could be the matter as we race toward the phone.

If, in asking for a date, the call is made the night before or even the same night as the expected date, it may communicate any number of things. Say Chris calls Pat Saturday afternoon for a date that evening. Calling at that particular time may communicate, for example, that Chris has another date who canceled, that Chris knew that Pat would be free and so there was no need to give notice, that Chris was such a catch that Pat would welcome Chris regardless of the time called, or the like. In turn, Pat's response communicates significant meaning to Chris. Pat's acceptance might confirm Chris's expectation that Pat was free or that Pat would welcome Chris's call at any time. Pat's rejection, depending on the kind of ego Chris had, might communicate that Pat really wanted to date Chris but could not appear too eager, that Pat didn't really want to date Chris and only used the short notice as an excuse, or that Pat had already made plans despite Chris's presumptuousness.

Any violation of accepted time schedules is determined; that is, it has a reason. As senders we may or may not be consciously aware of such reasons. As receivers we can only guess at the possible reasons, based on whatever other cues are available.

Silence, paralanguage, and time are three elements of nonverbal communication that often function below the level of conscious awareness. Nevertheless, when a speaker or listener misuses any of these unstated rules, it frequently identifies the individual as one lacking in some social communication skill. It often distinguishes a person we enjoy interacting with from someone with whom we feel uncomfortable and ill at ease. Through an understanding of the ways in which these three dimensions affect our communications, we are less likely to break these small but socially significant rules of interpersonal interaction. At the same time, we will be better able to understand the problems and consequences that arise when these rules are broken.

Summary: Contents in Brief

Silence Can:	Paralanguage Cues Are Used to:	Time Can:
provide thinking time	form impressions of others	signal a wide variety of feelings: • interest–disinterest • willingness–unwillingness to socialize • concern–lack of concern
hurt	identify emotional states of speakers	
allow one to isolate oneself		
prevent communication	maintain speaking position	
communicate feelings	pass on speaking position	
communicate "nothing" or a desire to say nothing	indicate desire to speak	signal status differences
	make credibility judgments	signal social awareness or lack of it
vary greatly in meaning from one culture to another	make intelligence judgments	
	make objectivity judgments	

Sources

On silence, see Max Picard. *The World of Silence* (Chicago: Gateway, 1952) for a philosophical perspective and Irving J. Lee, "When to 'Keep Still,' " in Joseph A. DeVito, ed. *Language: Concepts and Processes* (Englewood Cliffs, N.J.: Prentice-Hall, 1973) and Don Fabun, *Communication: The Transfer of Meaning* (New York: Macmillan, 1968) for a communications perspective. On silence among the Apache, see K. H. Basso, " 'To Give Up on Worlds': Silence in Western Apache Culture," in Pier Paolo Giglioli, ed., *Language and Social Context* (Baltimore: Penguin Books, 1972). For studies on the discomfort of silence, see Helen M. Newman, "The Sounds of Silence in Communicative Encounters," *Communication Quarterly* 30 (Spring 1982): 142–149 and Margaret L. McLaughlin and Michael J. Cody, "Awkward Silences: Behavioral Antecedents and Consequences of the Conversational Lapse," *Human Communication Research* 8 (1982): 299–316.

For a classification of and introduction to paralinguistic phenomena, see George L. Trager, "Paralanguage: A First Approximation," *Studies in Linguistics* 13 (1958): 1–12 and "The Typology of Paralanguage," *Anthropological Linguistics* 3 (1961): 17–21. Mark Knapp, *Nonverbal Behavior in Human Interaction,* 2d ed. (New York: Holt, Rinehart and Winston, 1978) provides an excellent summary of research findings. For a collection of research studies on paralanguage, see Joel R. Davitz, ed., *The Communication of Emotional Meaning* (New York: McGraw-Hill, 1964). For the study by T. H. Pear, see his *Voice and Personality* (London: Chapman and Hall, 1931). For a thorough review of paralanguage, see Albert Mehrabian, *Silent Messages,* 2d ed. (Belmont, Calif.: Wadsworth, 1981) and W. P. Robinson, *Language and Social Behavior* (Baltimore: Penguin Books, 1972). The study of English and Scottish speakers and listeners can be found in W. M. Cheyne, "Stereotyped Reactions to Speakers with Scottish and English Regional Accents," *British Journal of Social and Clinical Psychology* 9 (1970): 77–79.

For the research reported in relation to speech rate, persuasion, and comprehension, I relied on John MacLachlan, "What People Really Think of Fast Talkers," *Psychology Today* 13 (November 1979): 113–117.

An excellent transitional article connecting the area of nonverbal communication and interpersonal relationships is provided by Judee K. Burgoon, David B. Buller, Jerold L. Hale, and Mark A. deTurck, "Relational Messages Associated with Nonverbal Behaviors," *Human Communication Research* 10 (Spring 1984): 351–378.

Part 4. Skills in Brief

Context
Assess the context in which nonverbal behavior takes place and interpret that behavior in its proper context; avoid seeing nonverbal behaviors as independent of context.

Packages or Clusters
Assess the entire package or cluster of nonverbal behaviors and interpret any nonverbal behavior as part of the cluster; avoid interpreting nonverbal behaviors in isolation.

Mixed-Message Detection
Detect mixed messages in other people's communications and avoid being placed in double-bind situations by seeking clarification from the sender.

Mixed-Message Sending
Avoid emitting mixed messages by focusing clearly on your purposes when communicating and by gaining more conscious control over your nonverbal behaviors.

Communication Inevitability
See all nonverbal behavior as communication and respond to the nonverbal as well as the verbal messages.

Cultural Rules
Respond to nonverbal behaviors according to the cultural rules of the sender; avoid interpreting the nonverbal behaviors of others exclusively through your own culture in order to avoid misinterpreting the intended meanings.

Nonverbal Meanings
Formulate hypotheses about the meanings of nonverbal behaviors; avoid drawing too definite conclusions about the meanings of any nonverbal behaviors.

Believability Judgments
Weigh both verbal and nonverbal messages before making believability judgments; increase sensitivity to cues to nonverbal (and verbal) deception, for example, too little movement, long pauses, slow speech, increased speech errors, mouth guard, nose touching, eye rubbing, the use of few words, especially monosyllabic answers. Use such cues to formulate hypotheses (rather than conclusions) concerning deception.

Adaptor Interference
Avoid adaptors that interfere with effective communication.

Emotional Communication
Increase your ability to communicate emotions nonverbally and decode emotional expression in others.

Eye Contact
Use eye contact effectively to monitor feedback, to signal conversational turns, to signal the nature of a relationship, and to compensate for physical distance.

Pupil Dilatation
Detect pupil dilatation and constriction and formulate hypotheses concerning their possible meanings.

Touch
Use touch to express consolation and support, power, and dominance. Never touch when "taking," as when criticizing or punishing.

Nonverbal Dominance
Resist nonverbal expressions of dominance when these are inappropriate, for example, when these behaviors are sexist.

Touch Rules
Respond to touch patterns of others in light of their gender and culture and not exclusively through your own.

Proxemic Distances
Adjust spatial (proxemic) distances as appropriate to the specific interaction (for example, distances that are too far, too close, or otherwise inappropriate); avoid inappropriate proxemic distances that might convey false impressions of your being too distant or too aggressive, for example.

Territoriality
Establish and maintain territory nonverbally by marking or otherwise indicating temporary or permanent ownership. Become sensitive to the territorial behavior of others.

Arrangement of Physical Setting
Arrange the physical setting of communication to stimulate effective and satisfying interactions; avoid creating spaces that make communication difficult and tedious (for example, seats that are too far apart or awkwardly aligned); arrange seating positions that are most conducive to the task at hand, for example, for conversing, cooperating, coacting, and competing.

Aesthetics
Make the physical context of communication as aesthetically pleasing as possible in order to make interpersonal interactions more effective and more satisfying.

Color Communication
Use colors (in clothing, in room decor, for example) to convey desired meanings.

Personality and Color
Avoid drawing conclusions about personality from color preferences.

Silence
Use silence to communicate feelings or to prevent communication about certain topics.

Silence Interpretation
Interpret silences of others through their culturally determined rules rather than your own.

Emotional Communication
Use paralanguage cues to encode and decode a wide variety of emotions.

Speaker and Listener Roles
Use paralanguage cues to maintain speaker and listener roles and to signal a desire for role change.

Speech Rate
Use variations in rate to increase communication efficiency and persuasiveness as appropriate.

Interpreting Time Cues
Interpret time cues from the point of view of the other's culture rather than your own.

Using Time Cues
Use time cues to signal your degree of interest or disinterest, willingness or unwillingness to communicate and socialize, and concern or lack of concern—for example, by arriving on time or by asking if it is an appropriate time to discuss an issue.

Leave-taking Cues
Increase your sensitivity to leave-taking cues; pick up on the leave-taking cues of others and communicate such cues tactfully so as not to insult or offend others.

Status Differences
Avoid inappropriate use of time cues in establishing and maintaining status differences.

Interpersonal Relationships

In this fifth part, we consider interpersonal relationships and the factors that influence their development and their deterioration. Attraction, power, and conflict are some of the more important factors involved in any and every interpersonal relationship. Each of these is considered in terms of its nature and, especially, in terms of what it means to our own relationships with others. Friendship, love, and primary relationships and families are singled out as our most important relationships and are covered in some detail. We examine the factors that influence these relationships for good or ill and consider ways in which these relationships may be made more effective and more rewarding. In the final two units we define relational deterioration and consider how to manage it most effectively.

In this largest part of the text, we raise a lot of questions:

Why and how do we develop relationships? ■ How can we more effectively initiate relationships? ■ What makes us attracted to another person? ■ What makes others attracted (or not attracted) to us? ■ Can we make ourselves more attractive to others? ■ How does power operate in an interpersonal relationship? ■ How can we increase our own power? ■ How can we prevent others from using power over us? ■ How does conflict operate interpersonally? ■ Are there benefits to be derived from conflict? ■ How and why do people fight unfairly? ■ How can we learn to fight more productively? ■ What is friendship? ■ How does friendship develop? ■ What is love? ■ How does love develop? ■ What conditions are most conducive to love? ■ How do we express our love verbally? ■ Nonverbally? ■ How do men and women differ as friends? ■ As lovers? ■ What keeps a family or a primary rela-

241

tionship together? ■ How might family communication be improved? ■ Why do relationships break down? ■ How do we communicate in relational deterioration? ■ Can we reverse relational deterioration? ■ What should we do if the relationship does end? ■ How can we manage the end of a relationship more effectively? ■ What skills can one master to become a more effective and more responsive relational partner? ■ What skills can one master to develop and manage relationships at all stages more effectively?

Universals of Interpersonal Relationships and Relational Development

OBJECTIVES

Upon completion of this unit, you should be able to:

1. identify at least four reasons for the development of interpersonal relationships
2. explain social exchange theory as it relates to relationship development
3. explain the five-stage model of relationships
4. identify the steps involved in initiating relationships
5. identify and explain at least eight suggestions for communicating in first encounters
6. define *breadth* and *depth* and illustrate how these concepts can be used to describe interpersonal relationships

There is probably nothing as important to you or me as contact with another human being. So important is contact with another person that when this is absent for prolonged periods of time, depression sets in, self-doubt surfaces, and one finds it difficult to conduct even the very basics of daily living. Research demonstrates clearly that the most important contributor to happiness—outranking money, job, and sex— is a close relationship with one other person.

This entire part of the text is devoted to interpersonal relationships. In this unit we focus on the development of interpersonal relationships: reasons for relational development, the stages characterizing relational development and deterioration, initiating relationships, and the breadth and depth of interpersonal relationships.

WHY INTERPERSONAL RELATIONSHIPS DEVELOP

Each person pursues a relationship for unique and individual reasons; no two relationships are pursued for exactly the same reason. Consequently, there are millions of reasons for seeking contact. Here we consider just four.

243

To Alleviate Loneliness

Contact with another human being helps to alleviate loneliness. At times we experience loneliness because we are physically alone, although being alone does not necessarily produce loneliness. Many can experience closeness with others though separated by long distances. At other times we are lonely because we have a need for close contact—sometimes physical, sometimes emotional, and most often both—that is, at least at the time, unfulfilled. From a different perspective, Chester Bennett makes a similar observation: ''Psychological studies of ship-wrecked sailors and prisoners in solitary confinement [and] experimental investigations of people who are closeted with their own thoughts for relatively brief periods of time . . . show how difficult it is for most of us to cope with isolation. We like solitude in small doses—if we can find a place to be alone in today's world. But mostly we seek companionship. We want to share experiences, even the private ones, with someone.''

We want to feel that someone cares, that someone likes us, that someone will protect us, that someone ultimately will love us. Close relationships assure us that someone does care, does like us, and will just be there when we need human contact.

Some people, in an attempt to alleviate loneliness, seek to surround themselves with numerous acquaintances. Sometimes this helps; often it only serves to make the loneliness all the more real. One close relationship usually works a lot better. Most of us know this, and that is why we seek to establish close, meaningful relationships.

To Secure Stimulation

Human beings, not unlike experimental monkeys and rats, need stimulation; if they are not stimulated, they withdraw; sometimes they die. Murray Davis, in *Intimate Relations*, refers to humans as *stimulotropic*. Like plants are heliotropic and orient themselves to light, humans orient themselves to sources of stimulation. Human contact is one of the best ways to be stimulated. We are composites of many different dimensions, and all our dimensions need stimulation. We are intellectual creatures, so we need intellectual stimulation. We talk with people about ideas, attend classes, argue about different interpretations of a film or novel. We thus exercise our analytical and interpretative abilities. In so doing we sharpen and expand them.

But we are also physical creatures and need physical stimulation as well. We need to touch and be touched; we need to hold and be held; we need to look at people and have them look at us—not through us or around us or at our new jacket, but at *us*. Perhaps we need to be assured that we are physical beings.

We are also emotional creatures and need emotional stimulation. We need to laugh and cry. We need to feel hope and surprise, to experience warmth and affection. We need exercise for our emotions as well as for our intellectual capacities. In our culture men have been taught that it is wrong to cry or show fear. Women have been taught that it is wrong to be aggressive or to feel sexual. Both sexes need to be retaught, because both need the emotions once culturally assigned only to one sex.

To Establish Contact for Self-knowledge

We need contact with other human beings because through them we learn about ourselves; that is, we acquire essential knowledge of self largely through interaction with others. We see ourselves in part through the eyes of others. If our friends see us as warm and generous, for example, we will probably also see ourselves as warm and generous. Our self-perceptions are greatly influenced by what we think others think of us, so contact with others enables us to see ourselves in a somewhat different way, from a somewhat different perspective.

Social comparison theory, for example, holds that we evaluate and assess ourselves—our attitudes, talents, values, accomplishments, abilities—primarily through comparing ourselves with others. These comparisons are, in large part, accomplished through our interpersonal interactions and relationships.

245

Unit 18:
Universals of
Interpersonal
Relationships and
Relational
Development

To Maximize Pleasures and Minimize Pain

The most general reason we establish relationships, and one that could include all the others, is that we seek human contact so that our pleasures may be maximized and our pain minimized. We have a need to share our good fortune with other people—perhaps to earn their praise, perhaps to assure us that we are in fact fortu-

Our interpersonal relationships help us to alleviate loneliness, secure stimulation, gain self-knowledge, maximize our pleasures, and minimize our pains. When these reasons for relational development are diminished, the relationship begins to deteriorate and may eventually dissolve. The communication choices we make during both relational development and relational deterioration will determine in great part the further course of the relationship as well as the satisfaction that we derive from the relational processes.

nate, perhaps to participate with us in enjoying the newfound pleasures. We also have a need to seek out relationships when we are in emotional or physical pain. Perhaps this goes back to when we were children and ran to mother to kiss our wounds or tell us everything was all right. We now find it difficult to run to mother, so we go to others, generally to friends who will provide us with the same kind of consolation that mother did.

A significant complication is introduced when we realize that in the satisfaction of one need, another need may of necessity go unsatisfied. For example, consider the person who forms a close primary relationship out of a need for security, social status, and economics but who also needs to be independent and to interact intimately with a number of different people. The two classes of needs contradict each other. If one of these groups of needs is satisfied, the other must go unsatisfied. Whether one develops and maintains the relationship or terminates it depends on how strong the various needs are. For example, some of us have a very strong need to affiliate with others; some of us have a strong need for independence. Which needs will prevail and whether the relationship develops or deteriorates will depend on the relative strength of these needs. But the fact that our needs so often do conflict is perhaps one of the reasons so few people are entirely satisfied with their relationships. Often such dissatisfaction is not the ''fault'' of our partner or of ourselves but is simply in the nature of our complicated and often conflicting system of needs.

SOCIAL EXCHANGE

Put in terms of the *social exchange theory,* we would say that we develop relationships in which our rewards or profits will be greater than our costs. We involve ourselves in relationships that provide us with rewards or profits—basically, the things that fulfill our needs for security, sex, social approval, financial gain, status, and so on. But rewards or profits involve some cost or ''payback.'' For example, in order to acquire the reward of financial gain, an individual might have to give up some degree of freedom. The cost of gaining parental approval might be a loveless marriage or giving up a relationship that provided other types of rewards or gains. Using this basic economic-oriented model, the social exchange theory puts into clearer perspective our tendency to seek profit (gain or reward) while incurring the least cost (punishment or loss). If you think about your current or past relationships, you will be able to see clearly that the relationships you pursued and maintained have been those that provided you with greater profit and greater need fulfillment than cost. Relationships you did not pursue or that you terminated were probably ones whose costs or loses exceeded the rewards or profits; these were the relationships in which there was more dissatisfaction than satisfaction, more unhappiness than happiness, more problems than pleasures.

STAGES IN INTERPERSONAL RELATIONSHIPS: DEVELOPMENT AND DETERIORATION

Most relationships, possibly all, are established in stages. We do not become intimate friends immediately upon meeting someone; rather we grow into an intimate relationship gradually, through a series of steps or stages. And the same is probably true

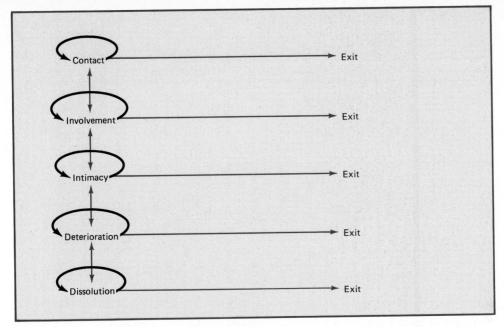

FIGURE 18.1: A Five-Stage Relationship Model.

247

Unit 18:
Universals of
Interpersonal
Relationships and
Relational
Development

with most other relationships as well. "Love at first sight" seems to create a problem for a stage model of relationships, so rather than argue that such love cannot occur (my own feeling is that it can and frequently does), it seems wiser to claim that the stage model of relationships characterizes *most* relationships for *most* people *most* of the time.

The five-stage model presented in Figure 18.1 seems a suitable one for describing at least some of the significant stages in the development of relationships. For each specific relationship, you might wish to modify and revise the basic model in various ways. But as a general description of relationship development, the stages seem fairly standard. Several additional attempts to identify relationship stages are presented in Table 18.1. Because the development of these models is, in many ways, in its infancy, these models are best viewed as initial and tentative explanations of this most complex of interpersonal processes.

The Five Stages

The five stages to be identified here are contact, involvement, intimacy, deterioration, and dissolution. These stages describe relationships as they are; they are not intended to evaluate or to prescribe how relationships should be.

CONTACT

At this first stage we make contact; there is some kind of sense perception—we see the person, we hear the person, we smell the person. This is the stage of "Hello, my name is Joe"—the stage at which we exchange basic information that is preliminary to any more intense involvement. This is the stage at which we initiate interaction ("May I join you?") and engage in invitational communication ("May I buy

TABLE 18.1: Models of Relational Development

DeVito	Levinger	Knapp	Wood	Altman and Taylor	Krug	Swensen
Contact	Zero contact Awareness Surface contact	Initiating	Individuals alone and receptive Invitational communication	Orientation	Initiation	Sampling
Involvement	Mutuality Moderate interaction	Experimenting Intensifying	Explorational communication Intensifying Revising	Exploratory affective exchange	Experimentation Liking Trial	Bargaining
Intimacy	Major intersection	Integrating Bonding	Bonding Navigating	Affective exchange Stable exchange	Coupling Stabilization—nurturance	Commitment Institutionalization
Deterioration		Differentiating Circumscribing Stagnating Avoiding	Differentiating Disintegrating Stagnating		Stabilization—conflict development	
Dissolution		Terminating	Terminating Individuals		Termination Avoidance Maintenance	

Note: Many writers on interpersonal communication have developed models of the stages in relationships. I present several of these here. My purpose is not to add complexity to an already complex area but rather to provide a sampling of additional perspectives and to enable you to see how any of the stages noted here could be differentiated further. For example, Levinger differentiates three levels of contact: zero or no contact, awareness, and surface contact. Knapp identifies two stages of involvement: experimenting and intensifying. Complete references to these models are provided in the source note at the end of this unit.

you a drink?''). According to some researchers, it is at this stage—within the first four minutes of initial interaction—that we decide if we want to pursue the relationship or not.

It is at this stage that physical appearance is so important because it is the physical dimensions that are most open to sensory inspection. Yet through both verbal and nonverbal behaviors, qualities such as friendliness, warmth, openness, and dynamism are also revealed at this stage. If we like the individual and want to pursue the relationship, we proceed to the second stage, the stage of involvement.

249

Unit 18:
Universals of
Interpersonal
Relationships and
Relational
Development

INVOLVEMENT

At this stage a sense of mutuality, of connectedness develops. During this stage we experiment and attempt to learn more about the other person.

The involvement stage is the stage of acquaintances, the stage at which we commit ourselves to getting to know the other person better and also to revealing ourselves to the other person. It is at this stage that we begin to share, in a preliminary way, our feelings and our emotions. If this is to be a romantic relationship, we might date at this stage: if it is to be a friendship relationship, we might share our mutual interests—go to the movies or to some sports event together.

INTIMACY

At the intimacy stage we commit ourselves still further to the other person and, in fact, establish a kind of relationship in which this individual becomes our best or closest friend, lover, or companion. This is the stage of bonding or coupling, when the individuals integrate and become a unit, an identifiable pair.

The commitment may take many forms; it may be an engagement or a marriage; it may be a commitment to help the person or to be with the person, or a commitment to reveal our deepest secrets. It may consist of living together or an agreement to ''become lovers.'' The type of commitment varies with the relationship and with the individual, but the important characteristic is that the commitment made is a special one; it is a commitment that we do not make lightly or to everyone. This intimacy stage is reserved for very few people at any given time—sometimes just one, sometimes two, three, or perhaps four. Rarely do we have more than four intimates, except in a family situation.

DETERIORATION

This stage and the next (dissolution) focus on the weakening of bonds between the parties and represent the down side of the relationship progression.

At the deterioration stage we begin to feel that this relationship may not be as important as we had previously thought. We grow further and further apart. We share less of our free time together, and when we are together there are awkward silences, fewer self-disclosures, less physical contact, and a lack of psychological closeness. There seems to be a general self-consciousness in our communication exchanges. Conflicts become more and more common, and their resolution becomes more and more difficult. In many cases we allow the conflicts to go unresolved, perhaps not caring enough to go through the trouble.

At this stage we are not exactly sure what to call our ''intimate.'' The person is not quite a lover or an ex-lover, not really a close friend but not an ex-friend either. This deterioration stage is that awkward in-between stage of neither here not there. If this deterioration stage continues unaltered, we enter the stage of dissolution.

The dissolution stage is the cutting of the bonds tying the individuals together. In a marriage, dissolution takes the form of establishing separate and different lives away from each other and eventually perhaps divorce. Avoidance of each other and a return to being or at least feeling "single" are among the primary identifiable features of this stage.

In some cases the former partners change the definition of their relationship, and, for example, the ex-lovers become friends or "just" business partners.

This is the point of "good-bye," the point at which we become ex-lovers, ex-friends, ex-husbands, ex-wives. At times this is a stage of relief and relaxation—finally it is over and done with. At other times this is a stage of intense anxiety and frustration, of recriminations and hostility, of resentment over the time ill-spent and now lost. In more materialistic terms, it is the stage where property is divided, where legal battles ensue over who should get the Mercedes and who should get the Rolls-Royce. It is the time of child-custody battles.

But it is also the time during which the ex-partners begin to look upon themselves as individuals, rather than as part of a pair, and to the establishment of a new and different life, either alone or with another person. Some people, it is true, continue to live psychologically with a relationship that has already been dissolved; they frequent old meeting places, reread old love letters, daydream about all the good times, and, in general, dwell on the ended relationship and thus fail to extricate themselves from a relationship that has died in every way except in their minds.

Movement Among the Stages

Figure 18.1 contains three types of arrows. The "exit" arrows indicate that each stage offers the opportunity to exit the relationship. After saying "hello" we can say "good-bye" and exit. The vertical or "movement" arrows going to the next stage and back again represent the fact that we can move to another stage, either one that is more intense (say, from involvement to intimacy) or one that is less intense (say, from intimacy to deterioration). We can also go back to a previously established stage. For example, you may have established an intimate relationship with someone but did not want to maintain it at that level. At the same time, you were relatively pleased with the relationship, and it was not really deteriorating. You just wanted it to be less intense, so you might go back to the involvement stage and reestablish the relationship at that more comfortable level. Similarly, if problems and differences are worked out in the deterioration stage, the people may reestablish an intimate relationship. And of course we may skip stages, although instances of this are probably not as common as one might think. Often people in a relationship appear to be skipping a stage when they are merely passing through it very quickly. Often, for example, a couple seems to skip from the initial stage of contact to the stage of intimacy. It is likely that they have not bypassed involvement; it is probably that the involvement stage lasted for only a very short time and to outsiders was not apparent. This is not to say, however, that in certain instances a stage could not be skipped. The stages, then, may last for different periods of time; there is no fixed time period that any stage must occupy. Stages may be extremely short or extremely long in duration.

The "self-reflexive" arrows—the arrows that return to the beginning of the same level or stage—signify that any relationship may become stabilized at any point. We may, for example, continue to maintain a relationship at the intimate level without its deteriorating or going back to a less intense stage of involvement. Or we might remain at the "Hello, how are you?" stage—the contact stage—without getting involved any further.

Movement through the various stages is usually a gradual process; we don't jump from contact to involvement to intimacy, for example. Rather, we progress gradually, a few degrees at a time. And yet, there are leaps that must and do take place. For example, during the involvement stage of a romantic relationship, the first kiss or the first sexual encounter requires a leap; it requires a change in the kind of communication and in the kind of intimacy to be experienced by the two people. Before these leaps are taken, we try to test the waters gradually. Before the first kiss, for example, we may hold each other, look longingly into each other's eyes, and perhaps caress each other's face. We do this in part to discover if the leap—the kiss, for example—will be responded to favorably or will be resisted. No one wants rejection—especially rejection of our romantic advances.

251

Unit 18:
Universals of
Interpersonal
Relationships and
Relational
Development

INITIATING RELATIONSHIPS: THE FIRST ENCOUNTER

Perhaps the most difficult and yet the most important aspect of relationship development is the process of initiating relationships—meeting the person, presenting yourself, and somehow moving to another stage, which, in our earlier model, would be to exit or to progress to a stage that is somewhat more intimate. Murray Davis, in *Intimate Relations,* notes that the first encounter consists of six steps. In addition to presenting these six steps we will also consider some communication guidelines or principles that should help make the first encounter more effective.

EXAMINE THE QUALIFIERS

The first step is to examine the qualifiers, those qualities that make the individual you wish to encounter an appropriate choice. Some qualifiers are manifest or open to easy inspection such as beauty, style of clothes, jewelry, and the like. Other qualifiers are latent or hidden from easy inspection such as personality, health, wealth, talent, intelligence, and the like. These qualifiers tell us something about who the person is and help us to decide if we wish to pursue this initial encounter.

DETERMINE CLEARANCE

Try to determine if this person is available for an encounter. Is the person wearing a wedding ring? Does the person seem to be waiting for someone else?

OPEN THE ENCOUNTER

Open the encounter, both nonverbally and verbally. Davis suggests that we look for two things: (1) a topic that will interest the other person (and you) and that could be drawn out of the opener and (2) indications by the other person of a readiness to engage in a more protracted encounter. If yes/no answers are given to your questions or if eye contact is not maintained then you have some pretty good indication that this person is not open to an extended encounter with you at this time. If, on the other hand, the person responds at length or asks you questions in return, then you have some positive feedback that says "continue."

An integrating topic is one that will interest the other person and you and will serve to integrate or unite the two of you. Generally, such topics are found through an analysis of free information and questions and answers. Look, therefore, for free information—information about the person that you can see or that is dropped into the conversation. For example, a college ring or jacket, a beeper, or a uniform will tell you something about the person and will suggest a possible topic of conversation. Similarly, a casual remark may include the person's occupation or area of study or sports interests—all of which can be used as take-off points for further interaction. Look and listen, therefore, for the free information that will enable you to continue the interaction and that will suggest additional communication topics. Further, ask questions (none that are too prying, of course) to discover more about this person and to communicate your interest.

CREATE A FAVORABLE IMPRESSION

Display what is called a "come-on self," a part of you that is inviting, engaging, and otherwise interesting to another person. Display a part of you that will make the other person want to continue the encounter.

ESTABLISH A SECOND MEETING

If you and your new partner seem to be getting along then a second meeting should be established. This may be a very general type of meeting—"Do you always eat here on Friday's?"—to a very specific type of meeting—"How about going to the beach next Saturday?"

During this first encounter, put into operation all the interpersonal communication principles you have already acquired. Here, however, are a few additional suggestions geared specifically to this first encounter. Although we divide this into the "nonverbal encounter" and the "verbal encounter," recognize that these must be integrated into any effective encounter.

The Nonverbal Encounter

Nonverbal communication concerns all and every aspect of yourself that sends messages to another person. On the basis of these messages, this other person forms an impression of you—an impression that will be quickly and firmly established.

1. Establish eye contact. Eye contact is the first nonverbal signal to send. The eyes communicate an awareness of, an interest in the other person.
2. While maintaining eye contact, smile and further signal your interest in and your positive response to this other person.
3. Concentrate your focus. The rest of the room should be nonverbally shut off from awareness. Be careful, however, that you do not focus too directly so as to make the person uncomfortable.
4. Establish physical closeness or at least lessen the physical distance between the two of you. Approach, but not to the point of discomfort, so that your interest in making contact is obvious.
5. Maintain an open posture. Throughout this nonverbal encounter, maintain a

posture that communicates an openness, a willingness to enter into interaction with the other person. Hands crossed over the chest or clutched around your stomach are exactly the kind of postures that you want to avoid. These are often interpreted to signal an unwillingness to let others enter your space.

6. Respond visibly. Assuming that your nonverbal communication is returned, respond to it visibly with a smile, a head nod, a wink.
7. Reinforce positive behaviors. Reinforce those behaviors of the other person that signal interest and a reciprocal willingness to make contact. Reinforce these by responding positively to them; again, nod or smile or somehow indicate your favorable reaction.
8. Avoid overexposure. Nonverbal communication works to make contact or to signal interest, but it can cause problems if it is excessive or if it is not followed by more direct communication. Consequently, if you intend to make verbal contact do so after a relatively short time or try another time.

253

Unit 18:
Universals of
Interpersonal
Relationships and
Relational
Development

The Verbal Encounter

1. Introduce yourself. Try to avoid trite and cliché opening lines. Don't become identified with "Haven't I seen you here before?" Actually, these openers are legitimate and would be more than appropriate if others understood that these lines are merely ways of saying "Hello." But, many do not; many think that these lines are a measure of your intelligence and wit. Given that sorry state of affairs, it is probably best to simply say, "Hi, my name is Pat."
2. Focus the conversation on the other person. Get the other person involved in talking about himself or herself; no one enjoys talking about anything more. Also, it will provide you with a opportunity to learn something about the person you want to get to know.
3. Exchange favors-rewards. Compliment the other person; be sincere but complimentary and positive. If you can't find anything to compliment the person about then it is probably wise to reassess your interest in this person and perhaps move on.
4. Be energetic. No one likes a lethargic, slow-moving, nondynamic partner. Demonstrate your high energy level, not by dancing all around but by responding facially with appropriate affect, smiling, talking in a varied manner, being flexible with your body posture and gestures, asking questions as appropriate, and otherwise demonstrating that you are really here.
5. Stress the positives. In the discussion of interpersonal effectiveness we noted that positiveness was one of the major qualities of effectiveness. It also contributes to a positive first impression simply because we like and are attracted more to a positive than to a negative person.
6. Avoid negative and too intimate self-disclosures. Enter a relationship gradually and gracefully. Disclosures should come gradually and along with reciprocal disclosures. Anything too intimate or too negative early in the relationship will create a negative image. If you cannot resist self-disclosing then try to stick to the positives and to those matters that would not be considered overly intimate.
7. Establish commonalities. Seek to discover in your interaction those things you have in common with the other person—attitudes, interests, personal qualities, third parties, places, and in fact anything that will stress a oneness.

BREADTH AND DEPTH OF INTERPERSONAL RELATIONSHIPS

Relationships may be described in terms of the number of topics talked about and the degree of "personalness" to which these topics are pursued. The number of topics about which the individuals communicate is referred to as *breadth*. The degree to which the inner personality, the inner core of an individual, is penetrated in the interpersonal interaction is referred to as *depth*.

Let us represent an individual as a circle and divide that circle into various parts. These parts would represent the topics or areas of interpersonal communication or breadth. Further, visualize the circle and its parts as consisting of concentric inner circles. These would represent the different levels of communication or the depth. Representative examples are provided in Figure 18.2. The circles are all divided into eight topic areas (identified A through H) and five levels of intimacy (represented by the concentric circles). Note that in circle A, only three of the topic areas are penetrated. Two of these are penetrated only on the first level, and one of them is penetrated to the second level. In this type of interaction, three topic areas are talked about, and they are discussed at rather superficial levels. This is the type of relationship we might have with an acquaintance. Circle B represents a more intense relationship, a relationship that is broader (here four topics are discussed) and in which the topics are discussed to a deeper level of penetration. This is the type of relationship we might have with a friend. In circle C we have a still more intense relationship. Here there is considerable breadth (seven of the eight areas are penetrated) and depth (note that most of the areas are penetrated to the deepest levels). This is the type of relationship we might have with a lover or a parent.

All relationships—friendships, loves, families—may be profitably described in terms of these concepts of breadth and depth, concepts central to the theory of *social penetration* developed by Irwin Altman and Dalmas Taylor. In its initial stage a relationship would normally be characterized by narrow breadth (few topics would be discussed) and shallow depth (the topics that are discussed would be discussed only superficially). If early in a relationship topics are discussed to a depth that would normally be reserved for intimates, we would probably experience considerable

FIGURE 18.2: Social Penetration with (A) an Acquaintance, (B) a Friend, and (C) an Intimate.

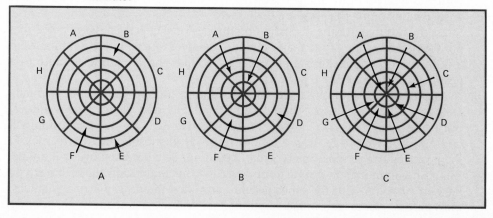

discomfort. As already noted (in Unit 8, "Self-disclosure"), when intimate disclosures are made early in a relationship, we feel something is wrong with the disclosing individual. As the relationship grows in intensity and intimacy, both the breadth and the depth increase, and these increases are seen as comfortable, normal, and natural progressions.

Depenetration

255

Unit 18:
Universals of
Interpersonal
Relationships and
Relational
Development

When a relationship begins to deteriorate, the breadth and depth will, in many ways, reverse themselves—a process of *depenetration*. For example, while in the process of terminating a relationship, you might eliminate certain topics from your interpersonal interactions and at the same time discuss the topics you discuss in less depth. You would, for example, reduce the level of your self-disclosures and reveal less and less of your innermost feelings. This reversal does not always work, of course. In some instances of relational deterioration, both the breadth and the depth of interaction increase. A good example of this is seen in the film *Making Love*. Here the relationship between Michael Ontkean and Kate Jackson is breaking up because after eight years of marriage he realizes that he is attracted to men. But during the breakup we see a process of penetration rather than depenetration; they each reveal themselves to each other to a much greater depth and discuss more topic areas than they had previously. Usually, however, relational deterioration is characterized by a decrease in both breadth and depth.

Summary: Contents in Brief

Reasons Interpersonal Relationships Develop	Stages	Initiating Realtionships	Breadth and Depth
To alleviate loneliness	Contact	Examine the qualifiers	*Breadth:* the number of topics about which the individuals communicate; increases as relationship develops and decreases in deterioration
To secure stimulation	Involvement	Determine clearance	
To establish contact for self-knowledge	Intimacy	Open the encounter	
	Deterioration	Select and put into operation an integrating topic	*Depth:* the degree to which the inner personality is penetrated; increases as relationship develops (penetration) and decreases as relationship deteriorates (depenetration)
To maximize pleasures and minimize pain	Dissolution	Create a favorable impression	
		Establish a second meeting	

Sources

In approaching the study of interpersonal relationships, you may wish to consult the following works to gain an additional and somewhat different perspective: Murray S. Davis, *Intimate Relations* (New York: Free Press, 1973) and Mark L. Knapp, *Interpersonal Communication and Human Relationships* (Boston: Allyn & Bacon, 1984). Also see Chester C. Bennett, "Secrets Are for Sharing," *Psychology Today* 2 (February 1969): 31–34 on the need for interpersonal contact. For different views on the stages of a relationship, see, for example, Knapp's *Interpersonal Communication;* Linda Krug, "Alternative Lifestyle Dyads: An Alternative Relationship Paradigm," *Alternative Communications* 4 (May 1982): 32–52; Julia T. Wood, "Communication and Relational Culture: Bases for the Study of Human Relationships," *Communication Quarterly* 30 (Spring 1982): 75–83; George Levinger, "The Embrace of Lives: Changing and Unchanging," *Close Relationships: Perspectives on the Meaning of Intimacy,* ed., George Levinger and Harold L. Raush (Amherst: University of Massachusetts Press, 1977), pp. 1–16; and C. H. Swensen, *Introduction to Interpersonal Relations* (Glenview, Ill.: Scott, Foresman, 1973).

On social penetration, see Irwin Altman and Dalmas Taylor, *Social Penetration: The Development of Interpersonal Relationships* (New York: Holt, Rinehart and Winston, 1973). In this connection also see Leslie A. Baxter, "Relationship Disengagement: An Examination of the Reversal Hypothesis," *Western Journal of Speech Communication* 47 (Spring 1983): 85–98. On different relationships and the names we use to label them, see Mark L. Knapp, Donald G. Ellis, and Barbara A. Williams, "Perceptions of Communication Behavior Associated with Relationship Terms," *Communication Monographs* 47 (November 1980): 262–278.

On social exchange theory, see, for example, J. W. Thibaut and H. H. Kelley, *The Social Psychology of Groups* (New York: Wiley, 1959) and H. H. Kelley and J. W. Thibaut, *Interpersonal Relations: A Theory of Interdependence* (New York: Wiley/Interscience, 1978). A thorough and insightful review of research in relationships is provided by Arthur Bochner, "The Functions of Human Communication in Interpersonal Bonding," Carroll C. Arnold and John Waite Bowers, eds., *Handbook of Rhetorical and Communication Theory* (Boston: Allyn & Bacon, 1984), pp. 544–621. On approaches to studying interpersonal relationships, see Steve Duck and Robin Gilmour, eds. *Personal Relationships. 1: Studying Personal Relationships* (New York: Academic Press, 1981). For a somewhat different approach to interpersonal relationships, see Donald P. Cushman and Dudley D. Cahn, Jr., *Communication in Interpersonal Relationships* (Albany: State University of New York, 1985).

UNIT 19

Attraction in Interpersonal Relationships

OBJECTIVES

Upon completion of this unit, you should be able to:

1. define *interpersonal attraction*
2. define *attractiveness* and explain its influence in interpersonal attraction
3. explain the relativity of physical and personality attractiveness
4. identify some of the sex differences in attractiveness
5. define *proximity* and explain the ways in which it influences interpersonal attraction
6. explain the *"mere exposure"* hypothesis
7. define *reinforcement* and explain how it enters into interpersonal attraction
8. explain the *"gain-loss"* theory of attraction
9. define *similarity* and explain how it operates in interpersonal attraction
10. explain the *"matching"* hypothesis
11. define *complementarity* and explain the ways in which it influences interpersonal attraction

We are all attracted to some people and not attracted to others. In a similar way, some people are attracted to us and some people are not. This seems to be the universal human condition. If we were to examine the people we are attracted to and the people we are not attracted to, we would probably see patterns in the decisions or judgments we make, even though many of these decisions seem subconsciously motivated.

We are all probably attracted to a "type" of person or to "types" of people. This ideal type (which differs for each person) can probably be found, in varying degrees, in each of the people we are attracted to and its opposite, in varying degrees, in each of the people we are not attracted to. Most people are attracted to others on the basis of five major variables: attractiveness (physical and personality), proximity, reinforcement, similarity, and complementarity.

ATTRACTIVENESS (PHYSICAL AND PERSONALITY)

When we say, "I find that person attractive," we probably mean either that (1) we find that person physically attractive or (2) we find that person's personality or ways of behaving attractive. For the most part we like physically attractive people rather than physically ugly people, and we like people who possess a pleasant personality rather than an unpleasant personality. Few would find fault with these two generalizations. The difficulty arises when we try to define *attractive*.

Defining Attractiveness

A good way to illustrate the difficulty in defining attractiveness is to look at some old movies, newspapers, or magazines and compare the conceptions of beauty portrayed there with those popular now. Or examine the conceptions of beauty in different cultures. At some times and in some cultures, people who are fat by our standards would be considered attractive, but in other cultures they would be considered unattractive. At one time fashion models were supposed to be extremely thin, whereas they are now allowed to have some flesh on their bones. The same difficulty besets us when we attempt to define "pleasant personality." To some this would mean an aggressive, competitive, forceful individual; to others it might mean an unassuming, shy, and bashful individual.

Similarly, we probably look for different physical and personality characteristics depending on the situation in which we are interacting. In a classroom it might be important to sit next to someone who knows all the answers, so regardless of this person's physical appearance, this "answer machine" is perceived as attractive. To go on a swimming date, however, we might select someone with a good body and not be too concerned with the person's intellectual abilities. When inviting someone to join a football team we might choose someone heavy and strong.

Although attractiveness (both physical and personality) is difficult, if not impossible, to define universally, it is possible to define it for any one individual for specific situations. Thus a person who was interested in dating someone would choose someone who possessed certain characteristics. For this person, then, in this situation, these are the characteristics that are considered attractive. In all probability, this same person in another, similar situation would again look for someone who possessed these same characteristics. We are relatively consistent in the characteristics we find attractive.

Forming Impressions

Generally, we attribute positive characteristics to people we find attractive and negative characteristics to people we find unattractive. If people were asked to predict which qualities a given individual possessed, they would probably predict the possession of positive qualities if they thought the person attractive and negative characteristics if they thought the person unattractive. Numerous studies have supported this commonsense observation. In a Vanderbilt University study, young male psychologists who were training to be therapists responded with greater warmth and supportiveness to attractive women than to unattractive women. These soon-to-be therapists also judged that the less attractive clients would more likely discontinue therapy. Perhaps we have here wishful thinking that develops into a self-fulfilling prophecy.

In another investigation of attractiveness and ugliness in mental adjustment, researchers compared the attractiveness of hospitalized women with university employees and shoppers. It was found that lower levels of adjustment (for example, general satisfaction with life and with personal relationships) characterized the early lives of ugly subjects. The researchers concluded that "it is not mental illness that makes people ugly, but rather ugliness and its social consequences that drive some of them crazy."

When photographs of men and women varying in attractiveness were viewed by both men and women who were asked to assess these persons, the more attractive persons were judged to be sexually warmer and more responsive, more sensitive, kinder, more interesting, stronger, more poised, more modest, more sociable, more outgoing, to make more competent husbands and wives, to have happier marriages, and to secure more prestigious jobs. The less attractive persons were judged to make better parents.

When 400 teachers were shown identical report cards but with different pictures attached, some of attractive students and some of unattractive ones, the teachers rated the report cards with the attractive students' pictures attached as having higher educational potential, higher IQs, better social relationships with peers, and parents who were more interested in their education.

Even children have prejudices and are subject to attractiveness bias. For example, children between the ages of 4 and 6 believed that aggressive, antisocial behavior was more characteristic of unattractive than of attractive children. And female students, given a written description of some delinquent act and a photograph of the

The Venus de Milo, the ancient statue of the goddess Aphrodite, carved around 150 B.C., not only captured the then accepted standard of beauty but also influenced standards of beauty for hundreds of years, in ways not too different from contemporary actors and models (and body builders) influencing our conception of what makes one attractive.

person who supposedly committed the act, judged the unattractive child as having more antisocial impulses and as more likely to misbehave in the future. Attractive female college students received more favorable evaluations from fellow male students on essays they supposedly wrote and "earned" higher overall grade-point averages in college than did unattractive females.

When students were asked to rate a man in terms of intelligence, self-confidence, likability, and talent, he was rated more favorably on all four variables when he was pictured with an attractive girlfriend than when the very same man was pictured with an unattractive girlfriend.

It seems clear from these studies and from hundreds of others that attractiveness is an asset for both men and women but is especially important for women. It also seems clear that his is a cultural phenomenon; we have been conditioned throughout our lives to look at women in terms of attractiveness and at men in terms of ability. This difference is well illustrated in one study in which men and women were asked to rate the qualities they find most important in the opposite sex. The results are presented in Table 19.1.

It also seems clear that such findings as these (as well as the findings reported earlier on the relative importance of attractiveness in both men and women) are undergoing considerable change and will in the next decade or two change even more. Women are now beginning to be evaluated more in terms of their abilities and men more in terms of their physical attractiveness. And this trend seems likely to continue.

PROXIMITY

Some 200 years ago, Henry Carey, in *Sally in Our Alley,* expressed the concept of proximity:

> Of all the girls that are so smart
> There's none like pretty Sally;
> She is the darling of my heart,
> And lives in our alley.

TABLE 19.1: Qualities Judged Most Important in a Potential Partner

For Men	For Women
1. achievement	1. physical attractiveness
2. leadership	2. erotic ability
3. occupational ability	3. affectional ability
4. economic ability	4. social ability
5. entertaining ability	5. domestic ability
6. intellectual ability	6. sartorial ability
7. observational ability	7. interpersonal understanding
8. common sense	8. art appreciation
9. athletic ability	9. moral and spiritual understanding
10. theoretical ability	10. art and creative ability

SOURCE: From R. Centers, "The Completion Hypothesis and the Compensatory Dynamic in Intersexual Attraction and Love," *Journal of Psychology* 82 (1972): 111–126.

How Proximity Works

If we look around at the people we find attractive, we would probably find that they are the people who live or work close to us. This is perhaps the one finding that emerges most frequently from the research on interpersonal attraction. In one of the most famous studies, Leon Festinger, Stanley Schachter, and Kurt Back studied friendships in a student housing development. They found that the development of friendships was greatly influenced by the distance between the units in which the people lived and by the direction in which the units faced. The closer the students' rooms were to each other, the better the chances that they would become friends. Also, the students living in units facing the courtyard had more friends than the students living in units facing the street. The people who became friends were the people who had the greatest opportunity to interact with each other.

In college dormitories and in city housing projects with a number of floors, most friendships develop between people living on the same floor; few develop between people on different floors. In fact, proximity influences not only who become friends but also how close the friendships come to be: the closer the living quarters, the closer the friendships. It is interesting to note that the vast majority of marriages are between people who have lived very close to each other.

Asked to name their friends, cadets at the training academy of the Maryland State Police named persons who sat in class and roomed in close proximity and with whom they therefore had more frequent interaction. Again, it appears that proximity leads to attraction.

As might be predicted, physical distance is most important in the early stages of interaction. For example, during the first days of school, proximity (in class or in dormitories) is especially important. It decreases (but always remains significant) as the opportunity to interact with more distant others increases.

The importance of physical distance also varies with the type of situation. For example, in anxiety-producing situations we seem to have more need for company and hence are more easily attracted to others than when we are in situations with low or no anxiety. It is also comforting to be with people who have gone through (or who will go through) the same experiences as we have. We seem especially attracted to these people in times of stress. We are also more attracted to someone else if we have previously been deprived of such interaction. If, for example, we were in a hospital or prison without any contact with other people, we would probably be attracted to just about anyone. Anyone seems a great deal better than no one. We are also most attracted to people when we are feeling down or when our self-esteem is particularly low.

Why Proximity Works

When we attempt to discover the reasons for the influence that physical closeness has on interpersonal attraction, we can think of many. We seem to have positive expectations of people and consequently fulfill these by liking or being attracted to those we find ourselves near. Proximity also allows us the opportunity to get to know the other person—to gain some information about him or her. We come to like people we know because we can better predict their behavior, and perhaps because of this they seem less frightening to us than complete strangers.

Still another approach argues that *mere exposure* to others leads us to develop positive feelings for them. In one study women were supposedly participating in a taste experiment and throughout the course of the experiment were exposed to other people. The subjects were exposed to some people ten times, to others five times, to others two times, to others one time, and to others not at all. The subjects did not talk with these other people and had never seen them before this experiment. The subjects were then asked to rate the other people in terms of how much they liked them. The results showed that they rated highest the persons they had seen ten times, next highest those they had seen five times, and so on down the line. How can we account for these results except by mere exposure? Consider another study. Three groups of rats were selected at random. One group listened to recordings of Mozart for 12 hours a day for 52 days. Another group listened to recordings of Schoenberg for 12 hours a day for 52 days. A third group listened to no music. After these 52 days, each rat was placed in a specially designed cage so that it could select its own music. The music the rats selected was written by the same composer as the music they had been exposed to for the 52-day period. Thus the rats raised on Mozart selected Mozart; the rats raised on Schoenberg selected Schoenberg. (By the way, Mozart was also preferred by the rats raised without music.) The music the rats heard during the 52-day period was not the same as that selected by the rats in the specially designed cages; it was only written by the same composer. Again, can we account for these findings in any way other than mere exposure?

Of course, if our initial interaction with a person is unpleasant, repeated exposure may not increase attraction. Mere exposure seems to work when the initial interaction is favorable or neutral; in these cases exposure increases attraction. When the initial interaction is negative, however, repeated exposure may actually decrease attraction.

Connected to this "mere exposure" concept is the finding that the greater the contact between people, the less they are prejudiced against each other. For example, whites and blacks living in the same housing development become less prejudiced against each other as a result of living and interacting together.

REINFORCEMENT

We tend to like people who reward or reinforce us. The reward or reinforcement may be social, as in the form of compliments or praise of one sort or another, or it may be material, as in the case of the suitor whose gifts eventually win the hand of the beloved.

But reward can backfire. When overdone, reward loses its effectiveness and may even lead to negative responses. The people who reward us constantly soon become too sweet to take, and in a short period we come to discount whatever they say. Also, if the reward is to work, it must be perceived as genuine and not motivated by selfish concerns. The salesperson who compliments your taste in clothes, your eyes, your build, and just about everything else is not going to have the effect that someone without ulterior motives would have. In all probability, the salesperson is acting out of selfish concerns. Hence this person's "reinforcements" would not lead to attraction since they would not be perceived as genuine.

The order in which reinforcement occurs and whether or not it is coupled with negative evaluations also affects its influence. Researchers investigated this issue by having subjects "overhear" conversations by others about themselves. Four conditions were established, each consisting of overhearing seven conversations. In the positive condition, all seven conversations the subjects overheard were positive. In the negative condition, all conversations were negative. In the negative-positive condition, the first three conversations were negative and the last four were positive. In the positive-negative condition, the first three conversations were positive and the last four were negative. After overhearing these conversations, the subjects were asked to indicate the extent to which they liked the "gossiping" individual on a scale ranging from -10 to $+10$. The most liked persons were the ones who first spoke negatively and then spoke positively; that is, the negative-positive condition produced the greatest amount of attraction ($+7.67$). The next most liked persons were those in the positive condition ($+6.42$). The third most liked were the persons in the negative condition ($+2.52$). The least liked were the persons who first spoke positively and then spoke negatively, the positive-negative condition ($+0.87$).

Gain–Loss Theory

Elliot Aronson has proposed that a *gain-loss theory* can account for such findings as these. Basically, the theory states that increases in rewards have greater impact than constant invariant rewards. We like a person more if that person's liking (rewards) for us increases over time than if that person constantly rewards us indiscriminately. This holds true even if the number of rewards given by the person who always likes us are greater than those given by the person whose liking for us increases over time. Conversely, decreases in rewards have a greater impact than constant punishments; we dislike the person whose rewards decrease over time more than the person who always punishes us or who never has anything good to say about us.

Intuitively this seems satisfying. We seem to have a greater attraction for the person who changes his or her mind toward us, as long as the final evaluation is positive. The person who first evaluates us positively and then negatively may well be perceived as a traitor, as an ally who later deserts us, and as such is less liked than even the person who speaks consistently of us in the negative.

Rewarding Others

We also become attracted to persons we reward. We come to like people for whom we do favors. Although our initial reaction might be to say that we give rewards to people because we like them—and this is certainly true—it also works in reverse. Giving others rewards increases our liking for them as well. It seems we justify going out of our way by convincing ourselves that the person is worth the effort and is a likable person. In an experiment in which subjects won money, one-third were asked to give it back as a special favor to the experimenter, one-third were asked to give it back for the psychology department's research fund, and one-third were not asked to return it at all. The subjects were later tested on how much they liked the experimenter. The subjects who gave back the money to the experimenter indicated the greatest liking for him. By liking him, the subjects justified giving back the money they won. You may have noticed this same phenomenon in your own interactions. You have probably increased your liking for persons after buying them an expensive present or going out of your way to do them a special favor. In these and numerous similar instances, we justify our behavior by believing that the person was worth our efforts; otherwise, we would have to admit to being poor judges of character and to spending our money and our effort on people who do not deserve it.

SIMILARITY

If people could construct their mates, the mates would look, act, and think very much like themselves. By being attracted to people like ourselves, we are in effect validating ourselves, saying to ourselves that we are worthy of being liked, that we are attractive. Although there are exceptions, we generally like people who are similar to ourselves in nationality, race, ability, physical characteristics, intelligence, attitudes, and so on. We are often attracted to mirror images of ourselves.

We have often heard people say that the pets of people come to look and act like their owners. This misses the point. Actually, the animals do not change. Rather, the owners select pets that look and act like them at the start. Look around and test this out on people who have dogs and cats.

The Matching Hypothesis

If you were to ask a group of friends, "To whom are you attracted?" they would probably name very attractive people; in fact, they would probably name the most attractive people they know. But if we were to observe these friends, we would find that they go out with and establish relationships with people who are quite similar to themselves in terms of physical attractiveness. Useful in this connection is the *matching hypothesis,* which states that although we may be attracted to the most physically attractive people, we date and mate with people who are similar to ourselves in physical attractiveness. Intuitively this too seems satisfying. In some cases, however, we notice discrepancies; we notice an old person dating an attractive younger partner or an unattractive person with a handsome partner. In these cases, we will probably find that the less attractive partner possesses some quality that compensates for the lack of physical attractiveness. Prestige, money, intelligence, power, and various personality characteristics are obvious examples of qualities that may compensate for being less physically attractive.

Attitude Similarity

Similarity is especially important when it comes to attitudes. We are particularly attracted to people who have attitudes similar to our own, who like what we like and who dislike what we dislike. The more significant the attitude, the more important the similarity. For example, it would not make much difference if the attitudes of two people toward food or furniture differed (though even these can at times be significant), but it would be of great significance if their attitudes toward children or religion or politics were very disparate. Marriages between people with great and salient dissimilarities are more likely to end in divorce than are marriages between people who are very much alike.

Generally, we maintain balance with ourselves by liking people who are similar to us and who like what we like. It is psychologically uncomfortable to like people who do not like what we like or to dislike people who like what we like. Our attraction for similarity enables us to achieve psychological balance or comfort.

Agreement with ourselves is always reinforcing. The person who likes what we like in effect tells us that we are right to like what we like. Even after an examination it is helpful to find people who wrote the same answers we did. It tells us we were right. Notice the next time you have an examination how reinforcing it is to hear that others have given the same answers.

Another reason we are attracted to similar-minded people is that we can predict that since they think like us, they will like us as well. We like them because we think they like us.

COMPLEMENTARITY

Although many people would argue that "birds of a feather flock together," others would argue that "opposites attract." This latter concept is the principle of complementarity.

Take, for example, the individual who is extremely dogmatic. Would this person be attracted to people who are high in dogmatism or to those who are low in dogmatism? The similarity principle predicts that this person will be attracted to those who are like him or her (that is, high in dogmatism), while the complementarity principle predicts that this person will be attracted to those who are unlike him or her (that is, low in dogmatism).

It may be found that people are attracted to others who are dissimilar only in certain situations. For example, the submissive student may get along especially well with an aggressive teacher rather than a submissive one but may not get along with an aggressive spouse. The dominant wife may get along with a submissive husband but may not relate well to submissive colleagues.

Theodore Reik in *A Psychologist Looks at Love* argues that we fall in love with people who possess characteristics that we do not possess and that we actually envy. The introvert, for example, if displeased with being shy, might be attracted to an extravert.

There seems intuitive support for both complementarity and similarity, and certainly neither can be ruled out in terms of exerting significant influence on interpersonal attraction. The experimental evidence, however, seems to favor similarity. Glenn Wilson and David Nias, in *The Mystery of Love*, review evidence demonstrating that similarity in attitudes, physical attractiveness, self-esteem, race, religion, age, and social class increase attraction and therefore support the similarity theory.

Complementarity finds less support. The most obvious instance of complementarity is found in the fact that most persons are heterosexual and are attracted to persons of the opposite sex. One of the most interesting supports for complementarity appears in the finding that when one person in a relationship is "witty," the other person is "placid." It seems so much easier being witty with a placid listener than with a competing wit—something we have probably all observed in our own interpersonal relationships.

Summary: Contents in Brief

Qualities of Interpersonal Attraction

Attractiveness	when the person is physically appealing and has an appealing personality
Proximity	when the person is physically close to us over a period of time The *mere exposure hypothesis* claims that exposure alone leads to an increase in attractiveness
Reinforcement	when the person rewards us and when we reward the person *Gain-loss theory* claims that increases in rewards have greater impact than constant nonvarying rewards
Similarity	when the person possesses characteristics similar to our own (especially attitudes) The *matching hypothesis* claims that in dating and mating we tend to select people who are about as attractive as we are
Complementarity	when the person possesses characteristics unlike or opposite to our own or that we wish we had

Sources

The area of interpersonal attraction is thoroughly surveyed in Ellen Berscheid and Elaine Hatfield Walster, *Interpersonal Attraction,* 2d, ed. (Reading Mass.: Addison-Wesley, 1978). I profited from the review and the insights provided by Patricia Nikes Middlebrook, *Social Psychology and Modern Life* (New York: Random House, 1974). Zick Rubin, *Liking and Loving: An Invitation to Social Psychology* (New York: Holt, Rinehart and Winston, 1973) covers the area of interpersonal attraction in an interesting and insightful manner. The experiments on ''mere exposure'' (the women in the taste experiment and the rats listening to music) are discussed by Rubin. The original references are Susan Saegert, Walter Swap, and Robert B. Zajonc, ''Exposure, Context, and Interpersonal Attraction,'' *Journal of Personality and Social Psychology* 25 (1973): 234–242 and Henry A. Cross, Charles G. Halcomb, and William W. Matter, ''Imprinting or Exposure Learning in Rats Given Early Auditory Stimulation,'' *Psychonomic Science* 7 (1967): 233–234. The most authoritative source for the mere exposure hypothesis is Robert B. Zajonc, ''Attitudinal Effects of Mere Exposure,'' *Journal of Personality and Social Psychology Monograph* Suppl. 9, No. 2 (1968), Pt. 2.

The studies cited in the discussion of attractiveness may be found in *Human Behavior* 7 (July 1978): 26; in Glen Wilson and David Nias, *The Mystery of Love* (New York: Quadrangle/The New York Times Book Co., 1976); and in M. W. Segal, "Alphabet and Attraction: An Unobtrusive Measure of the Effect of Propinquity in a Field Setting," *Journal of Personality and Social Psychology* 30 (1974): 654–657.

The analysis of attractiveness and the comparison between similarity and complementarity owes much to the Wilson and Nias discussion. The study of friendships in college housing was conducted by Leon Festinger, Stanley Schachter, and Kurt W. Back, *Social Pressures in Informal Groups: A Study of Human Factors in Housing* (New York: Harper & Row, 1950). Also see L. Nahemow and M. P. Lawton, "Similarity and Propinquity in Friendship Formation," *Journal of Personality and Social Psychology* 32 (1975): 205–213 and E. B. Ebbesen, G. L. Kjos, and V. J. Konecni, "Spatial Ecology: Its Effects on the Choice of Friends and Enemies," *Journal of Experimental Social Psychology* 12 (1976): 505–518. For the study on the influence of the order of reinforcement and the gain-loss theory, see E. Aronson and D. Linder, "Gain and Loss of Esteem as Determinants of Interpersonal Attractiveness," *Journal of Experimental Social Psychology* 1 (1965): 156–171 and Elliot Aronson, *The Social Animal,* 3d ed. (San Francisco: Freeman, 1980). On the matching hypothesis see, for example, Elaine Walster and G. William Walster, *A New Look at Love* (Reading, Mass.: Addison-Wessley, 1978). A useful overview of attraction from the point of view of the psychologist is provided in Herbert Harari and Robert M. Kaplan, *Psychology: Personal and Social Adjustment* (New York: Harper & Row, 1977).

The study on doing favors for others may be found in Jon Jecker and David Landy, "Liking a Person as a Function of Doing Him a Favor," *Human Relations* 22 (1969): 371–378 and is discussed in Aronson's *Social Animal.* Also see the articles on attraction, dealing with some of the issues discussed in this unit, in Elliot Aronson, ed., *Readings About the Social Animal,* 3d ed. (San Francisco: Freeman, 1981), pp. 341–406.

Judy Cornelia Pearson, *Gender and Communication* (Dubuque, Iowa; Wm. C. Brown, 1985), provides an insightful review of interpersonal attraction and the relevant gender differences.

UNIT 20

Power in Interpersonal Relationships

OBJECTIVES

Upon completion of this unit, you should be able to:

1. define *power*
2. identify and explain at least five general principles of power
3. explain the ways in which the following power games are played and how we might effectively deal with them: Nobody Upstairs, You Owe Me, and Metaphor
4. identify and define the six bases of power
5. identify at least four consequences of using reward versus coercive power
6. identify and explain the five suggestions offered for managing power interpersonally

Of all the interpersonal relationships existing between or among people, that of power is surely one of the most significant. Power permeates all our interpersonal relationships and interactions. It influences what we do, when, and with whom. It influences the employment we seek and the employment we get. It influences the friends we choose and do not choose and those who choose us and those who do not. It influences our romantic and our family relationships—their success, their failure, their level of satisfaction or dissatisfaction.

Interpersonal power is a relationship between or among people such that the one with power has the ability to control the behaviors of the others. Thus, if A has power over B and C, then A, by virtue of this power and through the exercise of this power or the threat of its being exercised, can control the behaviors of B and C.

SOME PRINCIPLES OF POWER

Power in interpersonal relationships may best be introduced by identifying some of its most important principles. These principles identify some of the basic characteristics of power and should aid considerably in our understanding of how power operates interpersonally and how we may effectively and efficiently deal with power.

Some People Are More Powerful than Others

All people may be equal under the law and therefore equal in their entitlement to education, legal protection, freedom of speech, and so on. But all people are not equal when it comes to just about everything else. Some are born into wealth, others into poverty. Some are born physically strong, good-looking, and healthy; others are born weak, unattractive, and with a variety of inherited illnesses.

Most important to our purposes, some people are born into power, and some of the others, not born into power, have learned its intricacies and have managed to achieve control over it. In short, some people control and others are controlled. Of course, the world is not quite that simple. Actually, some people exert power in certain areas, others in other areas. Some exert power in many areas, others in few areas. There are many people—for example, teachers and psychiatrists—who exert power in the limited and narrow areas of their specialization, in the classroom and in the therapeutic encounter. Some people know what to do with power, how to wield it to derive the benefits they want; others do not know the first thing about manipulating power.

Power Can Be Increased or Decreased

Although we differ greatly in the amount of power we wield at any time and in any specific area, all of us can increase our power in some ways. We can lift weights and increase our physical power; we can learn the techniques of negotiation and increase our power in group situations; we can learn computer technology and increase our power to manipulate data; we can learn the principles of communication and increase our power to persuade.

Power can also be decreased. Perhaps the most frequent way in which power is decreased or lost entirely is through ineffective attempts to control another's behavior. For example, the person who threatens us with punishment and then fails to carry out the threat, loses power. Similarly, the person who attempts to use legitimate power (for example, that power we assign to a person by virtue of one's position or authority, see below) outside one's area or realm of authority, loses power. Thus, for example, the police officer who attempts to dictate moral behavior or the doctor who attempts to dictate religious principles loses power through these ineffective attempts to control behavior.

General rules or principles of interpersonal power can be learned so that we may increase our own interpersonal power. Michael Korda, in his influential and highly readable *Power! How to Get It, How to Use It,* for example, proposes five rules of power that he argues will help to increase an individual's power.

ACT IMPECCABLY

Every act you engage in, everything you do, should be done if it were the most important thing in the world. Excellence should become a way of life, a manner of acting in all endeavors.

NEVER REVEAL ALL OF YOURSELF TO OTHERS

The more we reveal about ourselves to others, the more we can be attacked for; the more others know about us, the more they can use against us. Furthermore, when others know a great deal about us, they can predict our behaviors with considerable accuracy; we thus lose the element of surprise and also provide others with the ability to get ahead of us. After all, if they can predict where we are going or what we are going to do, they can more easily get there before us. Along with this suggestion, consider the evidence and argument for (and against) self-disclosure (Unit 8).

USE TIME; DON'T WASTE TIME

Time is the most precious resource we have. If we squander it or waste it, we will have lost our most valuable asset. Learn to use time to develop your abilities, to improve your skills, to accomplish the work that needs to be done. Only people with unimportant work (hence people of little power) can afford to waste time. People who have important work, whose responsibilities are significant, and who deal with important issues and important people must make every minute count. These are the people who read such books as *The Management of Time*, *The Time Trap*, and *Do It!*, who attend time management seminars, and who keep daily schedules of activities in front of them at all times.

ACCEPT YOUR MISTAKES

Only people with little power are afraid to accept their mistakes. When they make a mistake, they go through elaborate scenes to justify their error and to make it seem that the mistake was either not made or not their fault. When it is obvious to others that a mistake was made and that these people were in fact at fault, their credibility is severely damaged. Furthermore, only people of little or no power would care about other people's impressions enough to be unable to admit their own mistakes. It is the new worker, the low-status employee who has to worry about making mistakes; the chief executive officer or the president of the company can readily admit a mistake. And, generally, as a result of this admission, people gain rather than lose respect for the individual. As a result, that person's power grows rather than diminishes.

DON'T MAKE WAVES

Power people move slowly without disturbing what is around them. The logic of the principle is that the more waves a person makes, the more chance that person has of meeting defeat, of being proved wrong, of running into someone more powerful. Only when an issue is extremely important do powerful people fight for it. Further, most issues are not worth the studied notice of a truly powerful person. Only persons of little power concern themselves with the trivia around them.

Power Is a Function of the Transaction of Internal and External Forces

Power is, in part, in the individual—in the wealth controlled, in the position occupied, in the number of followers. Power is also, however, in the perception of others. If someone thinks you have a great deal of power, then for many situations and for most practical purposes you have that power. For example, if someone thinks I know a great deal about real estate investments, for all practical purposes I have the power to influence that person's attitudes and perhaps financial resources in matters concerning real estate. In part, power is a function of the relationship between two people; it is not absolute or logical. For example, person A may have power over person B and person B may have power over person C, but it does not follow that person A has power over person C. The power that A, B, and C have may be in the unique relationship that exist between each pair and cannot necessarily be predicted from knowing the power relationships of other pairs.

It is interesting to note in this connection that power is, in part, conferred by the less powerful on the more powerful—a situation that may at first seem paradoxical. But consider an employee who desperately wants to get promoted. This employee gives power to the employer because of this desire to get promoted. If this individual did not want to get promoted, the employer would not have that power. If you want to use the family car on Saturday, you give your parents the power to grant or not to grant your request. If, on the other hand, you did not want the car, they would have less power over you; they would not have, in this instance, a perfect reward for your desired behavior.

All Interpersonal Communication Encounters Involve Power

No interpersonal relationship exists without a power dimension. Consequently, our interpersonal interactions invariably involve power maneuvers and consequences.

A number of researchers have identified and clarified some of the power games that are played in interpersonal interactions. Here are three discussed by Claude Steiner in *The Other Side of Power.*

NOBODY UPSTAIRS

In this power play, the individual refuses to acknowledge your request. The game takes the form of not listening to what you are saying, regardless of how you say it or how many times you say it. One common form is to refuse to take no for an answer and is clearly seen in the stereotypical man who persists in making advances to a woman despite her repeated refusals.

Sometimes Nobody Upstairs takes the form of ignoring socially and commonly accepted (but unspoken) rules such as knocking when you enter a person's room, not opening another person's mail, or not going through another person's wallet. The power play takes the form of expressing ignorance of the rules: "I didn't know you didn't want me to look in your wallet" or "Do you want me to knock the next time I come into your room?"

In dealing with this power play, the best strategy is to confront the game player directly, saying something like, "I'm sorry you persist in not hearing me. I'm not sure why you are doing it, but when I say I don't want you to hold me, I mean it. I'm not saying this to play hard to get; I'm saying it because I don't want you to hold me."

YOU OWE ME

In this power play, an individual does something for you and then demands something in return. The maneuver puts you in the position of owing this individual something.

This game is played frequently by men who take a woman on an expensive date. The objective is to make the woman owe something, usually sex. It is also seen in the woman who gives a man a great deal—sexually, emotionally, financially—and then demands something in return, for example, marriage. These two examples are of course stereotypes; they occur a great deal in the movies, in popular fiction, and on television dramas. But they probably occur in real life as well.

Another common example is the parents who sacrifice for the child and who later let the child know that now the child owes them. Whenever the child wants to do something that would be against the wishes of the parents, they remind the child that they are owed something for their sacrifice: "How can you quit college after all we sacrificed?,""How can you get such low grades when we worked so hard for your education?," "Why don't you want to wear that jacket? I spent two hours fixing it."

Again, the best strategy is to confront the game player: "I'm angry that you're doing this to me; I don't want to be put in the position of being made to feel guilty for doing something I want to do. Please don't do things for me because you want something in return. I don't want to feel obligated. I want to do what I want because I think it is best for me and not because I would feel guilty about paying you back for your sacrifices."

METAPHOR

Metaphor is an interesting power play that is at times difficult to identify and see as a power maneuver. For example, consider the situation in which one member of a group is going out with someone the other members do not like, and they respond with such comments as "How can you go out with her? She's a real dog" or "How can you date him? He's such a pig." *Dog* and *pig* are metaphors. Metaphors are figures of speech in which one word is used in the place of another. In these examples, *dog* and *pig* are used in place of the persons referred to with the intention of identifying the most obvious characteristics of these animals (ugliness and sloppiness, for example) with the people. The object here is to put down the individual and not allow you a chance to defend the person. After all, it is difficult to defend dating a dog or a pig!

One way to confront metaphors is to point out their inaccuracy: "Oh, no, Jane's not a dog; she's a New Yorker" or "John isn't a pig; he's a sophomore." Responses such as these often have the effect of calling the unfairness of the metaphor to the individual's attention and may well result in the retraction of the put-down. A more direct way, of course, is to call the metaphor to the attention of the individual and say, for example, "I really resent your calling Jane a dog; I like her and enjoy going out with her. If you don't like her, I would rather you told me that you didn't like her than call her names."

Some Resources Are More Powerful than Others

Generally, the power of any characteristic or asset depends on the context; what is perceived as powerful in some contexts is not perceived as powerful in another context. For example, physical strength is extremely important among teenaged boys; consequently, power is greatly influenced by physical strength. Among a bridge club or surgical team or group of lawyers or teachers, physical strength may be irrelevant. Here skill in bridge, surgery, and so on may be the significant determinants of power.

Despite this relativity of the resources of power, however, some resources are still generally more powerful than others. For example, rewards are generally more powerful in influencing behavior than are punishments. This has been repeatedly in experiments. If you want to influence human behavior, rewards work better than punishments. Rewarding compliance works better than punishing noncompliance. In our culture, certain rewards are seen by the vast majority of people as power resources. Money, social position, occupation, love, affection, and sex are among the most powerful rewards. If you are in control of these resources and can dole them out to others as rewards (or deny them to others as punishments), you have power over them. If, on the other hand, you seek these from another person, this other person has power over you.

Power Follows the Principle of Least Interest

In any interpersonal relationship, the person who maintains the power—the person who is able to control the behavior of the other person—is the one who is less interested in the rewards and punishments controlled by the other person. Consider the following relationship: Pat and Chris are involved in an interpersonal relationship; each wants something from the other. Who controls the power? Who is able to control the behavior of the other? The one who controls the power is the one who is less dependent on the rewards and punishments controlled by the other. If Pat, for example, can walk away from the rewards that Chris controls or can suffer the punishments that Chris can mete out, Pat controls the relationship. If, on the other hand, Pat needs the rewards that Chris controls or is unable or unwilling to suffer the punishments that Chris can administer, Chris maintains the power and controls the relationship.

The more a person needs a relationship, the less power that person has in the relationship. The less a person needs a relationship, the greater the power possessed. In a love relationship, for example, the person who maintains the greater power is the person who would find it easier to walk out the door, to break up the relationship, to get a divorce or separation. The person who is unwilling (or unable) to walk out or break up has little power, precisely because he or she is dependent on the relationship being maintained and on the rewards provided by the other person.

Another way of looking at this principle is in terms of social exchange theory (see Unit 18). With this perspective, power may be viewed as the control of the more significant rewards and costs in the relationship. The person who controls the rewards and punishments, controls the relationship. The person who needs to receive the rewards and needs to avoid the costs or punishments controlled by the other person is the less powerful and is controlled by the other. Alternatively, the person who can effectively ignore both the rewards and the costs of the other, is the less interested party, and therefore possesses the controlling power in the relationship.

THE BASES OF POWER

Power is present in all relationships and in all communication interchanges. But the type of power exerted and responded to varies greatly from one situation to another and from one person to another. Here we identify these types of power using a system proposed by John French and Bertram Raven and later modified by Raven and his associates. Six power bases or types of power are identified.

One of the clearest examples of referent power is seen when a younger brother or sister wants to be like the older sibling. The older sibling has power over the younger precisely because the younger wishes to be like or identified with the older.

Referent Power

Person A has referent power over person B when B wishes to be like A or to be identified with A. For example, an older brother may have power over a younger brother because the younger brother wants to be like the older brother. The assumption made by the younger brother is that he will be more like his older brother if he behaves and believes as his older brother does. The younger brother has already made the decision to do as the older brother does and to believe as the older brother believes. Once that is established, it takes little effort for the older brother to exert influence or power over the younger. Referent power depends greatly on attractiveness and prestige; as these increase, so does identification and consequently power.

The operation of referent power is also seen in the tendency of an individual to follow rather than to contradict others. There is a wealth of evidence, well summarized by Barry Collins and Bertram Raven, that indicates that an individual is much more likely to follow the group than not. For example, we will be more likely to go against a traffic signal or sign a petition if others are seen to have done it. The influence will be especially strong if the influencing agent is well-liked and well-respected. Further, the influence of referent power is greatest when the influencing agent is similar to the person being influenced in sex, attitudes, and experience.

Legitimate Power

Person A has legitimate power over person B when B believes that A has a right—by virtue of A's position—to influence or control B's behavior. If I believe that someone has a right to control my behavior, that person may be said to have power over me. Legitimate power stems from our belief that certain people should have power over us, that they have a right to influence us, because of who they are. Usually legitimate power is found in the role that people occupy. Teachers are often perceived to have legitimate power because of their role as teachers, and this is doubly true for religious teachers. Parents, by virtue of their being parents, are seen as having legitimate power over their children. Employers are often seen as having legitimate power over their employees.

There are numerous sources for legitimate power. One obvious source is cultural values. In our culture, for example, persons who are older or more intelligent or knowledgeable are often granted legitimate power. A second major source is found in the acceptance of the social structure or "office" that the individual holds. Thus judges, religious leaders, chairpersons, and managers are granted legitimate power because we accept the social structure and grant power to the office held by these individuals. Note that we do not have to agree with the person's decisions to grant that person legitimate power over us. For example, even if we disagree with a politician, we would probably still accept the right of this person to enact certain laws and thus to exert power over us. A third source for legitimate power is designation by a legitimating agent. For example, if the president of a company appoints Pat Creep manager, we accept Pat's power because it has been designated by an agent whose power we consider legitimate, in this case the president. Similarly, we accept the legitimacy of a politician or class president because we accept the legitimacy of the voting system.

Reward Power

Person A has reward power over person B if A has the ability to reward B. Rewards may be material (for example, money, promotion, jewelry) or social (for example, love, friendship, respect). If I am in a position to grant you some kind of reward, I have control over you to the extent that you want what I am in a position to give you. The degree of power wielded by A is directly related to the value or desirability of the reward as seen by B. Teachers have reward power over students because teachers control grades, letters of recommendation, social approval, and so on. Students, in turn, have reward power over teachers because students control social approval, student evaluations of faculty, and probably various other rewards. Parents control rewards for children—food, television privileges, rights to the car, curfew times, and the like—and thus possess reward power.

Coercive Power

Person A has coercive power over person B when A has the ability to administer punishment to or remove rewards from B should B not yield to the influence of A. I have coercive power over you if I can administer punishment to you or remove the things you want and value. Usually, people who have reward power also possess coercive power. Teachers may not only reward with high grades, favorable letters of recommendation, and social approval but may also punish with low grades, unfavorable letters, and social disapproval. Parents may deny as well as grant extended privileges concerning time or recreation and hence possess coercive as well as reward power.

The strength of the power depends on two factors: (1) the magnitude of the punishment that can be administered and (2) the likelihood that it will be administered as a result of noncompliance. When threatened by mild punishment or by punishment we think will not be administered, we are not as likely to do as directed as we would be if the threatened punishment is severe and if its likelihood of being administered is high.

REWARD VERSUS COERCIVE POWER: SOME CONSEQUENCES

A few consequences of using reward and coercive power should be noted. First, reward power seems to increase one's attractiveness; we like people who have the power to reward us and who then do in fact reward us. But coercive power decreases attractiveness; we dislike those who have the power to punish us and who threaten us with punishment, whether they actually do follow through and punish us or not.

Second, users of reward do not incur the same costs that users of punishment do. When exerting power by reward, we have a contented and happy individual with whom to deal. But with coercive punishments, we must be prepared to incur the costs of anger and hostility, which may well be turned against us in the near or distant future.

Third, when a reward is given, it is a sign that the power has been exercised effectively and that there has been compliance. That is, we reward the individual for doing as we wished. But note that in the exercise of coercive power, the reverse is true. When punishment is given, it is a sign that the coercive power has been ineffective and that there has been no compliance. That is, if we are consistent and true to our threats, we must follow through and punish the individual for not doing as we wished.

Fourth, when coercive power is exerted, other bases of power are frequently lost or decreased. There seems to be a kind of boomerang effect operating here; when coercive power is exercised, we frequently see that person as possessing less expert, legitimate, and referent power. Alternatively, when reward power is exerted, other bases of power are increased.

In an investigation of power in the classroom, Virginia Richmond and her colleagues have found a fifth consequent of coercive power: a decrease in both cognitive and affective learning. In classrooms where the teacher is seen by the students to exercise coercive power (and the same applies to legitimate power), students learn less effectively and have more negative attitudes toward the course, course content, and teacher, and are less likely to take additional similar courses and to perform the behaviors taught in the course. Richmond and her colleagues also report that coercive and legitimate power have negative impact when used by supervisors on subordinates in business organizations.

All in all, coercive power seems a last resort and one whose potential negative consequences should be carefully weighed before applying.

Expert Power

Person A has expert power over person B if A is regarded by B as having expertise or knowledge; the knowledge that A has gives A expert power. Persons with expert power influence us in ways that persons without such power do not. Further, that power is usually subject-specific. For example, if we have an illness, we are influenced by the recommendation of someone with expert power that is related to our illness—say, a doctor. But we would not be influenced by the recommendations of someone to whom we do not attribute expert power—say, the mail carrier or a plumber. We give the lawyer expert power in matters of law and psychiatrists expert power in matters of the mind, but we do not mix them up; we are not influenced by the lawyer's recommendations on depression or anxiety or the psychiatrist's recommendations on the legal dimensions of filing for divorce or writing a will. This is the ideal situation. At times, however, the "sleeper effect" operates. It goes something like this: A person with little or no expert power says X is Y. Because of the person's lack of expert power, we think we forget the information. Actually, we haven't really forgotten it; it has only been "sleeping." At a later time, we remember the information but forget its source. The negative source is no longer associated with the information, and we believe it. Thus we frequently give expert power to nonexperts because we dissociate the content of the message from its source.

Expert power is increased when we feel the source (expert) is unbiased and has nothing to gain personally from influencing us. Expert power decreases if we see the expert as biased and as having something to gain from the advice or recommendation.

Information or Persuasion Power

Person A has information or persuasion power over person B when B attributes to A the ability to communicate logically and persuasively. I give information power to another person by believing that this other person has the ability to persuade me. We generally attribute persuasion power to someone we see as possessing the significant information and the ability to use that information in presenting a well-reasoned, well-thought-out argument.

In the first five bases of power, it is the personal qualities of the power-holder that are significant. In informational power, it is the content of the communication that is the important element and not the influencing agent's personal qualities. Thus, for example, the speaker who presents convincing argument or the teacher who explains a logical problem will exert influence over the listener regardless of his or her personal qualities.

In any given situation, it would be rare to find that only one base of power has been used to influence another individual; in most situations a number of power bases are used in concert. If I possess expert power, it is likely that I also possess information power and perhaps legitimate power as well. If I want to control your behavior, it is likely that I would use all three bases of power rather than rely on just one.

As can be appreciated from this discussion, certain individuals have a number of power bases at their disposal, while others seem to have none. And this brings us back to our first principle: Some people are more powerful than others.

A Note on Negative Power

We normally think of the attempts to influence others as having some effect in the desired direction. At times, however, negative power operates; here the influence attempt backfires with results that may be in direct contrast to that desired by the agent of power or may increase the differences between the agent and the individual influenced. Each of the six power bases may, at times, have such negative influence. For example, negative referent power would occur when a son rejects his father and wants to be the exact opposite of the father. Negative coercive power may be seen when a child is warned against doing something under threat of punishment and then does exactly what he or she was told not to do; the threat of punishment may have made the behavior seem exciting or challenging.

MANAGING POWER INTERPERSONALLY

If power is an integral part of interpersonal communication and if we are to learn how to become effective interpersonal communicators, we must learn how to deal with power—as both "exerter" and "exertee." Here are five rules to add to the five presented earlier in connection with the principle "Power can be increased or de-creased."

Acquire the Skills of Power

It is impossible to control or manipulate power to any meaningful degree without knowing what power is, the various bases from which power may be exercised, and the way it is used in a variety of situations. This unit can only be a first step; there is much more that can and should be learned. A good second step is to consult the references listed in the source note at the end of this unit. I especially recommend Michael Korda's *Power!*, Clause Steiner's *The Other Side of Power*, and R. G. H. Siu's *The Craft of Power*. Together these books provide a thorough grounding in the ways and means of power. The one major principle that should be kept in mind in approaching the literature on power is to recognize that your power is inseparable from your general behavior and attitude. Power is a way of life; powerful people act powerfully in all their dealings and in all their thinking.

Communicate Power

Earlier we noted the principle of communication inevitability, that one cannot not communicate. That principle is particularly important in dealing with power. Everything you do communicates about your power—raising it or lowering it. When in an interactional situation, therefore, it is essential to recognize that assessments of your power will be made along with your assessments of competence, trustworthiness, honesty, openness, and so on.

People who are powerful communicate verbally with declarative sentences; they are definite and conclusive. They avoid sentences containing weak modifiers ("this is *pretty* good," "that was *about* right"), disqualifiers ("I'm not sure of this but . . .," "I may be wrong about this but . . ."), and markers that ask for permission or agreement ("Is six o'clock OK?" "That was a good book, don't you think?"). Powerful persons don't yell or scream, even when angry; to do so is to admit to having little power over yourself and consequently over others as well.

It should come as no surprise that the powerful persons in our culture are generally the rich. These are the persons who control our jobs, our government policy, our economic system. These people not only have money, they also have had the best education and the best training. Their speech reflects this; powerful people do not talk like they came from Tobacco Road. They talk like they went to prep schools and Ivy League colleges because they probably did.

Much as we communicate our power or lack of it verbally, we also communicate our power nonverbally. Trendiness is powerless; cheap is powerless. Conservative is powerful; expensive is powerful. It is actually all very logical. Truly powerful people have no time for new trends that come and go every six months. Further, they don't wear or have anything cheap because they have money to buy the real thing. The cheap, trendy watch with 27 different gadgets to tell the time in ten different parts of the world, the date, lap time, alarms, and various other bits of information says that this person has little power. The powerful person probably wears a watch with an hour and a minute hand—a Rolex, Cartier, Gucci, or the like, but always plain, without frills; one that cries out, "I'm rich; I'm powerful."

Similarly, our nonverbal behavior often betrays our lack of power, as when we fidget or shuffle at a meeting, indicating discomfort. A powerful person may be bored but would not be uncomfortable or ill at ease.

Your territory also reflects your power or lack of it. It is difficult for the junior executive who operates out a cubbyhole in the basement of some huge office building to appear powerful with an old metal desk and beat-up filing cabinet. Often, however, we are more in control of our territory than we realize. Clutter, metal ashtrays, and "cute" statues with signs like "Kiss me now," "The doctor is in," or "Place your butt here" all signify a lack of power.

But perhaps the most important aspect of communicating power is to evidence your knowledge, your preparation, your organization over whatever you are dealing with. If you can exhibit control over your own responsibilities, it is generally concluded that you can and do also exhibit control over others.

Associate with Power

This is sure to sound crass and unfeeling. In some ways it is, yet it is one of the facts of power. You may or may not wish to follow it. We are judged by the people with whom we associate. If we associate with powerful people, we are judged powerful; if we associate with competent people, we are judged competent. On the other hand, if we associate with clods, we are judged clods ourselves. After all, it can reasonably be asked why we would associate with clods unless we ourselves were clods. R. G. H. Siu, in *The Craft of Power,* puts it this way: "Join the right groups and people will think you right and fit; join nobodies and people will think you a nobody."

John Molloy, in his discussion of office politics in *Molloy's Live for Success,* observes that men and women behave very differently when they rise in the corporate structure. When a male salesperson, say, rises to become an executive, his associates change; he now associates not with the sales staff but with his new colleagues, the executives. Women behave differently; when a woman rises to a higher level, she retains the associates she had at the lower level. In doing this she thus loses the tremendous advantage that the new associations could bring her but also communicates to others that perhaps she is not ready to serve fully as an executive. One foot seems still to be on the lower level.

Although I would not go so far as to argue that women should abandon their former associates and co-workers, it does seem warranted to suggest that if power is desired then new associates and co-workers should not be ignored and, in fact, should be actively cultivated for both the social and professional benefits they may produce.

Reinforce Your Power

If power is to be exercised, it needs to be periodically revitalized and reinforced. Power, as noted earlier, is largely in the minds of those with whom we deal; if they do not see our power exercised, they are likely to conclude that it doesn't exist, that it was all a myth, or that we somehow lost it. Whatever the real reason, their perception is that we have it no longer.

Protect Your Power

Power is a funny thing. When we allow others to exercise power over us unfairly, we lose our own power. If someone makes a fool of us at the office and we do nothing about it, we are seen to have lost power. The reason seems logical enough: Who but a powerless fool would allow others to make a fool of him or her?

Further, when we allow that to happen, we are in effect telling ourselves that we have no power. If we let others play the power games that we noted earlier without any form of retaliation, we communicate that we have no power, no resources with which to hit back. We are telling others and ourselves that we are powerless.

One further corollary: When we allow others to do that to us, we not only lose our own power but also contribute to the enhancement of the power of the louse who is playing these power games on us.

Summary: Contents in Brief

Principles of Power	Bases of Power	B has power over A when:	Management Principles
Some people are more powerful than others.	*Referent:*	A wants to be like B	Acquire the skills of power.
Power can be increased or decreased.	*Legitimate:*	A believes B has a right to control A's behavior	Communicate power.
Power is a function of the transaction of internal and external forces.	*Reward:*	B has the ability to reward A	Associate with power.
	Coercive:	B has the ability to punish A	Reinforce your power.
All interpersonal encounters involve power and power plays such as	*Expert:*	A regards B as having knowledge or expertise	Protect your power.
• Nobody Upstairs	*Information or Persuasion:*	A attributes to B the ability to communicate logically and persuasively	
• You Owe Me			
• Metaphor			
Some resources are more powerful than others.			
Power follows the principle of least interest.			

Sources

The literature on power is extensive. Three excellent, popular, and well-written overviews are Michael Korda, *Power! How to Get It, How to Use It* (New York: Ballantine, 1975); John Kenneth Galbraith, *The Anatomy of Power* (Boston: Houghton Mifflin, 1983); and Claude M. Steiner, *The Other Side of Power* (New York: Grove Press, 1981). The power games are based on Steiner's analysis. A thorough discussion of power from a number of points of view is provided in R. G. H. Siu, *The Craft of Power* (New York: Quill, 1984). Sex differences are thoroughly surveyed in Hilary M. Lips, *Women, Men, and the Psychology of Power* (Englewood Cliffs, N.J.: Prentice-Hall [Spectrum], 1981). The bases of power are taken from the analyses of John R. P. French Jr., and Bertram Raven, "The Bases of Social Power," in Dorwin Cartwright and Alvin Zander, eds., *Group Dynamics: Research and Theory*, 3d ed. (New York: Harper & Row, 1968), pp. 259–269, and B. Raven, C. Centers, and A. Rodrigues, "The Bases of Conjugal Power," in R. E. Cromwell and D. H. Olson, eds., *Power in Families* (New York: Halsted Press, 1975), pp. 217–234. An excellent discussion of power in the family may be found in Kathleen M. Galvin and Bernard J. Brommel, *Family Communication: Cohesion and Change*, 2d ed. (Chicago: Scott, Foresman, 1986).

For a review of research on power and communication see Barry E. Collins and Bertram H. Raven, "Group Structure: Attraction, Coalitions, Communication, and Power," *The Handbook of Social Psychology*, 2d ed., eds. Gardner Lindzey and Elliot Aronson (Reading, Mass.: Addison-Wesley, 1969), Vol. IV, pp. 102–204 and Wally D. Jacobson, *Power and Interpersonal Relations* (Belmont, Calif.: Wadsworth, 1972).

For power and its relevance to teaching and learning see James C. McCroskey and Virginia P. Richmond, "Power in the Classroom I: Teacher and Student Perceptions," *Communication Education* 32 (April 1983): 175–184; Virginia P. Richmond and James C. McCroskey, "Power in the Classroom II: Power and Learning," *Communication Education* 33 (April 1984): 125–136; Patricia Kearney, Timothy G. Plax, Virginia P. Richmond, and James C. McCroskey, "Power in the Classroom III: Teacher Communication Techniques and Messages," *Communication Education* 34 (January 1985): 19–28 and "Power in the Classroom IV: Alternatives to Discipline," *Communication Yearbook 8*, ed. Robert N. Bostrom (Beverly Hills, Calif.: Sage, 1984), pp. 724–746. For the use of power in organizations see Virginia P. Richmond, Leonard M. Davis, Kitty Saylor, and James C. McCroskey, "Power Strategies in Organizations: Communication Techniques and Messages," *Human Communication Research* 11 (Fall 1984): 85–108.

Conflict in Interpersonal Relationships

OBJECTIVES

Upon completion of this unit, you should be able to:

1. define *interpersonal conflict*
2. explain the distinction between content and relationship conflict
3. identify at least three potential negative aspects of conflict
4. identify at least three potential positive aspects of conflict
5. identify and explain at least four unproductive conflict strategies
6. explain the five stages of the process model of conflict resolution
7. explain the interpersonal effectiveness model as a conflict strategy by identifying the five qualities of interpersonal effectiveness and explaining the suggestions made for using these qualities in conflict encounters.

Some years ago, a group of 11-year-old boys at a summer camp unknowingly became subjects in a most interesting study of conflict. There were three main stages in this simulated war, devised by Muzafer Sherif and his colleagues. In the first stage the boys were divided into two groups, and each group was isolated from the other. The boys developed close interpersonal relations with members of their own group and a strong feeling of group cohesiveness. The groups called themselves the Eagles and the Rattlers.

The second stage involved the creation of friction between the two groups. The groups were placed in a number of competitive and mutually frustrating activities. A high level of intergroup hostility was thus developed.

The third stage focused on attempts to reduce the conflict. At first the experimenters brought the groups together for mutually satisfying activities such as seeing a movie, eating, and participating in a series of experiments. The effect of these activities was to produce outward displays of conflict and hostility, both verbal and nonverbal. The experimenters then set up a series of goals that required mutual cooperation between the groups. In one situation the researchers staged a water shortage. The cooperation of all the boys was needed if the water was to be turned on again. In another situation both groups had to contribute money to obtain a movie they all wanted to see but for which neither group had enough cash by

283

themselves. In the third situation the two groups were removed from the camp and had to perform a number of cooperative tasks, such as using their combined efforts to start a stalled truck.

The outcome of these situations was that the hostility between the two groups was significantly reduced, attributed by the experimenters to the interpersonal experiences of cooperation between the two groups. It seems universally agreed that if conflict is to be reduced, it is to be reduced through interpersonal interaction. The corollary to this seems equally agreed upon: If conflict is to be generated and maintained, it is to be done through interpersonal interaction as well. Conflict, both its generation and its resolution, seems largely an interpersonal communication process.

In this unit we examine three areas of conflict: (1) the nature of conflict: the definition of conflict, the ways in which conflict is manifested, and some of the problems and some of the values to be derived from conflict; (2) some popular and widespread but unproductive conflict strategies; and (3) productive conflict strategies—approaches to conflict engagement and conflict management that should help make conflict a more positive experience.

THE NATURE OF CONFLICT

Conflict is one of the most complex of all interpersonal processes. Consequently, we need to examine in some depth what interpersonal conflict is, the area on which the conflict might center, and the negative and positive dimensions of conflict.

What Is Conflict?

Conflict, in its most basic form, refers to a disagreement. Interpersonal conflict, then, refers to a disagreement between or among connected individuals. By including the word *connected* we emphasize that each person's position affects the other person; the positions in conflict are to some degree interrelated and incompatible. Interpersonal conflict most often refers to disagreements among persons who are closely connected with one another: close friends, lovers, family members. But interpersonal conflicts are also seen between, for example, teacher and student, employer and employee, neighbors, and other persons who interact within the same space and whose position or stance influences others.

As experience teaches us, the disagreements can be of various types: goals to be pursued ("We want you to go to college and become a teacher or a doctor, not a disco dancer"); allocation of resources such as money or time ("I want to spend the tax refund on a car, not on new furniture"); decisions to be made ("I refuse to have the Jeffersons over for dinner"); behaviors that are considered appropriate or desirable by one person and inappropriate or undesirable by the other ("I hate it when you get drunk, pinch me, ridicule me in front of others, flirt with others, dress provocatively, . . .").

Content and Relationship Conflicts

Using concepts developed earlier, we may distinguish between content conflict and relationship conflict. *Content conflict* centers on objects, events, and persons in the world that are usually (but not always) external to the parties involved in the conflict. These include the millions of issues that we argue and fight about every day—the value of a particular movie, what to watch on television, the validity of a grade received on a term paper, the fairness of the last examination, the job promotion, the way to spend our savings, and how our false teeth look.

Relationship conflicts are equally numerous and include the conflict between two brothers that develops because the younger brother does not obey the older brother, the conflict between husband and wife because each wanted to have an equal say before vacation plans were made, and the conflict between mother and daughter when each wants to have the final say concerning the daughter's life-style. Here the conflicts are not so much concerned with the outside world or with some external object as with the relationships between the individuals, with such issues as who is in charge, the equality of a marital relationship, and who has the right to set down rules of behavior.

Content and relationship conflicts are always easier to separate in a textbook than they are in real life, where many conflicts contain elements of both content and relationship conflict. But it helps a great deal if we can recognize which issues pertain to content and which to relationship. Only by doing this can we understand the conflict well enough to manage it effectively and productively.

The Negatives and Positives of Conflict

The kind of conflict we focus on here is interpersonal conflict, conflict among or between intimates. Interpersonal conflict occurs frequently between husband and wife, between lovers, between best friends, between siblings, and between parent and child. Interpersonal conflict is made all the more difficult because, unlike many conflict situations, here we care for, like, even love the individual with whom we are in conflict.

There are both negative and positive aspects or dimensions to interpersonal conflict, and each of these should be noted.

NEGATIVE ASPECTS

Conflict often leads to increased negative regard for the opponent, and when this opponent is someone we love or care for very deeply, it can create serious problems for the relationship. The problem here is that many conflicts involve unfair fighting and are based largely on hurting the other person. To the extent that an individual succeeds in hurting the other, increased negative feelings are almost inevitable. Even the strongest relationship has limits.

Conflict frequently leads to a depletion of energy, energy that could better be spent on other and perhaps more productive areas. This is especially true when unproductive conflict strategies are used.

At times conflict leads us to close ourselves off from the other individual—a popular (but not necessarily productive) strategy. Though it would not be to our advantage to reveal our weaknesses to our "enemy," to the extent that we hide our true selves from our intimate, we prevent meaningful and productive communication from taking place. One possible consequence of this is that because the need for intimacy and interpersonal interaction is so strong, frequently one or both parties seek this intimacy elsewhere. This, as can easily be appreciated, often leads to further conflict, mutual hurt, and resentment—qualities that add mightily to the costs carried by the relationship. As these costs increase, the conflict situation is often such that rewards become difficult and perhaps impossible to exchange. Here, then, we are left with a situation in which the costs increase and the rewards decrease—a situation that often results in relationship deterioration and eventual breakdown.

POSITIVE ASPECTS

I think the major value of interpersonal conflict is that it forces the individuals to examine a problem and to work out a potential solution together. If productive conflict strategies are used, the relationship may well emerge from the conflict encounter stronger, healthier, and more mutually satisfying than before. Even if conflict served no other function, it would still be of significant value to every interpersonal relationship. But conflict does have additional positive benefits. In *Interpersonal Conflict Resolution*, Alan Filley considers four major values of conflict:

1. Many conflict situations have the effect of diffusing more serious conflicts. This is especially the case when the conflicts (perhaps more accurately described as competitive exchanges) are played out according to a system of rules. The disagreements that result often reduce the probability of more significant conflicts arising.
2. Conflict situations lead us to acquire new information, new ways of looking at things. They energize our creativity and force us to explore new ideas and new ways of behaving.
3. When the conflict is an intergroup one, conflict functions to increase group cohesiveness. One of the most powerful ways to encourage members of a group to interact cooperatively and efficiently is to put the group into conflict with another group.
4. Conflict provides an opportunity for individuals or groups to measure their power, strength, or ability, since it is in conflict situations that such qualities are mobilized to their peak.

Brent Ruben affirms the positive value of conflict:

> Although conflict may be associated with feelings of stress and pain, it must nevertheless be viewed as a sine qua non of learning, creativity, and biological and psychological growth and differentiation for the individual. And, as social conflict may be a precondition for war and political and economic strife, so, also, should it be regarded as the lifeblood of social change, choice, and social revolution.

When we attempt to resolve conflict within an interpersonal relationship, we are saying in effect that the relationship is worth the effort. To confront such a conflict we must care, at least to some degree, about the relationship; otherwise we would walk away from it. Although there may be exceptions—as when we confront conflict to save face or to gratify some ego need—it seems generally true that confronting a conflict indicates concern, commitment, and a desire to preserve the relationship.

UNPRODUCTIVE CONFLICT STRATEGIES

In dealing with conflict, keep in mind the following law of conflict: *Any conflict is easier to create than to resolve.* This law is simple enough, but there are some rather spiteful corollaries. For example, the time it takes to create an interpersonal conflict is always shorter than the time it takes to resolve the conflict. Alternatively, the energy needed to create a conflict is often minor; the energy expenditure to resolve that conflict is major.

Although many such unproductive strategies might be identified, we concentrate here on seven that seem most important. Understanding these unproductive fight strategies will enable us to deal more effectively with them when they occur in the behavior of others and to eliminate them from our own conflict resolution arsenal.

Avoidance or Redefinition

Avoidance may take the form of actual physical flight (whereby the individual leaves the scene of the conflict), falling asleep, or just mentally withdrawing. Or it may take the form of emotional or intellectual avoidance, whereby the individual leaves the conflict psychologically by not dealing with any of the arguments or problems raised.

Avoidance often takes the form of changing the subject or talking about the problem so abstractly or in such incomprehensible language that mutual understanding is impossible. A similar method is to redefine the conflict so that it becomes no conflict at all or so that it becomes irrelevant to the individuals and hence unnecessary to deal with.

Force

When confronted with a conflict, many people prefer not to deal with the issues but rather simply to force their way of thinking or behaving on the other person by physically overpowering the individual or by threatening the use of such physical force. At other times the force used is more emotional than physical. In either case, however, the issues are avoided and the individual who "wins" is the individual who exerts the most force. This is the technique of warring nations, children, and even some normally sensible and mature adults.

Minimization

Sometimes we deal with conflict by making light of it, by saying and perhaps believing that the conflict, its causes, and its consequences are really not important. We might argue that if left alone, time will resolve it. But time does absolutely nothing; over time *we* may do something, but time itself never acts in one way or the other.

Sometimes we minimize a conflict with "humor" (usually sarcasm or ridicule) and may literally laugh at it. But notice that this technique does nothing to resolve the problem; it merely uses the conflict situation as an opportunity to ridicule the other person. When the laughter dies, the conflict is still very much alive, probably energized further by these personal attacks.

Note that humor can be productive when appropriately used. When the humor is designed to ease the tension or provide a temporary break in the seriousness of the interaction, it may actually help resolve the conflict or at least put the individuals into a more receptive frame of mind.

Blame

Sometimes conflict is caused by the actions of one individual; sometimes it is caused by clearly identifiable outside forces. Most of the time, however, it is caused by such a wide variety of factors that any attempt to single out one or two factors is doomed to failure. Yet a frequently employed fight strategy is to avoid dealing with the conflict by blaming someone for it. In some instances we blame ourselves. This may be the result of a realistic appraisal of the situation, or it may be an attempt to evoke sympathy or to gain pity from the other individual. More often, however, we blame the other person. If a couple has a conflict over a child's getting into trouble with the police, for example, the parents may start blaming each other for the child's troubles instead of dealing with the conflict itself. As can easily be appreciated (at least when we are not parties to the conflict), blaming solves nothing other than temporarily relieving a degree of intrapersonal guilt.

Silencers

One of the most unfair but most popular fight strategies is the use of silencers—a wide variety of fighting techniques that literally silence the other individual. One frequently used silencer is crying. When confronted by a conflict and unable to deal with it or when winning seems unlikely, the individual cries and thus silences the other person. Another silencer is to feign extreme emotionalism, to yell and scream and pretend to be losing control of oneself. Still another is to develop some ''physical'' reaction; headaches and shortness of breath are probably the most popular. One of the major problems with silencers is that we can never be certain that they are strategies to win the argument and not real physical reactions that have to be attended to. Regardless of what we do, the conflict remains unexamined and unresolved.

Gunnysacking

Gunnysacking refers to the practice of storing up grievances—as if in a gunnysack—and holding them in readiness to dump on the person with whom you are now in conflict. Instead of dealing with and resolving conflicts as they come along, the gunnysacker saves them up for future use. When a conflict occurs, the sack is unloaded: ''You always forget our dates. Remember last year, it was my birthday; you forgot completely. And what about my parents anniversary? You forgot that too. You always forget my parents. But you always have time for your friends.'' Going farther into the past and farther away from the source of the present conflict, gunnysacking opens old wounds, avoids coming to grips with the immediate conflict, and never results in resolving differences and disagreements.

Beltlining

Each of us has a ''beltline'' that separates what we can tolerate effectively from what we cannot. In an interpersonal relationship, we know where that beltline is because we know the other person so well. The task is not to go below that line in conflict encounters. When we do hit below the belt—focus on the other's baldness, impotence, previous failures, low salary, history of mental illness, alcoholic parent—we aggravate the conflict and move farther away from any resolution. Beltlining is used by persons who want to win the fight and destroy the opponent, a strategy that quickly and effectively damages the interpersonal relationship.

PRODUCTIVE CONFLICT STRATEGIES

The art of effective and productive conflict engagement and management may be approached in at least two ways. First, we look at the formal stages that we might go through in attempting to understand and resolve a specific conflict; we call this a *process model* because it focuses on the processes or stages one goes through in seeking conflict resolution. Second, we return to five qualities of effective interpersonal communication discussed earlier and apply them to conflict encounters; we call this an *interpersonal effectiveness model.*

A Process Model of Conflict Resolution

Any conflict situation may be approached as would a problem requiring a decision. The methods suggested for dealing with conflict are very similar to the methods of

Relational conflicts are inevitable in any intimate relationship. Conflict resolution, however, is frequently aided by a third party who can often see the problem from a different point of view and can often suggest remedies that the involved parties cannot see.

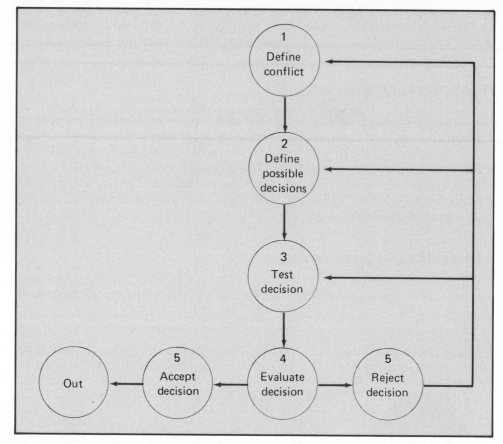

FIGURE 21.1: Stages in Conflict Resolution.

reflective thinking long taught as educational techniques and in small group communication classes. Five principal stages in conflict resolution are distinguished here. A diagram of these essential stages is presented in Figure 21.1. This diagram and the discussion that follows should not be taken to imply that all conflicts may be resolved in this way or in any other prescribed way. Some conflicts may not be amenable to solution; some differences may be irreconcilable. Communication can help us understand and resolve many conflicts, but unfortunately not all.

1. DEFINE THE CONFLICT

Defining the conflict is perhaps the most essential step of conflict resolution, yet many people omit this stage entirely. We need to ask ourselves what the specific nature of the conflict is and why this conflict exists. It is at this stage that we should collect as much relevant data and as many opinions as we possible can. Special care should be taken to ensure that we collect data and opinions that may disagree with our position as well as supportive data and opinions.

In defining the conflict, "operationalize" it to make it as concrete as possible. Conflict defined in the abstract is difficult to deal with and resolve. For example, the husband who complains that his wife is "cold and unfeeling" is defining the problem in such abstract terms that it will be difficult to reach agreement as to the nature of the conflict, let alone its resolution. There should be an attempt to deal with conflicts in behavioral terms, if possible. It is one thing for a husband to say that his wife is "cold and unfeeling" and quite another to say she does not call him at the office or kiss him when he comes home or hold his hand when they are at a party. These behaviors can be dealt with, whereas the abstract "cold and unfeeling" is most difficult to handle. Further, it is useful to operationalize our conflicts because it forces us to be specific and to spell out exactly what we are fighting about. For a wife to say that her husband does not make her feel attractive but then fail to provide concrete examples of such behaviors is saying something quite different from the wife who can easily rattle off 20 recent specific situations in which he criticized her appearance, laughed at her clothes, whistled at other women, and so on.

2. DEFINE POSSIBLE DECISIONS

For any conflict, a number of possible decisions can be made. In some instances any one of three or four possible decisions will resolve the conflict; in other cases only one possible decision will work. But in all cases we need first to analyze all possible alternatives.

The word *decision* is used deliberately instead of the more common *solution*. To say that we will find a solution to a conflict assumes that we will eliminate the conflict. Very probably this is not what will happen—we actually strive to lessen the conflict. To imply that we will actually solve a conflict as we solve a mathematical equation is assuming too simplistic a view of human behavior and human interpersonal relationships. More likely we are attempting to make a decision so that future interactions may be undertaken in a somewhat more productive setting. For example, if one spouse discovers that the other spouse is having an affair with a neighbor and the couple move to another city or neighborhood, they have not solved the problem; they have made a decision so that future interactions may take place in a more productive atmosphere. In short, the word *decision* seems more descriptive of what actually goes on in conflict resolution.

In analyzing the possible decisions to resolve the conflict, we should attempt to predict the consequences of each of them. This is impossible to do with complete accuracy, but some attempts should be made. We should guard against any tendency to dismiss possible decisions before we give them a fair hearing. Many excellent decisions are never put into operation because they at first seem strange, incorrect, or too difficult to implement.

3. TEST THE DECISION

The true test of any decision can only be made when the decision is put into effect. And so we play the odds—we select the decision that seems most logical and try it out. Although each decision put into effect should be given a fair chance, we should recognize that if a particular decision does not work, another decision should be put to the test. It is self-destructive to put a decision into effect with the idea that if it does not work, conflict resolution is impossible.

4. EVALUATE THE DECISION

When the decision is in effect, we need to evaluate it, examining the ways in which it acts to resolve (or aggravate) the conflict. Does it feel right? Does it make for improved interpersonal communication? Does it significantly lessen the conflict?

5. ACCEPT OR REJECT THE DECISION

As a result of our evaluation, we move to accept or reject the decision. If we accept the decision, we are ready to put the decision into effect or perhaps to move on to consider other conflict situations and problems. If we move to reject the decision, there are three alternatives: First, we might attempt to test another decision. Perhaps the decision we ranked as number two will prove more satisfactory, so we should try it out. A second possibility is to redefine the various decisions and then test one of them. The third course of action is to go back and reanalyze and redefine the conflict itself. That is, we can reenter the conflict resolution process at any of the first three stages. In any case, another decision must eventually be put into effect, one that promises to work better than the previous one. And perhaps we will have learned something from the last decision-making process that will prove useful in subsequent conflict resolution attempts.

An Interpersonal Effectiveness Model

In Unit 6, "Effectiveness in Interpersonal Communication," five characteristics in a humanistic model of effective interpersonal communication were identified and defined. These same qualities should characterize conflict encounters. Their specific application to conflict situations should enable us to fight more productively, with less hurt and with a greater chance of resolving differences and disagreements.

OPENNESS

1. State your position, your feelings, your thoughts openly, directly, and honestly without attempt to hide or disguise the real object of your disagreement. Only by bringing the conflict out into the open is an eventual and meaningful resolution possible.

2. React openly to the messages of your combatant. Even though this will be difficult—especially if the messages are hostile or personally insulting—it is important that each person listens to and reacts appropriately and honestly to the messages of the other.

3. Own your own thoughts and feelings. Don't attribute your negative statements about your combatant to others ("Everybody thinks you're cheap; even your mother says you're stingy"). Take responsibility for what you feel and for what you say. Use I-messages: "I feel. . . , I want. . . ."

4. Address the real issues that are causing the difficulties, at least insofar as you can identify and describe them. Don't focus your conflict on the burnt toast when the real source of anger is that you don't want your in-laws to vacation with you. Center your attention on the present; don't dredge up the past or gunnysack by recalling all your past hurts and your partner's past indiscretions. If there is a specific source of conflict, address it squarely and directly.

EMPATHY

5. Demonstrate empathic understanding. Try to feel what your intimate is feeling even though this may be drastically different from what you feel. Try to see the situation from the other person's point of view as clearly and as honestly as you can.

6. Once you have empathically understood your opponent's feelings, validate those feelings where appropriate. If your partner is hurt or angry, and you feel that

such feelings are legitimate and justified (from the other person's point of view), say so; say, "You have a right to be angry; I shouldn't have called your mother a slob. I'm sorry. But I still don't want to go on vacation with her." Note that in expressing validation you are not necessarily expressing agreement on the issue in conflict; you are merely stating that your partner has feelings that are legitimate and that you recognize them as such.

SUPPORTIVENESS

7. Concentrate on describing the behaviors with which you have difficulty (for example, drinking, joke telling, lateness for appointments) rather than jumping quickly to evaluation. Make sure that you are both considering the same behaviors before you make any attempt to pin a label on them.

8. Express your feelings with spontaneity rather than with strategy. Remember that there is no need in interpersonal conflict situations to plan a strategy to win a war. The objective is not to win but to increase mutual understanding and to reach a decision that both parties can accept.

9. State your positions tentatively, provisionally. Demonstrate flexibility and a willingness to change your opinion or position should appropriate reasons be given. There is little hope of reaching agreement—and a good chance that the conflict will escalate—if you approach the conflict with the idea that things must be seen your way and only your way.

POSITIVENESS

10. In any conflict situation there are areas and issues of agreement. Capitalize on these agreements and perhaps use them as a basis for approaching disagreements and impasses. Little is accomplished by emphasizing disagreement and minimizing agreement. This is not an invitation to avoid differences and disagreements; it is, rather, a suggestion to be sure that you do not overlook real and important similarities and areas of agreement that may pave the way for greater understanding.

11. View the conflict experience, at least in part, in positive terms. Try not to see the conflict as an attempt to hurt each other or to get back at your partner for having hurt you. Rather, recall the positive values of conflict and especially the ultimate aim of the conflict, the achievement of greater understanding.

12. Express positive feelings for the other person and for the relationship between the two of you. Throughout any conflict, many harsh words will probably be exchanged, later to be regretted. The words cannot be unsaid or uncommunicated, but they can be partially offset by the expression of positive statements. If you are engaged in combat with someone you love, remember that you are fighting with a loved one and express that feeling. "I love you very much, but I still don't want your mother on vacation with us. I want to be alone with you."

EQUALITY

13. Regardless of how right you feel you are and how wrong you think your partner is, remember the principle of equality; even in combat situations, treat the other person as an equal. The other has feelings that have to be dealt with and understood, and these must be treated with the same respect that you want shown your feelings.

14. Involve yourself on both sides of the communication exchange. Be an active

TABLE 21.1: Conflict Behavior Score Sheet

Conflict Behaviors	Score		Evidence and Reasoning
	P_1	P_1	
OPENNESS			
1. states position openly and without disguise			
2. reacts openly to incoming messages			
3. owns own thoughts and feelings; uses I-messages			
4. addresses real, here-and-now issues			
EMPATHY			
5. demonstrates empathic understanding			
6. expresses validation			
SUPPORTIVENESS			
7. describes other's behavior			
8. expresses feelings spontaneously			
9. states position provisionally			
POSITIVENESS			
10. emphasizes agreement			
11. views conflict positively			
12. expresses positive feelings for other			
EQUALITY			
13. treats other as equal			
14. is involved as both speaker and listener			
TOTAL SCORE			
OVERALL EVALUATION			

Scoring system:
+2 = definitely demonstrates this characteristic
+1 = demonstrates this characteristic
 0 = not clear or doubtful on the basis of the evidence
−1 = does not demonstrate this characteristic
−2 = definitely does not demonstrate this characteristic

participant as a speaker and as a listener; voice your own feelings and listen carefully to the voicing of your opponent's feelings. This is not to say that periodic moratoriums are not helpful; sometimes they are. But you must be willing to communicate as both sender and receiver—to say what is on your mind and to listen to what the other person is saying.

Analyzing Conflict Behaviors

Every fight can be analyzed in terms of the extent to which the parties involved followed or did not follow these specifics. An analysis form is presented in Table 21.1. The specific conflict behaviors are noted, in abbreviated form, on the left. In the center is a place for indicating a score for each of the parties. A simple five-point scoring system is suggested. For each of the 14 conflict behaviors, each combatant should be scored somewhere from a high of $+2$ (indicating a clear demonstration of effective communication behaviors) to a low of -2 (indicating a clear demonstration of ineffective communication behaviors). On the right is space for recording evidence, both verbal and nonverbal, that led you to score as you did. The scoring is usually done by each combatant for his or her own behavior, but may also be done by each combatant for the behavior of the other or by some third party, say a therapist or mutual friend. The important thing is that ratings be assigned *and discussed*.

If you wish to practice with this analysis method, a suitable dialogue for analysis is presented in Experiential Vehicle 41 in the handbook at the back of this book.

Summary: Contents in Brief

Nature of Conflict	Unproductive Conflict Strategies	Process Model of Conflict	Interpersonal Effectiveness Model
Content and/or relationship disagreement between or among connected individuals resulting in negative or positive consequences	Avoidance/ redefinition	Define the conflict	Openness
	Force	Define possible decisions	Empathy
	Minimization	Test decision	Supportiveness
	Blame	Evaluate decision	Positiveness
	Silencers	Accept/reject decision	Equality
	Gunnysacking		
	Beltlining		

Sources

Excellent overviews of conflict are plentiful. See, for example, Alan C. Filley, *Interpersonal Conflict Resolution* (Glenview, Ill.: Scott, Foresman, 1975); Joyce Hocker Frost and Wiliam W. Wilmot, *Interpersonal Conflict* (Dubuque, Ia.: Brown, 1978); and Joseph P. Folger and Marshall Scott Poole, *Working Through Conflict: A Communication Perspective* (Glenview, Ill.: Scott, Foresman, 1984).

George R. Bach and Peter Wyden, *The Intimate Enemy* (New York: Avon Books, 1968) is a popular, well-written account of conflict and productive and unproductive ways of fighting. Gunnysacking and beltlining were drawn from Bach's work, as was the idea for the conflict behavior analysis. The study of the boys at camp can be found in M. Sherif, O. J. Harvey, B. J. White, W. E. Hood, and C. W. Sherif, *Intergroup Conflict and Cooperation: The Robber's Cave Experiment* (Norman, Okla.: University of Oklahoma Book Exchange, 1961). For an analysis of conflict and communication, see Brent D. Ruben, "Communication and Conflict: A System-Theoretic Perspective," *Quarterly Journal of Speech* 64 (1978): 202–210.

Perhaps the best single source on conflict is Fred Jandt's insightful *Win-Win Negotiating: Turning Conflict into Agreement* (New York: Wiley, 1985).

Friendship in Interpersonal Relationships

OBJECTIVES

Upon completion of this unit, you should be able to:

1. define *friendship*
2. identify and explain at least six characteristics that seem essential to all friendships noted in the "friendship profile"
3. identify the functions that friendships serve
4. define the types of friendships identified by Aristotle and Reisman
5. explain the three conceptualizations of friendship identified by James and Savary
6. identify the five stages of friendship development and characterize the communications at each stage
7. identify at least two gender differences in friendship

Friendship has engaged the attention and imagination of poets, novelists, and artists of all kinds. In the movies and on television, friendships have become almost as important as romantic pairings—E.T. and Elliott, Rocky Balboa and Apollo Creed, Admiral Kirk and Mr. Spock, Kate and Allie, Felix and Oscar, Hawkeye and B.J., Trapper and Gonzo, Hardcastle and McCormick, and Cagney and Lacey, (not to mention the "Love Boat" crew) are just a few of those we readily recognize and illustrate how important we think friendship is.

Although important and central to much of our lives, friendships are extremely selective. Throughout our lives we meet numerous people, but out of this wide array we develop relatively few relationships we could call friendships. At times we seem afraid to develop friendships, to extend ourselves, to risk the possibility that we will be rebuffed and rejected in our overtures of friendship. Our increased mobility—in both living and working—has contributed further to the difficulty in establishing friendship relationships, which admittedly take considerable time to develop. This difficulty is seen most clearly in college classrooms, where you may develop a relationship with an individual in one class and then not have another opportunity to interact with that person for two or three semesters.

In the discussion to follow, I begin by briefly noting the stages of friendship development in the child. Then I present a definition of friendship and attempt to isolate the elements that constitute the essence of this type of relationship. Three approaches to, or theories of, friendship are next examined to clarify further the nature of friendship. I then focus on some of the functions friendships serve, which are at the same time the reasons we develop friendships. Next, I attempt to define the stages of friendship development from the initial meeting to the creation of an intimate friendship. Throughout these discussions I focus on friendship as a relationship between two people who may be of the same sex or the opposite sex, of the same age or separated by generations. Sexual interest may or may not be present. Finally, some gender differences in friendship are considered.

CHILDREN'S FRIENDSHIPS

When we were children, say around 3 to 7 years of age, our friendships might have been characterized as "momentary playmateship": We valued friends for what they had (the ball, the rope, the tree house) and what they could do (play ball, run fast, jump rope). At this stage of development friends (as we think of them now) really did not exist. As we grew older, say between the ages of 4 and 9, we still had no real understanding of the mutual-assistance nature of friendship. A friend, in the young "one-way assistance" relationship, was valued or desired basically for what he or she could give us or for doing what we wanted. Later, around the ages of 6 to 12, we entered our "two-way fair-weather cooperation" stage, where friendship existed to serve our own self-interests rather than interests that were mutually beneficial. Around ages 9 to 15 we developed "intimate, mutually shared relationships"; we were able to step outside the friendship and view it as a separate entity— a thing of value for its own sake. Friendship now became a collaborative effort, entered into to achieve some common goals. Here we shared not only objective information but our feelings as well, and we helped each other with problems and conflicts. But at this stage we were also possessive and resented third parties, disturbing these friendships. Still later, from around age 12 on, we developed "autonomous interdependent friendships." These friendships—the ones we now have and the ones from the recent past—were developed and maintained to give mutual emotional and psychological support. Unlike the previous stage, however, the friendships here are not possessive and exclusive; rather, each friend is seen as able to develop other independent relationships, and these relationships do not affect the basic structure of the original friendship.

These several stages, identified by psychologists Robert L. Selman and Anne P. Selman, illustrate the development and growth from immature to mature and productive friendships and provide an excellent starting point for examining friendship as an interpersonal relationship.

FRIENDSHIP: DEFINITIONAL ASPECTS

To analyze friendships and their stages of development, we need to examine a working definition of *friendship* and identify some of the more popular types.

What Is Friendship?

Friendship may be defined as an interpersonal relationship between two persons that is mutually productive, established and maintained through perceived mutual free choice, and characterized by mutual positive regard.

Friendship, as defined here, is an interpersonal relationship. Communication interactions must have taken place between the people. Further, as Paul Wright notes, the interpersonal relationship involves a "personalistic focus." The individuals see and react to each other as complete persons, as unique, genuine, and irreplaceable individuals. Although we may view ourselves as having established a bond of friendship with the entire human race or with some subgroup, that is a different kind of bond and is probably more correctly designated "concern," "regard," or even "universal love."

Friendships must be mutually productive. I include this qualifier to emphasize that friendship by definition cannot be destructive either to oneself or to the other person. Once destructiveness enters into a relationship, it can no longer be characterized as one of friendship. Love relationships, marriage relationships, parent-child relationships, and just about any other possible relationship can be destructive or productive. But friendship can only be productive. By definition, friendship enhances the potentials of the individual.

Friendships are established and maintained through perceived mutual free choice. At least they seem to be; we think we are choosing freely. Sometimes we may be justified in this assumption; at other times it may be an illusion. This is a particularly troublesome concept. We do not choose our brothers and sisters, our aunts and uncles, our parents, sometimes even our marital partners. Similarly, we do not have complete choice in the people we work with or live next to or go to school with. There are probably unconscious factors that exert some influence on our selection of friends, so it may be misleading to say that friendships are established entirely by free choice. This notion applies not just to the establishment of the relationship but also to its day-to-day interactions. As Paul Wright notes, "Good friends often contrive to spend time together even if it entails 'arranging' or inconvenience. They allow their lives to overlap; the plans, decisions, and activities of one person are contingent upon those of the other. A high level of voluntary interdependence is one mark of a strong friendship."

Finally, friendships are characterized by mutual positive regard. Liking people is essential for our calling them friends. Although this surely seems a reasonable inclusion, most definitions omit it entirely—perhaps because they fail to distinguish true friendships from relationships that merely bear the label.

A Friendship Profile

Psychologist Keith Davis has recently drawn an interesting profile of the characteristics that seem essential in a friendship relationship. Davis identifies eight such characteristics.

Enjoyment. Friends enjoy each other's company.

Acceptance. Friends accept each other as each is now; a friend does not attempt to change a friend into another person.

Trust. Friends trust each other to act in the other's best interest.

Respect. Friends respect each other; each assumes that the other will demonstrate good judgment in making choices.

Mutual assistance. Friends can count on each other for assistance and support.

Confiding. Friends share feelings and experiences with each other.

Understanding. Friends understand what is important and why friends behave as they do. Friends are good predictors of their friends' behaviors and feelings.

Spontaneity. Friends do not have to engage in self-monitoring; friends can express their feelings spontaneously, without worrying that these expressions will create difficulties for the friendship.

Types of Friendships

Another way of approaching friendship is to look, at least briefly, at some of the different types of friendships that have been defined. We know that not all friendships are the same, but we are often vague about how one friendship differs from another. I discuss here the friendship types as distinguished by Aristotle, Reisman, and James and Savary in order to give you a clear picture of the variety of friendships that can and do exist. In reviewing these friendship types, you should be able to see more clearly how you function as a friend and how your friends function with you.

ARISTOTLE: UTILITY, PLEASURE, VIRTUE

In *Nicomachean Ethics*, Aristotle identified three kinds of friendly relationships, each of which was motivated by a different purpose. Friendships based on *utility* were those in which the individuals formed a relationship in order to profit from the association, for example, financial advantage, prestige, professional advancement, and so on. Self-interest rather than mutual interest motivated the friendship. Friendships based on *pleasure* were those in which the individuals associated for the purpose of increasing their pleasures—physical, emotional, intellectual, sexual, and so on. Both of these types of friendships, of course, are motivated by the desire to gain something. Friendships based on *virtue,* however, grew out of a recognition by each person of the good qualities (the virtues) of the other. When we see a person's essential goodness, we grow to like them and wish to form a bond of friendship with them.

REISMAN: RECIPROCITY, RECEPTIVITY, ASSOCIATION

John M. Reisman, in *Anatomy of Friendship,* also distinguishes three types of friendships. The friendship of *reciprocity* is the ideal type, characterized by loyalty, self-sacrifice, mutual affection, and generosity. A friendship of reciprocity is a friendship based on equality, where each individual shares equally in the giving and in the receiving of the benefits and rewards of the relationship. The friendship of *receptivity,* on the other hand, is characterized by an imbalance of giving and receiving; one person is the primary giver and one the primary receiver. This imbalance, however, is a positive one because each person gains something from the relationship—the individual (but different) needs of both the person who receives affection and the person who gives affection are satisfied. This is the friendship that often develops between a teacher and a student or between a doctor and a patient; in fact, a difference in status is, according to Reisman, an essential factor for the friendship of receptivity to develop. The friendship of *association* is a transitory one, sometimes more aptly described as a friendly relationship rather than a friendship. Associative friendships are the kind we have with fellow classmates or with neighbors or co-workers. There is no great loyalty, no great trust, no great giving or receiving; the association is cordial but not very intense.

JAMES AND SAVARY: HALF-TO-WHOLE, NOURISHMENT, THIRD SELF

Muriel James and Louis Savary, in their insightful *Heart of Friendship*, distinguish among three viewpoints or theories concerning the nature and effects of friendship. These viewpoints provide considerable insight into what friendship is and what it does to people.

The first approach, which we might label the *half-to-whole view*, conceives of friendship as a process of making people whole. People without friends, in this view, are incomplete individuals, and it is only through the establishment of a friendship that these people are made whole. At the same time, it also leads the individual to supplant his or her own identity. Traditional marriages are often viewed in this way; the husband and wife become one; they are no longer as much individuals as they are a team. Here there is no "I" or "you"; there is just "we" and "us."

The second approach, which we might label the *nourishment view*, conceives of friendship as enhancing, developing, and nourishing each individual. According to this view, friendship does not destroy individuality but rather heightens it. This approach, as James and Savary note, is clearly typified in the famous and often-repeated observation of Fritz Perls from *Gestalt Therapy Verbatim*:

> I do my thing, and you do your thing. I am not in this world to live up to your expectations, and you are not in this world to live up to mine. You are you, and I am I: if by chance we find each other, it's beautiful. If not, it can't be helped.

Whereas traditional views of marriage aligned themselves with the half-to-whole approach, Perls's view of friendship allows the uniqueness and the individuality of each person to grow and to progress. Here they remain "I" and "you."

The third view that James and Savary distinguish is called the *third-self theory* and views friendship as having a life of its own. It is an extension of the nourishment point of view and is not incompatible with it. When two persons experience friendship, a third self emerges—a metaself, a higher-order self. In this view friendship does not destroy or even detract from the uniqueness and individuality of each person but actually enhances it; at the same time, a new self—a third self—emerges. A similar situation occurs with individual notes played on a piano. Each is unique and individual, but when they are played together, something new emerges without destroying the integrity or individuality of the individual notes.

According to this view—which James and Savary feel is the most meaningful—each friendship should be treated like a new person, much as a corporation is treated legally as a person. This is similar to teams and gangs having their own identity and even their own names.

One of the implications of this view is that concern and attention must be directed not only to each other but to the relationship as well, that is, to the metaself, the third self. The problem created by the neglect of this third self is seen clearly in those parent-child relationships in which the parent cares for the child's biological and physical needs but ignores the relationship between them. This relationship—this third self—must be cared for and acknowledged, just as the individual must be. In this view there are "I," "you," and "we" (the third self).

The definition and types of friendships may also be seen in the responses of people who were asked to identify the qualities they felt most important in a friend. The responses, presented in Table 22.1 are derived from a *Psychology Today* survey of 40,000 respondents. If you examine the list, you will find it easy to fit each one of these qualities into one of the types of friendship noted in this discussion.

TABLE 22.1: The Most Frequently Mentioned Qualities of a Friend

Friendship Qualities	Percentage of Respondents
1. Keeps confidence	89%
2. Loyalty	88
3. Warmth, affection	82
4. Supportiveness	76
5. Frankness	75
6. Sense of humor	74
7. Willingness to make time for me	62
8. Independence	61
9. Good conversationalist	59
10. Intelligence	57

SOURCE: Based on Mary Brown Parlee and the Editors of *Psychology Today,* "The Friendship Bond," *Psychology Today* 13 (October 1979): 43–54, 113.

FRIENDSHIP FUNCTIONS

In the *Psychology Today* survey, the 40,000 respondents indicated from a wide number of activities which ones they had engaged in over the past month with friends. Table 22.2 presents the ten most frequently noted activities. As can be appreciated from this list, friendship seems to serve the same functions that all relationships serve but in a unique way. Friendships serve the functions of alleviating loneliness; providing physical, intellectual, and emotional stimulation; and presenting an opportunity to gain self-knowledge. Two general functions—need satisfaction and pleasure/pain functions—are considered by most theorists as basic functions of friendship. These, then, are the functions that friendships serve, as well as the reasons we develop and maintain them.

Need Satisfaction

Friendships develop and are maintained to satisfy those needs that can only be satisfied by certain people. We select as friends those who, on the basis of our

TABLE 22.2: The Ten Most Frequently Identified Activities Shared with Friends

1. Had an intimate talk
2. Had a friend ask you to do something for him or her
3. Went to dinner in a restaurant
4. Asked your friend to do something for you
5. Had a meal together at home or at your friend's home
6. Went to a movie, play, or concert
7. Went drinking together
8. Went shopping
9. Participated in sports
10. Watched a sporting event

SOURCE: Based on Mary Brown Parlee and the Editors of *Psychology Today,* "The Friendship Bond," *Psychology Today* 13 (October 1979):43–54, 113.

experiences or our predictions, will help to satisfy our basic needs or growth needs, and we cultivate and strive to preserve these relationships.

Selecting friends on the basis of need satisfaction is similar to our choosing a marriage partner, an employee, or any person who may be in a position to satisfy our needs. Thus, for example, if we have the need to be the center of attention or to be popular, we select friends who provide fulfillment of these needs—that is, people who allow us, and even encourage us, to be the center of attention or who tell us, verbally and nonverbally, that we are popular.

As our needs change as we grow older or develop in different ways, the functions that we look for in our friendships also change, and in many instances old friends are dropped from our close circle to be replaced by new friends who better serve these new needs.

FIVE FRIENDSHIP VALUES

Psychologist Paul H. Wright has identified more specifically the needs that we seek to have satisfied through friendships. We establish and maintain friendships, Wright observes, because they provide us with certain "direct rewards."

First, friends have a *utility value*. A friend may have special talents, skills, or resources that may prove useful to us in achieving our specific goals and needs. We may, for example, become friends with someone who is particularly bright because such a person might assist us in getting better grades, in solving our personal problems, or in getting a better job.

Second, friends have an *affirmation value*. The behavior of a friend toward us acts as a mirror that serves to affirm our personal value and enables us to recognize our attributes. A friend may, for example, help us to recognize more clearly our leadership abilities, our athletic prowess, or our sense of humor.

Third, friends have an *ego-support value*. By behaving in a supportive, encouraging, and helpful manner, friends enable us more easily to view ourselves as worthy and competent individuals.

Fourth, friends have a *stimulation value*. A friend introduces us to new ideas and new ways of seeing the world and helps us to expand our world view. A friend enables us to come into contact with issues and concepts with which we were not previously familiar—modern art, foreign cultures, new foods, and hundreds of other new, different, and stimulating things.

Fifth, friends have a *security value*. A friend does nothing to hurt the other person or to emphasize or call attention to the other person's inadequacies or weaknesses. Because of this security value, friends can interact freely and openly without having to worry about betrayal or negative responses.

Pleasure and Pain Functions

The other function of friendship is to maximize pleasure and minimize pain. This view is actually a special case of the need-satisfaction function.

If you were to ask people to complete the statement "I most need a friend when . . .," I think they would answer in two ways. One would be to say, "I most need a friend when I'm down," "I most need a friend when I'm feeling sorry for myself," or "I most need a friend when I'm depressed." Such statements typify the function that friendships serve in the avoidance or the lessening of pain. We want a friend to be around when we are feeling down so that he or she will make us feel a little better, lift our spirits, or in some way alleviate the pain we are feeling.

The other would be to say, "I most need a friend when I'm happy," "when I want to share my good news," or "when I want someone to enjoy something with me." These statements typify the general function friendships serve to augment one's pleasure. A great part of the pleasure in winning a game, in receiving good news, and in experiencing some good fortune is in telling someone else about it and in many cases sharing it with them.

In the language of operant conditioning, friends provide reinforcement. Friends may provide us with positive reinforcement by complimenting us, giving us presents, and providing social support for our ideas and our decisions. Friends provide negative reinforcement by removing painful stimuli, nursing us when we are sick, getting us out of our depressions, alleviating loneliness, and in general minimizing our pain. Goethe expressed much the same idea when he wrote:

> The world is so empty
> if one thinks only
> of mountains, rivers, and
> cities; but to know someone
> who thinks and feels with me,
> and who, though distant,
> is close to me in spirit,
> this makes the earth for me
> an inhabited garden.

STAGES AND COMMUNICATION IN FRIENDSHIP DEVELOPMENT

Friendship at first sight is even more rare than love at first sight—if it is possible at all. Though you may like a person at first sight, you could hardly call that person a friend, at least until there has been some opportunity for interaction and communication. Friendship, like most worthwhile things, takes time to develop. It may be described according to a number of stages or phases and is best viewed as existing on a continuum. At one end are "strangers" or two persons who have just met, and at the other end are "intimate friends." We need to consider what happens between these two extremes so that we might be in a better position to move from initial meetings to real friendships, to encourage the growth of friendship in the right direction, and to introduce correctives in the process should problems, obstacles, or breakdowns occur.

One way in which the communication behaviors at the various stages of friendship might be characterized is by reference to the concepts of depth and breadth considered earlier (in Unit 18). As we progress from the initial contact stage to the intimate friendship, the depth of our communications increases; we talk about issues that are closer and closer to our inner core. Similarly, the breadth, or number of communication topics, increases as our friendship becomes closer. As depth and breadth increase, so, it seems, does the enjoyment that we derive from the friendship. Most of us prefer intimate to casual interaction.

The five stages of friendship development are discussed with the ten characteristics of effective interpersonal communication identified in Unit 6. The assumption

Opposite-sex friendships, although still not as common as same-sex friendships, seem to be increasing. One of the major difficulties in such relationships arises when one person wants to retain the friendship status of the relationship and the other wants to change it to a romantic one.

made here is that as the friendship progresses from initial contact, through acquaintanceship, casual friendship, and close friendship, to intimate friendship, the qualities of effective interpersonal communication are increased and enhanced.

Many friendships stabilize themselves at some stage before reaching the intimate stage. The friendship does not progress or deteriorate; it reaches a level that seems mutually satisfying for both individuals and remains at that level, neither person caring to dissolve it or to see it grow beyond this level. This type of situation is often seen among college students, especially among those who commute to school. The two students may be good friends within the context of college; they may take courses together and perhaps study and eat lunch together, but after the school day, they each go their own ways. One may spend nonschool time with a boyfriend or girlfriend, while the other may stay with neighborhood friends. People who work together often develop friendships that stabilize themselves in this same way. Should one individual want the relationship to progress when the other is content with its current stage, conflict can arise.

Initial Contact

The first stage of friendship development is obviously an initial meeting of some kind. It may be a meeting by accident or by strategy, planned or unplanned, self-initiated or brought about by some third party, face to face or by letter or telephone. In any event, some interpersonal encounter must take place. This does not mean that what has happened prior to the encounter is unimportant—quite the contrary. In fact, one's prior history of friendships, one's personal needs, and one's readiness or lack of readiness for friendship development are extremely important in determining whether a relationship will develop into a close friendship, will end soon after the first encounter, or will continue for a long period as a mere acquaintanceship.

At this initial contact stage we find the characteristics of effective interpersonal communication to only a small degree. We are guarded, rather than open or expressive, lest we reveal aspects of ourselves that might be viewed too negatively. Because we do not really know the other person, our ability to empathize or to orient ourselves significantly to the other are extremely limited, and the "relationship"—at this stage at least—is probably viewed as too temporary to be worth the energy and effort that such empathy and other-orientation would entail. Because we really do not know the other person, supportiveness, positiveness, and equality would all be difficult to manifest in any meaningful sense. The characteristics that are demonstrated are probably done so more out of good manners than out of any genuine expression of positive regard for this relative stranger or this tentative relationship. When conflicts arise, they often function to terminate the relationship rather than to stimulate us to work them through. At this stage the relationship is not important enough for us to work through differences; it is often easier to move on to someone else.

There seems at this stage little genuine immediacy; the individuals see themselves as separate and distinct rather than as a unit; there is no real sense of "we-ness," and consequently few verbal or nonverbal immediacy behaviors are in evidence. The confidence that is demonstrated is probably more a function of the individual personalities than of the relationship. Because the relationship is so new and because the individuals do not know each other very well, the interaction is often characterized by a certain awkwardness—overlong pauses, uncertainty in the selection of topics to be discussed, frequent nonfluencies, ineffective exchanges of speaker and listener roles, verbal and nonverbal behaviors that may be misinterpreted, and a general lack of the smoothness of interaction that characterizes more intimate relationships.

Acquaintanceship

If the initial meeting proves productive, the individuals progress to the acquaintanceship stage. At this stage personality attractiveness becomes significant and in fact greatly determines whether or not the relationship will progress. The dimension of physical attractiveness, however, probably never fades completely.

At this stage there is a clear recognition of each other, a consistent exchange of phatic messages, and a definite memory for name, face, and other identifying data.

Put differently, at this stage each person is clearly defined in the mind of the other person and clearly distinguished from other persons.

At the acquaintanceship stage, and in fact at all subsequent stages, a process of testing goes on that most people seem reluctant to admit to. At this stage we attempt to determine whether this acquaintanceship should be developed into a closer relationship or whether it should be terminated. The entire dating system of our culture is essentially one in which each person tests the other person and attempts to determine whether a long-term or even a lifetime relationship should be established.

At this acquaintanceship stage we begin to respond more openly and expressively, but still in a mostly guarded manner. The communications are still essentially impersonal. There is little attempt to talk about personal problems, fantasies and unfulfilled desires, family problems, one's financial situation. In short, there is little attempt to engage in self-disclosure of any significance. In fact, should significant self-disclosures occur, they immediately call attention to themselves and seem intuitively out of place. Empathy and other-orientation are still extremely difficult to achieve because of our limited knowledge of the other person. If our initial contact and our acquaintanceship have been positive, we would probably demonstrate supportiveness and positiveness toward the other person. We begin to see this person as a potential friend, and our positive affect manifests itself in our communications. Similarly, as we get to know the other person, we begin to see him or her as a unique and contributing individual, and equality becomes evident.

Although confidence is somewhat greater here than at the earlier stage, it is still relatively low and, again, more a product of the individuals than of the relationship. There is still no genuine immediacy, although a sense of "we-ness" may be at a very early stage. The interaction is smoother here than at the earlier stage, yet there is still a decided lack of synchrony; questions may be awkwardly phrased and perhaps inappropriate, eye glances are uncoordinated, many of the other's verbal and nonverbal signals are still not completely or correctly understood.

Casual Friendship

In this stage there is a dyadic consciousness, a clear sense of "we-ness," of togetherness; we communicate with a sense of immediacy. At this stage the individuals participate in activities as a unit rather than as separate individuals. Most important, each person sees the dyad as a unit, a whole.

A casual friend is one we would call to go to the movies, sit with in the cafeteria or in class, or ride home from school with. The loss of such a friendship would disturb us, but only for a relatively short period of time. We might feel diminished, but only slightly so.

At this casual friendship stage the qualities of effective interpersonal interaction begin to be seen more clearly. We start to express ourselves openly, and we become interested in the other person's disclosures. Prior to this time, disclosures seem unnatural and premature. We begin to own our own feelings and thoughts with this person and respond openly to his or her communications. Because we are getting to understand this individual, we can begin to empathize and demonstrate significant other-orientation. We also demonstrate supportiveness and develop a genuinely positive attitude toward the other person and toward the general communication situation. We know what this person's needs and wants are—to some extent at least—

and so can stroke effectively. As we get to know the other person more and more, we see ourselves as both contributing to and deriving benefit from the developing relationship.

Perhaps the most significant change at this stage is that there is now a smoothness, a coordination in the interaction between the two persons. The awkward pauses, the nonfluencies, the misinterpretations of the other's behaviors are now few and, for the most part, go unnoticed. The individuals communicate with confidence; eye contact is appropriately maintained, there is flexibility in body posture and in gesturing, and there are few irrelevant responses and few adaptors signaling discomfort.

Close Friendship

The close friendship is an intensification of the casual friendship; it is a logical progression along the lines of intimacy from the casual friendship. At this stage the individuals know each other well and as a result are able to predict the behaviors of each other with considerable accuracy. In part our predictions are based on our having seen the other person in similar situations, and assuming some consistency, we predict that the person will again behave in the same way. But our predictions are also based on knowing things about the person that enable us to extrapolate beyond anything we have observed. We may know the person's values, attitudes, and opinions about specific issues, so when decisions are to be made or when actions are to be taken, we use our knowledge of these values and attitudes to predict future and probable behaviors. Because of this knowledge, significant interaction management becomes possible.

At this stage we become willing to make significant sacrifices for the other person. We will go far out of our way for the benefit of this friend, and the friend in turn does the same for us. Touching and other nonverbal expressions of immediacy become accepted parts of our friendship behavior. Depending on the sex of the individuals, close friends may kiss, hug, slap each other on the back or on the buttocks, put their arms around each other's shoulders, and so on. Touching is not uncomfortable, as it often is with a stranger or a mere acquaintance. Instead, it serves a comforting function for both parties; it assures each of the closeness between them. It is nonverbal testimony that this is indeed a close friendship.

Similarly, we begin, at this level, to read the other's nonverbal signals accurately, and we use these signals as guides to our interactions—avoiding certain topics at certain times, offering consolation before any verbal expression, and, in general, responding appropriately on the basis of mutually shared nonverbal signs.

At this stage we exchange significant messages of affection, messages that express fondness, liking, loving, caring for the other person. Openness and expressiveness are clearly in evidence. Women exchange more affectional messages than do men. In part this difference seems due to the fact that we expect such messages from women and treat such expressions positively, whereas in men they are unexpected and are often treated negatively. Fortunately, the situation seems to be changing somewhat, and perhaps in the not too distant future men will feel comfortable expressing affection for another man or for a woman friend.

At the level of close friendship we see all of the characteristics demonstrated at the previous stage but in increased proportions. The depth of our self-disclosures increases considerably, and we disclose things about ourselves and our families, for example, that we normally keep hidden from persons at less intimate levels. We feel that whatever we disclose will not only be kept in confidence but will be accepted. The friendship is felt to be strong enough that our disclosures will not weaken it or damage it in any significant way. This confidence is demonstrated in both verbal and nonverbal behaviors. This is not to say that we are not at times proved wrong, but generally we make the correct assumption that we will be accepted and that the relationship will withstand any disclosures. As humanistic philosopher George Santayana put it, "One's friends are that part of the human race with which one can be human."

We empathize and exchange perspectives a great deal more, and we expect in return that this friend will also empathize with us. With a genuinely positive feeling for this individual, our supportiveness and our positive stroking become spontaneous. We view this friend as one who is important in our lives; as a result, conflicts—inevitable in all close relationships—become important to work out and resolve through compromise and empathic understanding rather than, for example, a refusal to negotiate or a show of force.

Intimate Friendship

An intimate friendship is that very special kind of relationship we might have with one or perhaps two other people at any given time. Rarely can we sustain more, largely because intimate friendships take so long to develop and a great deal of time and energy to nurture and maintain.

An intimate friendship possesses all the qualities of the close friendship but goes beyond these. For example, the sacrifices each friend is willing to make at this stage are more extreme than those normally seen at the close friendship stage. A classic example of this is found in the Old Testament, in Ruth's expression of friendship for Naomi (Ruth 1:16–17):

> *Do not ask me to abandon or forsake you! For wherever you go I will go, wherever you lodge I will lodge, your people shall be my people, and your God my God: Wherever you die I will die, and there be buried. May the Lord do so and so to me, and more besides, if aught but death separates me from you!*

The touching that is permitted among close friends is naturally permitted here, as is more intimate touching, again, depending for specifics on the sex of the individuals. Touching between intimates may be more prolonged and more frequent and may focus on more intimate body parts. We may touch each other's faces, breasts, thighs, and so on without any self-consciousness, without any granting of permission. In fact, many of the societal rules that govern touching behavior in our culture, as well as the rules governing other forms of verbal and nonverbal behavior, are disregarded by intimates. Intimates create their own rules of interpersonal interaction. The rules are formed from mutual agreement rather than societal edict. And even the rules that the intimates themselves create may be broken, normally without fear of offending.

At this level of intimate friendships, the characteristics of effective interpersonal interaction are seen almost in their idealized form—total openness, expressiveness, empathy, other-orientation, supportiveness, confidence, immediacy, interaction management, positiveness, and equality. Almost, but not quite. There are still matters that we may keep entirely to ourselves and hidden from this intimate, but these would be few in number. Generally, the amount of self-disclosure is considerable; the disclosures themselves are more revealing than those made at the previous levels, and an even greater amount of acceptance is expected and is (generally) received. These disclosures pose less of a threat to the friendship than did those disclosed at the level of the close friendship. "A friend," noted Ralph Waldo Emerson, "is a person with whom I may be sincere. Before him I may think aloud." We are willing to respond openly, confidently, and expressively to this person and to own our own feelings and thoughts. We see the relationship as a strong one and one that will withstand the temporary difficulties and differences that arise from time to time. Empathy is at its height in the intimate friendship. We feel what the other person is feeling with great intensity and great similarity. If he or she fails a course or loses a job or has a fight, we know what that friend is going through because we can feel as he or she feels. Sometimes, our empathic abilities are so good that the other person hardly has to talk; we can feel how this person feels solely on the basis of nonverbal cues. Our supportiveness and positiveness are genuine expressions of the closeness we feel for this person. We want to avoid hurting this person because we care but also because it hurts us when our intimate is hurt. Each person in an intimate friendship is truly equal; each can initiate and each can respond; each can be active and each can be passive; each speaks and each listens.

GENDER DIFFERENCES IN FRIENDSHIP

Many have theorized about the differences between men and women as friends, but little reliable research evidence is available to support these conclusions. Perhaps the most well-documented finding—already noted in our discussion of self-disclosure—is that women self-disclose more than do men. This difference holds throughout male and female friendships. Male friends disclose less often and with less intimate details than female friends.

Psychologist Robert Hays has recently reported that women engage in significantly more affectional behaviors with their friends than do males. This difference, Hays notes, may account for the greater difficulty men experience in beginning and in maintaining close friendships. Women engage in more casual communication and also share greater intimacy and more confidences with their friends than do men. Communication, in all its forms and functions, seems a much more important dimension of women's than of men's friendships.

Men's friendships are often reported to be built around shared activities—attending a ball game, playing cards, working on a project at the office. Women's friendships, on the other hand, are reported to be built more around a mutual sharing of feelings, support, and personalism. And yet, when we examine the activities men and women report they share with their friends, there seems much greater similarity than difference. Some evidence for the greater similarity was presented in Table 22.2.

The ways in which men and women develop and maintain their friendships will undoubtedly undergo considerable changes—as will all sex-related variables—in the next several years. At one time I would have felt confident predicting the direction of these changes; today, I'm not so sure.

Summary: Contents in Brief

FRIENDSHIP IN INTERPERSONAL RELATIONSHIPS

Definition	Types	Functions	Stages
An interpersonal relationship between two persons that is mutually productive, established and maintained through perceived mutual free choice and characterized by mutual positive regard	Aristotle: utility, pleasure, virtue Reisman: reciprocity, receptivity, association James and Savary: half-to-whole, nourishment, third self	Satisfaction of needs: • utility value • affirmation value • ego-support value • stimulation value • security value Maximize pleasure, minimize pain	Initial contact Acquaintanceship Casual friendship Close friendship Intimate friendship

Sources

A cross-cultural perspective on friendship is provided by Robert Brain, *Friends and Lovers* (New York: Basic Books, 1976). Muriel James and Louis Savary, *The Heart of Friendship* (New York: Harper & Row, 1976) provides some interesting insights into friendship relations. Jerry Gillies, *Friends: The Power and Potential of the Company You Keep* (New York: Harper & Row [Barnes & Noble Books], 1976) covers the various aspects of friendship thoroughly and provides useful and interesting experiences for investigating our own friends and friendship relationships. For more scholarly accounts of friendship, see S. B. Kurth, "Friendships and Friendly Relations," and G. D. Suttles, "Friendship as a Social Institution," both in G. J. McCall, ed., *Social Relationships* (Chicago: Aldine, 1970). For an excellent summary of theory and research on friendship, see Paul H. Wright, "Toward a Theory of Friendship Based on a Conception of Self," *Human Communication Research* 4 (Spring 1978): 196–207. Also see Wright's "Self-reference Motivation and the Intrinsic Quality of Friendship," *Journal of Social and Personal Relationships* 1 (March 1984): 115–130 for a model of friendship based on a conception of the self. For an alternative, but not contradictory, view of friendship development, see Robert B. Hays, "The Development and Maintenance of Friendship," *Journal of Social and Personal Relationships* 1 (March 1984): 75–98. The stages in friendship development in children were taken from Robert L. Selman and Anne P. Selman, "Children's Ideas About Friendship: A New Theory," *Psychology Today* 13 (October 1979): 71–80, 114. For an insightful analysis of close friendships, see William K. Rawlins, "Negotiating Close Friendship: The Dialectic of Conjunctive Freedoms," *Human Communication Research* 9 (Spring 1983): 255–266. A useful, well-written overview is provided in Alan Loy McGinnis, *The Friendship Factor* (Minneapolis: Augsburg Publishing House, 1979). For the friendship profile and some of the differences between friendship and love, see Keith E. Davis, "Near and Dear: Friendship and Love Compared," *Psychology Today* 19 (February 1985): 22–30. A number of valuable articles on friendship appear in *Personal Relationships. 2: Developing Personal Relationships*, ed. Steve Duck and Robin Gilmour (New York:

Academic Press. 1981). See especially, Wenda Dickens and Daniel Perlman, "Friendship Over the Life-Cycle," pp. 91–122; Ignor S. Kon, "Adolescent Friendship: Some Unanswered Questions for Future Research," pp. 187–204; John Reisman, "Adult Friendships," pp. 205–230; and Sheila M. Chown, "Friendship in Old Age," pp. 231–246

312

Part 5:
Interpersonal
Relationships

Love in Interpersonal Relationships

OBJECTIVES

Upon completion of this unit, you should be able to:

1. identify the five dimensions or variables of love identified by Pitirim Sorokin
2. identify the two behavior clusters of love noted by Keith Davis
3. define *ludus*, *storge*, *mania*, *pragma*, *eros*, and *agape*
4. explain at least three conditions under which love is more likely to occur
5. explain the theory of love as *labeled arousal*
6. explain the theory of love as imprinting
7. explain at least three ways in which women and men differ in their loving behavior
8. explain the relationship between loving and communication

Of all the types of interpersonal relationships, none seems as important as love. "We are all born for love," noted Disraeli; "It is the principle of existence and its only end." Cyril Bibby, in "The Art of Loving," suggests that *loving* may be a better term to use than *love* and in so doing gets at some of the important qualities of this interpersonal relationship. So long as love is treated as a thing, to be built up mechanically by the addition of this piece of social relationship to that piece of amatory technique, it can never really flourish. To make the most of the human capacity for loving, it is necessary to treat it as an activity of the whole person, in which body, mind, and emotions are all actively involved.

THE NATURES OF LOVE

Loving and *love* are not easy terms to define. Unlike concepts such as attraction or conflict, which can be defined and measured with some ease, *love* and *loving* resist such approaches. On the one hand, we have poets who extol love's virtues: "Come live with me and be my love, / And we will all the pleasures prove," wrote Christopher Marlowe, and who could resist the promise of such a reward? On the other hand, there are cynics, spoken for eloquently by Ambrose Bierce in *The Devil's Dictionary*. Love, says Bierce, is "a temporary insanity curable by marriage or by removal of the patient from the influences under which he incurred the disorder. This disease, like caries and many other ailments, is prevalent only among civilized races living under

313

artificial conditions; barbarous nations breathing pure air and eating simple food enjoy immunity from its ravages."

Perhaps it is the variety of ways in which people may love that makes definition difficult. In *How Do You Feel?* four different approaches to loving are presented. Among the words the writers use in describing the feelings and the behaviors of loving are *warmth, contentment, excitement, oneness, limitless, infinite, boundless, totally encompassing, lucky, faith, trust, dynamic, effort, commitment, tender, multicolored, active, healthy, energetic, courageous, forward-looking, patient, robust, openness, honesty, understanding,* and *fun.* Throughout these words there is a clear emphasis on activity rather than passivity. Loving is an active process. Larry Carlin, in one of the essays in *How Do You Feel?*, puts it this way: "When I feel loving it seems like I can't keep what's inside inside; I have to reach out, touch, embrace, hold, kiss."

Five Dimensions of Love

Pitirim Sorokin further explains love by identifying five major dimensions or variables.

Intensity. Loving feelings or behavior can vary in intensity from nothing to slight to some undefined extreme. Love can vary in intensity from giving a dime to a beggar to sacrificing one's life for one's loved ones.

Extensity. Love can vary in terms of the degree to which it extends from outside the individual and may be solely a love of oneself (low extensity) or may range to the love of all humankind (high extensity).

Duration. Like any emotion, loving can vary in duration from seconds to a lifetime.

Purity. By purity Sorokin means the degree to which the love is motivated by considerations for the self or by considerations for the other person. "Impure" love, in this system, refers to love motivated by selfish considerations without concern for the other person. Pure love is the love of an individual for the sake of the beloved.

Adequacy. Love may vary from wise to blind. In inadequate or blind love there is a huge difference between the purposes or motives in loving and the consequences. An example of inadequate or blind love might be the excessive love a father and a mother have for their child that leads the child to become totally dependent on them. Adequate or wise love, on the other hand, has consequences that are positive for the beloved.

Two Behavior Clusters of Love

Psychologist Keith Davis clarifies love further by identifying two general categories or clusters of behaviors that characterize love: the passion cluster and the caring cluster.

THE PASSION CLUSTER

This cluster consists of fascination, exclusiveness, and sexual desire. Fascination is seen in the lovers' preoccupation with each other, their difficulty in concentrating on issues or people other than the loved one. Exclusiveness is seen in the commitment each lover has toward the other and in their giving to this relationship priority over all others. Sexual desire is seen in the lovers' desire to touch and be touched and to engage in sexual intimacy.

THE CARING CLUSTER

This cluster consists of giving the utmost and being a champion or an advocate. Giving the utmost is seen by the sacrifices one lover makes for the other, in the willingness of one to give all for the loved one. Being a champion or an advocate is seen in the lovers' "active championing of each other's interests and in a positive attempt to make sure that the partner succeeds."

Love and Friendship

Although there are surely many differences and similarities between friendship and love, the findings of Keith Davis are especially helpful along these lines. Davis claims that love possesses higher levels of fascination, exclusiveness, sexual desire, caring, and the willingness to give one's utmost. Love also possesses the potential for the heightened experience of a variety of positive emotions and simple enjoyment. Unfortunately, there is also a negative side to love. In love relationships, notes Davis, there is a greater potential for conflict, criticism, and distress. In short, love, when compared to friendship, offers a greater chance for both satisfaction and frustration, for both happiness and pain.

Psychologist Paul Wright identifies different characteristics separating friendship and love. Love is a more exclusive relationship; we can have a variety of friends but only one (maybe two) lovers. Love is more intense: Emotions are higher in love than in friendship. Love is more permanent: Love, at least in many ideal conceptions, is a permanent relationship; friendship is more temporary. Last, love relationships, notes Wright, are governed by the expectations and the rules established by the society or culture.

TYPES OF LOVE

In *The Colors of Love,* John Alan Lee distinguishes six types of love: ludus, storge, mania, pragma, eros, and agape, as well as various combinations of these.

Ludus

Ludus love is experienced as a game. The ludic lover sees love as fun, a game to be played. The better he or she can play the game, the more the love is enjoyed. To the ludic lover, love is not to be taken too seriously; emotions are to be held in check lest they get out of hand and make trouble; passions never rise to the point at which they get out of control. Ludic love is a self-controlled love—a love that the lover carefully manages and controls rather than allowing it to control him or her. This lover is consciously aware of the need to remain in control and uses this awareness to guide his or her own behaviors.

The ludic lover retains a partner only so long as the partner is interesting and amusing. When the partner is no longer interesting enough, it is time to change. And ludic lovers do change partners frequently. Perhaps because love is a game, sexual fidelity is not something that is of major importance in a ludic love relationship. The ludic lover expects his or her partner to have had (and probably to have in the future) other partners and does not get upset if this happens occasionally during their relationship.

Dating patterns seem greatly influenced by ludic conceptions of love. In ludic love (as in dating) there is no mutual claim and no long-time commitment agreed upon by the partners. Instead it is experienced because it is fun, and when it stops being fun, the relationship is terminated. As one might rate a date (on a ten-point scale, for example), one also rates one's ludic partner. When one partner's rating gets too low or when one or more others are available with higher ratings, the ludic relationship is ready to end.

Storge

Like ludus, *storge* lacks passion and intensity. But whereas the ludic lover is aware of passion but keeps it under control, the storgic lover is unaware of any intensity of feeling. The storgic lover does not set out to find a lover but to establish a storge relationship with someone whom he or she knows and with whom he or she shares interests and activities. Storgic love develops over a period of time rather than in one mad burst of passion. Sex in storgic relationships comes late, and when it comes it assumes no great importance. One advantage of this is that storgic lovers are not plagued by sexual difficulties, as are so many other types of lovers.

Storgic lovers rarely say "I love you" or even remember what many would consider romantic milestones such as the first date, the first weekend alone, the first verbalization of feelings of love, and so on. Storgic love is a gradual process of unfolding thoughts and feelings; the changes seem to come so slowly and so gradually that it is often difficult to define exactly where the relationship is at any point in time. Storgic love is sometimes difficult to separate from friendship; it is often characterized by the same qualities that characterize friendship: mutual caring, compassion, respect, and concern for the other person.

Not only is storgic love slow in developing and slow-burning, it is also slow in dissolving. Storgic lovers can endure long periods of time away from each other without feeling that there is any problem with the relationship. Similarly, they may endure long periods of relative inactivity or lack of excitement without feeling there is any relationship problem.

Mania

The quality of *mania* that separates it from all others is its extremes of highs and lows, of ups and downs. The manic lover loves intensely and at the same time intensely worries about and fears the loss of the love. This intense fear prevents the manic lover in many cases from deriving as much pleasure as might be derived from the relationship. At the slightest provocation, for example, the manic lover experiences extreme jealousy. Manic love is obsessive; the manic lover has to possess the beloved completely—in all ways, at all times. In return, the manic lover wishes to be possessed, to be loved intensely. It seems almost as if the manic lover is driven to these extremes by some outside force or perhaps by some inner obsession that cannot be controlled.

Manic lovers are often unhappy with life and so devote a great deal of energy to love. The manic lover's poor self-image seems capable of being improved only by being loved; self-worth seems to come only from being loved rather than from any sense of inner satisfaction. Because love is so important, danger signs in a relationship are often ignored; the manic lover really believes that if there is love, nothing else matters.

There is a spiral effect in the manic relationship brought on by the manic lover's need to possess and be possessed completely and wholly. When, for example, the manic lover expresses commitment and intensity of feelings, he or she expects a more intense expression of commitment in return. This is responded to with even greater commitment, and so on. The manic lover needs to give and to receive constant attention and constant affection. When this is not given or when an expression of increased commitment is not returned, such reactions as depression, jealousy, and self-doubt are often experienced and can lead to the extreme lows characteristic of the manic lover.

Pragma

The *pragma* lover is the practical lover who seeks a relationship that will work. Pragma lovers seek compatibility and a relationship in which their important needs and desires will be satisfied. Computer matching services seem based largely on pragmatic love. The computer matches persons on the basis of similar interests, attitudes, personality characteristics, religion, politics, hobbies, and a host of likes and dislikes. The assumption is that persons who are similar will be more apt to establish relationships than will persons who are different.

In its extreme, pragma may be seen in the person who writes down the qualities wanted in a mate and actively goes about seeking someone to match these stated qualities. As might be expected, the pragma lover is concerned with the social qualifications of a potential mate even more than personal qualities; family and background are extremely important to the pragma lover, who relies not so much on feelings as on logic. The pragma lover wants to marry and settle down and get on with the business of living. In pragma, a love relationship is a means to the achievement of other ends, unlike the manic lover, to whom love is the end and all else are means to its attainment. The pragma lover views love as a necessity—or as a useful relationship—that makes the rest of life easier. So the pragma lover asks such questions of a potential mate as "Will this person earn a good living?," "Can this person cook?," and "Will this person help me advance in my career?"

Not surprisingly, pragma lovers' relationships rarely deteriorate. This is true in part because pragma lovers have chosen their mates carefully and have emphasized similarities. Perhaps they have intuitively discovered what experimental research has confirmed, namely, that relationships between similar people are much less likely to break up than are relationships among those who are very different. Another reason for the less frequent breakups seems to be that their romantic expectations are realistic. They seem willing to settle for less and, consequently, are seldom disappointed.

Eros

One version of the Narcissus legend is that Narcissus, a beautiful Greek boy, fell in love with his own reflection in the water. So absorbed was he with his own beauty that he ignored the love of the beautiful nymph Echo. One day, while admiring his own reflection and attempting to get closer and closer to it, he fell into the water and drowned. Another way of looking at this legend, as John Lee suggests, is to look at Narcissus as the classic erotic lover. In this view Narcissus was punished for his total absorption with a beauty and perfection that he could never possess. His own reflection was more beautiful than the fountain nymph Echo or anyone else he could possibly love. The *erotic* lover focuses on beauty and physical attractiveness, sometimes to the exclusion of qualities we might consider more important and more enduring. And like Narcissus, the erotic lover often has an idealized image of beauty that is unattainable in reality. Consequently, the erotic lover often feels unfulfilled. Erotic lovers are particularly sensitive to physical imperfections in their beloveds—a nose that is too long, a complexion that is blemished, a figure that is a bit too full, and so on. And this is one reason why the erotic lover wants to experience the entire person as quickly in the relationship as possible.

Eros is an ego-centered lover, a love that is given to someone because that person will return the love. It is in this sense a utilitarian, rational love because it is a calculated love with an anticipated return. Eros is essentially hedonistic; it is a sensual love of the physical qualities of an individual where physical attraction is paramount. Eros is a discriminating type of love; it is selective in its love objects. It is directed at someone because he or she is valuable and can be expected to return equally valuable love.

Agape

Agape (ah-guh-pay) is a compassionate love, an egoless, self-giving love. Agape is nonrational and nondiscriminative. Agape creates value and virtue by its love rather than bestowing love only on that which is valuable and virtuous. The agapic lover loves even people with whom he or she has no close ties. This lover loves the stranger on the road, and the fact that they will probably never meet again has nothing to do with it. Jesus, Buddha, Gandhi, and similar people practiced and preached agape, an unqualified love.

Agape is a spiritual love. One cannot love altruistically if one loves with the thought that one will be rewarded in some way for this love or compassion. Agapic love is offered with no concern for any kind of personal reward or gain. The agapic lover loves without expecting that the love will be returned or reciprocated.

The agapic lover gives to the other person the kind of love the person needs even though there may be great difficulties or personal hardships involved. Thus, for example, if one person in a love relationship would prefer to be free and to be living with another person, the true agapic lover will leave the relationship for the sake of the beloved with no thought that this altruistic act will result in his or her love being returned. Furthermore, the true agapic lover will want this new relationship to succeed and will be hurt if it brings unpleasantness or unhappiness to the beloved. Most often when relationships break up and one of the parties is hurt, the hurt individual wants the new relationship to fail, as a kind of punishment. But the agapic lover responds differently; even if hurt, the agapic lover wants only the best for the beloved.

In one sense agape is more of a philosophical kind of love than a love that most of us have the strength to achieve. In fact, John Lee notes that "unfortunately, I have yet to interview any respondent involved in even a relatively short-term affiliative love relationship which I could classify without qualification as an example of agape. I *have* encountered brief agapic episodes in continuing love relationships."

Each of these loves can combine with others to form new and different patterns. These six, however, should be sufficient to delineate some of the major types of love and to illustrate the complexity of a love relationship. It is perhaps obvious to say that different people are satisfied by different things—that each person seeks satisfaction in a unique way. When it comes to love, however, this "obvious" point needs to be highlighted. The love that may seem to you to be "lifeless" or "crazy" or "boring" may to someone else be ideal. At the same time, another person may see the very same negative qualities in the love you are seeking that you might see in theirs. With an understanding of these various kinds of love, we may become more tolerant and empathic. A real problem does arise, of course, when a person seeking one type of love falls in love with a person seeking a very different type of love; there is no easy path to a mutually productive relationship in such a case.

THE DEVELOPMENT OF LOVE

Love is an extremely difficult emotion to deal with in terms of its development or the conditions conducive to its occurrence. How do you make someone love someone? What makes one person love another? It would be a gross understatement to say that these are difficult questions. And so it is with considerable hesitancy that I attempt to characterize the ways in which love develops. First, I offer some tentative propositions concerning the conditions under which love is more likely to occur. Second, I put forth two theories concerning the development of love.

Conditions Conducive to the Development of Love

Loving, it seems, is more likely to occur under the following general circumstances.

1. *When there is mutual respect.* Both research and folk wisdom attest to the difference between loving and liking. One can be present without the other. We can like someone we do not love, and we can love someone we do not like. Yet it seems that in most situations we like and respect the person we love, with the liking and respecting coming first.

2. *When the individuals have positive self-images.* Engaging in a loving relationship is easier if a person has a positive self-image. If one does not love oneself, it is extremely difficult, if not impossible, to love another person. Psychologist and family therapist Virginia Satir has argued that a positive self image is essential to all meaningful communication in close relationships. Love, as well as compassion, honesty, and integrity flow easily from persons with positive self images since these persons feel that they matter and that their compassion and love, for example, also matter.

3 *When there is a physical attraction.* There is a physical component in almost all love relationships. When we love someone, we want to be with that person, and generally we choose not to be with people we find unattractive. And attractiveness is at least in part physical.

4. *When the individuals are relatively free of significant problems.* It is difficult to love or be loving when we have nothing to eat and no prospects of getting a job, for example. If we are on the verge of being convicted and sentenced to jail for life, it is understandable that we would think very little, if at all, about love and loving. We may, of course, worry about our loved ones and what will happen to them, but we would not be in a very good position to establish a new love relationship. These examples are purposely far removed from our own experiences. But consider individuals who constantly worry about a business, money, or grades. Their available energy for love is greatly reduced.

Theories on the Development of Love

While literary and poetic explanations of love and loving are varied and numerous, there are few scientific explanations that seem to have any merit. Two exceptions to this general rule are discussed here with the intention of stimulating you to reflect on the nature of love in interpersonal relationships rather than convince you that these are in fact the ways in which love develops.

LOVE AS LABELED AROUSAL

One of the most interesting theories of emotion, proposed by Stanley Schachter, hypothesizes that two factors are essential for emotion. The first factor is physiological arousal, which may take various forms, for example, increased heart rate, sweating, increased breathing rate, facial flush, and so on. The second essential factor is that this physiological arousal must be labeled or named in terms of its cause. If you experience intense physiological arousal when someone forces you to address an audience of several hundred people, you might label that *apprehension*. Neither factor by itself is sufficient for the development of emotion; both arousal and labeling must be present.

A number of researchers have attempted to apply this basic theory to love. One such example is that of Ellen Berscheid and Elaine Walster, who expanded the two-factor theory to three factors. Three factors (or three components) are necessary, say Berscheid and Walster, for love to develop. First, there has to be some knowledge of how the culture defines love; that is, one has to know what love is. By knowing what love is—even if the individual has not yet experienced it—the person is in a ready state to find it, recognize it, and perhaps expect it. The more one thinks about love, the greater the chances of experiencing it. Second, there must be some appropriate person available to whom this love can be directed. (Naturally it helps if this available person possesses qualities that you find attractive or that meet with your expectations.) Third, there must be some physiological arousal that has been labeled *love*.

The process of the development of love, then, would have three stages: (1) We know what love is, are looking for it, and are ready to experience it; (2) we spot a likely love object; and (3) we experience a physiological arousal that we label *love*. The arousal may be stimulated by some love-related activity, such as kissing or by some unrelated activity, such as running or fighting.

One of the interesting implications of this theory is that love may be encouraged by disco dancing, viewing a boxing match, seeing a horror movie, hearing a rock concert, or winning or losing money on the horses. All lead to physiological arousal. However, the individual must then label the arousal *love*. Needless to say, this labeling is more likely to take place when the initial physiological arousal seems logically related to what we normally think of as love.

This theory very satisfactorily explains why women are reportedly more prone to fall in love after an intense relationship than are men. The intense relationship, we may assume, leads to physiological arousal of both sexes, so the first factor is present for both. But note that women have been conditioned to associate this type of arousal with love and so will be more apt to label the experience *love* than will males, who traditionally have been taught that there is a definite separation between physiological arousal and love. These sex differences are growing smaller, but, some difference still survives and perhaps accounts—at least in part—for the different love experiences of men and women.

LOVE AS IMPRINTING

The concept of imprinting was developed by Konrad Lorenz, who used it to refer to the behavior of ducklings who would follow just about any animal or object that moved in front of them as they hatched. Normally this is the mother duck, but when it was Lorenz himself, the ducklings treated him as if he were their mother; even in the presence of the natural mother, the ducklings would follow Lorenz.

Imprinting is a form of one-shot conditioning; it occurs once, and, apparently, the behavior is learned for all time. First, there is a specific time in the life of the individual in which imprinting occurs. The time varies with the behavior and with the specific animal, but there seem to be critical periods for different behaviors. Second, imprinting does not seem to be influenced by rewards or punishments extrinsic to the behavior; apparently an animal may be imprinted even if it is being punished at the same time. Third, the imprinting occurs without rewards or punishments occurring after the behavior is emitted. The behavior itself is apparently the reward.

Edward Brecher has argued that this concept of imprinting and particularly these three characteristics may be used to explain love. According to Brecher, falling in love is essentially an imprinting process. It occurs not so much because of the individual one meets but rather because of the time in the life of the individual. Usually a boy or girl will fall in love at puberty, and the object of the love is not particularly relevant. What is important is that it was the right time in life to fall in love, and so the person did so. As Brecher put it:

> Just as the mallard duckling follows the first moving object that happens by when it is thirteen hours old, so the boy or girl freshly arrived at adolescence falls in love with the first potential love object who happens past at the critical period of puberty. The object imprinted may be too old or too young, too fat or too thin, too bashful or too domineering; it doesn't much matter if he or she comes past when the moment for falling in love is ripe.

This theory seems to explain well why it is that we never seem to get over our first love, why our first love and our first lover always seem to have a special place in our thoughts and in our feelings.

A COMBINED VIEW

If we attempted to combine these two positions, we would propose a five-factor theory which would take the "labeled arousal" theory as a basis and add to it two "imprinting" elements: (1) the actual presence of the appropriate love object or some clear symbolic representation, for example, a photograph or film, and (2) a specific time in life that love is apt to develop most readily. According to this synthesized theory, then, the entire process would go something like this:

1. We learn about love from our culture; we know what love is; we look for love; we expect love to happen to us.
2. We reach a particular point in our lives when we are ready for love—we are at the stage where imprinting is possible.
3. We see an appropriate love object or some symbolic representation.
4. We are physiologically aroused from kissing, fighting, or some other physical activity.
5. We label the physiological arousal *love* and attribute that arousal, that love, to the "appropriate love object."

GENDER DIFFERENCES IN LOVING

In our culture, the differences between men and women in love are considered great. In poetry, in novels, and in the mass media, women and men are depicted as acting very differently when falling in love, being in love, and ending a love relationship. Women are seen as totally absorbed with love, whereas men are seen as relegating love to one part of their lives. Or, as Lord Byron put it in *Don Juan*, "Man's love is of man's life a thing apart, / 'Tis woman's whole existence." Women are portrayed as emotional, men as logical. Women are supposed to love intensely, while men are supposed to love with detachment. Military leader Giorgio Basta noted, "Man loves little and often, woman much and rarely." Though the folklore on sex differences is extensive, the research is meager.

DEGREE OF LOVE

In their responses to a questionnaire designed to investigate love, social psychologist Zick Rubin found that men and women were quite similar; men and women seem to experience love to a similar degree. Women do, however, indicate greater love for their same-sex friends than do men. This may reflect a real difference between the sexes, or it may be a function of the greater social restrictions under which men operate. Men are not supposed to admit their love for another man, lest they be thought homosexual or somehow different from their fellows. Women are permitted greater freedom to communicate their love for other women.

ROMANTIC EXPERIENCES AND ATTITUDES

In an attempt to investigate the number of romantic experiences and the ages at which these occur, sociologist William Kephart surveyed over 1,000 college students from 18 to 24 years of age. The women indicated that they had been infatuated more times than the men. The median times infatuated for the women was 5.6 and for the men, 4.5. For love relationships, there is greater similarity. The median number of times in love for these same women was 1.3 and for the men, 1.2. As expected, women had their first romantic experiences earlier than men. The median age of first infatuation for women was 13 and for men was 13.6; median age for first time in love for women was 17.1 and for men was 17.6.

In this same study men, contrary to popular myth, were found to place more emphasis on romance than women. For example, the college students were asked the following question: "if a boy (girl) had all the other qualities you desired, would you marry this person if you were not in love with him (her)?" Approximately two-thirds of the men responded no, which seems to indicate that a high percentage were concerned with love and romance. However, less than one-third of the women responded no. Further, when sociologist D. H. Knox surveyed men and women concerning their views on love—whether it is basically realistic or basically romantic—it was found that married women had a more realistic (less romantic) conception of love than did married men. It is also interesting to note that married persons had a more realistic view of love than did unmarrieds.

ROMANTIC BREAKUPS

Popular myth would have us believe that when love affairs break up, the break-ups are the result of the man's developing some outside affair. But the research does not seem to support this. When surveyed on the reasons for breaking up, only 15 percent of the men indicated that it was because of their interest in another partner, but 32 percent of the women noted this as a reason for the breakup. And these findings are consistent with the perceptions of the partners regarding the causes of the breakups as well: 30 percent of the men but only 15 percent of the women noted that their partner's interest in another person was the reason for the breakup. The most popular reason reported was a mutual loss of interest: 47 percent of the men and 38 percent of the women noted this as a reason for breaking up.

In their reactions to broken romantic affairs, there are both similarities and differences between women and men. For example, both women and men tended to remember only the pleasant things and to revisit places with past remembrances about equally. On the other hand, men engaged in more dreaming about the lost partner and in more daydreaming generally as a reaction to the breakup.

What will happen in the next decades with regard to sex differences in loving is hard to gauge. On the one hand, as the sexes become more equal socially and economically, the differences in love and loving may be lessened considerably, maybe even eliminated. On the other hand, as the socioeconomic differences are eliminated, the sexual-romantic-loving differences may be accentuated and may well take on added significance and relevance.

LOVING AND COMMUNICATION

Herbert A. Otto, one of the leaders in the human potential movement, notes in *Love Today* the paradoxical conclusions made about communication in love. Communication in love, says Otto, is characterized by two features: ''(1) confusion and lack of clarity; and (2) increased clarity and comprehension.'' While some lovers note the extreme difficulty in understanding what the other person means, many others note the exceptional ability they now seem to possess in understanding the other person.

Ron Lunceford, in *How Do You Feel?*, expresses clearly the strong desire to communicate love and the difficulties in doing so.

> The one thing I think I wish for myself is that I could express my love more. I can express my love, but sometimes I have the fear of talking about it too much. I like being loved and I like giving love and sometimes talking about it changes that feeling for me. Sometimes too it is sad for me to talk about love and loving feelings to people who don't have someone to love or anyone to love them; that's sad.
>
> I want to say sometimes to people, ''Hey, you can love me and we don't have to make promises to each other.'' Some people can handle that and some can't. Some just need permission to express love and be open to it; sometimes it helps to begin to take that risk.
>
> But for me, I want to say, ''I love you'' more. I don't want anyone I love to go without knowing that.

Effectiveness Characteristics and Love

Empathic communication is naturally increased in any love relationship since, on the basis of our more open communication, we can understand how the other feels and want to feel what he or she feels. This increased empathy enables us to know much more accurately what messages are appropriate and when. We know what

This love relationship is signaled nonverbally with intimate proxemic distance, touching, smiling, looking longingly into each other's eyes, and a lack of awareness of others.

arouses our loved one into anger and into ecstasy. Consequently, we can easily offend, not only because we are important to our loved one and hence have great power to hurt but also because we know the person's soft spots, the forbidden areas that can only be discussed at great risk. Fortunately, we also know how to soothe and calm our loved one. In short, when people become lovers and develop a strong empathic ability, they learn what buttons to push with what effect. In many ways, to love someone is to support him or her. We naturally support those we love, in part because we want them to be secure and unafraid. Our supportiveness helps them and theirs helps us. Love is an emotion that is not only good to receive but good to give as well; it makes us feel pleased to love and, consequently, the positiveness we feel for ourselves, for our beloved, and for the relationship itself is increased. Normally, we love persons whom we respect and regard as good; we like them as well as love them. If we love someone, we want to become a part of that person. This is perhaps the best way to encourage the feeling of equality.

But loving implies taking risks, as Lunceford mentions. We run the risk of not having our love returned or being rejected outright. The alternative we often take is to conceal our love or perhaps never even admit it to ourselves. Communicating our love also involves the risk of self-disclosure. In any love relationship, mutual self-disclosure is important. As Otto says, "This helps to establish a relationship characterized by optimal personality growth for both lovers."

Much as loving relationships are helped by self-disclosure, love also encourages openness and honesty. We seem to have a need to express ourselves, to let other people know who we "really" are. Yet perhaps because of the fear of rejection, we conceal our "true selves." In a love relationship, we have someone to whom we can reveal ourselves without fear of being rejected or thought foolish. Not every relationship is quite so simple, of course. In many instances it is with the people we love that we are most on guard. If, for example, we initially pretended to be strong, we might conceal weakness for fear that it was our strength that made us attractive.

Verbal Indicators of Love

In addition to these general communication characteristics, we may also note a number of more specific ways in which we communicate when in love. Verbally, there is an exaggeration of the virtues and a minimization of the faults of the one we love. We share emotions and experiences and speak tenderly and with an extra degree of kindness to each other, "please," "thank you," and similar terms abound. Murray Davis, for example, identifies three major types of endearing names lovers use: (1) names that place the beloved above others, for example, "angel"; (2) names that place the beloved lower than others but in an innocent and caring way, for example, "baby"; and (3) names that identify the beloved with a special taste sensation, for example, "honey" and "sweetie."

Lovers also develop private codes; they speak in a way that only each other can understand, a phenomenon that Truman Capote referred to when he defined love as never having to finish your sentences. Likewise, lovers have private names for each other, pet names that are sometimes sweet and sometimes silly but always appropriate to the lovers exclusively. When outsiders use these terms—as they sometimes do—they seem inappropriate, at times an invasion of privacy.

Nonverbal Indicators of Love

We have all seen movies of the star-struck lovers staring into each other's eyes. This prolonged and focused eye contact is perhaps the clearest nonverbal indicator of love. Lovers lean toward each other in an attempt, it would seem, to keep physical distance at a minimum and any possible intruders outside the privacy of the relationship. The physical closeness (even, a spatial overlap) echoes the emotional closeness. In deteriorating relationships, when emotional closeness fades, so does physical closeness—both the closeness of bodies and the closeness that is achieved psychologically by direct and prolonged eye contact.

Lovers not only become more conscious of their loved one but also of their physical selves. There seems a certain muscle tone that is heightened when people are in love, a tendency to engage in preening gestures, especially immediately prior to meeting the loved one, and an arrangement of the body (to the extent possible) into its most attractive position—stomach pulled in, shoulders square, legs arranged in masculine or feminine positions.

Lovers may even talk with a somewhat different vocal quality. For example, Murray Davis, in *Intimate Relations*, notes that there is some evidence to show that sexual excitement enlarges the nasal membranes which gives the speech of lovers a certain nasal quality.

And perhaps the most obvious nonverbal behavior of all is the elimination of the socially taboo adaptors (at least in the presence of the loved one): scratching one's head, picking one's teeth, cleaning one's ears, and passing wind are avoided. Interestingly enough, these adaptors often (though foolishly, I think) return after the lovers have achieved a permanent relationship.

Summary: Contents in Brief

Types of Love	Conducive Conditions	Theories of Love Development	Communication in Love
Ludus: love as a game	Mutual respect	Labeled arousal	Confusion and clarity
Storge: love as companion-ship	Positive self-image	Imprinting	Empathy increased
Mania: love as obsession and possession	Physical attraction	Arousal + imprinting:	Supportiveness increased
Pragma: love as a practical relation	Freedom from problems	• We know what love is	Openness increased
Eros: love as sensuous and erotic		• We are at the imprinting stage	Exaggeration of virtues
Agape: love as self-giving, al-truistic		• We see an appropriate love object	Tenderness and politeness
		• We are physiologically aroused	Private codes
		• We label the arousal *love* and attribute it to the "ap-propriate love object"	Endearing names
			Prolonged and focused eye contact
			Physical closeness
			Consciousness of physical self
			Preening behaviors
			Elimination of taboo adapt-ors

Sources

Pitirim A. Sorokin, "Altruistic Love," and Cyril Bibby, "The Art of Love," in Albert Ellis and Albert Abarbanel, eds., *The Encyclopedia of Sexual Behavior* (New York: Hawthorn Books, 1967) were particularly helpful in defining and characterizing love and loving. John Wood, ed., *How Do You Feel?* (Englewood Cliffs, N.J.: Prentice-Hall, 1974) contains interesting articles by Ron Lunceford and Larry and Kay Carlin, both cited here, as well as by John Wood and Bill and Audry McGraw. All four articles, and in fact the entire book, are worth reading. Zick Rubin, *Liking and Loving* (New York: Holt, Rinehart and Winston, 1973), is especially insightful. On the clusters of love and the ways love and friendship differ, see Keith E. Davis, "Near and Dear: Friendship and Love Compared," *Psychology Today* 19 (February 1985): 22–30.

On types of love, see John Alan Lee, *The Colors of Love* (New York: Bantum Books, 1977). For the theories of love as physiological arousal, see Stanley Schachter, "The Interaction of Cognitive and Physiological Determinants of Emotional State," in Leonard Berkowitz, ed., *Advances in Experimental Social Psychology*, vol. 1 (New York: Academic Press, 1964) and the explanation of the Berscheid-Walster adaptation in Robert A. Baron and Donn Byrne, *Exploring Social Psychology*, 2d ed. (Boston: Allyn & Bacon, 1982). Also see Ellen Berscheid and Elaine Walster, "A Little Bit About Love," in T. L. Huston, ed., *Foundations of Interpersonal Attraction* (New York: Academic Press, 1974). For the theory of love as imprinting, see Edward M. Brecher, *The Sex Researchers* (Boston: Little, Brown, 1969). Herbert A. Otto, "Communication in Love," in *Love Today: A New Exploration* (New York: Dell [Delta Books], 1972), is perhaps the best single source on love and communication. Two excellent works offer thorough summaries of research on love and insight into our own loving behavior: Elaine Walster and G. William Walster. *A New Look at Love* (Reading, Mass.: Addison-Wesley, 1978) and Glenn Wilson and David Nias, *The Mystery of Love* (New York: Quadrangle/The New York Times Book Co., 1976). Murray Davis, *Intimate Relations* (New York: Free Press, 1973) and Virginia Satir, *Peoplemaking* (Palo Alto, Calif.: Science and Behavior Books, 1972) offer wide-ranging insights on love and its development. Research and theory is well presented in John D. Cunningham and John K. Antill, "Love in Developing Romantic Relationships," *Personal Relationships. 2: Developing Personal Relationships*, ed. Steven Duck and Robin Gilmour (New York: Academic Press, 1981), pp. 27–51.

The studies reported on sex differences in loving were taken from Wilson and Nias's *Mystery of Love*. Original references are as follows: William M. Kephart, "Some Correlates of Romantic Love," *Journal of Marriage and the Family* 29 (1967): 470–479 and D. H. Knox, "Concepts of Love by Married College Students," *College Student Survey* 4 (1970): 28–30. For the study on frequency and age of first romantic experiences, see C. Kirkpatrick and T. Caplow, "Courtship in a Group of Minnesota Students," *American Journal of Sociology* 51 (1945): 114–125. Also see Clyde Hendrick, Susan Hendrick, Franklin H. Foote, and Michelle J. Slapion-Foote, "Do Men and Women Love Differently?" *Journal of Social and Personal Relationships* 1 (1984): 177–195.

UNIT 24

Primary Relationships, Families, and Interpersonal Communication

OBJECTIVES

Upon completion of this unit, you should be able to:

1. define *family* and *primary relationship*
2. identify five characteristics common to all primary relationships
3. identify five of the reasons discussed here for the maintenance of primary relationships
4. define and explain the four communication patterns that characterize primary relationships
5. explain the operation of manipulation, nonnegotiation, emotional appeal, personal rejection, and empathic understanding as conflict strategies in primary relationships
6. identify and explain the five suggestions for improving communication within the primary relationship and the family

All of us are now or were at one time part of a family. Some of our experiences have been pleasant and positive and are recalled with considerable pleasure. Other experiences have been unpleasant and negative and are recalled only with considerable pain. Part of the reason for the pleasure or the pain rests with the interpersonal communication patterns that operate within the family. This unit is designed to provide a better understanding of the interpersonal communication patterns that operate within the family and some insight into how these interactions can be made more effective, more productive, and more pleasant.

Five issues relating to these goals are discussed. First, we consider the nature and characteristics of families and primary relationships in order to spell out some of the universals common to these relationships. Second, we look into the reasons people establish and maintain such relationships. Third, we identify the patterns of communication that operate within these interpersonal units. Fourth, we examine some conflict strategies popular in primary relationships and families. Fifth, we offer some suggestions for improving interpersonal communication within primary relationships and families.

PRIMARY RELATIONSHIPS AND FAMILIES: NATURE AND CHARACTERISTICS

If you had to write a definition of what constitutes a family, you would probably note that a family consists of a husband, a wife, and one or more children. When pressed you might also note that some of these families also consist of other relatives—in-laws, brothers and sisters, grandparents, aunts and uncles, and so on. But there are other types of relationships that are, to its own members, "families." Perhaps the most obvious example is people living together in a marriagelike state but who are not in fact married. For the most part, these "cohabitors" live as if they were married. For example, there is an exclusive sexual commitment, there may be children, there are shared financial responsibilities, shared time and space, and so on. These relationships are like traditional marriage unions except that in one case the union is recognized by church or state and in the other it is not.

Sociologists Philip Blumstein and Pepper Schwartz, in their comprehensive *American Couples,* report that although the number of such couples is only around 2.0 to 3.8 percent of all couples, their number is increasing. For example, if we examine couples where the male is under 25, the percentage of cohabiting couples increases to 7.4 percent. In Sweden, 12 percent of all couples are cohabitors. Further, these researchers note that the judicial system, by considering the claims of cohabitors against each other (remember the famous Lee Marvin–Michele Triola case in which the term "palimony" was introduced and Ms. Triola was awarded $104,000) have given this relationship a new kind of legitimacy.

Another obvious example is the gay male or lesbian couple who live together as "lovers" with all the other characteristics of a "family" but who are not legally married. Many of these unions too have children from previous heterosexual unions or by adoption. Although accurate statistics are difficult to secure, primary relationships among gays and lesbians seem more frequent than the popular media leads us to believe. Research studies put the number of gay or lesbian couples at 70 to over 80 percent of the gay population (itself estimated variously at between 4 and 16 percent of the total population, depending on the definitions used and the studies cited). In summarizing these previous studies and their own research, Blumstein and Schwartz conclude, " 'Couplehood,' either as a reality or as an aspiration, is as strong among gay people as it is among heterosexuals."

The communication principles that apply to the traditional nuclear family (the mother-father-child family) also seem to apply to these nonmarried relationships. In the following discussion the term *primary relationship* is used to designate the two principal parties involved—the husband and wife, for example—and the term *family* to designate the broader constellation that includes children, relatives, and assorted significant others. All primary relationships have a number of characteristics in common, and these will be identified.

Defined Roles

There is a relatively clear perception of the roles each person is expected to play in relation to each other and to the relationship as a whole. Each knows approximately what are his or her obligations, duties, privileges, and responsibilities. This does not mean that the individuals do not fight over the roles or that they are completely satisfied with them, just that the roles are fairly clear to the parties. Such roles might include wage earner, cook, house cleaner, child watcher, social secretary, home decorator, plumber, carpenter, food shopper, money manager, and so on. At times the roles may be shared, but even in the sharing it is generally assumed that one person has primary responsibility for certain tasks and the other person for others.

Commitment to Preservation

In a primary relationship there is a commitment to the preservation of the relationship. Again, this does not mean that each party is always satisfied with the relationship or that there are not times when one party might long to be alone or with someone else. But the individuals usually have an intellectual and emotional commitment to maintain this particular relationship. They seek its preservation, its continuance. Along with this commitment is a strong bond between the individuals; generally they care for and like (perhaps even love) each other.

Recognition of Responsibilities

The parties see themselves as having certain obligations and responsibilities to each other. In the single state, the individual does not have the same kinds of obligations to another person as in a primary relationship. For example, individuals have an obligation to help each other financially—on a day-to-day basis as well as on a more long-term basis, for example, in insurance, hospitalization, and retirement planning. Relationships today are more than ever characterized by this economic interdependence. As medical costs, taxes, and inflation erode our earnings and savings and as the desire to accumulate goods and to improve one's living conditions increase, this economic interdependence will become even more significant in defining our primary relationships.

There are also emotional responsibilities: to comfort the individual when distressed, to take pleasure in their pleasures, to feel their pain, to raise their spirits. Temporal obligations must also be considered, since each person is obligated to reserve some large block of time for the other. Time sharing seems important to all relationships, though each couple will define this differently. With some couples temporal commitments and obligations are extensive; they do everything together and rarely do anything alone or with third or fourth parties. Other couples sleep together but do little else with each other. Between these two extremes lie most primary relationships. Sexual obligations are another factor: The individuals in a primary relationship are more or less committed to achieving a substantial part of their sexual gratification (in some relationships, all of it) with each other.

Shared History and Future

Primary relationships have a shared history and the prospect of a shared future. For a relationship to become a primary one, there must be some history, some significant past interactions. Primary relationships do not emerge full-blown: they develop over a period of time. During this time the members get to know each other, to understand each other a little better, and ideally to like and even love each other. Similarly, the individuals view the relationship as having a potential future. In fact, this is one of the main reasons relationships are developed—so that each individual will have a special partner tomorrow, the day after that, and perhaps forever.

Despite the fact that researchers predict that 50 percent of first marriages now being entered will end in divorce (the rate is higher for second marriages) and that 41 percent of all persons of marriageable age will experience divorce, most couples entering a relationship such as marriage view it—ideally at least—as permanent. In contrast, casual sexual encounters do not have a history and usually do not have a prospect of a future—at least this is not the individuals' primary orientation. In such casual encounters the object is a purely sexual and emotional one and does not involve the same temporal commitment or the same mutuality that a primary relationship does. This is not to say that casual relationships cannot be intense or satisfying; nor is it to say that such casual relationships may not develop into significant and lasting relationships—some can and do. Nevertheless, at the point of the encounter, the casual relationship does not have a significant shared past or a prospect of a shared future, which in itself functions to alter the relationship a great deal. When individuals in a primary relationship have a shared history and a commitment to a shared future, they respond to each other, to relational problems, and to significant others in very different ways than do partners who have no history or prospect for a future.

Shared Living Space

In our culture, persons in primary interpersonal relationships usually share the same living space. When living space is not shared, it is generally seen as "abnormal" or as temporary by both the culture as a whole and by the individuals involved in the relationship. For example, one of the parties may work out of town or may be in prison, in the armed forces, or in a hospital. But this situation is generally seen as a deviation from the normal pattern. There are cases, of course, where a man or woman who lives with a partner, parents, children, or even alone may have a lover with whom he or she does not share living space. They probably perceive a shared space, however, as the ideal and, in fact, usually do share some special space at least part of the time.

In some cultures, men and women do not share the same living space—the women may live with the children while the men live together in a commune-type arrangement. Today, in our culture, many couples are choosing to live apart, each maintaining an apartment. Usually they do this with a view to sharing the same space at some more appropriate time, for example, when the level of commitment of one or both parties is higher or when other problems or difficulties have been resolved.

THE MAINTENANCE OF PRIMARY AND FAMILY RELATIONSHIPS

The reasons for maintaining primary relationships are as numerous and varied as the reasons for beginning such relationships. Some of the more popular and frequently cited reasons are mentioned here.

EMOTIONAL ATTACHMENT

The most obvious reason is that the individuals love each other and want to preserve their relationship. They wish to maintain what they have because alternative

This family, like most families, is probably held together by a combination (and interaction) of factors. Among the most important are emotional attachment, convenience, children, fear, financial considerations, and inertia.

couplings do not seem as inviting or as potentially enjoyable—the individuals' needs are being satisfied and so the relationship is continued. In some cases these needs are predominantly love and mutual caring, but in other cases the needs being met may not be quite so positive. For example, one individual may maintain a relationship because it provides a means of exercising control over another person. Another might continue the relationship because it provides ego gratification or some form of humiliation, each according to his or her specific need.

CONVENIENCE

Often the relationship neither involves great love nor great need satisfaction but is maintained because it is convenient. Perhaps both partners work together—they may jointly own a business or a house—or have certain mutual friends that are important to them. In these cases it may be more convenient to stay together than to break up and go through the difficulties involved in finding another person to live with or another business partner or another social escort. At times both feel the same way about the relationship, and here there is seldom any difficulty; neither is "fooling" the other. At other times, the relationship is one of great love for one partner and one of convenience for the other.

CHILDREN

Relationships are often kept together because there are children involved. Children are often (fortunately or unfortunately) brought into the world to save a relationship. In some cases they do—or at least the union is preserved. The parents stay together because they feel, rightly or wrongly, that it is in the best interests of the children to preserve the relationship. In other cases, the children are just a socially acceptable excuse for the fear of being alone, for convenience, for financial advantage, and so on. In childless relationships, both parties can be more independent and can make life choices based more on individual needs and wants. These individuals, therefore, are less likely to remain in relationships they may find unpleasant or uncomfortable.

FEAR

Fear motivates many to stay together. The individuals may fear the outside world; they may be fearful of being alone and of facing others as "singles." They may remember the horrors of the singles bars, the "one-night stands," and the loneliness of the weekends and may elect to preserve their current relationship as the better alternative. For example, in the United States women outnumber men. The 1980 census noted that for people in their forties, there are 233 single women for every 100 single men. This relative lack of opportunity for women to enter another relationship may deter some from exiting a current relationship.

Sometimes the fear may be of social criticism: "What will our friends say? They always thought we were such a great couple. They'll think I'm a failure because I can't hold on to another person." Sometimes the fear concerns the consequences of violating some religious or parental tenet.

FINANCIAL CONSIDERATIONS

Financial advantages may motivate many couples to stick it out. Divorces and separations are expensive both emotionally and financially. "Palimony" and "galimony" (recall the Billie Jean King case) are as much feared as alimony, so people with considerable amounts of money are fearful of breaking up because they fear losing half their wealth or even more. Also, depending on where the individuals live and their preferred life-style, being single can be expensive. The cost of living in New York, Philadelphia, Houston, Chicago, San Francisco, Boston, and many other cities is almost prohibitive for single people, and many couples stay together to avoid facing additional economic problems.

INERTIA

Still another reason is inertia—perhaps a major reason for the preservation of many relationships. Many people just "go along with the program," and it hardly occurs to them to consider changing their status; change seems too much trouble. Inertia—the tendency for a body at rest to remain at rest and a body in motion to remain in motion—is greatly encouraged by the media. It is easier for many individuals to remain in their present relationship and to seek vicarious satisfactions from situation comedies, dramas, and especially soap operas wherein the actors do all the things the viewer would do if he or she were not so lazy and resistant to change.

Few relationships stay together for a single reason. Rather, there are usually a multiplicity of reasons that vary in terms of intensity and from one relationship to another. Obviously, the more intense the reasons, the more likely the relationship will be preserved. But because so many of the reasons for relational preservation are subconscious, it is difficult to discover why a particular couple stays together or breaks up or to predict which relationships will last and which will not.

COMMUNICATION PATTERNS IN PRIMARY RELATIONSHIPS AND FAMILIES

Each primary relationship functions with a unique set of communication patterns. No two relationships evidence exactly the same interpersonal communication structures. But amid this diversity and uniqueness, there are general patterns that can be identified and that may serve as general classifications or types. Each interpersonal relationship may then be viewed as a variation on one of these basic types. To this end, four major patterns are identified.

The Equality Pattern

The equality pattern probably exists more in theory than in reality, but it is a good starting point for examining communication in primary relationships. In the *equality* pattern each party shares in the communication transactions equally; the roles played by each are equal. Thus each party is accorded a similar degree of credibility by the other; each is equally open to the ideas, opinions, and beliefs of the other; each engages in self-disclosure on a more or less equal basis. The communication that takes place is open, honest, direct, and free of the power plays that characterize so many other interpersonal relationships. Here there is no leader or follower, opinion giver or opinion seeker; rather, both parties play these roles equally. Because of this basic equality, the communication exchanges themselves, over a substantial period of time, are equal. For example, the number of questions asked, the depth and frequency of self-disclosures, the nonverbal behavior of touching and eye gaze would all be about equal.

Both parties share equally in the decision-making processes—the insignificant ones about which movie to attend as well as the significant ones about where to send the child to school, what church to attend, what house to buy, and so on. Conflicts in equality relationships may occur with some frequency, but they are not seen as threatening to the individuals or to the relationship. They are viewed, rather, as exchanges of ideas, opinions, and values. Even when these individuals disagree, they disagree agreeably. The disagreement is not seen as due to one's being stupid and the other's being smart but to the inevitable clash of ideas and the differences in values and preceptions that are a part of long-term relationships. Put in terms of the content-relationship postulate discussed in Unit 2, these conflicts are content rather than relational in nature. This couple has few power struggles within the relationship domain.

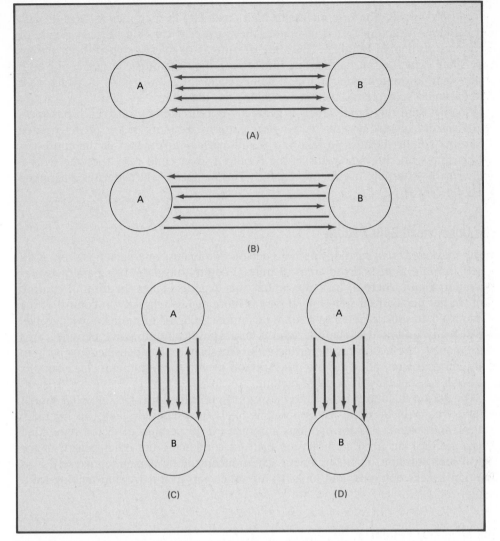

335

Unit 24: Primary
Relationships,
Families, and
Interpersonal
Communication

FIGURE 24.1: Communication Patterns in Primary Relationships.

If a communication model of this relationship were drawn in which arrows were used to signify individual messages, there would be an equal number of arrows emanating from each person. Further, if the arrows were classified into different types, the types would likewise be similar. A representation of this is given in Figure 24.1(A).

The Balanced Split Pattern

In the *balanced split* communication pattern, an equality relationship is maintained, but here each person is in control of or has authority over different domains. Each person, for example, is seen as an expert, but in different areas. For example, in the traditional nuclear family, the husband maintains high credibility in business matters and, say, in politics. The wife maintains high credibility in such matters as child care and cooking. Although this is changing, these patterns can still be seen clearly in numerous traditional families. There are also areas of overlap where both parties have some expertise but neither one much more than the other. For example, both parties may know the same amount about religion, health, or art, in which case neither would be perceived as more credible than the other.

Conflict with these individuals is generally nonthreatening since each has specified areas of expertise and so the win–lose patterns are more or less predetermined before the conflict begins. To take our traditional example again, if the conflict is over business, the husband wins; if the conflict is over child care, the wife wins—neither party is terribly hurt by the conflict. This balanced split pattern is diagrammed in Figure 24.1(B).

The Unbalanced Split Pattern

In the *unbalanced split* relationship, one person dominates; one person is seen as an expert in more than half the areas of mutual communication. This pattern is diagramed in Figure 24.1(C). In many unions this expertise takes the form of control. Thus, in the unbalanced split, one person is more or less regularly in control of the relationship. In some cases this person is the more intelligent or more knowledgeable, but in many unions it is the one who is more physically attractive or who earns more money. The less attractive or lower-income partner compensates by giving in to the other person, allowing the other person to win the arguments, for example, or have his or her way in decision making.

The person in control makes more assertions, tells the other person what should be and what will be done, gives opinions freely, plays power games to maintain control, and seldom asks for opinions in return except perhaps to secure some kind of ego gratification from confirmation or from convincing the other person of the logical sophistication of the argument. The noncontrolling person, conversely, asks questions, seeks opinions, and looks to the other person for decision-making leadership.

The Monopoly Pattern

In a *monopoly* relationship, one person is seen as the authority. This person lectures rather than communicates, pontificates rather than converses. Rarely if ever does this person ask questions to seek advice, and he or she reserves the right to have the final say. In this type of union, the arguments are few because both individuals already know who is boss and who will win the argument should one arise. When the authority is challenged, perhaps from outside instigation—"Don't let him walk all over you," "Be a man; stand up to her"—there are arguments and bitter conflicts. One reason the conflicts are so bitter is that these individuals have had no rehearsal for adequate conflict resolution. They do not know how to argue or how to disagree agreeably, so their arguments frequently take the form of hurting the other person.

The controlling person tells the partner what is and what is not to be. The noncontrolling person looks to the other for permission, for opinion leadership, for decisions to be made, almost as would a child to an all-knowing, all-powerful parent.

In many cases these unions are more like child-parent relationships. One individual (the "parent") gains gratification from playing the parental role, from ordering, guiding, and caring for the other person, while the "child" gains gratification from having his or her needs met and from not having to make decisions and consequently having to suffer any negative consequences attendant upon wrong or inadequate decisions. This pattern is diagrammed in Figure 24.1(D).

In thinking about these four types of communication patterns, it is easy to identify with the equality or balanced split pattern, and surely most of us would consciously wish to be a part of these unions rather than either of the others. But many of our decisions are based on subconscious factors, and our motivations are not always "logical" and "mature." Further, many people clearly opt for the unbalanced split and monopoly patterns, some viewing themselves as the controlling agents, others viewing themselves as the controlled. What makes for happiness, satisfaction, and productivity in a relationship varies with the individuals. An equality pattern that might produce satisfaction in one relationship may lead to dissatisfaction among individuals who need either to control another person or to be controlled. The pattern that makes you happy might make your father and mother or your son and daughter unhappy. A clear recognition of this relativity is a prerequisite to understanding other people's relationships and the role that communication plays in the maintenance of those relationships.

CONFLICT STRATEGIES IN PRIMARY RELATIONSHIPS AND FAMILIES

In Unit 21 we examined conflict, some of the productive and some of the unproductive methods of conflict resolution. Here we examine, in brief, a few additional conflict strategies that have been found to be particularly prevalent in primary relationships. I follow the analysis of Mary Anne Fitzpatrick and Jeff Winke, who identify five main strategies: manipulation, nonnegotiation, emotional appeal, personal rejection, and empathic understanding.

MANIPULATION

In *manipulation* there is an avoidance of open conflict. The individual attempts to divert the conflict by being especially charming (disarming, actually) and getting the other individual into a receptive and noncombative frame of mind before disagreeing. That is, the conflict situation and the other individual are manipulated so that the manipulating individual may eventually win the battle, argument, or disagreement.

NONNEGOTIATION

Nonnegotiation is a type of conflict avoidance in which the individual refuses to discuss the conflict or disagreement and even refuses to listen to the other person's argument or point of view. Actually, of course, one cannot really avoid a conflict, since avoidance is in itself a way of dealing with the conflict, much like not responding to another's request is itself a response. At times this nonnegotiation takes the form of hammering away at one's own point of view until the other person gives in, a technique that has been called *steamrolling*.

EMOTIONAL APPEAL

The *emotional appeal* strategy involves crying, sulking, pouting, demonstrating anger, and in fact any means that will succeed in arousing the emotions of the other person. The individual may, for example, appeal to the other person's love and affection—"How could you do this and say you still love me?"—or may promise to behave in the future or to be more loving or more caring.

PERSONAL REJECTION

In *personal rejection* the individual withholds love and affection and seeks to win the argument by getting the other person to break down under this withdrawal. The individual acts cold and uncaring, attempting to demoralize the other person. In withdrawing affection, the individual hopes to make the other person question his or her own self-worth. Once the mate is demoralized and feels less than worthy, it is relatively easy to get one's own way by simply making the restitution of love and affection contingent upon resolving the conflict in the individual's favor.

EMPATHIC UNDERSTANDING

In *empathic understanding* we have the one strategy of conflict resolution that would be called "adult" and "mature" by most individuals. Here there is an emphasis on cooperating and understanding the other person's point of view. Each person attempts to state the position calmly, with reason, with a degree of tentativeness, and with a willingness to change and bend. The emphasis here is not on winning a war, but on achieving a mutually satisfying peace.

How the Strategies Are Used

In preliminary research based on reported usage of these conflict strategies, a number of differences have been identified depending on the sex of the individual and on the type of relationship involved. In Table 24.1 the conflict strategies are given for opposite-sex and for same-sex relationships in order of frequency of usage. In opposite-sex relationships we attempt to manipulate more and to use emotional appeal more. Perhaps the most interesting fact about the usage of these strategies is the relative infrequency of empathic understanding for both relationships. Men, it has been found, generally favor nonnegotiation as a strategy; women seem to favor personal rejection, empathic understanding, and emotional appeal, all of which require considerable understanding of the other individual to employ successfully. In casual relationships manipulation and nonnegotiation are used a great deal, whereas emotional appeal and empathic understanding are used very little. With marrieds, emotional appeals and personal rejections are used a great deal, but unfortunately empathic understanding is used little.

How can we explain these results? We might attempt to explain each one individually by noting, for example, that marrieds may feel they know each other a great deal better and hence do not have to enter a conflict ready to understand the other's point of view; they already know it and disagree with it. A generalization that might account for all these results is that we use what works; the strategies that work are the ones that are used with greatest frequency, with no apparent concern for their ultimate effect on the relationship. Thus, for example, marrieds who know

TABLE 24.1: Rank Order of Frequently Used Conflict Strategies

FOR OPPOSITE-SEX RELATIONSHIP CONFLICTS
1. Manipulation
2. Nonnegotiation
3. Emotional appeal
4. Personal rejection
5. Empathic understanding

FOR SAME-SEX RELATIONSHIP CONFLICTS
1. Nonnegotiation
2. Personal rejection
3. Manipulation
4. Empathic understanding
5. Emotional appeal

SOURCE: Mary Anne Fitzpatrick and Jeff Winke, "You Always Hurt the One You Love: Strategies and Tactics in Interpersonal Conflict," *Communication Quarterly* 27 (Winter 1979): 3–11.

339

Unit 24: Primary
Relationships,
Families, and
Interpersonal
Communication

each other well and who have a great deal invested in the relationship can effectively hurt the other person with emotional appeals and personal rejection, and hence "win the argument" with these strategies. Empathic understanding will not allow us to win as many conflicts as we would like and so we use it little. Further, because marrieds know each other well, they can effectively manipulate the emotions and perceived self-worth of the other person. They are in a powerful position and most likely to win their battles with these strategies. In casual relationships we do not know enough about the other individual to manipulate him or her and consequently cannot use emotional appeal very effectively. Furthermore, we usually do not care a great deal about the casual relationship and so we employ the strategies that will simply enable us to win the battle or get out of the conflict situation—namely, manipulation and nonnegotiation.

Clearly we would need a great deal more research before we would be able to say with any degree of confidence that the strategies we employ are not the result of our intelligence, our education, and our concern for the other person, but rather the result of our desire to win the battle, to have our way, and to remain in control. Nevertheless, it does appear from the little research and evidence available that we select the strategies that will enable us to win.

IMPROVING COMMUNICATION WITHIN PRIMARY RELATIONSHIPS AND FAMILIES

Communication is improved in primary interpersonal relationships by the application of the same principles that improve communication in any other context. But to be most effective, these principles need to be adapted to the uniqueness of the primary relationship context. The purpose of this section is to suggest how the general principles of effective communication may be best applied to primary interpersonal relationships. Additional suggestions for improving communication within relationships are presented in Unit 26 (see the section "Communication Patterns in Relational Deterioration").

Empathic Understanding

If meaningful communication is to be established, we must learn to see the world from the other person's point of view, to feel that person's pain and insecurity, to experience the other person's love and fear. Empathy is an essential ingredient if a primary relationship or a family is to survive as a meaningful and productive union. It is essential, for example, that the individuals be allowed—and in fact encouraged—to explain how and why they see the world, their relationship, and their problems as they do.

Self-disclosures

The importance of self-disclosure in the development and maintenance of a meaningful interpersonal relationship has been noted repeatedly. The research on self-disclosure, however, suggests that total self-disclosure may not always be rewarding and effective. In fact, research indicates that at times it may be expedient to omit, for example, past indiscretions, certain fears, and perceived personal inadequacies if these disclosures may lead to negative preceptions or damage the relationship in some way. In any decision as to whether or not to self-disclose, the possible effects on the relationship should be considered. But it is also necessary, it seems to me, to consider the ethical issues involved, specifically the right of the other person to know about behaviors and thoughts that may influence the choices he or she makes. Certainly, these decisions are not easy to make, but they must be faced by all individuals involved in intimate relationships.

If we survey the relationships around us, we would probably find too little self-disclosure as well as too little acceptance of disclosures made by others. Carefully reversing this process would seen effective; most relationships would profit from increased self-disclosures and from a greater acceptance of disclosures in general. The type of self-disclosures I am advocating are disclosures of present feelings rather than the details of past sexual experiences or past psychological problems. The sharing of present feelings also helps a great deal in enabling each person to empathize with the other; each comes to understand better the other's point of view if these self-disclosures are made. It has been found, for example, that the length of time a couple spends together is not related to the amount of understanding they have of each other, indicating that self-disclosure is not a normal and accepted part of daily interaction in most relationships.

When self-disclosures are made, it is particularly important that clear and unmistakable support for the person be demonstrated—nonverbally and verbally. This does not mean that you have to agree with the disclosure itself, only that you should support the act of disclosing and the person as a whole.

Openness to Change

If there is one general quality that seems essential to effective interpersonal relationships, I think it is openness to change, to experimentation. Throughout any significant relationship there will be numerous and significant changes in each of the individuals and in the relationship as a whole. The person who is open to these changes, who accepts them as a normal and natural part of life, is better able to adjust to and control the changes as they occur. Again, I am not suggesting that we should uncritically accept the results of any specific change but that we accept the process of change and realize that change is normal and that lack of change is the exception.

Fighting Fair

341

Unit 24: Primary
Relationships,
Families, and
Interpersonal
Communication

Conflict, as already noted, is inevitable; it is an essential part of every meaningful interpersonal relationship. The goal should not be to have a relationship free of conflict but rather to manage conflict effectively and productively. Perhaps the most general rule to follow is to *fight fair*. Winning at all costs, beating down the other person, getting one's own way, and the like are perhaps appropriate in business, politics, and the boxing ring, but they have little use in a primary relationship or family. Instead, cooperation, compromise, and mutual understanding must be substituted. If we enter a conflict with a person we love with the idea that we want to win and we want the other person to lose, the conflict has to have the effect of hurting at least one partner, though very often both get hurt in the process. In such situations the loser gets hurt and in response frequently retaliates to hurt the winner, with the effect that no one wins in any meaningful sense. On the other hand, if we enter a conflict with the idea of resolving the conflict and of reaching some kind of mutual understanding, neither party need be hurt, and in fact both parties may benefit from the clash of ideas or desires and from the airing of differences.

Acceptance of Less than Perfection

When we look at other people's relationships, we often see only the surface, and on the surface most relationships look pretty good. We do not see the day-to-day hassles over money, the snoring during the night, the disagreements. Instead we are presented with a picture of near harmony. Few couples or families, for example, fight openly in front of others; in most primary relationships, fighting takes place in private. We do, however, see these day-to-day problems in our own relationships—usually all too vividly.

Consequently, other relationships often appear to be a great deal better than our own, but in actual fact, they are probably much like our own. The major difference is in our perception of the two relationships. If we look upon our own relationship as unsatisfying (regardless of how good or bad it may appear to others), this may become a self-fulfilling prophecy and we *will* be unhappy in it. If, on the other hand, we realize that no relationship is perfect, it may help us to stay in touch with reality and not be discouraged when problems occur. No mate—however attractive, wise, urbane, sexy, and charming—is perfect. To aim for or expect perfection can only result in disappointment.

Again, to be accepting of less than perfection does not mean that we should not try to improve ourselves and our relationships or that we should be content to have relationships filled with problems. Rather, it is to emphasize that any meaningful relationship *will* have problems and that is is best to deal with these problems—to correct or to alleviate them in some way—rather than to long for a utopian relationship that does not really exist.

Summary: Contents in Brief

Characteristics of Primary Relationships	Reasons for Relationship Maintenance	Communication Patterns	Conflict Strategies	Communication Improvement
Defined roles	Emotional attachment	Equality	Manipulation	Empathy
Commitment to preservation	Convenience	Balanced split	Nonnegotiation	Self-disclosure
Recognition of responsibilities	Children	Unbalanced split	Emotional appeal	Openness to change
Shared history and future	Fear	Monopoly	Personal rejection	Fighting fair
Shared living space	Financial considerations		Empathic understanding	Acceptance of less than perfection
	Inertia			

Sources

A great deal of research and theory is being directed at understanding family communication. Useful popular sources include Sven Wahlroos, *Family Communication* (New York: New American Library, 1974); Jane Howard, *Families* (New York: Berkley Books, 1978); and Harvey White, *Your Family Is Good for You* (New York: Berkley Books, 1980). Perhaps the best overview of the area is presented by Kathleen M. Galvin and Bernard J. Brommel, *Family Communication,* 2nd ed. (Glenview, Ill.: Scott, Foresman, 1986). An interesting analysis of family communication and the strategies on lessening problems is presented in Edwin J. Thomas, *Marital Communication and Decision Making: Analysis, Assessment, and Change* (New York: Free Press, 1977). The relationship between the time a couple spends together and their mutual understanding is covered in J. Richard Udry, Harold A. Nelson, and Ruth O. Nelson, ''An Empirical Investigation of Some Widely Held Beliefs About Marital Satisfaction,'' *Marriage and Family Living* 23 (1961): 338–390. A useful summary of this and related studies may be found in Edgar W. Butler, *Traditional Marriage and Emerging Alternatives* (New York: Harper & Row, 1979). For an interesting discussion of the different types of families, see Mary Anne Fitzpatrick and Julie Indvik, ''The Instrumental and Expressive Domains of Marital Communication,'' *Human Communication Research* 8 (Spring 1982): 195–213.

Statistical data on a wide variety of relational issues and types of relationships are presented by Philip Blumstein and Pepper Schwartz, *American Couples* (New York: Morrow, 1983). Relevant to the contents of this unit are the discussions of Michael D. Newcomb, ''Heterosexual Cohabitation Relationships,'' and Robert L. Burgess, ''Relationships in Marriage and the Family,'' *Personal Relationships. 1: Studying Personal Relationships* (New York: Academic Press, 1981), pp. 131–164, 179–196.

343

Unit 24: Primary
Relationships,
Families, and
Interpersonal
Communication

UNIT 25

Understanding Relational Deterioration

OBJECTIVES

Upon completion of this unit, you should be able to:

1. explain the nature of relational deterioration
2. explain how psychological, behavioral, contextual, and status changes might account for relational deterioration
3. explain the operation of at least six causes of relational deterioration

Just as a relationship may grow and progress, becoming stronger and more meaningful, it can also wane and regress, becoming weaker and less meaningful. Some dimensions of relational deterioration are considered here, specifically, the nature of relational deterioration and some of the causes of this deterioration. Our purpose here is to further our understanding of the processes operating when a relationship experiences difficulty.

THE NATURE OF RELATIONAL DETERIORATION

Relational deterioration refers to the weakening of the bonds holding people together. At times the relationship may be weakened only mildly and may appear normal to outsiders; to the participants, however, it is clear that the relationship has weakened significantly. The obvious extreme of relational deterioration is the complete termination of the relationship. Between these two extremes are an infinite number of variations. Relational deterioration occurs on a continuum from just a little bit less than intimate to total separation and total dissolution.

The Process of Deterioration

The process of deterioration may be gradual or sudden. Murray Davis, in *Intimate Relations*, uses the terms "passing away" to designate gradual deterioration and "sudden death" to designate immediate or sudden deterioration. An example of

344

"passing away" is when one of the parties in a relationship develops close ties with a new intimate and this new relationship gradually pushes out the old intimate. An example of "sudden death" is when one or both of the parties break a rule that was essential to the relationship (for example, the rule of complete fidelity), and both realize that since the rule has been broken, the relationship cannot be sustained and, in fact, must be terminated immediately.

Responsibility for Deterioration

The deterioration or termination of a relationship may be the primary responsibility of both parties, one of the parties, or neither party—a possibility that we often fail to consider. In the first case, both parties may wish to go their separate ways, perhaps each with a new intimate or perhaps alone. In either case they both agree that separation is the best choice. In the second case, one of the parties wants to leave while the other party wants to remain in the relationship. These are the types of relationships movies and romantic novels are made of—the struggle to hold together a family, a marriage, or a friendship. In the third case, neither party wants the relationship to deteriorate, but perhaps one of the parties says or does something that is so detrimental to the other person and to the relationship, to use Murray Davis's example, that it becomes apparent that the relationship cannot survive.

All relationships are different; what pulls one relationship apart may well hold another together. The death of a child, for example, can destroy one marriage but solidify another. Outside threats usually strengthen a relationship, though at times they have the effect of tearing it apart.

The Negatives and the Positives

Not all relationships should be retained. Not all breakups are bad, and few, if any, bad breakups are entirely bad. In the midst of a breakup this may be difficult to appreciate, but in retrospect it seems almost always to be true.

At times relationships are unproductive for one or both parties, and a breakup is often the best alternative. Such a termination may provide a period for the individuals to regain their independence and to become self-reliant again. Some relationships are so absorbing that there is little time available for reflection on oneself, on others, and on the relationship itself. Sometimes distance helps.

One of the major problems with some relationships is that they prevent one or both parties from developing new relationships, from becoming involved with new intimates, from developing new friends and associations. A termination of such a relationship provides the individuals with opportunities to develop these new associations and to explore different types of relationships with different types of people.

These are obviously not the only redeeming characteristics of terminating a relationship that might be mentioned; each relationship is different, and each individual is different. The freedom to explore new relationships may be viewed by one person as a challenging and exciting opportunity; to another person it may be threatening and frightening. It would be foolhardy to state with any degree of authority what the specific benefits may be to specific people in specific relationships. The only point I want to make here is that relational deterioration does not have to

Interpersonal relationships deteriorate for a wide variety of reasons. Sometimes the reasons for establishing the relationship have diminished: the loneliness is still present, the stimulation is weak, the self-knowledge and self-growth expected are insufficient, and attractiveness has faded. Sometimes, the intimacy claims are too great for comfortable interaction, third party relationships intrude, relational changes create adjustment difficulties, undefined expectations create conflicts, sexual incompatibilities develop, work-related problems absorb time and energy, and financial difficulties create stress and inequalities.

have only negative consequences. For the most part, it is up to the individual to draw out of any decaying relationship some positive and productive characteristics, a lesson earned that can be used later on.

SOME CAUSES OF RELATIONAL DETERIORATION

In all interpersonal interactions, the causes of relational deterioration are as numerous as the individuals involved, and so it is with considerable modesty that I even attempt to identify some of them. Having offered this qualification, perhaps the best place to start is to look at some of the reasons relationships are developed and see how changes in these factors may lead to deterioration.

Reasons for Establishing the Relationship Have Diminished

In Unit 18 I noted some factors that are important in establishing relationships. When these are no longer operative or when they are changed drastically, it may be a cause of relational deterioration.

LONELINESS IS NOT REDUCED

One of the major reasons people seek relationships is to alleviate loneliness. When loneliness is no longer lessened by the relationship, when one or both of the individuals experience loneliness for prolonged or frequent periods, the relationship may well be on the road to decay.

STIMULATION IS WEAK

If relationships are established and maintained in part because they are stimulating to the individuals, then relationships will decay when that stimulation is removed or significantly lessened. This is often seen in marriages. Before marriage they said, "I love you," held each other's hands, hugged each other tight, and otherwise demonstrated their affection for each other. After some years of marriage that emotional and physical stimulation often fades. Such shows of affection were among the important reasons why the relationship was established and maintained; to allow them to become just memories jeopardizes the relationship.

SELF-KNOWLEDGE AND SELF-GROWTH ARE INSUFFICIENT

We are extremely complex creatures, and regardless of how long we live we will probably never fully understand ourselves. We need constantly to learn more about ourselves and grow, and we often establish a relationship to these ends. When we cease to gain self-knowledge and to grow, the relationship is not fulfilling one of its major functions and may soon show signs of decay.

ATTRACTIVENESS HAS FADED

The reason most often mentioned for relational deterioration is that the initial attractiveness that brought the individuals together is gone—the pot belly, the baldness, the sagging buttocks, the lines in the face, the extra weight, and so on all contribute to the loss of attractiveness. Similarly, in long-term relationships people have a tendency to ignore or drop the social niceties they once thought essential when the relationship was in its formative stages. The common courtesies—the phone call to say "I'll be late," the card on a birthday or anniversary, the flowers for no reason at all—are often forgotten or considered unimportant, and this attitude contributes to the loss of attractiveness. People who assume that physical and personality attractiveness is no longer important after 5, 10, or 20 years of a relationship are probably fooling themselves. They seem to be attempting to find an excuse for sloppiness, for not exercising, for not keeping to a diet, for not being considerate. Or perhaps they are trying to convince themselves that they are still desired despite the physical changes. Perhaps they are right—if so, it is probably in spite of themselves.

Research tells us that men who place a great deal of emphasis on physical attractiveness are less likely to stay in a relationship a long time. Such men quit a relationship when the physical attractiveness of their partners, a major contributor to the development of their relationship, fades. Further, when relationships break up, it is the more attractive partner who leaves. There is no denying the power of attractiveness in the development of relationships and the influence of its loss in the deterioration of relationships.

Intimacy Claims

At times intimacy claims may create problems (or at least be at the base of some relationship conflicts). In most relationships—especially those of considerable intensity—the members make extensive intimacy claims on each other. Such claims may include, for example, expectations that the partner will sympathize and empathize, attend to self-disclosures with total absorption, or share the other's preferences with equal intensity. These intimacy claims often restrict personal freedom and often take the form of possessiveness when one member of the relationship becomes defined (functionally as well as verbally) as a part of the other person—"*my* woman," "*my* husband," "*my* child." Intense intimacy claims often put people under pressure that some find difficult to live with on a day-to-day basis. To be always responsive, always sympathetic, always loving, always attentive is more than many people can manage.

Third-Party Relationships

Relationships are established and maintained because in such a relationship pleasures are maximized and pains are minimized. When that ceases to be the case, the relationship stands little chance of survival. The reason, I think, is obvious. These needs are so great that when they are not met within the existing relationship, their satisfaction and fulfillment will be sought elsewhere. When a new relationship serves these needs better, the old relationship may deteriorate. At times this may be a romantic interest (more on this under "Sex"); at other times it may be a parent or, frequently, a child. When an individual's needs for affection or attention were once supplied by the other party in the primary relationship and are now supplied by a friend or a child, the primary relationship is in for alteration and sometimes deterioration.

Relational Changes

In addition to those factors that in one form help to establish a relationship and in another form help to dissolve it, there are a number of relationship changes that might be mentioned as causes of relational deterioration.

PSYCHOLOGICAL CHANGE

Psychological change in one or both parties may contribute to relational deterioration. Prominent among psychological changes would be the development of incompatible attitudes, vastly different intellectual interests and abilities, and major goal changes. To the extent that these are incompatible with those of the other individual, the relationship will by shaky. This does not mean that one person cannot be a Democrat and the other a Republican. It does mean, however, that a staunch atheist and a devout fundamentalist are going to have some problems. When one party in a marriage believes in open marriage and the other does not, the marriage is probably heading for difficulties.

BEHAVIORAL CHANGE

Behavioral change, like psychological change, is also significant. For example, the individual who once devoted much time to the other person and to the development of the relationship and who then becomes totally absorbed in business or in school and devotes all free time to business activities or studying is going to encounter significant repercussions. The individual who becomes addicted to drugs or alcohol will likewise present the relationship with a serious problem.

CONTEXTUAL CHANGE

Contextual change may also exert considerable influence on the relationship. Some relationships cannot survive separation by long distances as when, for example, one of the parties is forced to move far away. When I moved to Illinois from New York to pursue graduate work, my primary relationship survived two years of long-distance separation because it was particularly strong and because it continued to serve many of the needs already mentioned. But I witnessed many other relationships decay and terminate because the individuals were not able to surmount the physical distance barriers. This is a particularly difficult problem for people in the military. The physical separation is too stressful for many people, so many such relationships deteriorate, as stereotyped in the ''Dear John'' letters of war years. Long incarceration or long hospital confinement are also context changes that may lead to severe trouble.

STATUS CHANGE

When there is a significant status change between two people or between one member and a third party, the relationship may undergo considerable change and possibly deteriorate. This type of situation is seen, for instance, when students and teachers develop a romantic relationship. The relationship develops as a student-teacher relationship and is maintained for some time as that. But as the student matures and perhaps becomes a teacher too or otherwise assumes a position equal to or superior in status to that of the teacher, their relationship undergoes considerable change; frequently, this results in some kind of deterioration. In F. Scott Fitzgerald's *Tender Is the Night* we see the same kind of situation, though here it is between a young psychiatrist, Dick Diver, and a wealthy and beautiful patient, Nicole Warren. While Nicole is mentally ill and in need of Dick's care, the relationship flourishes for both; each apparently serves the needs of the other. But as Nicole gets stronger, Dick gets weaker; the relationship changes drastically and ultimately deteriorates. In *The Blue Angel*, the famous German movie with Marlene Dietrich and Emil Jannings, we see a similar relationship between a sophisticated and well-respected schoolteacher, Professor Immanuel Rath, and a low-class cabaret entertainer, Lola Frohlich. Their relationship prospers as long as she is able to look up to him and respect him. When their relationship changes and he becomes her servant, a willing victim of Lola's humiliation and abuse, their relationship becomes a mockery and dies.

Undefined Expectations

At times conflicts center on ''trivial'' issues such as who will do the dishes and the wash, who will cook, who will iron, or who will use the new car and who will use the old one. To an outsider these are trivial issues, but we need to recall that in these conflicts the content is often not the true focus of the conflict; often such conflicts center on relational dimensions. The fact that there are frequent conflicts over who will do the dishes may mean that the individuals have problems that go beyond the dishes and perhaps center on more significant issues such as who is the boss or whose time is less valuable and should therefore be devoted to the trivial. "Unresolved disputes over 'who is in charge of what,' " notes William Lederer in *Creating a Good Relationship*, "is one of the most powerful and prevalent causes of conflicts and divorces." Often conflicts over such "trivial" issues mask resentment and hostility concerning some general dissatisfaction or unhappiness. At times these conflicts are generated because some other more significant conflict has not been adequately resolved and the ill feeling one person feels toward the other has not yet dissipated.

At times the expectations each person has of the other may be unrealistic, and when reality enters the relationship, conflict may ensue. This type of situation often occurs early in a relationship where, for example, the individuals think that they will want to spend all their time together. When it is discovered that neither one does, each resents this "lessening" of feeling in the other. Unrealistic sexual expectations are also a frequent source of conflict. In our culture, the man is supposed to be always ready and always in a sexually aggressive mood. Many women believe this stereotype and are soon rudely instructed in the reality of the male sex drive. On the other hand, men who perceive women basically as sexual gratifiers will accuse them of withholding love when the women are not continually receptive to their overtures. The resolution of such conflicts lies not so much in meeting these expectations as in demonstrating that the original ones were unrealistic and in substituting satisfying and attainable expectations.

Sex

Few relationships are free of sexual problems and differences that cannot easily be resolved and that often generate conflicts of considerable magnitude. In fact, sexual problems rank among the top three problems in almost all studies of newlyweds. When these same couples are surveyed later in their relationship, the sexual problems have not gone away; they are just talked about less. Apparently the individuals resign themselves to living with the problems. In one survey, for example, 80 percent of the respondents identified their marriages as either "very happy" or "happy," but some 90 percent of these said that they had sexual problems.

Although sexual frequency is not related to relational breakdown, sexual satisfaction is. Research clearly shows that it is the quality, not the quantity of a sexual relationship that is crucial. When the quality is poor, affairs outside the primary relationship may be sought. And although there is much talk of sexual freedom within and outside primary relationships, the research is again clear: Extrarelational affairs contribute significantly to breakups for all couples, whether married or cohabiting. Interestingly enough, even "open relationships"—ones in which the individuals permit each other sexual freedom outside the primary relationship—create problems and are more likely to break up than the traditional closed relationship.

Work

Unhappiness with work often leads to difficulties with relationships. Problems at and with work cannot, it seems, be separated from one's relationships. Dissatisfaction with work is often associated with relationship breakup. This is true for all types of couples. With heterosexual couples (both marrieds and cohabitors), if the man is disturbed over the woman's job—for example, if she earns a great deal more than he does or she devotes a great deal of time to the job—the relationship is in for considerable trouble, and this is true whether the relationship is in its early stages or is a well-established one. Often the man expects the woman to work but does not reduce his expectations concerning her household responsibilities. The man becomes resentful if the woman does not fulfill these expectations, and the woman becomes resentful if she takes on both outside work and full household duties. It is a no-win situation, and the relationship suffers as a result.

Although the stability of a relationship is not hampered by the husband's doing little or no housework, stability is hampered when the husband perceives that the wife is doing less than he thinks she should. Another instance of inequality in heterosexual couples concerns ambition. Women want their partners to be ambitious in their work; men who are not ambitious are less appreciated by their partners, and their relationship loses stability. However, men do not appreciate ambitious women; relationships with ambitious women are less stable than those with unambitious women. Further, it is found that the more ambitious, more work-devoted partner is the one more likely to leave the relationship.

A further work-related issue (closely related to contextual change) that contributes to relationship dissolution is the time couples spend together. Blumstein and Schwartz observe, "Spending too much time apart is a hallmark of couples who do not stay together." If couples take separate vacations, meet with different friends, eat separately, and spend a great deal of time at work and away from home, their relationships are less likely to survive. Time spent away from each other is both a cause and an effect of relationship deterioration: The more time spent apart, the more a relationship tends to deteriorate, and as the relationship deteriorates, we feel less desire to spend time together and look for other ways to gain satisfaction. It is a spiral that often grows larger and larger until the relationship dissolves.

Financial Difficulties

In surveys of problems among couples, financial difficulties loom large. Money is perhaps the major taboo topic for couples beginning a relationship, yet it proves to be one of the major problems faced by all couples as they settle into their relationship. One-fourth to one-third of all couples rank money as their primary problem; almost all rank it as one of their major problems. Financial difficulties are perhaps most obvious when the family is large; when the children are young, expensive, and noncontributing; and when only one spouse can work. But even when both individuals work, financial problems do not cease. Rather, the conflict centers on the amount of money each brings in.

Perhaps the major reason money is so important in relationships is its close connection with power. Money brings power; this is true in business and in relationships. The person bringing in the most money wields the most power. This person has the final say on, for example, the purchase of expensive items as well as on decisions having nothing to do with money. The power that money brings quickly generalizes to nonfinancial issues as well.

The unequal earnings of men and women create further problems regardless of who earns more. In most heterosexual relationships, the man earns more money than the woman. Because of this, men possess a disproportionate share of power. This creates, as Shulamith Firestone points out in *The Dialectic of Sex*, a situation in which the woman, because of her lack of power, will often turn to manipulative and underhanded tactics to get what she wants. This type of tactic also generalizes, resulting in a relationship in which dishonesty and deception are the normal modes of interpersonal interaction.

When the woman earns more than the man, the problems are different. Though our society has finally taught women to achieve in business and the professions, it has not taught men to accept this very well, and as a result the higher-earning woman is often resented by the lower-earning man. This is true for both married and cohabiting couples.

Financial difficulties often interact with other relationship dimensions to create further problems. For example, men who earn little or less than their female partners or who worry about not being good providers often avoid sex at payday, when their self-perceived inadequacy is particularly salient. This avoidance feeds back and causes other difficulties, especially when the man is not aware of why he is avoiding sexual intimacy. Often partners perceive this decreased drive as an indication that they are no longer interesting to their mates or that they have found someone outside the relationship. Jealousy and suspicion may quickly follow.

Money also creates problems by virtue of the fact that men and women view it differently. To men, money is power; to women, it is security and independence. To men, money is accumulated to exert power and influence; to women, money is accumulated to achieve some sense of security and to reduce dependence on others. Conflicts over how the couple's money is to be spent or invested can easily result from such different perceptions.

The most general equation we could advance would be this:

Dissatisfaction with money = dissatisfaction with the relationship

This is true for married and cohabiting couples and gay male couples but not for lesbian couples, who seem to care a great deal less about financial matters. This difference has led some researchers to postulate (though without conclusive evidence) that the concern over money and its equation with power and relational satisfaction are largely male attitudes.

Inequitable Distribution of Rewards and Costs

Earlier we noted that, according to social exchange theory (Unit 18), we stay in relationships that are rewarding and leave relationships that are punishing. We may now add the concept of equity to this general notion. Equitable relationships are those in which the rewards and the costs are almost equally distributed between the two individuals; each person derives about equal rewards, and each person pays or suffers about equal costs. When a relationship becomes inequitable; that is, when one person derives a disproportionate share of the rewards or one person suffers an excessive share of the costs, the relationship suffers.

Research demonstrates that when partners perceive their relationship to be equitable, they will continue to date, live together, and marry. The partners will be more content with each other and with the relationship and will derive greater satisfaction from the relationship. Sexual fulfillment and relational stability are greater in equitable relationships. When the relationship is not equitable, these benefits are not obtained and the relationship suffers and may well deteriorate.

A Note on Commitment

An important factor influencing the course of relational deterioration is the degree of commitment the individuals have toward each other and toward the relationship. All our relationships are held together, in part, by our degree of commitment. And the strength of the relationship, including its resistance to possible deterioration, is often directly related to the degree of commitment of the individuals. When relationships show signs of deterioration and yet there is still a strong commitment to the relationship—a strong desire to keep the relationship together—the individuals may well surmount the obstacles and reverse the process of deterioration. When their commitment is weak and the individuals doubt that there are good reasons for staying together, relational deterioration seems to come faster and stronger.

Financial Commitment. Commitment is closely related to financial considerations. On the one hand, it is only after a couple develops a strong commitment to each other and to the relationship that they will pool their financial resources. "Failure to pool," note Blumstein and Schwartz, "often indicates that couples have not given up their independence and may never have visualized the relationship as lasting into the indefinite future." With cohabitors, where there are few legal bonds, the fact that such pooling of finances comes only after a strong commitment has been made clearly illustrates this natural sequence of events. Conversely, the pooling of finances often increases the commitment of the individuals to each other and to the relationship. People may feel committed because they have invested all their money together or because they have established a business or own real estate together.

Temporal Commitment. At other times the commitment is based on time considerations. People may feel that since they have lived together for these past 10 or 15 years, all that time would be lost if the relationship were terminated. College students who have dated the same person for three or four years often feel that the time investment has been so great that they might as well continue the relationship and often allow and encourage it to progress to a permanent relationship, perhaps marriage. Although much could be said for this attitude, it seems to me that time is never wasted if something is learned from it or, more important, if we have lived in the present and enjoyed the relationship for its day-to-day value rather than for what it will mean 10 or 20 years from now. It is far better to terminate a four-year-old relationship that is unsatisfactory than to continue it for the rest of one's life. Unfortunately, only to those who are not now or who have never been in such a relationship will this seem obvious.

Emotional Commitment. Sometimes the commitment is based on emotional investment; so much emotional energy may have been spent on the relationship that the individuals find it difficult even to consider dissolving it. Or people may feel committed because they care for each other and for the relationship and feel that for all its problems and difficulties, the relationship is more good than bad, more productive than destructive, more pleasurable than painful. This, it seems to me, is the kind of commitment that will function to stem and perhaps reverse relational deterioration. Other bases for commitment (for example, materialism, time, and emotional investments) may function to preserve the surface features of the relationship, but these factors will probably have little influence on preserving its meaning and intimacy.

All these "causes" of relational deterioration are also the effects of relational deterioration. For example, just as the contextual changes may influence the deterioration of a relationship, they may also be an effect of the deterioration. Thus when things start to go sour, the individuals may remove themselves physically from one another in response to the deterioration. This physical separation in turn functions as a cause of further deterioration by driving the individuals farther apart emotionally and psychologically. Similarly, the degree of commitment that the individuals have for each other may lessen as other signs of deterioration manifest themselves. In turn, the lack of commitment may also function as a cause of deterioration in, for example, lessening the need the individuals may feel to resolve conflicts or to leave the channels of communication open.

Summary: Contents in Brief

What is relational deterioration?	the weakening of the bonds holding people together
Who is responsible for relational deterioration?	one of the parties, both of the parties, or neither of the parties
How does relational deterioration occur?	suddenly ("sudden death") or gradually ("passing away")
What effects does relational deterioration have?	positive as well as negative effects; from the freedom to pursue other meaningful relationships to added financial difficulties and a loss of self-esteem
Why does relational deterioration occur?	reasons for establishing the relationship have diminished
	intimacy claims
	third-party relationships
	relational changes (psychological, behavioral, contextual, and status)
	undefined expectations
	sex
	work
	financial difficulties
	inequitable distribution of rewards and costs
	lack of commitment

Sources

On relational deterioration, see Murray S. Davis, *Intimate Relations* (New York: Free Press, 1973); Michael D. Scott and William G. Powers, *Interpersonal Communication: A Question of Needs* (Boston: Houghton Mifflin, 1978); and Mark L. Knapp, *Interpersonal Communication and Human Relationships* (Boston: Allyn & Bacon, 1984). Relational deterioration within a family context is well covered in Kathleen M. Galvin and Bernard J. Brommel, *Family Communication: Cohesion and Change,* 2d ed. (Glenview, Ill.: Scott, Foresman, 1986). Michael J. Cody has presented an interesting five-stage model of relationship breakdown; see "A Typology of Disengagement Strategies and an Examination of the Role Intimacy, Reactions to Inequity, and Relational Problems Play in Strategy Selection," *Communication Monographs* 49 (September 1982): 148–170. The research findings and many of the insights concerning sex, money, and work were reported by Philip Blumstein and Pepper Schwartz, *American Couples* (New York: Morrow, 1983).

On relationship development and improvement see William J. Lederer, *Creating a Good Relationship* (New York: Norton, 1984). On commitment see Michael P. Johnson, "Social and Cognitive Features of the Dissolution of Commitment to Relationships," *Personal Relationships. 4: Dissolving Personal Relationships,* ed. Steve Duck (New York: Academic Press, 1982), pp. 51–73. For equity see Ellen Berscheid and Elaine Hatfield Walster, *Interpersonal Attraction,* 2d ed. (Reading, Mass.: Addison-Wesley, 1978) and Elaine Hatfield and Jane Traupmann, "Intimate Relationships: A Perspective from Equity Theory," *Personal Relationships 1: Studying Personal Relationships,* ed. Steve Duck and Robin Gilmour (New York: Academic Press, 1981), pp. 165–178.

UNIT 26

Managing Relational Deterioration

OBJECTIVES

Upon completion of this unit, you should be able to:

1. identify at least five patterns of communication that characterize relational deterioration
2. explain how negative communication patterns may be reversed when one wishes to improve or repair a deteriorating relationship
3. define *cherishing behaviors*
4. explain three steps for a positive action program
5. identify at least five suggestions for dealing with a relationship that ends

Managing relational deterioration is here viewed from two major perspectives. First, we focus on the role of communication in relational deterioration and examine the communication patterns that characterize relationship deterioration and some of the ways in which we might reverse relational deterioration through communication. Second, we consider some suggestions that may prove useful if the relationship ends.

When a relationship goes bad, there are three basic alternatives: (1) to keep it as it is and make no change, (2) to dissolve the relationship, and (3) to change one or more of the elements to attempt to make the relationship different and better. Of these three possibilities, only the first is illogical; the second and third are both candidates for serious consideration. Therefore, I offer suggestions not for keeping a relationship intact but rather for managing deterioration, whether that entails an attempt to save the relationship or an attempt to terminate it as quickly as possible.

COMMUNICATION PATTERNS IN RELATIONAL DETERIORATION

Like relational development, relational deterioration involves unique and specialized communication patterns. Here we describe and analyze some of the ways in which we communicate during relational deterioration. These patterns are in part a response to the deterioration; we communicate the way we do because of the way we feel our relationship is deteriorating. However, these patterns are also causative; the communication patterns we employ determine in a large sense the fate of our relationship. Seven major patterns that characterize communication during relational deterioration are considered: withdrawal, self-disclosure, supportiveness, deception, evaluative responses, request behaviors, and exchange of favors.

Withdrawal

Perhaps the easiest communication pattern to see is that of a general withdrawal. As Gerald Miller and Malcolm Parks note: "We would expect dissolution to be characterized by both a decrease in the duration of encounters and an increase in the time between encounters." Nonverbally, this withdrawal is seen in the greater space each person seems to require and the ease with which tempers and other signs of disturbance are aroused when that space is encroached upon. When people are close emotionally, they can occupy close physical quarters. But when they are growing apart, they need wider spaces. Other nonverbal signs include the failure to engage in direct eye contact, the failure to look at each other generally, and the lessening of touching behavior. All these changes seem to be part of the desire to withdraw physically from the emotional pairing.

Verbally, withdrawal is seen in a number of ways. Where once there was a great desire to talk and to listen, there is now less desire, perhaps none. At times phatic communication is also severely limited since the individuals do not want any of its regular functions served. At other times, however, phatic communication (or what would appear to be phatic communication) is engaged in as an end in itself. Whereas phatic talk is usually a preliminary to serious conversation, here phatic communication is used as an alternative or to forestall serious talk. And so people in the throes of dissolution may talk a great deal about insignificant events—the weather, a movie on television, a neighbor down the hall. The topics are not important. What is important is that by focusing on these topics, the individuals are able to avoid confronting the serious issues that might be raised if the silence were to become too unpleasant.

Withdrawal of another kind may be seen, as Mark Knapp notes, in the decrease in similarities in clothing and in the display of "intimate trophies" such as bracelets, photographs, and rings.

Self-disclosure

Self-disclosing communications decline significantly. Self-disclosure may not be thought worth the effort if the relationship is dying. We only wish to self-disclosure to people we feel close to, and when a relationship is deteriorating, we feel less close to the other person and naturally have no desire to self-disclose. We also limit our self-disclosures because we feel that the other person may not be accepting of our disclosures—an essential assumption if disclosures are to be made in the first place.

In our discussion of self-disclosure in Unit 8, I noted that self-disclosure generally leads to increased trust, which in turn leads to increased self-disclosure, and so on. The result is a spiral with ever-increasing self-disclosure and trust. It seems almost universal that in relationships that are experiencing difficulty, one of the first changes is a marked decrease in trust. When we witness bitter divorce proceedings in which the parties battle over every asset, it is easy to see why some people withdraw trust at the first signs of relational deterioration. We may fear that the trust we put in the other person will soon be used against us.

Supportiveness

Where once supportiveness characterized the relationship, defensiveness is now the more prevalent characteristic. In many deteriorating relationships, one party blames the other; neither wants to assume the blame for the failure of the relationship, and it seems difficult to believe that no one really caused the breakup. Instead, it is easier to blame the other person. The primary method available for dealing with accusations of blame is defensiveness. We want to protect our egos; we want to continue believing that we are not to blame, that it is not our fault. And perhaps we want especially to believe that we are not the cause of another person's and our own pain.

Deception

Deception increases as relationships break down. Sometimes this takes the form of clear-cut lies that may be used to avoid getting into added arguments over the reasons for staying out all night or for not calling or for being seen in the wrong place with the wrong person. At other times lies may be used because of some feeling of shame; we do not want the other person to think less of us even though we fully realize that the relationship is deteriorating. Perhaps we want to save the relationship and do not want to add another obstacle. At other times, although we may wish to see the relationship terminated, we do not want to appear to be the cause of the problem. So we lie. Sometimes the deception takes the form of avoidance—the lie of omission. We talk about everything we did last night except the crux of the difficulty. Whether by omission or commission, deception runs high in relationships that are deteriorating. One of the problems with this is that deception has a way of escalating. And although we may tell ourselves that we lied to protect the other person or to avoid some greater problem (both of which may be true), we have at the same time created a climate, in our own minds and ultimately in the mind of the other person, of distrust, disbelief, and falsity rather than truthfulness.

Evaluative Responses

One of the most obvious communication changes is an increase in negative evaluation and a decrease in positive evaluation. Where once we praised the other's behaviors or talents or ideas, we now criticize them. Often the behaviors have not changed significantly; what has changed is our way of looking at them. What was once a cute habit now becomes annoying, even repulsive. What was once "different" now becomes eccentric or inconsiderate. When we like someone, we seem able to tolerate almost anything. When we dislike someone and want to terminate the relationship, we seem able to tolerate very little. This negative evaluation frequently leads to outright fighting and conflict, and although conflict is not necessarily bad, it often happens that in relationships that are deteriorating the conflict is not resolved. Neither party may care enough to go through the effort of resolving the conflict, so it resurfaces the next day or perhaps escalates into an all-out battle. Seldom does it go away. One of the characteristics of such conflicts is that a great deal of time is needed to resolve them, and the cooling-off period lasts much longer.

Request Behaviors

During relational deterioration, as William Lederer points out, there is a marked change in the types of requests made. When a relationship is deteriorating, there is a decrease in requests for pleasurable behaviors ("Will you fix me my favorite desert? The one with the whipped cream and nuts?" or "Hug me real tight"). At the same time, there is an increase in requests to stop unpleasant or negative behaviors ("Will you stop bragging about your ex-husband's money?" or "Will you stop monopolizing the phone every evening?").

Another symptom is the sometimes gradual, sometimes sudden decrease in the social niceties that accompany requests, a progression from "Would you please make me a cup of coffee, honey?" to "Get me some coffee, will you?" to "Where's my coffee?"

Exchange of Favors

Earlier we noted that one of the main reasons relationships were developed and maintained was that the rewards exceeded the costs. When a relationship deteriorates, the costs begin to exceed the rewards, until a point is reached when the individuals feel that the costs are too high (and the rewards too low), at which point the relationship is terminated. In relational deterioration there is little favor exchange; compliments, once given frequently and sincerely, are now rare. Positive stroking is minimal. Nonverbally, we avoid looking directly at the other, smile seldom, and touch, caress, and hold each other infrequently (if at all).

REVERSING RELATIONAL DETERIORATION: RELATIONSHIP REPAIR

If we wish to salvage a relationship, we may attempt to do so by changing our communication patterns and, in effect, putting into practice the insights and skills learned in this course. Some of the more significant areas for relationship repair are noted briefly.

Reversing Negative Communication Patterns

The first step in reversing relational deterioration is to stop withdrawal. We need to talk not about insignificant events as we do in withdrawal, but about the causes of and possible cures for our problems and disagreements.

We must reverse the tendency to hide our inner selves; we need to disclose our feelings. Most important, we must express support for the other's disclosures, to demonstrate trust and understanding and a willingness to expose our own vulnerability.

We need to express supportiveness for the other person's feelings, to validate their perspective and their opposing point of view. We have to resist the temptation to blame the other person, knowing that blaming only aggravates rather than alleviates problems and makes achieving compromise and regaining mutual respect all the more difficult.

We need to avoid deception, to be honest with ourselves, about ourselves and about the relationship. We need to be honest with our partner and about our partner. Most important, we need to be honest about the problems facing the relationship. As with alcoholics, before we can work on a cure, we have to admit we have problems. And we have to be honest about what these problems are. We need a certain degree of detachment and objectivity to see the alternatives available for improving the relationship, for reversing the negative spiral.

We must increase the expression of positive evaluations and decrease the expression of negative evaluations. This is not to say that we should hide our true feelings, only that we should make a special effort to notice and to comment on positive characteristics of the other person and perhaps soften our negative evaluations or postpone these to a more opportune time.

We must make a conscious effort to increase our requests for pleasurable behaviors, decrease our requests to cease unpleasurable behaviors, and perhaps most important, bring back the social courtesies that characterized our requests at a more positive stage in the relationship.

We need to increase the exchange of favors; compliments, positive stroking, and all the nonverbals that say "I care" become especially important when we wish to reverse negative communication patterns.

Cherishing Behaviors

One way in which increasingly negative evaluations can be reversed is to incorporate a specific kind of favor exchange, namely, "cherishing behaviors." Cherishing behaviors are those small behaviors that we enjoy receiving from our relational partner (a smile, a wink, a squeeze, a kiss). Cherishing behaviors should be (1) specific and positive, (2) focused on the present and future rather than related to issues about which the partners have argued in the past, (3) capable of being performed daily, and (4) easily executed.

William Lederer suggests that the individuals make a list of the cherishing behaviors they each wish to receive and then exchange lists. Each person then performs the cherishing behaviors desired by the partner. At first these behaviors may seem self-conscious and awkward. In time, however, they will become a normal part of interaction.

Adopting a Positive Action Program

We now have a great deal of insight into deteriorating relationships and a wealth of suggestions for improvement, but these would count for little if we did not incorporate them into some meaningful program of action. Each person should develop an action program tailored to the individuals and the relationship. Here are three general principles that should prove useful in developing and implementing this program.

IDENTIFY THE PROBLEMS

Specify what is wrong with your present relationship (in concrete, specific terms) and what changes would be needed to make it better (again, in concrete, specific terms). Without this first step there is little hope for improving any interpersonal relationship. Put differently, create a picture of your relationship as you would want it to be and compare that picture to the way the relationship looks now. Specify the changes that would have to take place to have the idealized picture replace the present picture.

APPLY THE REQUISITE SKILLS

Apply the skills and insights you have acquired to the task of relationship improvement. In this course you have covered a wide variety of suggestions for improving interpersonal communication and relationships. Put these ideas into practice; make them a normal part of your interactions. Here, for example, is just a handful of suggestions designed to refresh your memory:

- look closely for relational messages that will help clarify motivations and needs; respond to these messages as well as to the content messages
- exchange perspectives with your relational partner and see the sequence of events as punctuated by each other
- exchange favors and cherishing behaviors, especially when costs are running high
- practice empathic and supportive responses even in conflict situations
- eliminate unfair fight habits and substitute productive conflict strategies
- be descriptive when discussing grievances, being especially careful to avoid troublesome terms such as *always* and *never*
- listen to your partner actively, empathically, and with an open mind
- own your feelings and thoughts; use I-messages and take responsibility for these feelings
- remember the principle of irreversibility; think carefully before saying things you may regret later
- keep the channels of communication open; be available to discuss problems, to negotiate solutions, and to practice new and more meaningful interaction patterns

TAKE RISKS

Take risks in attempting to improve any relationship. Risk giving favors without any certainty of reciprocity. Risk rejection; make the first move to make up or say you are sorry. Be willing to change, to adapt, to take on new tasks and responsibilities.

IF THE RELATIONSHIP ENDS

Even with the best intentions and skills, some relationships end. Sometimes there is simply not enough to hold the couple together. Sometimes there are problems that cannot be resolved. Sometimes the costs are too high and the rewards too few. Sometimes the relationship is recognized as destructive and escape seems the only alternative. Given the inevitability that some relationships will breakup, I offer some suggestions to ease the difficulty that is sure to be experienced. These suggestions can apply to the termination of any type of relationship, between friends or lovers, through death, separation, or breakup. I use the language of romantic breakups because these are the ones college students deal with most frequently.

Break the Loneliness–Depression Cycle

Perhaps the two most experienced feelings following the ending of a relationship are loneliness and depression. Realize at the outset that these feelings are not insignificant and should be treated with seriousness. Recognize, for example, that depression often leads to serious illness. Ulcers, high blood pressure, insomnia, stomach pains, and sexual difficulties frequently accompany or are seriously aggravated by depression. Wallowing in self-pity and playing the role of the abandoned lover may provide a certain degree of romanticism but such actions create more problems than they solve.

In most cases loneliness and depression are temporary. Seldom does depression, for example, last for more than three or four days. Similarly, the loneliness that follows a breakup is generally linked to this specific situation and will fade when the situation changes. Our task then is to change the situation to eliminate or lessen these uncomfortable and potentially dangerous feelings.

Take Time Out

Be neither a "leaper" nor an "abstainer." Resist the temptation to jump into a new relationship while the current relationship is still warm or before the new relationship can be assessed with some degree of objectivity. Also resist swearing off all relationships. Neither extreme works well.

Rather, take some time out for yourself. Renew your relationship with yourself. If you were in a long-time relationship, you probably saw yourself as part of a team, as part of a couple. Now get to know yourself as a unique individual, standing alone now but fully capable of entering a meaningful relationship in the near future.

Bolster Self-esteem

When relationships fail, we often experience a lowering of self-esteem. We may feel guilty for having been the cause of the breakup; we may feel inadequate for not holding on to a permanent relationship. We may feel unwanted and unloved. All of these feelings contribute substantially to a lowering of self-esteem. Our task is to bolster that self-esteem, to regain the positive self-image that we need to function effectively as individuals and as members of another interpersonal relationship.

Recognize, first, that having been in a relationship that failed—even if you view yourself as the primary cause of the breakup—does not mean that you are a failure. It does not mean that you cannot succeed in a new and different relationship. It merely means that something went wrong with this one relationship.

Further, take positive action to raise your self-esteem. Oddly enough, helping others is one of the best ways to raise our own self-esteem. When we do things for others, we feel good about ourselves, and we generally get the positive stroking from others that helps us to feel better about ourselves. Positive and successful experiences are most helpful in building self-esteem, so engage in activities that you enjoy, that you do well, and that are likely to result in success.

Bolster your self-esteem by focusing on yourself as a physical person. Now is a perfect time to lose those few pounds you've been meaning to get rid of—go to the gym, work out, and tighten up. It will release a great deal of pent-up energy and at the same time will make you feel a lot better about yourself as a physically attractive individual.

Remove or Avoid Uncomfortable Symbols

After any breakup there are a variety of reminders—photographs, gifts, letters, places you went to together. Resist the temptation to burn all the old photographs and love letters. Just remove them. Give them to a friend to hold or put them in a drawer or in a closet where you won't see them. Similarly, if possible, avoid places you frequented together. These symbols will merely remind you of your relationship and will bring back memories that will be uncomfortable to deal with. After you have achieved some emotional distance, you can go back and enjoy these as reminders of a once pleasant relationship.

Seek Support

Although many people feel they should bear their burdens alone—men, in particular, have been taught that this is the only "manly" way to handle things—seeking the support of others is one of the best antidotes to the discomfort and unhappiness caused when a relationship ends. Avail yourself of your friends and family for support. Most people enjoy giving support to someone who suffered in a relationship. Allow them this satisfaction and at the same time gain a great deal from their closeness, their positive expressions, their willingness to be there when you need them. You would be supportive of them, so let them now be supportive of you.

Tell your friends of your situation—in only general terms, if you prefer—and make it clear that you need support right now. Seek out people who are positive and nurturing. Avoid negative individuals who will paint the world in even darker tones.

Make the distinction between seeking support and seeking advice. If you feel you need advice, seek out a professional. For support, friends are best.

Avoid Extreme Statements

Extreme statements—for example, allness statements—must be avoided. When a relationship ends, there is a tendency to talk in extremes (and usually in the negative)—about the relationship, about the former partner, about the problems. One reason for avoiding such extremes is that in retrospect these will appear foolish and will be a cause for embarrassment. Another reason is that these extreme statements influence the way in which you think and behave. These statements will distort your memory of the relationship. If you say your partner never really did care for you, was parasitic, and was a horrible lover, these statements will influence how you remember your relationship and this individual. In effect, you will come to believe your own statements.

Avoid Repeating Negative Patterns

Although the divorce rate is high for first marriages, it is even higher for second marriages. It seems that many of us repeat our mistakes. We enter second and third relationships with the same blinders, faulty preconceptions, and unrealistic expectations with which we entered earlier relationships.

We need to learn from failed relationships and not repeat the same patterns. Of course, this is easy to say; it is quite another thing to put it into practice. But even a little learning is better than nothing, so we should ask ourselves at the start of a new relationship if we are entering a relationship modeled on the previous one. If the answer is yes, we must be especially careful that the same problems are not repeated.

At the same time, do not become a prophet of doom. Do not see in every new relationship vestiges of the old. Do not jump at the first conflict and say, "Here it goes all over again." Treat the new relationship as the unique relationship it is and do not evaluate it through past experiences. Past relationships and experiences should be guides, not filters.

Resist Comparisons

Comparisons are inevitable. But there are times when we must resist comparing our new relationships with our old ones. One of the major comparisons people make is in terms of the adequacy of the new partner as a lover. The problem here is that the memory usually wins. It works this way, I think, because there is a human tendency to remember the good and forget the bad. Especially avoid voicing comparisons to the new partner. This injunction is very obvious, yet it is frequently violated. Listen to your friends discuss their past and present relationships and you will probably hear comparisons flow with great fluency.

All interpersonal communication involves choices and these choices involve risks. The greater the potential gain, the greater the risk. Without risk there is little chance of meaningful gain. Throughout this book I have tried to provide you with information that would guide you to choices that would be effective and personally satisfying and thus reduce the potential risk. But there is still risk. And that is perhaps what makes interpersonal communication—its practice and its study—exciting, frustrating, challenging, disheartening, satisfying, depressing, fulfilling. . . .

Summary: Contents in Brief

Management Guidelines for Relational Dissolution	Communication Patterns in Deteriorating Relationships	Relational Repair
Break the loneliness–depression cycle	Partners withdraw	Reverse negative communication patterns
Take time out	Self-disclosure declines	Increase cherishing behaviors
Bolster self-esteem	Supportiveness decreases	Adopt a positive action program, for example:
Seek support	Deception increases	• identify the problem
Avoid extreme statements	Negative evaluations increase; positive evaluations decrease	• apply the requisite skills
Avoid repetition of negative patterns	Requests for pleasurable behaviors decrease; requests to stop negative behaviors increase	• take risks
Resist comparisons	Exchanges of favors decrease	

Sources

On communication and relational deterioration, see, for example, Mark L. Knapp, *Interpersonal Communication and Human Relationships* (Boston: Allyn & Bacon, 1984) and Gerald R. Miller and Malcolm R. Parks, "Communication in Dissolving Relationships," *Personal Relationships. 4: Dissolving Personal Relationships*, ed. Steve Duck (New York: Academic Press, 1982), pp. 127–154. The discussion of positive action was inspired and influenced by William J. Lederer, *Creating a Good Relationship* (New York: Norton, 1984). Lederer's work is an excellent source for couples who are experiencing relationship difficulties or who simply wish to improve their relationship. For research and theory on this issue see Steve Duck, "A Perspective on the Repair of Personal Relationships: Repair of What, When?" *Personal Relationships. 5: Repairing Personal Relationships*, ed. Steve Duck (New York: Academic Press, 1984), pp. 163–184. Loneliness and the loneliness cycle are discussed by Carin Rubenstein and Philip Shaver, *In Search of Intimacy* (New York: Delacorte, 1982). For a thorough discussion of research and theory on loneliness see Letitia Anne Peplau and Daniel Perlman, eds., *Loneliness: A Sourcebook of Current Theory, Research and Therapy* (New York: Wiley/Interscience, 1982). The connection between loneliness and interpersonal relationships is considered by Daniel Perlman and Letitia Anne Peplau, "Toward a Social Psychology of Loneliness," *Personal Relationships. 3: Personal Relationships in Disorder,* ed. Steve Duck and Robin Gilmour (New York: Academic Press, 1981), pp. 31–56.

Part 5: Skills in Brief

Interpersonal Needs

Identify the needs that led you to seek your interpersonal relationships and the needs that led others to seek interpersonal relationships with you in order to understand and deal with the nature and function of these relationships.

Communication Adjustment

Adjust your own communications as appropriate to the stage of your interpersonal relationship.

Interest

Demonstrate interest in and acceptance of another person through appropriate verbal and nonverbal means.

Initiating Relationships

In initiating relationships, remember the following steps: examine the qualifiers, determine clearance, open the encounter, select and put into operation an integrating topic, create a favorable impression, and establish a second meeting.

Integrating Topics

In selecting an integrating topic, look for free information and ask relevant (but not prying) questions.

Nonverbal Encounter

In initiating relationships, keep the following nonverbal guidelines in mind: establish eye contact, signal interest and positive responses, concentrate your focus, establish physical closeness, maintain an open posture, respond visibly, reinforce positive behaviors, and avoid overexposure.

Verbal Encounter

In initiating relationships, keep the following verbal guidelines in mind: introduce yourself, focus the conversation on the other person, exchange favors-rewards, be energetic, stress the positives, avoid negative and too intimate self-disclosures, and establish commonalities.

Attractiveness

Use physical distance to increase interpersonal attractiveness.

Reinforcement
Reinforce others as a way to increase interpersonal attractiveness and general interpersonal satisfaction.

Attitudinal Similarity
Identify the attitudes for which attitudinal similarity is important and the attitudes for which such similarity is unimportant.

Complementarity
Identify the qualities or characteristics that you do not find in yourself but that you admire in others and that therefore might be important in influencing your perception of complementarity.

Power Increase
Increase your interpersonal power by acting impeccably, controlling your self-disclosures, using rather than wasting time, accepting your own mistakes, and not making waves.

Power Games
Identify the power games that people play on you, especially Nobody Upstairs, You Owe Me, and Metaphor, and respond to these power plays so as to stop them.

Power Bases
Increase your sources or bases of power (referent, legitimate, reward, coercive, expert, and information).

Power Communication
Communicate power through forceful speech, the avoidance of weak modifiers and excessive body movement, and evidencing your knowledge, preparation, and organization of the matters at hand.

Power Protection
Protect your power by preventing others from taking unfair advantage of you and by practicing assertiveness.

Unproductive Conflict Strategies
Avoid unproductive conflict strategies such as avoidance or redefinition, force, minimization, blame, silencers, gunnysacking, and beltlining.

Conflict Resolution
Resolve conflict situations by following the standard problem-solving steps: defining the conflict, defining the possible solutions or decisions, testing the decisions, evaluating the decisions, and accepting or rejecting the decisions on the basis of the evaluation.

Productive Conflict
Follow these guidelines to fight more productively: (1) State your position directly and honestly. (2) React openly to the messages of your combatant. (3) Own your

own thoughts and feelings. (4) Address the real issues that are causing the conflict. (5) Demonstrate empathic understanding. (6) Validate the feelings of your interactant. (7) Describe the behaviors causing the conflict. (8) Express your feelings spontaneously rather than strategically. (9) State your position tentatively, provisionally. (10) Capitalize on agreements. (11) View conflict in positive terms to the extent possible. (12) Express positive feelings for the other person. (13) Treat your combatant as an equal, avoiding ridicule or sarcasm, for example. (14) Involve yourself in the conflict; play an active role as both sender and receiver.

Friendship

Adjust your verbal and nonverbal communication as appropriate to the stages of your various friendships.

Love

Share meaningful emotions and experiences with a significant other.

Empathic Understanding

Increase empathic understanding for your primary partner by sharing experiences, role playing, and seeing the world from his or her perspective.

Relationship Stimulation

Keep a relationship stimulating by changing routines and exposing yourselves to new experiences.

Intimacy Claims

Reduce the intensity of intimacy claims when things get rough; give each other space as appropriate.

Expectations

Define and discuss the expectations each has of the other, the nature of sexual satisfaction as each sees it, and the role and function of work and money in the relationship as a way of preventing unrealistic and unfulfilled expectations from creating conflicts.

Relationship Repair

When you wish to repair a relationship: (1) Avoid withdrawal (keep the channels of communication open at all times). (2) Avoid the sudden decrease in self-disclosure that often signals distrust. (3) Increase supportiveness. (4) Avoid deception. (5) Avoid excessive negative responses. (6) Increase cherishing behaviors to create an environment conducive to compromise and rebuilding.

Relational Improvement

If it is desired to preserve or repair a deteriorating relationship, take positive action by specifying what is wrong with the relationship, apply the skills and insights you have acquired to the task of relationship improvement, and be willing to take risks in attempting to improve your relationship in order to maximize the chances of finding a satisfactory solution to the relationship difficulty.

Dealing with the End of a Relationship

If the relationship ends: (1) Break the loneliness-depression cycle. (2) Take time out to get to know yourself as an individual. (3) Bolster your self-esteem. (4) Remove or avoid uncomfortable symbols that may remind you of your past relationship and may make you uncomfortable. (5) Seek the support of friends and relatives. (6) Avoid extreme statements. (7) Avoid repeating negative patterns. (8) Resist comparisons of new and present relationships with old and ended relationships.

The Experiential Vehicles:

In Part I of this handbook are grouped a series of Experiential Vehicles—exercises designed to enable you to work actively with the concepts and processes discussed throughout this book. Each Experiential Vehicle is prefaced with the unit number and title to which it is most appropriate.

The Review Quizzes:

In Part II of this handbook are grouped five "Review Quizzes"—one for each of the five major parts of the text—designed to enable you to review and recall to memory some of the major terms and principles discussed in the text.

A Handbook of Experiential Vehicles and Review Quizzes in Interpersonal Communication

Handbook Part I. Experiential Vehicles

1. MODELING SOME UNIVERSALS OF INTERPERSONAL COMMUNICATION

Unit 1. Universals of Interpersonal Communication

The following concepts are generally considered to be essential ingredients in even the most basic model of interpersonal communication. Read over the terms and their definitions (in Unit 1 and in the glossary) and construct an original visual representation of the process of interpersonal communication that includes (as a minimum) the concepts noted below. In constructing this model, be careful that you do not fall into the trap of visualizing interpersonal communication as a linear or simple left-to-right process. Remember that all elements are interrelated and interdependent.

source-receiver   context
messages   noise
channels   feedback
encoding-decoding   effect
competence   field of experience
performance

When everyone has completed the model, form groups of five or six to pool your insights in order to construct one improved model of communication. After this is completed, all models should be shared with the entire class.

You may wish to consider some or all of the following issues:

1. Why is it important to speak of a source-receiver rather than of a source and a receiver? Why is it important to speak of encoding-decoding rather than encoding and decoding?

2. Most models of communication do not include the concepts of competence and performance. Do these concepts help to clarify the nature of interpersonal communication? If so, in what ways?

3. Some theorists have argued that it is not necessary to consider feedback as a separate and distinct element. They argue that feedback is just another message and does not differ in any essential way from "regular" messages. Do you think

that the concept of feedback helps in understanding the nature of interpersonal communication? If so, in what ways?

4. Could your model also serve as a model of intrapersonal communication? Explain it as a description of the intrapersonal communication process.

5. What elements or concepts other than those noted above might be added to the model? Why would they help us to understand interpersonal communication better?

2. FIRST IMPRESSIONS

Unit 1. Universals of Interpersonal Communication
Unit 3. Perception in Interpersonal Communication
Unit 7. Universals of the Self and Self-awareness

This exercise is designed to raise a variety of issues concerning first impressions and to sensitize you to the wide range of cues you give off and receive and on the basis of which first impressions are formed.

A variety of procedures may be used in putting this exercise into practice. One procedure is for students to form dyads with someone they have never spoken to before. Without any initial interaction, the students are to discuss a specific topic (such as sports, politics, movies, television, economics, college life) for a specified amount of time. Five minutes is usually sufficient.

At the end of this time, the interaction is to stop. The "First Impressions" forms are distributed; students should complete them as accurately and as specifically as possible. After these forms are completed, the "First Impressions: Self-report" forms are distributed and completed. After both forms are completed, students should exchange forms and discuss what they have written. Special care should be taken to see that students are specific in identifying the cues they used to make their inferences and predictions. "I just felt you were conservative" or "You just seemed like you would like disco" or "You looked assertive" are inadequate responses. These responses merely restate the conclusion the students reached; they are not *reasons* for the conclusions, and it is these reasons, these verbal and nonverbal cues, that we want to identify.

From these discussions a number of points should be clear:

1. Regardless of what we talk about, we inevitably talk about ourselves; we are forever telling others who we are, what we like and don't like, and a great deal more—some of which are identified in the questions asked on the "First Impressions" forms.

2. We cannot not communicate. From the moment the interaction begins, we communicate; we send messages to the other person about ourselves, our communication patterns, and our interpersonal relationship. (See Unit 2 for a discussion of this axiom.)

3. We use a wide variety of cues in drawing inferences about others. Clothing, hair, posture, hand gestures, jewelry, tone of voice, vocabulary, eye movements, facial

movements, and many other cues are used to draw inferences about who the person is and what the person is like. At the same time, others are using these same cues to draw inferences about us.

4. First impressions are formed very quickly. In this exercise, five minutes of interactional time is used as a base for drawing first impressions, but in many situations we draw inferences in much less interaction time and on the basis of a much less intense interaction experience. Often we draw inferences about a person from merely seeing that person smile or spit or chew gum. And others are just as quick to draw such inferences and formulate such first impressions about us.

5. First impressions often stay with us long after we have had much more extensive interactions. First impressions are difficult to change; the first impressions we derive of someone often serve as filters through which everything else about that person is seen. First impressions are thus extremely important in a wide variety of situations—in an interview, on a first date, on meeting your prospective in-laws for the first time, on the first day of class when you meet teachers and fellow students.

First Impressions

Respond to the following questions about the person with whom you just interacted as specifically and as accurately as you can.

Identifying data

1. Name _____

2. Age _____

3. Occupation and/or college major _____

4. Relational status _____

5. Political orientation (liberal, conservative, Democrat, Republican, etc.) _____

6. Music preferences (rock, disco, jazz, popular, classical, etc.) _____

Identify some of the cues (verbal and nonverbal) you used in "learning" these identifying data.

_____

_____

_____

Some Attitudes

Using the scale presented below, indicate the extent to which you think the person with whom you just interacted agrees or disagrees with each of the following propositions.

SCALE

1 = strongly agrees
2 = agrees
3 = is relatively neutral
4 = disagrees
5 = strongly disagrees

1. Legalization of marijuana: _____

2. Gay and lesbian rights bills: _____

3. Mandatory retirement at age 65: _____

4. Setting the legal drinking age at 21: _____

5. Equal Rights Amendment (ERA): _____

Identify the cues (verbal and nonverbal) you used in drawing these inferences.

_____

_____

_____.

Interpersonal Communication Patterns

Respond to the following questions concerning the interpersonal communication behavior patterns of the person with whom you just interacted.

SCALE

1 = definitely
2 = probably
3 = can't say
4 = probably not
5 = definitely not

1. This person is apprehensive when communicating in most situations: _____

Cues: _____

_____

2. This person is normally dominant in interpersonal interactions: _____

Cues: _____

_____

3. This person is normally assertive in most interpersonal interaction: _____

Cues: _____

_____

4. This person is relaxed and comfortable at the present time: _____

Cues: _____

_____

5. This person feels good about herself or himself at the present time: _____

Cues: _____

_____

6. This person readily reveals her or his inner self to other people: _____

Cues: _____

_____

Relationship Predictions

1. This person would like to get to know me better and perhaps have a drink with me at some later time: _____

Cues: _____

_____

2. This person enjoyed our brief interaction: _____

Cues: _____

_____

First Impressions: Self-Report Form

Respond to the following questions about yourself.

Identifying Data

1. Name _____
2. Age _____
3. Occupation and/or college major _____
4. Relational status _____
5. Political orientation (liberal, conservative, Democrat, Republican, etc.) _____
6. Music preferences (rock, disco, jazz, popular, classical, etc.)

_____

Some Attitudes

Using the scale presented below, indicate the extent to which you agree or disagree with each of the following propositions.

SCALE

1 = strongly agree
2 = agree

3 = am relatively neutral
4 = disagree
5 = strongly disagree

1. Legalization of marijuana: _____

2. Gay and lesbian rights bills: _____

3. Mandatory retirement at age 65: _____

4. Setting the legal drinking age at 21: _____

5. Equal Rights Amendment (ERA): _____

Interpersonal Communication Patterns

Respond to the following questions concerning your interpersonal communication behavior patterns.

SCALE

1 = definitely
2 = somewhat
3 = can't say
4 = not really
5 = definitely not

1. I am apprehensive when communicating in most situations: _____

2. I am normally dominant in interpersonal interactions: _____

3. I am normally assertive in most interpersonal interactions: _____

4. I am relaxed and comfortable at the present time: _____

5. I feel good about myself at the present time: _____

6. I readily reveal my inner self to other people: _____

Relationship Predictions

1. I would like to get to know this person better and perhaps have a drink with her or him at some later time: _____

2. I enjoyed this brief interaction: _____

3. ANALYZING A TRANSACTION

Unit 2. Axioms of Interpersonal Communication

The axioms of human communication proposed by Watzlawick, Beavin, and Jackson and discussed in Unit 2 should prove useful in analyzing any interpersonal transaction. To understand these axioms better and to obtain some practice in applying them to an actual interaction, a summary of Tennessee Williams's *Cat on a Hot Tin Roof* is presented.* Ideally, all students would read the entire play or see the movie and then apply the six axioms to the interpersonal interactions that take place. This brief summary is presented, then, more in the nature of a "mental refresher." (Note that the original play, as it has been published, differs from the film, particularly in the last act. The film version of the play is somewhat more positive. The summary presented here is from the original stage play, the version Williams preferred.)

Big Daddy and Big Mama Pollitt, owners of a huge estate, have two sons: Brick (married to Maggie, the cat), an ex–football player who has now turned to drink, and Gooper (married to Mae), a lawyer and the father of five children, with one more on the way. All are gathered to celebrate Big Daddy's sixty-fifth birthday. The occasion is marred by news that Big Daddy may have cancer, for which there is no hope of a cure. A false report is given to Big Mama and Big Daddy stating that the test proved negative and that all that is wrong is a spastic colon—a sometimes painful but not fatal illness. It appears to Maggie, and perhaps to others as well, that Gooper and Mae are really here to claim their share of the inheritance.

The desire to assume control of Big Daddy's fortune (estimated at some $10 million and 28,000 acres "of the richest land this side of the valley Nile") has created considerable conflict between Gooper and Mae, on the one hand, and Maggie, on the other. Brick, it appears, does not care about his possible inheritance.

Throughout the play there is conflict between Brick and Maggie. Brick refuses to go to bed with Maggie although Maggie desperately wants him. This fact is known by everyone, since Mae and Gooper have the adjoining room and hear everything that goes on between Brick and Maggie. The cause of this conflict between Brick and Maggie goes back to Brick's relations with Skipper, his best friend. Brick and Skipper were football players on the same team and did just about everything together. So close were they that rumors about their love for each other began to spread. While Brick is in the hospital with a football injury, Maggie confronts Skipper and begs that he either stop loving Brick or tell him of his love. In an attempt to prove Maggie wrong, Skipper goes to bed with her but fails and as a result takes to drink and drugs. Maggie repeatedly attempts to thrash this out with Brick, but he refuses to talk about it or even to listen to Maggie. All he wants to do is drink—waiting for the little click in his head that tells him he can stop.

In a confrontation with Big Daddy, Brick talks of his disgust with lying and his using liquor to forget all the lies around him. Under pressure from Big Daddy, Brick admits that Skipper called to make a drunken confession after his attempted relationship with Maggie but that Brick hung up and refused to listen. It was then that Skipper committed suicide. And this, it appears, is what Brick uses alcohol to forget. In his anger, Brick tells Big Daddy that he is dying of cancer.

Gooper and Mae confront Big Mama with the news that Big Daddy has cancer and attempt to get Big Mama to sign some papers concerning the disposition of the property

---

* An interesting discussion of *Cat on a Hot Tin Roof* in terms of communication problems is provided by Philip C. Kolin, "Obstacles to Communication in *Cat on a Hot Tin Roof*," *Western Speech Communication* 39 (Spring 1975): 74–80. For alternative views of Maggie, Kolin recommends the following articles, both of which should prove useful in analyzing the role of Maggie and in understanding the communication dimension of the play as a whole: James Ray Blackwelder, "The Human Extremities of Emotion in *Cat on a Hot Tin Roof*," *Research Studies* 38 (1970): 13–21, and Paul J. Hurley, "Tennessee Williams: The Playwright as Social Critic," *Theatre Annual* 21 (1964): 40–56.

now that Big Daddy has not much longer to live. Perhaps Gooper and Mae's major argument is that they are responsible (as shown by their five children), while Brick and Maggie are not responsible (as shown by Brick's drinking and by his refusal to sleep with Maggie and have a child, something Big Daddy wants very much). At this point Maggie announces that she is pregnant. Big Mama is overjoyed and seems to be the only one who believes her. This, Big Mama reasons, will solve all the problems, even the problem of Brick's drinking. Brick of course knows that Maggie is lying but says nothing to betray her.

In the final scene, Maggie locks up all the liquor and pressures Brick into going to bed with her in order to make her lie become truth. Afterward she promises to unlock the liquor so that they may both get drunk. She sobs that she really loves Brick, while Brick thinks, If only that were true.

After reading the play or viewing the film, identify instances and explain the importance of the following.

1. Communication is inevitable.
   a. Do the characters communicate significant messages even though they may attempt not to communicate?
   b. In what ways do the characters communicate simply by their physical presence?
   c. What alternatives does Brick use in attempting to avoid communicating with Maggie?
   d. What alternatives does Brick use in attempting to avoid communicating with Big Daddy?

2. Communication is irreversible.
   a. Are any messages communicated that the characters would have preferred not to communicate?
   b. Do any of the characters attempt to reverse the communication process, that is, to uncommunicate?

3. Communication involves content and relationship dimensions.
   a. How does Brick deal with the self-definitions of Maggie and Big Daddy? Is he effective or ineffective? Explain.
   b. How does Big Daddy deal with Big Mama's definition of herself?
   c. Are any problems caused by the failure to recognize the distinction between the content and the relationship levels of communication? Explain.

4. Communication is a process of adjustment.
   a. Can any of the failures to communicate be traced to the lack of adjustment?
   b. Throughout the interaction, how do the characters adjust to one another? How is communication affected by the changes in the characters throughout the play?

5. Communication sequences are punctuated for processing.
   a. How do Maggie and Brick differ in their punctuation of the events?
   b. Why do they punctuate the sequences differently?
   c. How do Brick and Gooper differ in their punctuation of their relationship with each other and of their individual relationships with Big Daddy?

6. Communication involves symmetrical and complementary transactions.
   a. What type of relationship exists between Brick and Maggie? Gooper and Mae? Big Daddy and Big Mama? Big Daddy and Brick? Big Daddy and Gooper? Maggie and Mae?
   b. Can any instances of rigid complementarity be found?
   c. Do any of the relationships change from symmetrical to complementary or from complementary to symmetrical during the course of the play? Explain.

As an alternative to analyzing *Cat on a Hot Tin Roof*, the entire class may watch a situation comedy show, television drama, or film and explore these six communication postulates in these presentations. The questions used in this exercise should prove useful in formulating parallel questions for the television program or film. Another way of approaching this topic is to have all students watch the same television programs for an entire evening and have groups of students focus on the operation of different postulates. Thus one group would focus on examples and illustrations of the impossibility of not communicating, one group on the content and relationship dimensions of messages, and so on. Each group can then report their findings and insights to the entire class.

4. THE STRANGER

Unit 3. Perception in Interpersonal Communication
Part 3. Verbal Messages
Part 4. Nonverbal Messages

The purpose of this exercise is to explore the bases you use in perceiving and judging people you see for the first time. Since we all make judgments of people on seeing them, we need to investigate the ways and means we use in making these judgments.

A stranger (someone you have not seen before) will be brought into the class. Look the stranger over and answer the questions below. For this phase of the exercise, no interaction between you and the stranger should take place. Use the number "1" to mark your answers.

After answering all the questions you will be able to interact with the stranger for 5 or 10 minutes. Ask him or her any questions you wish, though none can be directly related to the questions asked below. The stranger should answer any questions posed as fully as he or she thinks necessary. The stranger should not, however, answer any questions that relate directly to the questions posed on the following pages. After this interaction, again answer the questions, this time using "2" to mark your answers.

After these answers have been recorded, the stranger or the instructor will go over each of the questions, specifying which answers the stranger thinks are most appropriate.

The stranger would most likely:

1. read

   _____ a comedy

   _____ a classic Russian novel

2. see

   _____ a mystery movie

   _____ a romantic movie

_____ a sex-improvement manual   _____ a western

_____ a philosophical essay   _____ a comedy

_____ a current popular novel   _____ an erotic movie

_____ a Gothic romance   _____ a foreign film

3. participate in   4. listen to

_____ baseball   _____ classical music

_____ tennis   _____ rock music

_____ golf   _____ country and western

_____ skiing   _____ popular music

_____ none of these   _____ disco

5. watch on television   6. prefer to be

_____ a situation comedy   _____ alone

_____ the news   _____ in a crowd

_____ an educational show   _____ with one person

_____ a detective show

_____ a sports show

_____ a soap opera

7. go to   8. look for in a mate

_____ a rock concert   _____ intelligence

_____ an art museum   _____ looks

_____ a baseball game   _____ personality

_____ an opera   _____ money

_____ a play

_____ a movie

9. subscribe to   10. behave

_____ _Playboy/Playgirl_   _____ as an extrovert

_____ _National Geographic_   _____ as an introvert

_____ _Time/Newsweek_   _____ as an ambivert

_____ _Popular Mechanics_

_____ _Modern Bride_

11. act

_____ aggressively

_____ assertively

_____ nonassertively

12. be

_____ very energetic

_____ very lazy

_____ fairly energetic

_____ fairly lazy

13. behave in most situations

_____ very emotionally

_____ very rationally

_____ fairly emotionally

_____ fairly rationally

14. What is the stranger's

Age _____

Occupation _____

Educational level reached _____

Relational status _____

Financial status _____

Describe the stranger's personality in two, three, or four adjectives. How does the stranger feel now? Explain.

Discussion should focus on at least the following:

1. What cues (verbal and nonverbal) were most significant in revealing what the stranger was like?

2. Has your implicit personality theory enabled you to make inferences about the stranger's personality or behaviors? Explain.

3. Did primacy-recency influence your impressions? Did, for example, your first impressions serve as a kind of filter through which you examined and evaluated further and later information?

4. Did members of the class respond very differently to this stranger? To what can you attribute these different perceptions? For example, did the male and female students see the stranger differently?

5. Did the self-fulfilling prophecy operate here in any way? Did stereotyping? How?

5. PERCEIVING MY SELVES

Unit 3. Perception in Interpersonal Communication
Unit 7. Universals of the Self and Self-awareness

The purposes of this Experiential Vehicle are to get us to understand better how we perceive ourselves, how others perceive us, and how we would like to perceive ourselves. In some instances and for some people, these three perceptions will be the same; in most cases and for most people, however, they will be different.

Following this brief introduction are nine lists of items (animals, birds, colors, communications media, dogs, drinks, music, sports, and transportation). Read over each list carefully, attempting to look past the purely physical existence of the objects to their "personalities" or "psychological meanings."

Instructions

1. First, for each of the nine lists indicate the one item that best represents how you perceive yourself—not your physical self, but your psychological and philosophical self. Mark these items *MM* (Myself to Me).
2. Second, for each of the nine lists select the one item that best represents how you feel others perceive you. By "others" is meant acquaintances—neither passing strangers nor close friends, but people you meet and talk with for some time—for example, people in this class. Mark these items *MO* (Myself to Others).
3. Third, for each of the nine lists select the one item that best represents how you would like to be. Put differently, what items would your ideal self select? Mark these items *MI* (Myself as Ideal).

After all nine lists are marked three times, discuss your choices in groups of five or six persons in any way you feel is meaningful. Your objective is to get a better perspective on how your self-perception compares with the perceptions of others and your ideal perception. In discussions you should try to state as clearly as possible why you selected the items you did and specifically what each selected item means to you at this time. You should also welcome any suggestions from the group members as to why they think you selected the items you did. You might also wish to integrate consideration of some or all of the following questions into your discussion.

1. How different are the items marked *MM* from *MO*? Why do you suppose this is so? Which is the more positive? Why?

2. How different are the items marked *MM* from *MI*? Why do you suppose this is so?

3. What do the number of differences between the items marked *MM* and the items marked *MI* mean for personal happiness?

4. How accurate were you in the items you marked *MO*? Ask members of the group which items they would have selected for you.

5. Which of the three perceptions (*MM, MO, MI*) is easiest to respond to? Which are you surest of?

6. Would you show these forms to your best same-sex friend? Your best opposite-sex friend? Your parents? Your children? Explain.

ANIMALS	BIRDS	COLORS
_____ bear	_____ albatross	_____ black
_____ cobra	_____ chicken	_____ blue
_____ deer	_____ eagle	_____ brown
_____ fox	_____ hawk	_____ green

_____ hyena
_____ leopard
_____ lion
_____ monkey
_____ rabbit
_____ turtle

_____ ostrich
_____ owl
_____ parrot
_____ swan
_____ turkey
_____ vulture

_____ gray
_____ pink
_____ purple
_____ red
_____ white
_____ yellow

COMMUNICATIONS MEDIA

_____ body language
_____ book
_____ film
_____ fourth-class mail
_____ gossip
_____ radio
_____ smoke signals
_____ special delivery
_____ telephone
_____ television

DOGS

_____ Afghan
_____ boxer
_____ Dalmatian
_____ Doberman
_____ German shepherd
_____ greyhound
_____ husky
_____ mutt
_____ poodle
_____ St. Bernard

DRINKS

_____ beer
_____ champagne
_____ coffee
_____ milk
_____ prune juice
_____ scotch
_____ sherry
_____ water
_____ wine
_____ hot chocolate

SPORTS

_____ auto racing
_____ baseball
_____ boxing
_____ bullfighting
_____ chess
_____ fishing
_____ ice skating
_____ skydiving
_____ tennis
_____ yachting

TRANSPORTATION

_____ bicycle
_____ bus
_____ jet plane
_____ horse and wagon
_____ kiddy car
_____ motorcycle
_____ Rolls-Royce
_____ skateboard
_____ van
_____ Volkswagen

MUSIC

_____ broadway/film
_____ country and western
_____ disco
_____ folk
_____ hymns
_____ jazz
_____ opera
_____ popular
_____ rock
_____ synthesized

6. CAUSAL ATTRIBUTION

Unit 3. Perception in Interpersonal Communication

For each of the following examples, indicate whether you think the behavior of the individual was due to *internal* causes—for example, personality characteristics and traits or various personal motives—or *external causes*—for example, the particular situation one is in, the demands of others who might be in positions of authority, or the behaviors of others. The behavior in question appears underlined.

1. Pat has just quit his job. No one else that we know has quit that job. Pat has quit a number of jobs in the last five years and has in fact quit this same job once before.
2. Mary has just failed her chemistry test. A number of other students (in fact, some

40 percent of the class) have failed the test. Mary has never failed a chemistry test before and, in fact, has never failed any other test in her life.

3. <u>Liz tasted the wine, rejected it, and complained to the waiter.</u> No one else in the place seemed to complain about the wine. Liz has complained about the wine before and has frequently complained that her food was seasoned incorrectly, that the coffee was not hot enough, and so on.

4. <u>Russel took the children to the zoo.</u> Russel works for the board of education in a small town, and taking the children on trips is one of his major functions. All people previously in the job have taken the children to the zoo. Russel has never taken any other children to the zoo.

5. <u>John ran from the dog.</u> A number of other people also ran from this dog. I was surprised to see John do this because he has never run from other animals before and never from this particular dog.

6. <u>Donna received all A's on her film projects.</u> In fact, everyone in the class got A's. This was the first A that Donna has every received in film and in fact the first A she has ever received in any course.

After you have responded to all six examples, identify the information contained in the brief behavioral descriptions that enabled you to make judgments concerning (1) consensus, (2) consistency, and (3) distinctiveness. What combination of these three principles would lead you to conclude that the behavior was internally motivated? What combination would lead you to conclude that the behavior was externally motivated?

7. SEQUENTIAL COMMUNICATION

Unit 4. Listening and Feedback in Interpersonal Communication

This exercise is designed to illustrate some of the processes involved in what might be called "sequential communication"—communication that is passed on from one individual to another.

This exercise consists of both a visual and a verbal part; both are performed in essentially the same manner. Taking the visual communication experience first, six subjects are selected to participate. Five of these leave the room while the first subject is shown the visual communication. He or she is told to try to remember as much as possible, as he or she will be asked to reproduce it in as much detail as possible. After studying the diagram, the first subject reproduces it on the blackboard. The second subject then enters the room and studies the reproduced diagram. The first diagram is then erased, and the second subject draws his or her version. The process is continued until all subjects have drawn the diagram. The last reproduction and the original drawing are then compared on the basis of the processes listed below.

The verbal portion is performed in basically the same way. Here the first subject is read the statement once or twice or even three times; the subject should feel comfortable that he or she has grasped it fully. The second subject then enters the room and listens carefully to the first subject's restatement of the communication.

The second subject then attempts to repeat it to the third subject, and so on until all subjects have restated the communication. Again, the last restatement and the original are compared on the basis of the processes listed below.

Members of the class not serving as subjects should be provided with copies of both the visual and the verbal communications and should record the changes made in the various reproductions and restatements.

Special attention should be given to the following basic processes in sequential communication.

1. *Omissions.* What kinds of information are omitted? At what point in the chain of communication are such omissions introduced? Do the omissions follow any pattern?

2. *Additions.* What kinds of information are added? When? Can patterns be discerned here, or are the additions totally random?

3. *Distortions.* What kinds of information are distorted? When? Are there any patterns? Can the types of distortions be classified in any way? Are the distortions in the direction of increased simplicity? Increased complexity? Can the sources of or reasons for the distortions be identified?

NONVERBAL COMMUNICATION

VERBAL COMMUNICATION

A verbal communication that works well comes from William Haney's "Serial Communication of Information in Organizations":

Every year at State University, the eagles in front of the Psi Gamma fraternity house were mysteriously sprayed during the night. Whenever this happened, it cost the Psi Gams from $75 to $100 to have the eagles cleaned. The Psi Gams complained to officials and were promised by the president that if ever any students were caught painting the eagles, they would be expelled from school.

8. PRACTICING ACTIVE LISTENING

Unit 4. Listening and Feedback in Interpersonal Communication

A few situations are identified briefly. For each one, indicate appropriate and effective active listening responses, including paraphrases, expressions of understanding of feelings, and questions.

1. After breaking an engagement, a friend tells you of his loneliness and depression: *"I feel so alone, so depressed. I just can't think of what I'll do."*

2. A friend just won $20,000 on a quiz show but is depressed because she lost the championship and the chance to compete for the grand prize of $100,000: *"I knew the answer, but I just couldn't think fast enough. That money could have solved all my problems."*

3. One of your grandparents has just lost the lottery by one number and tells you of all the things that the money could have bought: *"I wanted to buy your father that new car he needs so badly and put something away for each of the grandchildren. I was so close."*

4. Your professor has just been notified that his contract for next year has not been renewed: *"I guess I thought I'd always be teaching here, and now—in just two months—I'll be on the unemployment line. I can't believe they would not renew my contract."*

5. Your friend has just received a rejection from the graduate school of her choice: *"I guess I'll just have to go to Podunk with the rest of the idiots."*

6. Your brother has just found out that his girlfriend is seeing his best friend: *"I hear they're serious about each other. And nobody has said a word to me. Everybody must know about them. I'm the only fool. I can't believe it. But I still love her. I must be crazy."*

7. In the last game, a member of the college baseball team struck out with bases loaded in the bottom of the ninth inning with a tie score. In extra innings the game was lost: *"I'm going to quit the team. I've had it. No more sports for me. I'm just wasting my time. I must have been stupid to think I could play professionally."*

8. Your classmate has to give a speech in one of her classes and is extremely nervous: *"I just can't give that speech. I'm going to drop the course. I could never get up in front of a whole class. They'd laugh at me."*

9. Your friend has just gotten engaged and is overjoyed: *"I can't believe it. I'm engaged. I'm so happy I could scream."*

10. Your mother has just broken a favorite vase that has been in the family for three

generations and is depressed: *"How could I have done such a thing, such a stupid clumsy thing?"*

9. SOME ETHICAL ISSUES

Unit 5. Ethics in Interpersonal Communication

This exercise is designed to raise only a few of the many questions that could be raised concerning the ethics of interpersonal communication and to encourage you to think in concrete terms about some of the relevant issues. The purpose is not to persuade you to a particular point of view but rather to encourage you to formulate your own point of view.

The exercise consists of a series of cases, each raising somewhat different ethical questions. This exercise will probably work best if you respond to each of the cases individually and then discuss your decisions and their implications in groups of five or six. In these small groups, simply discuss the cases that you found most interesting. The most interesting cases for small group discussion will probably be those that were the most difficult for you to respond to, the ones that involved the most internal conflict. A general discussion in which the various groups share their decisions and insights may conclude the session.

Guidelines

1. Carefully read each of the following cases and write down your responses. By writing your decisions, many issues that may be unclear will come to the surface and may then be used as a basis for discussion.

2. Your responses will not be made public, your papers will not be collected, and your decisions will be revealed only if you wish to do so. If individuals wish not to reveal their decisions, do not attempt to apply any social pressure to get them to make these decisions public.

3. Do not attempt to avoid the issues presented in the various cases by saying, for example, "I'd try other means." For purposes of these exercises, other means are ruled out.

4. Focus some attention in the small group discussions on the origin of the various values implicit in your decisions. As a starting point, you might consider how your parents would respond to these cases. Would their decisions be similar to or different from yours?

5. Devote some attention to the concept of change. Would you have responded in similar fashion five years ago? If not, what has led to the change? Would you predict similar responses five or ten years from now? Why? Why not? This concept of change is also significant in another respect. Focus attention on the changes or possible changes that might occur as a result of your acting in accordance with any of the decisions. That is, is the student who sells drugs the

same individual he or she was before doing this? Can this student ever be the same individual again? How is this student different? If we accept the notion, even in part, that how we act or behave influences what we are, how does this relate to the decisions we make on these issues?

6. Consider the concept of acceptance. How willing is each group member to accept the decisions of others? Are you accepting of your own decisions? Why? Why not? Would you be pleased if your children would respond in the same way you did?

7. Three questions are posed after each case. The first two focus on what you *should* do and what you *would* do. The distinction between these two questions is crucial and is particularly significant when your answers for the two questions are different. If they differ, try to analyze the intrapersonal dynamics. How do you account for the difference? Is there intrapersonal conflict? Are these differences the result of changes you are going through? How pleased or displeased are you with the differences in these answers? The third question asks you to consider the implications of your choices on the first two questions; that is, what do your answers to the first two questions mean in a more general sense?

IMMINENT DEATH

You have a very close friend or relative who has a fatal illness that is sure to result in the person's death within the next six months. The person knows that the illness is a progressive one but does not know that death is imminent. Assume that there is no possibility of an error having been made in the diagnosis or prognosis; the person is sure to die within the next six months. Since you are the closest friend (or relative), the doctors have left up to you the decision as to whether or not this person should be informed.

1. What should you do?

2. What would you do?

3. What are the implications of your choices?

SELF-DISCLOSURE

You are currently dating a wonderful person whom you eventually hope to marry, perhaps in the next year or so. You get along in every way. You have similar interests and values, you are supportive of each other—in short, you just enjoy being with each other. There seems to be only one problem: You were married for a short time and then quietly divorced. You have a 3-year-old child who lives with your ex-spouse and whom you have not seen for over two years. You fear that if your previous marriage, child, and divorce were made known, the relationship might break up. You do not want to keep this information secret, nor do you want to endanger the relationship.

1. What should you do?

2. What would you do?

3. What are the implications of your choices?

CHILDREN'S HOSPITAL

You have been put in charge of raising money for your town's new children's hospital, a hospital that is badly needed. There are a number of crippled children who are now wearing heavy braces and who must walk with crutches. These children, you reason, would be very effective in influencing people to give to the hospital fund. As a conclusion to a program of speeches by local officials and entertainment, you consider having these children walk through the audience and tell the people how desperately they need this hospital. An appeal by these children, you feel, would encourage many of the people to make donations, which they would not make if a more reasoned and logical appeal were presented. You know from past experience that other available means of persuasion will not be effective.

1. What should you do?

2. What would you do?

3. What are the implications of your choices?

THE RIGHT TO PRIVACY

You are a counselor at a local high school and for the past three years have been counseling students in both academic and personal and social matters. Although your job is to counsel students in all areas, a great deal of your time is taken up with counseling them in the area of sex education and especially in the area of birth control. You have given the students information of all sorts—about the various types of birth control devices, where to obtain them, how to use them, and so on. You have also, on occasion, given the students the birth control devices. The Parents Association now wants you to inform the parents as soon as a student requests birth control information. The Parents Association argues that it is the parents' right to give or to refuse to give their children such information. Teenagers living at home and supported by their parents do not, their parents argue, have the right to privacy that has often been mentioned in situations like these. On the one hand, you do not want to assume the role of the parent, but you know that the students come to you because you do respect their privacy. They come to you because they will not or cannot go to their parents. Your job is not in jeopardy; you may do whatever you think is right without suffering any sort of harm. Your problem is to decide what is the right thing to do.

1. What should you do?

2. What would you do?

3. What are the implications of your choices?

BUYING A PAPER

You are now taking an elective course in anthropology. You need an A in this course to maintain the average you think you will need to graduate. Although you have done the required work, you are running only a B − at best. The instructor has told you that you will get an A in the course if you write an extra paper and get an

A on it. You want to write this paper but are too pressed for time; you need to put what time you do have available into your other courses. You hear about one of those "paper mills" that, for approximately $100, will provide you with a paper that should get you the A in the course. You can easily afford the $100 fee.

1. What should you do?

2. What would you do?

3. What are the implications of your choices?

10. A TENTATIVE THEORY OF INTERPERSONAL ETHICS

Unit 5. Ethics in Interpersonal Communication

Formulate here what you might call "My Tentative Theory of Interpersonal Ethics." Formulate a theory that you feel is reasonable, justified, internally consistent, and consonant with your own system of values. Construct your theory so that it incorporates, at a minimum, all of the situations presented in Experiential Vehicle 9. That is, given this statement of ethical principles, another individual should be able to predict accurately how you would behave in each of the situations presented in the cases in Experiential Vehicle 9.

11. PETER AND BARBARA

Unit 6. Effectiveness in Interpersonal Communication

Presented here is a dialogue between two college students, Peter and Barbara. Carefully read the dialogue, noting especially their use or misuse of the principles of effective interpersonal interaction. Read the dialogue at least twice.

This exercise is designed to enable you to see more clearly how the principles of effective interpersonal interaction operate in actual practice. The exercise consists of two parts. First, analyze the brief interaction in terms of the ten principles of effective interpersonal interaction. Identify specific verbal behaviors that violate the principles of effectiveness or that demonstrate their effective application. Second, write a continuation of the dialogue. Assume that Peter and Barbara meet a week later and that neither has seen or spoken to the other throughout the week. Your continuation should illustrate the ways in which both Peter and Barbara might correctly apply the principles for effective interpersonal interaction. These continuation dialogues may be written independently or in small groups of four or five.

After this dialogue has been analyzed and completed, discuss in small groups or with the class as a whole the principles of effective interpersonal interaction and how they may operate to facilitate mutual understanding or to hinder it, to aid in the development of an interpersonal relationship or to contribute to its dissolution.

[Peter and Barbara have been dating for the past two years and are now in their senior year of college. The scene takes place in Peter's apartment near campus.]

Barbara: I really think you and I should sit down and talk about it. About you and me. I feel something is wrong but you just won't talk about it.

Peter: Nothing's wrong. I just don't have anything to say. You always want to talk about it. Well, what do you want to say?

Barbara: I just want to know what is going to happen with us. We're going to graduate in June—five months from now. What's going to happen then?

Peter: Nothing. I mean the same as now.

Barbara: Do you want to talk about plans for after graduation? You want to talk about marriage?

Peter: No. I don't see any reason to talk about that now. You always seem to start an argument when we do that. Can't we just continue going along like we have been?

Barbara: It's Nancy, isn't it?

Peter: Nancy? What are you talking about? Nancy was six months ago.

Barbara: Well, you lied about her then, and you're probably lying about her now.

Peter: I'm not. Take my word for it. I'm not.

Barbara: What good is your word? You lied before and you'll lie again. And anyway, Nancy is still after you.

Peter: She's not after me.

Barbara: Then you're after her.

Peter: Neither of us is after the other. We're just friends. Can't I have a friend? Must I be with you 24 hours a day? I have my own life, you know. Or rather, I had my own life two years ago.

Barbara: Then you don't care for me. We might as well break up.

Peter: Well, if that's what you want, then fine.

Barbara: But I don't want that. You know I don't. I want us to be together.

Peter: So we're together. What more do you want?

Barbara: I want to know you care for me.

Peter: I care.

Barbara: I want to know more than that.

Peter: I care. I care. What else do you want me to say?

Barbara: Even Carol and Donald say we should talk about the relationship. Even my mother said we should. I should know where I stand.

Peter: I'm not going out with Carol and Donald and I'm certainly not going out with your mother. She's your real problem.

Barbara: You always say that. You never did like my mother.

Peter: Correct I never did. And I don't now.

Barbara: And your mother is so great? Always calling up to find out if your're living with me. Always calling to see if you need anything. She treats you like a real baby. Maybe that's why you're the way you are—never wanting to make a decision or a commitment. Maybe you're afraid of leaving the womb, of leaving mother.

Peter: I'm not afraid of leaving my mother. I'm afraid of *you* becoming my mother. I've had enough of my mother. I don't want to marry my mother.

Barbara: Oh, so that's it. You don't want to marry me.

Peter: I didn't say that.

Barbara: But that's what you meant. Well, if that's the case, I might as well leave.

Peter: Fine. If that's the way you feel.

Barbara: Maybe that is better. Maybe I'll find someone who doesn't always have a headache.

Peter: What is that supposed to mean?

Barbara: It means that you never seem to want to do anything.

Peter: I would if you gave me a chance. I'm supposed to be the one to make the first moves, not you. I'm the man, remember? And I wasn't as experienced as you were.

Barbara: Sometimes I'm not so sure you're the man. Sometimes I really wonder. [After an extended pause.] Don't I have needs too? Why can't I make the first move?

Peter: I don't know. But I'm supposed to be the aggressor.

Barbara: Then why don't you?

Peter: I would if you gave me a chance. Anyway, if that's all you want, maybe you should find somebody else. Who cares?

Barbara: I guess nobody.

[Barbara walks out in anger as Peter turns up the stereo and falls onto the couch.]

12. "I'D PREFER TO BE"

Unit 7. Universals of the Self and Self-Awareness

This exercise should enable members of the class to get to know each other better and at the same time get to know themselves better. The questions asked here should encourage each individual to think about and increase awareness of one or more facets of her or his thoughts or behaviors.

Rules

"I'd Prefer to Be" is played in a group of four to six people. The general procedure is as follows.

1. Each member individually ranks each of the three traits in the 20 groupings listed, using 1 for the most preferred and 3 for the least preferred choice.

2. Then the group considers each of the 20 categories, with each member giving her or his rank order.

3. Members may refuse to reveal their rankings for any category by saying "I pass." The group is not permitted to question the reasons for any member's passing.

4. When a member has revealed rankings for a category, the group members may ask questions relevant to that category. These questions may be asked after any individual member's account or may be reserved until all members have given their rankings for a particular category.

5. The group may establish any additional rules it wishes, for example, appointing a leader or chairperson or establishing time limits.

"I'D PREFER TO BE"

1. _____ intelligent
   _____ wealthy
   _____ physically attractive

2. _____ a movie star
   _____ a senator
   _____ a successful businessperson

3. _____ blind
   _____ deaf
   _____ mute

4. _____ on a date
   _____ reading a good book
   _____ watching television

5. _____ loved
   _____ feared
   _____ respected

6. _____ bisexual
   _____ heterosexual
   _____ homosexual

7. _____ applying for a job by letter
   _____ applying for a job by face-to-face interview
   _____ applying for a job by telephone interview

8. _____ adventurous
   _____ scientific
   _____ creative

9. _____ successful in social life
   _____ successful in family life
   _____ successful in business life

10. _____ a traitor to my friend
    _____ a traitor to my country
    _____ a traitor to myself

11. _____ living yesterday
    _____ living today
    _____ living tomorrow

12. _____ angry
    _____ guilty
    _____ fearful

13. _____ introverted
    _____ extraverted
    _____ ambiverted

14. _____ traveling in uncharted areas
    _____ traveling in Europe
    _____ traveling in the United States

15. _____ the loved
    _____ the lover
    _____ the good friend

16. _____ a lion
    _____ an eagle
    _____ a dolphin

17. _____ a tree
    _____ a rock
    _____ a flower

18. _____ the sun
    _____ the wind
    _____ the waters

19. _____ a leader
    _____ a follower
    _____ a loner

20. _____ married (10 years from now)
    _____ single (10 years from now)
    _____ living with someone but unmarried (10 years from now)

Areas for Discussion

1. What are the reasons for the individual choices? Note that the reasons for the least preferred choice may often be as important as, or even more important than, the reasons for the most preferred choice.

2. What do the choices reveal about the individual? Can persons be differentiated on the basis of their choices among these and similar alternatives?

3. What is the homogeneity or heterogeneity of the group as a whole? Do the members evidence relatively similar choices or wide differences? What does this mean in terms of the members' ability to communicate with each other?

4. Do the members accept or reject the choices of other members? Are some members disturbed by the choices other members made? If so, why? Are some apathetic? Why? Did hearing the choices of one or more members make you want to get to know them better?

5. Did any of the choices make you aware of preferences you were not aware of before?

6. Are members reluctant to share their preferences with the group? Why?

13. COMMUNICATIONS OF DIFFERENT LIFE POSITIONS

Unit 7. Universals of the Self and Self-awareness

How would you respond to each of the following situations? Write down what you think your initial response would be.

1. being offered a promotion to a position of responsibility

2. being fired from a job you have held for the past five years
3. being asked out on a date
4. being robbed
5. being designated leader in a small group situation
6. being complimented for something you made
7. being criticized for something you did
8. being asked a favor that will take about an hour of your time
9. being assigned an unpleasant job that will last about a month
10. being given the opportunity to vote for or against the promotion of your interpersonal communication instructor

Respond again to the ten situations, but this time identify how each of the four life positions would respond in the same situation. Try not to refer to or even think about your initial responses.

Analyze your own responses in terms of the four life positions. Do you see any patterns in your responses? How would these responses influence your day-to-day experiences?

As an alternative, this exercise may be conducted by collecting students' response sheets (without names). The instructor or some member of the class would read the responses aloud, and the class would classify these into the four life positions. More important than mere classification, however, would be a discussion of what these responses mean in terms of our views of ourselves and of others.

14. DISCLOSING THE HIDDEN SELF

Unit 8. Self-disclosure

On an index card, write a statement of information that is currently in the hidden self. Do not put your name on the card; the statements are to be dealt with anonymously. The cards will be collected and read aloud to the entire group.

Discussion of Statement and Model

1. Classify the statements into categories: sexual problems, attitudes toward family, self-doubts, and so forth.

2. Why do you suppose this type of information is kept in the hidden self? What advantages might there be to hiding this information? What disadvantages?

3. How would you react to people who disclosed such statements to you? For example, what difference, if any, would it make in your closest interpersonal relationship?

4. What type of person is likely to have a large hidden self and a small open self? A large open self and a small hidden self?

5. In relation to the other group members, would your open self be larger? Smaller? The same size? Would your hidden self be larger? Smaller? The same size?

	Would Definitely Self-disclose	Would Probably Self-disclose	Don't Know	Would Probably Not Self-disclose	Would Definitely Not Self-disclose
1. My religious beliefs					
2. My attitudes toward other religions					
3. My attitudes toward different nationalities and races					
4. My political beliefs					
5. My economic status					
6. My views on abortion					
7. My views on pornography					
8. My views on premarital relations					
9. My major pastime					
10. My parents' attitudes toward other religions					
11. My parents' attitudes toward different nationalities and races					
12. My parents' political beliefs					
13. My parents' economic status					
14. My relationship with my parents					
15. My sexual fantasies					
16. My past sexual experiences					
17. My perceived sexual attractiveness					
18. My desired physical attractiveness					
19. My most negative physical attribute					
20. My physical condition or health					
21. My ideal mate					
22. My drinking behavior					
23. My drug-taking behavior					
24. My gambling behavior					
25. My personal goals					
26. My most embarrassing moment					
27. My unfulfilled desires					
28. My major weaknesses					
29. My major worries					
30. My major strengths					
31. My present happiness or unhappiness					
32. My major mistakes					
33. My general attractiveness					
34. My general self-concept					
35. My general feelings of adequacy					

15. SELF-DISCLOSURE QUESTIONNAIRE

Unit 8. Self-disclosure

Complete the questionnaire on page 398 by indicating in the appropriate spaces your willingness or unwillingness to self-disclose these matters to members of a group of students chosen at random from those in this class.

In a group of five or six persons, discuss the questionnaires, self-disclosing what you wish to self-disclose and not disclosing what you do not wish to disclose. Consider at least the following:

1. Are there any discrepancies between what you indicated you would self-disclose and what you were actually willing to self-disclose?

2. What areas were people most unwilling to self-disclose? Why?

3. After the group got going and a number of people self-disclosed, did you feel more willing to self-disclose? Explain your feelings. Relate this to the dyadic effect.

4. Were negative qualities (or perceived negative qualities) more likely to remain undisclosed? Why?

5. How would the results of your questionnaire have differed if this information were to be disclosed to your parents, a stranger you would never see again, a counselor, and a best friend? Would the results differ depending on the sex of the individual to whom the disclosures were to be made? Explain why.

16. ASSERTIVENESS QUESTIONNAIRE

Unit 9. Apprehension and Assertiveness

Indicate how you would respond to each of the 20 situations presented. Use the following keys:

AS = assertively
AG = aggressively
NO = nonassertively

Respond instinctively rather than in the way you feel you should respond.

After each person has responded individually, discuss these situations and the responses in groups of five or six in any way you feel is meaningful.

1. _____ A fellow student borrowed a book and has not returned it in two weeks.
2. _____ The people behind you in a movie are talking loudly.
3. _____ Your neighbor is playing a stereo so loud you have difficulty studying.
4. _____ You are shortchanged by 25 cents at a supermarket.
5. _____ Your meal in a restaurant arrives cold instead of hot.

6. _____ A neighbor's dog repeatedly defecates in front of your house.

7. _____ A neighbor's dog barks constantly during the day when the owner is out.

8. _____ A friend borrows $5 but does not show any interest in returning it.

9. _____ A neighbor repeatedly drops by for coffee without being invited.

10. _____ A fellow student does not work on a group project for which each member will receive the same grade.

11. _____ A teacher gives you a grade that you feel is unfair.

12. _____ You are attracted to someone in class and want to ask the person for a date.

13. _____ Your business partner does not do half the work.

14. _____ A friend is continually late for appointments.

15. _____ A group of fellow students is unfairly speaking against someone you know.

16. _____ A persistent salesperson keeps showing you merchandise you do not want to buy.

17. _____ Your friend wants to borrow your expensive watch and you are afraid he or she will lose it.

18. _____ Your boss takes advantage of you by asking you to take on all sorts of extra responsibilities.

19. _____ You are at a party where you know no one but the host.

20. _____ Someone asks you for a date but you do not want to go.

17. ROLE-PLAYING ASSERTIVENESS

Unit 9. Apprehension and Assertiveness

In groups of five or six, role-play each of the four situations so that each situation is played by an assertive, an aggressive, and a nonassertive behavior type. The roles should be rotated so that each person in the group gets an opportunity to demonstrate each of the three behavior patterns. The role of the initiator or stimulator should also be rotated.

Discussion should center on the following questions.

1. What nonverbal behaviors accompany each of the three behavior patterns?

2. What types of verbal statements are used to demonstrate the three behavior patterns?

3. Do some people have difficulty playing certain roles? Explain.

4. What kind of feelings accompany the playing of the various behavior types? Explain as specifically as possible.

5. Does assertiveness seem to come easier as the role playing progresses? Would this hold in the "real world"?

6. How might a hierarchy (as explained in the fourth principle for increasing assertiveness) be created for any one of the situations?

"CHEATING" ON AN EXAMINATION

You and another student turn in examination papers that are too similar to be the result of mere coincidence. The instructor accuses you of cheating by allowing the student behind you to copy your answers. You were not aware that anyone saw your paper.

DECORATING YOUR APARTMENT

You have just redecorated your apartment, expending considerable time and money in making it exactly as you want it. A good friend of yours brings you a house gift—the ugliest poster you have ever seen. Your friend insists that you hang it over your fireplace, the focal point of your living room.

BORROWING MONEY

A friend borrows $30 and promises to pay you back tomorrow. But tomorrow passes, as do 20 other tomorrows, yet there is no sign of the money. You know that the person has not forgotten about it and you also know that the person has more than enough money to pay you back.

NEIGHBOR INTRUSIONS

A neighbor has been keeping a stereo at an extremely high volume late into the night. This makes it difficult for you to sleep.

18. MEANINGS IN PEOPLE

Unit 10. Universals of Verbal Messages

Five sets of semantic differential scales, headed by various concepts, are presented. Rate each of these concepts as you see them.

After the ratings are completed, small groups of five or six (or the class as a whole) should discuss the meanings of the words as they are defined in a dictionary (the denotation) and as they are defined by the ratings on these scales (the connotation).

From this experience (the collection of the data and the ensuing discussion), the following should be clear:

1. Disagreement over the meaning of a word usually centers on the connotative meaning rather than on the denotative meaning.

2. Connotative and denotative meanings are very different aspects of a word's total meaning.

3. People are different and hence define words differently.

4. Different people can use the same word but mean very different things by it.

5. Meanings are not in words but in people.

INSTRUCTIONS FOR COMPLETING SEMANTIC DIFFERENTIAL SCALES

Rating a concept on the kind-cruel scale as an example, the seven positions should be interpreted as follows.

If you feel that the concept being rated is extremely kind or extremely cruel, mark the end positions as shown here:

Kind __X__:_____:_____:_____:_____:_____:_____: Cruel

or

Kind _____:_____:_____:_____:_____:_____:__X__ Cruel

If you feel that the concept is *quite* kind or *quite* cruel, mark the scale as follows:

Kind _____:__X__:_____:_____:_____:_____:_____ Cruel

or

Kind _____:_____:_____:_____:_____:__X__:_____ Cruel

If you feel that the concept is *slightly* kind or *slightly* cruel, mark the scale as follows:

Kind _____:_____:__X__:_____:_____:_____:_____ Cruel

or

Kind _____:_____:_____:_____:__X__:_____:_____ Cruel

If you feel that the concept is neutral in regard to kindness or cruelty mark the center of the scale as follows:

Kind _____:_____:_____:__X__:_____:_____:_____ Cruel

Note: Mark each scale in order, do not omit any scales; mark each scale only once; mark each scale on one of the seven scale positions; do not put a mark between positions.

LOVE

Good	_____:_____:_____:_____:_____:_____:_____						Bad
Pleasant	_____:_____:_____:_____:_____:_____:_____						Unpleasant
Ugly	_____:_____:_____:_____:_____:_____:_____						Beautiful
Weak	_____:_____:_____:_____:_____:_____:_____						Strong
Active	_____:_____:_____:_____:_____:_____:_____						Passive
Sharp	_____:_____:_____:_____:_____:_____:_____						Dull

Large ____:____:____:____:____:____ Small
Light ____:____:____:____:____:____ Heavy
Hot ____:____:____:____:____:____ Cold

COLLEGE

Good ____:____:____:____:____:____ Bad
Pleasant ____:____:____:____:____:____ Unpleasant
Ugly ____:____:____:____:____:____ Beautiful
Weak ____:____:____:____:____:____ Strong
Active ____:____:____:____:____:____ Passive
Sharp ____:____:____:____:____:____ Dull
Large ____:____:____:____:____:____ Small
Light ____:____:____:____:____:____ Heavy
Hot ____:____:____:____:____:____ Cold

RELIGION

Good ____:____:____:____:____:____ Bad
Pleasant ____:____:____:____:____:____ Unpleasant
Ugly ____:____:____:____:____:____ Beautiful
Weak ____:____:____:____:____:____ Strong
Active ____:____:____:____:____:____ Passive
Sharp ____:____:____:____:____:____ Dull
Large ____:____:____:____:____:____ Small
Light ____:____:____:____:____:____ Heavy
Hot ____:____:____:____:____:____ Cold

WOMEN'S LIBERATION

Good ____:____:____:____:____:____ Bad
Pleasant ____:____:____:____:____:____ Unpleasant
Ugly ____:____:____:____:____:____ Beautiful
Weak ____:____:____:____:____:____ Strong
Active ____:____:____:____:____:____ Passive
Sharp ____:____:____:____:____:____ Dull
Large ____:____:____:____:____:____ Small
Light ____:____:____:____:____:____ Heavy
Hot ____:____:____:____:____:____ Cold

GAY LIBERATION

Good ____:____:____:____:____:____ Bad
Pleasant ____:____:____:____:____:____ Unpleasant
Ugly ____:____:____:____:____:____ Beautiful
Weak ____:____:____:____:____:____ Strong
Active ____:____:____:____:____:____ Passive
Sharp ____:____:____:____:____:____ Dull
Large ____:____:____:____:____:____ Small
Light ____:____:____:____:____:____ Heavy
Hot ____:____:____:____:____:____ Cold

19. SOME SUBLANGUAGES

Unit 11. Language, Sublanguage, and Culture

Presented below are a few brief lexicons of several sublanguages. Note how these terms serve the functions discussed in Unit 11. Many of them are in the process of passing into the general language.

Assuming that you might like to test your knowledge of the various sublanguages, these lexicons are presented as matching quizzes. Write the number of the sublanguage term (left column) next to the letter of the corresponding general-language term or example (right column).

CRIMINAL TALK: THE ARGOT OF THE "UNDERWORLD"

1. maker, designer, scratcher, connection	a. bank burglar
	b. false key
2. paper, scrip, still	c. racket involving violence
3. jug stiff, cert	d. forger
4. beat, sting, come-off	e. wallet
5. buttons, shamus, fuzz	f. a parcel with a trap inside for hiding stolen merchandise
6. mark, hoosier, chump, yap	
7. poke, leather, hide	g. burglar alarm
8. cold poke, dead skin	h. iron safe
9. gun, cannon, whiz	i. forged check
10. booster	j. pickpocket
11. booster box	k. dynamite
12. bug	l. forged bank check
13. dinah, noise	m. shoplifter
14. double	n. watchman
15. gopher	o. policeman
16. hack	p. negotiable security
17. soup, pete	q. pickpocket victim
18. jug heavy	r. nitroglycerine
19. stiff	s. empty wallet
20. heavy racket	t. picking a pocket

CB TALK: THE CANT OF THE CB OPERATOR

1. green stamps	a. unmarked police car
2. good buddy	b. other CB owners or operators
3. seat covers	c. state police
4. X-ray machine	d. overnight stop
5. plain wrapper	e. radar unit ahead
6. ranch	f. diner
7. bear cave	g. FCC (Federal Communications Commission)
8. cut some Z's	

  9. clean
 10. ground clouds
 11. boy scouts
 12. handle
 13. bean store
 14. green stamp road
 15. keep your nose between the ditches and smokey out of your britches
 16. mama bear
 17. big daddy
 18. invitations
 19. haircut palace
 20. brush your teeth and comb your hair

 h. fog
 i. money
 j. toll ahead
 k. low overhead
 l. get some sleep
 m. traffic tickets
 n. passengers
 o. drive safely; watch for speed traps
 p. no police in sight
 q. CB transmission
 r. police station
 s. police radar
 t. policewoman

WORDS ABOUT WORDS: THE JARGON OF THE LANGUAGE SCHOLAR

  1. onomatopoeia
  2. spoonerism
  3. cliché
  4. metaphor
  5. ideogram
  6. anagram
  7. simile
  8. kangaroo word
  9. eponym
 10. ambiguity

 a. "right as rain," "the whole ball of wax"
 b. "he was a lion on the field"
 c. #, $, ¢, &
 d. "the real McCoy"
 e. "ding, snap, babble"
 f. "the star sang like an angel"
 g. "cat, tac, act"
 h. "our queer old dean" for "our dear old queen"
 i. "bat, run, ball"
 j. "evacuate" ("vacate")

COMMUNICATION TALK: THE JARGON OF THE COMMUNICOLOGIST

  1. argot
  2. codifiability
  3. credibility
  4. paralanguage
  5. batons
  6. immanent reference
  7. endomorphy
  8. empathy
  9. homophily
 10. ideographs
 11. elementalism
 12. intensional orientation
 13. Machiavellianism
 14. metacommunication
 15. phatic communion
 16. proxemics

 a. the characteristic of communication by which it always refers to the immediate situation
 b. the degree of similarity among individuals
 c. the fatty dimension of a body
 d. vocal but nonverbal dimension of communication
 e. a kind of sublanguage, generally of a criminal class
 f. the process of dividing verbally what cannot be divided nonverbally (in reality)
 g. the degree to which a message is predictable
 h. techniques by which control is exerted by one person over another
 i. a perspective in which primary attention is given to labels
 j. communication that is primarily social; communication that opens the channels of communication
 k. communication about communication

17. redundancy
18. emblems
19. specialization
20. stereotype

l. nonverbal behaviors that directly translate words or phrases
m. bodily movements that sketch the path or direction of a thought
n. the fixed impression of a group through which one then perceives specific individuals
o. bodily movements that accent or emphasize a specific word or phrase
p. the feature of language that refers to the fact that human language serves no purpose other than communication
q. the study of how space communicates
r. feeling as another feels
s. believability
t. the ease with which certain concepts may be expressed in a given language

20. FEMALE AND MALE LANGUAGE USAGE

Unit 11. Language, Sublanguage, and Culture

Here are ten examples of language usage. For each, indicate whether this usage is more characteristic of women or of men.

1. *–in'* instead of *–ing* suffixes on such words as *doing, fishing, going*
2. swear and curse words
3. words such as *charming, sweet, lovely,* and *precious*
4. sentence qualifiers such as "This may not be the place to say this, but . . ." or "I may be wrong about this, but it seems to me that . . ."
5. tag questions (questions carrying tags at the ends that ask for the listener's agreement) such as "That's a terrible thing to do, isn't it?" or "This teacher is brilliant, don't you think?"
6. the use of rising intonation to change answers into questions, as in saying "Seven?" instead of "Seven" to the question "When will you be ready?"
7. joke telling
8. speech defects (especially stuttering) among children
9. speech onset and development at an earlier age and more rapid development of language generally
10. talk more in mixed-sex dyads

After responding to all ten language examples, answer these questions.

1. What were your reasons for each response?

2. What do you feel might cause the sex differences?

3. What other sex-related language differences do you observe?

21. WORD COINAGE

Unit 11. Language, Sublanguage, and Culture

Although language and culture are closely related, and although the language closely reflects the culture, there often seem to be concepts important to a culture or a subculture for which the language does not provide a convenient one-word label.

Sometimes slang or "substandard" forms fill this void, for example, *youse* or *you all* for *you* (plural) or *screw* for *prison guard*. Sometimes words are created because of some social issue, for example, *Ms.* as a form of address for women equivalent to *Mr.* for men.

To gain greater insight into the relationship between language and culture or subculture and to become more familiar with the dimensions and functions of words, perform the following exercise in groups of five or six.

1. Create a new word for some concept that is important to the culture or to a particular subculture and for which a single-word label does not exist.

2. Define the word as it would be defined in a dictionary and identify its part of speech.

3. List its various inflectional forms and definitions.

4. Provide two or three sentences in which the word is used.

5. Justify the coinage of this new word, considering, for example, why this word is needed, what void it fills, what it clarifies, what its importance is, what its effects might be should it be used widely, and so forth.

22. I, YOU, AND HE AND SHE TALK

Unit 12. Seven Pitfalls and Principles of Language and Verbal Interaction
---

The way in which we phrase something often influences the way in which it is perceived. This is especially true when dealing with and talking about people. We do not talk about ourselves in the same way that we talk about the people we are with or about the people we know but are not with.

Recognizing this simple language habit, Bertrand Russell, the British philosopher and mathematician, proposed a conjugation of "irregular" verbs. One example he used was:

I am firm.
You are obstinate.
He is a pig-headed fool

The *New Statesman* and *The Nation* picked up on this and offered prizes for contributions in the style of these irregular verbs. One of the best ones was:

I am sparkling.

You are unusually talkative.

He is drunk.

Here are ten sentences phrased in the first person. Following Russell's lead, "conjugate" these irregular verbs.

1. I speak my mind.
2. I believe in what I say.
3. I take an occasional drink.
4. I smoke.
5. I like to talk with people about people.
6. I am frugal.
7. I am concerned with what other people do.
8. I have been known to get upset at times.
9. I am concerned with my appearance.
10. I will put off certain things for a few days.

23. *E–PRIME*

Unit 13. Barriers to Verbal Interaction

E-prime (E') is normal English minus the verb *to be*. The expression refers to the mathematical equation $E - e = E'$, where E = the English language and e = the verb *to be*. E', therefore, stands for normal English without the verb *to be*.

D. David Bourland Jr., suggests that if we wrote and spoke without the verb *to be*, we would describe events more accurately. The verb *to be* often suggests that qualities are in the person or thing rather than in the observer making the statement. We often forget that these statements are evaluative rather than purely descriptive. For example, we say, "Johnny is a failure," and imply that failure is somehow *in* Johnny instead of in someone's evaluation of Johnny. This type of thinking is especially important in making statements about ourselves. We say, for example, "I'm not good at mathematics" or "I'm unpopular" or "I'm lazy," and imply that these qualities are *in* us. But these are simply evaluations that may be incorrect or, if at least partly accurate, may change. The verb *to be* implies a permanence that is simply not true of the world in which we live.

To appreciate further the difference between statements that use the verb *to be* and those that do not, try to rewrite the following sentences without using the verb *to be* in any of its forms—*is, are, am, was*, or any other tenses.

1. I'm a poor student.
2. They are inconsiderate.
3. What is meaningful communication?
4. Is this valuable?
5. Happiness is a dry nose.
6. Love is a useless abstraction.
7. Is this book meaningful?

8. Was the movie any good?
9. Dick and Jane are no longer children.
10. This class is boring.

24. FACTS AND INFERENCES

Unit 13. Barriers to Verbal Interaction

Carefully read the following report and the observations based on it. Indicate whether you think the observations are true, false, or doubtful on the basis of the information presented in the report. Circle T if the observation is definitely true. F if the observation is definitely false, and ? if the observation may be either true or false. Judge each observation in order. Do not reread the observations after you have indicated your judgment, and do not change any of your answers.

A well-liked college teacher had just completed making up the final examinations and had turned off the lights in the office. Just then a tall, dark, broad figure appeared and demanded the examination. The professor opened the drawer. Everything in the drawer was picked up and the individual ran down the corridor. The dean was notified immediately.

1. The thief was tall, dark, and broad.	T	F	?
2. The professor turned off the lights.	T	F	?
3. A tall figure demanded the examination.	T	F	?
4. The examination was picked up by someone.	T	F	?
5. The examination was picked up by the professor.	T	F	?
6. A tall, dark figure appeared after the professor turned off the lights in the office.	T	F	?
7. The man who opened the drawer was the professor.	T	F	?
8. The professor ran down the corridor.	T	F	?
9. The drawer was never actually opened.	T	F	?
10. Three persons are referred to in this report.	T	F	?

25. BREAKING NONVERBAL RULES

Unit 14. Universals of Nonverbal Messages

The general objective of this exercise is to become better acquainted with some of the rules of nonverbal communication and to analyze some of the effects of breaking such rules.

Much as we learn verbal language (that is, without explicit teaching), we also learn nonverbal language—the rules for interacting nonverbally. Among such rules might be:

1. Upon entering an elevator, turn to the door and stare at it or at the numbers indicating where the elevator is until your floor is reached.

2. When sitting next to or near someone, do not invade the person's private space with your body or your belongings.

3. When strangers are talking, do not enter their group.

4. When talking with someone, do not stand too close or too far away. You may move closer when talking about intimate topics. Never stand close enough so that you can smell the other person's odor. This rule may be broken only under certain conditions, for example, when the individuals involved are physically attracted to each other, when one individual is consoling another, or when engaged in a game whose rules require this close contact.

5. When talking in an otherwise occupied area, lower your voice so that other people are not disturbed by your conversation.

Procedure

Form student pairs, with one student in each pair designated the rule breaker and the other the observer. The task of the rule breaker is simply to enter some campus situation in which one or more rules of nonverbal communication would normally be operative and to break one or more rules. The task of the observer is to record mentally (or in writing, if possible) what happens as a result of the rule breaking.

Each pair should return after a specified amount of time and report what happened to the entire class.

Note: No rules should be broken if it means infringing on the rights of others.

26. INSTRUCTING NONVERBALLY

Unit 15. Body Communication

The purpose of this exercise is to heighten your awareness of nonverbal communication, particularly communication with the body.

The class is broken up into groups of five or six. One member from each group leaves the room for approximately one minute. While these "subjects" are out of the room, each group is given an instruction that they must communicate to the subject using only the nonverbal cue or cues to which they are restricted. All groups should of course be given the same instruction and be limited to the same verbal cue or cues so that the task will be equally difficult for all groups.

The first group to get the subject to comply with their instruction wins the round and gets 10 points. Then the process is repeated, this time with another subject chosen from the group, another instruction, and another nonverbal cue (or cues). The exercise is completed when one group wins 50 points, when time is up, or when some other predetermined point is reached.

Some sample instructions and types of nonverbal cues follow. Instructors may wish to compile their own list of instructions to ensure that they have not been seen by any member of the class.

SAMPLE INSTRUCTIONS

Leave the room; give the teacher a pat on the back; shake hands with each member of the group; open (close) all the windows; open (close) the door; bring into the class someone who is not a member of the class; write the time on the board; find a red pen; raise your hand; clap hands; sit on the floor; put your shoes on the wrong feet; get a drink of water; hold up a notebook with a name of the school on it; comb your hair.

NONVERBAL CUES

Vocal (but nonverbal) cues; hand and arm movements; eye movements (but not head movements); head movements; movements of the entire body; manipulation of the entire body; tactile cues; manipulation of objects in the room; leg movements (including feet movements).

27. WHO?

Unit 3. Perception in Interpersonal Communication
Part 3. Verbal Messages
Part 4. Nonverbal Messages

The purpose of this exercise is to explore some of the verbal and nonverbal cues that people give off and that others receive and use in formulating assumptions about the knowledge, ability, and personality of another. The exercise should serve as a useful summary of the concepts and principles of verbal and nonverbal communication and of perception.

The entire class should form a circle so that each member may see each other member without straining. If members do not know all the names of their classmates, some system of name tags should be used for this exercise.

Each student should examine the following list of phrases and should write the name of one student to whom he or she feels each statement applies in the column labeled "Who?" Be certain to respond to all statements. Although one name may be used more than once, the experience will prove more effective if a wide variety of names are chosen. Unless the class is very small, no name should be used more than 4 times.

Next to each student's name, record a *certainty rating* in the column labeled "CR," indicating how sure you are of your choices. Use a 5-point scale with 5 indicating great certainty and 1 indicating great uncertainty.

After the names and certainty ratings have been written down for *each* statement by *each* student, the following procedure may prove useful. The instructor or group leader selects a statement and asks someone specifically, or the class generally, what names were written down. (There is no need to tackle the statements in the order they are given here.) Before the person whose name was put down is asked if the phrase is correctly or incorrectly attributed to him or her, some or all of the following questions should be considered.

1. Why did you select the name you did? What was there about this person that led you to think that this phrase applied to him or her? What *specific* verbal or nonverbal cues led you to your conclusion?

2. What additional verbal and/or nonverbal cues would you need to raise your degree of certainty?

3. Is your response at all a function of a stereotype you might have of this individual's ethnic, religious, racial, or sexual identification? For example, how many women's names were put down for the questions or phrases about the saws or pistons? How many men's names were put down for the statements pertaining to cooking or using a sewing machine?

4. Did anyone give off contradictory cues such that some cues were appropriate for a specific phrase and others were not appropriate? Explain the nature of these contradictory cues.

5. How pleased or disappointed are the people whose names have been proposed? Why? Were there any surprises? Why were some of these guesses unexpected?

6. How do you communicate your "self" to others? How do you communicate what you know, think, feel, and do to your peers?

WHO?	CR	
_____	_____	1. goes to the professional theater a few times a year
_____	_____	2. has taken a vacation outside the country in the last 12 months
_____	_____	3. likes to cook
_____	_____	4. watches soap operas on a fairly regular basis
_____	_____	5. wants lots of children
_____	_____	6. knows the function of a car's pistons
_____	_____	7. knows how to knit
_____	_____	8. would vote against the ERA
_____	_____	9. has a pet
_____	_____	10. has seen a pornographic (XXX rated) movie within the last 3 months
_____	_____	11. knows how to wire a lamp
_____	_____	12. has been to an opera
_____	_____	13. is a member of an organized sports team
_____	_____	14. watches television for an average of at least 3 hours per day
_____	_____	15. knows who played Superman in the television series
_____	_____	16. has cried over a movie in the last few months
_____	_____	17. fluently speaks a foreign language
_____	_____	18. is married
_____	_____	19. has many close friends

_____	_____	20. knows how potatoes should be planted
_____	_____	21. knows who Edward R. Murrow was
_____	_____	22. knows the differences among a hacksaw, a jigsaw, and a copingsaw
_____	_____	23. knows the ingredients for a bloody Mary
_____	_____	24. knows how to make a hollandaise sauce
_____	_____	25. knows the function of the spleen
_____	_____	26. knows what an armoire is
_____	_____	27. can name all 12 signs of the zodiac
_____	_____	28. has a car in his or her immediate family costing over $20,000
_____	_____	29. would come to the aid of a friend even at great personal sacrifice
_____	_____	30. is frequently infatuated (or in love)
_____	_____	31. would like, perhaps secretly, to be a movie star
_____	_____	32. knows how to play bridge
_____	_____	33. enjoys reading poetry
_____	_____	34. knows where Liechtenstein is
_____	_____	35. knows the legal status of Puerto Rico
_____	_____	36. keeps a diary or a journal
_____	_____	37. knows how many members are on a soccer team
_____	_____	38. knows what SALT stands for
_____	_____	39. knows who the heavyweight boxing champion is
_____	_____	40. knows what the prime rate means
_____	_____	41. was a member of the Boy Scouts or Girl Scouts
_____	_____	42. is very religious
_____	_____	43. would describe himself or herself as a political activist
_____	_____	44. wants to go to graduate, law, or medical school
_____	_____	45. would vote in favor of gay rights legislation
_____	_____	46. is planning to get married within the next 12 months
_____	_____	47. is going to make a significant contribution to society
_____	_____	48. is going to be a millionaire
_____	_____	49. is a real romantic
_____	_____	50. would emerge as a leader in a small group situation

28. FACIAL COMMUNICATION

Unit 15. Body Communication

Working in dyads or small groups, test the conclusion of Ekman, Friesen, and Ellsworth, discussed in Unit 15, that the face is capable of communicating the following eight "emotion categories": happiness, surprise, fear, anger, sadness, disgust, contempt, and interest.

On index cards, write the names of these emotion categories, one to a card. Place the cards face down on the desk and have one person select a card at random and attempt to communicate the emotion using only facial gestures. Keep a record of accurate and inaccurate guesses. Play until each emotion has been demonstrated at least twice. Then consider the following questions.

1. Do you agree with Ekman, Friesen, and Ellsworth that the face can communicate these eight emotion categories?

2. Are some emotions easier to communicate than others? Why do you suppose this is true?

3. Dale Leathers, in *Nonverbal Communication Systems*, suggests that in addition to the eight emotions noted here, the face is also capable of communicating bewilderment and determination. Test out this suggestion in any way that seems useful and valid to you.

4. Are some members of your small group better facial communicators (encoders) than others? Are some better decoders than others? How might you account for these differences in ability?

29. EYE CONTACT

Unit 15. Body Communication

Form dyads and talk about any topic of mutual interest—sports, film, politics. For the first two minutes, the conversation should be conducted without any special rules. At an agreed-upon signal, eye-face contact is to cease. The conversation should continue for another two minutes as before, ideally without interruption. At another signal, focused eye-eye contact is to be established. Each person is to maintain direct eye contact for two minutes and continue the conversation as usual. At another signal, the participants should return to their customary means of communication for the final two minutes. Each person should share her or his feelings during the four periods:

1. normal interaction situation
2. no-eye-contact situation
3. focused eye contact
4. normal situation but with heightened awareness and perhaps some awkwardness carried over from the two periods of abnormal interaction.

Specifically, members may address themselves to the influence of changes in eye contact on such variables as:

1. fluency, nonfluencies, and silences
2. general body movements, especially of head, hands, and legs
3. comfort or discomfort
4. interest in the other person and in the conversation
5. time perception (did some eye-contact situations seem longer than others?)

What suggestions for effective interpersonal interaction might we derive from this brief experience?

30. SPATIAL RELATIONSHIPS AND COMMUNICATION FUNCTIONS

Unit 16. Space Communication

Presented here are diagrams of tables and chairs. Imagine that the situation is the school cafeteria and that this is the only table not occupied. For each of the diagrams, place an X where you and a friend of the same sex would seat yourselves for each of the four conditions noted. Do this for *both* the round and the rectangular tables.

1. Conversing, for example, to talk for a few minutes before class

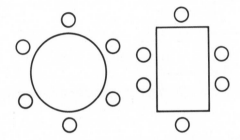

2. Cooperating, for example, to study together for the same exam or to work out a math problem

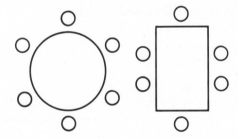

3. Coacting, for example, to study for different exams

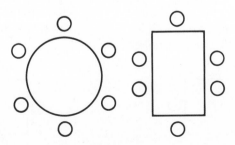

4. Competing, for example, to see who would be the first to solve a series of puzzles

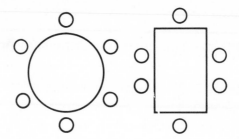

For Discussion

1. Why did you select the positions you did?

2. Explain the differences in the opportunity for nonverbal interaction that the different positions chosen allow.

3. How do these different positions relate to verbal communication?

4. Would you have chosen the same positions if you were romantically interested in the other person? Explain.

5. Compare your responses with the responses of others. How do you account for the differences in seating preferences?

6. Are there significant differences in choices between the round and the rectangular tables? Explain.

31. INTERPERSONAL INTERACTIONS AND SPACE

Unit 16. Space Communication

Presented here are diagrams of tables and chairs. Imagine that the situation is the school cafeteria and that this is the only table not occupied. In the space marked X is seated the person described above the diagram. Indicate by placing an X in the appropriate circle where you would sit.

1. A young man or woman to whom you are physically attracted and whom you would like to date but to whom you have never spoken

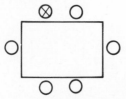

2. A person whom you find physically unattractive and to whom you have never spoken

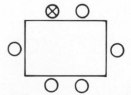

3. A person you dated once and had a miserable time with and whom you would never date again

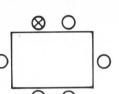

4. A person you have dated a few times and would like to date again

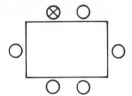

5. An instructor who gave you an undeserved F in a course last semester and whom you dislike intensely

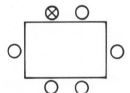

6. Your favorite instructor, whom you would like to get to know better

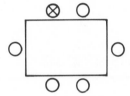

For Discussion

1. Why did you select the positions you did? For example, how does the position you selected better enable you to achieve your purpose?

2. Assume that you were already seated in the position marked X. Do you think that the person described would sit where you indicated you would (assuming that the feelings and motives are generally the same)? Why? Are there significant sex differences? Significant status differences? Explain.

3. What does the position you selected communicate to the person already seated? In what ways might this nonverbal message be misinterpreted? How would your subsequent nonverbal (and perhaps verbal) behavior reinforce your intended message? That is, what would you do to ensure that the message you intended to communicate is in fact the message communicated and received?

32. AESTHETICS AND COLOR COMMUNICATION

Unit 16. Space Communication

The purpose of this exercise is to explore the influence that our physical environment has on interpersonal communication. Form groups of five or six at random. The task of each group is to redesign your classroom so that it is more conducive to the aims of this course. Allow 15 to 20 minutes for the groups to come up with a new design.

("Redesign" should be taken to mean anything that is possible to do within the rules or restrictions imposed by the school and would include changing, adding, or removing any materials that may and can be changed, added, or removed by the group.)

After each group has planned the "new" classroom, the designs should be shared with the other members of the class. From all the suggestions, a composite redesigned classroom should be constructed and put into actual operation for at least a week of classes.

Before this design is put into effect, discussion should cover at least the following areas:

1. In what ways will this new design facilitate interpersonal communication? Be as specific as possible.

2. How would the classroom be designed if a party were to be held in it? Why? A formal lecture? Why?

3. If you could paint the classroom any color you wanted to, what color would you select? Why?

33. COLOR MESSAGES

Unit 16. Space Communication

The purpose of this exercise is to sensitize us to some of the messages communicated (or thought to be communicated) by various colors.

The class is broken down into seven groups; each group is assigned a specific color (blue, red, green, yellow, brown, white, and black are perhaps the easiest to work with). In order that each member of the group visualizes the same shade, paint chips or pictures illustrating a particular shade of the color should be used. Before any interaction among group members takes place, each person should individually complete the following questionnaire for the specific color assigned (noted here as "X").

Color Questionnaire

1. The personality of a person whose favorite color is X may best be described as

   _____, _____, and _____.

2. The personality of a person who has an extreme dislike for X may best be described as _____, _____, and _____.

3. When I visualize X, my thoughts and feelings can best be described as

   _____, _____, and _____.

4. My first impression of a book whose cover is X is that the book is

   _____.

5. My first impression of a man who wears X a great deal is that the man is

   _____.

6. My first impression of a woman who wears X a great deal is that the woman is

   _____.

7. Do certain colors appear masculine (or communicate masculinity in some way) and certain colors appear feminine (or communicate femininity in some way)? Which colors would you categorize as masculine? Why? Which colors would you categorize as feminine? Why?

8. My first impression of a room decorated in X is that the room is

   _____.

9. What colors would you use to package the following products? Why?

   a. A new and powerful detergent _____

   b. An expensive line of chocolate chip cookies _____

   c. An extremely powerful personal computer _____

   d. A mild liquid laxative _____

   e. An expensive gold watch _____

10. What colors would you use to communicate the following feelings and characteristics? Why?

   a. Friendliness _____

   b. Hostility _____

   c. Warmth _____

   d. Sex appeal _____

   e. Love _____

   f. Satisfaction _____

   g. Anger _____

   h. Strength _____

   i. Weakness _____

   j. Happiness _____

After all persons have filled out this brief questionnaire, group members should share their responses and attempt to derive some general statements concerning the messages that their color seems to communicate. When this is completed, all groups should compare their results, considering such issues as the following.

1. How much agreement or lack of it was evidenced in identifying the messages these colors communicate? Was there greater agreement for some colors than for others? Why?

2. How accurate do you think your inferences about personality and color preferences would be? How accurate do you think your first impressions of a book would be? Of men and women? Of a room?

3. How universal do you think the impressions that people get from various colors are? For example, do men and women get the same impressions on the basis of color? Would young and old derive the same impressions? Would members of different cultures? Explain.

4. In what ways is color important to the manufacturer and the advertiser? Are they successful in getting their message across to you? Explain.

34. PARALANGUAGE COMMUNICATION

Unit 17. Silence, Paralanguage, and Temporal Communication

In this exercise a subject recites the alphabet while attempting to communicate each of the following emotions:

anger	nervousness
fear	pride
happiness	sadness
jealousy	satisfaction
love	sympathy

The subject may begin the alphabet at any point and may omit and repeat sounds, but the subject may use only the names of the letters of the alphabet to communicate these feelings.

The subject should first number the emotions in random order so that he or she will have a set order to follow that is unknown to the audience, whose task it will be to guess the emotions expressed.

As a variation, have the subject go through the entire list of emotions: once facing the audience and employing any nonverbal signals desired and once with his or her back to the audience without employing any additional signals. Are there differences in the number of correct guesses depending on which method is used?

For Discussion

1. What are some of the differences between encoding and decoding "emotional meaning" and "logical meaning"?

2. Davitz and Davitz found the number of correct identifications for these emotions to be as follows: anger (156), nervousness (130), sadness (118), happiness (104), sympathy (93), satisfaction (75), love (60), fear (60), jealousy (69), and pride (50). Do these figures correspond to those you obtained? What conclusions would you draw about the relative ease or difficulty of expressing these emotions?

3. Do you think there is a positive relationship between encoding and decoding ability in situations such as this? Is the person who is adept at encoding the emotions also adept at decoding them? Explain.

4. What variables might influence encoding ability? Decoding ability?

5. What personality factors seem relevant to the encoding and decoding of emotions?

35. SOME NONVERBAL SEX DIFFERENCES

Unit 15. Body Communication
Unit 16. Space Communication
Unit 17. Silence, Paralanguage, and Temporal Communication

The following statements summarize some of the research findings on sex differences in nonverbal communication. For each statement, insert *men* or *women* in each blank space. After completing all 15 statements, consider the questions for discussion.

1. _____ seem to be slightly more accurate at judging emotions from observing facial expressions than _____.

2. _____ seem better able to communicate emotions by facial expressions than _____.

3. _____ smile more than _____.

4. _____ are generally approached more closely than _____.

5. _____ reveal their emotions facially more readily than _____.

6. _____ extend their bodies, taking up greater areas of space, than _____.

7. _____ maintain more eye contact than _____ in mixed-sex dyads.

8. Both men and women, when speaking, look at _____ more than at _____.

9. In mixed-sex dyads, _____ interrupt _____ more often.

10. Some research indicates that _____ speak with greater volume than _____.

11. If a man and a woman are walking toward each other, the _____ will be more apt to move out of the _____'s way.

12. Unattractive _____ seem to be less accepted than are unattractive _____.

13. _____ both touch and are touched more than _____.

14. _____ engage in greater mutual eye contact with a same-sex partner than _____.

15. Same-sex pairs of _____ sit more closely together than do same-sex pairs of _____.

Questions for Discussion

1. On what basis did you think that the nonverbal behavior was more accurately ascribed to one sex than the other?

2. What do you think might account for the differences in nonverbal behavior?

3. Are there types of women or men in which these differences are especially pronounced? Almost absent? Totally absent? On what basis do you make these predictions?

4. How would you go about testing one of these statements for accuracy?

5. After learning the answers given by research findings, do these seem to be consistent with your own observations? Note each that is not. How might you account for this discrepancy?

36. EXTRAORDINARY PEOPLE: RELATIONAL ANALYSIS

Unit 18. Universals of Interpersonal Relationships
and Relational Development

The dialogue that follows is an abbreviated account of the development and disso-lution of a relationship. Consequently, the five stages of relationships, for example, are easy to see and are quite clearly differentiated. In reality and in longer dialogues, these divisions would not be so obvious. The main purpose of this dialogue is to provide a focus for the discussion and analysis of the universals of interpersonal relationships.

Examine the dialogue, taking into consideration some or all of the following questions:

1. *Reasons for relational development.* Are there any indications of why Chris and Pat sought a relationship with each other? What reasons seem to account for the development of relationships among most college students?

2. *Stages in interpersonal relations.* Identify the stages in the dialogue. What specific phrases in the dialogue cue you to the stages of the relationships? What conver-sational cues signal movement from one stage to another?

3. *Initiating Relationships.* Illustrate (by actual or hypothetical examples) how the six steps identified in Unit 18 for initiating relationships might have been fol-lowed: examine the qualifiers, determine clearance, open the encounter, discover and put into operation an integrating topic, create a favorable impression, and establish a second meeting.

Identify specific verbal messages (and hypothetical nonverbal messages) that influenced (or might have influenced) the development of this initial relationship.

4. *Breadth and depth of relationships.* What would you expect the breadth and depth of the relationship to be at each of the five stages? At what stage is there greatest breadth? The least? At what stage is there greatest depth? The least? On what specific conversational cues do you base your responses? Draw diagrams similar to those presented in Figure 18.2 to represent any two stages in the relationship. Explain these diagrams with reference to specific messages in the dialogue.

THE SAGA OF CHRIS AND PAT

Pat: Hi. Didn't I see you in English last semester?

Chris: Yeah. I'm surprised you noticed me. I cut that class more than I attended. I really hated it.

Pat: So did I. Higgins never did seem to care much about whether you learned anything or not.

Chris: That's why I think I cut so much. Your name's Pat, isn't it?

Pat: Yes. And you're Chris. Right?

Chris: Right. What are you doing in Interpersonal Communication?

Pat: I'm majoring in communication. I want to go into television production—maybe editing or something like that. I'm not really sure. What about you?

Chris: It's required for engineering. I guess they figure engineers should learn to communicate.

Pat: You gonna have lunch after this class?

Chris: Yeah. You?

Pat: Yeah. How about going over to the Union for a burger?

[At the Union Cafeteria]

Chris: I'm not only surprised you noticed me in English, I'm really flattered. Everyone in the class seemed to be interested in you.

Pat: Well, I doubt that but it's nice to hear.

Chris: No, I mean it. Come on. You know you're popular.

Pat: Well, maybe . . . but it always seems to be with the wrong people. Today's the exception, of course.

Chris: You sure know the right things to say.

Pat: OK, then let me try another. What are you doing tonight? Want to go to a movie? I know it's late and all, but I thought just in case you had nothing to do. . . .

Chris: I'd love to. Even if I had something else planned, I'd break it.

Pat: That makes me feel good.

Chris: That makes me feel good, too.

[Six months later]

Pat: I hope that this doesn't cause problems but I got you something.

Chris: What is it?

Pat: Take a look. I hope you like it.

Chris: [*Chris opens the package and finds a ring.*] I love it. I can't believe it! You know, a few weeks ago when we had to write up a recent fantasy for class, I wrote one I didn't turn in. And this was it. My very own fantasy coming true. I love you.

Pat: I love you . . . very much.

[*Chris and Pat have now been living together for about two years.*]

Pat: It's me. I'm home.

Chris: So am I.

Pat: That's not hamburgers I smell, is it?

Chris: Yes, it is. I like hamburgers. We can afford hamburgers. And I know how to cook hamburgers. Make something else if you don't want to eat them.

Pat: Thanks. It's nice to know that you go to such trouble making something I like. I hate these damn hamburgers. And I especially hate them four times a week.

Chris: Eat out.

Pat: You know I have work to do tonight. I can't go out.

Chris: So shut up and eat the burgers. I love them.

Pat: That's good. It's you for you. Whatever happened to us and we?

Chris: It died when I found out about your little side trips upstate.

Pat: But I told you I was sorry about that. That was six months ago anyway. I got involved, I know, but I'm sorry. What do you want to do, punish me for the rest of my life? I'm sorry, damn it. *I'm sorry!*

Chris: So am I. But I'm the one who was left at home alone while you were out fooling around.

Pat: Is that why you don't want to make love? You always have some kind of excuse.

Chris: It's not an excuse. It's a reason. And the reason is that I've been lied to and cheated on. How can I make love to someone who treats me like dirt?

Pat: But I don't. I love you.

Chris: But I don't love you. Maybe I never have.

Pat: I *will* eat out.

[*Two weeks later*]

Pat: Did you mean what you said when you said you didn't love me?

Chris: I think I did. I just lost my feelings. I can't explain it. When I learned about your upstate trips, I just couldn't deal with it. And I guess I tried to protect myself and, in the process, lost my feelings for you.

Pat: Then why do you stay with me? Why don't you leave?

Chris: I don't know. Maybe I'm afraid to be alone. I'm not sure I can do it alone.

Pat: So you're going to stay with me because you're afraid to be alone? That's crazy. Crazy. I'd rather see us break up than live like this—a loveless relationship where you go out on Tuesdays and I go out on Wednesdays. What kind of life is that?

Chris: Not much.

Pat: Then let's separate. I can't live with someone who stays with me out of fear of being alone, who doesn't want to be touched, who doesn't want to love me. Let's try to live apart and see what happens. Maybe we need some distance. Maybe you'll want to try it again.

Chris: I won't, but I guess separation is the best thing.

Pat: Why don't you stay here and I'll go to my brother's place tonight. I'll pick up my

things tomorrow when you're at work. I don't think I can bear to do it when you're here.
Chris: Goodbye.

37. THE QUALITIES OF INTERPERSONAL ATTRACTION

Unit 19. Attraction in Interpersonal Relationships

Complete the following questionnaire and answer the two questions that follow it before reading any further.

Characteristics of the Person to Whom You Would Be Most Attracted

Age   _____

Sex   _____

Height   _____

Weight   _____

General physical attractiveness   _____

Race   _____

Religion   _____

Nationality   _____

Intelligence level   _____

Years of formal education   _____

Profession or professional goal   _____

Religious attitudes   _____

At least three major personality characteristics   _____

_____

Name five people to whom you are very attracted. _____

_____ _____ _____ _____

Name five people to whom you are not attracted. _____

_____ _____ _____ _____

Consider the following questions relevant to your responses.

1. Concerning the characteristics of the person you chose as being most attractive:
   a. Would the person whose characteristics you described be considered phys-

ically attractive? Physically unattractive? Would this person have an attractive personality? An unattractive personality?

    b. What specific characteristics did you emphasize in terms of attractiveness (physical or personality)?

    c. How similar are the characteristics you see yourself as possessing?

    d. Were the attitudinal characteristics especially important?

    e. Could instances of complementarity be identified? That is, did you list characteristics that would complement your own?

2. Concerning the persons you listed as being very attracted to:

    a. Are these persons attractive in terms of physical and personality characteristics?

    b. Do they live or work close to you?

    c. Do they reinforce you frequently? Socially? Materially?

    d. Are they similar to you in what they like and what they dislike? Are they similar to you in terms of physical and personality characteristics? Especially, are their attitudes toward significant issues similar to yours?

    e. Do they complement you in any way? How are they different from you? Are these differences complementary?

3. Concerning the persons you listed as being not attracted to:

    a. Are they generally unattractive? Physically? In terms of personality? What specific behaviors do you find unattractive?

    b. How does proximity enter into your choices? Do any of the persons listed live or work very close to you?

    c. Do these people reinforce you? If so, how do they do this? Why does their "reinforcement" not have a positive effect?

    d. How similar or dissimilar to you are the persons listed? Physically? Intellectually? Attitudinally?

    e. In what ways are you and they complementary? That is, do these persons have characteristics that would complement your own?

4. How valuable are the five variables discussed in Unit 18 in explaining the bases for those you find interpersonally attractive? What other variables seem significant to you?

38. HEROES

Unit 19. Attraction in Interpersonal Relationships

At the end of this exercise is a list of 100 noted personalities. Some of these persons you will recognize and will probably know a great deal about. Others, however, may seem totally unfamiliar. Your task is to select the five persons you would nominate for your personal hall of fame. That is, select the five people you feel could serve as your personal heroes.

Either of two general procedures will prove useful. After each person has selected five people from the list, the names should be written on index cards and collected anonymously. A tabulation of the number of votes for each person should be made, and the ten persons receiving the highest number of votes should be noted. This method will provide an anonymous procedure and will probably result in a much more candid final list.

An alternative procedure is to form groups of five or six after each person has selected her or his own choices from the list. The task of each group is to select a final list of five persons that the group would nominate for its hall of fame. After each group has selected its "heroes," the names should be put on the blackboard. This procedure, although the easier and more efficient to follow, does not allow for anonymity and hence will probably result in the selection of more socially acceptable heroes.

DO NOT READ ANY FURTHER UNTIL YOU HAVE WRITTEN DOWN AND TURNED IN THE FIVE NAMES.

Discussion may then center on some or all of the following questions.

1. The "Heroes" list contains the names of 50 men and 50 women. Are there more men or women represented in the final list(s)? If there are differences, how do you account for them? Is the original list weighted unfairly in terms of one sex by featuring more prominent males than females or vice versa? If so, how might that imbalance have been corrected? Did anyone feel an obligation to select both males and females? An obligation to select only one sex? Explain.

2. Did men's and women's selection patterns differ significantly? If so, why do you think this happened?

3. On the "Heroes" list of 100 people there are 20 blacks. How did blacks do in the final list(s)? Explain. What other blacks might have been included on the list?

4. If sexual preference (gay or straight) had been listed along with the name, or if the information had been known (as with sex and race), would the gays have been selected?

5. What areas of accomplishment are represented most frequently in the final list(s)? Why do you feel this is so?

6. How do you think the votes given here would differ if, say, your parents or your teachers did the voting? Explain.

7. Of the names on the "Heroes" list, which were the least well known? From what areas of accomplishment are these? How do you account for this?

8. What values do the class members hold that can be deduced from the final list of heroes? Are there any surprises?

HEROES

Bella Abzug	Joan Baez	Marlon Brando
Muhammad Ali	Pearl Bailey	Helen Gurley Brown
Idi Amin	James Baldwin	Anita Bryant
Neil Armstrong	Christiaan Barnard	Carol Burnett
Mary Kay Ash	Julian Bond	César Chávez

Julia Child
Shirley Chisholm
Mario Cuomo
Salvador Dali
Angela Davis
Sammy Davis, Jr.
Doris Day
Jeane Dixon
Clint Eastwood
Queen Elizabeth II
Werner Erhard
Jane Fonda
Betty Friedan
Boy George
Nikki Giovanni
Mikhail S. Gorbachev
Billy Graham
Wayne Gretzky
Patty Hearst
Lillian Hellman
Xaviera Hollander
Larry Holmes
Lee Iacocca
Jesse Jackson
Michael Jackson
Mick Jagger
Barbara Jordan
Ted Kennedy
Billie Jean King
Coretta King

Jeane Kirkpatrick
Ruhollah Khomeini
Ted Koppel
Cyndi Lauper
Sophia Loren
Shirley MacLaine
Charles Manson
Maharishi Mahesh Yogi
Liza Minnelli
Sun Myung Moon
Mary Tyler Moore
Patricia Murphy
Bill Murray
Ralph Nader
Louise Nevelson
Richard Nixon
Joyce Carol Oates
Sandra Day O'Connor
Jacqueline Kennedy Onassis
Dolly Parton
Pope John Paul II
Norman Vincent Peale
Isabel Perón
Sylvia Porter
Ayn Rand
Ronald Reagan
Vanessa Redgrave
Harry Reems
Mary Lou Retton
Jonas Salk

Phyllis Schlafly
Arnold Schwarzenegger
George P. Shultz
Bobby Seale
Tom Seaver
Fulton J. Sheen
Brooke Shields
O. J. Simpson
Frank Sinatra
B. F. Skinner
Margaret Chase Smith
Alexander Solzhenitsyn
Steven Spielberg
Sylvester Stallone
Elizabeth Taylor
Shirley Temple
Mother Teresa
Margaret Thatcher
John Travolta
Pauline Trigère
Margaret Truman
Tina Turner
Abigail van Buren
Gore Vidal
Barbara Walters
Lina Wertmuller
Roy Wilkins
Vanessa Williams
Stevie Wonder

39. THE EXERCISE OF POWER

Unit 20. Power in Interpersonal Relationships

Examine your most important interpersonal relationships in terms of (1) the power that you exert and (2) the power that is exerted on you.

Select one significant other and state the amount of power you exert over her or him and the amount that she or he exerts over you. Express the amount of power in terms of percentages; the total should add up to 100 percent for each column.

YOU EXERT OVER OTHER	POWER	OTHER EXERTS OVER YOU
_____	Referent	_____
_____	Legitimate	_____
_____	Reward	

_____	Coercive	_____
_____	Expert	_____
_____	Information	_____

Consider the following questions.

1. Research suggests that we would like the person who has reward power over us and dislike the person who has coercive power over us. Is this true in your situation? Explain why you think the relationships prevail in your case.

2. On what bases do most people attribute expert power to you? That is, in what fields or areas do you have expert power? How might you increase your expert power?

3. What type of power seems to work best when exerted on you? That is, what type of power enables people to control your behavior? Explain.

4. What power is least effective when exerted on you? Explain.

5. In what ways are reward and coercive power exerted over you? In what ways do you exert reward and coercive power over others?

6. To whom do you attribute legitimate power? Why?

7. Do you exercise legitimate power? Who attributes legitimate power to you? Explain.

8. What power is least effective when exerted on you? Why?

9. In what ways might you increase your interpersonal power?

10. Are you satisfied or dissatisfied with your responses to power and with your use of power? How would you like to change? What might you do to effect these changes?

40. SANDY

Unit 21. Conflict in Interpersonal Relationships

Sandy is a beautiful young woman, age 21, a senior in college. Sandy is majoring in biology and is an honor student; she plans to work toward her master's degree in biology at night while teaching high school during the day.

At the high school where Sandy has applied for a job, a committee of five members plus the school principal make all the hiring decisions. After reviewing Sandy's record—outstanding in every respect—the committee asks her in for a personal interview. This is a standard procedure with this high school. In this case, however, because Sandy's records and recommendations are so outstanding, the personal interview is regarded by the members of the committee and the principal as a formality. They are clearly eager to hire Sandy. Although there are other qualified applicants, none seems as outstanding as Sandy.

At the specified time, Sandy appears to meet the committee. The members look at each other in shocked amazement; it seems obvious to them that Sandy is _____.*
There is just no doubt that Sandy is, in fact, _____.

Thinking quickly, the principal, as committee chairperson, tells Sandy that the committee has fallen behind schedule and that they will see her in 15 minutes. Sandy leaves the room and sits outside, waiting to be called back in. Sandy is well aware of their reactions and knows why they asked her to wait outside. She has seen those reactions before and is not surprised. She is _____, and as she sits waiting she ponders what the committee will do.

The committee, now alone for 15 minutes, comes quickly to the point. The applicant is _____. "What should we do?" the principal asks.

Students should role-play members of the committee and reach a decision as to what they should do with regard to Sandy. The members of the committee are:

Mrs. Markham, the school principal
Mr. Ventri, the biology department chairperson
Miss Colson, teacher of physical education
Mr. Garcia, teacher of chemistry
Ms. Goldstein, teacher of Romance languages
Mr. Jackson, teacher of art

Approximately 10 to 20 minutes should be allowed for the discussion. After this time, the class members should discuss the interactions that took place in the role-playing session in terms of conflict and conflict resolution. This discussion should have no rigid structure and may focus on any of the concepts considered under conflict and conflict resolution.

41. WIN AS MUCH AS YOU CAN

Unit 21. Conflict in Interpersonal Relationships

This exercise is designed to explore conflict. Form "clusters" of eight persons. Each cluster consists of four teams of two members each. Visualizing the area as a clock, the four teams are placed at 12, 3, 6, and 9 o'clock. The teams should be far enough apart from each other so that they can communicate without the other teams' hearing them.

The game consists of ten rounds. In each round, each team selects X or Y. The selection is made on the basis of each team's prediction of what the other teams will select and the itemized "payoffs" as presented in the "Payoff Table." For each round, each team must select either X or Y. Both team members must agree on which letter to select.

The sequence of events should follow the "Score Sheet." For each round, the teams are allowed a certain amount of time (listed in the column headed "Time")

* Your instructor will fill in the blanks.

in which to make their selection of *X* or *Y.* After they reach their decision, the *X* or *Y* is recorded in the column headed "Choice." Only after each team has recorded its choices are the choices revealed. When the choices are revealed, refer to the Payoff Table to determine how many points each team wins or loses. For example, if two teams selected *X* and two teams selected *Y,* according to the Payoff Table the teams selecting *X* would each win 2 points and the teams selecting *Y* would each lose 2 points. Another example: If one team selected *Y* and three teams selected *X,* the team that selected *Y* would lose 3 points and the teams that selected *X* would win 1 point each.

The amount won or lost for each round should be noted in the appropriate column, and a balance should be noted in the column headed "Balance."

Note that for rounds 5, 8, and 10, the game is played a bit differently. Before conferring with one's partner, all teams in the cluster confer for three minutes. The teams may talk about anything they wish, but they may not mark their choices at this time. They can mark their choices only after private consultations with their partners, which take place immediately after the cluster conferences. Note also that these three rounds are bonus rounds; the amount won or lost in that round is multiplied by 3 in round 5, by 5 in round 8, and by 10 in round 10.

PAYOFF TABLE

4 *X*'s	lose 1 point each
3 *X*'s 1 *Y*	win 1 point each lose 3 points
2 *X*'s 2 *Y*'s	win 2 points each lose 2 points each
1 *X* 3 *Y*'s	win 3 points each lose 1 point each
4 *Y*s	win 1 point each

Consider the following questions only *after* you have played the game.

1. How would you describe the behavior of the members of the cluster? How would you describe your own behavior?

2. Is this behavior typical? That is, did you behave here as you would in a real-life situation?

3. How do you feel about the way you played the game? Are you pleased? Disappointed? Sorry? Guilty? Explain the basis for your feelings.

4. If you were playing for points on an examination or even for points toward your final grade in the course, would you have played differently? Explain. What if you were playing for money—say, $1 per point?

5. Were you surprised at the way in which other members of your cluster played? Explain.

Round	Time	Conference	Choice	Points Won	Points Lost	Balance
1	2 min.	partner				
2	1 min.	partner				
3	1 min.	partner				
4	1 min.	partner				
5	3 min. 1 min.	cluster partner		× 3 =	× 3 =	
6	1 min.	partner				
7	1 min.	partner				
8	3 min. 1 min.	cluster partner		× 5 =	× 5 =	
9	1 min.	partner				
10	3 min. 1 min.	cluster partner		× 10 =	× 10 =	Total =

42. PAT AND CHRIS: A CASE IN INTERPERSONAL CONFLICT

Unit 21. Conflict in Interpersonal Relationships
Unit 2. Axioms of Interpersonal Communication
Unit 6. Effectiveness in Interpersonal Communication
Unit 25. Understanding Relational Deterioration
Unit 26. Managing Relational Deterioration

The following brief dialogue was written to illustrate the seven unproductive conflict strategies discussed in the text (avoidance or redefinition, force, minimization, blame, silencers, gunnysacking, and beltlining) and to provide a stimulus for the consideration of alternative and more productive methods of conflict management.

Locate examples of each of the seven unproductive strategies and write or discuss alternative responses that represent more effective and more productive approaches to conflict management.

This dialogue may also be analyzed in terms of at least four principles of interpersonal communication discussed earlier, and you may wish as well to locate examples of the failure to recognize and act on these principles: (1) the irreversibility of communication; (2) the distinction between content and relationship messages and, particularly, the failure to hear and respond to relational messages; (3) the punctuation of communication events, especially the failure to see the sequence of events punctuated in any other way but one's own; and (4) owning one's own thoughts and feelings instead of attributing these to others. Explain how these combatants might have taken these principles into consideration in this particular conflict.

PAT AND CHRIS IN CONFLICT

Pat: It's me. Just came in to get my papers for the meeting tonight.

Chris: You're not going to another meeting tonight, are you?

Pat: I told you last month that I had to give this lecture to the new managers—on how to use some new research methods. What do you think I've been working on for the past two weeks? If you cared about what I do, you'd know that I was working on this lecture and that it was especially important that it go well.

Chris: What about shopping? We always do the shopping on Friday night.

Pat: The shopping will have to wait; this lecture is important.

Chris: Shopping is important too, and so are the children and so is my job and so is the leak in the basement that's been driving me crazy for the past week and that I've asked you to look at every day since then.

Pat: Get off it. We can do the shopping any time. Your job is fine and the children are fine and we'll get a plumber just as soon as I get his name from the Johnsons.

Chris: You always do that. You always think only you count, only you matter. Even when we were in school, your classes were the important ones, your papers, your tests were the important ones. Remember when I had that chemistry final and you had to have your history paper typed? We stayed up all night typing *your* paper. I failed chemistry, remember? That's not so good when you're pre-med! I supposed I should thank you for my not being a doctor? But you got your A in history. It's always been that way. You never give a damn what's important in my life.

Pat: I really don't want to talk about it. I'll only get upset and bomb out with the lecture. Forget it. I don't want to hear any more about it. So just shut up before I do something I should do more often.

Chris: You hit me and I'll call the cops. I'm not putting up with another black eye or another fat lip—never, never again.

Pat: Well, then, just shut up. I just don't want to talk about it anymore. Forget it. I have to give the lecture and that's that.

Chris: The children were looking forward to going shopping. Johnny wanted to get a new record, and Jennifer needed to get a book for school. You promised them.

Pat: I didn't promise anyone anything. You promised them and now you want me to take the blame. You know, you promise too much. You should only promise what you can deliver—like fidelity. Remember you promised to be faithful? Or did you forget that promise? Why don't you tell the kids that? Or do they already know? Were they here when you had your sordid affair? Did they see their loving parent loving some stranger?

Chris: I thought we agreed not to talk about that. You know how bad I feel about what happened. And anyway, that was six months ago. What has that to do with tonight?

Pat: You're the one who brought up promises, not me. You're always bringing up the past. You live in the past.

Chris: Well, at least the kids would have seen me enjoying myself—one enjoyable experience in eight years isn't too much, is it?

Pat: I'm leaving. don't wait up.

43. FRIENDSHIP FEELINGS

Unit 22. Friendship in Interpersonal Relationships

This experiential vehicle asks you to examine your feelings about being a friend. In responding to this "quiz," try to avoid thinking of what would be the "right" or the "best" choice; answer with your true feelings. Select only one alternative for each question. Respond to these questions now, before reading any further.

1. If Friend won a $1 million lottery, you would
   a. be extremely pleased.
   b. be pleased but feel it should have been you.
   c. be displeased but not exceptionally so.
   d. be resentful.

2. If you and Friend—who knew about the same as you—studied together for an examination and Friend got an A and you got a C, you would
   a. be pleased that Friend did so well but displeased that you did not do so well.
   b. be displeased at the wide discrepancy in grades.
   c. be resentful that Friend did well and you did not

3. If Friend called you up in the middle of the night because Friend was depressed, you would
   a. listen as long as Friend wanted you to.
   b. tell Friend that you were sleeping and that you will call back in the morning.
   c. tell Friend that this is not an appropriate time to call and hang up.

4. If Friend called you up in the middle of the night because Friend wanted to share the good news that Friend was going to be married, you would
   a. listen as long as Friend wanted you to.
   b. tell Friend that you were sleeping and that you would call back in the morning.
   c. tell Friend that this is not an appropriate time to call and hang up.

5. If you were eager to see a particular movie but Friend wanted to see another film, you would
   a. insist on seeing the movie you preferred.
   b. express your preference but give in to Friend's choice.
   c. discuss the merits of each movie and be amenable to whichever one seems best.
   d. not express your preference but simply agree to see the movie of Friend's choice.

6. If Friend sought you out for an hour or so, you would be most responsive, helpful, and willing to spend the time with Friend
   a. in sharing Friend's joy at having just received an important promotion.
   b. in consoling Friend over just being fired.
   c. in helping Friend accomplish some important work-related task.

Unlike most tests, there are no correct or incorrect answers here. These questions were designed to assist you in bringing to a more conscious awareness some of your feelings about what friendship involves. Each response entails a very different definition of what a friend is and what a friend should be. For example, in number 6, I think the "best" choice is *a* because I think that the most important function a friend can serve is unselfishly to share a friend's joy. Alternative *c*, I think, is the next best choice since we are again helping a friend to do something that will benefit only Friend. Alternative *b*, while still a respectable and worthwhile choice, is the least defining of friendship largely because it is relatively easy to console someone. In fact, we readily console people who are not our friends. Many take a kind of pleasure in sharing the grief of another; we have been conditioned to do this since we were children. But our competitive natures have led us to compete even with our closest friends. Therefore, to select either alternative *a* or *c* means that we must put our friend above this very natural, well-learned competitive response. Obviously with different assumptions about friendship, different alternatives will be selected.

In a manner similar to that offered for question 6, in groups of four to six, consider each of the alternatives for each of the questions.

44. FRIENDSHIP BEHAVIORS

Unit 22. Friendship in Interpersonal Relationships

Five specific situations are presented here. For each situation indicate (1) how you, as a friend, would respond, by writing the word *would* in the appropriate space, (2) how you think a good friend should respond, by writing *should* in the appropriate space, and (3) the qualities or characteristics you feel a good friend should have relevant to these six situations, by completing the sentence, ". . . because a good friend should . . ."

After completing all five situations, respond to the questions presented at the end of this exercise—alone, in dyads, or in small groups of five, six, or seven persons.

FRIENDSHIP AND LOVE

Two of your close friends have been going together for a few months. They seem to care for each other a great deal, and the relationship seems to be a mutually productive one. The only problem is that you are in love with one of them. At times you feel the love is returned, but perhaps because you have been silent about your feelings, nothing has been said. You wonder what you should do.

_____ _____ a. Confess your love to the one you love.
_____ _____ b. Say nothing.
_____ _____ c. Confess your love to both friends.
_____ _____ d. Confess your love to the friend you are not in love with and see the reaction before doing anything else.
_____ _____ e. (Other—you suggest an alternative.)

. . . because a good friend should _____.

FRIENDSHIP AND MONEY

Your closest friend has just gotten into serious debt through some misjudgment. You have saved $2,500 over the past few years and plan to buy a car on graduating from college. Your friend asks to borrow the money, which could not be repaid for at least four or possibly five years. Although you do not need the car for work or for any other necessity, you have been looking forward to the day when you could get your own car. You've worked hard for it and feel you deserve the car, but you are also concerned about the plight of your friend, who would be in serious trouble without the $2,500 loan. You wonder what you should do.

———— ———— a. Lend your friend the money.

———— ———— b. Tell your friend that you have been planning to buy the car for the last few years and that you cannot lend him or her the money.

———— ———— c. Give your friend the money and tell your friend that there is no need to pay it back; after all, your friend already has enough problems without having to worry about paying it back.

———— ———— d. Tell your friend that you already gave the $2,500 to your brother but that you would certainly have lent him or her the money if you still had it.

———— ———— e. (Other—you suggest an alternative.)

... because a good friend should _____.

FRIENDSHIP AND ADVICE

Two friends, Pat and Chris, have been dating for the past several months. They will soon enter into a more permanent relationship after graduating from college. Pat is now having second thoughts and is currently having an affair with another friend, Lee. Chris tells you that there is probably an affair going on (which you know to be true) and seeks your advice. You are the only one who is friendly with all three parties. You wonder what you should do.

———— ———— a. Tell Chris everything you know.

———— ———— b. Tell Pat to be honest with Chris.

———— ———— c. Say nothing; don't get involved.

———— ———— d. Suggest to Chris that the more permanent relationship planned should be reconsidered, but don't be specific.

———— ———— e. (Other—you suggest an alternative.)

... because a good friend should _____.

FRIENDSHIP AND DEPRESSION

One of your close friends had been having problems and seems to be constantly depressed. For the past month your friend has been calling you or visiting you to tell you all about these problems and depression, asking your advice, and rehashing everything imaginable. These discussions have succeeded only in depressing you, but this seems to have gone unnoticed by your friend. Although you have recommended professional help, your friend won't listen. You wonder what you should do.

_____ _____ a. Continue to listen in the hope that the depression will lessen.

_____ _____ b. Tell your friend that you just cannot continue to listen to all these problems because they are depressing you and getting nothing accomplished.

_____ _____ c. Tell your friend to seek professional help or you will withdraw from the relationship.

_____ _____ d. Lay some of your depression on your friend and see what happens.

_____ _____ e. (Other—you suggest an alternative.)

. . . because a good friend should _____.

FRIENDSHIP AND CHEATING

Your anthropology instructor is giving a midterm and is grading it on a curve. Your close friend somehow manages to secure a copy of the examination a few days before it is scheduled. Since you are a close friend, the examination is offered to you as well. You refuse to look at it. The examination turned out to be even more difficult than you had anticipated, the highest grade being a 68 (except for your friend's, which was a 96). According to the system of curving used by this instructor, each grade will be raised 4 points. But this means that the highest grade (aside from your friend's) will be only a 72, or a C−. A few students will receive C−, about 30 to 40 percent will receive D, and the rest (over 50 percent) will receive F. Although only you and your friend know what happened, you know that the instructor and the entire class are wondering why this one student, never particularly outstanding, did so well. After curving, your grade is 70 (C−). You wonder what you should do.

_____ _____ a. Tell your friend to confess or you will tell the instructor yourself (although you could not prove it).

_____ _____ b. Tell the instructor what happened (even though you could not prove anything).

_____ _____ c. Say nothing; don't get involved.

_____ _____ d. (Other—you suggest an alternative.)

. . . because a good friend should _____.

For Discussion

1. Were there significant differences between the *would* and the *should* responses? How do you account for these differences?

2. What values or standards or models did you use in making the *should* responses? Why did you choose them?

3. With which situation did you experience the greatest difficulty in making a decision as to what you would do? Can you explain why?

4. Does friendship necessarily entail the willingness to make sacrifices?

5. How would you define *friend*?

45. GIFT GIVING

Unit 23. Love in Interpersonal Relationships

This exercise is an excellent one to use at the end of the semester as a kind of final parting "gift" that one member of the class gives to another.

In groups of five or six persons, each member indicates a "gift" that he or she would wish to obtain for each of the other members of the group. (It is sometimes helpful to write down the names of each person in the group and, next to each name, the gift you would want these people to have.

These gifts are symbolic gifts and are not actually given. They are more like wishes for the other person. As such the gifts may be material or spiritual, concrete or abstract, expensive or inexpensive, general or specific. In all cases, however, they must be positive gifts.

Discussion may center on the reasons for the selections made, their appropriateness or inappropriateness, what they say about the person for whom the gift is intended, what they say about the relationship between the persons, and so on.

46. POSITIVE WORDS

Unit 23. Love in Interpersonal Relationships

This exercise is performed by the entire class. One person is "it" and takes a seat in the front of the room or in the center of the circle. (It is possible, though not desirable, for the person to stay where she or he normally sits.) Going around in a circle or from left to right, each person says something positive about the person who is "it."

For this exercise, only volunteers should be chosen. Students may be encouraged but should not be forced to participate. It is best done when the students know each other fairly well.

Persons must tell the truth; that is, they are not allowed to say anything about a person that they do not believe. At the same time, however, all statements must be positive. Only positive words are allowed during this exercise. Persons may, however, "pass" and say nothing. No one may ask why something was said or why something was not said. The positive words may refer to the person's looks, behavior, intelligence, clothes, mannerisms, and so on. One may also say, "I don't know you very well, but you seem friendly," or "You seem honest," or whatever. These statements, too, must be believed to be true.

After everyone has said something, another person becomes "it." After all volunteers have been "it," consider the following questions individually.

1. Describe your feelings when thinking about becoming "it."

2. How did you feel while people were saying positive words?

3. What comments were the most significant to you?

4. Were you "it"? If so, would you be willing to be "it" again? If not, why not?

5. How do you feel now that the exercise is over? Did it make you feel better? Why do you suppose it had the effect it did?

6. What implications may be drawn from this exercise for application to everyday living?

7. Will this exercise change your behavior in any way?

After you have completed all these questions, share with the entire class whatever comments you would like to make.

47. ANALYZING A FAMILY TRANSACTION

Unit 24. Primary Relationships, Families, and Interpersonal Communication
Unit 21. Conflict in Interpersonal Relationships
Unit 25. Understanding Relational Deterioration
Unit 26. Managing Relational Deterioration

Carefully read the transaction, paying particular attention to the following communication issues:

1. the communication problems facing this family
2. the strategies that this family uses in communicating and in dealing with its problems
3. the effectiveness or ineffectiveness of their strategies
4. the alternative strategies that might prove more effective in dealing with these problems—that is, if you were called in by this family to analyze their communication patterns and make suggestions for their improvement, what would you say?

Small groups may be formed in which each student pools insights and recommendations concerning the interaction. Each small group may then report to the entire class concerning the problems identified and the recommendations they would make for the improvement of the family's communications. An alternative procedure is to have a discussion in which the class as a whole seeks to identify the major communication problems and to offer solutions for the improvement of the interpersonal communication process in this particular family.

In either case, some attention should be directed to the formulation of general principles that might be advanced for effectively communicating within families. That is, what general rules should members of a family follow in order to make their communications more effective?

An Interpersonal Transaction

Participants

Margaret: mother, housewife, junior high school history teacher; 41 years old
Fred: father, gas station attendant; 46 years old
Diane: daughter, receptionist in an art galley; 22 years old
Stephen: son, college freshman; 18 years old

Margaret is in the kitchen finishing preparing dinner—lamb chops, Fred's favorite, though she does not care much for them. Diane is going through some records. Stephen is reading one of his textbooks. Fred comes in from work and throws his jacket over the couch; it falls to the floor.

Fred (*bored but angry, looking at Stephen*): What the hell did you do with the car last night? It stunk like hell. And you left all your damn school papers all over the back seat.

Stephen (*as if expecting the angry remarks*): What did I do now?

Fred: You stunk up the car with your damn pot or whatever you kids smoke, and you left the car looking like hell. Can't you hear?

Stephen (*says nothing; goes back to looking at his book but without really reading*).

Margaret: Dinner's almost ready. Come on. Wash up and sit down.

[At dinner]

Diane: Mom, I'm going to go to the shore for the weekend with some friends from work.

Margaret: OK. When will you be leaving?

Diane: Friday afternoon, right after work.

Fred: Like hell you're going. No more going to the shore with *that* group.

Margaret: Fred, they're nice people. Why shouldn't she go?

Fred: Because I said so, OK? Finished. Closed.

Diane (*mumbling*): I'm 22 years old and he gives me problems. You make me feel like a kid, like some stupid little kid.

Fred: Get married and then you can tell your husband what to do.

Diane: I wish I could.

Stephen: But nobody'll ask her.

Margaret: Why should she get married? She's got a good life—good job, nice friends, good home. Listen, I was talking with Elizabeth and Cara this morning and they both feel they've just wasted their lives. They raised a family and what have they got? They got **nothing?** (*to Diane*): And don't think sex is so great either; it isn't, believe me.

Fred: Well, they're idiots.

Margaret: *They're* idiots? (*snidely*) Yeah, I guess they are.

Diane: Joanne's getting married.

Margaret: Who's Joanne?

Stephen: That creature who lives with that guy Michael.

Fred: Watch your mouth, wise-ass. Don't be disrespectful to your mother or I'll teach you how to act right.

Margaret: Well, how do you like the dinner?

[Prolonged silence]

Diane: Do you think I should be in the wedding party if Joanne asks me? I think she will; we always said we'd be in each other's wedding.

Margaret: Sure, why not. It'll be nice.

Fred: I'm not going to no wedding, no matter who's in it.

Stephen: Me neither.

Diane: I hope you'll both feel that way when I get married.

Stephen: By then I'll be too old to remember I got a sister.

Margaret: How's school?

Stephen: I hate it. It's so big. Nobody knows anyone. You sit in these big lecture halls and listen to some creep talk. I really feel lonely and isolated, like nobody knows I'm alive.

Fred: Listen to that college talk bullshit. Get yourself a woman and you won't feel lonely, instead of hanging out with those pothead faggots.

Diane (*looking to Margaret, giving a sigh as if to say, "Here we go again"*).

Margaret (*to Diane, in whisper*): I know.

Diane: Mom? Do you think I'm getting fat?

Stephen: Yes.

Fred: Just don't get fat in the stomach or you'll get thrown out of here.

Margaret: No, I don't notice it.

Diane: Well, I just thought I might be.

Stephen (*pushing his plate away*): I'm finished; I'm going out.

Fred: Sit down and finish your damn supper. You think I work all day for you to throw the food away? You wanna go smoke your dope?

Stephen: No. I just want to get away from you—forever.

Margaret: You mean we both work all day; it's just that I earn a lot more than you do.

Fred: *No,* I mean I work and you baby-sit.

Margaret: Teaching junior high school history isn't baby-sitting.

Fred: What the hell is it then? You don't teach them anything.

Margaret (*to Diane*): You see? You're better off single. I should've stayed single. Instead . . . Oh, well. I was young and stupid. It was my own fault for getting involved with a loser. Just don't you make the same mistake.

Fred (*to Stephen*): Go ahead. Leave the table. Leave the house. Who cares what you do?

48. PRIMARY RELATIONSHIP COMMUNICATION

Unit 24. Primary Relationships, Families, and
        Interpersonal Communication
Unit 25. Understanding Relational Deterioration

This exercise is designed to encourage you to examine more closely the communication patterns operative in your own primary relationship(s). The exercise is divided into a number of related phases.

1. Select the primary relationship on which you wish to focus for this experience.

The primary relationship may be within your immediate family, you and your closest intimate, you and your husband or wife, your extended family, or any other primary relationship. Before progressing any further, it will help if you record all the names of the individuals in this relationship and their relationship to you.

2. For each of the 14 communication characteristics listed in the "Primary Relationship Communication Questionnaire," indicate the member of the primary relationship to whom this characteristic applies most closely. Do this for all 14 characteristics before reading any further.

Primary Relationship Communication Questionnaire

For each characteristic, indicate the name of the member of the primary relationship to whom it most closely applies.

1. Has the greatest general credibility: _____

2. Self-discloses the most: _____

3. Self-discloses the least: _____

4. Is the most open-minded: _____

5. Is the most closed-minded: _____

6. Has the final say in making the important decisions: _____

7. Is the most authoritarian: _____

8. Is the most apt to avoid conflict rather than confront it: _____

9. Is the most apt to become emotional and to use an emotional strategy in conflict situations: _____

10. Tries hardest to achieve empathic understanding: _____

11. Is the most apt to use unfair methods in conflict: _____

12. Has the greatest commitment to the preservation of the relationship: _____

13. Has changed the most since the relationship began: _____

14. Has the most intrapersonal conflicts: _____

3. After all 14 statements have been answered, write down one or more implications of your answers for the relationship as a whole or for the other members of the relationship as individuals. For example, let us assume that you are concentrating on your immediate family (you, your mother, and your father). For "has the highest general credibility," you might note that this applies foremost to your father. This attribution of credibility to your father has various implications. One implication might be that your father is the one who is looked to for information or advice and the one who is expected to make most of the decisions. Another implication might be that you resent this unchallenged credibility that your mother attributes to him, and this in turn causes you purposely to avoid asking his advice.

4. After each person has completed the questionnaire and has indicated one or more implications for each characteristic, discuss your responses in groups of five or six. In discussing your responses, try to develop hypotheses that might be applicable to primary relationship communication in general. Such hypotheses would be based on reasonable assumptions as to the general principles operating in primary relationship communication. From our example, we might formulate the hypothesis that "in a nuclear family, it is the father who has the greatest credibility." Another hypothesis might be, "The most credible person is resented the most by the second most credible person or by the person who is growing intellectually at the most rapid rate." Each group should keep a list of their hypotheses.

5. After all groups have discussed the characteristics and have developed a set of hypotheses, share these with the entire class and consider, for example:

a. Which hypotheses seem most reasonable? Which seem to be agreed upon by most groups?

b. How might you go about testing the validity of the various hypotheses? That is, how might you go about discovering if these hypotheses are true or false?

49. THE TELEVISION RELATIONSHIP

Unit 24. Primary Relationships, Families, and
Interpersonal Communication
Unit 25. Understanding Relational Deterioration

This exercise is designed to enable you to gain some insight and experience in the difficult task of analyzing family communication. The class should be divided into several small groups, each of which should select a different television program that centers on a family. Suitable examples are "The Jeffersons," "Who's the Boss?," "Webster," "Dallas," "Dynasty," "Knots Landing," and "Falcon Crest."

Each member should watch the assigned television show and respond to the questions in this exercise. After viewing the show and completing the questions, members should meet in their small groups and discuss their responses, working toward consensus in their answers. After recording the group's responses (noting any significant differences of opinion), each small group should report to the entire class the results of its discussions. A general class discussion should then follow and might concentrate on the implications of the responses to question 8.

1. Who constitutes the "family"? List the members of the family or primary relationship and identify their major roles within the family structure. Are there some persons on the show whose status in the family is not quite clear? That is, is there doubt as to whether some persons are or are not members of the family? Identify these and explain the reasons for the lack of a clear status.

2. In the text we identified several characteristics that all primary relationships or families had in common: relatively clear definition of roles, commitment to the

preservation of the relationship, a recognition of responsibilities to each other, a shared history and future, and a shared living space. Are these characteristics evident in the family portrayed in the program you viewed? Are there other characteristics that might be offered to define their relationships? Are there characteristics mentioned in the text that are not evident in the program?

3. What factors seem to hold this family together? Identify specific elements of plot or dialogue that demonstrate these factors.

4. What type of communication pattern best seems to describe this particular family? You may find it convenient to begin by singling out selected dyads within the family and identifying the type of communication pattern that best describes their interactions. You may then expand the dyad to include more and more people until the entire family is included. Diagram the communication pattern(s). Can you identify specific elements of dialogue that led to your conclusions? Do the communication patterns used most frequently in the show cause any difficulties? Explain.

5. In the text, a number of reasons were cited as potential causes of conflict development in primary or family relationships: intimacy claims, intimacies outside the primary relationship or family, undefined expectations, sexual problems and differences, work and financial difficulties. Others, briefly noted, were intrapersonal conflicts, privateness, change, and different standards and role expectations. Were the causes of conflict noted here operative in the conflicts in the episode viewed or more generally in the program's history? What other causes might be noted? Are there causes noted here that do not seem to operate in television shows? Why?

6. Identify the conflict strategies used most often by the central characters in this show. Are these strategies effective as used?

7. If the characters on this television show constituted a real family and wished to improve their family communication, what suggestions would you make? It is particularly important here that you fit the suggestions to the specific individual and to the specific family situation. For this question, draw not only on the suggestions noted in Units 6, 24, and 26 (empathic understanding, self-disclosure, openness to change, fighting fair, and the acceptance of less than perfection) but also on those discussed elsewhere in the text.

8. It is often difficult to see what these shows teach us about families and primary relationships and about the communication that goes on within them because it is difficult for us to separate what we gain from television from that gained through other means. Further, we probably internalize a great deal from watching television that we fail to recognize consciously as having its origin in television. So it may prove helpful to fantasize a bit and imagine a Martian coming to earth, trying to discover something about what a family is and how it operates. For the purposes of this exercise, assume that this Martian has no information other than that gained from this television series. What would our Martian conclude about earth families and primary relationships? State this information in the form of principles or statements about what constitutes a "family" and about what takes place in a family or primary relationship. Cover the major areas discussed in this unit: the characteristics that all families have in common, the factors that keep the family together, the communication pattern that best describes the family's interactions, the sources of conflict, the conflict strategies used, and the application of the principles of effective interpersonal interaction.

50. MALE AND FEMALE

| Unit 25. Understanding Relational Deterioration |
| Unit 26. Managing Relational Deterioration |

This exercise is designed to increase your awareness of matters that may prevent meaningful interpersonal communication between the sexes. It is also designed to encourage meaningful dialogue among class members.

The women and the men are separated, and one group goes into another classroom. The task of each group is to write on the blackboard all the things that they dislike having the other sex think, believe, do, or say about them in general. Group members should write on the board all the things that members of the opposite sex think, believe, say, or do in reference to them that they dislike and that prevent meaningful interpersonal communication from taking place.

After this is done, the groups should change rooms. The men discuss what the women have written and the women discuss what the men have written. After satisfactory discussion has taken place, the groups should get together in the original room. Discussion might center on the following questions.

1. Were there any surprises?

2. Were there any disagreements? That is, did the members of one sex write anything that the members of the other sex argued they do not believe, think, do, or say?

3. How do you suppose the ideas about the other sex got started?

4. Is there any reliable evidence in support of the beliefs of the men about the women or the women about the men?

5. What is the basis for the things that are disliked? Put differently, why was each statement written on the blackboard?

6. What kind of education or training program (if any) do you feel is needed to eliminate these problems?

7. In what specific ways do these beliefs, thoughts, actions, and statements prevent meaningful interpersonal communication?

8. How do you feel now that these matters have been discussed?

Sources

The general idea for Experiential Vehicle 2 owes its formulation to an exercise that appeared in Jon A. Blaubaugh and Jim Quiggins, *Instructor's Manual to Accompany Patton and Griffin's* Interpersonal Communication in Action, 3d ed. (New York: Harper & Row, 1981), pp. 28–31. Experiential Vehicle 4, "The Stranger" (though in a somewhat different form) was suggested by James C. McCroskey, Carl E. Larsen, and Mark L. Knapp in their *Teacher's Manual* for *An Introduction to Interpersonal Communication* (Englewood Cliffs, N.J.: Prentice-Hall, 1971).

Experiential Vehicle 7 was inspired by William V. Haney, "Serial Communication of Information in Organizations," in *Communication: Concepts and Processes*, 3d ed., Joseph A. DeVito, ed. (Englewood Cliffs, N.J.: Prentice-Hall, 1981).

The general idea for Experiential Vehicle 14 comes from Gerard Egan, *Encounter: Group Processes for Interpersonal Growth* (Belmont, Calif.: Brooks/Cole, 1970). The questionnaire presented in Experiential Vehicle 15 is modeled after those developed by Sidney M. Jourard in *Disclosing Man to Himself* (New York: Van Nostrand Reinhold, 1968) and *The Transparent Self*, rev. ed. (New York, Van Nostrand Reinhold, 1971).

The nature of *E*-prime, featured in Experiential Vehicle 23, is discussed in detail in D. David Bourland, Jr., "A Linguistic Note: Writing in *E*-Prime," *General Semantics Bulletin* 32 and 33 (1965–1966). Experiential Vehicle 24 is taken from Joseph A. DeVito, *General Semantics: Guide and Workbook*, rev. ed. (DeLand, Fla.: Everett/Edwards, 1974), p. 55, and is modeled on exercises developed by William V. Haney.

Experiential Vehicle 25 was suggested by Professor Jean Civikly.

Experiential Vehicles 30 and 31 are based on Robert Sommer, *Personal Space: The Behavioral Basis of Design* (Englewood Cliffs, N.J.: Prentice-Hall, 1969).

Experiential Vehicle 34 is based on Joel R. Davitz, *The Communication of Emotional Meaning* (New York: McGraw-Hill, 1964). Although most books on nonverbal communication discuss sex differences, I relied for Experiential Vehicle 35 on the excellent summaries in Judee K. Burgoon and Thomas Saine, *The Unspoken Dialogue* (Boston: Houghton Mifflin, 1978) and Barbara Eakins and Gene Eakins, *Sex Differences in Communication* (Boston: Houghton Mifflin, 1978).

Experiential Vehicle 39 was inspired by the research of James McCroskey, Virginia Richmond, and their colleagues reported in Unit 20. Experiential Vehicle 40 owes its formulation to an exercise by William Gellerman in *A Handbook of Structured Experiences for Human Relations Training*, vol. 2, J. William Pfeiffer and John E. Jones, eds. (LaJolla, Calif.: University Associates, 1974).

Handbook Part II. Review Quizzes

1. TERMINOLOGICAL MAZE: REVIEW QUIZ FOR PART 1, INTERPERSONAL COMMUNICATION PRELIMINARIES

Fifteen terms used in the study of interpersonal communication are hidden in the "Terminological Maze," p. 448. The terms may be read forward, backward, up, down, or diagonally but are always in a straight line. The terms may overlap, and individual letters may be used more than once. The terms are those used in the first six units; their definitions and some identifying clues follow.

1. a relationship in which one person's behavior is the stimulus for similar behavior from the other person
2. what effective communication is
3. the moral dimension of communication
4. feeling what another person feels
5. has physical, temporal, and social-psychological dimensions
6. is always present in a communication interaction and interferes with one's receiving the message sent
7. present in all communications but often difficult to locate and measure
8. a type of message that provides the source with information as to the effect she or he is having; may be positive or negative
9. a basis for ethics
10. may be either verbal or nonverbal
11. language is one example
12. a postulate or commonly accepted truism
13. most prefer the positive type but seem to prefer even a negative one to none at all
14. the geometric figure that seems best to describe communication
15. when there is great overlap, there is a greater likelihood of effective communication (field of ———)

2. DEFINING DEFINITIONS: REVIEW QUIZ FOR PART 2, THE SELF IN INTERPERSONAL COMMUNICATION

Here are some of the significant concepts introduced in Part Two. Identify the concept defined in each of the following statements.

1. A model of the self, consisting of the open, blind, hidden, and unknown selves.

L	A	C	I	R	T	E	M	M	Y	S
A	X	I	Y	O	Q	T	Y	L	E	T
B	I	R	A	U	E	H	E	D	E	R
C	O	C	A	F	T	I	O	K	L	O
M	M	L	U	A	U	C	I	Z	O	K
P	W	E	P	M	E	S	S	A	G	E
T	N	M	O	T	X	E	T	N	O	C
C	E	S	I	O	N	P	I	D	E	I
E	A	E	I	U	Y	Q	C	V	I	O
F	B	I	P	U	W	M	P	S	L	H
F	E	E	D	B	A	C	K	A	B	C
E	X	P	E	R	I	E	N	C	E	E

2. This person sees others as well adjusted and generally effective but sees himself or herself as maladjusted and ineffective.

3. "The position of genuine heroes and princes, heroines and princesses." These people approach and solve problems constructively. They have valid expectations about themselves and others and accept themselves and others as basically good, worthy, and significant human beings.

4. From out of all our early experiences, particularly from the verbal and nonverbal messages received from our parents, we develop these, and for the most part follow them throughout our lives.

5. A type of communication in which information about the self that is normally kept hidden is communicated to another person.

6. The mode of noninvolvement; a manner of revealing the self that is only pseudo self-disclosure; an approach that details some facts of the individual's life but does not really invite involvement from listeners.

7. The generalizing of virtue from one area to another; a process whereby we perceive a person as credible or knowledgeable in several areas because of that person's credibility or knowledge in one area.

8. A lack of assertiveness in only certain kinds of contexts, for example, those that create a great deal of anxiety or those in which authority must be exercised.

9. Individuals who are willing to stand up for their own rights, who speak their minds and welcome others' doing likewise; people who act in their own best interest, stand up for themselves without undue anxiety, express their feelings honestly and comfortably, and exercise their own rights without denying these rights to others.

10. A fear of communication that is specific to a situation rather than a fear of communication in all its forms.

3. MATCHING LANGUAGE JARGON: REVIEW QUIZ FOR PART 3, VERBAL MESSAGES

Match up the definitions with the concepts.

1. a system whose "direct energetic consequences are biologically irrelevant"
2. openness, creativity
3. the characteristic of language that enables us to communicate about matters remote in time and space
4. vocabulary terms that are derived particularly from cant and argot that are understood by most persons but would not normally be used in formal communications
5. the principle of verbal interaction that refers to the notion that communication may take place only to the extent that the communicators share the same system of signals
6. the specialized vocabulary of a disreputable or underworld subculture
7. the technical language of a professional class, for example, professors, doctors, or lawyers
8. verbal behavior that is forbidden by a society or social group
9. "nice" words that are designed to make unpleasant topics seem less unpleasant
10. the emotional, subjective, personal meaning

a. polarization
b. slang
c. connotation
d. adjustment
e. euphemism
f. specialized system
g. jargon
h. indiscrimination
i. taboo
j. productivity
k. denotation
l. semantic differentiation
m. argot
n. intensional orientation
o. displacement

11. an objective definition; the type of definition found in a dictionary
12. a measurement of connotative meaning that uses seven-point bipolar scales and measures the evaluation, potency, and activity dimensions of terms

13. the tendency to view and describe the world in terms of opposite extremes
14. the tendency to view people, objects, and events in terms of their labels rather than in terms of the way they actually exist and operate
15. a misevaluation resulting from a failure to see each individual, object, or event as unique and different

4. NONVERBAL TRUTHS AND FALSEHOODS: REVIEW QUIZ FOR PART 4, NONVERBAL MESSAGES

Indicate whether each of the following statements is true or false. If a statement is false, explain why it is false and rewrite it so that it is true.

1. All contradictory (or mixed) messages are double-binding.

2. Nonverbal behavior sometimes serves a metacommunicational function.

3. Emblems are nonverbal behaviors that translate words or phrases rather directly, for example, the OK sign or the peace sign.

4. Regulators are nonverbal behaviors that accompany and literally illustrate the verbal messages.

5. Generally, fathers touch their children more than mothers do.

6. College students report that they are touched more by their same-sex friends than by their opposite-sex friends.

7. The closest proxemic distance Edward Hall identifies is personal distance.

8. Territoriality refers to a possessive or ownership-like reaction to an area of space.

9. All cultures seem to treat silence in the same way; all cultures seem to attribute the same meanings to silence.

10. Paralanguage is the verbal but nonvocal dimension of speech.

11. Generally, it has been found that slow talkers are more persuasive than fast talkers.

12. Two reasons why speakers should speak at a rate slower than normal are that comprehension is improved and that listeners prefer slower-than-normal speech.

13. Affect displays are always unintentional.

14. While verbal language is governed by rules, nonverbal communication is not.

15. The relative status of the individuals in a dyad has no influence on who is permitted to touch whom.

5. RESEARCH FINDINGS AND THEORIES ON INTERPERSONAL RELATIONSHIPS: REVIEW QUIZ FOR PART 5, INTERPERSONAL RELATIONSHIPS

Here are 20 statements dealing with interpersonal relationships that have been discussed in the text. Some are supported by research findings and well-conceived theories; others are contradicted by the research findings and theories. Which are true? Which are false? For those that are false, indicate why they are false and rewrite them so that they are true.

1. In most instances, when a relationship deteriorates there is a process of depenetration in which the breadth and the depth of the relationship become more narrow and shallow, more closely resembling relationships in their beginning stages.

2. Although attractive people will be given preference by uneducated individuals, both attractive and unattractive persons are treated in the same way by educated individuals.

3. Children younger than, say, 6 or 7 do not have preferences based on physical attractiveness.

4. The qualities that men and women judge as important in a partner are, for the most part, the same.

5. On the basis of the gain-loss theory we would hypothesize that increases in rewards will have less impact than will constant invariant rewards. That is, we will like a person more if that person has always liked us and less if that person's liking for us increases over time.

6. On the basis of the matching hypothesis we would predict that when people are given the opportunity to ask a person for a date, they will select the most attractive person to ask first, the second most attractive person to ask next, and so on until a yes response is obtained.

7. Generally, there is more research evidence supporting similarity than complementarity in attraction.

8. Friendship, when compared with love, offers a greater chance for both satisfaction and frustration, for both happiness and pain.

9. According to the two-factor theory of love, we would expect physiological arousal from running or fighting to increase the likelihood of love occurring.

10. Although men and women seem to experience love to a similar degree, men indicate greater love for their same-sex friends than do women.

11. Research on conflict resolution in primary relationships supports the conclusion that men and women are today using the same strategies for resolving such conflicts.

12. When a relationship breaks up, it is generally the more physically attractive person who exits first.

13. Sexual frequency is closely related to a couple's chances of survival.

14. Open relationships are more likely to survive than closed (sexually exclusive) relationships.

15. The stability of a relationship is endangered if the husband does little or no housework.

16. Generally, the partner who leaves a relationship is the more ambitious, the one who is more devoted to work.

17. Couples who spend a great deal of time apart and, say, take separate vacations are more likely to stay together; absence makes the heart grow fonder.

18. Money arguments create problems for cohabitors but not for same-sex couples.

19. Marriages in which the wife is financially independent are more likely to break up than marriages in which the wife is financially dependent.

20. Married couples and cohabitors who are dissatisfied with their income level or living standard are more likely to separate than those who are satisfied.

Glossary

Listed here are definitions of the technical terms of interpersonal communication—the words that are peculiar or unique to this discipline. These definitions should make new or difficult terms a bit easier to understand. For the most part, the words included here are used in this text. Also included are other terms that may be used in the conduct of a course in interpersonal communication. All italicized terms in definitions appear as entries in the glossary. For more extensive coverage of the terminology of communication, see my *The Communication Handbook: A Dictionary* (New York: Harper & Row, 1986).

Abstraction. A general concept derived from a class of objects; a part representation of some whole.

Abstraction process. The process by which a general concept is derived from specifics; the process by which some (never all) characteristics of an object, person, or event are perceived by the senses or included in some term, phrase, or sentence.

Accent. The stress or emphasis that is placed on a syllable when pronounced.

Accommodation. A state of cold-war conflict; a condition in which the parties, though still in conflict, agree not to battle; a state in which the conflicting individuals have adjusted to each other's position and in which interpersonal communication may take place although real cooperation is absent.

Action language. Movements of the body—for example, the way in which one walks, runs, or sits.

Active listening. A process of putting together into some meaningful whole the listener's understanding of the speaker's total message—the verbal and the nonverbal, the content and the feelings.

Adaptors. Nonverbal behaviors that, when emitted in private or in public without being seen, serve some kind of need and occur in their entirety—for example, scratching one's head until the itch is eliminated.

Adjustment (principle of). The principle of verbal interaction that claims that communication may take place only to the extent that the parties communicating share the same system of signals.

Affect displays. Movements of the facial area that convey emotional meaning—for example, anger, fear, and surprise.

Agapic love. Compassionate love; self-giving love; spiritual love; altruistic love.

Allness. The assumption that all can be known or is known about a given person, issue, object, or event.

Alter adaptors. Nonverbal movements (see *adaptors*) learned in the manipulation of material things, for example, changing a tire.

Ambiguity. The condition in which a word or phrase may be interpreted as having more than one meaning.

Analogic communication. Communication consisting of continuous rather than discrete signals; nonverbal communication systems are in most instances analogic. See *digital communication.*

Arbitrariness. The feature of human language that refers to the fact that there is no

453

real or inherent relationship between the form of a word and its meaning. If we do not know anything of a particular language, we could not examine the form of a word and thereby discover its meaning.

Argot. A kind of *sublanguage; cant* and *jargon* of a particular class, generally an underworld or criminal class, which is difficult and sometimes impossible for outsiders to understand.

Assertiveness. A willingness to stand up for one's rights but with respect for the rights of others.

Assimilation. A process of message distortion in which messages are reworked to conform to our own attitudes, prejudices, needs, and values.

Attention. The process of responding to a stimulus or stimuli; usually some consciousness of responding is implied.

Attitude. A predisposition to respond for or against an object, person, or position.

Attraction. The state or process by which one individual is drawn to another, by having a highly positive evaluation of that other person.

Attractiveness. The degree to which one is perceived to be physically attractive and to possess a pleasing personality.

Attribution theory. A theory concerned with the processes involved in attributing causation to a person's behavior.

Balance. A state of psychological comfort in which all the attitude objects in our minds are related as we would want them to be or as we would psychologically expect them to be.

Barriers to communication. Those factors (physical or psychological) that prevent or hinder effective communication.

Batons. Bodily movements that accent or emphasize a specific word or phrase.

Belief. Confidence in the existence or truth of something; conviction.

Beltlining. An unproductive conflict strategy in which one hits below the level of tolerance of the other person.

Blindering. A misevaluation in which a label prevents us from seeing as much of the object as we might see; a process of con-

centrating on the verbal level while neglecting the nonverbal levels; a form of *intensional orientation.*

Blind self. The part of the self that contains information about the self that is known to others but unknown to oneself.

Body language. A form of nonverbal communication in which messages are communicated by gesture, posture, spatial relations, and so forth; a popular term covering all aspects of nonverbal communication.

Breadth. The number of topics about which individuals in a relationship communicate.

Bypassing. A misevaluation caused when the same word is used but each of the individuals gives it a different meaning.

Cant. A kind of *sublanguage;* the conversational language of a special group (usually, a lower-social-class group), generally understood only by members of the subculture.

Censorship. Legal restrictions imposed on one's right to produce, distribute, or receive various communications.

Certainty. An attitude of closed-mindedness that creates a defensiveness among communication participants; opposed to *provisionalism.*

Channel. The vehicle or medium through which signals are sent.

Channel capacity. The maximum amount of information that a communication channel can handle at any given time.

Chemistry binders. A class of life characterized by the ability to combine chemicals in order to grow and survive; plants are chemistry binders.

Cherishing behaviors. Small behaviors we enjoy receiving from others, especially from our relational partner.

Civil inattention. Polite ignoring of others so as not to invade their privacy.

Cliché. An expression that is overused and calls attention to itself; "tall, dark, and handsome" as a description of a man would be considered a cliché.

Closed-mindedness. An unwillingness to receive certain communication messages.

Code. A set of symbols used to translate a message from one form to another.

Codifiability. The ease with which certain concepts may be expressed in a given language.

Coercive power. *Power* dependent on one's ability to punish or to remove rewards from another person.

Cognitive complexity. The state of having numerous concepts for describing people.

Cohesiveness. The property of togetherness; as applied to group communication situations, it refers to the mutual attractiveness among members, a measure of the extent to which individual members of a group work together as a group.

COIK. Acronym for *clear only if known*, referring to messages that are unintelligible for anyone who does not already know what the messages refer to.

Communication. (1) The process or act of communicating; (2) the actual message or messages sent and received; (3) the study of the processes involved in the sending and receiving of messages. (The term *communicology* is suggested for the third definition.)

Communication apprehension. Fear or anxiety over communicating; trait apprehension refers to fear of communication generally, regardless of the specific situation; state apprehension refers to fear that is specific to a given communication situation.

Communication gap. The inability to communicate on a meaningful level because of some difference between the parties—for example, age, sex, political orientation, religion.

Communication network. The pathways of messages; the organizational structure through which messages are sent and received.

Communicology. The study of communication, particularly the subsection concerned with human communication.

Competence. *Language competence* is a speaker's ability to use the language, a knowledge of the elements and rules of the language. *Communication competence* refers to the rules of the more social or interpersonal dimensions of communication and is often used to refer to the qualities that make for effectiveness in interpersonal communication. See *performance*.

Competition. An interpersonal process in which persons strive to attain something and at the same time to prevent others from attaining it.

Complementarity. A principle of *attraction* holding that one is attracted by qualities one does not possess or one wishes to possess and to people who are opposite or different from oneself; opposed to *similarity*.

Complementary relationship. A relationship in which the behavior of one person serves as the stimulus for the complementary behavior of the other; in complementary relationships, behavior differences are maximized.

Conditioning. An approach to the control of behavior in which the learning or unlearning of behaviors is dependent on their consequences.

Confidence. A quality of interpersonal effectiveness; a comfortable, at-ease feeling in interpersonal communication situations.

Conflict. An extreme form of competition in which a person attempts to bring a rival to surrender; a situation in which one person's behaviors are directed at preventing or interfering with or harming another individual. See *interpersonal conflict*.

Congruence. A condition where both verbal and nonverbal behaviors reinforce each other.

Connotation. The feeling or emotional aspect of meaning, generally viewed as consisting of the evaluative (for example, good–bad), potency (strong–weak), and activity (fast–slow) dimensions; the associations of a term. See *denotation*.

Consensus. A principle of attribution through which we attempt to establish if other people react or behave in the same way as the person on whom we are now focusing; if the person is acting in accordance with the consensus, we seek reasons for the behavior outside the individual; if the person is not acting in accordance with the consensus, we seek reasons that are internal to the individual.

Consistency. (1) A perceptual process that influences us to maintain balance among our perceptions; a process that influences us to see what we expect to see and to be uncomfortable when our perceptions are contrary to our expectations; (2) A principle of attribution through which we attempt to establish if this person behaves the same way in similar situations; if there is consistency, we are likely to attribute the behavior to the person, to some internal motivation; if there is no consistency, we are likely to attribute the behavior to some external factor.

Consonance. A psychological state of comfort created by having two elements (for example, cognitions or beliefs), one of which follows from the other. For example, consonance would exist for the following two cognitions: (1) X is healthy; (2) I engage in X.

Content and relationship dimensions. A principle of communication that messages refer both to content (the world external to both speaker and listener) and to relationship dimensions (the relationship existing between the individuals interacting).

Context of communication. The physical, psychological, social, and temporal environment in which communication takes place.

Cooperation. An interpersonal process by which individuals work together for a common end; the pooling efforts to produce a mutually desired outcome.

Credibility. The degree to which a receiver perceives the speaker to be believable. See *ethos.*

Credibility gap. A tendency between or among people to disbelieve each other and to doubt the honesty and integrity of each other; the difference between the image a person tries to convey (highly positive) and the image a receiver perceives (usually less positive), which is often taken as a measure of the extent to which the public image is disbelieved.

Culture. The body of knowledge concerning the appropriate and inappropriate patterns of thoughts and behaviors of a group.

Date. An *extensional device* used to emphasize the notion of constant change and symbolized by a subscript: for example, John Smith$_{1973}$ is not John Smith$_{1986}$.

Decoder. Something that takes a message in one form (for example, sound waves) and

translates it into another form (for example, nerve impulses), from which meaning can be formulated (for example, in vocal-auditory communication). In human communication, the decoder is the auditory mechanism; in electronic communication, the decoder is, for example, the telephone earpiece. See *encoder.*

Decoding. The process of extracting a message from a code—for example, translating speech sounds into nerve impulses. See *encoding.*

Defensiveness. An attitude of an individual or an atmosphere in a group characterized by threats, fear, and domination; messages evidencing evaluation, control, strategy, neutrality, superiority, and certainty are assumed to lead to defensiveness. Opposed to *supportiveness.*

Deictic movements. Bodily movements that point to an object, place, or event.

Delayed reactions. Reactions that are consciously delayed while a situation is analyzed.

Denotation. Referential meaning; the objective or descriptive meaning of a word. See *connotation.*

Depenetration. A reversal of *penetration;* a condition where the *breadth* and *depth* of a relationship decreases.

Depth. The degree to which the inner personality—the inner core of an individual—is penetrated in interpersonal interaction.

Determinism (principle of). The principle of verbal interaction that holds that all verbalizations are to some extent purposeful, that there is a reason for every verbalization.

Dialect. A specific variant of a language used by persons from a specific area or social class; dialects may differ from the "standard" language in phonology, semantics, or syntax, but they are intelligible to other speakers of the language.

Dialogue. A form of *communication* in which each person is both speaker and listener; communication characterized by involvement, concern, and respect for the other person; opposed to *monologue.*

Digital communication. Communication signals that are discrete rather than continuous; opposed to *analogic communication.*

Directive function of communication. Communication intended to persuade; communication that serves to direct the receiver's thoughts or behaviors.

Directive language. Language that directs us to focus on or see certain things to respond in certain ways.

Direct speech. Speech in which the speaker's intentions are stated clearly and directly.

Disconfirmation. The process by which one ignores or denies the right of the individual even to define himself or herself.

Displaced speech. Speech used to refer to something that is not present or in the immediate perceptual field.

Dissonance. A psychological state of discomfort created by having two elements (for example, cognitions and beliefs), one of which would not follow, given the other. Two such elements might be "X is harmful" and "I engage in X." These two elements represent dissonance, since given one of them, the other would not follow. See *consonance*.

Distinctiveness. A principle of attribution in which we ask if this person reacts in similar ways in different situations; if the person does, there is low distinctiveness, and we are likely to conclude there is an internal cause or motivation for the behavior; if there is high distinctiveness, we are likely to seek the cause in some external factors.

Dogmatism. Closed-mindedness in dealing with communications.

Double-bind message. A particular kind of contradictory message possessing the following characteristics: (1) The persons interacting share a relatively intense relationship; (2) two messages are communicated at the same time, demanding different and incompatible responses; (3) at least one person in the double bind cannot escape from the contradictory messages; (4) there is a threat of punishment for noncompliance.

Downward communication. Communication in which the messages originate at the higher levels of an organization or hierarchy and are sent to lower levels—for example, management to line worker; more generally, the habit of some people to address others as if these listeners were subordinate or ignorant; opposed to *upward communication*.

Duality of patterning. The feature of language that refers to the fact that language consists of two levels, the level of individual sounds (phonemic) and the level of individual meaningful units or morphemes (morphemic). Duality of patterning makes it possible for a language to consist of relatively few phonemes (about 45), which can be combined in various different ways or patterns to form an extremely large number of morphemes.

Dyadic communication. Two-person communication

Dyadic consciousness. An awareness of an interpersonal relationship or pairing of two individuals; distinguished from situations in which two individuals are together but do not perceive themselves as being a unit or twosome.

Dyadic effect. The tendency for the behaviors of one person to stimulate behaviors in the other interactant; usually, used to refer to the tendency of one person's *self-disclosures* to stimulate the listener to self-disclose also.

Dynamic judgments. Perceptual judgments that refer to the characteristics of another person that change relatively rapidly. See *static judgments*.

Ectomorphy. The skinny dimension of body build.

Effect. The outcome or consequence of an action or behavior; communication is assumed always to have some effect.

Ego states. More or less stable patterns of feelings that correspond to patterns of behaviors; in transactional analysis, three such ego states are defined: Parent ego state, Adult ego state, and Child ego state.

Elementalism. The process of dividing verbally what cannot be divided nonverbally— for example, speaking of body and mind as separate and distinct entities.

Emblematic movements. Elements used to illustrate a verbal statement, either repeating or substituting for a word or phrase.

Emblems. Nonverbal behaviors that directly

translate words or phrases—for example, the signs for "OK" and "peace."

Emotive function of communication. Communication that tells us something about the speaker as opposed to the external world or serves some personal need of the speaker.

Empathy. The feeling of another person's feeling; feeling or perceiving something as does another person.

Encoder. Something that takes a message in one form (for example, nerve impulses) and translates it into another form (for example, sound waves). In human communication, the encoder is the speaking mechanism; in electronic communication, the encoder is, for example, the telephone mouthpiece. See *decoder*.

Encoding. The process of putting a message into a code, for example, translating nerve impulses into speech sounds. See *decoding*.

Endomorphy. The fatty dimension of body build.

Entropy. A measure of the extent of disorganization or randomness in a system. Entropy is a measure of the degree of uncertainty that a destination has about the messages to be communicated by a source. Entropy is high if the number of possible messages is high and low if the number of possible messages is low.

E-**prime.** A form of the language that omits the verb *to be* except when used as an auxiliary or in statements of existence. Designed to eliminate the tendency toward *projection*.

Equality. An attitude that recognizes that each individual in a communication interaction is equal, that no one is superior to any other; encourages *supportiveness*; opposed to *superiority*.

Erotic love. A sexual, physical love; a love that is ego-centered and is given because it will be returned; a calculated love that is given because of an anticipated return.

Etc. An extensional device used to emphasize the notion of infinite complexity; since one can never know all about anything, any statement about the world or event must end with an explicit or implicit *etc.*

Ethics. The branch of philosophy that deals with the rightness or wrongness of actions; the study of moral values.

Ethos. The aspect of persuasiveness that depends on the audience's perception of the character of the speaker; to Aristotle, *ethos*, or ethical proof, depended on the speaker's perceived goodwill, knowledge, and moral character. Ethos is more commonly referred to as *speaker credibility*.

Euphemism. A polite word or phrase used to substitute for some taboo or otherwise offensive term.

Evaluation. A process whereby a value is placed on some person, object, or event.

Experiential limitation. The limit of an individual's ability to communicate, as set by the nature and extent of that individual's experiences.

Expert power. *Power* dependent on a person's expertise or knowledge; knowledge gives an individual expert power.

Expressiveness. A quality of interpersonal effectiveness; genuine involvement in speaking and listening expressed verbally and nonverbally.

Extensional devices. Linguistic devices proposed by Alfred Korzybski to keep language a more accurate means for talking about the world. The extensional devices include *etc.*, *date*, and *index* (the working devices) and the *hyphen* and *quotes* (the safety devices).

Extensional orientation. A point of view in which the primary consideration is given to the world of experience and only secondary consideration is given to the labels. See *intensional orientation*.

Fact-inference confusion. A misevaluation in which one makes an inference, regards it as a fact, and acts upon it as if it were a fact.

Factual statement. A statement made by the observer after observation and limited to the observed. See *inferential statement*.

Faith. A type of attitude or belief that is primarily emotional.

Fear appeal. The appeal to fear to persuade an individual or group of individuals to believe or to act in a certain way.

Feedback. Information that is given back to the source. Feedback may come from the source's own messages (as when we hear what we are saying) or from the receiver(s) in the form of applause, yawning, puzzled looks, questions, letters to the editor of a newspaper, increased or decreased subscriptions to a magazine, and so forth. See *negative feedback, positive feedback.*

Field of experience. The total of an individual's experiences, which influences that person's ability to communicate. In some views of communication, two people can communicate only to the extent that their fields of experience overlap.

Friendship. An interpersonal relationship between two persons that is mutually productive, established and maintained through perceived mutual free choice and characterized by mutual positive regard.

Frozen evaluation. See *static evaluation.*

Gain-loss theory. A theory hypothesizing that increases in rewards have greater impact than constant invariant rewards.

Game. A simulation of some situation with rules governing the behaviors of the participants and with some payoff for winning; in transactional analysis, *game* refers to a series of ulterior transactions that lead to a payoff; the term also refers to a basically dishonest kind of transaction in which participants hide their true feelings.

General semantics. The study of the relationships among language, thought, and behavior.

Ghostwriting. The procedure by which one writes or prepares messages for someone else and the identity of the real author is kept hidden.

Grammar. The set of rules of *syntax, semantics,* and *phonology.*

Gossip. *Communication* about someone not present, some third party, usually about matters that are private to this third party.

Gunnysacking. An unproductive conflict strategy of storing up grievances—as if in a gunnysack—and holding these in readiness to dump on the person with whom one is in conflict.

Halo effect. The tendency to generalize an individual's virtue or expertise from one area to another.

Heterophily. The degree of difference between individuals. See *homophily.*

Hidden self. The part of the self that contains information about the self known to oneself but unknown to (hidden from) others.

High-order abstraction. A very general or abstract term or statement; an inference made on the basis of another inference. See *level of abstraction.*

Homophily. The degree of similarity between individuals. See *heterophily.*

Honorific. Expressing high regard or respect. In some languages certain pronouns of address are honorific and are used to address those of high status. In English such expressions as "Dr.," "Professor," and "the Honorable" are honorific.

Hyphen. An *extensional device* use to illustrate that what may be separated verbally may not be separable on the event or nonverbal level; although one may talk about body and mind as if they were separable, in reality they are better referred to as body-mind.

Iconicity. The condition of a term or symbol's bearing a real or nonarbitrary relationship to its referent; opposed to *arbitrariness.*

Identification. In general semantics, a misevaluation whereby two or more items are considered as identical; according to Kenneth Burke, a process of becoming similar to another individual; a process of aligning one's interests to those of another. Burke sees identification as a necessary process for persuasion.

Ideographs. Bodily movements that sketch the path or direction of a thought.

Idiolect. An individual's personalized variation of the language.

Illustrators. Nonverbal behaviors that accompany and literally illustrate the verbal messages—for example, upward movements that accompany the verbalization "It's up there."

I-messages. Messages in which the speaker accepts responsibility for personal thoughts and behaviors; messages in which the speaker's point of view is stated explicity. Opposed to *you-messages*.

Immanent reference (principle of). The principle of verbal interaction that holds that all verbalizations make some reference to the present, to the specific context, to the speaker, and to the receivers.

Immediacy. A quality of interpersonal effectiveness; a sense of contact and togetherness; a feeling of interest and liking for the other person.

Implicit personality theory. A theory of personality that each individual maintains, complete with rules or systems, through which others are perceived.

Imprinting. An attachment established at a specific time in the life of the individual that seems unrelated to rewards and punishments; imprinted attachments are extremely difficult to reverse.

Impromptu speech. A speech given without any direct prior preparation.

Index. An *extensional device* used to emphasize the notion of nonidentity (no two things are the same) and symbolized by a subscript—for example, politician$_1$ is not politician$_2$.

Indirect speech. Speech that hides the speaker's true intentions; speech in which requests and observations are made indirectly.

Indiscrimination. A misevaluation caused by categorizing people or events or objects into a particular class and responding to specific members only as members of the class; a failure to recognize that each individual is an individual and is unique; a failure to apply the *index*.

Inevitability. A principle of communication referring to the fact that communication cannot be avoided; all behavior in an interactional setting is communication.

Inferential statement. A statement that can be made by anyone, is not limited to the observed, and can be made at any time. See *factual statement*.

Information interview. A type of interview in which the interviewer asks the interviewee, usually a person of some reputation and accomplishment, questions designed to elicit the person's views, predictions, perspectives, and the like on specific topics.

Information overload. A condition in which the amount of information is too great to be dealt with effectively or the number or complexity of messages is so great that the individual or organization is not able to deal with them.

Information power. *Power* dependent on one's ability to communicate logically and persuasively. Also called *persuasion power*.

In-group talk. Talk that is understood only by members of a particular group; the sublanguage of a group.

Inoculation principle. A principle of persuasion that states that persuasion is more difficult to achieve when beliefs and attitudes that have already been challenged previously are attacked, because the individual has built up defenses against such attacks in a manner similar to inoculation.

Intensional orientation. A point of view in which primary consideration is given to the way in which things are labeled and only secondary consideration (if any) to the world of experience. See *extensional orientation*.

Interaction management. A quality of interpersonal effectiveness; the control of interaction to the satisfaction of both parties; managing conversational turns, fluency, and message consistency.

Interchangeability. The feature of language that makes possible the reversal of roles between senders and receivers of messages. Because of interchangeability, all adult members of a speech community may serve as both senders and receivers; people may produce any linguistic message they can understand.

Interpersonal communication. Communication between two persons or among a small group of persons and distinguished from public or mass communication; communication of a personal nature and distinguished from impersonal communication; communication between or among intimates or those involved in a close relationship; often, intrapersonal, dyadic, and small group communication in general.

Interpersonal conflict. A conflict between two connected persons; a conflict within an individual caused by that individual's relationships with other people.

Interpersonal perception. The perception of people; the processes through which we interpret and evaluate people and their behavior.

Interview. A particular form of interpersonal communication in which two persons interact largely through questions and answers for the purpose of achieving specific goals.

Intimate distance. The closest proxemic distance, ranging from touching to 18 inches.

Intrapersonal communication. Communication with oneself.

Intrinsic credibility. The credibility or believability a listener perceives a communicator to possess, based on what takes place during the actual communication encounter.

Irreversibility. A principle of communication referring to the fact that communication cannot be reversed; once something has been communicated, it cannot be uncommunicated.

Jargon. A kind of *sublanguage;* the language of any special group, often a professional class, which is unintelligible to individuals not belonging to the group; "shop talk."

Kine. An individually produced bodily movement.

Kineme. The range of bodily movements that are functionally important or that communicate different meanings.

Kinesics. The study of the communicative dimensions of facial and bodily movements.

Kinetographs. Nonverbal movements that depict a bodily action or some nonhuman physical action.

Language. The rules of *syntax, semantics,* and *phonology;* a potentially self-reflexive structured system of symbols that catalog the objects, events, and relations in the world. *A language* refers to the infinite set of grammatical sentences generated by the grammar of any language—for example, English, Italian, Bantu, Chinese.

Learnability. The feature of language that refers to the fact that any normal human being is capable of learning any language as a first language. Learnability is dependent on and follow from languages being traditionally or culturally transmitted.

Legitimate power. *Power* dependent on the belief that a person has a right, by virtue of position, to influence or control the behavior of another.

Leveling. A process of message distortion in which a message is repeated, but the number of details is reduced, some details are omitted entirely, and some details lose their complexity.

Level of abstraction. The relative distance of a term or statement from the actual perception; a low-order abstraction would be a description of the perception, whereas a high-order abstraction would consist of inferences about inferences about descriptions of a perception.

Life positions. The sets of directions or scripts by which people live their lives; in transactional analysis, four such scripts are defined, each of which describes how one views oneself and how one views others: "I'm OK, you're OK"; "I'm OK, you're not OK"; "I'm not OK, you're OK"; and "I'm not OK, you're not OK."

Linguistic determinism. A theory that holds that language determines what we do, say, and think and in fact limits what we are able to do, say, and think.

Linguistic relativity. A theory that argues that the language we speak influences what we perceive and think. Since different languages catalog the world differently, speakers of different languages see the world differently.

Linguistics. The study of language; the study of the system of rules by which meanings are paired with sounds.

Listening. An active process of receiving aural stimuli.

Loving. An interpersonal process in which one feels a closeness, a caring, a warmth, and an excitement for another person.

Low-order abstraction. A description of what is perceived. See *level of abstraction.*

Ludus love. Love as a game, as fun; the position that love is not to be taken seriously and is to be maintained only as long as it remains interesting and enjoyable.

Machiavellianism. The techniques or tactics by which control is exerted by one person over another.

Macroscopic approach to communication. The focus on broad and general aspects of communication.

Manic love. Love characterized by extreme highs and extreme lows; obsessive love.

Matching hypothesis. An assumption that we date and mate with people who are similar to ourselves—who match us—in physical attractiveness.

Meaningfulness. A principle of perception that refers to the fact that we assume that the behavior of people is sensible and stems from some logical antecedent and that it is consequently meaningful rather than meaningless.

Mere exposure hypothesis. The theory that holds that repeated or prolonged exposure to a stimulus may result in attitude change toward the stimulus object, generally in the direction of increased positiveness.

Mesomorphy. The muscular dimension of body build.

Message. Any signal or combination of signals that serve as a *stimulus* for a receiver.

Metacommunication. Communication about communication.

Metalanguage. Language used to talk about language.

Microkinesics. The area of *kinesics* concerned with bodily movements that communicate different meanings.

Micromomentary expressions. Extremely brief movements that are not consciously controlled or recognized and that are thought to be indicative of an individual's real emotional state.

Microscopic approach to communication. The focus on minute and specific aspects of communication.

Minimization. An unproductive conflict strategy in which one makes light of the objections or complaints of another person, stating that the conflict, its causes, and its consequences are really insignificant.

Model. A representation of an object or process.

Monologue. A form of *communication* in which one person speaks and the other listens; there is no real interaction among participants; opposed to *dialogue*.

Multiordinality. In general semantics, a condition whereby a term may exist on different levels of abstraction.

Multivalued orientation. A point of view that emphasizes that there are many sides (rather than only one or two sides) to any issue.

Negative feedback. Feedback that serves a corrective function by informing the source that his or her message is not being received in the way intended. Negative feedback serves to redirect the source's behavior. Looks of boredom, shouts of disagreement, letters critical of newspaper policy, and the teacher's instructions on how to approach a problem better would be examples of negative feedback.

Negative reinforcement. The strengthening of a particular response by removing an aversive stimulus. See *positive reinforcement*.

Neutrality. A response pattern lacking in personal involvement; encourages *defensiveness;* opposed to *empathy.*

Noise. Anything that distorts the message intended by the source. Noise may be viewed as anything that interferes with the receiver's receiving the message as the source intended the message to be received. Noise is present in a communication system to the extent that the message received is not the message sent. Noise may originate in any of the components of the communication act—for example, in the source as a lisp, in the channel as static, in the receiver as a hearing loss, in written communication as blurred type. Noise is always present in any communication system, and its effects may be reduced (but never eliminated completely) by increasing the strength of the signal or the amount of redundancy, for example.

Nonallness. An attitude or point of view in which it is recognized that one can never know all about anything and that what we know or say or hear is only a part of what there is to know or say or hear.

Nondirective language. Language that

does not direct or focus our attention on certain aspects; neutral language.

Object adaptors. Nonverbal behaviors (see *adaptors*) that make use of some kind of prop that itself does not serve any instrumental function—for example, scratching your head with a pencil or chewing on your necklace.

Object language. Language used to communicate about objects, events, and relations in the world; the structure of the object language is described in a *metalanguage*; the display of physical objects—for example, flower arranging and the colors of the clothes we wear.

Object level. The nonverbal level of sense perception, which we abstract from the event level; the level on which we live our lives.

Objective abstracting. A form or type of abstracting in which we group individual units into a class of which they are all members—as, for example, the grouping of all chapters into a book.

Obstinate audience. A view of the audience, particularly the public and mass communication audience, as critical, selective, and active.

Olfactory communication. Communication by smell.

Openness. A quality of interpersonal effectiveness referring to (1) a willingness to interact openly with others, to self-disclose as appropriate; (2) a willingness to react honestly to incoming stimuli; and (3) a willingness to own one's feelings and thoughts. Also see *productivity.*

Open self. The part of the self that contains information about the self that is known to oneself and to others.

Operant. A response emitted without a clearly identifiable prior stimulus; a bit of behavior controlled by its consequences.

Operant conditioning. A process whereby reinforcement is contingent upon a particular response, with the effect that the response is strengthened, or a process whereby punishment is contingent upon a particular response, with the effect that the response is weakened. See *negative reinforcement, positive reinforcement.*

Opinion. A tentative conclusion concerning some object, person, or event.

Opinion leader. Persons looked to for opinion leadership; those who mold public opinion.

Other orientation. A quality of interpersonal effectiveness involving attentiveness, interest, and concern for the other person.

Other talk. Talk about the listener or some third party.

Packaging. See *reinforcement.*

Paralanguage. The vocal (but nonverbal) aspect of speech. Paralanguage consists of voice qualities (for example, pitch range, resonance, tempo), vocal characterizers (laughing or crying, yelling or whispering), vocal qualifiers (intensity, pitch height), and vocal segregates (*uh-uh*, meaning "no," or *sh*, meaning "silence").

Passive listening. *Listening* that is attentive and supportive but occurs without talking and without directing the speaker in any nonverbal way; also used negatively to refer to inattentive and uninvolved listening.

Perception. The process of becoming aware of objects and events from the senses.

Perceptual accentuation. A process that leads us to see what we expect to see and what we want to see; for example, we see people we like as better-looking and smarter than people we do not like.

Performance. The actual utterances a speaker speaks and a hearer hears. See *competence.*

Performative. A statement whose utterance is itself an action; includes such verbal acts as voting, delivering verdicts, apologzing, and cursing.

Personal distance. The second-closest proxemic distance, ranging from $1\frac{1}{2}$ feet to 4 feet.

Persuasion. The process of influencing attitudes and behavior.

Persuasion power. See *information power.*

Phatic communion. Communication that is primarily social; communication designed to open the channels of communication rather than to communicate something about the external world; "Hello," and "How are you?" in everyday interaction are common examples.

Phonology. The area of linguistics concerned with sound.

Pictics. The study of the pictorial code of communication.

Pictographs. Bodily movements that draw pictures in the air of the general shape of the thing being talked about.

Pitch. The highness or lowness of the vocal tone.

Polarization. A form of fallacious reasoning by which only the two extremes are considered; also referred to as "black-or-white" and "either-or" thinking or two-valued orientation.

Polymorphism. The tendency to serve as a leader for a number of topics; generally characterizes local opinion leaders.

Positive feedback. *Feedback* that supports or reinforces behavior along the lines it is already proceeding in—for example, applause during a speech.

Positiveness. A characteristic of effective communication involving positive attitudes toward oneself and toward the interpersonal interaction. Also used to refer to positively *stroking* another person through compliments and expressions of acceptance and approval.

Positive reinforcement. The strengthening of a particular response by making a reward contingent upon it. The process may be visualized in three stages: (1) A response is emitted—for example, a child says "Daddy"; (2) a reward is given—for example, a smile or candy or touching; (3) the response, "Daddy," is strengthened—that is, it is more likely to recur under similar circumstances. See *negative reinforcement.*

Power. The ability to control the behaviors of others.

Pragmatic love. Practical love; love based on compatibility; love that seeks a relationship in which each person's important needs and desires will be satisfied.

Pragmatics. In communication, an approach that focuses on behaviors, especially on the effects or consequences of communication.

Prevarication. The feature of human language that makes lying possible. This feature depends on and is a function of *displacement, openness* or *productivity,* and *semanticity.*

Primacy effect. The condition by which what comes first exerts greater influence than what comes later. See *recency effect.*

Problem orientation. A focus on a problem and its possible solutions rather than on controlling the group processes; encourages *supportiveness;* opposed to *control.*

Process. Ongoing or nonstatic activity; communication is referred to as a process to emphasize that it is always changing, always in motion.

Productivity. The feature of language that makes possible the creation and understanding of novel utterances. With human language we can talk about matters that have never been talked about before, and we can understand utterances we have never heard before. Also referred to as *openness.*

Progressive differentiation. A relational problem caused by the exaggeration or intensification of differences or similarities between individuals. Also see *Schismogenesis.*

Projection. A psychological process whereby we attribute characteristics or feelings of our own to others; often used to refer to the process whereby we attribute our own faults to others.

Pronouncements. Authoritative statements that imply that the speaker is in a position of authority and the listener is in a childlike or learner role.

Provisionalism. An attitude of open-mindedness that leads to the creation of *supportiveness;* opposed to *certainty.*

Proxemics. The study of the communicative function of space; the study of how people unconsciously structure their space—the distance between people in their interactions, the organization of space in homes and offices, and even the design of cities.

Proximity. As a principle of *perception,* the tendency to perceive people or events that are physically close as belonging together or representing some unit; physical closeness; one of the qualities influencing interpersonal *attraction.*

Public distance. The farthest proxemic distance, ranging from 12 feet to over 25 feet.

Public speaking. Communication that occurs when a speaker delivers a relatively prepared, continuous address in a specific setting to a large audience that provides little immediate feedback.

Punctuation of communication. The breaking up of continuous communication sequences into short sequences with identifiable beginnings and endings or stimuli and responses.

Punishment. Noxious or aversive stimulation.

Pygmalion effect. The condition in which one makes a prediction and then proceeds to fulfill it; a type of self-fulfilling prophecy but one that refers to others and to our evaluation of others rather than to ourselves.

Quotes. An *extensional device* used to emphasize that a word or phrase is being used in a special sense and should therefore be given special attention.

Rapid fading. The evanescent or nonpermanent quality of speech signals.

Rate. The speed with which we speak, generally measured in words per minute.

Receiver. Any person or thing that takes in messages. Receivers may be individuals listening or reading a message, a group of persons hearing a speech, a scattered television audience, or a machine that stores information.

Recency effect. The condition in which what comes last (that is, most recently) exerts greater influence than what comes first. See *primacy effect*.

Recurrence (principle of). The principle of verbal interaction that holds that individuals will repeat many times and in many different ways who they are, how they see themselves, and in general what they think is important and significant.

Redundancy. The quality of a message that makes it totally predictable and therefore lacking in information. A message of zero redundancy would be completely unpredictable; a message of 100 percent redundancy would be completely predictable. All human languages contain some degree of built-in redundancy, generally estimated to be about 50 percent.

Referent power. *Power* dependent on one's desire to identify with or be like another person.

Reflexiveness. The feature of language that refers to the fact that human language can be used to refer to itself; that is, we can talk about our talk and create a *metalanguage*, a language for talking about language. See *self-reflexiveness*.

Regulators. Nonverbal behaviors that regulate, monitor, or control the communications of another person.

Reinforcement. The strengthening of a particular response. See *positive reinforcement*, *negative reinforcement*.

Reinforcement or packaging (principle of). The principle of verbal interaction that holds that in most interactions, messages are transmitted simultaneously through a number of different channels that normally reinforce each other; messages come in packages.

Rejection. A response to an individual that rejects or denies the validity of that individual's self-view.

Relational abstracting. A form or type of abstracting in which relationships among items are abstracted and represented in some kind of formula, equation, or diagram; for example, the formula $a^2 = b^2 + c^2$ expressing the relationship among the sides of a right triangle is the result of relational abstracting.

Relational communication. Communication between or among intimates or those in close relationships; used by some theorists as synonymous with *interpersonal communication*.

Relational deterioration. The stage of a relationship during which the connecting bonds between the partners weaken and the partners begin drifting apart.

Reliability. The degree of agreement that can be obtained from a number of observers; the degree to which an instrument or observers will yield the same results on repeated observations.

Resemblance. As a principle of *perception*, the tendency to perceive people or events that are similar in appearance as belonging together.

Response. Any bit of overt or covert behavior.

Reward power. *Power* dependent on one's ability to reward another person.

Rhythmic movements. Body movements that depict or visually imitate the rhythm or pacing of an event.

Rigid complementarity. The inability to break away from the complementary type of relationship that was once appropriate and now is no longer.

Role. The part an individual plays in a group; an individual's function or expected behavior.

Schismogenesis. The *progressive differentiation* of relationships; in complementary relationships, the relationships become even more different and more clearly distinguished; in symmetrical relationships, the similar responses become more and more intense.

Selective exposure (principle of). A principle of persuasion that states that listeners actively seek out information that supports their opinions and actively avoid information that contradicts their existing opinions, beliefs, attitudes, and values.

Self-acceptance. Being satisfied with ourselves, our virtues and vices, and our abilities and limitations.

Self-adaptors. Nonverbal behaviors (see *adaptors*) that serve some personal need—for example, autoerotic activity.

Self-attribution. A process through which we seek to account for and understand the reasons and motivations for our own behaviors.

Self-concept. An individual's self-evaluation; an individual's self-appraisal.

Self-disclosure. The process of revealing something significant about ourselves to another individual or to a group, something that would not normally be known by them.

Self-fulfilling prophecy. The situation in which we make a prediction or prophecy and fulfill it ourselves—for example, expecting a class to be boring and then fulfilling this expectation by perceiving it as boring.

Self-monitoring. The manipulation of the image one presents to others in interpersonal interactions so as to give the most favorable impression of oneself.

Self-reflexive abstracting. A form or type of abstracting in which the abstraction is of itself—as when, for example, we think about our thinking, love our love, or fear our fear.

Self-reflexiveness. The property of being able to refer to itself; for example, language is self-reflexive because it can be used to refer to itself. See *reflexiveness.*

Self-serving bias. A bias that operates in the self-attribution process and leads us to take credit for the positive consequences and to deny responsibility for the negative consequences of our behaviors.

Self talk. Talk about oneself.

Semantic differential. A device for measuring connotative meaning consisting of seven-point, bipolar scales; generally three dimensions of meaning are measured: evaluation, potency, and activity.

Semanticity. The feature of human language that refers to the fact that some words have denotations in the objective world. All human languages possess semanticity, but not all words have denotations (for example, *of, the,* and *is* do not have objective referents in the real world).

Semantics. The area of language study concerned with meaning.

Semantogenic. Caused by semantics or labels; used most widely in reference to a problem or disorder whose origin may be found in the labels. For example, stuttering has been called semantogenic; because some particular behavior was labeled "stuttering," according to the semantogenic theory, that behavior became stuttering.

Sequential communication. Communication in which messages are passed from A to B, B to C, C to D, and so on; linear communication.

Sexist language. Language derogatory to one sex, generally women.

Sharpening. A process of message distortion in which the details of messages, when repeated, are crystalized and heightened.

Shyness. The condition of discomfort and uneasiness in interpersonal situations.

Sign. Something that stands for something else and that bears a natural, nonarbitrary relationship to it—for example, dark clouds as a sign of rain. See *symbol*.

Sign language. Gesture language that is highly codified—for example, a hitchhiker's gesture.

Signal and noise (relativity of). The principle of verbal interaction that holds that what is signal (meaningful) and what is noise (interference) is relative to the communication analyst, the participants, and the context.

Signal reaction. A conditioned response to a signal; a response to some signal that is immediate rather than delayed. See *symbol reaction*.

Silence. The absence of vocal communication; often misunderstood to refer to the absence of any and all communication.

Silencers. A tactic (such as crying) that literally silences one's opponent—an unproductive conflict strategy.

Similarity. A principle of *attraction* holding that one is attracted to qualities similar to those possessed by oneself and to people who are similar to oneself; opposed to *complementarity*.

Slang. The language used by special groups that is not considered proper by the general society; the language made up of the *argot*, *cant*, and *jargon* of various subcultures, known by the general public.

Small group communication. Communication among a collection of individuals, few enough in number so that all members may interact with relative ease as both senders and receivers, who are related to each other by some common purpose and with some degree of organization or structure among them.

Social distance. The third proxemic distance, ranging from 4 to 12 feet; the distance at which business is usually conducted.

Social exchange theory. A theory hypothesizing that we develop relationships in which our rewards or profits will be greater than our costs and that we avoid or terminate relationships in which the costs exceed the rewards.

Social kinesics. The area of *kinesics* concerned with the role and meanings of different bodily movements.

Social penetration theory. A theory concerned with relationship development from the superficial to the intimate levels and from few to many areas of interpersonal interaction.

Somatotype. Body type measured in terms of the degree to which one is fat, muscular, and skinny.

Source. Any person or thing that creates messages. A source may be an individual speaking, writing, or gesturing or a computer solving a problem.

Spatial movements. Body movements that depict spatial movements—for example, rapid hand motions to depict the passing of a speeding car.

Speaker apprehension. A fear of engaging in communication transactions; a decrease in the frequency, strength, and likelihood of engaging in communication transactions.

Specialization. The characteristic of serving no purpose other than that for which something is designed.

Specialized communication system. A communication system that serves no other function than that of communication; human language is a specialized system.

Speech. Messages conveyed via a vocal-auditory channel.

Speech community. A group of persons using the same language.

Spontaneity. The communication pattern in which one verbalizes what one is thinking without attempting to develop strategies for control; encourages *supportiveness*; opposed to *strategy*.

Stability. The principle of perception that refers to the fact that our perceptions of things and of people are relatively consistent with our previous conceptions.

State apprehension. Speaker apprehension for specific types of communication situations—for example, public speaking or interview situations.

Static evaluation. An orientation that fails to recognize that the world is characterized by constant change; an attitude that sees people and events as fixed rather than as constantly changing.

Static judgments. Perceptual judgments that refer to those characteristics of another person that are relatively unchanging—for example, race, occupation, age, and nationality. See *dynamic judgments*.

Status. The relative level one occupies in a hierarchy; status always involves a comparison, and thus one's status is only relative to the status of another. In our culture, occupation, financial position, age, and educational level are significant determinants of status.

Step theories of mass communication. A group of theories that hold that the media have their effects on viewers and listeners in steps. The one-step theory holds that the media influence people directly; the two-step theory holds that the media influence opinion leaders, who in turn influence the majority of others; the multistep theory holds that the media's influence is a reciprocal one, a process that goes back and forth between the media to the people.

Stereotype. In communication, a fixed impression of a group of people through which we then perceive specific individuals; stereotypes are most often negative (Martians are stupid, uneducated, and dirty) but may also be positive (Venusians are scientific, industrious, and helpful).

Stimulus. Any external or internal change that impinges on or arouses an organism.

Stimulus-response models of communication. Models of communication that assume that the process of communication is a linear one, beginning with a stimulus that then leads to a response.

Storge love. Love based on companionship, similar interests, and mutual respect; love that is lacking in great emotional intensity.

Strategy. The use of some plan for control of other members of a communication interaction that guides one's own communications; encourages *defensiveness;* opposed to *spontaneity.*

Stroking. Verbal or nonverbal acknowledgment of another person; positive stroking consists of compliments and rewards and, in general, behaviors we look forward to or take pride in receiving; negative stroking is punishing and would consist of criticisms, expressions of disapproval, or even physical punishment.

Structural differential. A model of the abstraction process consisting of an *event level*, an *object level*, and first, second, third, and further *verbal levels*.

Subjectivity. The principle of perception that refers to the fact that one's perceptions are not objective but are influenced by one's wants and needs and one's expectations and predictions of the perceiver.

Sublanguage. A variation from the general language used by a particular subculture; *argot, cant,* and *jargon* are particular kinds of sublanguages.

Superiority. A point of view or attitude that assumes that others are not equal to oneself; encourages *defensiveness;* opposed to *equality.*

Supportiveness. An attitude of an individual or an atmosphere in a group that is characterized by openness, the absence of fear, and a genuine feeling of equality; messages evidencing *description, problem orientation, spontaneity, empathy, equality,* and *provisionalism* are assumed to lead to supportiveness. See *defensiveness.*

Symbol. Something that stands for something else but bears no natural relationship to it—for example, purple as a symbol of mourning. Words are symbols in that they bear no natural relationship to the meaning they symbolize. See *sign.*

Symbol reaction. A reaction that is made with some delay. See *signal reaction.*

Symmetrical relationship. A relation between two or more persons in which one person's behavior serves as a stimulus for the same type of behavior in the other person(s). Examples of such relationships include situations in which anger in one person encourages or serves as a stimulus for anger in another person or in which a critical comment by the person leads the other person to respond in like manner.

Syndicate method. This is a method used to improve some organizational function in which a committee is formed and charged with the investigation of a specific issue. The syndicate studies the issue, prepares a report, and delivers it to the organization.

Syntax. The area of language study concerned with the rules for combining words into sentences.

Taboo. Forbidden; culturally censored. Taboo language is language that is frowned upon by "polite society." Topics and specific words may be considered taboo—for example, death, sex, certain forms of illness, and various words denoting sexual activities and excretory functions.

Tactile communication. Communication by touch; communication received by the skin.

Territoriality. A possessive or ownership reaction to an area of space or to particular objects.

Theory. A general statement or principle applicable to a number of related phenomena.

Time binders. A class of life that survives by passing information on from one generation to another, thus making knowledge cumulative; human beings.

Total feedback. The quality of speech that refers to one's ability to receive all the communications one sends.

Traditional transmission. The feature of language that refers to the fact that human languages (at least in their outer surface form) are learned. Unlike various forms of animal languages, which are innate, human languages are transmitted traditionally or culturally. This feature of language does not deny the possibility that certain aspects of language may be innate. Also referred to as *cultural transmission.*

Trait apprehension. Speaker apprehension for communication generally; a fear of communication situations regardless of their kind or context.

Transactional. Characterizing the relationship among elements whereby each influences and is influenced by each other element; communication is a transactional process, since no element is independent of any other element.

Transactions. The patterns of interaction between people; in transactional analysis, three types of transactions are defined: complementary, crossed, and ulterior.

Trust. *Faith* in the behavior of another person; confidence in another person that

leads us to feel that whatever we risk will not be lost.

Undelayed reaction. A reaction that is immediate; a signal response; a reaction made without any conscious deliberation.

Universal language. A language understood by all people and that all people have the ability to use.

Universal of interpersonal communication. A feature of communication common to all interpersonal communication acts.

Universal of language. A feature of language common to all known languages.

Unknown self. The part of the self that contains information about the self that is unknown to oneself and to others but is inferred to exist on the basis of various projective tests, slips of the tongue, dream analyses, and the like.

Upward communication. In organizational communication, communication that originates from an individual who is low on the organizational hierarchy and directed to someone higher up; more generally, the habit of some people to address others as if these listeners were superiors or authorities; opposed to *downward communication.*

Value. Relative worth of an object; a quality that makes something desirable or undesirable; ideals or customs about which we have emotional responses, whether positive or negative.

Variable. A quantity that can increase or decrease; something that can have different values.

Vocal qualifiers. Aspects of *paralanguage*—specifically, intensity, pitch height, and extent of vocalizations.

Vocal segregates. Aspects of *paralanguage*—specifically, such vocalizations as *uh-uh, uh-huh, sh,* and pauses.

Voice qualities. Aspects of *paralanguage*—specifically, pitch range, vocal lip control, glottis control, pitch control, articulation control, rhythm control, resonance, and tempo.

Volume. The relative loudness of the voice.

Word association. A method for measuring connotative meaning; a way of measuring the meaningfulness of words; a projective technique in which associations to stimulus words are analyzed in terms of their psychological significance.

You-messages. Messages in which the speaker denies responsibility for his or her own thoughts and behaviors; messages that attribute what is really the speaker's perception to another person; messages of blame; opposed to *I-messages*.

INDEX

Page numbers in italics refer to the "Skills in Brief" sections.

About the Author

Joseph A. DeVito is Professor of Communication at Hunter College of the City University of New York. After earning his M.A. at Temple University and Ph.D. at the University of Illinois, he did postdoctoral studies at Illinois and at the University of Minnesota's Human Learning Institute. He has taught the interpersonal communication course for over fifteen years, and is a specialist in psycholinguistics. Dr. DeVito has written widely for major scholarly journals such as the *Quarterly Journal of Speech, Communication Monographs*, the *Journal of Communication, Communication Education*, and many others. He is the author of a number of textbooks, including *The Elements of Public Speaking* and *Human Communication*, both published by Harper & Row. His two newest books are the fourth edition of *The Interpersonal Communication Book* and *The Communication Handbook: A Dictionary*, both published in 1986.

BOOKS BY THE AUTHOR

The Psychology of Speech and Language: An Introduction to Psycholinguistics

Communication: Concepts and Processes (Third Edition)

General Semantics: Nine Lectures

General Semantics: Guide and Workbook (Revised Edition)

Language: Concepts and Processes

Psycholinguistics

Articulation and Voice: Effective Communication

The Elements of Public Speaking (Second Edition)

Human Communication: The Basic Course (Third Edition)

The Communication Handbook: A Dictionary